BENSON'S 2001 ROTISSERIE® BASEBALL ANNUAL

**DIAMOND
LIBRARY**

Managing Editor:
Douglas DelVecchio

Associate Editors:
James Benson, Tony Blengino, Marc Bowman, Lary Bump, Bill Gilbert, Bill Gray, Eric Marino, Fred Matos, Lawr Michaels, Karl Mordhorst, Kevin Wheeler, and Doug White

Layout and Design:
Wade Lunsford and Joe Palys

Copyright © 2001 by John Chapman Benson with licenses to Diamond Analytics Corporation

All rights reserved under International and Pan-American Copyright Conventions.

Library of Congress Cataloging-in-Publication Data:
Benson, John
Rotisserie Baseball Annual 2001
1. Baseball — United States — History
2. Baseball — United States — Records
I. Title

ISBN 1-880876-94-9

For information address: Diamond Library.

Published by Diamond Library, a division of Diamond Analytics Corporation, with offices at:
15 Cannon Road, Wilton, Connecticut, 06897.
Telephone: 203-834-1231.

PRINTED IN THE UNITED STATES OF AMERICA

Cover design by Digital Grafx

Rotisserie League Baseball is a registered trademark of The Rotisserie League Baseball Association, Inc. For information contact R.L.B.A. at 370 Seventh Avenue, Suite 312, New York, New York 10001.
Telephone: 212-629-4036.

Statistics are provided by STATS, Inc., 8131 Monticello Ave., Skokie, IL 60076
Telephone: 847-676-3322.

TABLE OF CONTENTS

Our Own All-Star Roster

James Benson
John Benson
Tony Blengino
Marc Bowman
Lary Bump
Bill Chastain
Douglas DelVecchio
Bob Gale
Bill Gilbert
Ken Gurnick
Peter Graves
David Luciani
Wade Lunsford
Jack Magruder
Eric Marino
Fred Matos
Lawr Michaels
Karl Mordhorst
LaVelle E. Neal III
Kevin Wheeler
Doug White

INTRODUCTION

We could keep adding late-breaking transactions until April, but we know you want your *2001 Rotisserie Baseball Annual* by spring training. The book is still the most up-to-date book out there.

The first edition of this book was titled *Winning Rotisserie Baseball*. We didn't know it was going to be an annual. We weren't even thinking about anything beyond 1989. But then things happened. The 500 copies sold out quickly on the basis of a quarter-page ad in *Baseball America*, plus a flyer to a few dozen people who had been buying my forecast stats and values from a classified ad in *The Sporting News* since 1986. The critics loved the book. Fan mail was encouraging, and two publishers approached me to bid for a 1990 edition before the end of July. By January 1990 we were in bookstores nationwide.

Nobody was forecasting anything about baseball in 1989, except team standings. Bill James had been publishing the *Project Scoresheet* writers' and scores' poll of the best players ranked at each position, and that poll came into this book when the *Abstract* series came to an end after 1989. But stats and values for individual players were a whole new world of content for publishing, and folks like you devoured them quickly.

I keep saying "*we*" because even in 1989 there was a separate writer for each major league team, even two writers for some teams. The forecast stats for each player were illuminated with serious explanations saying why we believed what we believed, and so it remains today in this, twelfth annual edition. Some of the original group remain in these pages; many new friends (and top baseball writers) have come on board in the decade that followed the first edition.

The world of baseball information is changing rapidly. Just ten years ago, we had no *Baseball Weekly*, no STATS Red Book (or Green Book or Blue Book), no Baseball Tonight, no STATS On Line, no cornucopia of websites spewing daily information and insight. *"The National"* had not yet appeared and disappeared. Box scores contained only the scantiest information.

Time management has become the big new question. A decade ago, the problem was that we had the time, but we didn't have enough information. Sure, we were frenzied in our pursuit of information, and it often seemed like we were short of time, but remember how many nights we stayed up — even those of us with "instant" on-line access to the news wires — waiting for the West Coast box scores. That's right: waiting. And at other times, we bought morning newspapers only to find they were missing half the previous night's games; often we had to wait for Tuesday's "late" box scores to appear in Thursday's papers. Again, notice the word: Today we don't wait.

Today, staying informed is relatively easy, raising three implications: (1) staying informed isn't such a competitive advantage, because everyone is doing it; (2) there is new challenge to find the information wisely, replacing the old challenge to find the information in the first place: and (3) tiny bits of information can amount to bigger competitive advantages.

Today, the main issue is to use time wisely — to get the most useful information, to get it faster than your opponents, and to avoid wasting time on second-hand or out-of-date information.

For my competitive purposes, I find STATS Online to be the best use of my time.

For numbers and scores and anything statistical in origin, STATS Inc. is the undisputed champ in the on-line world. I will give you four examples of what STATS Online can do for you. I could give a hundred.

In-progress Box Scores: Why wait for the conventional news services to file their results after the game is over? Often I need to make a pitcher decision, and I can't wait for the Seattle game to finish. So I log onto STATS and check to see how a certain pitcher is doing. If he's got a two-hit shutout going in the seventh inning, I feel good about him. If he left with one out in the fifth inning and six runs in, that tells me something important, too.

Merely seeing the starting lineups can be useful. And seeing that a player has already stolen a base in the second inning can tell you plenty about how his hamstring is feeling — hours before your competition has the same information.

Statistical Profiles: If you have seen the STATS Blue Book, with all those splits, home/road, grass/turf, day/night etc., you have only seen the tip of the iceberg, and you are looking at last year's numbers. How would you like to know how a given pitcher is doing against every team in the league, in June or July this year? It's there, in STATS On Line, update continuously as the season unfolds.

Daily Logs: Imagine going through every newspaper from April to August, to find out how and when a player's performance has changed. What is a player's batting average, since he came off the DL three weeks ago? When is the last time he stole a base? Is he striking out more than usual? Has he been drawing enough walks to downplay a low batting average? It's all there. You can scan the whole season, even a whole career, day by day, or you name the date and see everything that has happened since then.

Whenever I need to choose a pitcher, I look at his last three or four starts, and focus on strikeout/walk ratio. Give me five pitchers to choose from, and I can instantly tell you which one is on top of his game right now.

Player Portfolio: This one is my favorite, because I play in so many leagues that it can be difficult just to remember who's on what roster. I type my teams into STATS On Line (they save all the info for me) and then I can check each day's results, last week, or even look at the upcoming schedule and see instantly who's going to Colorado.

The Player Portfolio saves me literally dozens of hours every month, hundreds of hours every season. And here is a tip on how to get even more benefit than tracking your own players: put in each league's available list, and see instant comparisons when you need to choose a substitute. Sometimes I even put in an arch rival's roster, especially when he's got pitchers headed for Colorado.

With STATS On Line, I find that the piles of daily newspapers which used to inundate my office have now become largely superfluous. Of course I read Baseball America and Baseball Weekly for ongoing analysis of developing events, but day by day it is STATS that keeps me informed. I simply turn on my modem, and tap in.

The purpose of this book was, and is, winning Rotisserie baseball. In 2001 more than ever, that means wise use of time.

John Benson

THE HOT STOVE

OLD FACES, NEW PLACES AND HIDDEN MEANINGS

by Bill Gray

10-Dec
Fla
Jeff Abbott-OF
Traded from the White Sox after a second sub par year, Abbott will be hard pressed to find a starting job in Florida. Despite and impressive minor league career and a promising debut in 1998, Abbott lacks power, outfield range and he throws poorly. Abbott has the skill to bat .300 but he'll have to have a very strong spring training to earn a starters role. Despite his potential to hit for a high average, he is a one category player and not very useful for Rotisserie.

13-Dec
Atl
Kurt Abbott-IF/OF
Signed to a minor league contract, Abbott's dilemma is that he is on a contending team and that means it will be tougher to get playing time.

20-Dec
Cle
Scott Aldred-P
Signed to a minor league contract with Cleveland; his seventh team. 'Nuff said.

5-Dec
Det
Jermaine Allensworth-OF
Signed to a minor league contract, Allensworth surely realizes that he is running out of time. A strong minor league performance will earn him a mid season call up but he is a long way from regaining a starters job that was once handed to him.

18-Dec
CWS
Sandy Alomar Jr.-C
Signed as free agent through 2002. Cleveland offered Alomar, the player who was the heart and soul of their fruitless championship chase in the 1990s, a fair contract

for 2001. They also told him he would usually have a comfortable spot on the bench to watch Einar Diaz catch. Alomar was right to reject the Tribe's offer and he stuck it to them by signing on — as the number one catcher — with Cleveland's arch rival, the Chicago White Sox. The move is a boost for Sandy, and it's a huge win for the White Sox hurlers.

22-Nov
Cin
Clayton Andrews-P
A Jim Bowden special. Part of the Steve Parris deal. A young, (22) but crafty lefty who could make the Reds in situational match ups this year. He has the make up to be a quality starter and he is cheap.

10-Dec
NYM
Kevin Appier-P
Signed as free agent through 2004, Appier showed he is healthy but few pitchers ever come all the way back after such an injury. All the way back for Appier would mean he would again be considered one of the top five pitchers in the game. Such a return is unlikely but Appier is still a capable pitcher who could win 15 games for the Mets.

13-Dec
SD
Alex Arias-IF
Arias is signed through 2002. The journey continues for a journeyman utility infielder.

6-Dec
LA
Andy Ashby-P
Ashby signed as a free agent with an option year for 2004 and on the surface Los Angeles appears to be a good move. He was traded to the Phillies before last season but he never got it going in 2000. He was brilliant in July (5-0) but inadequate the rest of the season. Ashby had a rough time with lefthanded batters, which provides an

easy strategy for opposing managers and if they continue to load up a lineup with southpaws, Ashby will be hit hard.

21-Dec
SF
Rich Aurilia-SS
Signed through 2003, Aurilia is a late bloomer who should have been given a chance to be a regular sooner than 1999. AT age 29, Aurilia will not improve much over his last two seasons.

11-Dec
Hou
Brad Ausmus-C
Acquired by Houston from Detroit and a long time Capo in the Smith Family Mob, Ausmus begins his second tour with the Astros. It seems as if every Thanksgiving Day, the Smith's gather and just before the Turkey and stuffing is served, Brad Ausmus is traded to, or from Houston to, or from Detroit. Trading Brad Ausmus has become one of baseball's most enduring traditions and Ausmus has become the Smith's Family Thanksgiving Day Player-To-Be-Named-Sooner-or-Later. Over the years, Tal and Randy Smith — between bites of stuffing and gravy have peddled Ausmus to each other about forty times now. Brad has two nicknames: In Detroit, they call him "The Motor City Cowboy." In Houston, they call him "The Lone Star Lug Nut." Brad is getting on in years but he's hitting in a hitters paradise now. If you consider his 500 plus at bats while catching last year one must wonder when some important body part is going to give out. Regardless, at the lead-footed catching spot, Ausmus has stolen bases in double figures for five out of the last six years. He will steal a few bases again but can we be sure that Randy won't reacquire Ausmus in July at the annual Smith Family Fourth of July Picnic?

3-Nov
CWS
Harold Baines-DH
Baines declared free agency and spent the Holidays without a job. Baines was slipping in his late thirties but he had a rebound and hit well at age 40. That enforces that Baines was a fine hitter, but the negative is that age 40 is almost always the last hurrah for a good hitter. Nobody turns it around at age 42.

20-Dec
Atl
Paul Bako-C
Signed for 2001 but with Javy Lopez starring as Starto which means Eddie Perez plays Bako. Paul is stymied

unless Lopez or Perez get Hurto.

11-Dec
Bal
John Bale-P
Acquired in trade from Toronto, Bale is just an arm in the pen.

11-Dec
Ana
Kimera Bartee-OF
Signed as free agent for 2001 after Cincinnati released him, Kimera, whose first name should be Billy because he hits like a dwarf. The Angels are the latest team to take a flyer on Bartee. He is signed to a minor league contract . . . and there he stays. He's toast.

3-Nov
Ari
Miguel Batista
Signed as free agent for 2001, Batista has a live arm and live arms always get a chance but Batista is still struggling to find the plate. Batista is age 30 and the best hop is that Mother Nature will take something off his fastball, which may improve his control.

10-Nov
Bos
Rod Beck-P
Beck signed for 2001 and the fact that Boston resigned him rather quickly in the off season is meaningful. Despite the barbs tossed his way, Beck is still a good pitcher. Don't write him off as a closer just yet.

7-Dec
Ana
Tim Belcher-P
In spite being signed to a minor league contract, the 39 year old veteran will find a job as a fifth starter in Anaheim, or elsewhere.

10-Dec
Pit
Derek Bell-OF
Signed as free agent with an option for 2003, Bell and the Bucs have a new stadium and they are finally making a serious attempt to upgrade the offense. When traded in the past, Bell usually puts good numbers for a couple years and then he tails off. At age 32, Bell is still effective and he will have a good year in Pittsburgh.

20-Dec
Phi
Rigo Beltran-P
Signed to a minor league contract, Beltran can stick as a middle inning reliever only if he regains his control.

18-Dec
ChC
Jason Bere-P
Signed as free agent through 2002, Bere is OK when his curve is working and he gets ahead in the count but he'll fall victim to pitching too carefully in Wrigley. He'll fall behind in the count and then — he'll throw his straight not-so-fast-fastball — and it will get crushed.

22-Nov
TB
Sean Bergman-P
Signed to a minor league contract, Bergman is looking for a big league job after being cut loose by the Twins, which is not a good sign.

3-Nov
Det
Willie Blair-P
Declared free agency but despite a bit of a rebound in 2000, it appears that most MLB GMs are on to him. Blair has a deep bag of tricks but he has been able to fool hitters only for one year, never two in a row. His bag of tricks is about empty and his winter Holiday was uneventful. That said, somebody — in some front office — will push the bad move button.

14-Dec
NYY
Brian Boehringer-P
He actually signed to a minor league contract with the Yankees! Bo must really enjoy playing in the minor leagues.

9-Nov
Fla
Ricky Bones-P
Signed for 2001 Bones also got an option year. Wow. Hey, Willie Blair is still available!

22-Dec
Sea
Bret Boone-2B
Signed as free agent for 2001, now we wonder if he can beat out Mark McLemore? He's back with Seattle, his original team, but the fact that he's been traded three times in three years is a sign his future is in doubt. He'll probably start but if Seattle is out of contention, Boone will be on the bench by mid-season.

20-Dec
Bal
Mike Bordick-SS
Signed as free agent through 2002, Bordick returns to Baltimore after being rented by the Mets. It's a winning move for Bordick who would have been a backup in New York to Rey Ordonez. In Baltimore, Bordick will start at shortstop and he should be able to continue his late-in-life power surge.

25-Nov
Ana
Toby Borland-P
Signed to a minor league contract but the only way he'll be in a major league stadium is if buys a ticket.

15-Dec
Phi
Ricky Bottalico-P
Signed as free agent for 2001, Bottalico rehabbed for two years. Now he's relatively healthy and he could regain his old closers job with his old team but he's not the same pitcher as he was in his heyday and as a closer he's a risk, a rather large risk.

3-Jan
Hou
Kent Bottenfield-P
Signed as free agent for 2001, the 32 year-old Bottenfield pitched for two teams last year, Anaheim and Philadelphia. He was 8-10 with both teams after coming out of oblivion to post a stellar 18-7 record in 1999 with the Cardinals. Bottenfield quickly lost whatever it was that made him effective in 1999. Houston is not a good place for Bottenfield to recover his form. It's a hitters park and Bottenfield is a flyball pitcher. It's not a good mix.

3-Jan
Hou
Charlie Hayes-1B/3B
Signed to a minor league contract, The Astros will bring Hayes to spring training. Hayes no longer has the ability to help a club as a starter, and he has no business on a Rotisserie team.

2-Jan
Tex
Peter Munro-P
Signed to a minor league contract, Munro is 26 and clearly not prepared to pitch in the major leagues.

11-Dec
Hou
Doug Brocail-P
If you want a set up man, get the best.

13-Dec
Atl
Rico Brogna-1B
Signed as free agent for 2001. Pay attention to the one year contract. He's productive but he has peaked.

20-Nov
Cle
Ellis Burks
Signed as free agent with an option for 2004, Burks last played in the American League in 1993 and he is still a fine hitter. At age 36, Burks will be able to rest his aching knees occasionally while serving as a designated hitter. Make no mistake, the Indians want Burks to play the field as much as he can because he is a fine right fielder and a major defensive upgrade over Manny Ramirez.

23-Dec
Cle
Tim Byrdak-P
Signed to a minor league contract The Indians picked him up quickly after Kansas City cut him loose. He's headed for Buffalo, but somebody likes him.

27-Nov
FA
Miguel Cairo-IF
Tampa Bay released him—and his 28 stolen bases. Keep tabs on him.

10-Dec
Tex
Ken Caminiti-3B
Signed as free agent for 2001 with an option for 2003 Caminiti will have his moments but at age 38, Caminiti now has more pop in his knees than in his bat. He is a consensus pick to land on the disabled list and on the Rangers he's one of several newly-acquired, fortyish geezers battling for breathers as a designated hitter. The problem is that Caminiti will probably need to DH more than any other new old guys in Texas if he is to remain

whole all year. The bad news is Cammy doesn't have DH power anymore.

21-Dec
FA
Mike Caruso-SS
He was not offered contract and became free agent and maybe he got the message about humility. He has big league ability but he has to produce or learn to enjoy the minors.

7-Dec
Bos
Frank Castillo-P
Signed as free agent through 2002, Castillo's resurrection last year was not a fluke. After some decent years in the mid-1990s, Castillo stumbled in 1998-99 and he was universally written off. He has taken his lumps and he has learned from his past. Plus, he knows how to pitch. He regained his pinpoint control and confidence last year. With the exception of last season, Castillo has spent his entire career in pitchers purgatory: Wrigley Field, Tiger Stadium and Coors Field. Why should tiny Fenway bother him? It won't. Here, you have a sleeper.

20-Dec
Tex
Frank Catalanotto-MI/CI
Signed for 2001, Supersub qualifies at 1B, 2b and of course MI/CI. He is the only healthy, young player in the Ranger infield is A-Rod. At age 27, Catalanotto is ripe now and he will play more this year. Given the age and physical woes of the Randy Velarde, Ken Caminiti and even Andres Galarraga, Frank looks like a sleeper. Don't put him on a long term contract. His game is better suited to the National League and he is a free agent at the end of the year.

11-Dec
Det
Roger Cedeno-OF
Traded away after only one season year with Houston, Cedeno will flag down a lot of gap shots in Comerica Park, which is good news for all Detroit's hurlers. The good news for you is that Phil Garner will let him run. Cedeno missed two months with a hand injury last year but he still stole 25 bases. Highly recommended.

19-Dec
Sea
Norm Charlton-P
Signed to a minor league contract. Myers and Dibble are

still available, Lou.

14-Dec
CWS
Royce Clayton-SS
Traded from Texas, Clayton would have preferred to compete for his shortstop spot on the Rangers with that A-Rod kid, but he will gladly take the SS role with the White Sox. He will run more in Chicago than he did in Texas.

16-Nov
Cin
Michael Coleman-OF
Why didn't Jim Bowden just keep Chris Stynes?

20-Dec
Cle
Marty Cordova-OF
Signed to a minor league contract. Cordova is the kind of role player the Indians like — a fading big leaguer with a recognizable name who will make Triple A fans come to see him try to play.

27-Nov
Pit
Francisco Cordova-P
Signed for 2001, Cordova was disabled last year due to a bone spur on his elbow. He is supposed to be healthy but he has a lot to prove, hence the one year deal.

30-Nov
Phi
Rheal Cormier-P
Signed as free agent with an option for 2004,, it had better be bullpen work, please. If they make him a starter, something will break.

21-Dec
Ari
Craig Counsell-IF
Signed for 2001, it's just utility work for the hero of the 1997 World Series.

21-Nov
Col
Darron Cox-C
He's not a winner or a loser, unless you are interested in a 33 year old, career minor league catcher. Cox has been a catcher in the minors since 1989 and his only major league experience came in 1999 when he got 25 AB for the Expos and hit his only major league home run. Cox is a real life version of Crash Davis from the movie "Bull Durham." He's with the Colorado organization now and he is good at developing young pitchers. What does this mean to you? Nothing, really but Cox deserves our notice and respect. He is the kind of player who is truly the fabric of baseball and in that sense, he is a winner.

21-Dec
SF
Felipe Crespo-CI/1B/OF
A decent hitter with a little pop in his bat for a utility player. He can play infield or outfield. For Rotisserie he qualifies this year at corner, first base and outfield.

11-Dec
Hou
Nelson Cruz-P
Acquired by the Astros from Detroit (go figure). The Astros have an iffy closer situation and Cruz has the stuff to close but he's seems to be headed for more middle relief and he may spot start. He's a good pitcher who throws grounders. If you twist our arm we might suggest Cruz as a longshot special for more than a handful of saves.

15-Dec
Ari
Midre Cummings-OF
Signed as free agent for 2001, Cummings has settled into a small role as a pinch hitter and late inning sub.

20-Dec
Mil
Will Cunnane-P
Traded from San Diego to the Brewers Cunnane appears to have recovered his velocity after suffering from elbow trouble in 1998. He's a player who will slip the cracks but he has the ability to make a positive contribution to a Rotisserie team.

22-Dec
SF
Eric Davis-OF
Signed as free agent for 2001, Davis is 39 and he can't play a lot but he will play more than he has since 1998. The fact that he put off retirement to play for the Giants is telling. In the 1980s, Davis looked like the guy who would hit 500 homers and steal 500 bases. Now, he gets to play alongside of 37 year old Barry Bonds and watch as Barry reaches 500/500. Expect low end double digits in steals and home runs.

13-Nov
Tor
Jason Dickson-P
Signed to a minor league contract. Dickson is a longshot who is trying to rebuild an injury-riddled career.

8-Dec
SF
Shawon Dunston-IF
Signed as free agent with an option through 2002, Dunston is another new resident of Baker's Old Folk's Home. The Giants are a nice blend of age and, uh, age. Negotiations with Juan Marichal continue. Say Hey! Where's my glove?

21-Dec
FA
Todd Dunwoody - OF
Released by Kansas City after the Royals gave him a fair chance. He got lot of playing time in the second half but Dunwoody flopped. He can't hit lefties and few teams are interested in 25 year old platoon players.

6-Dec
Oak
Dave Eiland-P
Dave Eiland signing a minor league contract has become one of Baseball's Rites of Winter. Oakland doesn't seem to be a good fit for him.

22-Nov
Cin
Leo Estrella-P
He probably won't make the team in spring training but keep track of Estrella. He's a gifted young pitcher.

7-Nov
Tor
Scott Eyre-P
A lefty in the pen, but his pen will probably be in a minor league park.

20-Nov
Ana
Jorge Fabregas-C
Signed as free agent for 2001, J-Fab is a career back up catcher with a weak bat.

8-Dec
ChC
Jeff Fassero-P
Signed as free agent with an option for 2003, Fassero

won't be around much longer. He is out of gas and this will be a short, ugly year for Fassero.

5-Nov
Phi
P.J. Forbes-IF
Signed to a minor league contract and likely to play there, Forbes once looked like he had a big league future but he never improved.

27-Nov
FA
Ben Ford-P
Released by the Cubs, Ford can only be effective as a starter. At 6'7", Ford has trouble finding his rhythm. Making him come out of the bullpen only gives him more chances to have mechanical problems and not enough time to solve his problems. He's devastating when he's on but he needs to work a lot of uninterrupted innings somewhere in the minors and sound his ship. He is still worth watching

14-Nov
Bal
Brook Fordyce-C
Signed with option for 2004, Fordyce has a decent bat and he should be the starting catcher for Baltimore.

13-Dec
Tex
Kevin Foster-P
Signed to a minor league contract, this once interesting pitching prospect for the Cubs is 32 now and he has been in the minors since 1998. He still has a live arm but he never learned how to pitch.

20-Nov
Fla
Andy Fox-IF
Fox will try to win a utility role.

21-Dec
Ari
Hanley Frias
Signed for 2001 Good field — No hit — No play.

11-Dec
Tor
Jeff Frye-2B
Signed as a free agent for 2001, Frye is aging and injury prone but still solid enough to start, if Homer Bush is not able to play.

8-Dec
Tex
Andres Galarraga-DH/1B
Signed as free agent with an option for 2002, Galaragga appears to be ageless and apparently invulnerable. The 39 year old, power hitting first baseman will get to DH this year when he needs a breather. He'll face weaker pitching in the American League and the Big Cat will feast.

10-Dec
Col
Ron Gant-OF
Signed as free agent with an option for 2002, Gant can't hit a curve ball, or moving fastballs anymore but since nobody can throw them in Coors, Gant could hit 35 homers and bat .187.

22-Dec
Cle
Karim Garcia-OF
Signed to a minor league contract because he is a good minor league player. In The Show, hitters have to hit a curve ball and Garcia can't handle it.

27-Nov
CWS
Amaury Garcia-2B
Traded from Florida, he's a good young second base prospect but Ray Durham is in his way in Chicago. At best he'll be a back up middle infielder. Most likely he will be in Triple A.

9-Nov
TB
Derrick Gibson-OF
Signed to a minor league contract, Gibson has the tools but he hasn't learned how or when to use them.

11-Dec
Ana
Benji Gil-SS
Do you think the Angels have a problem at second and short? They are signing anybody with a glove

16-Nov
Atl
Marcus Giles-2B
Still young and destined for more minor league fine tuning. He is impressive and a potential Rotisserie gem.

14-Dec
ChC
Tom Gordon-P
Signed with the Cubs as a free through 2002. Coming off a major injury, it's questionable if he can still pitch, much less close.

8-Dec
Ari
Mark Grace-1B
Signed as free agent through 2002 with an option for 2003 Grace played 13 seasons with the Cubs and he freely admitted he made this move to Arizona for the money. Who can blame him? Money aside, he's a pro and this will be a great addition for the D-Backs. Grace has never had a bad year and even though he is age 37, he will have his best power season at the plate in several years. Think, "Luis Gonzales."

21-Dec
CWS
Tony Graffanino-IF
Signed for 2001. He'll fight for a utility infielder role with the White Sox, but most likely he will end up in the minors.

13-Dec
ChC
Scarborough Green-OF
Signed to a minor league contract. Green showed good speed in the Winter League play but he doesn't have the tools to help a major league team.

4-Nov
Tor
Todd Greene-DH
Signed for 2001, everybody missed the call on Greene. Now, at age 30, Green caught only one game last year. He is still considered a power hitter but he has never hit many homers. Injuries have wrecked a promising career.

6-Dec
TB
Ozzie Guillen-IF
Signed to a minor league contract and hanging on.

20-Dec
Cle
Eric Gunderson-P
Signed to a minor league contract and Buffalo bound.

22-Dec
Mil
Jeffrey Hammonds-OF
Signed as free agent through 2003, Hammonds arrival in Colorado for the 2000 season led us to conclude, correctly, that he would he the sleeper of the year. The Rockies have been through similar the "breakthrough-year-where's-my-money?" scenarios before and they just yawned at Hammonds asking price and wished him well but did not offer Hammonds salary arbitration after his big year. A year in Colorado usually does wonders for anybody with decent major league experience, basic hitting skills and playing time. Playing time was the key ingredient and Hammonds got it thanks to one huge month in May in which he belted eight home runs and had thirty-four RBI. Hammonds is talented but his wondrous season last year is, by far, the highest rung upon which he will stand in his career. The Brewers are hoping that they have a .330 hitting, 20 plus HR hitting, 100 RBI a year player. What Milwaukee has is a 30 year old player — strikeout prone and a one-year wonder — whose 2001 output will be about 70 percent of 2000. Ironically, last years stop sleeper candidate may play a part in finding another sleeper. A fellow named Marquis Grissom. According to Brewers General Manager Dean Taylor, the acquisition of Jeffrey Hammonds is supposed to send Grissom to the bench as the Brewers fourth outfielder. Grissom is 34 which is the only advantage the 30 year old Hammonds has on him. If Taylor's comment was meant to light a fire under Grissom, let's hope it does. Grissom hit .244 last year and he had a lousy on base percentage. This year, Grissom will move his average back up to the .270 range and he can outperform Jeffrey Hammonds in his sleep. Simply put, Grissom has more reason to bear down this year. He has grown a bit home run happy and undisciplined at the plate but he is still talented and too good a player to be a reserve. If the Brewers don't want him to play everyday, some other team will. Prediction: Hammonds will not be a starter by mid-season.

8-Dec
Col
Mike Hampton-P
Sentenced to an eight year contract with Colorado. Hampton is now rich as Hell — and he will now pitch in Hell.

5-Dec
KC
Doug Henry-P
Signed as free agent through 2002. He has a good opportunity to become the Royals closer.

19-Dec
Cin
Drew Henson-OF
Signed to a minor league contract but the NFL is still a possibility.

19-Dec
Bal
Pat Hentgen-P
Signed as a free agent with an option through 2003, Hentgen is the consummate workhorse. He's not the pitcher he was three years ago, but he will still give you thirty four starts a year and he'll win fifteen games. No pitcher in the game earns or deserves his success more than Pat Hentgen. He will fill the gap created by the departure of Mike Mussina and he will be nearly as effective as Mussina was for Baltimore.

14-Dec
StL
Dustin Hermanson-P
Traded from Montreal, Hermanson may have peaked as a starter but the Cardinals gave up a lot to get him which is intriguing enough to make him worth a shot.

20-Nov
Hou
Carlos Hernandez-IF
Fighting to win a back up middle infielder job for Houston.

20-Dec
Cle
Dave Hollins-3B
Signed a minor league contract. Hollins can still hit a little. Just what the Indians need. Another ancient hitter — for Buffalo.

11-Dec
Det
Chris Holt-P
The father and son Smith tandem were at it again this winter. What would the Hot Stove do without the blessed Smiths? Last year they traded Park Effects! Now, we actually want guys who pitch in Detroit and we pass on Astros hurlers. Holt emerges as a winner and he will have a good year for Detroit. What's next? Randy trades himself to Houston for his Pop?

20-Dec
Mil
Tyler Houston-IF
Signed through 2002, Houston qualifies at first, third and

catcher. Now, the bad part: He's unqualified at the plate.

21-Dec
Pit
Thomas Howard-OF
Signed to a minor league contract, the well traveled Howard hasn't had 300 at bats since 1996. The Pirates are his ninth organization since his rookie year in 1990.

12-Dec
ChC
Todd Hundley-C
Signed as free agent through 2004, Hundley caught 84 games (poorly) last year and he hit 24 homers in 299 at bats. Rotisserie doesn't count passed balls so go get him! For those of you who can fix your Rotisserie rosters every week, put all your speedy players on the active squad when they face the Cubs. Hundley can't throw, as you may know.

30-Nov
Phi
Brian Hunter (the slow one)-1B
Ask a manager about Hunter and he'll tell you Hunter has "decent power." Hunter has never hit more than 15 homers in a season. What else are they going to say? "Well, he's not as fat as I thought he was?"

14-Dec
Hou
Mike Jackson-P
Signed as free agent for 2001, the last organization to acquire arms at Houston's pace was Nazi Germany.

22-Nov
Det
Ryan Jackson-1B/OF
Signed to a minor league contract. He is age 30 and bouncing around looking for a major league job. His poor defense limits his chances to American League teams.

7-Dec
Ari
Jason Jacome-P
A former prospect trying to find a role in the D-Backs bullpen.

29-Nov
NYY
Domingo Jean-P
Signed to a minor league contract, Jean was once a decent prospect. Now he's on the fringe of oblivion.

21-Dec
LA
Marcus Jensen-C
Signed to a minor league contract.

21-Dec
LA
Brian Johnson-C
Signed to a minor league contract, Johnson was a starter until he was injured in 1998. He is relatively healthy and he remains acceptable on defense but he can't hit anymore. Johnson is not far removed from being a valued Rotisserie catcher. He is still a recognizable name and some bonehead in your league will draft him.

18-Dec
Fla
Charles Johnson-C
Signed as free agent through 2005, Johnson is back where it all began for him. He showed promise early in his career and last year he hit for average and with excellent power, a sure sign that he has reached and will remain at his new level. For value on both sides of plate, Johnson is probably the top catcher in baseball.

1-Dec
SD
Scott Karl-P
Signed as free agent for 2001, Karl pitched in Colorado last year. He has had his moments before and he is certainly worth a look in San Diego.

5-Dec
Col
Brooks Kieschnick
Signed to a minor league contract, The 29 year old Kieschnick is running out of time and he's not going to make it.

20-Nov
Bos
Sun-Woo Kim-P
Purchased from Triple-A Pawtucket, Kim started 25 games and was 11-7 with 116 Ks in 134 innings for Pawtucket in 2000.

14-Dec
StL
Steve Kline-P
Quality bullpen help. Will get some saves too.

2-Dec
StL
Rick Krivda-P
Signed to a minor league contract, Krivda is a level below Dave Eiland in the minor league pitchers rankings.

27-Nov
Cin
Brian L. (the fast one) Hunter-OF
His potential can tantalize GMs but up close, his flaws are glaring. At age 30, he'll get another chance or two but the curtain is coming down.

20-Dec
Cle
Tim Laker-C
Signed to a minor league contract and there he will stay. It's highly unlikely that he'll get playing time with the Indians.

21-Dec
LA
Aaron Ledesma-IF
Signed to a minor league contract but he should stick as a utility infielder with the Dodgers.

11-Dec
Tor
Cole Liniak-3B
Acquired from the Cubs just as he is starting to put it together.

19-Dec
Cin
Larry Luebbers-P
Former prospect now toiling in the minor leagues. He usually gets a callup at some point in the season.

22-Nov
SD
Keith Luuloa-IF
A 26 year old, aspiring to win a utility job with the Padres.

21-Dec
KC
Jeff M. D'Amico-P
Not offered a contract by the Royals which should make it easier for the unaware to avoid drafting the wrong Jeff D'Amico. The good one is with Milwaukee.

13-Dec
ChC
Robert Machado-C
Good catcher who has a little pop. Todd Hundley is a bad catcher who has a lot of pop. Machado might stick and he could end up catching a lot. Potential sleeper.

22-Nov
SD
Ron Mahay-P
Signed to a minor league contract, Mahay still can't find the plate. At age 29 he's part of the Padres winter cattle call. Nothing more.

20-Nov
Det
Mike Maroth-P
23 year old left handed starting pitcher for the Jacksonville Suns. Detroit wants him in Toledo.

10-Dec
Atl
Dave Martinez-OF
Signed as free agent through 2002. Wasn't he with the Braves in Milwaukee? Or was it Boston?

3-Jan
LA
Ramon Martinez-P
Martinez returns to the Dodgers after a year in Boston. On paper the injury-plagued, 33 year old Martinez looks risky. He started 27 games for the Red Sox last year and his ERA was 6.17, but in 12 seasons with the Dodgers, his ERA hit 4.00 only once. He was usually in the high 2.00 to low 3.00 range in ERA. His injuries have to have taken their toll, but the man has never pitched poorly as a Dodger. He is well worth a shot.

20-Nov
Mon
Sandy Martinez-C
Trying to win a backup catchers job.

22-Dec
StL
Quinton McCracken-OF
Signed as free agent through 2002, McCracken will battle to replace Eric Davis on the Cardinals bench.

2-Nov
Fla
Ryan McGuire-IB/OF
Signed to a minor league contract, the former prospect, now age 29, will fight to win the last spot on the Marlins bench.

2-Nov
Sea
Mark McLemore-2B
Signed for 2001. This is the way the Mariners retaliate against the Rangers for signing A-Rod?

11-Dec
Det
Mitch Meluskey-C
He should be the starting catcher for Detroit. He has improved as a hitter. Not great but passable for Rotisserie.

21-Nov
Phi
Jose Mesa-P
Signed as free agent through 2002 to be the Phils closer for at least the start of the 2001 season. Well, it should be fun to watch Larry Bowa deal with Mesa.

15-Nov
Cle
Ralph Milliard-IF
Signed to a minor league contract, Milliard is still young enough to make it but the Indians will keep him in the minors.

7-Nov
Ari
Mike Morgan-P
Signed for 2001, Morgan began pitching before Arizona was a state. Can you name another major league pitcher who has pitched in four different decades and two different centuries? And why only a one year contract? Scared?

7-Dec
Mil
James Mouton-OF
Signed to a minor league contract and darn well worth it.

27-Nov
Mil
Lyle Mouton-OF
Released by the Brewers. Obviously, Milwaukee isn't big enough for two Moutons.

19-Nov
ChC
Bill Mueller-3B
Good hitter with so-so power in San Francisco but Wrigley will yield a few more homers.

9-Dec
Pit
Terry Mulholland-P
Signed as free agent through 2002, Mulholland, 38, will spot start, relieve and help the ground crew drag the infield.

15-Dec
Mon
Bobby Munoz-P
Signed to a minor league contract, the 33 year old Munoz is a former power pitcher trying to hang on as a finesse pitcher.

13-Dec
Tex
Mike Munoz-P
Signed to a minor league contract, Munoz, if healthy, will pitch in relief for the Rangers.

30-Nov
NYY
Mike Mussina-P
Signed as a free agent through 2006. Repeat after Commissioner Bud, "Baseball is not a business. Baseball is not a business." For years the Atlanta Braves had the best rotation in the game. Adding Moose to a club that has looks like the greatest team in the history of baseball is simply an extra piece in a puzzle that they solved several years ago. Sure it's overkill, and George "Buy Buy Balboni" Steinbrenner plans to address that subject in his forthcoming autobiography, The Obsessive-Compulsive Baseball Executive.

9-Nov
FA
Randy Myers-P
He filed for free agency but he's been out of action for two years due to injuries. At age 38, a comeback is unlikely, but the fire still burns.

13-Dec
Tor
Jaime Navarro-P
Gaahhh! Toronto signed him to a minor league contract. Navarro lacks the heart and passion to work at his craft. Did we say, Gaaahhh!

4-Dec
Col
Denny Neagle-P
Neagle is slipping as a pitcher. It's been career suicide for every quality pitcher to sign with Colorado but for Neagle it could be a smart move. If he gets bombed, which he will, he can blame it on the thin air and everyone will agree. In a year or two, some other team will sign Neagle to a lucrative contract, thinking he'll recover his form in a normal atmosphere. He won't. He's done.

1-Dec
Sea
Jeff Nelson-P
Signed as a free agent through 2003, Nelson is still a good reliever. It's his second stint with the Mariners.

19-Dec
Cin
Chris Nichting-P
Signed to a minor league contract, Nichting is 34 but he's pitching well now and maybe better than at any time in his career. It could earn him a spot in the Reds bullpen.

15-Dec
Bos
Hideo Nomo-P
Cooked.

21-Nov
NYY
Joe Oliver-C
Signed as free agent for 2001. He will back Jorge Posada and probably wear a World Series Ring.

20-Dec
Phi
Kevin Orie-3B
Signed to a minor league contract. To make the Phillies all he needs to do is outplay Scott Rolen.

22-Nov
Tor
Steve Parris-P
Acquired from Cincinnati, Parris will get hammered in the American League.

21-Dec
LA
Yorkis Perez-P
Signed to a minor league contract. He's a lefty but he did not pitch in the majors last year. No reason to think this year will be any different.

20-Dec
Eduardo Perez-IB/OF
Released by the Cardinals. He will try it in Japan this year.

15-Dec
Det
Matt Perisho-P
Acquired from Texas, Perisho has good stuff and he looks like a sleeper in Detroit.

10-Dec
Tex
Mark Petkovsek-P
He beefs up the Rangers bullpen.

15-Nov
TB
Jim Pittsley-P
Signed to a minor league contract.

8-Dec
Tor
Dan Plesac-P
Signed through 2002, Plesac will be in the Jays bullpen and he'll face only one or two hitters in each appearance.

5-Dec
SD
Jeremy Powell-P
Signed to a minor league contract, the 25 year old Powell has good stuff and excellent control. He could break through in a big way when he learns how to set up hitters. Right now he's too easy for hitters to read.

21-Dec
Mon
Curtis Pride-OF
Signed to a minor league contract. He's 33 now and while he can still hit, he is a liability in the outfield. Best case: Reserve duty in Montreal.

19-Dec
Min
Tom Prince-C
Signed to a minor league contract, Prince, 36, will battle for a back up job with the Twins.

2-Nov
T B
Bill Pulsipher-P
Signed to a minor league contract. Worth watching. Pulsipher is not overpowering anymore due to his physical problems but he has enough more than enough stuff to get by and he has added "smarts" to his repertoire.

21-Dec
Mon
Tim Raines-OF
Signed to a minor league contract. You can bet that he won't play in the minors so his comeback may end in spring training. If he makes the Expos, there is nothing left in Raines tank.

13-Dec
Bos
Manny Ramirez-OF
Manny signed through 2008 with an option that can take him to 2010. He's a winner at the ATM but for what he'll cost you, he will be a losing proposition. Fenway is one of the worst scenarios for Ramirez. It's not that he's going to nose dive. He will have a good year but the expectations are for him to have a great year and lead the Sox to a championship. Faced with such high expectations, Ramirez can't win—unless they Sox win it all. If the team falters, Ramirez will get ALL of the blame. He's never shown any ability or resolve to become a team leader and he tends to get lazy. If the Sox do not overtake the Yankees — and they won't; fingers will point at Ramirez. Boston is the worst place in the game to be a scapegoat.

1-Nov
Pit
Alex Ramirez-OF
Signed to play in Japan.

11-Dec
Ana
Pat Rapp-P
Signed for 2001. He's not a great pitcher but he is a reliable workhorse who has started at least 20 games for six straight years.

15-Dec
NYM
Desi Relaford-IF
Signed for 2001. To this point, Relaford has been an underachiever at shortstop. Second base seems to be a better spot for him but he's not going to break into the Mets infield so it appears he's destined for reserve duty.

18-Dec
Sea
Frank Rodriguez-P
Released. Again. The older he gets, the worse he pitches.

11-Dec
Tex
Alex Rodriguez-SS
Signed through 2007 with options through 2010. With a contract valued at slightly over a quarter billion dollars, it will be hard to live up to because no baseball player has ever been paid so much. The Rangers bank account might be a loser, but A-Rod will hit like a god and he's poised for a breakout year. Rodriguez, 25, now in his prime, has already produced spectacular numbers. He flirted with fifty home runs in the mists of Seattle but in the broiling Texas sun, he'll threaten the 60 mark this year or next. Mark it down and then pay whatever you need to, to get him on your team. Up to now, Rodriguez' has been lumped together with Derek Jeter and Nomar Garciaparra, but Rodriguez has the best tools of the trio. He is a rare baseball talent and this year he will begin to distance himself from the pack. He will establish a new level and Nomar and Derek will remain a level below him.

17-Nov
NYM
Nerio Rodriguez-P
Signed to a minor league contract. This converted catcher is still a flame thrower but he knows more about catching than pitching.

16-Nov
Cin
Donnie Sadler-IF/OF
Acquired from Boston. He will try to win Chris Stynes' old job as a jack of all trades for the Reds.

21-Dec
Mon
Bob Scanlan-P
Signed to a minor league contract. The former major league closer is now trying to win any spot in the bullpen.

21-Dec
Bal
David Segui-1B
Signed as free agent through 2004. The former Oriole returns for a second tour. Segui is a career .308 hitter who hit a career best .334 last year. He is not going to have a bad year, but he won't hit .close to 334 again and he probably won't reach the .300 level. Segui hit so well last year because he played for two offensive powerhouses; Texas and Cleveland. While Segui improves Baltimore's lineup, he's on the weakest team since he his first tour with the Orioles in the early 1990s.

15-Nov
TB
Andy Sheets-OF
Signed to a minor league contract, which says it all.

11-Dec
NYM
Tsuyoshi Shinjo-OF
With Derek Bell gone, Shinjo has a chance to start with the Mets. Marginal American hitters — Lee Stevens come to mind — went to Japan to refine their hitting. Sometimes they return to the majors and make a statement in the Show, but Shinjo, regardless of his success in Japan, is not worth the gamble.

18-Nov
SEA
Ichiro Suzuki-OF
Suzuki, 28, is a seven time batting champion in Japan, so it's safe to assume that he will make the Mariners opening day roster.

15-Nov
CLE
Eddie Taubensee-C
On the surface, it appears that Taubensee will platoon with Einar Diaz. Given that Taubensee is a lefthanded hitter, it would seem that he would play more, but the opposite is true. Injuries limited Taubensee to 81 games in 2000 and that's a reasonable projection for 2001 with plenty of game activity coming as a DH.

15-Nov
NYM
Steve Trachsel-P
Signed as free agent through 2003, Trachsel has reached the point of his career where all he can do is go up, or out. He has shown flashes of competency in his career, and he will be working in a bona fide pitchers park. The question is, does Trachsel have the stones to exist, let alone thrive in the Big Apple? If he grows a new pair and he taps into his talent, he will be a pleasant surprise. If he craps out here, it's a severe blow to his future as a major league baseball player.

15 Nov
SD
Bubba Trammell-OF
Bubba's best prospects are in the AL as designated hitter. In the field he has no range and no wheels and his bat is not really all that strong. A few starts and a lot of pinch hitting lie ahead this year.

13-Dec
Tex
Ruben Sierra-OF
Here we go again. Signed to a minor league contract, Sierra is hanging on and wondering where it all went.

27-Nov
Det
Randall Simon-1B
Signed to a minor league contract, Simon's chances to play in Detroit are contingent upon Tony Clark's health.

17-Nov
Mon
Mark Smith-OF
Signed to a minor league contract. Time is running out.

13-Dec
ChC
Chris Snopek
A former White Sox who never reached his potential. He signed a minor league contract with the other team in Chicago with no clear role in hand. Whatever became of Robin Ventura?

27-Nov
FA
Jerry Spradlin-P
Released by the Cubs. Signed by the Phils.

8-Dec
SD
Ed Sprague-3B
Signed to a minor league contract. Has usually starts well but then he disappears in the second half.

9-Dec
ChC
Matt Stairs-OF
Signed for 2001. He's in an ideal park for his rightfield power. Wrigley did wonders for Henry Rodriguez and Stairs is a better hitter than Henry.

13-Dec
ChC
Rob Stanifer-P
Signed to a minor league contract, he'll compete for a bullpen job with the Cubs.

10-Nov
FA
Darryl Strawberry-DH
Straw declared free agency. Actually, his attorney made the declaration. Straw had nodded off....

16-Nov
Bos
Chris Stynes IF/OF
Acquired from
Cincinnati. His managers love his work ethic.

14-Dec
Mon
Fernando Tatis-3B
Acquired from St Louis, Fernando is now in his prime. One of the top 3B in the game with some upside. What were the Cards thinking?

16-Nov
ChC
Julian Tavarez-P
Signed through 2002, Tavarez pitched surprisingly well for the Rockies last year. His groundball stuff is helpful in Wrigley. Sleeper.

13-Dec
Tor
Ryan Thompson-OF
Signed to a minor league contract.

5-Jan
Ana
Ismael Valdes
Signed with the Angels. He will be in the top of the starting rotation. You have probably heard this before, but we will say it again: He has a lot of talent, but is weak mentally on the mound.

17-Nov
Tex
Randy Velarde
Acquired from Oakland. He's gritty, but nearly 40 years old which is not a good age for a second baseman. The words "fiery" and "leadership" are Velarde's strongest assets now. These attributes are always welcome but more so on a young team such as Oakland. With mostly veterans as teammates in Texas, Velarde won't need to do a lot of chest pounding and tail kicking. If you own him, have a contingency plan ready, especially for the second half.

15-Nov
Col
Ron Villone
Acquired by the Rockies from Cincinnati. Don't look.

20-Nov
Hou
Jose Vizcaino-IF
Signed for 2001. He won't start but he'll fill in everywhere.

20-Dec
Phi
Ed Vosberg-P
Signed to a minor league contract, Vosberg will compete for a bullpen job.

5-Dec
NYM
Paul Wagner-P
If you have been desperately wondering whatever happened to Paul Wagner, now you know. The Mets signed him to a minor league contract. Now, get a life!

13-Dec
ChC
Dave Wainhouse-P
Signed to a minor league contract. Years ago Wainhouse was used briefly by John Benson to win a Rotisserie pennant. It's a long story.

19-Dec
Cin
Matt Walbeck-C
Signed to a minor league contract: Bob Boone likes him.

11-Dec
NYM
Donne Wall-P
Acquired from San Diego, Wall is a former starter but in his present relief role, he looks like a guy who can be the team cherry picker. He's not worth a draft pick but he's a decent pickup who will give you six wins.

15-Dec
Cin
Mark Wohlers-P
Signed for 2001, Wohlers has recovered most of his velocity and confidence. The Reds have not kept him around to be a setup man. He will get a shot at closing.

19-Nov
SF
Tim Worrell-P
Acquired via trade from Chicago for Bill Mueller. Durable setup man.

LATE, LATE NEWS!

Oak - Miguel Cairo-2B
Cairo was expected to start as the A's second baseman.

Oak - Johnny Damon-OF
Damon was acquired in a 3-way trade with the Royals and D'Rays. Damon's role will stay the same in Oakland as it was in KC: starting left fielder and lead off man.

KC - Roberto Hernandez-P
Closer Hernandez was brought in from TB to be the Royals bullpen savior. The pen is now much improved and Hernandez is on a better team who will contend. Look for more saves in 2001.

TB - Ben Grieve-OF
Grieve will split time between the OF and DH. He is capable of much better numbers than what he showed in 2000 with the A's.

KC - A.J. Hinch-C
Forgotten in the 3-way trade was Hinch, who was once a top hitting/catching prospect with the A's. Look for

Hinch to get his shot to prove he belongs in 2001. If he takes advantage of a weak position on the Royals he could be a sleeper pick for the 2001 season.

Cin - Kelly Stinnett-C
Stinnett was expected to backup Jason LaRue.

Cin - Wilton Guerrero-OF
Look for Guerrero to be the Reds 4th OF. Taking at-bats away from the aging Michael Tucker.

ChC - Ron Coomer-1B/3B
Coomer will split time between 1st and 3rd as a backup.

Tex - Jeff Brantley-P
Jeff will get a shot at closing.

ChW - David Wells-P
Wells is the Sox ace. Injuries are a risk with him. He has a bad back, is overweight and is old. A very bad combo.

Tor - Mike Sirotka-P
Sirotka will be one of the top Jays starters. He is a under appreciated pitcher and may come as a bargain.

Tor - Kevin Beirne-P
Has some potential as a middle reliever, setup man.

Tor - Brian Simmons-OF
If healthy, Simmons has talent. Look for him to be in a 4th or 5th OF role.

Col - Roberto Kelly-OF
Kelly missed all of last season. He is in the right spot for a hitter to make a comeback. A reserve role is his best bet.

SF - Eric Davis-OF
Past his prime.

Ari - Reggie Sanders-OF
Talented, but injury prone.

Bos - David Cone-P
A comeback story would be nice, right? Don't bet on it!

Ana - Mo Vaughn-1B
Vaughn was expected to be out until the middle of the season while his bicep heals.

Ana - Jose Canseco-OF/DH
Jose still has something left. With Vaughn out, Jose's P.T. will go up.

LOOKING BACK AT 2000 AND FORWARD TO 2001

by Marc Bowman

Trends -

If anyone doubts that offense at the end of the millennium was on the upswing, they have to look no further than season totals in the two major leagues. Every primary offensive *hitting* category in both leagues was up except for National League batting average, which slipped two points to .266. Balance that slight downturn against increased batting average and hits in the American League, more doubles, triples, and homers in both leagues, and higher on-base and slugging averages in both leagues – and, most importantly, more runs in both leagues – and you can see the millennium-ending trend is, in a word: offensive.

2000 was especially offensive to the pitchers, who saw the composite major league ERA reach its highest point since the 1930 season. At 4.80, the major league ERA was easily the highest in Rotisserie baseball history, topping the 4.70 mark set one season earlier which was, itself, a new record high. For the major league teams themselves, getting outstanding – not just good – pitching was *the* crucial element towards reaching the post-season and succeeding once October arrived.

That lesson should not be lost on Rotisserie players, either. Whereas a 4.00 ERA might get you eight or ten points in a standard American League Rotisserie competition just a few years ago, it is now good enough to top the league. Look at it from the other angle: how much damage can one bad pitcher do to a Rotisserie team? Simply ask anyone who owned Jose Lima or Pat Rapp how many pitching points they earned last year (ask this question from a distance, for your own safety). Nearly all of their full-season owners finished in the second division as 200 innings of bad pitching cannot be overcome.

Look at it from the other angle. Just how valuable is a good starting pitcher? How many of Pedro Martinez's owners won their league? Martinez's 1.74 ERA was 3.18 runs better than the American League composite ERA, a new record, eclipsing his own record set in 1999. Likewise, Martinez's ERA bested second-place finisher Roger Clemens by 1.96 runs, also shattering his own record from 1999. Martinez was the only player in either league worth nearly $50 (conservatively estimated at a $46 value), and he was worth $15 more than any other starting pitcher in baseball last season. At no other position was there such a discrepancy between the best and second best players.

While it may be more fun to watch baseballs sail out of the park at a record pace and it may put more butts in the seats to have new offensive records set every year, it is pitching which makes the difference both in real baseball and on the Rotisserie stat sheets.

Another lesser trend, on the offensive side of the ledger, showed fewer stolen bases (excluding the strike-shortened seasons of 1981 and 1994) than any year since 1975, when there were six fewer major league teams than in the 2000 season. Again, baserunning is at an all-time low for Rotisserie players. The trend towards hitting the ball out of the yard has diminished the value of single-run strategies like basestealing.

There were 2923 stolen bases in the majors last year, down 17% from the 3421 from 1999. For Rotisserie players the significance of fewer steals is that fewer players are running, and those who do run less often, thus shrinking not only the pool from which to select those basestealers, but also reducing their individual impact. While it used to be possible to have a couple of top base thieves on a roster at the same time, it is now hard to find enough of them to go once around the league. The importance of stolen bases to Rotisserie teams is underscored by the fact that the most valuable Rotisserie hitters from each major league last year – Johnny Damon in the American League and Luis Castillo in the National League – were also their leagues' stolen base leaders.

Damon was the only American Leaguer to top 40 steals in 2000; it marked the first time since 1974 there was only one 40-plus base thief in either league (again, excepting the strike-shortened 1981 season). Castillo's 62 thefts would have placed him third the previous year and ranks, all-time, as one of the lowest totals for a stolen base leader in National League history.

It is certainly easier to survive a Rotisserie season without a top baserunner than it is without a staff ace on the mound, but it is not a recommended method. Look at your own league standings and you will likely see the winner finishing in the top third or quarter of the league in steals.

So, the primary lesson from 2000 is about the value of great starting pitching. The secondary lesson from 2000 is about the importance of having a top base thief on your roster.

Studs and Duds -

To further recap the 2000 season, lets review the top Rotisserie performers from the past season, and the worst. The following All-Star teams ("Studs") reflect players at each position who earned more in 2000 relative to their previous big-league season. The complementary lists of "Duds" are those whose earnings dropped the most in 2000. The rosters shown below are fashioned like standard Rotisserie rosters, with 14 hitters and nine pitchers and the values are figured using 12 teams for the American League and 14 teams for the National League.

STUDS

Po.	American League	Gain	Po.	National League	Gain
C	Charles Johnson	+$14	C	Mitch Meluskey	+$12
C	Jorge Posada	+$12	C	Jason Kendall	+$9
1B	Frank Thomas	+$15	1B	Andres Galarraga	+$21
2B	Delino DeShields	+$25	2B	Luis Castillo	+$14
3B	Troy Glaus	+$17	3B	Phil Nevin	+$11
SS	Jose Valentin	+$21	SS	Rafael Furcal	+$27
MI	Adam Kennedy	+$19	MI	Jose Vidro	+$15
CI	Travis Fryman	+$16	CI	Derrek Lee	+$16
OF	Darin Erstad	+$33	OF	Moises Alou	+$30
OF	Bobby Higginson	+$23	OF	Richard Hidalgo	+$27
OF	Terence Long	+$17	OF	Jim Edmonds	+$25
OF	Johnny Damon	+$15	OF	Jeffrey Hammonds	+$19
OF	Mark Quinn	+$14	OF	Cliff Floyd	+$18
UT	Cristian Guzman	+$16	UT	Julio Lugo	+$20
P	Kazuhiro Sasaki	+$39	P	Daryl Kile	+$32
P	Latroy Hawkins	+$27	P	Jose Jimenez	+$28
P	Jason Isringhausen	+$25	P	Antonio Alfonseca	+$21
P	Derek Lowe	+$16	P	Jeff D'Amico	+$20
P	Jim Mecir	+$15	P	Chan Ho Park	+$19
P	Keith Foulke	+$15	P	Armando Benitez	+$19
P	Cal Eldred	+$15	P	Robb Nen	+$19
P	Jeff Fassero	+$14	P	Gabe White	+$18
P	Frank Castillo	+$14	P	Curtis Leskanic	+$18

DUDS

Po.	American League	Loss	Po.	National League	Loss
C	Ivan Rodriguez	-$15	C	Eddie Taubensee	-$14
C	Dan Wilson	-$7	C	Michael Barrett	-$10
1B	Jose Offerman	-$15	1B	Rico Brogna	-$19
2B	Homer Bush	-$23	2B	Craig Biggio	-$15
3B	Vinny Castilla	-$17	3B	Fernando Tatis	-$21
SS	Omar Vizquel	-$12	SS	Rey Ordonez	-$10
MI	Randy Velarde	-$16	MI	Alex Arias	-$10
CI	Tony Clark	-$12	CI	Matt Williams	-$18
OF	Carlos Beltran	-$19	OF	Larry Walker	-$23
OF	Juan Gonzalez	-$15	OF	Roger Cedeno	-$20
OF	Albert Belle	-$15	OF	Reggie Sanders	-$17
OF	Marty Cordova	-$14	OF	Devon White	-$15
OF	Brady Anderson	-$14	OF	Tony Gwynn	-$15
UT	John Jaha	-$20	UT	Kevin Young	-$14
P	David Cone	-$27	P	Billy Wagner	-$35
P	Billy Taylor	-$25	P	Jose Lima	-$33
P	Jose Mesa	-$22	P	Mike Jackson	-$31
P	Roy Halladay	-$20	P	Ugueth Urbina	-$28
P	Bobby Howry	-$20	P	Omar Daal	-$27
P	Mike Trombley	-$20	P	Kevin Millwood	-$21
P	Omar Olivares	-$19	P	John Smoltz	-$20
P	Jeff Zimmerman	-$19	P	Shane Reynolds	-$17
P	Darren Oliver	-$19	P	Scott Williamson	-$17

The list of "Studs" is full of young hitters who got their first shot at regular play, such as Troy Glaus, Adam Kennedy, Terence Long, Mark Quinn, Mitch Meluskey, Rafael Furcal and Julio Lugo interspersed with veterans returning to full-time play following injury, such as Andres Galarraga, Moises Alou, Jim Edmonds. The "Stud" pitchers are mostly newly anointed closers, such as Kazuhiro Sasaki, Latroy Hawkins, Jason Isringhausen, Keith Foulke, Jose Jimenez and Curtis Leskanic.

The "Duds" are primarily players who suffered an injury and lost significant playing time, such as Ivan Rodriguez, Homer Bush, John Jaha, Fernando Tatis, Tony Gwynn, Billy Wagner, Mike Jackson, and Ugueth Urbina. Many other "Dud" pitchers are closers who lost their role in 2000, such as Billy Taylor, Jose Mesa, Bobby Howry, Mike Trombley, and Scott Williamson.

It is important to note that of the 36 pitchers on these lists, more than half are relievers, which should help stress the fleeting nature of this role. Rotisserie players know this already, of course, but it can't be emphasized too much that saves are very much a function of managerial choice. Thus it is always risky business to spend big money on closers. Attentive Rotisserie owners who pick up "closers in waiting" are often rewarded with new low-priced closers by mid-season.

Players on both lists are likely to return to more normal levels of play in 2001. That is to say that the "Studs" will be more likely to drop back towards the pack while the "Duds" will be more likely to improve. Pick your sleepers from the "Duds" – not the "Studs." Expect to pay top dollar to acquire players from the "Studs" list in 2001.

Welcome Back -

The following players each performed far below expectations or were injured – or sat out the season in order to compete in the Olympics, like Dave Nilsson – in the year 2000 and can be expected to bounce back to more consistent levels in 2001 –

Catchers: Ivan Rodriguez, Dave Nilsson, Eddie Taubensee, A. J. Hinch, and Michael Barrett.
First Basemen: Mark McGwire, John Olerud, Sean Casey, Tony Clark, Jose Offerman, Rico Brogna, and Doug Mientkiewicz.
Second Basemen: Craig Biggio, Chuck Knoblauch, Todd Walker, Warren Morris, Homer Bush, and Marlon Anderson.
Third Basemen: Vinny Castilla, Matt Williams, Fernando Tatis, Robin Ventura, and Aaron Boone.
Shortstops: Mike Caruso, Tim Bogar, Rey Ordonez.
Outfielders: Juan Gonzalez, Albert Belle, Tony Gwynn, Rusty Greer, Roger Cedeno, Darryl Hamilton, Carlos Beltran, Quinton McCracken, Karim Garcia, J. D. Drew, and Chad Allen.
Designated Hitter: John Jaha.
Starting Pitchers: John Smoltz, Francisco Cordova, Charles Nagy, Shane Reynolds, Wilson Alvarez, Andy Ashby, Juan Guzman, Jose Rosado, Pete Harnisch, Ismael Valdes, Omar Daal, Jason Schmidt, Sterling Hitchcock, Darren Oliver, Hideki Irabu, Justin Thompson, Matt Morris, Scott Elarton, Paul Byrd, Dave Mlicki, and Roy Halladay.
Relief Pitchers: Billy Wagner, Mike Jackson, Ugueth Urbina, Tom Gordon, Matt Mantei, Doug Brocail, and Jeff Zimmerman.

These players should form a separate list for Draft Day. If they are still available at a point in the draft long past when they should have been selected, chances are they have been forgotten and can be purchased at a fraction of their real value.

Out with the Old: Fading Stars -

For some, the slide began a few years ago and is continuing in earnest. For others, the slippery slope just became slippery. In any case, each of these players have peaked and will fade rapidly over the next few years. These players can be expected to perform below their 2000 value, significantly so in many cases. Be very careful not to bid more than a bare minimum for these players or, better yet, not at all:

Catchers: Darrin Fletcher, Todd Hundley, Benito Santiago, and Joe Girardi.

First Basemen: Rafael Palmeiro, Fred McGriff, Andres Galarraga, Todd Zeile, Jeff Conine, Mike Stanley, Hal Morris, Gregg Jefferies, and Will Clark.

Second Basemen: Mark McLemore, Mike Lansing, Luis Sojo, Luis Alicea, Mickey Morandini, Jay Bell, and Lenny Harris.

Third Basemen: Ron Coomer, Cal Ripken, Jr., Ken Caminiti, Jeff Huson, Mike Benjamin, and Dave Magadan.

Shortstops: Mike Bordick and Kevin Elster.

Outfielders: Dante Bichette, Ellis Burks, Paul O'Neill, Rickey Henderson, Brady Anderson, Troy O'Leary, Jay Buhner, Chad Curtis, Brian L. Hunter, Bobby Bonilla, Tom Goodwin, Larry Walker, Steve Finley, B. J. Surhoff, John VanderWal, Marquis Grissom, Davey Martinez, Bernard Gilkey, and Lance Johnson.

Designated Hitters: Edgar Martinez, Jose Canseco, and Harold Baines.

Starting Pitchers: Terry Mulholland, Willie Blair, Mike Morgan, John Burkett, Jeff Fassero, David Cone, Ken Hill and Dwight Gooden.

Relief Pitchers: Todd Jones, John Wetteland, Rick Aguilera, Mike Timlin, and Doug Jones.

In with the New: New Players and Roles for the New Millennium -

Who will be the newest Rotisserie star of the new millennium? If history is any guide, it'll be a new closer, probably in one of these cities: Cleveland, Tampa Bay, Minnesota, Texas, Atlanta, Chicago (Cubs), Milwaukee, Philadelphia, Pittsburgh or Arizona. While there are closers in the bullpens at some of these places, none are secure in their roles. Most likely, the saves will be split amongst several closers.

In Cleveland, Bob Wickman and Steve Karsay could each lay claim to the job, or it might go to Paul Shuey. In Tampa Bay, there is no clear favorite; it could be Doug Creek, or one of the club's many starters, such as Estaban Yan. Minnesota likes the look of LaTroy Hawkins in the bullpen heading into spring training, but he is far from being established in the role. After failing to re-sign John Wetteland, Texas is still hopeful of landing a full-time closer via trade or free agency.

John Rocker has seemingly put his past behind him to reclaim his closer job, but Kerry Lightenberg, Mike Remlinger and others are waiting in the wings should Rocker stumble again. Healthy again, Tom Gordon is the odds-on favorite for saves from the Cubs' bullpen, but only if he is truly healthy. Although Curtis Leskanic ended 2000 with the Brewers bullpen ace job, he hasn't yet proven able to handle it all season. Philadelphia could use any of four pitchers who have closed games in the past: Jose Mesa, Ricky Bottalico, Jeff Brantley or Wayne Gomes; only Mesa hasn't been a closer in Philadelphia at some point before the 2001 season. In Pittsburgh, Mike Williams has the job, for now, but is one of the shakier closers in the game. Arizona also shared the closer role in 2000 and may do so again in 2001.

Because there is such a great need for starting pitching, there will certainly be opportunity for young, unknown pitchers to step into important roles in 2001; some of them will succeed and become overnight sensations. In the American League, the best bets are: Matt Wise and Ramon Ortiz of Anaheim, Matt Riley of Baltimore, Tomokazu Ohka of Boston, Jon Garland and Kip Wells of the White Sox, C.C. Sabathia and Danys Baez of Cleveland, Chris George of Kansas City, Matt Kinney of Minnesota, Ted Lilly of the Yankees, Ryan Anderson of Seattle, Travis Harper of Tampa Bay, and Ryan Glynn or Doug Davis of Texas. Among this group Riley, Ohka, Garland, Lilly and Anderson are the cream of the crop.

In the National League, the best bets are: John Patterson of Arizona, Ed Yarnall of Cincinnati, Jason Marquis of Atlanta, A.J. Burnett of Florida, Eric Gagne of Los Angeles, Paul Rigdon and Ben Sheets of Milwaukee, Tony Armas, Jr. and Britt Reames of Montreal, Bronson Arroyo of Pittsburgh, Brian Tollberg and Wascar Serrano of San Diego, and Kurt Ainsworth of San Francisco. Among this group, look for Burnett, Armas, and Tollberg to have the best seasons in 2001.

Keep in mind that young starting pitchers are especially subject to wide performance fluctuations; the young phenom can go bust overnight. While most of the opportunities for young starters usually exist with struggling teams, those starters should be avoided as they often have to take their lumps as they learn on the job – an especially bad recipe for Rotisserie owners. The best kind of young starter to have is a fifth starter for a strong team. If the youngster does well, he stays in the rotation and keeps helping your team. If he goes bust, he heads back to the minors so the big club can stay in the pennant race and the kid doesn't wreck your pitching stats while he learns.

Of course, there will be plenty of position players emerging for the first time. At catcher in the American League Josh Paul of the White Sox is playing behind Sandy Alomar, Jr., who has missed many games over the years due to injury; Paul could get a real chance to play. Javier Cardona is an unknown power prospect for Detroit. A. J. Pierzynski and Matt LeCroy will battle for the catching duties in Minnesota, although they will probably each get a fair share of at-bats in 2001; Pierzynski is the better bet to come away with more playing time and better Rotisserie stats.

There will be several newcomers at second base in the American League. Jerry Hairston in Baltimore, Luis Rivas in Minnesota, and Jose Ortiz in Oakland are each expected to play a significant role in 2001; because Hairston can steal some bases and is a solid gloveman who won't losing playing time in the field he has the most to offer Rotisserie players. Should Cal Ripken, Jr., retire or miss games in Baltimore, look for Ivan on Coffie to get a shot at the majors. Russ Branyan should get 400 at-bats for the first time and could hit 30-35 homers. Highly touted Alfonso Soriano may join the Yankees as a third baseman; he is a long-shot to produce right away. Joe Crede only has to supplant Herbert Perry to play third base regularly for the White Sox.

Expect to see a lot of Luis Matos (Baltimore), Billy McMillon (Detroit), Dee Brown (Kansas City), Adam Piatt or Mario Valdez (Oakland), Jason Tyner (Tampa Bay), and Vernon Wells (Toronto) as newcomers to the American League outfield. McMillon, Brown, Piatt and Valdez could see significant time as DH, too. Wells is the best bet among this group to shine in 2001, although Tyner could become very valuable if he wins a leadoff spot as he can really run.

In the National League Jason LaRue will get to play regularly behind the plate in Cincinnati as will Ben Petrick in Colorado. Paul LoDuca has only Chad Kreuter ahead of him in Los Angeles; opportunity knocks. Rookie catchers are almost as bad for Rotisserie purposes as rookie pitchers as they often develop defensively long before they become useful major league hitters. Of these catchers LaRue and Petrick have the best potential to produce in 2001. In the National League, the best bets are at shortstop where Jimmy Rollins in Philadelphia and Santiago Perez in San Diego will each get a chance to play; both can run, so both can contribute to a Rotisserie team. Julio Zuleta has some pop in his bat and might get a full shot at the Cubs first base job. The departure of Ken Caminiti opens the door for Chris Truby to play regularly at hitter-friendly Enron Field. Personnel changes in St. Louis should give Placido Polanco and Chris Haas ample opportunity to get at-bats. Shortstop Timoniel Perez has speed and can hit; he may get 300 at-bats for the Mets. If Kevin Young keeps struggling, the Pirates could give Alex Hernandez a chance at first base.

Top prospects Corey Patterson (Cubs) and Milton Bradley (Expos), speedster Juan Pierre of Colorado, outfielder/ first baseman Daryle Ward of Houston, power/speed combo Alex Escobar of the Mets, and Mike Darr of San Diego will get plenty of chances in the outfield. Darr has the greatest opportunity due to sparse competition and has potential to produce in a variety of ways, although Patterson is the best long-range prospect of the bunch. Chad Hermansen of Pittsburgh could easily shake the "failed prospect" label to have a fine season in 2001.

Final Thoughts: Pitching, Pitching and More Pitching -

The unabated trend towards hitting has simplified the Rotisserie baseball game in many respects. Now the trick on Draft Day is to get quality pitching wherever you can find it and also acquire base thieves, and then fill in your remaining hitters from the vast player population that has power potential. You'll always be able to find power hitters at the end of the draft, so make sure you take care of your other needs first. Even if you don't really need the additional pitching or speed, be sure to get it where you can because a commodity in short supply can become very valuable as the pennant races heat up.

If you doubt this, try trading a power hitter at mid-season for that one base thief you need to put you over the top. The basestealer's owner will inevitably drive a hard bargain since he has access to a very limited supply of stolen bases. He can find power hitters anywhere: they are on every roster. You, on the other hand, have limited options when it comes to getting some additional steals. Its better to acquire those steals on Draft Day than have to go begging for them at the trade deadline.

This ideal of having more than you applies doubly to starting pitching. Inevitably pitchers get hurt. When they do you will be able to replace them from your own supply instead of having to trade for them. Or, you can use them as trade bait yourself to acquire the missing elements for your own pennant chase.

STRATEGY AND TACTICS
by John Benson

Where to begin?

If I start out by assuming that all of the readers here have been following my work for years, then I am going to leave some folks disoriented right out of the starting gate. On the other hand, if I start at the very beginning, some long-time readers are going to yawn and ho-hum and wish I would get to the point faster. And what about those who found this chapter a year ago?

This is, I suppose, no time to be modest. I could write a book on the subject of Rotisserie strategies, have written a book in fact, have written two books on the subject (*Rotisserie Baseball Volumes I and II* — see inside back cover). So for this current exercise, rather than roll out the encyclopedia, I will try to focus on selected items that seem to come up frequently in conversation, in calls to my advice line over the last couple of years, since those books first appeared. And I will try to focus mainly on items that are new, newly interpreted, possibly subject to misunderstanding or forgetfulness, or just newly verbalized.

GENERAL PLANNING CONSIDERATIONS

> Always have an objective

Consider these two calls from advice-seekers ...

Caller #1 - Should I trade a $15 Ray Durham for a $15 Dean Palmer?
JB - What's your objective?
Caller #1: I need more power and have excess speed.
JB - Yes, go ahead and do that. You could ask for more, but the deal accomplishes your objective.

And ...

Caller #2 - Should I trade a $15 Dean Palmer for a $15 Ray Durham?

JB - What's your objective?
Caller #2 - I need more speed and have excess power.
JB - Yes, go ahead and do that. You could ask for more, but the deal accomplishes your objective.

Whether you are working within the tiny context of a tactical trade negotiation, or designing your whole draft strategy for the coming year and beyond, you will do better if you clarify your objective before taking any steps. Winners tend to focus early and stay focused a long time. Losers tend to lack focus much of the time and to change their focus frequently.

Following are some examples of clear objectives for the coming season:

- "Finish first, no matter what it takes."

- "Finish in the money this year, and save enough future value to finish in the money again next year."

- "I just want to finish higher than this one chump who bugs the heck out me."

- "Build for 2001 and beyond."

As illustrated in some of the examples below, and in Tony Blengino's personal tips in this edition, finishing first is a goal which requires an early focus and constant attention. Becoming clear about the goal is the first step to achieving it.

> Stick with your determined objective as long as possible, even while it hurts.

After a winter of planning and strategizing based on the belief that your team is good enough to win this year, it's unlikely that your chances for winning can be ruined by a tough start. Even a lackluster draft and weak April performances by key players are unlikely to crush a team that was good enough to focus on first place on April 1. One of the wonderful aspects of the baseball season is its great length. Luck has a tendency to balance out, over time.

One helpful metaphor for me is to think of strategy as a large ship on a charted course. Concepts like putting on the brakes, making sharp turns, and reversing direction simply do not apply. The decisions that you make before and during the draft will have a definite momentum as the season unfolds. Very rarely is it a good idea to fight that momentum. Minor shifts in direction, yes. Major changes, no. Rarely.

> **Set your objective as early as possible.**

Like everything in life, starting early correlates with success when it comes to Rotisserie competition. If you weren't poring over 2000 minor league results as soon as they became available in September, you weren't doing everything you could to get ready for 2001 ... but some of your opponents might have been doing just that. Especially in a zero sum game, where it's important for you to get players before the opposition, and generally do unto them before they do it to you, waiting and waiting to formulate a clear objective will cost you, eventually.

> **Develop an integrated set of actions.**

To a large extent, this strategy will take care of itself once you have defined a clear objective. If you consider each tactical decision in terms of how it fits your grand plan, then the collected tactical maneuvers and each step along the way will become an integrated set of actions. Until this concept becomes habit, and even for us elderly veterans who think we never forget it, wisdom dictates thinking of detail actions collectively.

For example, if your plan is to finish first at all cost, then you can see a number of necessary steps before you get to them. You know you will be trading away some low price youngsters for some high price veterans as soon as the draft is over, so you may as well start thinking along those lines as soon as possible, even before the draft. You know you will need to make life difficult for your arch rival(s), so you better plan before the draft how to do that: bring up the players he needs early, when

everyone has lots of money and open roster slots (or in the case of a straight draft, put the squeeze on catcher or shortstop or ace reliever or whatever the other guy needs and you don't need).

Going for first place at all cost, you will need an information edge. If you are thinking about subscribing to a new periodical, or getting on-line access to box scores (STATS On Line and PSX are great), or adding any other weapons to your arsenal, do it as early as possible if your intention is to win. Especially on the information front, playing catch-up can be fatal.

> **You may change your objective once in each season, never twice.**

Simple as this rule sounds, it's amazing how frequently it gets violated, and by smart people who should know better. This rule is closely tied to the maxim of following an integrated set of actions.

The world has changed. Just ten years ago, it was possible for an astute owner to dominate a league year after year, cleaning up on draft day with superior knowledge that kept a steady flow of high-value players coming into the franchise at low prices. That kind of broad dominance is no longer possible, unless you play in one of those leagues that allow you to keep star players forever (which can be fun, but it sure isn't standard).

Every year, more and more, victory in each league goes to the one owner who is most single-minded about winning the current year. Once you become 100% clear that winning in the current year is your only objective, then all sorts of integrated actions begin to jump at you. Take freeze lists, for example. You look at all the marginal cases where you're not sure whether to extend a player for another year at an additional $5 salary, and all those cases where you're torn between two years at $10 or three years at $15.

To finish first this year, settle all freeze questions in favor of having more money on draft day (i.e. when in doubt, don't extend). If you can find just three cases where you save $5 apiece, that's $15 more for draft day, enough to buy one whole healthy everyday productive outfielder instead of a pure zero on your roster. That much value is enough to lift any team from third to first in the typical highly competitive league.

That single-minded focus will actually accelerate during the season. Undoubtedly anyone strong enough to set a goal of winning this year will emerge from the draft with some bargains here and there. Trading those bargains early, to get higher-priced stars in return, becomes a matter of some urgency. Why? Because the sooner you get the high-price stars onto your roster, the more impact those players will have for you. Getting a $55 Ken Griffey when his owner throws in the towel on July 31 isn't nearly as good (in fact, it's less than half as beneficial) as getting the high-priced Junior in mid May. Trading later, you get two months of benefit. Trading at the earlier date, you get four and a half months of benefit. How much is that two and a half month difference worth? Often about two and a half places in the standings!

Some of the following strategies will flesh out exactly which integrated actions should come into play, depending on your selected overall objective, but some examples are enough to show the theme. Obviously the owner who gets focused on his objective early and single-mindedly is going to do better than an owner who takes a "see what happens" approach on draft day and then sits on his roster inactively until late July when he finally decides whether to go for this year or next year; by then it's too late to do very well in either race, because others have already gotten off to big head starts in both directions.

Finally, on the question of when it's appropriate to change strategies, there has to be some break point. Playing for first place all year, when your best pitcher has gone out with a torn rotator cuff, and your best hitter has been traded to the other league, can be just plain stupid. But how do you know when to turn pessimistic? I look at it this way: all year, I keep asking myself, "What will it take to win?" If the answers are plausible, such as I need to trade one gem keeper for a $30 slugger within the next month, and I need a couple of my problem pitchers to start performing around their career norms, and then I can win, surely I will stick with the current year objective. But when I start getting answers like, I need John Flaherty to hit .300 with 20 homers and I need all

three of my setup relievers to inherit closer roles within the next week or so, then it's obviously time to get realistic and start thinking about the longer term.

Switching from a rebuilding strategy to a "win this year" strategy is a much rarer case of reversing direction than is the decision to give up and start rebuilding, but shifting your attention from next year to this year can sometimes be appropriate—and a lot of fun, too. The fundamental question is the same, and you should never avoid asking this question, even when you have already decided to dump: what will it take to win this year? Sometimes the answer is a lot more achievable than you guessed on draft day, especially if most owners have dumped and the teams going for this year have been running into bad luck.

BEFORE THE DRAFT

> Know the four stages of competition.

Long ago, I proposed that Rotisserie competition can be viewed in terms of four component parts:

(1) scouting and forecasting,

(2) player valuation and rankings,

(3) conduct of the draft, and

(4) managing your roster during the season. The roster management aspect (if you retain players) then continues through the winter and into the next year, starting the cycle again.

These four components will all be critical, no matter whether you are going for this year or building for the long-term future. The strategy just provides focus within each component. For example, when scouting and forecasting for the current year, you want to identify players likely to be high value in the current year, hopefully from opening day immediately. When working on a three-year plan, your scouting and forecasting time can be dedicated to rookies, prospects, and minor leaguers.

> **Spend the most time on scouting and forecasting.**

The "information edge" is the key to winning. That fact applies in midsummer as well as during draft preparation, but it's most important early in the season.

Even as our game has changed, so it's no longer easy to find any high-value players at low prices on draft day, still the information edge is as powerful as ever. Now that leagues are tight and "everybody has the same information," a tiny edge in information can yield a big edge in standings points. With all teams packed tightly together on the standings, finding an extra five stolen bases or a half a dozen home runs overlooked by the other owners, can have just as big an impact on standings as finding a $25 for $5 might have done a few years ago.

I urge everyone to look behind published dollar values, to understand as much as possible about what's happening in every player's career and—just as important — what's happening in every manager's and GM's mind. That's why we dedicate so much of the *Rotisserie Baseball Annual* to manager-viewpoint coverage of every position on every team. Even if the players change, management thinking about WHY these players were selected (or not) will carry over and be considered in handling whoever gets onto the roster, and in deciding who's on the roster.

Following are just a few of many methods that I employ to get an edge in scouting and forecasting. These illustrative examples will point the direction to other insights and considerations.

> **Look for meaning behind every winter deal.**

Even if Rotisserie owners change direction every month or two, real major league teams tend to stay on a steady course within each season and year after year. Teams that go for low budget .500 rosters will stick with that method and generally favor younger players and be extra willing to experiment. Teams that shell out big bucks to become contenders are likely to keep playing their high-priced veterans even after they are falling out of contention, and not give chances to rookie callups until after the team is mathematically eliminated.

Winter deals point the direction that each team is going. The Pirates and Expos were obviously building around low salaries long before the winter began, and the Marlins jumped on the same bandwagon as soon as the 1997 World Series was over. Some of the other teams are going to be hedging their bets right up through spring training, and the moves they make during the final week of spring games will tell you if they are going to favor youth or experience in 2001.

> **Be wary of emerging youngsters in spring training.**

Management "announcements" during spring training, especially when they relate to younger players challenging veterans, are often issued for reasons other than informing the public about who's really going to play. It is a widespread source of disinformation, to say that a bright young rookie is on his way to displacing a proven veteran, when the real situation is little more than management's desire to see the veteran become less complacent and work harder.

In 2000, we learned a corollary to this rule: don't be wary of youngsters emerging on low-salary teams. You would have missed Lance Berkman and Barry Zito.

> **Use spring training "games finished" to search for saves.**

It's flattering to see how many emerging experts have acquired this method, which I first published ten years ago. One problem with the spring training schedule is that it doesn't provide enough games for saves to be a meaningful statistic. Some ace relievers get zero saves, or one or two, during spring training. Some middle relievers can get three or four saves just by pitching in the right place at the right time, saving split squad games, pitching the day after the ace reliever pitched, etc.

One stat that does come up frequently enough to be meaningful, is the game finished stat. Every game has a "GF" while a save can only occur in a victory, with a close score. Besides being more common, the GF is also useful because it sheds light into each manager's thinking. During spring training, the manager will routinely send out his ace reliever to pitch the ninth inning (and only the ninth inning) every other day during the last two weeks before opening day. Thus an ace reliever can be expected to accumulate six or eight games finished.

On days when the ace reliever doesn't work, the manager will send out another short reliever, theoretically someone worth getting a look as a closer. These pitchers will accumulate GF stats and will stand out, by the end of spring training, as the obvious alternate closers in the manager's thinking. Such information is useful not only on draft day but throughout the season.

This method is as reliable as ever. In 2000 it would have put you on the trail of Antonio Alfonseca, Jose Jimenez, and just about anyone else you can think of in the emerging ace reliever population.

> **Scrutinize spring training box scores.**

Experimental and tune-up games in Florida and Arizona tell more about managers' thinking than any lengthy essays could accomplish. Who's batting cleanup, who's leading off, who's been relegated to batting eighth ... all these little clues speak volumes about future value.

During 1997 spring training there were magazine covers featuring the question of whether Scott Rolen or Todd Walker would be the best brekthrough rookie. Rolen was being given an honored place in the Phillies spring batting order (third/fourth) while the Twins had Todd Walker all over the place and often out of the lineup in Florida. Guessing which of the two top rookie third basemen would make it in 1997 was easy, based on box score usage signs.

> **Especially watch split squad games for clues.**

There is a definite culture at work when a manager decides which players are home when the team plays a split squad game, and which players get on a bus and ride to another stadium that day. The standard method is to send a famous starting pitcher and one top star on the bus, just so the fans in the other town can feel that they are watching real competition, not a "B" game. Sometimes one other obvious star will make the trip, but most of the established veterans will stay at home and play that day.

This tradition can help you see whether a marginal player is being viewed as a starter or a backup. If a player on the brink of a starting role rides the bus with the famous pitcher and the obvious superstar and the busload of backups, that's a bad sign.

Another clue for split squad games can be watching for pairs of middle infielders. Managers like to have the real shortstop and the real second baseman work together. So if you hear that a rookie is winning a starting job at one of these positions, but the two veterans keep playing together in every split squad game, you can suppose the manager is blowing smoke about the rookie breaking into the lineup.

> **Watch for batting order changes.**

The lion's share of team RBI usually belong to batters hitting in positions three, four or five. If a hitter is moved closer to 3-4-5 his opportunity to drive in runs will improve. Farther away from 3-4-5, the opportunity will diminish. When Barry Bonds hit leadoff for Pittsburgh he never had more than 59 RBI. The season he moved down in the order; 1990, he had 114 RBI, a 93% improvement over the previous year. Mike Stanley's career took off when he moved up from number eight to fifth/sixth in the Yankees' order in the mid—1990s.

Often the spring training box scores will tip you off to a change in batting order before it happens in games that count.

> **Look at your freeze list as part of the auction.**

It's amazing how many people follow separate lines of thinking for freezing versus buying players on draft day. It is the same question: do you want this player on your roster now, for $X? If you would gladly buy the player in a draft, then go ahead and freeze him. If you would hesitate early in the auction, because similar players at better prices are likely to be available later, then you should hesitate from freezing also.

The freeze and the auction are two parts of the same process: you give up money, to get players, to fill roster spots.

> **Build trade opportunities into your freeze list.**

As for setting your objective early, there is no better way to get started on next year, than to begin work before this year's auction. The two-year plan on draft day can put you in a race by yourself.

Often I have observed that, in all leagues that allow trading of players and allow retention of players from year to year, there are always two races going on simultaneously on the same race track: this year and next year. As fate would have it, the competitors who do best in each race are those who get started earliest and help each other during the season—and they get started early helping each other, too. For example, the faster the "next year" guy can trade away his high-priced stars, the more benefit will accrue to the "this year" owner who gets them. Remember: five months of Barry Bonds is worth more than twice as much as two months of Barry Bonds, so the price can (and will) be twice as high early in the year.

Trades will be fundamental to success, regardless which race you choose to run in, this year's or next year's. Visualizing these trades before the draft will ensure that you have a good draft.

Freezing a $50 Barry Bonds often makes fine sense when you're going for next year. Don't forget you can trade Bonds for three gem keepers right after the auction. Similarly, freezing a $10 rookie, who isn't expected to play much and might even get sent down, can be a fine move even when going for this year. If that youngster is likely to be attractive to the rebuilding teams, then he is a trade asset and merits consideration as a freeze.

There is an important trade consideration related to contract extensions. Earlier I said that "this year" teams would do best to save $5 wherever possible, by not extending contracts. That's true, but it doesn't mean avoiding all extensions. If you have Carlos Lee at $7 going into his option year, you cannot let him expire! He's obviously a gem keeper at $12 for 2002. So you extend Lee at $12. And then if you need more stats in 2001, you trade Lee for two high priced stars, with a team working on 2001. You know that Lee at $12 is

going to be extremely attractive to a rebuilding team. If you had let Lee play out the year at $7, you would have saved $5, but you would have nothing to trade for 2002 — and that loss would be bigger than the $5 you saved. Finally on this point, you do not raise Lee to $17 unless you are sure he is going to look like a gem keeper at $17 in May 2001. If Lee slumps in April-May 2001, he won't look like a gem keeper at $17. One or two owners might think he's OK at $17 for 2001, but you have a much less attractive trade asset than Lee at $12. And a $22 salary kills your trade asset completely.

So think of "freeze and trade" or "extend and trade" as integrated actions, not disjointed steps going in opposite directions. And on draft day, "buy and trade" can be one integrated action, started in early April and finished in mid May, as planned.

> **Watch roster size when freezing.**

Often people call me with a long list of possible keepers at low prices, and I say "yes" to each individual name, until we get so far down the list that we have, say, five outfielders being retained. The classic case is a bunch of solid $12 everyday players at prices of $1 to $9. Then when we get to the end of the list, I say wait a minute, we better go back and take another look at those guys.

The question can become one of using up roster slots, more than a question of using up money. Aside from the fact that it's a tactical advantage to have one outfield slot open until late in the auction, just in case a gem bargain floats by, it is also wise to make sure you get your fair share of high-value outfielders. Freezing five $12 players at $5 apiece could be a path to disaster, if there aren't enough high value players (and roster slots) available to get the benefit of that extra cash.

> **View your freeze list as a lifeboat.**

The freeze list allows you to carry a number of players from one year to the next. In most leagues, this number is limited, and in some leagues it is extremely limited. The key point is understanding that anyone who doesn't fit into your freeze list "lifeboat" cannot help your team, at least not actively. Yet there are many useful ways to get value from those wasting assets.

> **With a strong freeze list, make two-for-one and three-for-one deals.**

Say your 15th-best freeze has a $6 implicit profit, your 16th best has a $4 profit, and your 17th best has a $2 profit. You can only keep 15. So you trade all three of them to another team with a weak freeze list, and you get back in trade one freeze with a $10 profit. You're happy because your lifeboat has $4 more value (that 15th freeze's profit went from $6 to $10). The other trader is happy because (assuming he didn't have 15 good freezes but only 12 or 13) his lifeboat went up in value by $2 (the one +$10 freeze changed into a $6, a $4, and a $2).

> **If you can't trade away excess freezes, "place" them.**

Suppose in the above example you couldn't find any trade like the one illustrated. Do you give up and just release the +$4 freeze and the +$2 freeze? Heck, no. You trade them to your buddy Joe, for two overpriced bums (or better yet, not two bums, but two good yet overpriced players you would like to see coming back into the auction). Joe is happy to be getting two more freezes, and you're happy because those two players won't hurt you in the standings, especially if you pick the right kind of players to park on Joe's roster. And of course Joe might remember that you did him a favor, and be more inclined to trade with you rather than your arch rival in the coming year.

> **Offer marginal freezes around in trade.**

What you're doing here is collecting free information. Nobody says, just because you offer a player in trade to see what gets offered back, that you have to make any trade. So if you have a $12 Luis Castillo, and with inflation in your league, you figure Castillo is worth $15 and has upward possibilities, and the bottom line is you would be willing to pay $12 for Castillo if the auction was going on right now. Should you freeze him? Maybe. Offer Castillo to three owners who should appreciate his value. If they all scoff at you, then it appears you have a good chance to get Castillo for under $12 on draft day, so you may throw him back (I am assuming you have a good freeze list anyway). If you end up paying $13 for Castillo, so it cost you a buck. But if you buy him for $5 late in the draft, then you have gained $7. Play the odds.

> **Shark tip: deceive people who offer marginal freezes around in trade.**

In the above example, scoff at the guy who's thinking of freezing Dmitri Young for $14, then bid $15 or more after he's thrown back.

> **When in doubt, don't freeze.**

Consistent with the roster-slot-has-value theory, be aware that every roster slot filled is an opportunity lost. If you freeze (or buy) a player with a $1 profit, you are giving up any opportunity to get a $5 or $10 profit in that roster slot. Most of the people reading this book are pretty astute scouts and bidders, and roster slots are worth more in their hands than in the hands of less knowledgeable folks. So if you don't feel pretty sure that a freeze is a good idea, throw the player back and see what happens. You might like it a lot.

> **Avoid questions and problems on freeze lists.**

There is one critical difference between players frozen and players bought on draft day: you have all the time in the world to think about freezes, whereas the heat of bidding may lead you to take a player at auction when you wouldn't have taken him if given more time to think. Often someone will ask me if a certain injured player with a $7 salary is likely to come back and be worth $12 like he was a year or two ago. Should such a player be frozen? How about the $10 rookie who will probably be worth $12 but might get sent back to the minors if he struggles early. Is that player a good freeze? My general answer is "no" to close calls, when the player has some significant question or problem. The freeze list is a vehicle to transport sure things onto your draft day roster. The give-and-take of the auction will yield enough players with questions and problems on every roster. I like my freeze list to be refined as much as possible: obvious keepers only.

> **Follow the "double yes" rule before freezing.**

Implicit in all of the above points about when to freeze a

player is a simple test. If you can answer "yes" to both of the following questions, then you want to freeze the player:

(1) Do you like this player at this price?

(2) Do you expect that getting this type of player at about this price would be a major success on draft day?

You may think that Neifi Perez is worth $15, so when it comes to freezing him at $10, you answer "yes" to question number one. But if the other owners in your league all believe that Perez is worth about $10, then you must answer "no" to question number two, and take a pass on this freeze decision.

> Don't estimate inflation, calculate it.

It's astounding how many people pay me good money to go over their freeze lists and plan a draft strategy, and they don't know the inflation rate in their league. Rates commonly range from 10% to 50%. Many leagues, enough for you to consider the possibility, have negative inflation (everybody freezes everybody) and many have inflation over 80%!

If you're looking at a $30 player (and of course most leagues are won or lost based on the handling of $30 players) the normal range of inflation will be $3 to $15 on that player. Obviously, guessing can lead to disaster.

The numbers you need are all there. The Draft Software does this for you, but if you don't have it, then get out a paper and pencil and a calculator, and do this exercise:

(A) How much money is in your auction? Take (for example) $260 per team ($280 using the new NL salary limit, but we will stick with $260 in this example), times the number of teams, minus the salaries of frozen players.

(B) How much value is in your auction? Again, take salary per team (e.g. $260) times the number of teams, and subtract the value of frozen players. Then divide (A) by (B). An answer of 1.25 means 25% inflation, and you need to increase all values to 25% before your auction begins.

> Mark your values list up/down before the auction.

Even if you don't use my Draft Software, you can get a leg up on your opponents by tinkering with dollar values (in writing) to suit your league, before the draft. If your league counts runs, for example, don't just go to the auction with a vague notion that you are going to bid aggressively when leadoff batters come up for bid. Write your estimated values on the papers that you will bring to the auction with you, and those adjustments will be one less factor that you have to remember during the heat of the auction. If you're in a straight draft, rearrange priority lists before, not during, the auction.

> Keep studying right up until the last moment before your draft.

Having access to a good sports radio station and/or checking on-line wire services just before your draft will yield good results. Remember: tiny edges pay bigger dividends now than they did just a few years ago. Knowing who's hurt and who's healthy is critical. Even a tiny item, like knowing which backup catcher just hit a three-run home run, can make the difference between first place and second place, when it comes to October and you're tied in home runs with your arch rival.

> But don't overstudy.

There are really two points here: (1) get a good night's sleep before draft day, and (2) don't overload the info circuits. Think of draft day as something akin to taking the Law Boards. Staying up all night cramming may add a few words to your memorized vocabulary, but losing the edge from fatigue will more than offset the benefits. And topping off the knowledge tank with details like spring training caught stealing percentages will fill up valuable brain cells with useless data.

ON DRAFT DAY

> Watch the Littlefield Effect.

There is an implicit tip underlying this advice: go back and read every edition of Glen Waggoner's RLB books, if you haven't already. If you have done that homework, then you know about John Littlefield, the Padres reliever who got two blow-em-away saves during the first week of the 1981 season, and thus had two saves by draft day, and — you guessed it — never got another save in his entire career. Littlefield sold for the price of all other obvious ace relievers on draft day, about $30.

It isn't just the obscure hot-start players who manifest the Littlefield Effect. The biggest factor to watch isn't the little snares and pitfalls here and there. The biggest factor is the massive undervaluation of established stars in every league every year. And I do mean every league. Even the most experienced and most dispassionate competitors tend to pay too much attention to the first couple weeks of stats; it's a natural result following a winter of starving for stats and box scores. Whatever comes in first gets over-scrutinized, rather like the New Hampshire primaries.

In 1994 I won an all-champions invitational league, which drafted about three weeks into the season, by loading up with big stars off to slow starts: Barry Larkin, Bip Roberts, Tony Gwynn ... you get the idea. Eleven highly astute owners sat there and let me get away with it. It's just human nature to look in the paper and believe what you see.

> **Don't be afraid to pay top prices for top players.**

On draft day your two major goals are (1) profits — get bargain players at low prices, and (2) value — acquiring your fair share of reliable, high-value players. While engaged in bargain-hunting, too many competitors forget the fair share question. Consider this caricature: Filling a roster with 23 players worth $10 each, with salaries of only $5, might sound good, but you'll have $150 to spend on your 23rd player, and of course you will lose.

See the essay Practical Auction Budgeting for more (in that two-volume set).

> **Don't pursue specific players.**

It just amazes me how many well-prepared competitors blow months of study by losing perspective on draft day.

They call me and ask the question: "Who should I go after this year?" If you ever catch yourself thinking along the lines of "go after" when planning for draft day, and that's your main line of draft preparation, then you must stop yourself and rethink the purpose of the draft in your path to victory.

Targeting a specific player is only appropriate as a narrow tactical maneuver, after you have ensured having enough bargains on your roster, after you have thought through who is available at each position, after you have decided which positions and which stat categories offer the best and most opportunities for bargains, and after you have designed tactics to interfere with your arch rivals accomplishing their objectives. I won't say you should never target a specific player, because I have done it myself, but only after careful study.

> **For every purpose in the draft, list as many names as possible to help accomplish that purpose.**

Thinking of specific names is the final step of draft planning, and when you get to that step, you want to be making long lists of acceptable players, not short lists of must-get players. Whether you need speed, or saves, or a middle infielder, or a starting pitcher, always begin by thinking about that general need and probing everywhere before forming a plan to fulfill that need. The answer may be two players, not one. The answer may be a post-draft trade, not an acquisition on draft day. And whatever the answer is, it should be developed with a long list of players who can help.

> **Deviate from published dollar values when appropriate.**

There are two points here. Published dollar values are never precise. Would you take investment advice from a stock broker who tells you he is certain that the Dow Jones average a year from now is going to be 9549.67 because his computer model say so? Or would you be more comfortable with a guru who says that, based on his understanding of technical and fundamental trends (which he can explain, if you like) the DJIA is likely to be in the 9200 to 9900 range a year from now? The former expert is clearly deluding himself and anyone who listens to him. The latter has a better grip on reality.

All kinds of forces can operate to make calculated dollar values more or less appropriate in any auction, or at different moments within the same auction. Several of these are presented in our introduction to the forecast stats and values: optimal bidding, draft inflation, budgeting moves, etc.

My advice is NOT to disregard or disrespect published values, just put them into context. A dollar or two in any direction means nothing. A five dollar adjustment — even when you believe the underlying forecast stats and value calculation — may be perfectly appropriate for a given tactical situation, and I don't mean an inflation adjustment; I mean a deliberate departure from calculated value including inflation.

My advice is simply to have a reason, and to know it, and to be able to explain it to yourself (not to others, please) if you had to. Then it's OK to deviate from published values.

> **Early in the auction, nominate the type of players you don't need.**

If you go into the auction with two ace relievers, it should help your cause immensely to nominate all the remaining ace relievers before nominating any players you really need. This step will accomplish several purposes.

First, you will help the natural market forces to prop up the price of all remaining ace relievers, while everyone has plenty of money and plenty of vacant roster slots. No one will beat you by getting a proven ace for half of true value, as might happen later in the auction when money and roster slots have dried up.

Another purpose you will accomplish will be flushing money out from whoever has it, thus increasing your chances to get bargains on the types of players you do need.

Third, the maintaining of high prices on all ace relievers will prop up the trade value of your two aces; it wouldn't help if you freeze two aces at $35 apiece and then the auction makes it look like they were worth only $25 each. Finally, bringing up the type of players you don't need will put the squeeze on everyone who does need them.

This tactic works with any stat category and any position. Whatever you don't need, bring it up and make others pay. Whatever you do need, wait, save your money, and look for bargains.

> **Early in the auction, bring up players who are difficult to value.**

The wonderful aspect of this game is that people have different opinions. The same player may appear like a $20 star to one owner, while he's nothing more than a $5 speculation in the eyes of another owner. Obviously in such cases we are not talking about healthy, established star hitters; we are talking about players with questions or problems of some kind: rookies, players with insecure roles but high potential, players rehabbing from injuries, fading veterans possibly poised for a comeback, etc.

The more of these hard-to-value players you can bring up early, the more money you will flush out. Just bringing up all the rookie starting pitchers is a fine method to get you through the first ten rounds of any auction. Obviously, however, you don't want to bring up the guys you like yourself, the ones who might be real sleepers from your point of view.

> **Nominate players your arch rival needs, early.**

The flipside of nominating what you don't need is focusing on specific needs of your arch rival(s) and making sure they pay top dollar to fill their needs. If your toughest competitor is dying for a power hitter, and you're OK in that department, then just say the name of the top home run threat still available, every time it's your turn.

> **In 2001, pursue stolen bases.**

The offensive explosion of the expansion era has lifted every offensive category except one: stolen bases. Obviously, neither manager is going to be inclined to try one-run tactics when the score resembles a football game, like 7-0 or 10-3 or 14-7, as happened frequently since 1994. The relative scarcity of steals, versus home runs, simply hasn't sunk in yet. Most of the preseason forecasts and published values for 2001 don't fully reflect the new reality.

The rate of decrease in stolen bases slowed and then stopped in 1997. There were even some surprises in unexpected sources of speed. The players who steal five to ten bases had just about disappeared in 1995 to 1996, compared to a decade earlier, and they began to reappear in 1997. Why? Pitching has become so diluted, holding runners can be overlooked when the manager needs to find an arm which can throw strikes and keep the ball in the park most of the time. Mike Hargrove told me there are pitchers in the game today, where he could steal a base off them. Some catchers who don't throw well enough to discourage any runner are also part of the story.

Stolen bases remain rare, nonetheless.

> **Be ready to pay top dollar for premium starters.**

Expansion has put two dozen pitchers in the major leagues, who don't belong there. Everyone above them gets promoted: long relievers become fifth starters, and fifth starters become three/four men in their rotations in 2001.

The best meanwhile remain as good as ever. Greg Maddux and Pedro Martinez and their peers will be worth bids of $40 and up in many leagues. There just aren't many reliable starters left in the game.

> **When rebuilding, look at each player in terms of how good he might become.**

Here is a very important case where having an objective affects how you bid and build your roster. Everybody has the same $260 (or $280), but if you decide that you aren't going to spend any of your money for so-so mediocre middle-age talent at full prices, then you can allocate more money to young players for the future and high-price genuine stars whom you will trade away for more youngsters as the season unfolds.

One of the nice aspects of rebuilding is that a future star won't hurt you by flopping in his rookie season. You may decide to throw him back rather than keep him at the end of the year, but the harm done to you is minimal compared to what that player would have done to a contender who shelled out $15 for $2 worth of production.

> **Weakness loves risk; strength loves certainty.**

Rebuilding isn't the only viable strategy for a weak team. Surprises do happen. Some of the most satisfying victories in this game come from taking a weak freeze list and managing it all the way to first place. To succeed this year, weak teams need to take chances. Getting more rookie starters, more rehab cases, and more high-potential kids with weak track records, all increase your chances of getting lucky. They also increase your chances of getting burned, of course. Strong teams stay away from such players. But if you want to win this year, and the outlook is gloomy, buy a few players who could be characterized as lottery tickets: low price, slim chance of success, but with a big payoff if they do hit.

Strong teams lean the opposite way. The stronger your team, the more you want to get players who have no questions, no problems, no injuries, no controversies. A player who is worth about $10, and you know it, can be a better investment than a rookie who will be worth $20 if he clicks but only $2 if he flops.

> **Be contrary.**

Having a good draft is simple. Just refuse to move with the herd. When everyone is bidding up the price of power hitters, spend your money on speedy leadoff men. When everyone else is shunning expensive starters, buy a solid five-man rotation. Whatever everyone else is overvaluing, stay away from it. It's a fact that when too much money goes into one commodity, then other commodities must be available at bargain prices.

Having a solid foundation in valuation methods (or a wonderful, accurate list of values from a source authority) is the first half of being a successful contrarian. The other half of the battle is liberating your thinking about specific details concerning what you must accomplish on draft day.

> **You don't need a balanced roster on draft day.**

Often people approach the draft with unbearable anxiety about some scarce commodity. People often call me with comments like, "There are only three good starting pitchers available and everybody needs one, so I must plan on spending $30 or more to get one," or "With only two big home run hitters in this year's draft, I'm going to pay up to $55 for Mark McGwire because I need power badly." Such thinking misses the fact that each season is six months long.

You don't have to finish the draft with a balanced roster. You could finish the draft with only one starting pitcher, trade for two more starters in May-June, and then get more starters in July. One year I went through the month of September with eight starters, to reach a stringent IP minimum of 1,170. Just because your league rules steer you toward having at least five starters, doesn't mean you must have five starters on May 1.

Confined thinking is a major cause of suffering in Rotisserie baseball, and it's almost always self-imposed. Your opponents may help to create discomfort, but you can keep a clear mind by simply asking yourself "why" repeatedly, whenever you find yourself thinking about what you "must" do on draft day. It's a long, long season, offering plenty of time to shift your roster toward whatever you need.

After the draft, you can change your starter/reliever mix, or your power/speed balance, or whatever. You can spend 90% of your money on hitting, or 90% on pitching on draft day, and then trade for what you need later.

Understanding this flexibility is the key to the flexible strategy that guarantees a strong draft: be contrary. It astounds me how many smart competitors lock themselves into rigid thinking and then get battered on draft day, feeling at the mercy of external forces throughout the auction, not enjoying the draft, sweating and worrying, and not getting the young and improving players that make an owner feel good about his roster. Many people who fall into this trap come to the draft with excellent preparation and a deep knowledge of the player population, but then they get derailed on their way to picking a good team because they let the herd stampede them, and because they won't let go of their preconceived notion of what their post-draft roster must look like.

> **Spend whatever you want on hitting versus pitching.**

"But I must spend 65% of my money on hitting, and 35% on pitching; you say so yourself." Wrong. I never said that. What I have been saying for ten years is an observable fact: in all leagues as a group, worldwide, year after year, all owners as a group spend 65% of their money on hitting, consistently. And it doesn't vary much. Every year 99% of all leagues fall within the range 61% to 69%, and 80% of leagues fall within 63% to 67%. Within these leagues, however, there will be individual teams that may spend over 80% on hitting, or under 50%.

Opportunities present themselves in every draft, because not all owners will use exactly the same rational, dispassionate methods of valuation and bidding. In addition, each league tends to have a unique culture when it comes to valuation, generally following the personal prejudices of individual competitors who have been successful over the years. If the smartest and most successful competitors lean passionately toward home runs, the rest of the league will usually follow them, imagining they are pursuing the one true recipe for victory. If the perpetual winners favor stolen bases and saves, the other owners will shift their thinking along those lines, too, by observing and imitating.

> **You have to be lucky with starting pitchers.**

While it often makes fine sense to fill up your hitter slots with solid value at fair prices, it is rarely wise to do that with starting pitchers. The unspoken understanding of this fact of life is part of the reason why each league in total spends only 35% of its money on pitching every year.

If you pay full value ("fair value") for any player, you deny yourself the opportunity to get lucky with that player; the best you can do is to get what you pay for. Getting what you pay for is a worthy objective in the case of reliable star hitters; it is also a worthy objective for some (but not all) of your starting pitcher slots. Why? Look at any winning roster, and you find a big surprise in the starting pitcher department [if you don't believe me, go and look at the roster of last year's winner in your league]. Sometimes you find two or more big surprises among the starting pitchers on a first place roster.

Every year there is at least one starting pitcher who comes out of nowhere and produces $25 or more in value. In a tight league with everyone going for this year, the lucky owner who gets that pitcher for $6 is likely to finish first. A $19 windfall profit is usually just too big for the other contenders to overcome.

The windfall profit phenomenon among starting pitchers may occur in two or three cases, or even more, in each league each year, lifting two or three owners above the others. When there are multiple cases of windfall starting pitchers, having just one of them may not be enough to ensure victory; but you can say this much: any owner who does not get even one of them will have a darn hard time beating those who do get them. To win, you have to be lucky with starting pitchers. Filling all your starting pitcher slots with high value players at high (fair) prices, you cannot win, because you cannot get lucky. Always give yourself an opportunity or two to get lucky with starting pitchers.

> Know the valuation culture in your league.

Even if you're a new owner, you can tell which way the league is going to lean, by looking at prices paid in past auctions. Before you start bidding, you want a plan based on understanding of how those around you are going to conduct their auction. It would be nice to know each individual owner's tendencies and to use that information to your benefit; but even just knowing the general tendency of the league will help you is designing and building your roster. Some leagues love home runs. Others feast on rookies; they would rather prove their knowledge by getting this year's rookie-of-the-year, at any price, than by finishing in the money. Considering the culture ahead of time will help you be contrary, and thus help you win.

Study previous drafts. What are the various individual owners' draft tendencies? What conclusions can you draw? If a competitor has a history of going for a particular player or always tries to build his team around closers or power hitters, hit them where it hurts and bid aggressively for their "must have" players. You could

cause them to over-spend, which will hurt them later in the auction, or you may take their favorite player away. Even if you over spend they may become desperate and divert from their strategy. And if you have their favorite player it won't be long until they approach you for a trade. When they come to you, you own them.

> Downplay wins when bidding on starting pitchers.

More than any other stat, wins by pitchers are caused by factors other than the individual athlete's performance. The variability and unpredictability of wins are among the major factors that lead bidders to discount pitcher values. If you like wins, look for overlooked starters for teams that win a lot (Kevin Millwood is a good example). If you just want pure value, perk up when a starter with a consistently good B/I ratio comes up for bid.

> Look for the "Cherry Picker" of The Year.

Almost every year, some nondescript middle reliever ends up racking up seven or eight wins. Rarely do these middle relievers duplicate their success in consecutive years. It's a matter of managerial preference (using that pitcher in a tie game, or down by just a run) and in most cases these guys are found on a team with a very good offense, so they can score runs when your guy is in the game, and you get the cheap wins. Because they are middle relievers, they are almost always available cheap, or as a free agents during the season.

> Build around batting average.

Most people tend to downplay the importance of things they don't understand. Batting average is somewhat more difficult to value than home runs, stolen bases, and RBI, because you can't look at a player and see immediately that he has "twice as much batting average" compared to another player, as you can look at a 30-homer guy and see he gives you twice as much in that category as a 15-homer guy.

The minor mysteries surrounding batting average and its value can be easily removed with simple arithmetic, as you can see in my Volume Two, Playing for Blood. Unfortunately, not many competitors have the time or disposition to work through this arithmetic.

Even more unfortunate, some of the earliest writers who took a stab at BA valuation built their work upon a completely false premise, and so any useful arithmetic that may have applied, from that illogical starting point, shed no light on the subject but rather just obscured it further.

I am referring of course to the primitive notion that the "average batting average" must be worth zero. If the average batting average in a Rotisserie league is .265, with half the teams over .265 and half under, then a .265 hitter is utterly neutral, neither helping nor hurting, and "therefore his batting average must be worth zero." This theory suggests you could take the population of hitters on rosters in any standard league, and "see" that the upper half of this group is helpful by performing above average, and therefore adds value, while the lower half can be said to create a drag on batting average, and thus take away value. The conclusions of this theory are, therefore, that average batting average is worth zero, and the sum total of all hitters' contributions in BA must also add up to zero.

The clearest debunking of this myth was presented by Mike Dalecki, phrased in the form of a question printed by me ten years ago: if the average batting average is worth zero, then how do you explain the fact that a Rotisserie team with the average batting average doesn't score zero, but scores six points in that category? Obviously, the average batting average is not worth zero, and all arithmetic built on that premise is nonsense.

Value in batting average begins to accrue when your team gets lifted above the bottom of the league in the BA category, and your team begins to score points in batting average. The point of reference for zero value in batting average must therefore be the lowest TEAM batting average in your league, not the average team batting average.

Almost everyone now understands and accepts the Dalecki Principle of batting average valuation, but effects linger from the dark ages. While that ancient notion, that the sum of all batting averages must be zero and the whole category itself must be worth zero, has fled from the enlightening fact that even below-norm teams score positive points in the BA category, the lingering subjective impact of that notion, that batting average is a soft and suspect source of value, continues to affect perceptions and bidding.

I can suggest one more reason for the lack of appreciation of batting average, in addition to the effects of that old false premise which got into print, and the demands for somewhat more arithmetic to achieve full understanding of this category compared to others. The additional consideration is the fact that a player's batting average can go down, while his homers and RBI cannot. We have all known the experience of having a .295 hitter on our roster in July, and feeling the value from that asset, and then watched that hitter slump to .260 by year end, and we felt his value going down. A batter with 15 home runs in July may slump and finish the year with only 19, but we don't view that part of the slump as causing an actual drop in value (although we should because there was surely a standings impact there, too).

The disappointment of a shrinking BA is obviously akin to the feeling one gets when a pitcher's ERA goes up. The similarity of these feelings causes many to perceive the batting average category as unreliable, like ERA and B/I ratio, with the implication that batting average values should be discounted, the same as we do when assigning only 35% to pitchers in the total valuation picture. The facts, however, show that batting average is far more consistent than ERA from year to year. Batting average should not be discounted for this perceived risk, but in fact that discounting occurs every year.

The obvious strategic implication is that you can take advantage of everyone else's misunderstandings, by loading up with high average hitters. I do that every year, in every league (just by using my own calculated values and believing) and the method works marvelously.

> **The stronger your team, the more you need players with high batting average.**

One of the elusive aspects of batting average value is that every team has a different reference point. Because I love average so much (so many good things come with it!) often I have had teams with a .290 average as late as

June. With such a roster, I must view with disdain a player with a .270 average, because he will drag me down, closer to the next lower team with their .286. A .270 hitter may actually cost me points, while a low-standing team with a .255 average could get a lift of a couple of standings points by adding a solid .270 hitter in June.

The same logical arithmetic applies during the draft while you are building the roster that will produce those team stats. If you plan to build around strong hitting, then a .270 hitter is worth less to you than to another owner. Without getting too elaborate, just bid more aggressively on .290+ hitters and bid more passively on those expected to hit .265 or lower, and your roster will build itself rather nicely.

> **Watch park effects when pitchers change teams.**

Many successful pitchers owe much of their good fortune to their home ball park. A pitcher who induces hitters to hit flyballs for outs in a big stadium, could turn sour if traded to a smaller park. Sid Fernandez in 1994-95 was a vivid example. In spacious Shea Stadium, Fernandez was one of the league's best pitchers. When he moved to Baltimore and to the smaller parks of the American league his former flyball outs often left the park. Fernandez gave up 26 homers in only 109 innings in 1994 and he had the worst season of his career. Then back in the NL, he became a terrific pitcher again, before injuries set in. And I told you: Stay away from Darryl Kile in 1998. Starting pitchers crossing from the AL to the NL will generally be more effective because of the bigger parks and absence of designated hitters.

If you believe a pitcher might be affected by a change in venue, consider whether or not the pitcher in question is a fly ball pitcher who would be more effected by the distance to the fences, or if he is a ground ball pitcher who would be more affected by his new team's infield defense. A perfect example of this is the transformation of Tom Glavine into a Cy Young pitcher. In 1990, Glavine's ERA was 4.28. In 1991, the Braves installed Rafael Belliard at shortstop, Terry Pendleton at third base and Sid Bream at first base — Glavine's ERA dropped to 2.55, he won 20 games and a Cy Young award. So it isn't just the "ballpark" factor; it's also who's in the ballpark.

> **Get your last hitter from Colorado or Boston.**

Often when choosing a $1 middle infielder at the end of the draft, it's wise to pick a team rather than a player. Even a banjo hitting shortstop is capable of hitting a home run or two, and carrying a .280 average, in Colorado. The thin air makes it a hitters paradise, and a nightmare for pitchers. Wrigley Field is generous as well (lots of day games with sunshine to see the ball well, and close fences, and sometimes the wind is blowing out). Avoid Shea Stadium and Dodger Stadium. In the American league, the friendly parks include Detroit and Boston. So when in doubt about that last hitter, get Rockies or Red Sox.

CONCLUSION

The above tips will get you well-prepared for draft day and help you emerge from the draft with a solid team well on the path to your desired objective. There is more to the game, of course. We have just touched here and there on the subject of in-season roster management. (There will be plenty of advice on this subject, linked to current events as they unfold, during the regular season in the pages of my Baseball Monthly.) And there is a much-neglected aspect of strategy at ear-end: review and analyze. And that step of course gets you started again on planning for next year. But hey, just get through 2000 first!

HOW I WIN
30 Steps Toward Finishing First
by Tony Blengino

In past years, John Benson has encouraged me to write "How I Won" essays for the *Benson Baseball Monthly*, to illustrate the methods I used to come out on top in some of our highly competitive "invitation-only" leagues. After I won both our CompuServe Sports Forum NL and AL competitions in 1997, John's request changed but slightly. He asked me to change the tense of the verb in the title from the past to the present, and expand the scope of my analysis from a specific Rotisserie season to a comprehensive personal strategy.

My approach? I'll delve into some details in a moment, but it can be washed down to a handful of nouns. Knowledge, diligence, intensity and occasional calculated recklessness — all in the singleminded pursuit of winning championships — are prerequisites. There are no rebuilding seasons. There are no chucked categories. There are no self-imposed transaction budgets. There are no days off. Following is a look at my 30 Commandments of Rotisserie Success, broken down chronologically, beginning the day after the end of the World Series.

I. FALL/WINTER ANALYSIS

> Position Eligibility: Here's a big one, right off the top. As I will mention later, roster flexibility is a required trait of a winning Roti club. All but the luckiest owners get hit by injuries to their hitters over the course of a season, and you don't want to be forced to carry Craig Grebeck on your roster as a replacement. After the regular season ends, identify the players eligible at multiple positions immediately, with special attention to corner infielders and outfielders who also qualify in the middle infield.

> Transaction Logging: Welcome to baseball in the post-commissioner, Fehr-Orza Era. You simply can't take time off from baseball in late fall. Keep a simple spreadsheet or even a handwritten chart in a notebook detailing the comings and goings on each team, by league.

> Statistical Analysis (Minor Leagues): This is listed before major league statistical analysis simply because their season ends earlier. The key to interpreting numbers is to latch onto the right ones. Ignore batting average and RBI for hitters, and won-lost record and ERA for pitchers. Focus on on-base percentage and slugging percentage for hitters and strikeout/walk and strikeout/nine innings pitched ratios for pitchers. Most importantly, measure such stats RELATIVE TO THE LEAGUE. Give significantly more credit to players younger than their league average age who excel. Sound complicated? Buy my book, "*Future Stars*" -- I do it all for you. (End of plug.)

> Statistical Analysis (Major Leagues): After the major league season ends, build a simple spreadsheet. List all regular hitters in each league and group by position. Input their important numbers (all Roti numbers plus OBP and SLG), and find the average statistical output for each position in each league. Also list each player's age, and obtain the league average age at each position. This helps you identify not only "weak" and "strong" positions in both leagues, but also highlights positions where significant turnover is ready to take place. If all major league second basemen average 27 years old, for instance, it might not make much sense to stock up on second base prospects in your minors.

> Draft Software/Projections: Get your mitts on the "right" projections. That is, anything with John Benson's or Bill James' name on it. They are not only consistently accurate, they are also available relatively early in the offseason. Either use draft software, like John Benson's, or create a spreadsheet which allows you not only to calculate values for players by position, but also to break down players' values by category. You need to ensure that you're building a balanced roster on draft day. Draft software eliminates the guesswork at a nominal cost. A major point — also calculate players' values as A PERCENTAGE OF THE TOTAL VALUE AVAILABLE AT THEIR POSITION.

II. SPRING TRAINING

> **Limit Your Radar Screen:** It's March 3, and you notice that Jack Cust hit two triples to lead the D'backs to a spring victory. Who cares? Cust might be a decent intermediate-term prospect, but he has no chance to make a 2001 impact. Know going into spring training the 35 players most likely to secure a major league role on each club, along with the impact prospects who could break through (Jose Guillen, anyone?). Don't be swayed by anyone else's performance. You've got better things to do.

> **Temper Your Enthusiasm:** Do not overreact to huge spring training performances by known quantities. Former Phillie Ricky Jordan was notorious for roasting Grapefruit League pitching, especially minor leaguers looking to impress by throwing fastballs for strikes. Then Jordan would head north, face pitchers throwing breaking balls for strikes, and turn back into a pumpkin. If it looks like a duck and quacks like a duck, it's still a duck even if it's hitting .800 on March 10.

> **Watch Those Finishers:** The one exception to the previous rule. Saves are more subject to manager preference than raw talent. You too can get bundles of saves if you're given the ball with a three-run lead needing only three outs. Ask Norm Charlton, Dave Smith, Mitch Williams and others. Around mid-March, managers will begin settling into predictable bullpen patterns. At least a half-dozen clubs have uncertain closer plans on March 1, and are making major decisions two weeks later.

> **Managerial Tendencies:** Most teams will go with regular starters at six or more positions. However, identification of platoons and starters on shaky ground —for both health and performance reasons—need to be identified in the last seven to ten days of spring training.

> **The Lost Weekend:** Let's say you're drafting the Saturday night or Sunday afternoon before the season starts. Teams cut down the night before, and the West Coast cuts aren't in your newspaper. Hit the Internet right before you leave for your draft — ESPN.com, STATS and SportsWritersDirect.com are always up to date. The last minute cut information will save the bottom of your roster, where championships are won and lost.

III. THE DRAFT

> **The Night Before:** This might sound a bit hokey, but chill a little the night before the draft. You're ready — you've done your homework. Pay a little extra attention to your significant other, see "Titanic" for the 38th time, whatever. Get a good night's sleep, wake up early the next morning, hit the Internet, and drive safely to the draft.

> **Lists, Lists, Lists:** Bring your lists of players by position in descending order of value with you to the draft. Highlight starters and multipositional players, at the very least, with different colored markers. A laptop with draft software or your own spreadsheet takes you to the next level. You can track all teams' accumulated values by stat category and monitor all teams' remaining positional needs. You need to be in position to exploit the laws of supply and demand, and to anticipate the inevitable runs on players at specific positions.

> **Drain the Pool:** This is one of my favorite early draft strategies. Bring up big ticket players—trendy rookies, players coming off career years, hot spring performers, or even proven studs for whom you have no need or simply don't like — and watch the bucks fly. Make people overpay early, and some of the inflation will be drained out of the remaining pool of talent. This doesn't work as well, however, in the most competitive leagues.

> **Oh, Those Predictable Hitters:** Batting performance can be reliably projected from year to year, as first shown by Bill James in the mid-eighties. Pitching performance is much more subjective, due to factors such as injuries, mechanics, strength of team, among others. Only elite pitchers' performance can be projected with consistent precision. Therefore, seven of the ten most highly paid players on your club should generally be hitters — preferably filling at least two lean offensive positions (second base, shortstop, catcher) in the process. Obviously, focus on multicategory players. I have never, and will never own players like Otis Nixon or Brian Hunter; if their wheels go, their value goes. The three pitchers could include a closer, though that's not

always necessary, as we'll soon explore.

> **Who Needs a Top Closer:** OK, OK, I'd pay as much as the next guy for Trevor Hoffman, but after the very best closers, the inherent risk associated in investing a major chunk of a salary budget in some dude who pitches 50 innings is a bit steep for me. Each year, there are at least three affordable primary closers in each league. Snag one of them, plus two top setup men for low bucks, in the hope that one becomes a closer.

> **Every Team Has Overpaid Players:** Every team has a mix of over- and underpaid players. If you feel that you are developing a fiscally sound, potentially strong all-around team at the midway point of your auction, don't be afraid to significantly overpay for "The Last Piece". People thought I was nuts in 1998 when I broke out the checkbook for Biggio and Bagwell to the tune of nearly $70 dollars, forcing me to carry 10 $1 players.

> **Roster Flexibility:** The implementation of the aforementioned First Commandment. Every championship team needs to snag a couple of those multipositional guys so that you can make some of those nagging seven player moves at midseason which relieves you of the honor of picking up Rey Ordonez to replace Barry Larkin after he goes down.

> **Everyday Players Rule:** Remember three of the four offensive categories are additive—lots of at-bats generally mean lots of homers, RBI and steals. Draft 14 everyday players, if possible, unless number fourteen would be a lousy Kirt Manwaring-type backup catcher. Dig deep, and you'll find a Joe Randa or Scott Spiezio type who'll round out your roster nicely.

> **The Team With the Best $1 Players Wins:** Here's where the homework kicks in. Look for upside guys who just need a lucky break or opportunity to significantly help you, particularly in the sensitive steals and saves categories. Those speedy fourth (or fifth) outfielders, hard throwing setup guys caddying for shaky closers, can be had at the end of many drafts. Don't be overly swayed by a player's most recent performance; believe in his capabilities to a fault.

> **Read the Fine Print:** Each league's rules have their own quirks and nuances. Simply find the holes and exploit them. One of our writers' leagues featured unlimited free transactions and a reserve list, and other owners didn't become aware of my transactions until they received their weekly league report in the mail. I rolled over the bottom five players on my reserve list weekly, effectively making my roster five players larger than it appeared. Owners would claim the best available players, but I already had them. They didn't yet know which players I dropped, and by the time they did, I often had gotten them back.

> **Intimidation Via Intensity:** If I only had a dime for every time an owner in one of leagues complained about first come, first serve claims. You see, I'm always (OK, almost always) first. Put a claim in, even if you don't need a high profile callup early in the season. You will eventually wear down some of your opponents, who will say, "What's the use, Tony's already got him", down the homestretch.

> **Peer Review:** Get to know the personalities and tendencies of your potential trading partners. Send out an attractive trial balloon trade feeler to all owners early in the season. Some won't respond, some will insult your intelligence with their hilarious proposals, and some will actually talk turkey. Focus on the latter group, and don't be afraid to trade value for value. Trying to swindle people will eventually lose the trust of your fellow competitors.

> **Trade Value for Specific Value:** Down the stretch, don't be afraid to seemingly overpay in a trade for a specific need.

V. INTANGIBLES

> **Don't Chuck Categories:** Don't chicken out and write off a category unless you absolutely must. In 99 out of 100 leagues good enough to feel proud about winning, you will win if you finish second in every category.

> **Winning is an Attitude:** It sounds corny, but it's true. Never enter a league unless you expect to win it. Devise

a plan, implement it, and stick to it.

> **No Penny Pinching Allowed:** Don't skimp on personnel moves, even if it costs you cash. Yes, the prize money is nice, but the joy of winning must be paramount if you are to become a truly exceptional player.

> **Learn from Your Mistakes:** Two case studies here. In two separate leagues in 1996 — one of only two years that I had no first place finishes — I finished second by a half point. In one league, I would have won with a single RBI if I would have spent $10 and replaced a dormant Nelson Liriano in the season's last week. In the other, I sat around and watched the second place team — John Benson's — build up a pile of pitching points and trade them around the league for speed in the second half. I reacted, making my too-little trades too late in the season. I knew what he was going to do, and played not to lose instead of playing to win. I was simply not going to let it happen again.

> **The Big One:** Never write an article about your past success. It will only fire up your future opponents.

You don't have to be as maniacal as me to excel at Rotisserie baseball. Simply adopt a few of the above suggestions, rely on the best offseason publications ... if you're reading this, you know what they are — and, heck — give me a call if necessary. You need not be a rocket scientist, simply accumulate the right knowledge, respect the laws of supply and demand, stand by your educated perceptions, and compete relentlessly. Remember, those other owners will still be your friends in the morning.

_____

*Tony Blengino is the lead editor of **Future Stars 2001 - 2002**.*

HITTERS SECOND HALF 2000 STATS AND $ VALUES

AMERICAN LEAGUE

NAME	TM	VAL	AB	R	HR	RBI	SB	AVG	OBA	SLG
Johnny Damon	KC	$54	356	75	9	58	25	.374	.406	.567
Roberto Alomar	CLE	$40	307	60	10	54	18	.345	.411	.521
Kenny Lofton	CLE	$36	317	69	9	46	21	.303	.394	.448
Manny Ramirez	CLE	$34	256	60	25	75	0	.371	.483	.750
Darin Erstad	ANA	$33	326	59	9	41	13	.337	.389	.515
Bob Higginson	DET	$31	328	57	14	54	10	.311	.375	.512
Delino DeShields	BAL	$29	280	40	7	50	16	.296	.370	.457
Frank Thomas	CHW	$28	297	55	20	75	1	.323	.428	.613
Nomar Garciaparra	BOS	$28	300	65	13	52	3	.360	.426	.603
Magglio Ordonez	CHW	$28	307	47	13	57	10	.296	.337	.476
Derek Jeter	NYY	$27	322	68	8	43	6	.351	.448	.491
Alex Rodriguez	SEA	$27	256	56	20	61	7	.285	.398	.586
Garret Anderson	ANA	$27	320	49	13	59	3	.334	.357	.547
Ray Durham	CHW	$26	291	58	5	31	18	.282	.378	.412
Troy Glaus	ANA	$26	283	63	24	49	6	.272	.402	.590
Mike Sweeney	KC	$26	308	54	15	69	3	.312	.402	.477
Shannon Stewart	TOR	$25	340	68	11	37	9	.306	.355	.482
Carlos Lee	CHW	$25	290	56	9	36	9	.324	.362	.466
Mike Cameron	SEA	$25	276	48	8	38	17	.257	.362	.402
Jason Giambi	OAK	$24	241	47	21	61	0	.324	.473	.639
David Justice	NYY	$24	265	42	20	58	1	.313	.397	.604
Jose Valentin	CHW	$24	271	52	13	47	10	.277	.357	.487
Carlos Delgado	TOR	$23	270	48	14	65	0	.337	.483	.633
Gabe Kapler	TEX	$23	278	35	10	50	4	.335	.390	.529
Omar Vizquel	CLE	$23	315	62	5	34	11	.308	.404	.394
Jermaine Dye	KC	$22	320	57	13	56	0	.328	.390	.513
Damion Easley	DET	$22	297	52	11	43	11	.266	.350	.448
Miguel Tejada	OAK	$22	298	52	17	55	2	.299	.385	.527
Edgar Martinez	SEA	$22	296	44	14	61	3	.297	.404	.483
Juan Encarnacion	DET	$21	293	45	7	42	11	.280	.321	.444
Mark Quinn	KC	$21	296	48	12	46	3	.311	.353	.514
David Segui	CLE	$20	293	48	11	55	0	.331	.382	.512
Tim Salmon	ANA	$20	281	51	17	52	0	.306	.405	.573
Gerald Williams	TB	$20	333	45	13	45	7	.267	.308	.429
Travis Fryman	CLE	$20	303	46	8	60	1	.323	.380	.488
Rafael Palmeiro	TEX	$19	285	53	18	59	0	.288	.398	.551
Chris Singleton	CHW	$19	234	34	5	26	16	.244	.286	.350
Cristian Guzman	MIN	$18	314	42	2	23	18	.242	.287	.357
Terrence Long	OAK	$18	347	53	9	44	3	.300	.328	.455
Paul O'Neill	NYY	$18	270	36	9	53	7	.267	.314	.400
Chris Richard	BAL	$18	215	39	14	37	7	.265	.326	.544
Glenallen Hill	NYY	$18	171	28	18	36	0	.333	.375	.690
Bernie Williams	NYY	$18	233	48	12	45	5	.279	.383	.519
Rickey Henderson	SEA	$17	202	36	0	16	19	.238	.373	.317

NAME	TM	VAL	AB	R	HR	RBI	SB	AVG	OBA	SLG
Brad Fullmer	TOR	$17	234	32	18	54	0	.278	.306	.551
Mark McLemore	SEA	$17	230	34	2	23	14	.265	.355	.357
Tony Batista	TOR	$16	323	46	19	52	2	.248	.295	.483
Deivi Cruz	DET	$16	322	42	6	51	0	.317	.331	.475
Charles Johnson	CHW	$16	197	33	13	48	1	.305	.398	.563
Herbert Perry	CHW	$16	263	43	8	46	2	.308	.343	.483
Carl Everett	BOS	$16	233	39	11	40	5	.275	.350	.519
Eric Chavez	OAK	$16	252	44	14	45	2	.278	.348	.504
Fred McGriff	TB	$16	273	41	12	48	2	.282	.392	.440
Dean Palmer	DET	$16	287	38	13	62	4	.244	.318	.429
Paul Konerko	CHW	$15	246	40	10	47	1	.305	.370	.472
Jose Cruz	TOR	$15	281	42	13	32	7	.246	.328	.470
Torii Hunter	MIN	$15	196	30	5	35	4	.332	.371	.485
Joe Randa	KC	$15	320	47	7	54	1	.294	.319	.416
Rusty Greer	TEX	$15	240	41	6	42	4	.300	.393	.471
Jim Thome	CLE	$15	279	51	14	53	0	.276	.427	.487
Brook Fordyce	BAL	$15	228	31	11	33	0	.325	.365	.535
Adam Kennedy	ANA	$15	288	36	5	36	10	.250	.272	.399
Troy O'Leary	BOS	$14	304	37	8	53	0	.296	.345	.464
Darrin Fletcher	TOR	$14	249	25	11	30	1	.309	.349	.482
Matt Lawton	MIN	$14	258	37	7	38	6	.271	.369	.426
Miguel Cairo	TB	$14	159	27	1	18	14	.252	.307	.321
Dante Bichette	BOS	$14	291	37	10	45	0	.292	.345	.471
Brad Ausmus	DET	$14	256	45	2	24	8	.289	.377	.383
Brady Anderson	BAL	$13	239	50	10	23	7	.255	.394	.427
Jorge Posada	NYY	$13	266	49	15	48	0	.263	.391	.511
Jacque Jones	MIN	$13	253	29	7	35	5	.269	.310	.419
David Ortiz	MIN	$13	265	37	7	44	0	.302	.373	.472
Juan Gonzalez	DET	$12	199	32	9	34	1	.307	.353	.492
Mo Vaughn	ANA	$12	297	45	15	55	0	.246	.355	.448
Rey Sanchez	KC	$12	275	37	0	22	5	.309	.356	.345
Greg Vaughn	TB	$12	257	47	15	38	4	.226	.346	.459
Luis Matos	BAL	$11	167	20	1	17	12	.246	.301	.335
Dave Martinez	TOR	$11	243	37	2	27	4	.305	.384	.395
Tino Martinez	NYY	$11	282	35	9	46	2	.259	.331	.418
Ben Grieve	OAK	$11	284	42	12	42	1	.254	.358	.444
Jerry Hairston Jr.	BAL	$11	180	27	5	19	8	.256	.353	.367
Corey Koskie	MIN	$11	244	38	5	32	2	.295	.399	.439
Luis Polonia	NYY	$11	138	21	2	15	7	.312	.359	.442
Carlos Guillen	SEA	$10	225	37	7	37	1	.289	.348	.462
Melvin Mora	BAL	$10	267	32	3	23	6	.270	.332	.382
Chuck Knoblauch	NYY	$10	163	35	2	13	8	.276	.397	.368
Ron Gant	ANA	$9	154	32	12	28	2	.253	.372	.552
Denny Hocking	MIN	$9	203	28	2	21	3	.315	.383	.414
John Olerud	SEA	$9	283	30	7	54	0	.261	.361	.396
Randy Velarde	OAK	$9	304	51	6	21	3	.273	.327	.382
Ricky Ledee	TEX	$9	264	34	5	44	6	.227	.312	.345
Mark Lewis	BAL	$8	118	15	2	19	6	.288	.331	.441
Jay Buhner	SEA	$8	164	23	11	30	0	.268	.349	.543
Alex S. Gonzalez	TOR	$8	268	35	8	39	0	.261	.317	.422

NAME	TM	VAL	AB	R	HR	RBI	SB	AVG	OBA	SLG
Steve Cox	TB	$8	219	29	7	23	1	.279	.367	.452
Matt Stairs	OAK	$7	216	29	8	37	2	.241	.328	.421
Joe Oliver	SEA	$7	160	26	9	31	1	.256	.304	.506
Frank Catalanotto	TEX	$7	206	41	7	27	3	.248	.325	.408
Wil Cordero	CLE	$7	228	33	6	32	0	.276	.329	.443
Sandy Alomar	CLE	$7	210	27	4	26	2	.276	.299	.376
Trot Nixon	BOS	$7	191	24	4	21	4	.257	.358	.398
Al Martin	SEA	$6	204	30	5	14	4	.255	.314	.407
Gregg Zaun	KC	$6	150	23	4	20	2	.287	.404	.433
Billy McMillon	DET	$6	123	20	4	24	1	.301	.388	.472
Jose Canseco	NYY	$6	172	25	8	29	1	.244	.388	.436
Ben Molina	ANA	$6	243	28	6	36	0	.255	.303	.383
Luis Alicea	TEX	$6	267	44	3	28	0	.277	.342	.378
David Bell	SEA	$5	203	31	6	22	0	.276	.345	.433
Jeff Conine	BAL	$5	203	20	3	16	4	.256	.323	.350
Royce Clayton	TEX	$5	233	25	1	16	6	.245	.306	.326
Albert Belle	BAL	$5	254	24	5	39	0	.252	.299	.374
Bill Haselman	TEX	$5	162	21	6	23	0	.278	.335	.488
Luis Sojo	NYY	$5	132	20	2	17	2	.303	.333	.424
Mike Lamb	TEX	$5	282	31	3	23	0	.277	.322	.340
Scott Spiezio	ANA	$5	118	24	9	27	0	.237	.313	.508
Jay Canizaro	MIN	$5	173	19	3	21	2	.266	.306	.382
Jose Guillen	TB	$5	161	17	3	20	3	.255	.318	.391
David McCarty	KC	$4	162	19	5	32	0	.259	.307	.414
Orlando Palmeiro	ANA	$4	138	23	0	15	4	.275	.378	.377
Russ Branyan	CLE	$4	124	19	8	24	0	.242	.312	.500
Ron Coomer	MIN	$4	248	27	5	31	0	.250	.287	.367
Chad Curtis	TEX	$4	129	22	1	18	1	.310	.369	.403
Lou Merloni	BOS	$4	128	10	0	18	1	.320	.341	.438
Homer Bush	TOR	$4	83	17	1	4	5	.277	.337	.325
Carlos Febles	KC	$4	143	25	0	13	6	.238	.333	.266
Jason Varitek	BOS	$4	240	29	6	38	1	.225	.301	.363
Jeremy Giambi	OAK	$4	126	22	6	25	0	.254	.336	.468
Scarborough Green	TEX	$4	90	14	0	7	7	.222	.286	.244
Ramon Hernandez	OAK	$4	216	21	6	31	1	.231	.298	.370
Jose Vizcaino	NYY	$4	140	17	0	8	4	.279	.333	.329
Jose Offerman	BOS	$4	216	39	5	19	0	.264	.372	.389
Jason Tyner	TB	$3	83	6	0	8	6	.241	.281	.265
Scott Hatteberg	BOS	$3	137	13	5	19	0	.270	.395	.445
John Flaherty	TB	$3	184	14	6	18	0	.255	.289	.386
Benji Gil	ANA	$3	110	11	3	7	3	.264	.352	.355
Tony Graffanino	CHW	$3	103	18	2	10	5	.223	.339	.301
Adam Piatt	OAK	$3	124	19	3	15	0	.298	.412	.444
Scott Sheldon	TEX	$3	96	18	4	14	0	.302	.349	.542
Aubrey Huff	TB	$3	122	12	4	14	0	.287	.318	.443
Stan Javier	SEA	$3	169	26	2	21	0	.278	.340	.391
Randy Winn	TB	$3	68	9	1	8	4	.265	.363	.338
Jolbert Cabrera	CLE	$3	93	17	2	10	3	.258	.307	.344
Mickey Morandini	TOR	$3	186	17	0	12	3	.263	.315	.317
Brian Daubach	BOS	$2	243	23	8	29	0	.222	.276	.391

NAME	TM	VAL	AB	R	HR	RBI	SB	AVG	OBA	SLG
Hector Ortiz	KC	$2	88	15	0	5	0	.386	.443	.455
A.J. Pierzynski	MIN	$2	88	12	2	11	1	.307	.354	.455
Olmedo Saenz	OAK	$2	71	10	3	11	0	.338	.427	.507
Ozzie Timmons	TB	$2	41	9	4	13	0	.341	.357	.707
Rich Becker	DET	$2	153	31	4	22	1	.235	.378	.359
Wendell Magee	DET	$2	114	19	2	16	1	.272	.306	.368
Mike Stanley	OAK	$2	97	11	4	18	0	.268	.363	.464
Russ Johnson	TB	$2	135	21	1	8	3	.259	.342	.326
Carlos Beltran	KC	$2	77	6	1	12	3	.247	.302	.299
Scott Brosius	NYY	$2	266	33	9	34	0	.207	.281	.350
Craig Grebeck	TOR	$2	114	17	0	13	0	.316	.405	.421
Manny Alexander	BOS	$2	102	19	4	15	2	.216	.286	.363
Sal Fasano	OAK	$2	53	13	5	14	0	.264	.350	.623
Jose Macias	DET	$2	101	17	2	17	2	.238	.325	.396
Harold Baines	CHW	$1	101	7	3	14	0	.277	.381	.436
Jorge Fabregas	KC	$1	56	9	2	9	0	.357	.368	.518
Hal Morris	DET	$1	114	17	2	9	0	.298	.403	.412
Cal Ripken	BAL	$1	75	12	2	13	0	.307	.373	.480
Jeff Abbott	CHW	$1	100	17	1	13	1	.280	.342	.390
Raul Mondesi	TOR	$1	70	15	4	15	1	.229	.316	.457
Ivan Rodriguez	TEX	$1	58	9	3	13	1	.259	.281	.483
Einer Diaz	CLE	$1	102	12	1	9	2	.265	.318	.382
Luis Rivas	MIN	$1	58	8	0	6	2	.310	.323	.414
Shane Halter	DET	$1	127	16	2	22	0	.252	.302	.386
Morgan Burkhart	BOS	$1	52	12	4	14	0	.250	.412	.519
Darren Lewis	BOS	$1	148	23	1	11	3	.230	.296	.284
Chris Widger	SEA	$1	109	10	3	12	1	.239	.288	.404
Tony Clark	DET	$0	56	9	1	9	0	.339	.373	.482
Clay Bellinger	NYY	$0	100	19	2	12	3	.200	.281	.350
Ryan Thompson	NYY	$0	50	12	3	14	0	.260	.339	.500
Todd Dunwoody	KC	$0	138	11	0	20	3	.203	.228	.261
Trenidad Hubbard	BAL	$0	39	8	0	1	4	.179	.220	.231
Raul Ibanez	SEA	-$1	55	8	1	4	2	.236	.283	.327
Dan Wilson	SEA	-$1	121	15	2	14	1	.223	.291	.322
Brian Lesher	SEA	-$1	5	1	0	3	1	.800	.834	.376
Wilson Delgado	KC	-$1	84	17	0	7	1	.262	.308	.274
Luis Ordaz	KC	-$1	61	10	0	6	2	.230	.262	.246
Todd Greene	TOR	-$1	71	8	4	9	0	.211	.263	.408
Justin Baughman	ANA	-$1	13	3	0	0	2	.308	.357	.462
Israel Alcantara	BOS	-$1	29	6	3	6	0	.241	.267	.586
Ruben Sierra	TEX	-$1	60	5	1	7	1	.233	.281	.283
Donnie Sadler	BOS	-$1	33	7	0	2	2	.242	.297	.273
Eric Byrnes	OAK	-$1	10	5	0	0	2	.300	.364	.300
Rod Lindsey	DET	-$1	3	6	0	0	2	.333	.500	.667
Randy Knorr	TEX	-$1	34	5	2	2	0	.294	.294	.529
Robert Fick	DET	-$1	41	7	1	4	1	.244	.289	.415
Chad Allen	MIN	-$1	50	2	0	7	0	.300	.345	.360
Pedro Valdes	TEX	-$1	54	4	1	5	0	.278	.350	.426
Gene Kingsale	BAL	-$1	88	13	0	9	1	.239	.253	.284
John Barnes	MIN	-$2	37	5	0	2	0	.351	.415	.459

NAME	TM	VAL	AB	R	HR	RBI	SB	AVG	OBA	SLG
Mark L. Johnson	CHW	-$2	76	14	1	7	1	.224	.322	.316
Matt Walbeck	ANA	-$2	68	5	4	8	0	.191	.236	.382
Greg Myers	BAL	-$2	72	5	2	10	0	.222	.263	.347
Midre Cummings	BOS	-$2	96	10	1	10	0	.240	.330	.302
Doug Mientkiewicz	MIN	-$2	14	0	0	4	0	.429	.400	.429
Frankie Menechino	OAK	-$2	44	8	1	7	0	.250	.353	.409
Ryan Christenson	OAK	-$2	60	15	2	9	0	.217	.299	.383
Marty Cordova	TOR	-$2	60	7	2	7	1	.183	.279	.300
Dusty Allen	DET	-$2	27	5	2	2	0	.259	.355	.556
Shawn Wooten	ANA	-$2	9	2	0	1	0	.556	.556	.667
Ed Sprague	BOS	-$2	144	12	2	11	0	.222	.296	.306
Bernard Gilkey	BOS	-$2	91	11	1	9	0	.231	.327	.341
Ozzie Guillen	TB	-$2	49	8	1	3	1	.204	.235	.306
Ivanon Coffie	BAL	-$2	60	6	0	6	1	.217	.284	.317
Josh Paul	CHW	-$2	9	2	0	2	0	.444	.444	.556
Joe Crede	CHW	-$2	14	2	0	3	0	.357	.333	.429
Bobby Smith	TB	-$3	112	11	3	13	1	.170	.244	.277
John McDonald	CLE	-$3	9	0	0	0	0	.444	.444	.444
Edgard Clemente	ANA	-$3	23	3	0	2	0	.304	.304	.348
Dave Roberts	CLE	-$3	7	1	0	0	1	.143	.333	.143
Jason Maxwell	MIN	-$3	43	6	0	3	1	.209	.271	.302
Rico Brogna	BOS	-$3	71	8	1	9	0	.211	.253	.310
Mike DiFelice	TB	-$3	105	9	3	10	0	.190	.234	.352
Brian Buchanan	MIN	-$3	24	4	0	4	0	.250	.394	.292
Mike Kinkade	BAL	-$3	9	0	0	1	0	.333	.400	.444
Charles Gipson	SEA	-$3	6	2	0	2	0	.333	.500	.667
Bill Selby	CLE	-$3	46	8	0	4	0	.239	.271	.261
Anthony Sanders	SEA	-$3	1	1	0	0	0	.999	.1000	.999
Bo Porter	OAK	-$3	13	3	1	2	0	.154	.267	.385
Toby Hall	TB	-$3	12	1	1	1	0	.167	.231	.417
Vinny Castilla	TB	-$3	112	6	0	10	0	.223	.237	.268
Chad Mottola	TOR	-$3	9	1	0	2	0	.222	.300	.222
B.J. Waszgis	TEX	-$3	45	6	0	4	0	.222	.294	.244
Alfonso Soriano	NYY	-$3	8	0	0	1	0	.250	.250	.375
Damian Rolls	TB	-$3	3	0	0	0	0	.333	.333	.333
Greg Norton	CHW	-$3	42	8	1	7	0	.167	.327	.286
Willie Morales	BAL	-$3	3	0	0	0	0	.333	.333	.667
Felix Jose	NYY	-$3	10	1	0	2	0	.200	.333	.200
Jeff Reboulet	KC	-$3	65	9	0	4	2	.154	.225	.169
Vernon Wells	TOR	-$4	2	0	0	0	0	.000	.000	.000
Jose Ortiz	OAK	-$4	11	4	0	1	0	.182	.308	.182
Robert Machado	SEA	-$4	6	0	0	0	0	.167	.167	.167
Marcus Jensen	MIN	-$4	32	1	0	1	0	.219	.286	.219
John Jaha	OAK	-$4	10	2	0	0	0	.200	.385	.300
Jesse Garcia	BAL	-$4	6	2	0	0	0	.167	.286	.167
Shane Spencer	NYY	-$4	11	1	0	0	0	.182	.250	.182
Jeff Liefer	CHW	-$4	11	0	0	0	0	.182	.182	.182
Matt LeCroy	MIN	-$4	20	2	0	1	0	.200	.238	.250
Casey Blake	MIN	-$4	16	1	0	1	0	.188	.333	.313
Eric Munson	DET	-$4	5	0	0	1	0	.000	.000	.000

NAME	TM	VAL	AB	R	HR	RBI	SB	AVG	OBA	SLG
Javier Cardona	DET	-$4	36	1	1	2	0	.167	.184	.278
Dee Brown	KC	-$4	25	4	0	4	0	.160	.250	.200
Sean Berry	BOS	-$4	4	0	0	0	0	.000	.000	.000
Danny Ardoin	MIN	-$4	32	4	1	5	0	.125	.300	.250
McKay Christensen	CHW	-$4	14	2	0	1	0	.143	.250	.143
Mark Bellhorn	OAK	-$4	13	2	0	0	0	.154	.267	.154
Scott Pose	KC	-$4	16	1	0	0	0	.125	.176	.125
Alberto Castillo	TOR	-$4	56	4	0	3	0	.196	.308	.232
Chris Woodward	TOR	-$4	40	2	0	2	0	.175	.233	.225
Chad Moeller	MIN	-$4	97	10	1	7	0	.186	.238	.268
Chan Perry	CLE	-$4	14	1	0	0	0	.071	.071	.071
Kelly Dransfeldt	TEX	-$5	25	2	0	2	0	.120	.154	.200
Craig Wilson	CHW	-$5	12	1	0	0	0	.000	.143	.000
Mario Valdez	OAK	-$5	12	0	0	0	0	.000	.000	.000
Felix Martinez	TB	-$5	193	26	1	6	3	.176	.273	.264
Rob Ducey	TOR	-$5	82	10	0	10	0	.171	.278	.195
Chris Turner	NYY	-$5	56	5	0	2	0	.161	.254	.179
Kevin Stocker	ANA	-$5	191	16	0	15	0	.199	.290	.283
Karim Garcia	BAL	-$5	16	0	0	0	0	.000	.000	.000
Mike Lansing	BOS	-$5	209	15	0	15	1	.191	.223	.220
Fernando Lunar	BAL	-$6	31	1	0	1	0	.065	.147	.065
Ryan Minor	BAL	-$7	63	3	0	2	0	.095	.123	.111

NATIONAL LEAGUE

NAME	TEAM	VAL	AB	RUN	HR	RBI	SB	AVG	OBA	SLG
Preston Wilson	FLA	$41	291	46	14	61	24	.282	.344	.488
Todd Helton	COL	$37	308	58	21	78	3	.357	.446	.669
Jeff Bagwell	HOU	$36	283	82	26	73	4	.336	.453	.675
Luis Castillo	FLA	$36	300	46	1	13	28	.320	.387	.360
Richard Hidalgo	HOU	$36	298	67	21	62	8	.332	.393	.641
Rafael Furcal	ATL	$35	287	52	4	25	28	.289	.391	.380
Bob Abreu	PHI	$34	294	55	15	39	15	.316	.423	.575
Sammy Sosa	CHC	$34	291	51	29	69	1	.330	.417	.694
Tony Womack	AZ	$32	293	51	2	28	29	.259	.309	.362
Moises Alou	HOU	$32	278	53	19	76	1	.360	.420	.629
Andruw Jones	ATL	$32	340	55	15	54	13	.288	.329	.509
Eric Young	CHC	$30	288	44	1	19	28	.267	.334	.333
Chipper Jones	ATL	$29	303	63	17	51	9	.300	.390	.538
Sean Casey	CIN	$29	261	44	16	65	1	.372	.429	.659
Vladimir Guerrero	MON	$29	283	50	22	55	3	.325	.386	.622
Geoff Jenkins	MIL	$28	304	64	21	53	5	.299	.370	.589
Julio Lugo	HOU	$27	328	66	9	31	15	.284	.345	.445
Adrian Beltre	LA	$25	275	43	13	49	6	.316	.397	.516
Luis Gonzalez	AZ	$25	313	50	14	65	1	.319	.386	.546
Will Clark	STL	$24	250	42	16	53	1	.336	.412	.608
Todd Hollandsworth	COL	$23	235	45	12	31	11	.289	.349	.481
Barry Bonds	SF	$23	235	61	21	49	2	.302	.442	.643
Doug Glanville	PHI	$23	323	47	3	23	15	.291	.317	.390
John Vander Wal	PIT	$22	210	47	15	52	4	.314	.434	.590
Ellis Burks	SF	$22	218	45	15	59	0	.344	.416	.638
Jeffrey Hammonds	COL	$22	260	50	7	45	9	.304	.354	.435
Phil Nevin	SD	$22	238	40	15	47	1	.340	.421	.597
Jeff Kent	SF	$22	286	48	10	45	5	.311	.411	.497
Jim Edmonds	STL	$21	251	55	20	56	5	.247	.365	.522
Jason Kendall	PIT	$21	297	53	8	32	7	.310	.391	.465
Ryan Klesko	SD	$21	267	42	8	41	13	.251	.377	.404
Richie Sexson	MIL	$21	253	50	16	56	2	.292	.386	.553
Edgar Renteria	STL	$21	259	47	6	42	11	.278	.370	.425
Scott Rolen	PHI	$21	253	47	10	43	5	.312	.388	.538
Reggie Sanders	ATL	$21	154	24	8	26	12	.305	.382	.578
Brian Giles	PIT	$20	263	54	14	55	1	.308	.437	.551
Cliff Floyd	FLA	$20	155	26	7	37	9	.335	.395	.555
Gary Sheffield	LA	$20	221	43	16	38	3	.303	.424	.588
Damian Jackson	SD	$19	241	31	3	22	17	.253	.332	.378
Ken Griffey	CIN	$19	244	47	14	54	1	.303	.374	.553
Chris Stynes	CIN	$19	309	56	10	29	4	.311	.366	.472
Lance Berkman	HOU	$19	207	47	12	42	5	.300	.401	.570
Shawn Green	LA	$19	314	45	12	42	10	.236	.316	.424
Alex Ochoa	CIN	$19	174	35	10	42	5	.322	.379	.621
Tom Goodwin	LA	$18	278	34	2	20	20	.223	.295	.270
Dmitri Young	CIN	$18	268	39	9	48	0	.332	.375	.549
Edgardo Alfonzo	NYM	$18	266	46	13	39	1	.312	.415	.519
Danny Bautista	AZ	$18	227	39	5	44	5	.322	.374	.507

NAME	TEAM	VAL	AB	RUN	HR	RBI	SB	AVG	OBA	SLG
Mike Lowell	FLA	$17	265	38	10	48	4	.279	.366	.472
Jeff Cirillo	COL	$17	324	46	2	51	3	.306	.366	.401
Javy Lopez	ATL	$16	230	32	13	49	0	.300	.348	.517
Mark Kotsay	FLA	$16	260	49	5	25	9	.281	.339	.400
Steve Finley	AZ	$16	250	41	11	30	7	.260	.340	.476
Marvin Benard	SF	$16	289	47	6	25	11	.253	.336	.391
Rich Aurilia	SF	$16	270	36	13	46	1	.281	.352	.485
Jose Vidro	MON	$16	311	45	11	42	0	.296	.355	.482
Mike Piazza	NYM	$16	235	38	14	42	1	.285	.369	.498
Jeromy Burnitz	MIL	$16	270	39	15	50	2	.252	.374	.489
J.D. Drew	STL	$15	196	34	5	17	9	.296	.411	.423
Adrian Brown	PIT	$15	216	48	3	21	7	.315	.382	.412
Todd Walker	COL	$15	171	28	7	36	4	.316	.385	.544
Derrek Lee	FLA	$14	272	37	12	38	0	.290	.368	.493
Greg Colbrunn	AZ	$14	219	33	9	39	0	.320	.384	.511
Neifi Perez	COL	$14	358	59	6	32	1	.296	.322	.436
Ray Lankford	STL	$14	192	39	15	32	2	.266	.387	.563
Jay Payton	NYM	$14	291	36	9	35	2	.282	.319	.416
Andres Galarraga	ATL	$14	220	24	9	40	1	.300	.362	.477
Benny Agbayani	NYM	$13	219	38	8	34	3	.288	.413	.466
Mike Bordick	NYM	$13	278	35	7	31	4	.277	.337	.399
Geoff Blum	MON	$13	251	26	9	34	1	.295	.331	.470
Mike Darr	SD	$13	192	21	1	28	9	.281	.349	.411
Pokey Reese	CIN	$13	221	29	7	21	10	.235	.293	.371
J.T. Snow	SF	$13	266	44	12	55	0	.256	.356	.466
BJ Surhoff	ATL	$13	227	26	3	23	5	.308	.352	.436
Jay Bell	AZ	$13	266	36	9	37	4	.256	.321	.429
Matt Williams	AZ	$13	278	33	10	43	0	.277	.315	.446
Lenny Harris	NYM	$12	121	21	3	13	8	.331	.409	.496
Kevin Young	PIT	$12	202	34	9	34	4	.262	.318	.436
Juan Pierre	COL	$12	200	26	0	20	7	.310	.353	.320
Pat Burrell	PHI	$12	274	38	12	50	0	.252	.363	.445
Chris Truby	HOU	$12	206	23	10	53	2	.243	.281	.476
Eric Owens	SD	$12	281	37	2	21	10	.249	.296	.331
Michael Tucker	CIN	$12	146	28	6	15	9	.253	.375	.466
Ricky Gutierrez	CHC	$11	256	39	4	29	5	.273	.375	.375
Tyler Houston	MIL	$11	174	19	13	30	2	.253	.282	.534
Marquis Grissom	MIL	$11	270	29	6	21	9	.230	.283	.315
Mark Grace	CHC	$10	286	42	4	50	0	.276	.391	.416
Eric Karros	LA	$10	290	40	8	39	3	.241	.299	.372
Andy Tracy	MON	$10	144	25	9	26	1	.299	.376	.556
Roger Cedeno	HOU	$10	96	23	2	7	8	.323	.414	.406
Placido Polanco	STL	$9	155	25	2	23	3	.316	.363	.426
Todd Hundley	LA	$8	156	22	9	34	0	.269	.364	.487
Andy Fox	FLA	$8	130	16	2	7	8	.269	.358	.377
Jeff Frye	COL	$8	146	22	1	5	4	.342	.386	.425
Wally Joyner	ATL	$8	140	18	4	25	0	.336	.407	.479
Fernando Vina	STL	$8	242	39	1	11	2	.310	.377	.384
Mitch Meluskey	HOU	$8	148	19	6	28	0	.304	.419	.480
Barry Larkin	CIN	$8	163	31	3	13	4	.294	.382	.442

NAME	TEAM	VAL	AB	RUN	HR	RBI	SB	AVG	OBA	SLG
Orlando Cabrera	MON	$8	185	22	7	30	2	.249	.300	.438
Bill Spiers	HOU	$8	188	21	2	23	2	.298	.382	.399
Fernando Seguignol	MON	$7	153	22	10	20	0	.275	.325	.523
Brian Jordan	ATL	$7	240	28	4	27	6	.225	.288	.325
Benito Santiago	CIN	$7	135	13	5	29	2	.274	.320	.430
Daryle Ward	HOU	$7	107	17	8	19	0	.318	.342	.636
Wilton Guerrero	MON	$7	195	20	1	14	5	.277	.322	.344
Todd Zeile	NYM	$7	269	34	10	30	1	.234	.338	.416
Tony Eusebio	HOU	$7	102	15	5	21	0	.353	.411	.618
Mark Grudzielanek	LA	$7	276	39	3	20	4	.254	.322	.362
Peter Bergeron	MON	$7	248	35	2	17	5	.254	.335	.359
James Mouton	MIL	$7	67	17	1	9	8	.254	.398	.343
Craig Biggio	HOU	$7	92	16	4	10	4	.304	.356	.500
Brent Mayne	COL	$6	171	12	2	30	1	.287	.352	.368
Terry Shumpert	COL	$6	143	24	6	16	4	.238	.308	.413
Craig Paquette	STL	$6	162	21	7	23	2	.241	.262	.414
Warren Morris	PIT	$6	263	35	1	23	3	.262	.339	.357
Henry Rodriguez	FLA	$6	166	21	6	27	0	.271	.349	.446
Ben Petrick	COL	$6	131	29	3	20	0	.328	.406	.450
Butch Huskey	COL	$6	102	18	4	18	1	.324	.405	.529
Aramis Ramirez	PIT	$6	153	13	5	26	0	.281	.313	.464
Fernando Tatis	STL	$6	242	38	11	33	0	.219	.354	.409
Larry Walker	COL	$6	124	23	5	23	2	.258	.388	.460
Mike Matheny	STL	$6	212	22	3	27	0	.278	.323	.373
Tim Bogar	HOU	$6	168	22	5	22	1	.268	.342	.399
Brian L. Hunter	CIN	$5	126	27	1	6	7	.246	.309	.294
Desi Relaford	SD	$5	214	28	2	18	9	.192	.314	.238
Keith Osik	PIT	$5	95	8	2	17	3	.295	.391	.411
Terry Jones	MON	$5	122	18	0	9	5	.287	.320	.369
Lee Stevens	MON	$5	182	24	5	22	0	.275	.328	.429
Keith Lockhart	ATL	$5	184	19	0	20	3	.277	.338	.321
Derek Bell	NYM	$5	246	28	8	26	3	.211	.292	.358
Robin Ventura	NYM	$5	209	20	8	32	1	.220	.307	.373
Bill Mueller	SF	$5	276	49	4	20	2	.250	.322	.373
Glen Barker	HOU	$5	31	10	1	4	7	.258	.324	.452
Armando Rios	SF	$5	92	17	6	20	1	.261	.358	.565
Jose Hernandez	MIL	$5	170	19	2	22	2	.265	.326	.347
Damon Buford	CHC	$5	229	27	4	21	3	.236	.314	.345
Damian Miller	AZ	$5	181	24	4	21	0	.276	.348	.409
Alex Cora	LA	$4	241	21	3	26	4	.220	.278	.324
John Mabry	SD	$4	148	21	7	27	0	.236	.274	.439
Roosevelt Brown	CHC	$4	72	9	3	14	0	.375	.397	.583
Craig Counsell	AZ	$4	111	18	0	8	3	.315	.389	.387
Alex Gonzalez	FLA	$4	142	15	4	19	2	.246	.255	.394
Luis Lopez	MIL	$4	130	15	4	18	0	.285	.312	.438
Shawon Dunston	STL	$4	114	16	5	18	1	.254	.281	.474
Dave Magadan	SD	$4	75	8	2	17	0	.360	.495	.493
Pat Meares	PIT	$4	201	27	8	19	0	.234	.316	.398
Ramon E. Martinez	SF	$3	95	12	1	7	3	.295	.327	.411
Mike Lieberthal	PHI	$3	126	15	3	26	1	.246	.319	.381

NAME	TEAM	VAL	AB	RUN	HR	RBI	SB	AVG	OBA	SLG
Bret Boone	SD	$3	169	22	4	17	2	.237	.330	.355
Ruben Rivera	SD	$3	249	32	7	27	5	.177	.262	.329
Travis Lee	PHI	$3	213	25	2	23	3	.230	.365	.329
Rondell White	CHC	$3	89	11	3	12	0	.326	.375	.461
Felipe Crespo	SF	$3	78	11	3	16	2	.256	.330	.436
Alex Ramirez	PIT	$3	138	17	5	21	1	.232	.274	.413
Emil Brown	PIT	$3	116	13	3	16	3	.224	.300	.345
Eduardo Perez	STL	$3	90	9	3	10	1	.289	.343	.422
Kevin Millar	FLA	$3	107	16	6	20	0	.234	.336	.523
Ron Belliard	MIL	$3	261	34	2	21	3	.226	.311	.333
Calvin Murray	SF	$2	89	13	1	11	5	.202	.314	.303
Tomas De la Rosa	MON	$2	66	7	2	9	2	.288	.365	.455
Bubba Trammell	NYM	$2	104	12	3	23	1	.231	.314	.394
Darryl Hamilton	NYM	$2	90	20	1	5	2	.300	.394	.400
Jimmy Rollins	PHI	$2	53	5	0	5	3	.321	.345	.377
Russ Davis	SF	$2	88	10	6	15	0	.227	.281	.455
Joe Girardi	CHC	$2	174	17	2	21	0	.253	.298	.328
Jason Conti	AZ	$2	87	11	1	14	3	.230	.287	.379
Ben Davis	SD	$2	114	11	3	14	1	.246	.320	.377
Eric Davis	STL	$2	113	12	0	15	0	.301	.380	.327
Raul Casanova	MIL	$2	150	11	2	21	1	.233	.328	.373
Carlos Hernandez	STL	$2	60	8	1	11	2	.267	.348	.400
Kory DeHaan	SD	$1	54	11	2	7	3	.222	.250	.407
Shane Andrews	CHC	$1	74	9	4	12	0	.257	.341	.446
Juan Castro	CIN	$1	161	13	3	15	0	.248	.295	.360
Jason Larue	CIN	$1	98	12	5	12	0	.235	.299	.418
Chris Sexton	CIN	$1	100	9	0	10	4	.210	.310	.250
Enrique Wilson	PIT	$1	130	13	3	15	0	.246	.308	.377
Tom Prince	PHI	$1	86	10	2	14	1	.244	.323	.395
Mark Loretta	MIL	$1	152	20	2	17	0	.250	.337	.382
Chris Donnels	LA	$1	34	8	4	9	0	.294	.390	.735
Julio Zuleta	CHC	$1	33	6	2	8	0	.394	.444	.758
Milton Bradley	MON	$1	154	20	2	15	2	.221	.288	.325
Marlon Anderson	PHI	$1	162	10	1	15	2	.228	.282	.309
Brian R. Hunter	PHI	$1	82	8	5	13	0	.220	.333	.427
Dave Hansen	LA	$1	51	8	4	10	0	.255	.406	.529
Todd Pratt	NYM	$1	85	18	2	9	0	.282	.402	.388
Chad Kreuter	LA	$1	101	9	2	15	0	.257	.370	.386
Mike Benjamin	PIT	$0	96	11	1	10	2	.229	.288	.333
Gary Matthews	CHC	$0	144	19	3	12	3	.188	.259	.285
Willie Greene	CHC	$0	148	16	3	16	3	.176	.265	.311
Mark McGwire	STL	$0	23	2	2	7	0	.348	.500	.652
Damon Minor	SF	$0	9	3	3	6	0	.444	.546	.420
Charlie Hayes	MIL	$0	165	11	3	14	0	.230	.301	.303
Devon White	LA	$0	75	13	1	4	2	.240	.296	.347
Ramon Castro	FLA	$0	138	10	2	14	0	.239	.318	.312
Eddie Taubensee	CIN	$0	68	7	2	6	0	.279	.329	.412
Jeff Huson	CHC	$0	79	11	0	7	2	.241	.302	.291
Henry Blanco	MIL	$0	138	13	2	10	0	.246	.307	.399
John Wehner	PIT	$0	50	10	1	9	0	.300	.352	.420

NAME	TEAM	VAL	AB	RUN	HR	RBI	SB	AVG	OBA	SLG
Timoniel Perez	NYM	$0	49	11	1	3	1	.286	.333	.469
Keith McDonald	STL	$0	7	3	3	5	0	.429	.557	.690
Kevin Elster	LA	$0	65	5	4	11	0	.200	.342	.415
Bruce Aven	LA	$0	47	4	3	9	0	.234	.280	.468
Quilvio Veras	ATL	$0	26	4	1	3	1	.308	.419	.500
Wiki Gonzalez	SD	-$1	175	15	3	17	0	.217	.305	.331
Mark Smith	FLA	-$1	123	12	1	13	1	.220	.271	.309
Joe Vitiello	SD	-$1	52	7	2	8	0	.250	.365	.423
Matt Franco	NYM	-$1	63	5	2	9	0	.238	.338	.365
Alex Cabrera	AZ	-$1	66	7	4	8	0	.197	.239	.394
Kurt Abbott	NYM	-$1	57	6	3	5	0	.228	.241	.404
Adam Hyzdu	PIT	-$1	18	2	1	4	0	.389	.389	.667
Thomas Howard	STL	-$1	56	5	1	10	0	.250	.288	.357
Dave Berg	FLA	-$1	104	12	1	11	0	.240	.322	.308
George Lombard	ATL	-$1	39	8	0	2	4	.103	.146	.103
Gary Bennett	PHI	-$1	74	8	2	5	0	.243	.371	.392
Tike Redman	PIT	-$1	10	1	1	1	1	.300	.364	.600
Matt Mieske	AZ	-$1	28	5	2	5	0	.250	.290	.464
Walt Weiss	ATL	-$1	96	11	0	11	1	.219	.303	.260
Bobby Bonilla	ATL	-$1	93	7	2	11	0	.215	.315	.344
D.T. Cromer	CIN	-$1	19	1	1	2	0	.368	.368	.579
Tomas Perez	PHI	-$1	136	16	1	11	1	.213	.267	.294
Joe McEwing	NYM	-$1	79	9	1	12	1	.190	.205	.266
Darren Bragg	COL	-$2	21	3	0	2	1	.286	.375	.333
F.P. Santangelo	LA	-$2	27	6	1	2	1	.222	.344	.370
Kevin Jordan	PHI	-$2	151	12	3	19	0	.192	.233	.305
Alex Arias	PHI	-$2	77	10	1	10	1	.195	.270	.286
Raul Chavez	HOU	-$2	43	3	1	5	0	.256	.298	.372
Mike Bell	CIN	-$2	27	5	2	4	0	.222	.323	.444
Elvis Pena	COL	-$2	9	1	0	1	1	.333	.400	.444
Mike Mordecai	MON	-$2	84	7	1	6	0	.238	.289	.357
Bobby Estalella	SF	-$2	150	17	5	20	0	.167	.302	.340
Rube Durazo	AZ	-$2	51	7	1	6	0	.235	.310	.392
Dave Dellucci	AZ	-$2	48	2	0	2	0	.292	.333	.354
Alex Hernandez	PIT	-$2	60	4	1	5	1	.200	.200	.300
Corey Patterson	CHC	-$2	42	9	2	2	1	.167	.239	.333
Chris Clapinski	FLA	-$2	14	8	1	3	0	.286	.444	.571
Mike Redmond	FLA	-$2	90	7	0	9	0	.233	.311	.278
Jorge Toca	NYM	-$2	7	1	0	4	0	.429	.429	.571
Jeff Reed	CHC	-$2	124	12	1	10	0	.218	.336	.274
Pablo Ozuna	FLA	-$2	6	2	0	0	0	.667	.667	.833
Keith Ginter	HOU	-$2	8	3	1	3	0	.250	.300	.625
Abraham Nunez	PIT	-$2	52	6	1	7	0	.212	.293	.288
Rob Ryan	AZ	-$2	27	4	0	2	0	.296	.406	.407
Rod Barajas	AZ	-$2	13	1	1	3	0	.231	.231	.462
Frank Charles	HOU	-$2	7	1	0	2	0	.429	.429	.571
Kevin Sefcik	PHI	-$2	77	7	0	5	1	.208	.271	.247
Jose Nieves	CHC	-$2	97	8	1	8	1	.186	.225	.247
Lyle Mouton	MIL	-$2	7	0	0	1	0	.429	.500	.571
Angel Echevarria	MIL	-$2	48	3	1	5	0	.208	.309	.313

NAME	TEAM	VAL	AB	RUN	HR	RBI	SB	AVG	OBA	SLG
Lenny Webster	MON	-$2	38	2	0	5	0	.237	.341	.263
Hanley Frias	AZ	-$3	43	9	1	1	0	.233	.353	.372
Augie Ojeda	CHC	-$3	34	4	1	3	0	.206	.282	.324
Kim Bartee	CIN	-$3	4	2	0	0	1	.000	.200	.000
Lou Collier	MIL	-$3	32	9	1	2	0	.219	.333	.344
Brian Schneider	MON	-$3	82	4	0	8	0	.220	.253	.280
George Williams	SD	-$3	16	2	1	2	0	.188	.235	.375
Brady Clark	CIN	-$3	11	1	0	2	0	.273	.273	.364
Ross Gload	CHC	-$3	31	4	1	3	0	.194	.257	.355
Brant Brown	CHC	-$3	38	2	0	3	2	.105	.239	.105
Sandy Martinez	FLA	-$3	4	1	0	0	0	.500	.500	.750
Jim Leyritz	LA	-$3	54	3	1	7	0	.185	.279	.259
Mark Sweeney	MIL	-$3	39	6	1	2	0	.205	.340	.385
Mike Mahoney	CHC	-$3	7	1	0	1	0	.286	.444	.429
Adam Melhuse	COL	-$3	19	3	0	4	0	.211	.318	.316
Hiram Bocachica	LA	-$3	10	2	0	0	0	.300	.300	.300
Reggie Taylor	PHI	-$3	11	1	0	0	1	.091	.091	.091
Xavier Nady	SD	-$3	1	1	0	0	0	.999	.1000	.999
Doug Mirabelli	SF	-$3	108	6	0	10	0	.213	.315	.259
Eli Marrero	STL	-$3	16	2	0	0	1	.125	.222	.188
Rick Wilkins	STL	-$3	11	3	0	1	0	.273	.385	.273
Paul Bako	ATL	-$3	81	9	2	8	0	.173	.236	.309
Larry Sutton	STL	-$3	4	0	0	1	0	.250	.250	.250
Morgan Ensberg	HOU	-$3	7	0	0	0	0	.286	.286	.286
Talmadge Nunnari	MON	-$3	5	2	0	1	0	.200	.583	.200
Michael Barrett	MON	-$3	135	14	0	9	0	.215	.269	.267
Greg Larocca	SD	-$3	27	1	0	2	0	.222	.250	.296
Pedro Feliz	SF	-$3	7	1	0	0	0	.286	.286	.286
Kevin L. Brown	MIL	-$3	17	3	0	1	0	.235	.278	.412
Aaron Boone	CIN	-$3	6	0	0	1	0	.167	.143	.167
Mark DeRosa	ATL	-$3	0	5	0	0	0	.000	.000	.000
Jeff Branson	LA	-$3	17	3	0	0	0	.235	.278	.294
Mike Hubbard	ATL	-$3	1	0	0	0	0	.000	.000	.000
Clemente Alvarez	PHI	-$3	5	1	0	0	0	.200	.200	.200
Chad Hermansen	PIT	-$3	14	0	0	0	0	.214	.214	.286
Kevin Nicholson	SD	-$3	65	3	0	3	0	.215	.250	.323
Wes Helms	ATL	-$3	5	0	0	0	0	.200	.200	.200
David Lamb	NYM	-$3	5	1	0	0	0	.200	.333	.200
Pedro Swann	ATL	-$3	2	0	0	0	0	.000	.000	.000
Santiago Perez	MIL	-$3	13	1	0	0	1	.000	.188	.000
Chris Jones	MIL	-$3	16	3	0	1	0	.188	.235	.313
Trace Coquillette	MON	-$3	17	2	0	1	0	.176	.263	.294
Mark Johnson	NYM	-$3	8	1	0	0	0	.125	.300	.125
Mendy Lopez	FLA	-$3	3	0	0	0	0	.000	.250	.000
Tripp Cromer	HOU	-$3	8	2	0	0	0	.125	.222	.125
David Newhan	PHI	-$4	17	3	0	0	0	.176	.263	.176
Eddie Zosky	HOU	-$4	4	0	0	0	0	.000	.000	.000
Vance Wilson	NYM	-$4	4	0	0	0	0	.000	.000	.000
Gabe Alvarez	SD	-$4	13	1	0	0	0	.154	.214	.231
Steve Sisco	ATL	-$4	18	2	0	0	0	.167	.286	.167

2001 Rotisserie Baseball Annual   *Page 61*

NAME	TEAM	VAL	AB	RUN	HR	RBI	SB	AVG	OBA	SLG
Carlos Mendoza	COL	-$4	10	0	0	0	0	.100	.182	.100
Nate Rolison	FLA	-$4	13	0	0	2	0	.077	.125	.077
Scott Servais	SF	-$4	14	1	0	0	0	.143	.250	.143
Luis Saturria	STL	-$4	5	1	0	0	0	.000	.167	.000
Tim Unroe	ATL	-$4	5	0	0	0	0	.000	.167	.000
Paul LoDuca	LA	-$4	39	3	0	3	0	.179	.261	.205
Kelly Stinnett	AZ	-$4	90	6	0	5	0	.200	.280	.200
Jorge Velandia	NYM	-$4	7	1	0	0	0	.000	.222	.000
Terrell Lowery	SF	-$4	7	2	0	0	0	.000	.364	.000
Mike Metcalfe	LA	-$4	12	0	0	0	0	.083	.154	.083
Juan Melo	SF	-$4	13	0	0	1	0	.077	.077	.077
Yohanny Valera	MON	-$4	10	1	0	1	0	.000	.167	.000
Danny Klassen	AZ	-$4	20	3	0	1	0	.100	.250	.100
Chad Meyers	CHC	-$4	38	5	0	4	0	.132	.209	.132
Brooks Kieschnick	CIN	-$4	12	0	0	0	0	.000	.077	.000

PITCHERS SECOND HALF 2000 STATS AND $ VALUES

AMERICAN LEAGUE

NAME	TM	VAL	W	L	SV	IP	H	BB	K	ERA	RATIO
Derek Lowe	BOS	$45	2	1	25	44	50	10	39	2.44	1.35
Mariano Rivera	NYY	$39	5	1	18	40	26	13	32	2.48	0.98
Roberto Hernandez	TB	$39	2	5	21	36	30	14	28	2.02	1.24
Kazuhiro Sasaki	SEA	$39	1	0	21	32	17	14	40	2.50	0.96
Keith Foulke	CHW	$38	2	1	18	40	23	11	40	2.25	0.85
Pedro Martinez	BOS	$37	9	3	0	111	66	12	144	2.03	0.70
Billy Koch	TOR	$36	5	2	16	38	32	6	25	2.13	1.00
Todd Jones	DET	$30	2	3	19	35	38	19	37	4.15	1.64
Bob Wickman	CLE	$30	1	4	19	36	38	16	21	4.29	1.51
Jason Isringhausen	OAK	$24	3	2	14	34	34	16	28	4.46	1.46
John Wetteland	TEX	$23	3	3	14	28	32	12	27	4.45	1.55
Shigetoshi Hasegawa	ANA	$23	4	4	7	50	36	20	30	1.80	1.12
Troy Percival	ANA	$23	1	1	13	22	11	12	26	4.44	1.03
LaTroy Hawkins	MIN	$22	0	3	11	40	33	16	22	2.70	1.23
Ryan Kohlmeier	BAL	$21	0	1	13	26	30	15	17	2.40	1.71
Ricky Bottalico	KC	$20	2	4	11	35	27	18	23	4.32	1.27
Roger Clemens	NYY	$20	8	2	0	116	97	45	102	3.10	1.22
Barry Zito	OAK	$18	7	4	0	93	64	45	78	2.72	1.18
Jose Mercedes	BAL	$18	11	4	0	108	99	45	55	3.33	1.33
Mike Mussina	BAL	$18	6	8	0	111	105	19	110	3.73	1.12
Tim Hudson	OAK	$16	10	4	0	99	86	32	75	4.09	1.19
Bartolo Colon	CLE	$16	8	3	0	113	90	57	120	3.51	1.30
Steve W. Sparks	DET	$15	7	4	0	94	95	22	53	3.53	1.24
Freddy Garcia	SEA	$14	7	4	0	106	87	54	66	3.39	1.33
Jim Mecir	OAK	$14	4	2	5	50	47	22	48	3.24	1.38
Frank Castillo	TOR	$13	5	0	0	51	36	16	36	2.49	1.03
Bob Wells	MIN	$12	0	2	4	46	38	7	31	3.75	0.99
Albie Lopez	TB	$12	7	7	0	116	118	40	51	3.96	1.36
Jose Paniagua	SEA	$12	2	0	4	39	33	17	35	2.75	1.27
Orlando Hernandez	NYY	$11	5	7	0	97	91	21	68	4.55	1.15
Doc Gooden	NYY	$11	4	2	2	64	66	21	31	3.36	1.35
Mike Sirotka	CHW	$11	7	4	0	99	99	38	64	3.81	1.38
Andy Pettitte	NYY	$11	11	5	0	117	128	44	77	4.32	1.47
Bob Howry	CHW	$10	1	3	3	37	29	12	26	2.70	1.12
Eddie Guardado	MIN	$10	3	2	5	30	29	11	21	4.55	1.35
Tanyon Sturtze	TB	$10	4	0	0	43	35	11	31	2.30	1.07
Ramon Ortiz	ANA	$10	6	4	0	81	64	35	52	4.43	1.22
Dave Burba	CLE	$10	8	3	0	95	101	43	80	3.52	1.52
Jeff Weaver	DET	$10	6	9	0	105	113	26	76	4.37	1.32
Esteban Loaiza	TOR	$9	5	8	0	106	111	33	73	4.01	1.36
Steve Karsay	CLE	$9	4	4	4	38	42	16	33	4.22	1.51
David Wells	TOR	$9	7	6	0	114	135	17	72	4.80	1.33
Bryan Rekar	TB	$9	5	6	0	112	125	25	63	4.42	1.34
Tomokazu Ohka	BOS	$7	3	2	0	69	70	26	40	3.12	1.39
Paul Wilson	TB	$7	1	4	0	51	38	16	40	3.35	1.06
Blake Stein	KC	$7	8	5	0	108	98	57	78	4.68	1.44
Mark Redman	MIN	$7	7	6	0	74	77	21	52	4.97	1.32

NAME	TM	VAL	W	L	SV	IP	H	BB	K	ERA	RATIO
Jeff Suppan	KC	$7	8	3	0	110	124	44	59	4.32	1.52
Lorenzo Barcelo	CHW	$7	4	2	0	39	34	9	26	3.69	1.10
Hipolito Pichardo	BOS	$7	4	2	1	41	40	16	26	3.51	1.37
Chuck Finley	CLE	$7	9	6	0	103	111	46	80	4.56	1.53
Mark Petkovsek	ANA	$7	2	0	1	46	53	9	11	3.11	1.34
Aaron Sele	SEA	$6	7	7	0	105	113	37	72	4.81	1.43
Rick Helling	TEX	$6	8	6	0	108	109	50	71	4.82	1.47
Eric Milton	MIN	$6	5	8	0	97	106	24	75	4.92	1.34
Lue Pote	ANA	$6	1	1	1	34	31	10	30	2.89	1.20
Kelly Wunsch	CHW	$6	4	1	1	29	23	17	21	3.41	1.38
Tim Crabtree	TEX	$6	1	2	2	40	31	20	23	4.28	1.28
Gil Heredia	OAK	$6	6	5	0	96	112	31	45	4.33	1.49
Nelson Cruz	DET	$6	4	2	0	35	33	12	30	3.37	1.30
Sidney Ponson	BAL	$6	4	9	0	105	108	33	76	4.89	1.34
Rod Beck	BOS	$5	3	0	0	35	30	12	31	3.37	1.21
Mike Trombley	BAL	$5	0	3	3	43	41	25	42	3.77	1.53
Denny Neagle	NYY	$5	8	7	0	99	105	35	65	5.35	1.41
Steve Woodard	CLE	$5	3	4	0	67	68	14	42	4.94	1.22
Kelvim Escobar	TOR	$5	4	6	2	70	66	31	65	5.63	1.38
Paul Abbott	SEA	$5	4	5	0	100	94	49	41	4.42	1.43
Jarrod Washburn	ANA	$5	3	0	0	22	16	9	13	2.42	1.12
Rolando Arrojo	BOS	$5	5	5	0	96	95	34	66	5.23	1.34
Kevin Appier	OAK	$5	7	7	0	108	106	57	69	4.74	1.51
Brett Tomko	SEA	$5	3	3	1	46	43	22	20	4.14	1.43
Jeff Tam	OAK	$4	1	1	1	29	31	9	12	2.82	1.39
Hideo Nomo	DET	$4	5	5	0	78	83	32	77	4.60	1.47
Joey Hamilton	TOR	$4	2	1	0	33	28	12	15	3.55	1.21
Steve Reed	CLE	$4	1	0	0	30	26	9	18	2.97	1.16
Mark Buehrle	CHW	$4	4	1	0	51	55	19	37	4.21	1.44
Danny Patterson	DET	$4	3	0	0	26	25	5	13	4.50	1.15
Brian Meadows	KC	$3	6	5	0	103	126	23	40	5.24	1.45
Rich Garces	BOS	$3	5	1	0	33	36	13	25	4.40	1.50
Cory Lidle	TB	$3	3	3	0	48	52	14	24	4.50	1.38
Mike Venafro	TEX	$3	2	1	1	26	32	9	17	3.46	1.58
Dave Mlicki	DET	$3	4	2	0	44	51	14	22	4.30	1.48
Jim Parque	CHW	$3	5	4	0	91	100	38	52	4.73	1.51
Ben Weber	ANA	$3	1	0	0	15	12	2	8	1.84	0.95
Jeff Nelson	NYY	$3	2	2	0	26	19	15	24	3.41	1.29
Paul Shuey	CLE	$3	1	1	0	40	32	20	45	3.79	1.29
Paxton Crawford	BOS	$3	2	0	0	24	21	8	15	3.42	1.22
Mike Holtz	ANA	$3	3	2	0	25	21	9	24	4.98	1.19
Doug Jones	OAK	$3	2	1	0	36	38	13	25	3.29	1.43
Brad Radke	MIN	$3	7	7	0	101	134	23	67	5.06	1.55
B.J. Ryan	BAL	$3	1	0	0	23	14	10	20	4.23	1.03
Chad Bradford	CHW	$3	1	0	0	14	13	1	9	1.97	1.02
Sean Lowe	CHW	$3	2	0	0	38	32	16	21	4.74	1.26
Doug Brocail	DET	$2	1	1	0	13	10	3	11	2.13	1.02
Jeff Zimmerman	TEX	$2	3	1	1	37	45	18	39	4.14	1.70
John Halama	SEA	$2	7	5	0	85	113	21	43	5.16	1.57
Bryce Florie	BOS	$2	0	1	1	38	41	12	29	4.23	1.38
Justin Speier	CLE	$2	4	1	0	43	46	23	37	4.36	1.59
Doug Davis	TEX	$2	6	5	0	80	90	41	49	4.61	1.64
Brian Moehler	DET	$2	7	5	0	103	134	27	64	5.14	1.56

NAME	TM	VAL	W	L	SV	IP	H	BB	K	ERA	RATIO
Jose Santiago	KC	$2	2	4	1	23	26	10	15	4.70	1.57
Estaban Yan	TB	$2	3	2	0	52	55	13	52	5.57	1.32
John Frascatore	TOR	$1	1	2	0	35	40	13	16	3.60	1.51
Mike Fyhrie	ANA	$1	0	0	0	26	28	10	20	2.45	1.48
Dan Wheeler	TB	$1	1	0	0	13	11	8	12	2.71	1.43
C.J. Nitkowski	DET	$1	0	2	0	41	35	22	32	3.98	1.40
Buddy Groom	BAL	$1	3	0	0	27	32	8	27	5.08	1.50
Chuck McElroy	BAL	$1	2	0	0	37	37	18	27	4.43	1.50
Dan Murray	KC	$1	0	0	0	13	11	6	8	2.03	1.28
Arthur Rhodes	SEA	$1	3	6	0	33	28	14	39	6.35	1.29
Matt Wise	ANA	$1	3	3	0	37	40	13	20	5.55	1.42
Adam Bernero	DET	$1	0	1	0	34	33	13	20	4.20	1.34
Tim Belcher	ANA	$1	2	3	0	28	29	8	15	5.52	1.34
Mike Magnante	OAK	$1	1	0	0	23	27	8	12	3.91	1.52
Matt Anderson	DET	$1	0	1	1	40	34	25	33	4.77	1.49
Travis Harper	TB	$0	1	2	0	32	30	15	14	4.78	1.41
Tim Wakefield	BOS	$0	3	5	0	91	91	37	59	5.64	1.41
Sang-Hoon Lee	BOS	$0	0	0	0	11	9	5	6	2.45	1.27
Bryan Ward	ANA	$0	0	0	0	15	14	5	8	3.70	1.30
Jose Mesa	SEA	$0	2	2	0	42	44	22	37	4.71	1.57
Makoto Suzuki	KC	$0	5	7	0	100	116	49	62	4.75	1.64
Bill Simas	CHW	$0	1	2	0	27	34	8	20	4.27	1.53
Rheal Cormier	BOS	$0	1	2	0	33	35	9	23	5.41	1.32
Kris Wilson	KC	$0	0	1	0	34	38	11	17	4.20	1.43
Willie Blair	DET	$0	5	5	0	92	120	22	44	5.40	1.55
Cam Cairncross	CLE	$0	1	0	0	9	11	3	8	3.87	1.51
Hector Carrasco	BOS	$0	2	2	0	36	40	19	38	4.50	1.64
Mike Stanton	NYY	$0	1	2	0	29	29	11	37	5.33	1.39
Frank Rodriguez	SEA	$0	0	0	0	7	5	4	4	1.36	1.36
Ryan Rupe	TB	$0	5	2	0	60	80	18	40	5.52	1.63
Jaime Navarro	CLE	$0	0	0	0	7	3	2	4	5.45	0.76
Darrell Einertson	NYY	$0	0	0	0	6	9	1	3	1.50	1.67
Kevin Tolar	DET	$0	0	0	0	3	1	1	3	3.00	0.67
Scott Mullen	KC	$0	0	0	0	10	10	3	7	4.37	1.26
Matt Kinney	MIN	$0	2	2	0	42	41	25	24	5.11	1.56
Randy Choate	NYY	-$1	0	1	0	16	13	8	12	5.06	1.31
Aaron Myette	CHW	-$1	0	0	0	3	0	4	1	0.00	1.48
Jon Ratliff	OAK	-$1	0	0	0	1	0	0	0	0.00	0.00
Scott Service	OAK	-$1	0	2	1	17	20	8	17	6.21	1.61
Ariel Prieto	OAK	-$1	0	1	0	19	22	6	13	4.33	1.50
Robert Ramsay	SEA	-$1	0	0	0	24	23	19	18	3.33	1.73
Ricardo Rincon	CLE	-$1	0	0	0	11	9	9	10	4.21	1.68
Andrew Lorraine	CLE	-$1	0	0	0	3	4	2	1	3.00	2.00
Kenny Rogers	TEX	-$1	5	8	0	113	138	48	69	5.00	1.64
Luis Rivera	BAL	-$1	0	0	0	1	1	1	0	0.00	3.20
Jeff Fassero	BOS	-$1	2	5	0	62	68	28	59	5.25	1.56
Dan Reichert	KC	-$1	5	5	0	99	108	58	53	4.93	1.68
Joe Mays	MIN	-$1	3	5	0	58	73	20	42	5.43	1.60
Lance Painter	TOR	-$1	1	0	0	31	37	13	23	4.98	1.63
Sean Runyan	DET	-$1	0	0	0	3	2	2	1	6.00	1.33
Al Levine	ANA	-$1	2	4	0	38	42	23	18	4.93	1.70
Tom Martin	CLE	-$1	0	0	0	10	12	3	5	5.40	1.50
Jason Bere	CLE	-$1	7	4	0	78	88	40	64	6.00	1.64

NAME	TM	VAL	W	L	SV	IP	H	BB	K	ERA	RATIO
Chris Haney	CLE	-$1	0	0	0	1	1	1	0	9.00	2.00
Paul Spoljaric	KC	-$1	0	0	0	7	5	4	4	6.43	1.29
Ben Ford	NYY	-$1	0	0	0	3	3	2	0	6.67	1.85
Ramiro Mendoza	NYY	-$1	0	1	0	0	1	0	1	24.46	3.20
Steve Trachsel	TOR	-$1	2	7	0	93	115	32	46	5.01	1.57
Ted Lilly	NYY	-$1	0	0	0	8	8	5	11	5.63	1.63
Brett Laxton	KC	-$1	0	0	0	5	7	2	4	5.40	1.80
Rich Croushore	BOS	-$1	0	1	0	5	4	5	3	5.74	1.91
Todd Belitz	OAK	-$1	0	0	0	3	4	4	3	2.73	2.42
Leo Estrella	TOR	-$1	0	0	0	5	9	5	3	5.74	1.91
Erik Hiljus	DET	-$1	0	0	0	4	5	1	2	7.30	1.62
Jay Tessmer	NYY	-$2	0	0	0	7	9	1	5	6.72	1.49
Tim Young	BOS	-$2	0	0	0	0	1	0	0	32.00	3.20
Gil Meche	SEA	-$2	0	0	0	6	5	3	6	7.89	1.40
Mark Guthrie	TOR	-$2	0	2	0	29	34	12	29	5.03	1.61
Eric Weaver	ANA	-$2	0	0	0	1	2	1	0	13.85	2.31
Mike Duvall	TB	-$2	0	0	0	2	5	1	0	7.83	2.61
Jesus Pena	BOS	-$2	1	0	1	11	16	10	6	7.64	2.45
Seth Etherton	ANA	-$2	2	0	0	26	36	9	11	6.23	1.73
Jeff M. D'Amico	KC	-$2	0	0	0	2	3	2	0	13.50	2.50
Brian Williams	CLE	-$2	0	0	0	3	5	3	0	6.92	3.08
Travis Miller	MIN	-$2	1	1	0	29	39	11	27	5.53	1.71
Kevin Hodges	SEA	-$2	0	0	0	8	10	4	3	7.11	1.84
Matt Dewitt	TOR	-$2	0	0	0	4	5	3	4	10.23	1.82
Jay Spurgeon	BAL	-$2	1	1	0	24	26	15	11	6.00	1.71
Steve Ontiveros	BOS	-$2	1	1	0	5	9	4	1	10.19	2.45
James Baldwin	CHW	-$2	3	4	0	71	86	24	46	5.96	1.55
Kip Wells	CHW	-$2	2	2	0	24	33	12	11	6.00	1.88
Pasqual Coco	TOR	-$2	0	0	0	4	5	5	2	9.00	2.50
Alan Mills	BAL	-$2	2	0	0	13	16	14	9	6.77	2.26
Kevin Beirne	CHW	-$2	0	3	0	32	32	10	30	7.03	1.31
Danny Mota	MIN	-$2	0	0	0	5	10	1	3	8.49	2.08
Jack Cressend	MIN	-$2	0	0	0	14	20	6	6	5.26	1.90
Billy Taylor	TB	-$2	1	2	0	9	10	7	8	9.57	1.81
TJ Mathews	OAK	-$3	0	1	0	24	31	8	19	6.00	1.63
Paul Quantrill	TOR	-$3	2	2	0	37	51	12	23	5.89	1.72
Derrick Turnbow	ANA	-$3	0	0	0	24	24	20	15	4.81	1.81
Chris Nichting	CLE	-$3	0	0	0	9	13	5	7	7.00	2.00
Johan Santana	MIN	-$3	1	1	0	42	47	22	31	5.61	1.65
Marcus Jones	OAK	-$3	0	0	0	2	5	2	1	15.65	3.04
Joel Pineiro	SEA	-$3	1	0	0	19	25	13	10	5.60	1.97
Chris Fussell	KC	-$3	1	1	0	17	22	11	11	6.35	1.94
Jamie Moyer	SEA	-$3	7	7	0	98	118	40	63	6.23	1.61
Ed Yarnall	NYY	-$3	0	0	0	1	3	0	0	32.00	3.20
Doug Creek	TB	-$3	1	3	1	39	39	31	45	6.17	1.78
Tim Drew	CLE	-$3	1	0	0	8	14	8	5	7.88	2.75
Allen Watson	NYY	-$3	0	0	0	4	7	4	2	13.50	2.75
Jason Grimsley	NYY	-$3	0	0	1	38	40	20	19	7.11	1.58
Craig Dingman	NYY	-$3	0	0	0	8	17	1	6	8.67	2.17
Scott Schoeneweis	ANA	-$4	2	5	0	80	91	34	41	5.87	1.57
Doug Bochtler	KC	-$4	0	2	0	7	12	8	3	7.40	2.74
Tim Byrdak	KC	-$4	0	1	0	6	11	4	8	11.43	2.38
Tony Fiore	TB	-$4	1	1	0	15	21	9	8	8.40	2.00

NAME	TM	VAL	W	L	SV	IP	H	BB	K	ERA	RATIO
Jamie Brewington	CLE	-$4	2	0	0	32	48	13	26	6.41	1.89
Trevor Enders	TB	-$4	0	1	0	9	14	5	5	10.65	2.04
Rocky Biddle	CHW	-$4	1	2	0	23	31	8	7	8.33	1.72
Mark Mulder	OAK	-$4	4	7	0	74	97	33	42	5.62	1.76
Dave Eiland	TB	-$4	1	2	0	26	38	9	8	7.16	1.78
Jonathan Johnson	TEX	-$4	1	1	0	26	32	17	20	6.92	1.88
Brian Sikorski	TEX	-$4	1	3	0	38	46	25	32	5.73	1.88
Ramon Martinez	BOS	-$5	4	4	0	54	58	35	36	6.95	1.71
Randy Keisler	NYY	-$5	1	0	0	11	16	8	6	11.78	2.24
Jay Ryan	MIN	-$5	0	0	0	19	26	7	16	8.53	1.74
Darren Holmes	BAL	-$5	0	0	0	8	16	2	8	13.03	2.37
Pete Schourek	BOS	-$5	1	3	0	18	27	7	12	9.34	1.86
Cal Eldred	CHW	-$5	0	0	0	15	19	11	16	8.82	1.96
Lesli Brea	BAL	-$5	0	1	0	9	12	10	5	11.00	2.44
Juan Alvarez	ANA	-$5	0	0	0	6	14	5	2	13.50	3.17
Scott Erickson	BAL	-$5	2	2	0	29	37	18	11	8.07	1.90
Matt Ginter	CHW	-$6	1	0	0	9	18	7	6	13.55	2.69
Charles Nagy	CLE	-$6	0	3	0	11	16	7	2	12.62	2.15
Francisco Cordero	TEX	-$6	0	1	0	39	46	21	22	6.69	1.72
Chad Durbin	KC	-$6	0	2	0	22	32	12	8	7.77	2.00
Jon Garland	CHW	-$6	4	8	0	70	82	40	42	6.46	1.75
Andy Larkin	KC	-$6	0	3	1	24	34	16	22	8.63	2.08
Chris Carpenter	TOR	-$6	4	5	0	72	91	34	55	6.60	1.73
Pat Rapp	BAL	-$6	4	7	0	85	100	40	44	6.65	1.64
Omar Olivares	OAK	-$6	1	0	0	28	35	24	18	7.07	2.11
Mike Lincoln	MIN	-$6	0	2	0	14	22	10	9	10.51	2.34
Kent Mercker	ANA	-$7	1	2	0	26	35	21	12	7.73	2.19
Roy Halladay	TOR	-$7	1	2	0	23	36	14	18	8.72	2.20
Pedro Borbon	TOR	-$7	0	1	1	17	20	24	11	10.24	2.63
John Parrish	BAL	-$7	2	4	0	36	40	35	28	7.19	2.07
Ryan Glynn	TEX	-$7	4	7	0	71	95	35	26	6.55	1.82
J.C. Romero	MIN	-$8	2	7	0	58	72	30	50	7.02	1.77
Scott Karl	ANA	-$8	2	3	0	34	49	21	13	8.30	2.08
Jim Brower	CLE	-$8	0	1	0	20	34	14	11	9.14	2.44
Jason Johnson	BAL	-$9	1	4	0	41	50	26	30	8.34	1.85
Darwin Cubillan	TEX	-$9	0	0	0	18	32	14	13	10.74	2.61
Ken Hill	CHW	-$10	1	4	0	38	53	31	29	7.82	2.21
Darren Oliver	TEX	-$11	0	5	0	35	59	13	11	9.00	2.06
David Cone	NYY	-$11	3	8	0	71	90	41	61	7.51	1.85
Brian Cooper	ANA	-$12	1	6	0	33	56	19	13	9.91	2.29
Matt Perisho	TEX	-$17	0	5	0	57	80	36	42	9.16	2.04

NATIONAL LEAGUE

NAME	TM	VAL	W	L	SV	IP	H	BB	K	ERA	RATIO
Robb Nen	SF	$53	2	0	28	36	14	7	56	0.75	0.58
Armando Benitez	NYM	$42	2	1	23	36	18	17	53	1.49	0.96
Trevor Hoffman	SD	$40	3	4	22	37	28	5	36	2.68	0.89
Antonio Alfonseca	FLA	$31	2	2	20	30	31	11	16	3.56	1.39
Jeff Shaw	LA	$29	1	0	15	30	21	6	24	0.89	0.89
Greg Maddux	ATL	$27	10	6	0	124	104	16	86	2.62	0.97
Danny Graves	CIN	$27	1	4	18	40	45	18	21	3.60	1.58
Curt Leskanic	MIL	$26	9	1	11	39	29	22	38	1.85	1.31
Matt Mantei	AZ	$26	0	0	15	28	11	19	34	1.63	1.09
Octavio Dotel	HOU	$25	2	2	16	33	26	16	48	4.36	1.27
Dave Veres	STL	$23	2	3	13	35	29	14	32	2.59	1.24
Curt Schilling	AZ	$21	7	8	0	131	113	21	92	3.38	1.03
Tom Glavine	ATL	$21	13	4	0	117	112	24	60	3.16	1.17
Livan Hernandez	SF	$21	11	5	0	128	114	36	86	3.17	1.17
John Rocker	ATL	$21	0	2	12	30	23	15	41	1.21	1.28
Jeff C. D'Amico	MIL	$20	9	3	0	118	106	29	75	2.68	1.15
Kevin Brown	LA	$20	6	4	0	113	93	21	115	2.87	1.01
Mike Williams	PIT	$20	1	3	14	38	33	25	34	4.97	1.53
Chanho Park	LA	$19	9	6	0	118	89	58	124	2.44	1.25
Scott Strickland	MON	$19	2	3	9	34	22	14	36	2.38	1.06
Mike Hampton	NYM	$19	8	5	0	110	91	38	82	2.62	1.17
Daryl Kile	STL	$18	9	4	0	118	108	27	82	3.21	1.15
Jose Jimenez	COL	$18	1	2	10	37	31	15	24	3.19	1.25
Rick Aguilera	CHC	$18	0	1	12	19	18	5	18	4.64	1.19
Woody Williams	SD	$17	7	6	0	122	102	40	77	3.39	1.16
Mark Gardner	SF	$16	7	3	0	96	87	22	62	2.99	1.13
Gabe White	COL	$14	5	2	4	42	35	8	35	3.02	1.03
Andy Ashby	ATL	$14	10	6	0	113	113	28	60	3.82	1.25
Pete Harnisch	CIN	$14	7	2	0	100	91	26	45	3.52	1.17
Russ Ortiz	SF	$13	10	4	0	106	85	56	97	3.40	1.33
Rick Reed	NYM	$13	7	3	0	93	89	20	70	3.47	1.17
Al Leiter	NYM	$13	6	7	0	96	78	34	96	3.39	1.17
Scott Elarton	HOU	$13	10	4	0	115	103	47	83	3.90	1.30
Jeff Brantley	PHI	$13	1	6	12	32	45	15	34	6.69	1.86
Darren Dreifort	LA	$12	8	2	0	100	85	43	96	3.43	1.28
Brian Bohanon	COL	$12	9	5	0	111	107	45	59	3.41	1.37
Scott Sullivan	CIN	$12	2	3	1	56	36	17	50	2.40	0.94
Bobby J. Jones	NYM	$11	8	3	0	108	109	33	57	3.75	1.31
Rick Ankiel	STL	$11	5	4	0	89	67	37	108	3.55	1.17
Elmer Dessens	CIN	$11	11	5	0	105	115	29	53	4.04	1.38
Bruce Chen	PHI	$11	3	4	0	100	88	29	84	3.52	1.17
Matt Herges	LA	$11	6	3	1	62	57	20	30	3.06	1.25
Kerry Ligtenberg	ATL	$10	0	2	6	27	21	13	27	3.05	1.28
Brian Anderson	AZ	$10	3	5	0	109	113	22	51	3.62	1.24
Mike Remlinger	ATL	$10	3	1	5	32	27	19	29	3.38	1.44
Mike Timlin	STL	$10	3	1	5	40	38	21	33	3.63	1.49
Randy Johnson	AZ	$10	7	5	0	117	114	45	170	3.85	1.36
Kevin Millwood	ATL	$10	5	7	0	109	104	24	86	4.47	1.18
Glendon Rusch	NYM	$9	5	5	0	97	98	27	86	3.62	1.29
Jon Lieber	CHC	$9	6	6	0	125	127	25	100	4.81	1.21
Mike Fetters	LA	$9	3	1	4	30	24	13	22	3.64	1.25

NAME	TM	VAL	W	L	SV	IP	H	BB	K	ERA	RATIO
Chuck Smith	FLA	$9	6	5	0	95	87	45	93	3.41	1.39
Felix Rodriguez	SF	$8	1	2	2	36	27	15	43	1.73	1.15
Aaron Fultz	SF	$8	3	1	1	34	28	8	29	2.12	1.06
Tim Worrell	CHC	$8	3	3	3	45	48	18	39	2.78	1.46
Julian Tavarez	COL	$8	6	3	0	85	82	35	41	3.49	1.38
Ryan Dempster	FLA	$7	5	6	0	110	104	46	100	3.94	1.37
Pat Hentgen	STL	$7	9	6	0	102	108	43	64	3.99	1.49
Ray King	MIL	$7	3	2	0	27	17	10	18	0.99	0.99
Armando Reynoso	AZ	$7	6	6	0	92	89	30	52	4.60	1.29
Javier Vazquez	MON	$6	5	5	0	115	130	32	120	4.06	1.40
Juan Acevedo	MIL	$6	3	4	0	44	37	11	23	3.27	1.09
Turk Wendell	NYM	$6	4	3	1	35	24	17	35	3.89	1.18
Garrett Stephenson	STL	$6	7	5	0	98	103	32	57	4.70	1.38
Donne Wall	SD	$6	3	0	1	23	18	8	14	2.69	1.11
Mike James	STL	$5	2	1	1	32	23	15	23	2.79	1.18
Steve Parris	CIN	$5	9	6	0	107	129	38	66	4.12	1.56
Anthony Telford	MON	$5	0	1	2	36	34	9	35	3.50	1.19
Matt Morris	STL	$5	3	2	2	36	40	11	25	3.97	1.41
Alan Embree	SF	$5	3	3	1	26	22	8	18	3.42	1.14
Felix Heredia	CHC	$5	4	0	1	27	20	14	25	4.04	1.27
Kirk Rueter	SF	$4	5	5	0	95	118	24	31	3.98	1.49
Brian Tollberg	SD	$4	2	5	0	99	112	28	59	3.74	1.42
John Riedling	CIN	$4	3	1	1	15	11	8	18	2.35	1.24
Osvaldo Fernandez	CIN	$4	2	1	0	30	26	9	12	2.42	1.18
Britt Reames	STL	$4	2	1	0	41	30	23	31	2.87	1.30
Tony McKnight	HOU	$4	4	1	0	35	35	9	23	3.86	1.26
Cliff Politte	PHI	$4	3	1	0	37	33	17	31	2.92	1.35
Kerry Wood	CHC	$4	5	1	0	71	60	46	69	4.04	1.49
Paul Rigdon	MIL	$4	4	4	0	70	68	26	48	4.53	1.35
Scott Williamson	CIN	$4	3	3	0	59	51	33	58	3.37	1.43
Adam Eaton	SD	$4	6	4	0	96	104	39	63	4.49	1.48
Kevin Walker	SD	$4	4	1	0	34	21	23	32	3.74	1.31
Robert Person	PHI	$4	4	5	0	85	75	49	74	4.11	1.45
Joe Slusarski	HOU	$3	1	2	2	43	50	10	30	4.40	1.40
John Franco	NYM	$3	2	1	1	23	18	14	27	2.74	1.39
Rick White	NYM	$3	2	5	1	38	35	16	23	4.03	1.34
Josias Manzanillo	PIT	$3	2	2	0	39	31	22	27	2.97	1.35
Wade Miller	HOU	$3	6	6	0	105	104	42	89	5.14	1.39
Doug Henry	SF	$3	3	2	0	35	24	26	27	3.06	1.42
Steve Kline	MON	$3	0	3	5	35	51	10	26	5.86	1.73
Manny Aybar	FLA	$3	1	0	0	27	18	13	14	2.64	1.14
Kyle Farnsworth	CHC	$3	1	4	1	34	28	20	39	3.15	1.40
Tony Armas	MON	$3	4	4	0	45	39	22	27	4.63	1.36
Jesus Sanchez	FLA	$3	5	5	0	90	96	32	58	4.82	1.43
Tom Davey	SD	$3	2	1	0	13	12	2	6	0.71	1.10
Brad Penny	FLA	$2	4	0	0	37	36	14	23	4.81	1.34
Danny Miceli	FLA	$2	3	2	0	27	28	5	17	4.67	1.22
John Wasdin	COL	$2	1	3	1	45	48	10	40	4.97	1.28
Jose Cabrera	HOU	$2	2	1	2	23	28	5	17	6.26	1.43
Rob Bell	CIN	$2	3	2	0	65	59	31	53	4.69	1.38
Dan Plesac	AZ	$2	4	1	0	19	17	12	22	3.79	1.53
Shawn Estes	SF	$2	8	3	0	100	106	53	81	4.76	1.59
Antonio Osuna	LA	$2	3	2	0	36	36	16	39	4.00	1.44

NAME	TM	VAL	W	L	SV	IP	H	BB	K	ERA	RATIO
Bobby Chouinard	COL	$2	2	2	0	33	35	9	23	3.85	1.35
Guillermo Mota	MON	$2	1	0	0	19	15	6	18	2.89	1.12
Terry Adams	LA	$2	3	6	0	40	40	20	31	4.02	1.49
Chris Brock	PHI	$2	3	4	1	36	34	19	27	5.31	1.49
Mike Myers	COL	$2	0	1	0	27	16	16	24	3.00	1.19
Carlos Almanzar	SD	$2	3	2	0	27	33	11	19	3.00	1.63
Vic Darensbourg	FLA	$1	2	3	0	27	25	11	28	4.29	1.32
Jimmy Anderson	PIT	$1	4	6	0	86	96	33	42	4.80	1.49
Dennis Cook	NYM	$1	1	1	1	29	23	20	23	4.34	1.48
Dustin Hermanson	MON	$1	6	9	0	116	139	42	53	4.66	1.56
Luke Prokopec	LA	$1	1	1	0	21	19	9	12	3.00	1.33
Geraldo Guzman	AZ	$1	5	4	0	60	66	22	52	5.37	1.46
Scott Kamieniecki	ATL	$1	2	1	2	25	22	22	17	5.47	1.78
Matt Clement	SD	$1	6	10	0	104	97	61	88	5.03	1.52
Dave Weathers	MIL	$1	0	2	0	29	25	17	18	2.46	1.43
Alberto Reyes	LA	$1	0	0	0	7	2	1	8	0.00	0.45
Valerio De los Santos	MIL	$1	1	1	0	31	29	12	31	4.06	1.32
Ron Villone	CIN	$1	3	5	0	54	51	29	38	4.64	1.47
Kris Benson	PIT	$1	3	6	0	96	99	44	85	4.67	1.48
Chris Peters	PIT	$1	0	0	0	12	5	9	8	0.75	1.17
Rich Loiselle	PIT	$1	2	0	0	26	23	17	23	3.76	1.52
Kevin Tapani	CHC	$1	4	5	0	83	96	22	59	5.40	1.41
John Burkett	ATL	$1	4	3	0	68	80	23	48	4.90	1.51
Mark Wohlers	CIN	$1	1	2	0	28	19	17	20	4.50	1.29
Kent Bottenfield	PHI	$1	4	3	0	83	87	34	45	5.18	1.45
Everett Stull	MIL	$1	1	0	0	21	21	7	14	3.80	1.31
Todd Ritchie	PIT	$0	4	3	0	83	99	24	55	5.10	1.48
Scott Sauerbeck	PIT	$0	2	4	1	42	47	26	44	3.88	1.75
Dennis Reyes	CIN	$0	0	0	0	18	17	7	14	2.50	1.33
Greg Swindell	AZ	$0	1	5	0	39	42	13	31	4.35	1.40
Miguel Deltoro	SF	$0	2	0	0	17	17	6	16	5.20	1.33
A.J. Burnett	FLA	$0	3	7	0	83	80	44	57	4.79	1.50
Dave Maurer	SD	$0	1	0	0	15	15	5	13	3.67	1.36
Marc Wilkins	PIT	$0	3	2	0	45	38	32	30	4.80	1.56
Ryan Vogelsong	SF	$0	0	0	0	6	4	2	6	0.00	1.00
Will Cunnane	SD	$0	0	0	0	18	17	8	13	3.00	1.39
Chris Holt	HOU	$0	5	7	0	100	116	33	60	5.42	1.49
Terry Mulholland	ATL	$0	1	2	0	54	63	20	31	4.00	1.54
Brian O'Connor	PIT	$0	0	0	0	10	6	11	7	0.87	1.65
Jerry Dipoto	COL	$0	0	0	0	9	9	3	2	1.91	1.28
Keith Glauber	CIN	$0	0	0	0	7	5	2	4	3.70	0.96
Pedro Astacio	COL	$0	5	4	0	80	88	33	78	5.60	1.51
Vincente Padilla	PHI	$0	2	7	2	41	52	24	28	5.05	1.85
Russ Springer	AZ	-$1	0	2	0	29	29	11	31	4.34	1.38
Hector Mercado	CIN	-$1	0	0	0	7	6	4	7	1.34	1.49
Onan Masaoka	LA	-$1	1	1	0	12	10	6	13	5.25	1.33
Eric Cammack	NYM	-$1	0	0	0	4	2	4	5	0.00	1.50
Bronson Arroyo	PIT	-$1	2	4	0	53	53	24	37	5.39	1.44
Kevin McGlinchy	ATL	-$1	0	0	0	3	4	1	3	0.00	1.67
Hideki Irabu	MON	-$1	0	1	0	6	5	1	2	4.50	1.00
John Johnstone	SF	-$1	1	0	0	11	13	5	10	4.78	1.59
Ed Vosberg	PHI	-$1	1	1	0	24	21	18	23	4.13	1.63
Yorkis Perez	HOU	-$1	0	0	0	3	3	1	3	2.65	1.18

NAME	TM	VAL	W	L	SV	IP	H	BB	K	ERA	RATIO
Brian Powell	HOU	-$1	2	1	0	31	34	13	14	5.75	1.50
Mike Maddux	HOU	-$1	0	0	0	2	1	1	1	0.00	1.00
Jerrod Riggan	NYM	-$1	0	0	0	2	3	0	1	0.00	1.50
Chad Zerbe	SF	-$1	0	0	0	6	6	1	5	4.50	1.17
Horacio Estrada	MIL	-$1	1	0	0	5	5	5	4	5.09	1.89
Allen Levrault	MIL	-$1	0	0	0	1	2	0	0	0.00	2.00
Jamey Wright	MIL	-$1	3	8	0	110	119	53	53	4.68	1.57
Bobby M. Jones	NYM	-$1	0	1	0	21	18	12	18	4.35	1.45
Dan Serafini	PIT	-$1	2	5	0	62	70	27	32	4.91	1.56
Scott Winchester	CIN	-$1	0	0	0	4	6	1	2	2.25	1.75
Mike Buddie	MIL	-$1	0	0	0	6	8	1	5	4.50	1.50
Wayne Gomes	PHI	-$1	0	2	1	28	31	12	20	6.11	1.54
Omar Daal	PHI	-$1	2	10	0	77	90	32	56	4.66	1.58
Dave Coggin	PHI	-$1	1	0	0	16	21	7	12	4.50	1.75
Vladimir Nunez	FLA	-$1	0	0	0	8	6	7	7	4.50	1.63
Amaury Telemaco	PHI	-$1	0	3	0	15	15	6	13	4.93	1.44
Sean Spencer	MON	-$1	0	0	0	7	7	3	6	5.37	1.49
Mark Brownson	PHI	-$1	1	0	0	5	7	3	3	7.20	2.00
Will Ohman	CHC	-$1	1	0	0	3	4	4	2	8.18	2.42
Gregg Olson	LA	-$1	0	1	0	16	18	7	15	4.59	1.59
Randy Wolf	PHI	-$1	4	4	0	98	111	46	77	4.94	1.60
Chris Seelbach	ATL	-$2	0	1	0	2	3	0	1	10.59	1.76
Brian Rose	COL	-$2	4	5	0	64	72	30	40	5.51	1.60
David Lee	COL	-$2	0	0	0	3	3	3	1	6.67	2.22
Jeremy Powell	MON	-$2	0	1	0	9	11	3	5	6.00	1.56
Tom Jacquez	PHI	-$2	0	0	1	7	10	3	6	11.10	1.78
Matt Skrmetta	PIT	-$2	2	2	0	9	13	3	7	9.57	1.70
Felipe Lira	MON	-$2	4	8	0	65	80	23	29	5.68	1.58
Matt Whiteside	SD	-$2	0	2	0	9	10	3	3	6.00	1.44
Rich Rodriguez	NYM	-$2	0	0	0	8	10	2	2	8.18	1.56
Carlos Reyes	SD	-$2	0	0	0	4	4	2	4	11.25	1.50
Todd Van Poppel	CHC	-$2	2	3	0	54	54	34	44	5.00	1.63
Ismael Villegas	ATL	-$2	0	0	0	3	4	2	2	13.33	2.22
Steve Sparks	PIT	-$2	0	0	0	4	4	5	2	6.75	2.25
Gene Stechschulte	STL	-$2	0	0	0	17	16	10	9	5.93	1.56
Dave Stevens	ATL	-$2	0	0	0	3	5	1	4	12.00	2.00
Todd Stottlemyre	AZ	-$2	1	1	0	19	22	7	14	7.58	1.53
Brian Smith	PIT	-$2	0	0	0	4	6	2	3	10.47	1.86
Steve Montgomery	SD	-$2	0	1	0	4	5	3	2	9.73	2.16
Kevin Jarvis	COL	-$2	1	1	0	45	50	15	21	6.00	1.44
Ron Mahay	FLA	-$2	0	0	0	6	10	3	7	7.14	2.06
Doug Nickle	PHI	-$2	0	0	0	3	5	2	0	13.33	2.59
Paul Byrd	PHI	-$2	0	3	0	19	19	10	12	6.53	1.50
Francisco Cordova	PIT	-$2	1	2	0	14	21	5	10	6.92	1.82
Mike Matthews	STL	-$2	0	0	0	4	5	2	5	12.50	1.94
Steve Rain	CHC	-$2	2	4	0	38	38	27	40	5.25	1.72
Luther Hackman	STL	-$2	0	0	0	3	4	4	0	10.00	2.96
Nelson Figueroa	AZ	-$2	0	0	0	9	10	4	5	8.62	1.49
Joey Nation	CHC	-$2	0	2	0	12	12	8	8	6.92	1.71
Andy Benes	STL	-$2	4	6	0	66	72	36	39	5.62	1.64
Mike Dejean	COL	-$2	1	3	0	27	28	17	22	5.93	1.65
Larry Luebbers	CIN	-$2	0	2	1	20	27	12	9	6.21	1.92
Marc Valdes	HOU	-$2	4	4	0	38	48	16	22	6.68	1.70

NAME	TM	VAL	W	L	SV	IP	H	BB	K	ERA	RATIO
Jeff Williams	LA	-$3	0	0	0	3	4	4	1	13.33	2.96
Oswaldo Mairena	CHC	-$3	0	0	0	2	6	0	0	18.00	3.00
Braden Looper	FLA	-$3	3	0	1	28	35	20	14	7.31	1.94
Wayne Franklin	HOU	-$3	0	0	0	21	24	12	21	5.49	1.69
Todd Erdos	SD	-$3	0	0	1	30	32	17	16	6.67	1.65
David Moraga	COL	-$3	0	0	0	1	3	0	0	32.00	3.20
Scott Downs	MON	-$3	1	1	0	26	34	14	18	4.90	1.87
Rusty Meacham	HOU	-$3	0	0	0	5	8	2	3	11.49	2.13
Yovanny Lara	MON	-$3	0	0	0	2	5	3	2	15.00	3.20
Joe Nathan	SF	-$3	1	0	0	24	25	16	14	6.10	1.74
Mike Judd	LA	-$3	0	1	0	4	4	3	5	15.75	1.75
Bob Scanlan	MIL	-$3	0	0	0	2	5	0	1	26.47	2.94
Jamie Arnold	CHC	-$3	0	3	1	37	37	24	15	6.51	1.64
Johnny Ruffin	AZ	-$3	0	0	0	9	14	3	5	9.00	1.89
Joe Strong	FLA	-$3	0	0	0	2	8	0	2	18.75	3.20
Heath Slocumb	SD	-$3	0	1	0	28	28	20	20	5.70	1.69
Rigo Beltran	COL	-$3	0	0	0	1	4	0	1	32.00	3.08
Jose Lima	HOU	-$3	6	4	0	100	118	37	54	6.21	1.55
Jason Green	HOU	-$3	1	1	0	18	15	20	19	6.61	1.98
Jay Powell	HOU	-$3	0	0	0	4	10	2	4	11.25	3.00
Scott Linebrink	HOU	-$3	0	0	0	11	16	8	6	6.55	2.18
Jason Christiansen	STL	-$3	2	1	0	16	22	10	19	8.83	1.96
Eric Gagne	LA	-$3	3	2	0	40	48	23	26	6.08	1.78
Rafael Roque	MIL	-$3	0	0	0	5	7	7	4	10.19	2.64
Craig House	COL	-$3	1	1	0	14	13	17	8	7.23	2.19
Steve Schrenk	PHI	-$3	0	0	0	2	5	0	1	32.00	3.20
Mark Thompson	STL	-$3	0	0	0	8	14	3	8	9.35	2.21
Byung Kim	AZ	-$4	4	3	1	32	32	34	43	7.59	2.06
Grant Roberts	NYM	-$4	0	0	0	7	11	4	6	11.57	2.14
Pat Mahomes	NYM	-$4	3	2	0	42	42	30	33	6.64	1.71
Jason Boyd	PHI	-$4	0	0	0	15	19	10	15	7.20	1.93
Buddy Carlyle	SD	-$4	0	0	0	3	6	3	2	21.00	3.00
Ruben Quevedo	CHC	-$4	3	7	0	72	69	42	55	6.28	1.55
Reid Cornelius	FLA	-$4	1	8	0	75	87	34	35	5.38	1.61
Jason Marquis	ATL	-$4	0	0	0	9	15	6	7	9.68	2.26
Phil Norton	CHC	-$4	0	1	0	9	14	7	6	9.31	2.41
Julio Santana	MON	-$4	1	4	0	56	60	32	46	5.90	1.63
Pete Walker	COL	-$5	0	0	0	5	10	4	2	17.23	2.98
Gabe Molina	ATL	-$5	0	0	0	11	21	5	6	9.00	2.36
Scott Forster	MON	-$5	0	1	0	29	23	24	23	7.45	1.62
Mike Johnson	MON	-$5	2	3	0	58	60	31	35	6.88	1.58
Mike Morgan	AZ	-$5	2	3	0	39	57	18	27	6.00	1.92
Armando Almanza	FLA	-$5	3	2	0	19	25	18	20	9.79	2.23
Ismael Valdes	LA	-$6	1	5	0	57	75	19	39	6.35	1.66
Giovanni Carrara	COL	-$6	0	1	0	11	17	9	13	11.95	2.30
Jerry Spradlin	CHC	-$6	2	3	1	42	60	12	28	8.85	1.73
Kane Davis	MIL	-$6	0	2	0	8	17	8	3	13.01	3.01
Carlos Perez	LA	-$6	1	4	0	52	83	11	19	6.02	1.80
Alan Benes	STL	-$6	0	1	0	26	37	16	14	7.00	2.06
Mark Holzemer	PHI	-$7	0	1	0	14	25	7	9	11.88	2.22
Jay Witasick	SD	-$7	4	3	0	81	98	45	71	6.25	1.77
Masato Yoshii	COL	-$7	2	8	0	79	99	29	38	6.76	1.63
Jeff Wallace	PIT	-$7	0	0	0	16	21	18	15	10.69	2.44

NAME	TM	VAL	W	L	SV	IP	H	BB	K	ERA	RATIO
Stan Belinda	ATL	-$7	0	2	0	18	27	10	15	12.00	2.06
Trey Moore	MON	-$7	1	5	0	35	55	21	24	6.63	2.15
Shane Reynolds	HOU	-$8	1	3	0	23	35	11	16	11.10	2.03
Mike Thurman	MON	-$8	3	8	0	77	97	41	48	6.29	1.79
Ricky Bones	FLA	-$8	0	1	0	31	52	10	27	8.63	1.98
Daniel Garibay	CHC	-$8	0	5	0	46	60	24	25	7.29	1.84
Jose Silva	PIT	-$10	6	7	0	79	110	38	49	7.26	1.87
Jimmy Haynes	MIL	-$10	4	6	0	90	115	51	47	6.38	1.84
John Snyder	MIL	-$11	0	8	0	82	101	42	44	6.56	1.74

Who Were the Most Productive Offensive Players in 2000?

by Bill Gilbert

Since 1992, I have analyzed offensive performance each year using Bases per Plate Appearance (BPA) also referred to as Base Production Average. This measure accounts for the net bases accumulated by a player and is calculated as follows:

$$BPA = (TB + BB + HB + SB - CS - GIDP) / (AB + BB + HB + SF)$$

Where:
BPA = Bases per Plate Appearance
TB = Total Bases
BB = Bases on Balls
HB = Hit by Pitch
SB = Stolen Bases
CS = Caught Stealing
GIDP = Grounded into Double Plays
AB = At Bats
SF = Sacrifice Flies

The numerator accounts for all of the bases accumulated by a player, reduced by the number of times he is caught stealing or erases another runner by grounding into a double play. The denominator accounts for the plate appearances when the player is trying to generate bases. Sacrifice hits are not included as plate appearances, since they represent the successful execution of the batter's attempts to advance another runner rather than himself.

Major league BPAs for the past seven years are shown below:

Year	1992	1993	1994	1995	1996	1997	1998	1999	2000
Major League BPA	.423	.446	.467	.463	.471	.465	.463	.479	.481
Players over .550	13	29	38	37	41	34	41	50	50
Players over .600	4	8	16	15	21	15	22	29	30

The major league average BPA of .481 in 2000 was an all-time high, surpassing the record set in 1999. This table clearly illustrates the increase in offense beginning in 1993, the year that the Colorado Rockies entered the National League.

Below is a listing of the nineteen individual .700 BPA seasons since 1990. There were five in 2000, Barry Bonds (.745), Manny Ramirez (.726), Todd Helton (.720), Carlos Delgado (.707) and Jason Giambi (.706). The two players who were over .700 in 1999, Mark McGwire (.735) and Larry Walker (.731), were injured in 2000 and did not have enough plate appearances to qualify in 2000. Bonds has 5 seasons over .700 since 1990, McGwire has 3 and Walker has 2. No one else has more than one.

Player	Team	Year	BPA
Mark McGwire	St. Louis	1998	.799
Larry Walker	Colorado	1997	.770
Jeff Bagwell	Houston	1994	.768
Mark McGwire	Oakland	1996	.765
Frank Thomas	Chicago (A)	1994	.747
Barry Bonds	San Francisco	2000	.745
Albert Belle	Cleveland	1994	.741
Barry Bonds	San Francisco	1993	.740
Barry Bonds	San Francisco	1994	.738
Mark McGwire	St. Louis	1999	.735
Larry Walker	Colorado	1999	.731
Barry Bonds	Pittsburgh	1992	.730
Barry Bonds	San Francisco	1996	.730
Manny Ramirez	Cleveland	2000	.726
Todd Helton	Colorado	2000	.720
Rickey Henderson	Oakland	1990	.718
Ken Griffey, Jr.	Seattle	1994	.708
Carlos Delgado	Toronto	2000	.707
Jason Giambi	Oakland	2000	.706

The yearly leaders since 1992 are as follows:

1992	Bonds	.734
1995	Belle	.692
1998	McGwire	.799
1993	Bonds	.740
1996	McGwire	.765
1999	McGwire	.735
1994	Bagwell	.768
1997	Walker	.770
2000	Bonds	.745

The benchmark for an outstanding individual season is .600. Following is a list of 17 players with enough plate appearances to qualify for the batting title and with a BPA of .600 in both 1999 and 2000:

Bases per Plate Appearance (BPA) of .600+ in 1999 and 2000

Player	2000 BPA	LG	1999 BPA	LG	No. of .600+ Seasons	Comments
1 Ramirez, M.	.726	A	.689	A	4	Best in the AL.
2 Helton, T.	.720	N	.610	N	2	Gets better each year.
3 Delgado, C.	.707	A	.612	A	3	Joined elite class.
4 Giambi, J.	.706	A	.603	A	2	Oakland team leader.
5 Guerrero, V.	.669	N	.619	N	2	The sky's the limit.
6 Sosa, S.	.662	N	.646	N	3	Another big year.
7 Rodriguez, A.	.661	A	.625	A	4	May be best SS ever.
8 Bagwell, J.	.652	N	.676	N	6	Does it every year.
9 Giles, B.	.645	N	.651	N	2	Overlooked superstar.
10 Everett, C.	.631	A	.640	N	2	Explosive player.
11 Abreu, B.	.629	N	.630	N	2	Model of consistency.
12 Garciaparra, N.	.626	A	.639	A	2	Power down in 2000.
13 Martinez, E.	.621	A	.615	A	6	Still strong at 37.
14 Griffey, K. Jr.	.613	N	.646	A	7	Slipped in 2000.
15 Jones, C.	.609	N	.698	N	2	No MVP repeat.
16 Palmeiro, R.	.602	A	.656	A	6	Barely made the list.
17 Thome, J.	.601	A	.623	A	6	Six in a row, barely.

Thirteen other players had a BPA over .600 in 2000 but were not on the list in 1999:

Player	2000 BPA	LG	1999 BPA	LG	No. of .600+ Seasons	Comments
1 Bonds, B.	.745	N	.696*	N	10	Best year yet.
2 Sheffield, G.	.673	N	.585	N	3	Carried Dodgers.
3 Hidalgo, R.	.661	N	.489*	N	1	NL breakthrough year.
4 Thomas, F.	.659	A	.527	A	7	Big comeback year.
5 Glaus, T.	.653	A	.507	A	1	AL breakthrough year.
6 Edmonds, J.	.650	N	.485*	A	1	Strong comeback.
7 Piazza, M.	.631	N	.560	N	3	A superb hitter.
8 Kent, J.	.626	N	.550	N	1	Keeps getting better.
9 Jenkins, G.	.621	N	.588*	N	1	This guy can hit.
10 Justice, D.	.615	A	.536	A	2	Sparked the Yankees.
11 Alou, M.	.611	N	DNP*	N	3	Great comeback
12 Williams, B.	.606	A	.582	A	2	Best year yet.
13 Rolen, S.	.601	N	.590*	N	1	Should get better.

* Not enough plate appearances to qualify.

Twelve players were on the .600 BPA list in 1999 but failed to make the list in 2000. Injuries were a major factor as six failed to have enough plate appearances to qualify including Mark McGwire who was at the top of the list when he went down:

Player	2000 BPA	LG	1999 BPA	LG	No. of .600+ Seasons	Comments
1 McGwire, M.	.794*	N	.735	N	6	Third straight .700.
2 Walker, L.	.543*	N	.731	N	5	A lost season.
3 Green, S.	.543	N	.631	N	1	Didn't earn salary.
4 Burnitz, J.	.525	N	.624	N	2	Disappointing season.
5 Alomar, R.	.550	A	.622	A	1	1999 was career year.
6 Tatis, F.	.537*	N	.620	N	1	Injuries took toll.
7 Jaha, J.	.406*	A	.618	A	1	Only 97 at-bats.
8 Sanders, R.	.479*	N	.611	N	2	Huge disappointment.
9 Gonzalez, J.	.510*	A	.609	A	4	Never got going.
10 Jeter, D.	.546	A	.609	A	1	Slipped in 2000.
11 Vaughn, G.	.567	A	.600	N	2	On the decline.
12 Belle, A.	.481	A	.600	A	5	Worst in a decade.

* Not enough plate appearances to qualify.

Bonds has had a BPA of at least .623 every year since 1990. Frank Thomas and Ken Griffey Jr. each had six .600+ seasons in the 1990s. McGwire also has six .600 BPA seasons including his rookie year in 1987. Edgar Martinez and Jim Thome both have streaks of six straight .600 BPA seasons. Many prominent players, including Cal Ripken, Jr, Tony Gwynn, Wade Boggs, Joe Carter, Vinny Castilla and Mark Grace, didn't come close to having a .600 BPA season in the 1990s.

Of the newcomers to the 2000 list, the most interesting are Richard Hidalgo and Geoff Jenkins, who made it in the first year they had enough plate appearances to qualify for the batting title and Jeff Kent who made it for the first time in the 8th season he has qualified.

Looking at the other end of the spectrum, seven players who earned enough playing time to qualify for the batting title had BPAs under .400.

Warren Morris	.398	Marquis Grissom	.390
Mike Lamb	.394	Rey Sanchez	.336
Scott Brosius	.391		

The following eighteen players compiled a batting average over .300, an on-base average over .400, a slugging percentage over .500 and bases per plate appearance over .600 in 2000:

Player	BAVG	OBA	SLG	BPA
Barry Bonds	.306	.440	.688	.745
Manny Ramirez	.351	.457	.697	.726
Todd Helton	.372	.463	.698	.720
Carlos Delgado	.344	.470	.664	.707
Jason Giambi	.333	.476	.647	.706
Gary Sheffield	.325	.438	.643	.673
Vladimir Guerrero	.345	.410	.664	.669
Sammy Sosa	.320	.406	.634	.662
Alex Rodriguez	.316	.420	.606	.661
Frank Thomas	.328	.436	.625	.659
Jeff Bagwell	.310	.424	.615	.652
Brian Giles	.315	.432	.594	.645
Bobby Abreu	.316	.416	.554	.629
Nomar Garciaparra	.372	.434	.599	.626
Jeff Kent	.334	.424	.596	.626
Edgar Martinez	.324	.423	.579	.621
Moises Alou	.355	.416	.623	.611
Chipper Jones	.311	.404	.566	.609

Edgar Martinez has been on this list for the last six years and Bagwell has been on it for three. In 1999, there were twelve players on the list.

Another list of interest is one containing the names of players with a BPA of over .600 in 2000 who, for one reason or another, did not have enough plate appearances to qualify for the batting title. Following is a list of 12 players with 100 or more plate appearances who fell short of having enough playing time to qualify for the batting title:

Player	BPA	Comments
Mark McGwire	.794	On top when he went down with injury.
John Vander Wal	.633	Produced when given opportunity to start.
Ken Caminiti	.632	Having big year before injury.
Ellis Burks	.631	A regular on this list.
Ivan Rodriguez	.630	On target for best year when injured.
Dave Hansen	.619	Seven pinch-hit home runs.
Charles Johnson	.612	Finally put consistent offense with defense.
Cliff Floyd	.610	Productive when healthy.
Todd Hundley	.608	Big comeback year.
Alex Ochoa	.607	Strong finish playing every day.
Lance Berkman	.607	Potential superstar.
Glenallen Hill	.601	BPA of .741 after trade to Yankees.

Several other players, in addition to Hill, were exceptionally productive after mid-season trades. Will Clark deserves special mention, finishing his career with a flourish as he produced a BPA of .685 after his trade to St. Louis, compared to .548 with Baltimore. Clark's overall BPA in 2000 was .568. He never had a .600 BPA season. Charles Johnson produced a .652 BPA with the White Sox after a .592 BPA at Baltimore. David Justice was consistent with a .611 BPA at Cleveland followed by a .618 with the Yankees. A change of scenery was a big help for Richie Sexson as he went from .480 at Cleveland to .614 at Milwaukee (.535 overall).

Triple Milestones - 2000

by Bill Gilbert

While a number of team and league home run records were set in the 2000 season, for the first time in three years, no players hit over 60 home runs. Sammy Sosa had an even 50 and he was the only player to reach that level. However, 16 players hit 40 home runs, up from 13 last year. A record 47 players hit 30 or more breaking the previous high of 45 set in 1999.

There were more home runs hit in 2000 than in any previous year, an average of 2.34 per game breaking the record of 2.28 set in 1999. Offense was clearly up in 2000 as shown in the table below:

Year	Runs/Game	HR/Game	BAVG	OBA	SLG
1996	10.07	2.19	.270	.340	.427
1997	9.53	2.05	.267	.337	.419
1998	9.58	2.08	.266	.335	.420
1999	10.17	2.28	.271	.345	.434
2000	10.28	2.34	.271	.345	.437

The .437 slugging average in 2000 was the highest ever. The highest number of runs per game were scored in 1930 (11.10), a year that also accounted for the highest batting average (.296) and the highest on-base average (.356). Thus the records for all of the above categories were set in either 1930 or 2000.

A useful indicator for tracking offense is the number of players who reach the triple milestones of a .300 batting average, 30 home runs and 100 runs batted in. A total of 26 players reached all three milestones in 2000, easily surpassing the previous record of 21 set in 1996. Ten players reached triple milestones in both 1999 and 2000 and 5 others made it in previous years as well as 2000. The other 11 made it for the first time.

Following is a listing of players who achieved triple milestones in 1999 or 2000, separated into 4 categories: Players who made it in both 1999 and 2000 (10).

Player	Times	1999	2000	Comments
American				
Manny Ramirez	4	.333-44-165	.351-38-122	Finished strong after injury.
Jason Giambi	2	.315-33-123	.333-43-137	Getting even better.
Magglio Ordonez	2	.301-30-117	.315-32-126	Improved in each category.
National				
Mike Piazza	6	.303-40-124	.324-38-113	Fifth straight year.
Jeff Bagwell	5	.304-42-126	.310-47-132	New highs in HR and RBI.
Gary Sheffield	4	.301-34-101	.325-43-109	New high in HR.
Chipper Jones	4	.319-45-110	.311-36-111	Third straight year.
Vladimir Guerrero	3	.316-42-131	.345-44-123	Third straight year.
Todd Helton	2	.320-35-113	.372-42-147	New highs across the board.
Brian Giles	2	.315-39-115	.315-35-123	A model of consistency.

Repeaters from prior years (5).

Player	Times	1999	2000	Comments
American				
Frank Thomas	7	.305-15-77	.328-43-143	Back after 2-year absence.
Alex Rodriguez	3	.285-42-111	.316-41-132	Brought BAVG up in 2000.
National				
Barry Bonds	6	.262-34-83	.306-49-106	First time was 1990.
Moises Alou	2	Did not play.	.355-30-114	Great comeback.
Sammy Sosa	2	.288-63-141	.320-50-138	Career high BAVG.

Players who made it for the first time (11).

Player	Times	1999	2000	Comments
American				
Carlos Delgado	1	.272-44-134	.344-41-137	First year over .300.
Edgar Martinez	1	.337-24-86	.324-37-145	First year with 30+ HR.
Jermaine Dye	1	.294-27-119	.321-33-118	Close in 1999.
Bernie Williams	1	.342-25-115	.307-30-121	First year with 30 HR.
Carl Everett	1	.325-25-108	.300-34-108	First year with 30+ HR.
Bobby Higginson	1	.239-12-46	.300-30-102	Made it with big final week.
National				
Jeff Kent	1	.290-23-101	.334-33-125	First year over .300.
Richard Hidalgo	1	.227-15-56	.314-44-122	Breakthrough season.
Luis Gonzalez	1	.336-26-111	.311-31-114	First year with 30+ HR.
Andruw Jones	1	.275-26-84	.303-36-104	Still improving.
Phil Nevin	1	.269-24-85	.303-31-107	New highs in all 3 categories.

Players who failed to repeat in 2000 (9).

Player	Times	1999	2000	Comments
American				
Ivan Rodriguez	1	.332-35-113	.347-27-83	Well on his way when injured.
Juan Gonzalez	4	.326-39-128	.289-22-67	Not even close.
Rafael Palmeiro	2	.324-47-118	.288-39-120	BAVG slipped in 2000.
Fred McGriff	1	.310-32-104	.277-27-106	On downside of his career.
National				
Larry Walker	3	.379-37-115	.309- 9- 51	Injuries took toll.
Shawn Green	1	.309-42-123	.269-24-99	Didn't justify big contract.
Eric Karros	1	.304-34-112	.250-31-106	BAVG way down.
Matt Williams	1	.303-35-142	.275-12-47	Injury-filled season.
Robin Ventura	1	.301-32-120	.232-24-84	Lowest BAVG since 1989.

Some others just missed:

American	Team	2000	Comments
Mike Sweeney	KC	.333-29-144	Needed one more HR.
Brad Fullmer	TOR	.295-32-104	Missed last week with an injury.
National			
Andres Galarraga	ATL	.302-28-100	Tailed off in second half.
Jim Edmonds	STL	.295-42-108	.299 BAVG going into last week.

Some prominent players are missing from both the 1999 and 2000 lists. Mark McGwire has hit .300 only once in a full season, in 1996. Ken Griffey, Jr. has made the list 3 times but hasn't hit .300 since 1997. Albert Belle has made the list 4 times and has had 9 straight years with over 100 RBI but he had only 23 HR and a BAVG of .281 in 2000. Mo Vaughn has done it 3 times but his BAVG has fallen the last 2 years. Vinny Castilla made the list for 3 straight years in Colorado but hasn't come close the last 2 years

In one of his *Baseball Abstracts*, Bill James referred to triple milestone seasons as "Hall of Fame years". This is because all of the eligible players with 5 or more triple milestone seasons have been elected to the Hall of Fame. This correlation may not hold in the future since triple milestone seasons are much easier to achieve now than in the past. Among active players, Thomas has 7, Bonds and Piazza have 6 and Jeff Bagwell has 5 triple milestone seasons. All appear to be on the way to Hall of Fame careers. Ramirez, Sheffield and Chipper Jones are knocking on the door with 4, as are Belle and Juan Gonzalez. The only other players with 4 triple milestone seasons who are not in the Hall are Ted Kluszewski and Jim Rice.

The only team with 3 triple milestone players was Houston as Bagwell, Alou and Hidalgo led the Astros to a new National League record of 249 home runs.

In 1999, ten minor league players achieved triple milestones, a difficult feat in 140 games. While none of them repeated in 2000, five of them (Erubiel Durazo, Mark Quinn, Adam Piatt, D. T. Cromer and David Ortiz played in the major leagues in 2000. Eight more minor leaguers reached triple milestones this year:

Player	Team (Level)	Organization	Age	BAVG-HR-RBI
Alex Cabrera	El Paso (AA)	Arizona	28	.382-35- 82
	Tucson (AAA)			.282- 4- 12
	Arizona			.263- 5- 14
				.335-44-108
Jason Hart	Midland (AA)	Oakland	22	.326-30-121
Chad Mottola	Syracuse (AAA)	Cincinnati	28	.309-33-102
Phil Hiatt	Colo. Springs (AAA)	Colorado	31	.306-35-106
Ozzie Canseco	Newark (Ind.)		35	.304-48-127
Juan Silvestre	Lancaster (A)	Seattle	22	.304-30-137
Ozzie Timmons	Durham (AAA)	Tampa Bay	29	.300-29-104
	Tampa Bay			.341- 4- 13
				.303-33-117

Player	Team (Level)	Organization	Age	BAVG-HR-RBI
Ross Gload	Portland (AA)	Florida	24	.284-16-65
	Iowa (AAA)	Chicago Cubs		.404-14-39
		Chicago Cubs		.194-1-3
				.302-31-107

Three of the eight players finished the season in the major leagues (Cabrera, Timmons and Gload). Three others have played in the major leagues in past years (Mottola, Ozzie Canseco and Hiatt). Only Hart and Silvestre have not played in the major leagues.

Two former major league players had triple milestone seasons in the Mexican League:

Player	Team	Age	BAVG-HR-RBI
Warren Newson	Union Laguna	35	.386-39-121
Scott Bullett	Reynosa	31	.333-35-100

Newson played parts of eight seasons with the Chicago White Sox, Seattle Mariners and Texas Rangers, batting 250. Bullett played parts of four seasons with the Pittsburgh Pirates and Chicago Cubs, batting .233.

Another former major leaguer went to Japan to get his triple milestones:

Player	Team	Age	BAVG-HR-RBI
Sherman Obando	Nippon Ham Fighters	30	.332-30-101

Obando played parts of four seasons with the Baltimore Orioles and Montreal Expos, batting .239.

Only one college player had triple milestone season in 2000:

Player	School	BAVG-HR-RBI
Brad Cresse	Louisiana State	.388-30-106

Cresse's last RBI was the game winner in the final game at the College World Series.

Pitchers also strive for triple milestones -- 20 wins, 200 strikeouts and an earned run average under 3.00. Pedro Martinez achieved it in 1999 (23-4, 313, 2.07) but he fell short in 2000 with only 18 wins (18-6, 284, 1.74). Two National League pitchers came reasonably close, Randy Johnson (19-7, 347, 2.64) and Greg Maddux (19-9, 190, 3.00). There were only 7 pitcher triple milestone seasons in the 1990s. Roger Clemens did it three times and John Smoltz, Randy Johnson and Pedro and his brother Ramon Martinez each did it once. Clemens has done it 5 times, tying Christy Mathewson. Only Walter Johnson (7) and Juan Marichal (6) have more than five triple milestone seasons.

As an indication of how the game has changed, in the 1965-1969 period, there were 22 pitcher triple milestone seasons and only 11 hitter triple milestone seasons. An argument can be made that the game would be improved if there were a better balance between hitting and pitching. Such a balance might be difficult to attain but it could probably be approached by raising the pitcher's mound a couple of inches and calling the high strike the way it is defined in the rule book.

STRATEGIES FOR CATCHERS

Think "Damage Control"

by John Benson

Catchers are the most likely players to cause trouble on a Rotisserie roster. Catchers are not as dangerous as pitchers, of course, but pitchers are not really baseball players, at least not in the American League. What makes catchers a problem is their similarity to pitchers in this: catchers do many things, not reflected in hitting stats, which help their teams win. They watch the batters on opposing teams (most catchers now keep a notebook). They meet with the pitching coach and starting pitcher for pregame prep. They frame the strike zone. They call pitch selection and location. They go to the mound and tell pitchers things such as, "If you don't start throwing strikes, I think you might be in Buffalo tomorrow," and, "You can get this guy out with a high fastball because he was up late last night at the hotel bar." Catchers block low pitches. They field bunts. They throw out base-stealers (sometimes) and have about 2.05 seconds to catch the pitch, stand up, remove the ball from their mitt, cock their arm, and make the ball travel to second base which is 127 feet away. That's a lot to do in 2.05 seconds.

So there are many reasons why a catcher might be in the lineup, other than ability to hit. And catchers will take their turn at bat, just like pitchers in the NL (and like pitchers they might be removed for a pinch hitter when their team is losing in late innings). Two implications arise. First is that some catchers, who do all these other things well, can keep their jobs even while hitting .202, and that will hurt you. The other implication is that good-hitting catchers are premium assets on a Rotisserie roster.

Most Rotisserie owners know all these things, of course, which is why Ivan Rodriguez and Jason Kendall might be overbid or might be first-round picks. What most Rotisserie owners don't know is that paying top dollar for a good-hitting catcher can be a bad move — because catchers have yet another problem: they get injured a lot, more than any other position players. Ask Ray Fosse.

Going for a top catcher can be a good move for a weak team, a team that needs to take chances in order to win. For a strong team that goes into draft day with first placed locked up unless something weird happens, putting big money into a catcher can be taking an unnecessary risk. Since I always have a first-place roster (well, almost always) I rarely end up with a high-priced catcher at the end of the draft, because I try to stay away from all forms of risk.

Position scarcity is a pronounced reality for catchers and is much more important in draft leagues than in auction leagues. In the AL it's a $10 drop from Rodriguez down to the plateau of Mitch Meluskey, Jorge Posada, Darrin Fletcher and Ben Molina; and then there is another drop down to the others worth a bid over $3: Einer Diaz, Jason Varitek, Ramon Hernandez, Eddie Taubensee, Sandy Alomar and Greg Zaun.

In the NL the top tier is Mike Piazza and Jason Kendall, then the grade B types led by Javy Lopez and then Charles Johnson, Mike Lieberthal, Ben Petrick and Brad Ausmus.

If you don't get one of the above-mentioned names by paying attention and looking for a sneaky opportunity, the best policy is just to wait, wait some more, and keep on waiting. Don't look at the depth charts (please) with an idea that you have to get someone with playing time. If you get 250 at-bats with a .241 average, that can do more harm than a guy with 50 at-bats and a .270 average. The six or eight homers from a guy who plays won't be worth the damage done to the batting average.

Bring this list to your draft — guys who won't play (much) but won't hurt your batting average either: Kevin Brown, Edwards Guzman, Todd Pratt, Mike Redmond, Adam Melhuse (or any Rocky) in the NL; and in the AL, A.J. Pierzynski, Greg Zaun, Javier Cardona (don't be fooled by the .175), Scott Hatteberg, and Bill Haselman. The best time to get a second-string or third-string catcher is right after the starter has just been bought for $3; folks won't feel like bidding $2 for the also-ran, so you can get him for $1.

AMERICAN LEAGUE CATCHERS

ANAHEIM ANGELS

Bengie Molina has solidified his position as the number one catcher for the Angels with a break out season last year. Expect at least 450 at-bats from Molina, barring injury. Last season was significantly out of line with Molina's minor league performances, leading to one of two possibilities: it was an example of the "age 26" phenomenon, with Molina finally coming into his own; or, it was an aberration, in which case Molina could be expected to return to more modest levels of performance this season. While either could be the case, the truth probably lies somewhere in the middle. Expect the league's pitchers to catch up a little with Molina in 2001, with a .260-10-65 season a reasonable projection. Molina will hit seventh or eighth in the lineup.

Jorge Fabregas returns to Anaheim to back Molina up. Fabregas falls into the "veteran receiver" category of backup, the kind of player you really don't want accumulating stats for your Rotisserie team. He'll produce a low batting average with a couple of homers and not much else in 150 or so at-bats for the Angels.

Shawn Wooten is an interesting player. A utility type who can hit, Wooten may qualify at catcher in some leagues, having played four games at the position last season, and only three at first base. If he makes the Angels' roster as an all-purpose backup, Wooten would be a good $1 catcher, much better than the average no-hit good-field types (e.g. Fabregas) that dot the landscape.

Matt Walbeck became a free agent at the end of last season, and was not expected to return to Anaheim. Wherever he lands, he's on the "avoid" list, since he is likely to accumulate 200 or more at-bats with a very low batting average. Bret Hemphill is a 30-year-old minor leaguer who could see some time at the big league level, but is unlikely to hit well enough to contribute.

RECOMMENDATION REVIEW: Molina should deliver a decent season, but may be a little overpriced based on last season. If he makes the squad, Wooten is a good $1 pick if you can put him at catcher. Avoid Fabregas, Hemphill and Walbeck.

BALTIMORE ORIOLES

The Orioles liked what they saw of Brook Fordyce in the 53 games that he played with them following his acquisition from the White Sox and signed him to a multi-year contract. The Orioles are his fourth club, having previously been with the Mets, Reds, and White Sox. He's a solid hitter, but has never gotten into more than 105 games in a season. Last year he hit a career high .305-14-49 in 302 at-bats. Over the past two years, he's hit lefties in the .333-350 range and righties around .285. He now has 886 career at-bats, hitting an overall solid .282-27-121. As a starter over a full season, Fordyce could rap about 20 homers with 70-80 RBI. He has a defensive weakness in throwing out base stealers, so opposing runners can expected to pick up a lot of steals against Oriole pitching.

Greg Myers was the backup catcher last year behind Charles Johnson and Fordyce. He's 35, with a career average of .253. He doesn't have much power.

Mike Kinkade was acquired from the Mets in the Mike Bordick trade late last season. He's had some good years in the high minors, showing excellent power and stolen base speed while hitting for a good average. He's 27, and will be 28 in May, somewhat old to be still trying to make the majors. But his minor league stats and the leagues and locations where he's played all indicate that he will likely hit well in the majors if given regular play. Kinkade can also play third base and the outfield.

Fernando Lunar was acquired from Atlanta in the B.J. Surhoff trade. Except for 70 major league at-bats, he's spent the past two years in Double-A. His Double-A hitting was weak with averages around .220, with very little power. He's only 23, but he will have to improve his hitting soon to achieve prospect status and make the majors permanently.

Prior to last year, prospect Jayson Werth was thought to be another Jason Kendall. But hitting a weak .228-5-26 in Double-A earned a demotion to Single-A. The Orioles had been considering him as the successor to Charles Jackson, but his poor season caused them to rethink their plans. The acquisition of Kinkade, Fordyce and Lunar are clear indicators that Werth is not as high in the Orioles plans as he was before last year. He had difficulty with the more advanced pitching in Double-A, but he's only 21, and he could improve overnight.

RECOMMENDATION REVIEW: Fordyce can hit, and he's the starting catcher. Mike Kinkade is a good pickup because he may see playing time at DH or other positions.

BOSTON RED SOX

Both catchers from the 2000 Red Sox, Jason Varitek and Scott Hatteberg, were eligible for arbitration, so Boston figured to spend more on catchers for this season. The switch-hitting Varitek took playing time away from Hatteberg, but his production declined to .248-10-65. Varitek still is just 28. The 31-year-old Hatteberg (.265-8-36) had about half as many at-bats, partly as a designated hitter against righthanded pitchers. Even if Varitek doesn't hit as well as Hatteberg, the younger catcher is likely to play more because he's better defensively.

The catcher at Triple-A Pawtucket was Tim Spehr, a 34-year-old journeyman who batted just .150-5-25. He might be good for a home run now and again if he returned to the majors. But that wouldn't mean you should put him on your Rotisserie roster at any time.

Steve Lomasney's prospect status declined as he returned to Double-A. The 23-year-old batted .245-8-27.

The Sox still thought enough of him to send him to the Arizona Fall League.

RECOMMENDATION REVIEW: We can't give Varitek as high a recommendation as a year ago, but he provides above-average production for a catcher, even in a park that has been transformed into a poor place to hit. Hatteberg is way better than a $1 Rotisserie catcher, and he'll be forgotten in most auctions. Having both of them last year would have brought you 101 RBI at a modest price; that wouldn't be a bad strategy again.

CHICAGO WHITE SOX

Charles Johnson was acquired via trade by the White Sox during the 2000 season and he really gave them a nice push both as a receiver and as a hitter. He had a career year at the plate, hitting .304 with 31 home runs and 91 RBI while playing his usual Gold Glove caliber defense. He showed increased patience at the plate and a willingness to hit the ball to right and right-center field, which is why his numbers jumped so drastically. Johnson signed with the Marlins during the offseason. Johnson will be the everyday catcher and a valuable rotisserie player.

Sandy Alomar was signed to take Johnson's place. He cannot be expected to play everyday, but will see the majority of the time behind the plate; unless he gets injured, which is a high possibility with the injury prone Alomar. See more on Alomar in the Indians catchers section.

Mark Johnson spent the entire 2000 season as the Sox' number two catcher and struggled at the plate. His defense was respectable and he played a game or two each week, but he's not starter material. He hits lefthanded and catches well, which will keep him in the majors, but his lack of power and inability to make consistent contact will prevent him from being a good roto player.

Josh Paul only played in 36 games for the White Sox during the 2000 season, but he made a good impression. He showed that he could hit for average and he played very well defensively, which should give him the inside track for the backup catcher spot. He has no power and won't be much of a run producer early on in his career, but he runs well for a catcher and could wind up being a Brad Ausmus-like player.

The Sox have no real catching prospects other than Paul, who is their "catcher of the future."

RECOMMENDATION REVIEW: Charles Johnson will be a strong rotisserie player for his position and you really can't go wrong with him as your number one catcher. Paul was the favorite to be the backup, and has little value, but may be a smart pickup down the road if you have the often injured Alomar on your roster.

CLEVELAND INDIANS

Sandy Alomar is a great catcher — when he's healthy, which is rare. Looking over his career in the 11 years since he became a regular with the Indians in 1990, he's played in over 100 games four times. Last year it was 97 games, and in 1999, only 37 games. His career-best year was 1997 when he got into 125 games, hitting .324-21-83. His typical year is hitting .260-280 with about a dozen homers and 40-50 RBI. His career average is a solid .276. He is 34, and is still capable of being a number-one catcher on many teams. In Rotisserie, the injury factor will keep teams cautious, so he's likely to be underbid.

It's not surprising that the Tribe decided to let Alomar go and traded for Eddie Taubensee to achieve some dependability. But he also was slowed by a back injury last year, limiting him to only 81 games. His career-best year was 1999 when he hit .311-21-87 with Cincinnati. In other recent years he's hit .267-291 with 10-12 homers. He's 32 with a solid .274 career batting average. With the league change and a down season last year, Taubensee is likely to be underbid in many leagues.

Einar Diaz has filled in during Alomar's many DL times, and he's come through very nicely. He's not much of a power hitter and doesn't drive in many runs, but he hits for a solid average in the .270-280 area. With the Taubensee acquisition, Diaz will be perceived as a backup and will likely be underbid.

The Indians minor-league catchers include 33-year-old Mandy Romero and 30-year-old Bobby Hughes. They may get some playing time as a backup, getting called up when an injury occurs. They have no Rotisserie value.

Edgar Cruz was a top prospect a year ago, but too much weight lifting created tightness and ruined his swinging mechanics. His career progress took a step backwards with a poor .181 season in Class A. Casey Smith and Jeff DePippo are weak hitters in the minors, and many things need to happen before either gets to Jacobs Field.

RECOMMENDATION REVIEW: Alomar, Taubensee and Diaz are all expected to be undervalued in many Rotisserie leagues, and are good low-cost acquisitions. They are much better than the many poor hitting catchers.

DETROIT TIGERS

Starting catcher Brad Ausmus was traded to the Houston Astros in a six player deal during the offseason. One of the three players the Tigers got in return was young, good hitting catcher Mitch Meluskey. Meluskey was expected to get the majority of starts behind the dish. Look for a slow start with the bat from Meluskey while he adjusts to the AL. Once Meluskey becomes settled in the AL, he will be a solid offensive catcher. See more on Meluskey in the Astros catcher section.

The Tigers have an obvious number one catcher and he'll play almost every day during the 2001 season. Brad Ausmus is a pitcher's favorite. He calls a great game, is a well above average receiver and a very good thrower also. As a hitter, however, Ausmus is merely average. He makes contact, is a good hit-and-run man, and he has better than average speed for this position, but he's not an impact roto player. He'll give you a few extra steals at catcher, but his power numbers and batting average will be about average. Last year he hit .266 with 7 home runs and 51 RBI to go with 11 steals. The best thing about him is that he'll play everyday because of his defensive ability.

The Tigers have a couple of young catchers in their system that could have an impact at the major league level soon, though neither is ready to supplant Ausmus. Javier Cardona could very well be the Tigers' primary backup catcher in 2001. He's a solid defensive catcher with 20 home run potential, but he's an undisciplined hitter. He's done well against minor league pitching, demonstrating very good power, but he rarely walks and that could become a problem for him once he gets regular at-bats against major league pitchers.

The Tigers' top catching prospect is Brandon Inge, who is a Brad Ausmus clone by many accounts. He's a strong defensive catcher with solid leadership skills that makes contact. He doesn't have a lot of home run power, though he could develop a little more than Ausmus down the line, but he's beginning to show the ability to be a .300 hitter in the future. Inge is at least another year away from getting a shot at the majors, though a strong showing in the Arizona Fall League helped him this past offseason.

RECOMMENDATION REVIEW: If you're not looking for an impact player at catcher, Ausmus will be a nice fit for your team. He'll play every single day, barring injury, and he won't have a negative effect on your club. Neither Cardona nor Inge figure to have much roto value this season, though Inge might be worth picking up in deep leagues with minor league reserve rosters.

KANSAS CITY ROYALS

For the second straight season, the Royals relied on a group of second-string catchers to fill the role, again with no one player seeing regular duty for any significant length of time. The combined production of Brian Johnson, Jorge Fabregas and Gregg Zaun was good for the Royals' offense, although it didn't do much to end their pitching woes; and because the production was spread out so much, it didn't help Rotisserie players much, either.

Johnson got the bulk of catching chores early in the year, hit well for a couple of weeks, then went into an extended funk before being released at the end of June after refusing a minor league assignment. Johnson is a better hitter than he showed last year, but not much, and still not worth Draft Day dollars. Fabregas split time with both Johnson and Zaun and missed nearly half the season due to various injuries. His bat didn't warm up until the All-Star break, but by then he was relegated to a second-string role. Overall, he had a decent year, but with the injuries and slow start it is unlikely he helped many Rotisserie owners. It was his best season since 1997, but not enough to be worth more than a dollar on Draft Day.

Zaun also missed time due to injury, early in the season, then gradually took over more regular duty during the hot part of the year. He seemed to thrive on regular playing time and had the best year of his career at the plate, hitting for a decent average and with more power than ever before, stealing a few bases too. However, with his uncertain future, it is not wise to recommend Zaun at this time except as an emergency, midseason pickup. He's more likely to disappear altogether than to put up another plus-season for Rotisserie purposes. Hector Ortiz was a pleasant surprise following his midseason recall from Triple-A Omaha; Ortiz finished the year hitting .386 in 88 at-bats, but with virtually no extras; he was merely a singles hitter, although he certainly hit a lot of them! Despite little major league experience, Ortiz is hardly a prospect; he's 31-years-old and has spent a decade in the minors. If he can maintain that kind of batting average or hit for a little power (he has hit for moderate power in the

past) he can be a useful $1 catcher. That's a big IF, so treat him as you would any unproven career minor-leaguer; make him prove himself before dropping any Draft Day money on him.

Down on the farm, the Royals used retread Izzy Molina to handle a large part of their Omaha catching chores, plus Paul Phillips, Juan Brito, and Dave Ullery at Double-A Wichita; only Phillips is a prospect. Phillips batted .292 for Wichita, but with disappointing power and he is still trying to adapt to working behind the plate (he was a collegiate outfielder). The Royals will likely push Phillips to win a part-time big league job within the next year. For Rotisserie purposes, it's safe to give Phillips a miss; it's unlikely he'll be given enough playing time in 2001 to do anything significant. Besides, it often takes young catchers a couple of years in the majors before they begin to show much with the bat.

RECOMMENDATION REVIEW: While it is impossible to recommend any specific catcher for the Royals, it is wise to remember that Kauffman Stadium is now a hitter's park and the club is a much better hitting team, meaning more RBI and Runs are available to whomever plays regularly behind the plate in Kansas City. Look at who the Opening Day catcher was expected to be for Kansas City, and put that guy on your "$1 Catcher" list as a safety value should you be unable to win the bidding for Pudge or Posada. If you have room on your Ultra bench, consider Phillips for the end of it.

MINNESOTA TWINS

Terry Steinbach retired after the 1999 season, leaving the Twins with Javier Valentin, a backup for the last two seasons, as the most experienced catcher in the system. As the Twins head into the 2001 season, Valentin has played himself off the 40 man roster, and the Twins are even more unsettled at the position. It's the kind of situation that does not help the needy rotisserie owner. Matthew LeCroy is the best candidate to catch, if offensive potential was the key requirement to play the position. He's a stocky kid with a powerful stroke and has the potential to hit 30-35 homers in the majors.

That said, LeCroy is still learning the strike zone, how to take pitches and get aggressive when he's ahead in the count. In his brief stint in the majors last season, LeCroy fell behind in the count, lengthened his swing and chased pitches out of the strike zone. But he showed the ability to correct his flaw when he went to the minors and participated in the Arizona Fall League. High hopes remain for him.

LeCroy's catching skills, however, need even more refinement. He doesn't have a strong arm, and he has to improve his footwork behind the plate as well as learn to call better games. The Twins want him to succeed as a catcher because an offensive player behind the plate is a rarity, but the front office is already whispering about a move to first base if LeCroy continues to struggle defensively.

Of the five catchers the Twins used last season, A.J. Pierzynski made the best impression. His defense is sound and he bounces back from collisions well, which will help get him playing time in 2001. But his offense late in the season was a pleasant surprise. Pierzynski, in previous call-ups, had shown a slow bat and few thought he could hit major league pitching. But he swung more authoritatively when he was called up in 2000, driving the ball to center field. He goes into the 2001 season, at least, as a platoon player. He could increase his playing time if he continues to improve.

Chad Moeller is a option to start, too. He's a solid catcher who improved his game calling as the season went on. A knee injury in August ruined his year. He offers little at the plate at this point in his career, as there is still the question as to how much he will ever provide at the plate.

Danny Ardoin was acquired just before the trading deadline, and is the best catcher and thrower of all the candidates, but he was a backup in the minors when the Twins got him and he shows rough edges. At the plate, he provides little offense, a running theme with his group, but looked the farthest away among the candidates.

RECOMMENDATION REVIEW: One of the most unsettled aspects of the 2001 Twins is the catching situation. Any number of players could see time, and a 50/50 platoon situation is possible. There is no clear choice behind the plate. Unless you're a Twins fan or a relative of one of the catching candidates, there's no reason to choose any of these players.

NEW YORK YANKEES

We didn't follow some of our own advice with Jorge Posada last year. Though we noted that he had a relatively good second half of the 1999 season, we ignored that finish and wrote, "He is not worth a major investment."

The switch hitter wasn't worth A-Rod or Barry Bonds money, but only Pudge Rodriguez and the surprising Charles Johnson produced more among AL catchers than Posada's .287-28-86. Well, we did say he was likely to be closer to his 1998 totals of .268-17-63 than his .245-12-57 of 1999. His work load of catching 142 games did slow him down late in the season. Posada improved in throwing out basestealers. The 29-year-old clearly earned his All-Star Game berth.

The Yankees signed the Mariners Joe Oliver as Posada's 2001 backup. The veteran backstop will play rarely, and will not be much help offensively.

Chris Turner, 32, moved into the role of day-game-after-night-game catcher, and did nothing to earn additional playing time. He batted just .236-1-7, and has almost no Rotisserie value.

At Triple-A Columbus, the Yankees had two veteran catchers with strong track records as defenders. Tom Wilson, 30, has never played in the majors but he showed power potential (.276-20-71). Mosquera, 29, batted just .238-1-14.

The Yankees' 2000 first-round draft pick was David Parrish, the son of long-time Tiger Lance Parrish. At short-season Staten Island, the 21-year-old hit .240-4-29.

RECOMMENDATION REVIEW: Posada has moved up among the American League's best catchers. One factor that could reduce his playing time and production would be if the Yankees came up with a lefthanded-hitting catcher. Those listed here all bat righthanded.

OAKLAND ATHLETICS

Any guesses as to who holds the single season Athletics record for most games caught? "Ray Fosse," you say? No, not him. "How about Terry Steinbach," you ask? No, not Steiny, either. "Ramon Hernandez," you query with a skeptical look? Got it. 143 games behind the dish last season set a new single season mark for the team, and in a way that is the bad news.

The good news is that the .246 average Hernandez hit over those games was his career low. At 23, with a full time job in the majors essentially thrust upon him, Hernandez responded well, and that means better numbers' are ahead. Hernandez is on a team that stresses patience, and as a backstop, he will know how to work a count with the best of them; and he is on a team with a high offensive potential. Assemble those factors and there is a player (a catcher even) who is reliable, will improve, and based upon last year's totals, will be a relative bargain. Better stats (say numbers in the range of .265-15-65) are ahead, as Hernandez prepares for a break out season in 2002 or 2003.

Last year's backup backstop at The Net was Sal Fasano, an end of spring acquisition who nailed nearly half his 27 hits (six doubles and seven homers) for extra bases. Still not much value there for much of anything, as former top prospect A.J. Hinch is likely to grab the backup role. Though his bat has still not come through as anticipated when Hinch tore through the minors in 1997, the 26-year-old will likely move into a back up role following his .266-6-47 Triple-A campaign of last year. All things considered, it makes more sense to put Hinch, who has an upside, in the majors, and relegate a Fasano-type to the Sacramento taxi squad. Irrespective, Hinch's value on even an Ultra roster is questionable.

Cody McKay, son of former Athletic Dave McKay, leads the minor league prospects list, at least at the Triple-A level, but that is not saying much. First, Hernandez is entrenched for now, with Hinch in tow. Second, McKay, who did play in the AFL, is much of an answer.

Brian Luderer, a 22-year-old who was the 21st pick of the 1996 draft, did well though, hitting .301-4-23 at Modesto before advancing to Midland and going .315-4-16. He also walked 37 times, while whiffing just 33, a good sign, and one that fits in well with the Athletic's overall strategy.

RECOMMENDATION REVIEW: Ramon Hernandez is a young and improving hitter. You could do a lot worse than picking him as your catcher, though he might be better suited as a backup on your rotisserie team. He is most likely still a few years away from a career year, but should put up slightly improved numbers in 2001. The only other player worth looking at is A.J Hinch. He should only be considered if Hernandez gets injured, and even then don't expect much.

SEATTLE MARINERS

Dan Wilson has been the Mariners' catcher for years now, but his days as a full-time player may be coming to an end. Injuries and inconsistency at the plate have been the norm over the past couple of years. He's a top of the line receiver and thrower, but he has not been especially effective as a hitter recently. He played in just 90 games last year, hitting .235 with 5 home runs and 27 RBI. The Mariners entered the offseason looking for help at catcher, so Wilson could be expected to wind up a platoon player or else playing in another city.

Chris Widger was brought over from the Expos during the 2000 season, but he rarely played for the M's. His inability to carry an acceptable batting average has made him a reserve. Widger has some pop and isn't a horrible catcher, but wear and tear as the season always slows him down. He was expected to play a reserve role in 2001. Therefore Widger may stay healthy for a full year and be more productive.

Ryan Christianson has been considered the Mariners' catcher of the future since he was drafted a couple of years ago, but his name began to surface in trade rumors during the 2000 season as the M's searched for immediate catching or outfield help. Christianson is a good defensive player with excellent offensive potential, but he's at least two years away from the majors.

RECOMMENDATION REVIEW: None of the catchers on the Mariners' roster at press time had much roto value. You'd be better off looking elsewhere, though Widger has more offensive potential than Wilson -- if you have to choose.

TAMPA BAY DEVIL RAYS

The Devil Rays like the tandem of John Flaherty and Mike DiFelice, but they're always open to listening to offers from other teams for either since Toby Hall is in the picture. Flaherty dipped a from a stellar 1999 campaign that saw him hit .278 with 14 home runs and a career-high 71 RBI. In 2000 Flaherty hit .261 with 10 home runs and 39 RBI playing in just 109 games.

Meanwhile, DiFelice's numbers dropped as well. The Devil Rays' backup hit a career high .307 in 1999 and followed it with a disappointing .240 average in 2000 with six home runs and 39 RBI. Either catcher would likely put up average catcher numbers if given the chance to play everyday.

Hall is coming on strong and could be the force that pushes a trade of either Flaherty or DiFelice. Unlike the incumbents, Hall is known for his offense. Hall's bat carried him from stops at Double-A Orlando and Triple-A Durham before getting called up to the majors in September. The youngster's catching skills showed a marked improvement. Though he hit just .167 in 12 at-bats, Hall managed to give Devil Rays management a look at the future.

RECOMMENDATION REVIEW: Stay away from Flaherty and DiFelice as neither plays enough to have the quality numbers to make them worthwhile. However, if one of them gets hurt and the other sees everyday play, each is capable of putting up decent catcher numbers.

Hall isn't quite ready to take the starting job, so it's likely he'll start the season at Durham. However, if by some chance Hall manages to grab the catching job early in the season, jump on him as he's hit for average and power everywhere he's played. He's an up and comer.

TEXAS RANGERS

Pudge Rodriguez is The Man, easily the most valuable catcher in any American League Rotisserie league. Despite missing the last half of the season with a broken thumb, he was expected to be fully ready for spring training and should be stronger for the enforced rest. Rodriguez is a superbly conditioned athlete, and is capable of continuing to catch large numbers of games annually. For the upcoming season, expect Rodriguez to start nine out of every ten games for Texas, bat second or third, get 600 or more plate appearances and hit well over .300 with good power. The Rangers don't run much, especially toward the top of the order, but ten or so steals wouldn't be too much of a stretch. The time for Rodriguez to consider a positional move will eventually come, but it's at least a couple of years away at this point.

Bill Haselman re-signed with Texas and will serve as the little-used back up for Rodriguez. Starting a game every eight to ten days, Haselman won't play enough to have a positive impact on a Rotisserie team. However, unlike a lot of $1 catchers, he won't hurt you. Haselman is capable of hitting for a decent average, with occasional power. He hits lefthanded pitching particularly well. Since Rodriguez sits so infrequently, Texas almost never carries a third catcher.

In the event either Rodriguez or Haselman gets hurt, Mike Hubbard should get the call from Triple-A. A journeyman receiver, Hubbard would be a liability to a Rotisserie team. The Rangers have no major league catching prospects anywhere in the high minors. Scott Heard is an interesting long-term prospect, but is several years away and may ultimately need a position change.

RECOMMENDATION REVIEW: Rodriguez is expensive, but worth paying full price for. Haselman is an excellent choice for a $1 catcher. Stay away from any others.

TORONTO BLUE JAYS

The Jays decided immediately following the 2000 season to bring back veteran catcher Darrin Fletcher for another go-around in 2001.

Fletcher is a fan-favorite and reliable bat who can burn a team with his underrated power stroke. He is not prone to long slumps and is a good run-producer. Playing in 122 games last year, Fletcher enjoyed his best batting average in his career (.320) and set career marks for home runs. Though he doesn't throw well and will start this season thirty-four years old, he fits into the bottom third of the lineup as a smart hitter who calls a good game behind the plate. Whether catching or getting occasional work as a DH, Fletcher will get plenty of playing time.

Alberto Castillo was brought in as a backup last year and though he's not much of a threat with the bat, he has an outstanding arm and superb defensive skills, calling and blocking pitches. Because he hits for such a low average, he's never going to get a chance to play on a regular basis and chances are good that the 93 games he played for St. Louis two years ago will end up being a career high. His average last year is a concern and he should not be expected to rebound.

Todd Greene (covered in the DH section) can play behind the plate in an emergency and has openly stated his desire and readiness to play behind the plate a couple of times a week. A healthy Greene that could do this could surprise by moving ahead of Castillo on the team's depth chart. For now, he remains an emergency catcher at most and in most Rotisserie leagues, will not qualify at catcher to start the season.

Josh Phelps is the catching prospect closest to the big leagues, having actually made an appearance with the Jays last year. Phelps has a good arm and will develop into a superior offensive player over the next few seasons. In the long-term, he should become not only a regular catcher but a .300+ hitter with 20-30 home run ability. He needs to take more walks and continue his defensive improvement before we're likely to see him on a regular basis.

RECOMMENDED REVIEW: Fletcher is always a reliable hitter and never really has a bad season though he doesn't play everyday. Castillo has no Rotisserie value and Greene is unlikely to qualify at catcher in many leagues. Those who have in-season qualifying rules may want to take a second look at Greene as he should get some work behind the plate and could qualify there by mid season. Phelps is too far from the big leagues to be of any Rotisserie use in 2001.

TOP 2001 HOME RUN HITTERS

NAME	HR
Ivan Rodriguez	27
Jorge Posada	24
Darrin Fletcher	18
Mitch Meluskey	17
Brook Fordyce	15
Chris Widger	13
Jason Varitek	13
Ramon Hernandez	12
Ben Molina	12
Eddie Taubensee	11
John Flaherty	10
Javier Cardona	10

TOP 2001 RBI PRODUCERS

NAME	RBI
Ivan Rodriguez	87
Jorge Posada	83
Mitch Meluskey	80
Jason Varitek	65
Brook Fordyce	65
Ben Molina	64
Darrin Fletcher	62
Ramon Hernandez	61
Eddie Taubensee	48
John Flaherty	42
Chris Widger	39
Javier Cardona	37
Sandy Alomar	37

TOP 2001 RUN SCORERS

NAME	RUNS
Jorge Posada	84
Ivan Rodriguez	78
Mitch Meluskey	57
Jason Varitek	57
Josh Paul	54
Ben Molina	53
Brook Fordyce	51
Ramon Hernandez	48
Darrin Fletcher	43
Eddie Taubensee	41
Sandy Alomar	41

TOP 2001 BASESTEALERS

NAME	SB
Ivan Rodriguez	16
Gregg Zaun	6
Einer Diaz	6
Mark L. Johnson	5
Josh Paul	5
A.J. Pierzynski	4
Chris Widger	2
Dan Wilson	2
Joe Oliver	2
Jorge Posada	2
Mitch Meluskey	2

TOP 2001 BATTING AVERAGES

NAME	AVG
Ivan Rodriguez	.320
Mitch Meluskey	.304
Darrin Fletcher	.288
A.J. Pierzynski	.283
Brook Fordyce	.282
Eddie Taubensee	.280
Ben Molina	.279
Sandy Alomar	.275
Einer Diaz	.275
Josh Paul	.275
Jorge Posada	.269
Bill Haselman	.268
Scott Hatteberg	.268

NATIONAL LEAGUE CATCHERS

ARIZONA DIAMONDBACKS

Damian Miller moved a slight step or two ahead of Kelly Stinnett in the Diamondbacks' "revolving catcher" system last season, although it remains to be what philosophy new manager Bob Brenly — himself a former major league catcher — will employ.

Miller and Stinnett had alternated virtually on a game-by-game basis (barring injury, of course) since fellow expansion draftee Jorge Fabregas was sent to the New York Mets on the July 31, 1998, trading deadline.

Miller edged to the front just before the All-Star break last season and finished with 91 starts, the most of any catcher in the D'backs' three seasons. He might have hit triple figures if not for a sprained right foot in a Sept. 21 game against San Francisco that caused him to miss the final 11 games of the season. It was the second straight season in which a Sept. 21 injury (hairline fracture, lefthand) kept him out of the rest of the year.

He hit .312 in an eight-week stretch starting July 3 during a season in which he set career bests in at-bats, runs, hits and doubles. Miller has good power to both gaps.

Stinnett's batting average has dropped about 20 points in each of the last two seasons, and he suffered a severe power outage as the 2000 season progressed. Stinnett had eight homers in his first 96 at-bats last season but did not have another after taking Milwaukee's John Snyder deep on May 26.

Stinnett made only six starts in July and five in August as

Miller took over the main catching duties. Five of those July-August starts came when Randy Johnson pitched; Johnson typically told the D'backs which catcher he preferred, and that catcher started.

Miller played two games as a late-inning fill in at first base last season but does not appear likely to move around much this year. He has an accurate arm, and his defense was among the factors that moved him ahead of Stinnett last season. Miller threw out 31 percent of basestealers to Stinnett's 27 percent, but Stinnett was perceived as being more erratic.

Both strike out about once every four times and thus are likely to hit low in the order. Neither has basestealing speed.

Rookie Rod Barajas has homered in each of his two September callups. He led Triple-A Tucson in homers (13) and RBI (75) in his first season at the Triple-A level, but batted only .226 in 110 games in the Pacific Coast League, a hitter's league. Another Triple-A season is likely.

Fifth-round draftee Brad Cresse, the son of Dodgers' long-time bullpen coach Mark Cresse, homered in his first game at Class A High Desert of the California League and then took two more steps up the ladder at Double-A El Paso (Texas) and in the Arizona Fall League before finishing his first pro season. He showed impressive power and instincts for the game and might come fast, but he appears to be at least a year away.

RECOMMENDATION REVIEW: The improving

Miller moved ahead of Stinnett and could take the lion's share of the catching duties. He has a good bat for a catcher.

ATLANTA BRAVES

Javy Lopez has been about as consistent as any player over the past few seasons. Since he became Atlanta's full-time catcher in 1996, he has hit between .280 and .300 with 22 or 23 homers and about 70-80 RBI. His best year was 1998, when he clubbed 34 homers and drove in 109, but he is not quite that good.

A few years ago both Greg Maddux and Tom Glavine insisted that another catcher play when they were pitching. They were concerned about the ability of Lopez to call a good game and felt more comfortable with another backstop. However, those concerns have gone away in the past couple of years and Lopez has emerged with a better reputation.

Lopez is one player you should try to acquire. Unless he is hurt, as he was for half of 1999, he is a consistent producer who will hit about 25 homers, bat close to .300 and drive in some runs.

Eddie Perez is a competent reserve catcher who is popular with the pitching staff and skipper Bobby Cox. Perez is an outstanding defensive receiver, but he is limited offensively and offers no value to Rotisserie owners. He missed most of last season with a torn right rotator cuff, but was expected to be ready for the start of the 2001 season. He would do for a couple of weeks if Lopez were to have to make a short trip to the disabled list, but if Javy is out for any extended period of time the Braves would likely try to find a better hitter.

The Braves acquired Paul Bako late in the 2000 season, but he was around mainly for insurance. He has bounced around in his brief big league career, playing for Atlanta, Houston and Florida in 2000, and has proven to be a light hitter. He is a backup catcher at best.

Atlanta doesn't have any catchers on the horizon, having traded away Fernando Lunar to Baltimore late last season. Mike Hubbard and Pascual Matos were the club's primary receivers in Triple-A, but neither one is going to unseat Perez as the big league backup.

RECOMMENDATION REVIEW: Even if some of the pitchers complain about Lopez, he is still going to catch

five days a week because of his hitting ability. There is little doubt that he is the second best hitting catcher in the National League.

CHICAGO CUBS

The Cubs believed their platoon of Joe Girardi and Jeff Reed was a good one. However, that is just another reason why the Cubs were not a contending team.

The Cubs went out and signed free agent, slugging catcher Todd Hundley to improve their offensive production at the catcher position. He was expected to see most of the time behind the plate. In the cozy confines of Wrigley, expect Hundley's home runs, and RBI totals to increase. He is back from the elbow injury that sidelined him for most of the 1998 season. While his defense is still very weak behind the plate, his offensive production will keep him on the field more than the defensive minded Girardi.

Girardi may be a popular player with the fans and media and a strong influence in the clubhouse, but he is vastly overrated because of the time he spent winning world titles with the New York Yankees. He has never reached double figures in home runs in any season in the big leagues and has topped 20 doubles only twice. The Cubs brought him back to Chicago last season figuring he would be an improvement over Benito Santiago, but he wasn't. In 2000, Girardi had only 22 extra base hits and slugged only .375, which is an incredibly low figure.

Reed wasn't any better, though maybe he should get credit for perseverance. He made his big league debut in 1984 and has managed to keep a roster spot since then despite hitting an even .250 in 17 seasons with only 61 career home runs!

The main reason he is still around is because he is a lefthanded hitter and, like Girardi, he is popular with fans, broadcasters and management. But popularity doesn't help win Rotisserie leagues (or baseball games, for that matter), which means you should stay away from either of those two players.

The Cubs signed Mike Mahoney before the 2000 season and he got in a few games with the big league club last year, but the former Braves farmhand is no better than the incumbents. Like Girardi and Reed, Mahoney is a weak hitter who does not hit for average or power. He also is rather old for a prospect, having turned 29 over the winter.

RECOMMENDATION REVIEW: Look for Hundley to have one of his best overall offensive seasons in his career. There is nothing to recommend about any of the other Chicago catchers. You could do no worse settling for another team's reserve backstop.

CINCINNATI REDS

The Reds went into last season thinking they would have one of the best catching corps in the National League. Eddie Taubensee was supposed to be among the best hitting backstops in the league not named Piazza, while Jason LaRue and Benito Santiago were penciled in as more than competent backups.

That none of the three came up with anything close to a good season was only one of the reasons the club failed to live up to expectations. Taubensee was hitting above .300 through the first two months of the 2000 season before the back troubles which eventually ended his season in July robbed him of the ability to drive the ball. Santiago was well past the point in his career where he could be effective, and LaRue didn't get any kind of shot until the last three weeks of the season.

Taubensee, whose option for 2001 was picked up at the last minute, was expected to be fully recovered and will again be the starter. LaRue, who finally started to hit well in the last few games of last season, will be Taubensee's backup.

If you put the two catchers together you'd have an All-Star for sure. Taubensee is a gifted offensive player while LaRue is equally as adept defensively. While the Reds love LaRue and tout him as the team's "catcher of the future," Taubensee will get the lion's share of playing time based on what he can do with the bat. As long as he doesn't fall to pieces behind the plate and he has made solid improvement in recent years in that area, he will continue to play most of the time. It also helps his cause that he is a lefthanded hitter while LaRue swings from the right side.

If anything happens to Taubensee, LaRue should be able to hold his own. He isn't the offensive force that Taubensee can be, but he is not horrible either. While he has struggled in his first two tries in the big leagues, hitting .223 in a little less than 200 total at-bats, he improved tremendously at the end of last season. In his last 18 games of the 2000 season, LaRue hit .316 with three homers. Remember, just a couple of years ago he was regarded as an offensive player who needed much work on his defense.

Santiago made noise in the middle of last summer about his wanting to be an everyday catcher again, but he isn't that good any longer. He would have some value to a club as a mentor to a younger catcher, but it didn't appear that his ego would let him accept that kind of situation. Plus, his Rotisserie worth is next to nothing.

The Reds don't have much help coming soon in the minors. Guillermo Garcia, who spelled LaRue in Triple-A, would be a competent major league backup, but nothing more. Corky Miller started at Double-A, but he hasn't shown much at all at the plate. His claim to fame is that he has been hit by a pitch 82 times in three professional seasons, but that indicates he is not tremendously confident at the plate.

The club drafted Dane Sardinha last summer and signed him to a major league contract, partly to keep from having to pay him millions in a signing bonus. Most scouts regarded Sardinha, drafted out of Pepperdine, as being ready to play in the big leagues defensively now. However, he still has some work to do offensively and the Reds aren't counting on him being in Cincinnati for several more years. He'd be worth a gamble in keeper leagues.

RECOMMENDATION REVIEW: Taubensee will come much cheaper than he did last year, but expect him to provide plenty of value. All offseason reports indicated he was going to be 100 percent by the start of the season, and if he is healthy he is going to hit. He should hit close to .300 and approach 20 homers.

COLORADO ROCKIES

The Rockies once again appear set to use a platoon behind the plate with Brent Mayne this time sharing the job with Ben Petrick.

Petrick appears to be the Rockies' designated catcher of the future, but while he learns the defensive side of the game, Mayne and his veteran tutelage will come in handy.

Petrick, a second round draftee in 1995 who turned down several Pac-10 football scholarship offers to sign, spent three months with Colorado last season, his second and longest stint in the majors. He once again demonstrated he was not overmatched by big league pitching by hitting .322 with three homers 20 RBI in 52 games. He did not appear a product of Coors Field, either, hitting over .315 both home and road. He tattoos lefties, hitting .354 against them last year and .333 against them in a September callup in 1999.

A high school running back, Petrick stole 30 bases at Class A Salem in 1997 and had 13 in three tops in 1999, so a half-dozen stolen bases in semi-regular time are not out of the question.

While Petrick has shown no trouble at the plate, he still struggles behind it. He had eight passed balls in limited time last season and threw out only six of the 32 baserunners who attempted to steal off him, 19 percent.

Until Petrick learns a little more about the tools of ignorance, Mayne will share the job. Mayne, in the second year of a two-year contract, had a career offensive season, surprise, in his first year at Coors Field after spending time with Kansas City, Oakland and San Francisco.

Mayne hit a career-high .301 and nearly doubled his best RBI total with 64 in only 335 at-bats. Like Petrick, he seems perfect for a platoon role. Mayne hit .318 against righties while also showing good plate awareness, walking once every eight plate appearances. He will steal two bases. Catchers hit low in the Colorado order but still get plenty of chances with runners on base.

Mayne became the first major league position player to earn a victory since 1968 when he beat Atlanta with an inning of relief on Aug. 22. It was his first and probably last appearance as a pitcher.

Six-year free agent Darron Cox was signed as a veteran backup but is not likely to see major league time unless injuries strike.

RECOMMENDATION REVIEW: The Rockies appear to have a nice mix behind the plate the steady veteran Mayne, 33 the first month of the season, and up-and-comer Petrick. Both Mayne and Petrick should maintain their offensive production thanks to their home park. A platoon seems all but certain, not only because of Mayne's steady bat but also because of Petrick's current placement on the defensive learning curve.

FLORIDA MARLINS

The Marlins signed Charles Johnson during the offseason. He was slated to be their starting catcher. See more on Johnson in the White Sox catchers section.

The Marlins have a pair of catchers that could see some time this season. Of the holdovers, the Marlins would like Ramon Castro to step up as the backup. He was one of the best defensive catchers in the Triple-A Pacific Coast League last year and he's got power potential as well. He hit 14 home runs in just 218 at-bats at triple-A last year and has the ability to hit 20-plus in the majors someday. He's not a great hitter at this point, lacking patience and the ability to make consistent contact, but he's got a much better upside than Mike Redmond does.

Redmond has been a solid part-time catcher for the Marlins over the past couple of seasons, but he has no power at all and isn't the kind of guy they want to hand their catching job over to. He puts the ball in play, but isn't a threat and in the National League it's difficult to hide a catcher that can't hit much.

The Marlins have no offensive catchers in their minor league system.

RECOMMENDATION REVIEW: Johnson is the man you want here. He has come into his prime as an offensive threat. Returning home and being on a young and improving team will help. He is one of the top NL catchers for Rotisserie purposes. Castro and Redmond will see little time behind the workhorse Johnson and have no value at this point. Castro would step up if there was an injury to Johnson.

HOUSTON ASTROS

The Astros traded starting catcher Mitch Meluskey along with center fielder Roger Cedeno, and starting pitcher Chris Holt to the Tigers for catcher Brad Ausmus, reliever Doug Brocail, and swingman Nelson Cruz. Ausmus' role as a starting catcher will not change, however, due to the presence of backup catcher Tony Eusebio, Ausmus was expected to see more days off than if he was still with the Tigers. See more on Ausmus in the Tigers catchers section.

A shoulder separation early in the 1999 season delayed Mitch Meluskey's rookie season by a year. However, he made up for lost time with a stellar year in 2000. Four catchers in the National League stand out offensively (Piazza, Kendall, Lopez and Lieberthal) but, if Meluskey continues to improve, he could join this group in 2001. He batted .300 with 14 home runs and 69 RBI in only 337 at-bats. His .401 on-base average was also impressive, especially for a rookie.

Meluskey, a 27-year old switch-hitter, is firmly established as Houston's regular catcher. However, his playing time could be curtailed somewhat by his defensive deficiencies and a flaky personality that doesn't wear well with some pitchers. Two years ago, I asked former catcher, Alan Ashby, who managed Meluskey in the minors, if veteran pitchers would be comfortable with him. His response was that when they see the way he can hit, they will be very comfortable. After only one season, Meluskey appears to be the best hitting catcher the Astros have ever had.

Tony Eusebio, 34, has been Houston's nominal backup catcher for seven years, appearing in over 100 games only twice. He is a solid receiver who works well with pitchers and has hit at least .270 in all but one of his seven full seasons. He started slowly in 2000 but came on strong when Meluskey was injured in late July, putting together an improbable 28-game hitting streak, tying Art Howe's club record. He finished with a batting average of .280 and a career high seven home runs. Eusebio projects as Houston's backup catcher for at least one more year.

A possible eventual replacement for Eusebio is Carlos Maldonado, 22, who was obtained from Seattle in a trade for infielder, Carlos Hernandez, before the 2000 season. He had a solid .270-5-52-5 season for the Texas League champion Round Rock team. He should move up to Triple-A in 2000 and is probably a year or two away from challenging for a major league job.

In the lower minors, Houston's top prospect is John Buck, 20, who was .282-10-71 for the championship Michigan team in the low Class A Midwest League. If he can make a successful jump to Double-A in 2001, he could challenge for a major league job in a couple of years.

Veterans Raul Chavez and Frank Charles caught a few games for Houston late in the 2000 season but neither figure in the Club's plans for 2001.

RECOMMENDATION REVIEW: Meluskey, still relatively unknown, has a chance to move into the top echelon of National League catchers in 2001.

LOS ANGELES DODGERS

They have tried with big-name home-run hitters from the right side (Mike Piazza) and the left side (Todd Hundley), and with a perennial Gold Glove winner (Charles Johnson) wedged in between. No matter the big-ticket attempt, the Dodgers have not reached the promised land, so having let Hundley go they will try a low-budget platoon.

They stumbled upon this strategy almost by accident, having plucked Chad Kreuter off the scrap heap and finding his pitch-calling and backstop skills more than compensate for the high-priced reputations of his predecessors. Kreuter did everything a team would want from a catcher last year other than hit homers, especially when the Dodgers were able to keep him from going into the stands to choke hecklers.

Alas, nobody's perfect, and the real hole in Kreuter's game for a catcher is power. He handles the bat more than adequately, a switch-hitter whose .416 on-base percentage was enough to make the Dodger leadoff failures jealous. He had only 19 extra-base hits and 28 RBI in 80 games and is pretty much stuck in the seven hole of the batting order, although he did show more power righthanded than lefthanded.

Primary playing time will be his, however, as the club's first offseason maneuver was to re-sign him, a reward for generally being credited with milking an impressive comeback season out of Chan Ho Park. Fortunately for Kreuter, he was not blamed for the problems the Dodgers had with the fourth and fifth starters.

One of the lesser-known rites of spring is Paul LoDuca's annual pilgrimage to prove he is more deserving of a big-league job than Angel Pena. It seems each year management would prefer for Pena to beat out LoDuca for the backup job, and each year LoDuca emerges as the more reliable player.

He's 30 now and referred to by that dreaded tag of "insurance policy." He spent most of 2000 shuttling between Los Angeles and Albuquerque and had only 65 at-bats in three big-league visits. Frustrated with the crowd behind the plate, he started playing other positions in 2000 hoping the versatility might lead to a utility role. He's a line-drive hitter who is hard to strike out, a gamer whose attitude quickly wins over a coaching staff.

Pena is the opposite. More gifted, he's got a bad body and a worse reputation, although the organization is cautiously optimistic that being exiled to Albuquerque for an entire season will serve as a wake-up call. Pena has real offensive potential, and it is not too far fetched for him to blossom and win the job outright. But if the Dodgers were convinced that would happen, they might not have been so eager to re-sign Kreuter.

If Pena does not break through quickly, he will be passed by Geronimo Gil, a younger version who also could work a little harder but might be more fundamentally sound behind the plate.

RECOMMENDATION REVIEW: Kreuter was expected to get most of the playing time, but his production will not remind anyone of Piazza, or even Hundley. LoDuca and Pena are low-cost, potentially big payoff selections because at least one of them figures to back into considerable playing time. Of the two, Pena has the offensive tools to post the biggest numbers.

MILWAUKEE BREWERS

One of the first orders of business coming into the 2000 season for the new regime under GM Dean Taylor was to completely retool the catching corps, which defensively had been a laughingstock with David Nilsson the regular there in 1999. While Nilsson's numbers were fine offensively, Nillie threw out just 15% of runners attempting to steal in 1999, and the Big Aussie was off to the Far East in 2000 after an 8-year run with the Brew Crew.

Enter Henry Blanco. Brought on board specifically to contain the running game, Blanco left little doubt that there was a new sheriff in town, gunning down 58% of those doomed baserunners who were cavalier enough to test his rifle arm.

In this era of offensive-minded ball, Blanco is something of a throwback, being employed strictly for his defense. Of course in Rotisserie terms, this does virtually nothing for you. All you need to know in that regard is that Blanco went the entire month of July without an RBI!

But Blanco's cannon of an arm should be registered as a weapon, and Henry comes into the 2001 season as Davey Lopes' #1 receiver. An issue is that Blanco missed most of September with a sore shoulder, and arthroscopic surgery was considered. A slight tear in the rotator cuff (which was operated on once already a few years ago) is suspected, but the Brewers' medical staff decided against surgery.

Backing up Blanco is journeyman Raul Casanova, a switch-hitter with occasional pop. Casanova got into 86 games for the Brewers last season. He should see a fair amount of action in 2001 as Lopes looks to protect the golden-armed Blanco, who is prone both to injury and the occasional horrendous slump.

Tyler Houston is also likely to qualify at the catching position in 2001, and at the age of 30 will be coming off his most productive campaign, in which he hammered 18 home runs in just 284 at-bats.

Down in the minors, Milwaukee has (the other) Kevin Brown, who was acquired from Toronto late in the 2000 season to provide depth and got a September look. Robinson Cancel, who missed over half of the year due to an arm injury and has little power, is another Brewer receiver in the system. Career minor leaguer Creighton Gubanich went yard 16 times for Indianapolis last year. No significant prospects are on the immediate horizon.

RECOMMENDATION REVIEW: Since Rotisserie is an offensive-oriented game, steer absolutely clear of Henry Blanco, a virtual black hole when it comes to offense who will still get the majority of playing time because of his spectacular defensive ability. Houston is the best bet of the Brewer catchers in terms of offense. Be aware that he went over two months without venturing behind the plate after the acquisition of Casanova, although it's unlikely he's ready to disdain the tools of ignorance altogether. Once a fairly highly-regarded prospect in the Tigers' system, Casanova could surprise, but don't bet the house.

MONTREAL EXPOS

The Expos went into the winter with a relatively inexperienced group of receivers. Michael Barrett has been switched back to catcher and was expected to see the majority of the time behind the dish. His backup was slated to be the young Brian Schneider. Although the Expos were looking to bring in a veteran major league backup, they were looking for more of a defensive/good presence type catcher; similar to what they got from Lenny Webster and Charlie O'Brien last season.

Barrett is an interesting case and bares close attention during spring training. If he is comfortable behind the plate then his offense will follow and he will have a very good year. Last season he was never comfortable at third base and he let it affect him at the plate before being sent to the minors. He has always been a very good defensive catcher and it was probably a mistake to move him to third base in order to save his bat and body from the riggers of catching.

Pay attention to where he is hitting the ball. If he is hitting to all fields and not trying to pull everything he is at his best. Last season he was trying to pull the ball too much and was overly aggressive. It was similar to what happened with John Olerud in his last season with the Blue Jays.

Don't expect much power from Barrett, but if he rebounds, he will put up good numbers for a catcher.

Schneider should find himself on the big league roster for the full season in 2001. Batting lefty is a plus for him and one of the reasons he was expected to be around when the Expos head north. Although he is a backup at this point in his career, he is a good defensive catcher and has a good bat. While he has more power than Barrett, he is aggressive at the plate and strikes out a lot. He is still inexperienced and it would not be a shock to see him play part of the season at Triple-A. He will be a quality backup catcher in a year or so, who will be able to provide some offense.

Bob Henley was the Expos backup catcher of the future three years ago before he blew-out his elbow and subsequently missed most of the past two years. If he is healthy he will start in the minors, but is no longer a viable Rotisserie prospect at this point. Before his injury he had a good bat.

Look for the Expos to go after a major league veteran No. 2 or 3 catcher: just don't expect him to be of any Rotisserie value.

On the farm, and at least two to three years away is Scott Ackerman. Ackerman is a good offensive catching prospect. He has power and hits for average. His defense is below average at this point and needs to improve if he wants to get to the majors.

RECOMMENDATION REVIEW: Buy low, sell high as Peter Lynch or any of the great stock pickers might say. That is the route to take with Barrett who is still young and talented enough to have a bounce back year — you can't get much lower than his 2000 season. Expect for him to be the Expos everyday starter behind the plate who will hit around .280 with 10 homers and 60 RBI. He is well worth the risk.

NEW YORK METS

Mike Piazza remains the National League's best Rotisserie catcher. His batting average bounced back to .324, while his power numbers dropped to 38 and 113 — partly because his playing time dropped to 136 games. As much as the Mets try to spin that he's a good defensive catcher, he's not good at throwing out base stealers or blocking the plate. That's not of interest to you until Piazza is no longer eligible as a Rotisserie catcher. That could come when Todd Zeile (three years older at 35) leaves and Piazza moves to first base.

Behind Piazza is Todd Pratt, a young 34 because of a light workload — his 160 at-bats in 2000 were a major league career high. Pratt made the most of them by batting .275-8-25. His only pinch hit was a home run. Pratt has improved significantly at holding down opponents' running game.

Vance Wilson, considered a good defensive catcher, also batted .260-16-62 with Triple-A Norfolk. The 28-year-old isn't likely to earn much playing time with the Mets because, like Piazza and Pratt, he bats righthanded.

At Double-A Binghamton, the catchers were Jimmy Gonzalez, a 28-year-old journeyman who batted .278-8-30, and Jason "J.P." Phillips. He batted .388-0-13 in 27 games there after a .276-6-41 start at high Class A Port St. Lucie. At 24, Phillips is a bit old not to have succeeded above Double-A. Those two also bat righthanded.

RECOMMENDATION REVIEW: Piazza brings great value, but at a very high price. Even in limited duty, Pratt is better than many low-cost catchers. A year ago we likened him to Mike Macfarlane or Bill Haselman, and we're sticking to that story. Wilson could have some value with another team, or if there's an injury in New York.

PHILADELPHIA PHILLIES

In Mike Lieberthal, the Phils possess one of the premier all-around catchers in baseball — a dangerous power hitter and RBI man who controls the running game and handles his pitching staff well. He's not the Phils' best player, but considering his second half injuries in 1999 and 2000 and the Phils' horrible won-lost records while he was sidelined — he just might be their most valuable one.

Lieberthal, 29, was once scorned by Phils' fans as a misguided first round draft pick, a scrawny defensive specialist who would never match up against quality big league pitching. He has obviously proven such skeptics wrong. Lieberthal is a free swinger who makes consistent contact, and absolutely tears apart lefthanded pitching. He has ripped southpaws to the tune of .377 and .350 in the last two seasons, with respective slugging percentages of .697 and .575. He's less proficient against righties, often expanding his strike zone and getting himself out.

He has endured a fairly heavy workload over the last four seasons when healthy. He has broken down multiple times over that period, enduring hip and ankle injuries and, most recently, a right throwing elbow surgery that prematurely ended his 2000 season. His throwing elbow was expected to be fully healed in time for spring training, allowing him to remain one of baseball's best defensive receivers. As for his 2001 workload, new Phils' manager Larry Bowa has pledged to run out his starting eight almost every day, granting fewer non-injury-related days off than his predecessor, Terry Francona. He'll probably make some exceptions for Lieberthal, however, considering his value and second-half injury history.

Look for Lieberthal to continue to post above average offensive numbers for a catcher, though it would be foolish to ever expect him to again scale the .300, 31-homer mountain he climbed in 1998. He'll likely fit snugly into the #6 hole in a potentially potent Phils' lineup and bat .280 with 20-25 homers, and 80-90 RBI in 450 at bats.

Tom Prince was the Phils' primary backup catcher last year, for some reason. It was his last year of a two-year contract, and marked — believe it or not — his 14th straight year as a major league backup. Pitchers enjoy throwing to him, and his defensive skills are solid, but he flat out cannot hit. He's 36 now, became a free agent at the end of the season, and is unlikely to get big league job from the Phils or anyone else in 2001.

Gary Bennett is the most likely candidate to replace Prince as the Phils' backup. Bennett, 29, deserved better after replacing an injured Prince in 1999 and batting .273 with almost as many RBI (21) as hits (24). He made consistent contact and hit for average and power while playing solid defense at the Triple-A level in 2000 before again acquitting himself well at the major league level after Lieberthal's season-ending injury. He's no future starter, but Bennett is perfectly capable of batting .260 or so with a bunch of walks and three homers in 150 at bats as the Phils' backup. There are worse $1 backup catchers out there.

The Phils have just a little bit going at the catcher position in the minor leagues. Last year, they snagged former top Ranger prospect Cesar King, 23, off of waivers. Never a great hitter, he was once highly coveted because of exceptional defensive skills, which have been less in evidence as his conditioning has wavered in recent seasons. He's a longshot to help the Phils with the bat in the majors, but a worthwhile low-risk gamble nonetheless.

Widebody Andy Dominique, 25, was the Phils' Double-A catcher last season, and rates a mention only because of his power potential. He's not mobile enough to ever catch much in the majors, but could someday steal a job as a deep bench bat and multipositional reserve. Russ Jacobson, 23, is the Phils' only potential future starter in the system, but that's even a longshot. The 1999 third round pick has never batted above the Low-A level at his relatively advanced age, and though he has decent power potential and solid defensive skills, he's a wild swinger and low-average hitter. He needs to jump to Double-A in 2001 to stay on the "prospect" list.

RECOMMENDATION REVIEW: Mike Lieberthal, while he had a bit of a down year in 2000, is still young and in the upper echelon of NL catchers. Gary Bennett produces when he plays, but that's not often enough.

PITTSBURGH PIRATES

When the Pirates signed Jason Kendall to an expensive six-year contract during the offseason it appeared they had locked up one of the game's best catchers for a long time to come. But, they have indicated a desire to move Kendall to first base. This would reduce the wear and tear on Kendall and let the Bucs keep him in the lineup every day. If that happens it would be a boon to his Rotisserie owners as he would increase his at-bat total while decrease the injury risk associated with full-time catchers. Even if Kendall catches everyday he is an extremely valuable Rotisserie player who provides speed and batting average at a position where both are scarce. Kendall is very hard to acquire in a draft, however, as he is a known quantity, and somewhat of a rare combination of skills; all it takes is two owners who decide they NEED Kendall and the price goes through the roof.

Keith Osik is the backup backstop and plays less frequently than almost any other second-string catcher in the game. If the Pirates decide to move Kendall to first base occasionally, Osik may get a few more at-bats, or they may give those extra at-bats to a prospect. In any case, Osik only has value as injury replacement for Kendall; don't draft Osik.

Craig Wilson shared the catching duties with Tim Laker and Randy Knorr at Triple-A Nashville; Wilson is the prospect while Laker and Knorr are the re-treads. Wilson also played a lot at first base as the Sounds did their best to keep his bat in the lineup; it worked as Wilson in homers (33) and RBI (86) but he also fanned in almost a third of his at-bats. His batting skills are considered stronger than his catching skills, so he may end up at first base once he reaches the majors. Still, should the Pirates decide to shift Kendall to first base for any length of time, Wilson's use as a reserve catcher and first baseman might lead to a significant number of at-bats with a lot of power hitting to be earned for his Rotisserie owners. For Rotisserie purposes, Wilson is nearly unknown, and a fine choice for an Ultra squad.

Humberto Cota had the lion's share of catching duties for Double-A Altoona in 2000 with Yamid Haad and Lee Evans also seeing time behind the plate. Haad is a poor hitter and Evans is more likely to advance as a first baseman than a catcher. Cota is considered a decent prospect who has a bit of power and also has superior catching skills. If he advances to the majors he could fill a reserve catching role. There is no Rotisserie value here.

J.R. House is a very good prospect who had a fine season for Low-A Hickory in 2000, leading the Crawdads in batting average (.348), homers (23) and RBI (90). He's not an especially adept catcher and may lack the arm to play behind the plate at higher levels; House could shift to first base before reaching the majors.

RECOMMENDATION REVIEW: Kendall is one of the most valuable catchers in the game; having Kendall on your roster can have a big impact upon how you conduct your draft and upon what other kinds of players you acquire at other positions. However, he is very pricey and isn't likely to come down anytime soon. If you decide to chase Kendall, set a limit on what you will spend and make sure you have an alternate plan should you be unable to acquire him, both in terms of what kind of other catchers you'll get and how to replace Kendall's production in steals and batting average. Osik has value only as a long-term injury replacement, but not for drafting. Wilson and House are interesting choices for Ultra purposes, with Wilson being a more immediate candidate for Rotisserie production.

ST. LOUIS CARDINALS

The Cardinals' pitchers love Mike Matheny for the way he calls a game and for his throwing ability, but that won't help your roto team. After winning the Gold Glove last year, Matheny will almost surely be the Cardinals' number one catcher. He hit .261 with 6 home runs and 47 RBI in 128 games last year, which is about what you would expect from him. His bat has always been what has held him back, but since the Cards have such a potent lineup they can live with him as their starter.

Carlos Hernandez is a little bit more productive offensively and is fairly skilled behind the plate, but he appeared to be on course for duty as a backup or he appeared headed out of town at the end of 2000. It's hard to believe the Cards would want to pay someone what Hernandez earns to be a backup catcher, so there was a good chance they'd try to move him. His average season, when averaged out over 162 games, is .253 with 8 homers and 47 RBI. That won't help a rotisserie team much anyway.

Elisser Marerro could be the player that loses out the most in all of this. He's a talented player with some offensive potential to go with his outstanding defensive skills, but a bout with cancer weakened him and probably set him back two full seasons already. He was reportedly getting closer to where he was physically before the cancer and if so he could still be one heck of a player. He's got power potential and he runs exceptionally well for a catcher, but he's not been able to hit for average to this point in his career. His average season, when averaged out over 162 games, is .219 with 10 home runs, 47 RBI and 16 steals.

The Cardinals had absolutely no catching prospects on the horizon heading into this past offseason.

RECOMMENDATION REVIEW: Stay away from the Cardinals' catchers unless you're desperate, in which case you'll want Matheny because he figures to play the most of the three.

SAN DIEGO PADRES

Wiki Gonzalez surprised many expert observers by winning the Padres' regular catching job and then by starting the season on fire at the plate. The marvelous start and steady play behind the plate gave the Padres so much confidence they dealt away their nominal starter, Carlos Hernandez, to the Cardinals just before the trade deadline. The irony of Gonzalez taking Hernandez's job away is that the two are friends. After the trade, Gonzalez came back to Earth and finished the year poorly; he hit .219 after the All-Star break.

Perennial prospect Ben Davis began the season so poorly he was hitting under .100 at the All-Star break. After spending the bulk of the season at Triple-A Las Vegas, Davis returned to San Diego in a reserve role behind Gonzalez and had a much better second half, hitting .248 and slugging 300 points higher in the second half.

The comeback by prospect Davis and the slump by Gonzalez set up an interesting battle for the Padres' catching job in 2001. Gonzalez has the edge on defense, but the weak San Diego offense is crying out for the RBI potential Davis might have. The most likely scenario is that Gonzalez will begin the season catching most of the time with Davis a well-used reserve. What happens after that might just depend upon which of the two players progresses most over the first few months of the season.

For Rotisserie purposes both players present big risks. Since both could end up with 250-300 at-bats, it will be difficult for them to individually produce more than a couple of bucks worth of value. Since Gonzalez was such a quick and surprising producer in 2000, he's not likely to go for the minimum salary. Likewise, Davis' power potential make him a prospect who might command more than a buck, too. This lowers the likelihood of either player being a bargain in 2001. Get either of them at or near the minimum, or not at all.

Remember George Williams? He got the Vegas catching duties when Davis was in San Diego and he even got a handful of big-league at-bats, too. It would appear that this one-time big-league starter is now just injury insurance. Still, he's better than some major league reserve catchers and could wind up in the majors as a second-string catcher. In any case, he has no Rotisserie value.

When Williams or Davis weren't catching at Las Vegas, Mark Strittmatter and Steve Soliz got some work behind the plate. Strittmatter came over from Colorado Springs to finish the year in Las Vegas; overall he didn't play a lot and, having a season in the Pacific Coast League in which he didn't have a single homer indicates his status as a minor-league reserve. Soliz earned a promotion from Double-A Mobile despite hitting .204 with just ten RBI in 44 games. He didn't do much better in the hitting-rich PCL environment, batting .218 with just eight RBI in 34 games.

The better prospect in the Padres system is Wilbert Nieves who advanced from High-A Rancho Cucamonga at midseason and even got a single at-bat for Vegas, too. Nieves hit .257 with a very nice .350 on-base percentage at Rancho, then hit .266 for Mobile. He's the best of an otherwise weak minor-league crew.

RECOMMENDATION REVIEW: Avoid all Padres' catchers unless you can get either Gonzalez or Davis for the bare minimum. Gonzalez is recommended to teams that need more of a sure thing; Davis to teams that are willing to take a chance on power potential. Nieves is the only minor-leaguer worth consideration, but there are better prospects elsewhere.

SAN FRANCISCO GIANTS

The backstop platoon of Doug Mirabelli and Bobby Estalella did the Giants justice last year (.232-20-81, combined), although had you selected both as your backstop complements, you would have fallen short at the position.

Estalella certainly holds the upper hand of the two, and based upon the 14 homers he hit, mostly over the first half (.286-9-34 were his actual totals before the All Star break), as compared to his final season numbers, Estalella could be undervalued. He is certainly more than a $1 catcher at this point, but not worth much more than $5. The upside is that Estalella is capable of 20-plus homer seasons or better, and with a full and healthy season completed, he is poised to improve his numbers.

Slightly more adept at hitting lefties than Estalella, Mirabelli's second half totals were also disappointing. Mirabelli will continue to spell Estalella during slumps and injuries, but for now his only value is in an NL only league, or as a reserve player in an Ultra league.

The Giants minor league system has a pair of catchers worth tracking not merely because their stats are good, but because it would be great to see their names as part of a major league battery. First is Fresno State alum Giuseppe Chiramonte, who went .255-24-79 at Fresno, and second is Yorvit Torrealba, who went .286-4-32 at Shreveport.

RECOMMENDATION REVIEW: If you must choose between Estalella and Mirabelli choose Estalella. He has more of an upside and could put up decent numbers if he gets more playing time.

TOP 2001 HOME RUN HITTERS

NAME	HR
Mike Piazza	38
Charles Johnson	25
Javy Lopez	22
Todd Hundley	21
Mike Lieberthal	19
Jason LaRue	16
Tyler Houston	15
Bobby Estalella	14
Jason Kendall	14
Damian Miller	13
Ben Petrick	11
Kelly Stinnett	10

TOP 2001 RBI PRODUCERS

NAME	RBI
Mike Piazza	116
Javy Lopez	82
Charles Johnson	77
Mike Lieberthal	76
Jason Kendall	65
Todd Hundley	58
Damian Miller	54
Brent Mayne	53
Bobby Estalella	52
Brad Ausmus	51
Ben Petrick	45
Raul Casanova	44
Jason LaRue	44
Michael Barrett	41
Tyler Houston	38
Benito Santiago	38
Mike Matheny	37
Wiki Gonzalez	37
Kelly Stinnett	35

TOP 2001 RUN SCORERS

NAME	RUNS
Jason Kendall	113
Mike Piazza	93
Brad Ausmus	70
Charles Johnson	67
Ben Petrick	64
Mike Lieberthal	62
Javy Lopez	57
Damian Miller	49
Jason LaRue	47
Michael Barrett	46
Bobby Estalella	45
Todd Hundley	44

TOP 2001 BASESTEALERS

NAME	SB
Jason Kendall	26
Eli Marrero	11
Brad Ausmus	11
Jason LaRue	4
Bobby Estalella	3
Mike Piazza	3
Ben Petrick	3
Ben Davis	2
Wiki Gonzalez	2
Keith Osik	2
Raul Casanova	2
Tyler Houston	2
Angel Pena	2
Joe Girardi	2
Benito Santiago	2

TOP 2001 BATTING AVERAGES

NAME	AVG
Jason Kendall	.323
Ben Petrick	.320
Mike Piazza	.318
Javy Lopez	.292
Brent Mayne	.289
Mike Lieberthal	.280
Todd Pratt	.280
Michael Barrett	.280
Mike Redmond	.274
Damian Miller	.274
Brad Ausmus	.269
Charles Johnson	.269
Tony Eusebio	.266

STRATEGIES FOR FIRST BASEMEN

Let's Play Two

by John Benson

Most Rotisserie owners spend too much time and money on their first pick at first base, and not enough time or money on their second pick. Don't have any illusions about one first baseman being enough. By the time you fill your 1/3 slot and DH/UT, you will get two first basemen without trying. So the point is: don't agonize over the first, and spend more time on the second.

All first basemen can hit. The average major league first baseman's slot in the batting order in 2000 produced .289-29-110 in the AL and .282-30-110 in the NL, worth $17 and $18 respectively. In the NL Jeff Bagwell and Todd Helton are worth a lot more than that, and so is Sean Casey in 2001 (though not everyone has figured that out about Casey yet). After those three players, there are at least ten more who will provide 500 at-bats, 20-something homers, and around 100 RBI. That's what a first baseman is, by definition. In the AL Carlos Delgado, Mike Sweeney, Frank Thomas and Jason Giambi are notably more valuable than the imaginary average guy, while ten more are worth within $3 plus or minus of the average.

So the method is simple: wait while others shell out big bucks for the guys with glittering stats, while you sit back and wait to get roughly the same thing for half the money. If for some reason you don't want to nominate hard-to-value starting pitchers for the first ten rounds (the best way to flush out money) just bring up some glamour names in the first base population. This method serves two purposes. People will over-spend while they're sitting on a ton of cash, and they will also fill up their first base slots. The latter phenomenon is where the important part of the overall strategy begins to work. After people have filled their hole at first base, they will tend to doze off when other first basemen come up for bid. And that's where you cash in: you grab two first basemen, one after the other, in mid-draft. Taking any two full-timers after the first ten are gone, you will find low prices, little competitive interest, and two bargains. In my experience, the second and less expensive will often produce more than the one you thought was better.

Like any method, this idea won't work in every auction. Someone else may have read this book and decided to do the same thing, and when two people do the same thing in any auction, whether Rotisserie or antiques, it will produce high prices. So be ready to back off. The last thing you want to do is pay $16 for a $12 first baseman in the 15th round of the draft, just to prove you can get two good ones. A really easy way to know when to back off is to see people bidding full inflated value. Whenever that happens, wait and/or try something else later.

Your second pick at first base will be important however the draft unfolds. If all the regulars are gone, roll out these criteria: you want someone who bats left (if he gets platooned he will play enough); you want someone young (clear opportunity to improve); and you want someone who hasn't yet had a full productive season in the majors. This last item is a variation on the theme of taking guys who haven't yet had their career year: nobody really knows what they're worth, and most folks will underrate them. Since all first basemen are terrific hitters (it's a federal law) you can get real lucky with some of these cheapies.

Among the regulars in the AL, keep a draft-day eye on Paul Konerko and David Ortiz (the only youngsters) and for AL bargains consider Steve Cox, Mario Valdez, Doug Mientkiewicz and Chris Richard. In the NL, perk up when Sean Casey and Richie Sexson are up for bid, and be happy if Pat Burrell or Derrek Lee becomes your indifferent first pick. When the draft gets into the not-clearly-full-time guys, take some interest in Rube Durazo, Travis Lee and Fernando Seguignol.

Finally, whatever you do, don't make first base a big concern on draft day. If you end up with a bench jockey at first base and a third baseman for your 1/3, that means someone else is sitting on three good first-sackers, and that owner will have all kinds of unaddressed needs.

AMERICAN LEAGUE
FIRST BASEMEN

ANAHEIM ANGELS

Mo Vaughn's two seasons in Anaheim, while productive (69 homers, 225 RBI), did not live up to the high standards he had set previously as a member of the Boston Red Sox. The Angels believe that part of the problem is the 20-25 extra pounds that Vaughn is carrying compared to his Boston days. Part of the problem could be geographical, as Vaughn himself has expressed a desire to return to the East Coast. If Vaughn remains with Anaheim, he should continue to perform at current levels. He will be entering the third year of a six-year contract, with a limited no-trade clause. Vaughn is an established 30-homer, 100-RBI player, but has fallen well short of the .300 level with the Angels. At age 33, he has many productive years left. Vaughn would hit third in Anaheim's lineup.

Scott Spiezio is the primary backup, and will also play games at second and third base. Spiezio has good power but struggles to hit .250. With the Angels, Spiezio can expect 250-300 at bats. In most leagues, Spiezio will qualify only at first base on Draft Day, although he should qualify to be moved to other infield positions as the season progresses, which makes him somewhat more attractive. Shawn Wooten, discussed in the catcher section, is also a possible backup.

RECOMMENDATION REVIEW: Vaughn is a known commodity, who should perform at least as well as in the last two seasons. Spiezio should provide some power and roster flexibility at a low salary.

BALTIMORE ORIOLES

The Cardinals needed a veteran at first base for their stretch run last year, so rookie Chris Richard was traded to the Orioles for veteran Will Clark. Richard had been behind Mark McGwire and didn't get much playing time. Richard played a good first base for the Orioles.

The Orioles signed free agent David Segui during the winter from the Cleveland Indians. He was expected to start at first for the Orioles, but could also see some time in the outfield or DH. See more on Segui in the Indians outfield section.

Richard is 26, and has always hit well in the high minors, showing some power and stolen base speed. He hit .276-13-36 in 199 at-bats for the Orioles, with a healthy .563 slugging percentage, higher than Rafael Palmeiro's .558 and Dean Palmer's .471, putting him in the area of Edgar Martinez' .579. He bats left, but didn't hit against very many lefties, so a serious deficiency against southpaws can't be determined. His plate discipline needs improvement as he struck out too many times and walked much less than he should have. He should get better with experience.

Richard is 6-2, and 190 lbs, with long arms, and he looks lanky and in need of bulking up. He could get more power as he matures, and a year with 20-25 homers and 80-90 RBI could come this year or next.

Jeff Conine played first base in 39 games last year, and is the reserve first baseman. Oriole's management likes Conine, and he also plays third, the outfield, and DH's.

This has worked out to over 400 at-bats in each of the past two years. He's 34, and stays in shape year-round by playing racquetball where he's an outstanding player. Conine hits for a good average in the .280-.290 range with a dozen homers, although he's popped as many as 26 in a season of full-time play.

Calvin Pickering was once near the top of Orioles prospects, but ailments and being overweight has hampered him in the past two years. He's hit well in the high minors, but last year was a lost season in Triple-A hitting a weak .218, albeit in only 197 at-bats. Pickering looks like Mo Vaughn, and had good plate discipline up until last year. He expected to be the Orioles starter in 1999, but he was devastated when the Orioles signed Will Clark. Pickering needs to get into shape and play some good ball proving that he belongs in the majors. Chris Richard is now in front of him, so Pickering could flourish with another organization.

There is occasional talk of Cal Ripken shifting to first base, but with Richard and Conine doing an adequate job, there's no need to shift Cal to first.

Tommy Davis played the majority of games in Triple-A where he had a good year, but he's not in the Orioles long range plans. David Gibraltar was the key first baseman in Double-A where he hit for a good average and showed some power. Serious problems would have to occur to the Orioles before Davis and Gibraltar get major league time.

RECOMMENDATION REVIEW: Look for Segui's batting average to drop some. Closer to .300 is more realistic, but his overall offensive productions should stay the same since he is moving to another offensive ballpark. Chris Richard is only 26, and his future looks bright. He can grow into a 20-20 man in a year or two, and should be acquired in Rotisserie leagues before he gets too expensive. Jeff Conine is a solid hitter, who should go for less than he's really worth.

BOSTON RED SOX

Brian Daubach played a little more than half the schedule at first base in 2000. His 21 homers and 76 RBI's were nearly identical to last year's totals. However, he batted 114 times more than in 1999, so his batting average plunged to .248. An elbow injury bothered him. The 29-year-old was a late arrival in the majors, so even though he's a fan favorite, he could easily be replaced.

The Red Sox claimed Rico Brogna, 30, on waivers from the Phillies in August, but after barely a week in the lineup he was relegated to pinch hitting. A fractured wrist limited his season to 185 at-bats, and he batted just .232-2-21 after two seasons of 100 plus RBI. The Massachusetts native's time in Boston didn't work out, so he was a free agent during the offseason. Brogna was signed by the Braves during the offseason.

Morgan Burkhart may have an even better underdog story than Daubach's. After four years as the star of the independent Frontier League, the 29-year-old moved into the Red Sox organization in 1999. After a .255-23-77 start at Triple-A Pawtucket last year, he earned a promotion to Boston. There, the switch hitter played mostly as DH and pinch hitter, and produced a .288 average, four homers and 18 RBI in just 73 at-bats. He's 29, a couple of weeks older than Daubach, so Burkhart's future is limited.

The best first base prospect has been considered to be Dernell Stenson. He's 22 years old, and has had two similar seasons at Pawtucket (.268-23-71 in 2000). A converted outfielder, the lefthanded batter had defensive difficulty at first base. He's not as good a prospect as the Sox once thought -- and not likely to hit for average.

Juan Diaz, a 25-year-old righthanded batter, could sneak into Boston's lineup some time this season. With the top three Sox farm teams, the Cuban belted 28 homers and drove in 82 runs in fewer than 300 at-bats. A fractured ankle ended his season early.

Despite Diaz's success, Shea Hillenbrand, a converted catcher, was the Red Sox' Double-A Player of the Year. In his second season at Trenton, he improved to .323-11-79, 10 points above his minor league average. Hillenbrand is a 25-year-old righty batter, too old to be a good prospect.

RECOMMENDATION REVIEW: Boston's major league first basemen are not good Rotisserie picks, except perhaps as backup corner infielders. Diaz could be a high reward Ultra pick, possibly contributing in the majors.

CHICAGO WHITE SOX

The White Sox have a strong young starter at first base in Paul Konerko. He's a professional hitter that rarely gets himself out, hits for average and is going to hit for more power in the future. He hit .298 with 21 home runs and 97 RBI last year and that was no fluke. He rarely strikes out for someone with his power and run producing ability and he could develop into a .320 or .330 hitter in the future. Konerko will see some time as a designated hitter, but he's primarily a first baseman and should be entrenched as a starter for the foreseeable future.

Greg Norton's stock as really dropped over the past year and a half and he'll be lucky to make the major league roster in 2001. His best asset is his ability to switch-hit, but he's a bad hitter that strikes out a lot without providing much power. He also plays third base, but the White Sox have several better options there and Norton will have to settle for a small bench role if he can even win a job in Spring Training.

Jeff Liefer spent the 2000 season at Triple-A for the White Sox and he could become a factor at the major league level in the near future. The White Sox need more of a lefthanded presence in their lineup and Liefer can provide that. He hit .281 with 32 home runs and 91 RBI last year and can be a power hitter in the majors if given an opportunity.

RECOMMENDATION REVIEW: Konerko can be expected to perform at least as well as he did during the 2000 season and there's no doubt about his rotisserie value. Get him if you can, but not too early. Norton isn't worth much, though Liefer is someone worth paying attention to if he gets a shot at the major leagues.

CLEVELAND INDIANS

Slugger Jim Thome is the mainstay at first base. His average dropped a little last year, down to .269, the lowest he's hit since his .268 in 1994. He had some trouble with southpaws last year, hitting only .250 against them. His problem is strikeouts, as he whiffs around 30 percent of the time. He led the league with 171 strikeouts in 199, and came in second last year, again with 171. In contrast, he also gets a lot of walks, and has twice led the league. With the high number of strikeouts, it's a surprise that his on-base percentages are high, usually over .400, once reaching .450. Such on-base percentages are rare for big sluggers, and even premier leadoff man Rickey Henderson never achieved .450 in his career.

Thome is a patient hitter, and he was second in the league to Carlos Delgado in total pitches seen with 2869, and he ranked third in the league in average number of pitches per plate appearance with 4.19. Only 30 years old, it's surprising that Thome is already a 10 year veteran with a solid career batting average of .284. He's a valuable

Rotisserie player, and all winning Rotisserie teams need a few hitters like Thome. The only drawback is that he's likely to be overbid in many leagues.

Danny Peoples was a Triple-A first baseman last year, where he hit .260-21-74. He's 26, and will likely spend most of 2001 in Triple-A again.

RECOMMENDATION REVIEW: Jim Thome is the man to get to anchor the corner positions for your Rotisserie team. But be careful not to overbid unless you have sufficient margin in your other players.

DETROIT TIGERS

The Tigers had problems getting production at first base last year because Tony Clark spent the bulk of the year on the disabled list. He got a clean bill of health over the Winter and if the Tigers choose to keep him, Clark could be in for a good season. He's normally a slow starter that tears the cover off the ball in the second half of the season, but he showed signs of breaking out of that pattern last year. He only played in 60 games due to back problems, but hit 13 home runs and drove in 37 while hitting .274. If healthy, you can expect Clark to provide plenty of power and some run production, though his RBI totals will depend largely on how the players around him perform.

Robert Fick could also see some time at first for Detroit, though he will also see time at designated hitter and catcher. Fick is a good hitter that hasn't proven himself as a major league player yet, which places him in a reserve role at the moment. He has the ability to hit for some power and a respectable average, though he'll have to earn playing time.

The Tigers' top hitting prospect is Eric Munson and he could be ready for a shot at the full-time job in 2001, though a 2002 arrival seems more likely. He's got very good power and should hit for more average as he matures, but right now he strikes out too much. His defense is probably about average, meaning that if he hits enough he'll make it to the majors in the near future.

RECOMMENDATION REVIEW: If Clark is healthy during spring training, he could be a steal in many leagues. Pay attention to notes concerning his back, and make sure he plays regularly in spring games, before making a leap of faith. If you get him at a low cost or in the late rounds of a draft you will have done well. Fick has potential in really deep leagues, but otherwise should be more of a wait-and-see pick. Munson probably won't make it to Detroit this season, but he's a solid player to have if your league has a minor league taxi squad or a deep bench.

KANSAS CITY ROYALS

After Mike Sweeney's breakthrough season in 1999, there was some fear of a relapse in 2000. The "Plexiglass Principal" postulates that players (or teams) who have a wide variance from their established production level will sharply revert towards the norm again in the following season. Not so with Sweeney.

Instead, Sweeney built on his breakthrough season with yet another outstanding year at the plate, full of excellent power numbers and a great batting average. He was a Rotisserie owner's dream as he was consistently productive from wire to wire; you got good numbers from Sweeney week in and week out.

The only problem now for prospective Sweeney owners is to get him for the right price. He is difficult to accurately price as he can be both undervalued and overvalued. Keeping in mind how valuable a high batting average can be, Sweeney may give even more value to people who price him based primarily upon his homers and RBI, as most first basemen are often judged. On the other hand, because Sweeney can't quite knock the ball out of the park as regularly as, say, Carlos Delgado, Frank Thomas, Mo Vaughn, or Jim Thome, he can be underpriced if purchased solely because of his power hitting. Sweeney is still among the upper-tier first sackers, though, and should be priced accordingly. Look for about 30 homers and 130 RBI to go with an outstanding batting average. Talk up how Sweeney isn't a real home run hitter, then buy him for a little less than the going rate.

When Sweeney was DHing, the Royals turned to former Twins wash-out David McCarty. McCarty was so good in spring training that he beat out Paul Sorrento for the backup first baseman/DH/pinch-hitter job, a position which Sorrento was specifically acquired to fill. McCarty also played some in the outfield, helping pad his at-bat total, as he turned in a very useful season as a reserve and even earned more regular duty later in the season.

Still, unless Sweeney is shifted to a nearly full-time DH role (which isn't likely to happen), McCarty can't play enough to deliver much value to Rotisserie owners. There's no room in the outfield in Kansas City for McCarty to get more than a handful of at-bats. It would

be a surprise to see McCarty get 300 at-bats and in such a limited role he can't do much for a Rotisserie owner. He would be useful in a temporary, fill-in role, should Sweeney get hurt, or even for a Rotisserie team missing a player for a couple of weeks. But, don't use him more than briefly. On the farm, Kit Pellow shifted over from the hot corner to become one of Triple-A Omaha's best power bats. He managed 22 homers and a club-high 75 RBI, but also hit a disappointing .249 with 89 strikeouts in 421 at-bats. Pellow's power is interesting, but not enough to overcome his inability to make regular contact. If he reaches the majors in 2001 it will be due to injury in Kansas City and then only as a bench player. No value here and not much long range future, either, for Rotisserie purposes.

Dave Willis and Jose Amado split first-base duties for Double-A Wichita and neither is a top prospect, although Amado hit quite a bit better than Willis in 2000. The Royals' best first-base prospect is Ken Harvey, who was limited to just 45 games for High-A Wilmington last year although he acquitted himself well with a .335 batting average. Harvey is years away from the bigs and only a luke-warm prospect at best.

RECOMMENDATION REVIEW: Treat Sweeney as a top-of-the-line hitter in his prime, be willing to spend $30; his consistency and three-category production will serve as an offensive anchor on your club. Acquire McCarty as a deep reserve and as injury insurance if you own Sweeney. Ignore the existing Royals' prospects at this position.

MINNESOTA TWINS

The Twins are looking to upgrade their offense at this position. Chances are that Ron Coomer, who spent most of 2000 at this position will see fewer innings there in 2001.

So what's the solution? Barring a late trade or other acquisition, the Twins will have a couple of candidates who will have to prove they have the stick to stick at first base. This is not what the roto owner wants to read, but it does, at least, create a situation where a late-round, inexpensive reach on draft day could turn out to be the steal of 2001.

Coomer is a worthy starting point. He's the second longest tenured Twin, and has the support of manager Tom Kelly, who lobbied to have Coomer re-signed during the offseason. Coomer does not have gaudy numbers 16 homers, 82 RBI. And he always has the annual nagging that costs him a couple dozen games a season.

But Coomer rarely gives away an at-bat, and he will pound on a mistake by the pitcher. He can play first or third base, which gives him some flexibility. At 34, Coomer will not get much better than he already is. He will get his 500-plus at-bats, hit 15-18 homers and drive in 80 or so runs. That means he's a good reserve Rotisserie player, who will be worthy of a starting a assignment a couple times a season. It would be dangerous to rely on him for a full season when there are more prolific options.

David Ortiz has the type of power potential that excites coaches. He can drive a ball a long way. He'll take the outside pitch to the opposite field, and has enough power to drive it over the fence that way. Because he can hit to both sides of the field, he'll hit near .300.

Ortiz has shown the ability to carry the team at times, the only problem being is that he is better suited to do that as a designated hitter than as a first baseman. Ortiz is a below average first baseman. His footwork is poor, which leads to him making poor attempts at fielding grounders.

The roto owner could care less about errors; unless he/ she is in a league that does subtract for fielding flubs. But Ortiz will get a few a starts a month at first base, which means he can be slotted in that position. He'll likely spend most of 2001 as the designated hitter.

Doug Mientkiewicz, like Ortiz, is a lefthanded hitter. Unlike Ortiz, Mientkiewicz plays an excellent first base and has a good feel for the game there. The question is if he can hit well enough at a position that demands offensive capability. He's had success as the Twins' top first base prospect, but now has to prove himself in the majors.

Mientkiewicz has not shown the power that the prototypical first baseman has. He does have a good batting eye and an ability to get on base. He'll get his walks, and looks to be able to hit near .300.

That means Mientkiewicz has a chance to become the next Mark Grace; someone who, maybe, can hit 15 homers and drive in 80 runs. Does a roto owner really want that type of production from a first baseman with all kinds of hitters elsewhere? Perhaps not.

RECOMMENDATION REVIEW: There are much better places to look for a Rotisserie first baseman. If you must, Coomer is a solid backup for your team. Ortiz has a solid upside if you can afford to take a chance.

NEW YORK YANKEES

Tino Martinez, 33, may have saved his job, but put the Yankees in a difficult position, with a strong postseason showing. His production has tailed off in all Triple Crown categories the last three seasons, to .258-16-91 last year. Those were his lowest figures since 1993.

Martinez could keep his job because last year's first basemen at Triple-A Columbus were no more than journeymen. Randall Simon has a .315 major league career average in 248 at-bats for Atlanta, but he's a free-swinging singles hitter. He batted .266-17-74 for Columbus. Jon Zuber, 31, makes a lot more contact, but has even less power (.293-1-39). Both bat lefthanded.

Nick Johnson was supposed to be the Yanks' first sacker by this year, but he was limited last season to two at-bats in the Gulf Coast League because of a sprained right wrist. If the 22-year-old lefty batter can get his swing back in Triple-A ball, he could make it to the majors during the season. He's a very patient hitter with some power.

At Double-A Norwich, Nick Leach, still another lefthanded batter, finished at .277-7-49. He's a year older than Johnson, so Leach's future is limited.

RECOMMENDATION REVIEW: Check for any information you can get on Johnson during spring training. If he seems OK, he's worth a spot on an Ultra roster. If you have Yankees fans in your league, bring up Martinez early in the auction and hope they'll spend enough so you can get a better first baseman at a lower price.

OAKLAND ATHLETICS

There is not much you can say about Jason Giambi that his 2000 MVP title doesn't suggest. Well, he posted career highs in nearly every offensive category, and is now a top flight major leaguer and roto pick. Giambi is also consistent, and though it will be hard for him to top his tremendous 2000 numbers, "JG" will come close. In leagues that include walks and/or OBP, he's extremely valuable.

Backing Giambi up, when needed, will be the combo of Olmedo Saenz, John Jaha, and brother Jeremy Giambi. They are discussed in the third base, DH, and right field sections, respectively.

Oakland's top first base prospect is Jason Hart, a 23-year old who had excellent .326-30-121 totals at Midland last year. Giambi is a free agent at the end of the 2001 season, and though Oakland will make every effort to keep their leader, Hart is a player to watch in the event of an opening.

RECOMMENDATION REVIEW: If you can get Giambi, grab him, but be prepared to pay a hefty sum.

SEATTLE MARINERS

John Olerud came home to Washington state before the 2000 season and should be the Mariners' first baseman in the immediate future. Despite his .283 average last year, he is known as a .300 hitter with 15-20 home run power and unlimited RBI potential in the right lineup. Hitting behind Alex Rodriguez and Edgar Martinez last year Olerud was able to amass 103 RBI. He's an excellent defender as well, so there's no reason to expect him to lose his job any time soon. He's a dependable player with the ability to improve on his numbers from last season.

The Mariners don't have a true "backup" at first base. They've used Edgar Martinez and Raul Ibanez in the past and could use Chris Widger there as well. Brian Lesher, who also plays the outfield, hit well at Triple-A last season but isn't a prospect.

RECOMMENDATION REVIEW: Olerud is a known commodity for rotisserie owners and his standing heading into the 2001 season should be the same as it was heading into last season. He is not on the decline.

TAMPA BAY DEVIL RAYS

Fred McGriff isn't going anywhere, but there is a good chance he'll see less time at first base and more time at designated hitter. McGriff posted his second consecutive 100 RBI season for the Devil Rays in 2000 as he proved to be the only constant in the offense, driving home 106 runs and walking 91 times in 158 games. But McGriff is 37 and the .277 batting average and 27 home runs are proof, leaving open the opportunity for Steve Cox to play more at first base.

A year removed from International League MVP honors, the lefthanded hittting Cox was the team's rookie of the year after posting a .283 average with 11 home runs and 35 RBI. Cox is a slick fielder as well as a consistently patient hitter (he walked 46 times in 318 at bats). He's got good power, but it's used more often to drive the ball to gaps for doubles. There's no doubt he'll be in the lineup

more than the 116 games he played in 2000. There are no other bonifide firstbase candidates in the Rays' farm.

RECOMMENDATION REVIEW: Neither Cox or McGriff is going to carry a team, so don't invest a lot of money in either. McGriff will be the team's regular first baseman, though he'll get more starts at designated hitter this season with Greg Vaughn's return to left field. McGriff has enough left in him to be counted on for close to 100 RBI, but the home runs are not going to be there. Cox should finish with 20-30 home runs this season splitting time between first, DH and right field.

TEXAS RANGERS

Rafael Palmeiro is coming off a down year, by his high standards. Unlike in previous seasons, he did not have the benefit of hitting between Juan Gonzalez and Todd Zeile, and it did affect his output. So, one key factor for the 2001 season is whether the Rangers wind up acquiring another big bat to give Palmeiro a bit of company in the middle of the lineup. Even if that doesn't happen, Palmeiro should bounce back somewhat from his 2000 numbers. The Ballpark in Arlington is tailor-made for lefty power hitters, and Palmeiro was expected to be completely healthy for the start of the season. He'll bat fourth or fifth in the Ranger lineup, hitting .300 or better with more than 100 RBI, barring injury.

Unless Palmeiro gets hurt, Texas won't need much in the way of backups at first base. Andres Galarraga was signed to be the full-time DH and would be the primary backup to Palmeiro. He is discussed more fully in the DH section. Both backup infielders, Frank Catalanotto and Scott Sheldon, are capable of playing first base and would be the likely fill-ins. Catalanotto is discussed with the second basemen, and Sheldon with the shortstops.

The Rangers have a couple of excellent prospects at the position. Carlos Pena should reach Triple-A this season, and could get a September callup with the big club. In the majors, Pena should eventually hit in the high .200s with good power and a little speed. Travis Hafner is a solid long-term prospect who could reach the majors by late 2002. He has hit for average and power in the low minors, averaging more than 100 RBI per season.

RECOMMENDATION REVIEW: Palmeiro is a solid value at first base, and could be a small bargain coming off a slightly down year. Get Pena as an Ultra pick if you can. Hafner would be fine as a very late Ultra pick.

Thanks to new ownership and an improved budget, the Blue Jays signed Carlos Delgado to a long-term contract extension immediately following the conclusion of the 2000 season.

Delgado had an MVP-type year and would have won the award had the Blue Jays not collapsed in the final week of the season. Instead, he had to settle for team records in doubles and RBI and most significant was the increase in walks to 123. He has become one of the most feared sluggers in the league. The Jays were so committed to keeping him from becoming a DH that they shipped off David Segui prior to the start of the season to be sure there was no competition for Delgado's defensive position.

Delgado spent much of the summer chasing the Triple Crown and though he didn't finish first in any of the three categories, he finished in the top five in the league in all three of batting average, home runs and RBI. Considering that he is still in his twenties, he should enjoy many more 40 home run seasons though he will be hard-pressed to repeat the doubles and the .344 batting average of last year. He will continue to put up big RBI numbers as the Blue Jays' cleanup hitter.

If Delgado were to suffer an injury and be unable to play, the Jays would move Brad Fullmer (covered in the DH section) to first base. It was unclear as the 2000 season ended whether the Jays would be able to sign free agent Dave Martinez (covered in the OF section) but a 2001 Blue Jays' team with Martinez would have been able to play Martinez at first if Delgado went down.

One of the reasons the Jays signed Delgado is that there are really no viable first base prospects at the high end of the farm system and a Blue Jays team without Delgado would fill the position from the major league roster.

RECOMMENDATION REVIEW: Don't draft any minor league first basemen from the Blue Jays' system. Delgado is going to play every day and even if injured, his playing time would be distributed among major league players on the bench. A healthy Delgado will top 40 home runs and 130 RBI. There isn't another first baseman in the farm system likely to make any impact in the next three years.

TOP 2001 HOME RUN HITTERS

NAME	HR
Carlos Delgado	41
Rafael Palmeiro	40
Jason Giambi	38
Jim Thome	36
Mo Vaughn	36
Dean Palmer	32
Frank Thomas	32
Fred McGriff	27
Mike Sweeney	25
Tony Clark	25
Paul Konerko	22
Tino Martinez	20
David Segui	18
Andres Galarraga	17
Steve Cox	15
John Olerud	15
Brian Daubach	15

TOP 2001 RBI PRODUCERS

NAME	RBI
Carlos Delgado	132
Jason Giambi	130
Rafael Palmeiro	122
Mike Sweeney	121
Frank Thomas	116
Mo Vaughn	114
Jim Thome	109
Dean Palmer	103
Fred McGriff	99
John Olerud	96
Tino Martinez	93
Paul Konerko	87
David Segui	86
Andres Galarraga	73
David Ortiz	73
Tony Clark	73
Ron Coomer	61
Brian Daubach	54
David McCarty	51
Jeff Conine	51

TOP 2001 RUN SCORERS

NAME	RUNS
Carlos Delgado	110
Jason Giambi	109
Jim Thome	107
Frank Thomas	98
Mike Sweeney	97
Rafael Palmeiro	95
John Olerud	89
Mo Vaughn	85
David Segui	81
Dean Palmer	80
Fred McGriff	76
Paul Konerko	76
Tino Martinez	75
David Ortiz	70
Jose Offerman	69
Tony Clark	59
Steve Cox	55
Andres Galarraga	52

TOP 2001 BATTING AVERAGES

NAME	AVG
Carlos Delgado	.317
Mike Sweeney	.316
Frank Thomas	.315
David Segui	.312
Jason Giambi	.309
John Olerud	.296
Paul Konerko	.293
Mario Valdez	.290
Hal Morris	.287
David Ortiz	.286
Rafael Palmeiro	.284
Steve Cox	.281
Mo Vaughn	.281
Doug Mientkiewicz	.280
Tony Clark	.280

TOP 2001 BASESTEALERS

NAME	SB
Jose Offerman	8
Mike Sweeney	7
Shane Halter	5
Chris Richard	5
Tino Martinez	4
Dean Palmer	4
Andres Galarraga	3
Rafael Palmeiro	3
Robert Fick	3
Jeff Conine	3
Steve Cox	2
Fred McGriff	2
Jason Giambi	2

NATIONAL LEAGUE
FIRST BASEMEN

ARIZONA DIAMONDBACKS

Travis Lee is no longer the cornerstone of the D'backs' franchise, as he was billed when he signed for a record $10 million bonus in 1996. In fact, he is no longer on the team. He was sent to Philadelphia as part of a four-player package for Curt Schilling on July 27, 2000.

These days, first base is as muddled as any position on the Arizona team, although not for a dearth of talent. Both Greg Colbrunn and Erubiel Durazo have excelled in limited time at that position, and former Cubs first baseman Mark Grace was signed during the offseason.

The D'backs planned to use Grace in a platoon with Erubiel Durazo. See more on Mark Grace in the Cubs first basemen section.

Righthanded hitter Colbrunn and lefty Durazo were expected to be a strict platoon at first in 2000 after Lee was moved to right field in the offseason, but a right wrist injury kept Durazo off the field more than half the year. A platoon was a likely scenario this season, too.

Durazo, a 1999 late-season phenomenon, felt right wrist discomfort in spring training and underwent two operations to correct cartilage damage on the outside of the wrist last year, the first on May 30 and the second on August 24, that kept him out the rest of the season. He was productive while playing through the pain, driving in 33 runs with eight home runs in only 196 at-bats. He had a career-high 10 game hitting streak early in the season.

Colbrunn, who played mainly in platoon situations the first

four months, became the full-time starter at first on August 6 and responded with his most productive season since he was the everyday first baseman for Florida in 1996.

Colbrunn batted .349 in his final 50 starts, with 25 extra-base hits (16 doubles, nine homers) and 38 RBI in that run. He was the most valuable righthanded bat in the lineup the majority of the season as Matt Williams battled through foot and quadriceps injuries. Colbrunn moved into the cleanup position ahead of Williams on August 28 and stayed there for a month.

His numbers confused the platoon theorists -- he hit .337 against righthanders, .279 against lefties. At times, Colbrunn appears almost too good for his own good. The D'backs signed him to be their top righthanded hitter off the bench in 1999, and his inclusion in the starting lineup last season weakened the D'backs' reserves to the point that some in the organization would rather see Colbrunn return to the bench despite his day-in, day-out success.

In fact, Colbrunn did not start last season until the D'backs had tried both Lee and Cabrera at first base last July. Lee and Cabrera both made 11 starts there, mostly in July.

Cabrera, a minor league free agent signee in the offseason, earned a promotion to the big club on June 26 after hitting 35 home runs in 53 games at Double-A El Paso of the Texas League.

Cabrera homered as a pinch hitter in his first major league at-bat, one of 78 players in baseball history to do that. He tripled off the center field fence the next night, only the second player in major league history to go homer/triple in his first two plate appearances. But as he proved susceptible to breaking balls, his playing time decreased.

Cabrera's contract was sold to Japan during the offseason.

None of the three candidates -- Colbrunn, Durazo, or Grace will steal bases. And neither Colbrunn, or Durazo is considered above average defensively.

RECOMMENDATION REVIEW: While a quality hitter, Colbrunn is unlikely to repeat his 2000 numbers simply because he will not get the opportunity. Look for Grace and Durazo to share most of the time, while Colburnn goes back to his pinch-hitting, bench role. The D'backs are expected to again mix and match with a platoon this season.

ATLANTA BRAVES

There was no better feel-good story in 2000 than the return of Andres Galarraga from cancer. The Big Cat missed all of 1999 after having surgery and undergoing chemotherapy treatments. When he returned for the 2000 season, he returned in a big way, hitting a home run in his first game back and pounding out four dingers in his first six games.

All in all, Galarraga had a fine season, hitting .300 for the sixth time in seven seasons and driving in at least 100 for the fifth straight year. His hit fewer home runs in 2000 than he did in 1998 (28 to 44), although many of the big sluggers in the game saw their long ball production levels drop off as well.

Galarraga obviously tired in the second half of last season. He hit 10 homers in April and had 19 by the end of June, but managed only nine home runs in the final three months of the campaign. Still, his batting average remained constant most of the year, indicating that he still knows how to hit the ball. And with a full offseason to concentrate solely on getting stronger instead of beating cancer, Galarraga should be back to his dominating self by the start of the new season. He will hit in the neighborhood of .290-.310 with 30-35 homers and 100-120 RBI.

Galarraga was signed as a free agent by the Rangers during the offseason. The Braves signed first baseman Rico Brogna to fill Galarraga's starting spot. See more on Brogna in the Red Sox first basemen section.

Wally Joyner did a fine job of backing up Galarraga. Joyner, who was injured often while with the Padres, spent most of the first half of 2000 on the bench, but got to play more in the second half to give Galarraga more rest. He took advantage of the opportunity, hitting .350 after the All-Star break.

Joyner is not a starter at this point in his career. He never had a lot of power and now there is no way he will give you the kind of production you need at first base. However, like the Braves did last year, it wouldn't be bad having him around as an insurance policy.

The Braves are short on first basemen in the minor leagues. The players who saw significant action at that position in Double-A and Triple-A (Mike Glavine, Andy Barkett and Toby Rumfield) are in their upper-20s and would offer little in the way of offense with the big league club. A.J. Zapp was a first-round draft pick out of high school in 1996, but the 23-year-old is just learning how to hit and won't be ready to join the Braves for at least another year or two.

RECOMMENDATION REVIEW: One of these years the Big Cat is finally going to run out of steam. But until he proves on the field that he can't hit anymore there is no reason for you to shy away from making him your starting first baseman, especially if he winds up playing in a better ballpark for hitters than the spacious Turner Field.

CHICAGO CUBS

Mark Grace was lost to the D'backs during the offseason. Matt Stairs, acquired in the offseason from the A's, was expected to see the majority of the time at first now that Grace is gone.

Grace is what he is and nothing more. He has been the same type of player his entire career, one who hits for average as consistently as anybody in the game, walks some, but also one who does not hit for a lot of power. In the late 1980s Grace was a much better player than he is today. Before the offensive explosion, there were many more players who hit .300 with 15-20 home runs, something Grace has done all of his career. But now getting those numbers from a first baseman just doesn't cut it.

It's nothing personal against Grace. After all, there are several other players similar to him, Hal Morris' for example, who have gotten pushed out of the way in recent years.

Grace has far more value to a real baseball team than he does to Rotisserie owners. He is handsome and popular, which helps sell tickets and promote a positive image of his club. But like real teams, you can get away with having Grace as your starting first baseman, but only if you have enough other big boppers in your lineup. Otherwise he will kill your chances for winning a championship.

Soon after last season ended Grace and his agent popped off in the newspapers about the Cubs' management, so it appeared in November that there was no way he would be back with the club in 2001. Even if he surprised everyone and resigned with Chicago, he would only be holding the position until Hee Seop Choi is ready. Choi, a 22-year-old native of Korea, is the kind of prospect the Cubs haven't had in a long, long time. He can hit for average and power and has dominated all three leagues in which he has played.

After tearing up the Midwest League in 1999, he combined to hit 25 homers and drive in 95 runs for Single-A Daytona and Double-A West Tennessee last season, then posted the best power numbers of any hitter in the 2000 Arizona Fall League.

He might not start the season with the Cubs, especially considering Chicago's long history of not giving young players a chance, but it won't take him more than half a season in the minors to be knocking hard at the door. He is simply too good to be kept out of the big leagues for long.

Julio Zuleta performed well in a brief trial with the Cubs late in 2000 and could open the year as the starter, if the Cubs don't decide to go with Matt Stairs. Zuleta is a decent bat, but has his limitations. He is not a big thumper and he won't hit for a high average. If he gets regular playing time, expect something in the neighborhood of .280 with 20-25 homers and 70-85 RBI.

The Cubs acquired Stairs from the Oakland Athletics in late November. He was expected to start the season as the starting first baseman now that Grace is gone. Stairs had one big season in 1999 when he hit 38 homers, but other than that he has been unspectacular. There is no reason to think that he is going to explode for 45 long balls despite what Chicago's PR machine would have you believe. He will hit .250-.260 with 22-28 homers, which certainly is nothing special in this day and age.

RECOMMENDATION REVIEW: Take a chance with Choi. He has a chance to be a very special player, possibly by midseason. He will be inexpensive on draft day, meaning you will get a big value out of him over the long haul.

CINCINNATI REDS

The Reds seem to be set at first base for the next several years with Sean Casey. The popular lefthanded swinger has survived a couple of prolonged slumps in his first two years and has proven to be a productive hitter.

Casey is a big, strong guy, but he only started showing signs of being able to pound the ball in the last couple months of the 2000 season. Until then he was content to simply put the ball in play and get mostly singles and a few doubles. But something changed late last season. Casey started looking to pull the ball and wound up with 20 home runs in the second half, including 10 in September.

He looked like a completely different hitter in the second half of the 2000 campaign. After getting only 14 extra-base hits in the first three months of the season, he bounced back with one more than that in July alone, and had eight doubles to go with his 10 homers in September.

Casey is one of the slowest players in the major leagues, but don't let that scare you since first basemen who steal bases are very rare.

Casey was spelled last season by Dmitri Young, a switch hitter who often played first when the Reds were facing a lefthanded pitcher. Former Reds skipper Jack McKeon often preferred to put all righthanded hitters in the lineup in that situation, but that shouldn't be the case exclusively this year. For starters, Casey hit much better against lefties in the second half of the season. Also, the Reds will need Young to be in the outfield as much as possible. Still, Young will get in several games at first base, making him extremely valuable to Rotisserie owners.

If anything were to happen to Casey that would force him out of the lineup for an extended period of time, the club would turn to D.T. Cromer. Cromer is a decent hitter who has some power, but whose skills are just short of being good enough to play every day in the majors. He performed well last year when he filled in for Casey the first few weeks of the season, but there just isn't enough room on the club's roster to give him more than casual duty.

Further down in the minors, Samone Peters put up good power numbers for Single-A Clinton, clubbing 21 homers and hitting 22 doubles. But he batted just .204 and struck out 198 times in only 122 games, leaving the 22-year-old with plenty of work to do before he becomes a viable major league prospect.

RECOMMENDATION REVIEW: Casey has shown that he can hit for average, but this could be a breakout year for him. If you can't get one of the big thumpers like Jeff Bagwell or Frank Thomas, Casey would be an excellent second choice.

COLORADO ROCKIES

In Todd Helton, Colorado has arguably the most productive first baseman now and for the foreseeable future.

Helton was the best hitter in the major leagues last season, leading the majors in batting average (.372), RBI (147), doubles (59), extra-base hits (103), total bases (405) and slugging percentage (.698) while leading the National League in hits (216) and multiple-hit games (63).

He was the fifth player in baseball history -- and the first in the NL -- to record a season of 200 hits, 40 homers, 100 RBI, 100 runs, 100 extra-base hits and 100 walks. Babe Ruth, Lou Gehrig (twice), Jimmie Foxx and Hank Greenberg are the only others to have accomplished that.

Yes, Helton was abetted by the thin air in Denver's Coors Field. So what? His numbers do not get thrown out because they are wind-aided. And he will play half his games there again this year. Moreover, he still hit .353 on the road, the third-best road average in the NL.

Helton, 27, has improved his hitting numbers in each of his three seasons since replacing Andres Galarraga as the starter in Colorado, raising his batting average, hits, runs, doubles, home runs and walks each year since 1998.

A former starting quarterback at the University of Tennessee, Helton seemingly has left himself little more room for statistical improvement in 2001, although he is a determined worker who always strives to get the best out of himself.

Helton's work ethic has shown in his development in the field, where he has turned himself into a more than adequate fielder. He played 160 games last season and will play that many again this year.

He spent about half the season in the No. 3 spot in the order, replacing injured Larry Walker there, and fit well.

The Rockies are likely to keep Helton in the 'three' hole this season, guaranteeing him a few more run-producing opportunities. He does not have great speed but will steal a half-dozen bases a year.

Reserves Terry Shumpert and Butch Huskey are not first basemen, but they played there very, very occasionally last season.

RECOMMENDATION REVIEW: It would seem almost impossible for Helton to duplicate his 2000 season, when his numbers were comparable to the best seasons of the best hitters in the history of the game. But if the Livelier Ball Era has taught us anything, it is that virtually anything is possible, especially with Coors Field as your playground.

FLORIDA MARLINS

Derrek Lee broke through last season and began to show some of the offensive ability everyone raved about when he was a Padres' farmhand. He still struggled with strikeouts, but he drew a few more walks than he had in the past and managed to hit .281 with 28 home runs in 477 at-bats. If he improves even a little bit over last year, we're talking potential for 30 plus home runs and 90 RBI.

Kevin Millar is a fine reserve for a National League team because he can play both first and third base reasonably well and he can hit. He's not a power hitter, which is why he hasn't been a full-time player. He can, however, be a valuable part-time player and pinch hitter for a National League team.

The Marlins have a ton of first base prospects, but only Nate Rolison is even close to the Majors. Rolison tore up the Triple-A PCL last year, hitting .330 with 23 home runs and 88 RBI. He's a huge man, standing 6'6" and weighing nearly 240 pounds, but had never shown much power before last season. He had already shown the ability to hit for average, but last year he broke through with better power. If Lee struggles at all, Rolison could be in line for a shot at the first base job.

The Marlins other top first base prospects, Jason Stokes and Adrian Gonzalez, were both 2000 draft picks out of high school and are several years away from contributing.

RECOMMENDATION REVIEW: There is reason to be optimistic about Lee, but don't get too excited about him because he comes with some risk. If you can get him at a good price or relatively low in the draft, he could be a steal. Millar will be a good pickup in deep leagues or NL only leagues, but otherwise won't help a lot. Rolison would be a great pickup in leagues with a minor league reserve roster, but otherwise is someone to follow early in the season.

HOUSTON ASTROS

Jeff Bagwell has spent 10 seasons as the Astros' first baseman, averaging .305-31-109-17. In 2000, he exceeded all of these figures except for stolen bases (.310-47-132-9) suggesting that he is still in his prime years. The move to Enron Field helped his power numbers but cut down on his steals because of the type of baseball that is played there. For 2001, numbers in the range of .305-40-125-10 can be expected.

With his strong showing in 2000, Bagwell must now be considered better than an even bet to eventually be in the Hall-of-Fame. He turns 33 in May and, since he keeps himself in excellent condition, he should be able to perform at a very high level for several more years. He is the only active National League player with over 2000 at-bats and a career batting average over .300, an on-base average over .400 and a slugging average over .500.

While Bagwell puts up outstanding numbers every year, he is subject to prolonged slumps when his complex approach to batting gets out of kilter. In 2000, he had a two-month stretch (May and June) when he hit only .251 with 10 home runs and 34 RBI. His lack of production during this period was a significant factor in the Astros falling hopelessly out of the race.

A third baseman in the minor leagues, Bagwell has never played a major league game at a defensive position other than first base. He has excellent defensive instincts and is a better than average defensive player with one Gold Glove.

Bagwell's backup is Daryle Ward, a first baseman in the minors, who was moved to the outfield with Houston to get his bat in the lineup. Outfielder Lance Berkman is also a natural first baseman and is available to fill in. However, Bagwell rarely misses a game and, barring injury, does not need a backup.

The top first base prospect in the minors is 23-year old Aaron McNeal who followed a breakout .310-38-131 season for low Class A Michigan in 1999 with an injury-plagued .310-11-69 year at Double-A Round Rock. He played in the Arizona Fall League but was hurt again and missed most of the season. He is a still a raw talent who is at least two years away.

RECOMMENDATION REVIEW: There are a number of highly productive major league first basemen but none have Bagwell's record of consistency. While he is unlikely to again steal 30 bases as he has twice in the past, he can be expected to be among the leaders in that category among first basemen just as he is in the other categories.

LOS ANGELES DODGERS

The only difference in analyzing the Dodgers' first base position this year from any of the past five or six is that the chances of trading away Eric Karros are smaller than ever. In this era of mobility, Karros looks like a Dodger lifer. This will be his tenth big league season, and a multi-year contract signed last year will keep him planted on the bag a while longer.

He's also one of the easiest players in the game to project. He hits 30 homers and drives in 100 runs. If you like players who do that, Karros is your guy. He does it when he hits for high average (as in 1999, .304) and when he hits for low average (as in 2000, .250).

He was never one of manager Davey Johnson's biggest backers, and he lobbied loud and long for Rick Down to replace Johnson. Now Karros has to work for Jim Tracy, who will probably pencil the righthanded slugger into the fifth spot in the lineup behind Shawn Green, at least against righthanded pitching.

Karros had almost 500 at-bats last year batting fifth, but it's hard to make a case that Green's lefthanded bat helped Karros. Perhaps if Green's Toronto form returns, it will have an impact on Karros' numbers. As much as Karros likes to fancy himself as a cleanup hitter, he batted only .230 in that role. In every comparison of run-production category, Karros performed better batting fifth than fourth.

Last year was particularly streaky for Karros, as he struggled against righthanded pitching and disappeared the final six weeks. Some club officials believe his eyesight might be fading, as they look for reasons to explain a 121-point difference in average between day and night.

Despite a very bad knee, he is durable enough to play daily and, besides, who else would the Dodgers put over there?

Dave Hansen has first base experience, but after his record-breaking performance as a pinch-hitting home run specialist, he will start only if Karros is hurt or tired. Hansen, though, is truly a professional hitter who learned in Japan how to take a line-drive swing and get enough lift to go deep. He comes off the bench cold against the opposition's best relief pitcher, no easy task. And his seven pinch-homers are one more than he ever hit in any of nine previous big-league seasons.

RECOMMENDATION REVIEW: All decisions should be this easy. With Karros, you know what you're getting. If you're looking for 30/100, he'll deliver that and there's at least some reason to believe that if Shawn Green bounces back after a tough adjustment to the National League, Karros' batting average just might bounce back with him.

MILWAUKEE BREWERS

When Richie Sexson joined the Brewers in late July, it changed the dynamic and attitude of the entire Milwaukee organization. Suddenly the club had a viable cleanup hitter and righthanded hitting offensive force to fear. (Believe it or not, Charlie Hayes actually hit cleanup and started at first base on a number of occasions prior to the Sexson acquisition). Geoff Jenkins immediately went off on an offensive surge and Jeromy Burnitz followed with a September explosion of his own as the middle of the Milwaukee order featuring Jenkins-Sexson-Burnitz immediately went from joke to formidable weapon class.

GM Dean Taylor's acquisition of Sexson (along with pitchers Paul Rigdon and Kane Davis) in exchange for reliever Bob Wickman and beleaguered starting pitchers Steve Woodard and Jason Bere was easily one of the most astute moves by a baseball executive in the 2000 season, and bordered on grand larceny.

For the first time since John Jaha's career year in 1996, the Brewers have reason to be thrilled about their outlook at the first base position. And given that Jaha played in more than 100 games only twice in a Milwaukee career that spanned the 1992-98 seasons, you really need to go back to Cecil Cooper for a parallel to what the Brew Crew will boast heading into the 2001 season at this critical offensive position.

Sexson is a big-time hitter who combines enormous power with the ability to hit for average. While it may not be realistic to expect him to hit .300 again, as he did after coming over to Brew Town for most of the year before finishing at .296, it's not out of the question. Sexson combined to hit .272 between Cleveland and Milwaukee in 2000, with 30 home runs and 91 RBI, in 148 games. But his playing time for the Indians was more sporadic as he shuttled between left field and first base. In Milwaukee, Sexson can concentrate on playing first base exclusively, and hitting cleanup.

What that means for Kevin Barker, who flopped horrendously in Milwaukee in April and early May last season before being exiled to Triple-A Indianapolis for the remainder of the year, is very much an open question. And it wasn't as if Barker stepped it up once he returned to the minors, actually regressing badly to finish at a lowly .196 with just 11 home runs (.353 SLG) for Indianapolis. The best-case scenario for Barker is probably a new organization, unless a move back to the outfield is in the offing for the once-promising lefthanded hitter.

Utilityman Tyler Houston saw some action at first base (35 games) for Davey Lopes in 2000, prior to Sexson's arrival, and provides insurance and a lefthanded stick as an occasional option as well.

At the minor league level, the Brewers are anything but loaded at the first base position. Barker presumably returns in an attempt to salvage his career, unless he changes organizations or makes the varsity as an extra outfielder and part-time first baseman. At Double-A, the Brewers have converted outfielder Buck Jacobsen, a power hitter who belted 18 home runs in half a season before being sidelined for the year with a broken wrist.

RECOMMENDATION REVIEW: Richie Sexson is the real deal. He enters the 2001 season with a regular position and the knowledge that he is the Brewers' full-time cleanup hitter. At 26, he is positioned to just begin realizing his considerable promise. What sort of an offensive stadium Miller Park will be remains to be seen, but it won't be any more difficult than County Stadium, the most unyielding offensive ballpark in the National League in 2000. Comparisons to Jeff Bagwell may be premature, and Sexson needs to cut down on the strikeouts and improve his plate discipline to approach that level. In 2001, look for 40 plus home runs and 115 RBI from Sexson, and don't forget he hit .296 after the trade to Milwaukee. Playing in the anonymity of a small market and perhaps unproven in the minds of some, he could quite possibly be a huge bargain in your draft. Go for it.

MONTREAL EXPOS

Finally handing out long-term contracts again, the Expos made a curious move by signing first baseman Lee Stevens to a long-term deal after they acquired him in a three-way trade involving Brad Fullmer, who went to the Blue Jays, and David Segui who went to the Rangers. Although he adds a veteran bat and presence to the lineup and club house, the Expos have some younger players who could fill-in reasonably well; and of course at a lower salary.

Stevens is a lower rung rotisserie first baseman who will give you good power numbers and a middle of the road batting average. He played every day after he arrived in Montreal and was expected to continue as the starter. On his way to a career year with the Expos, Steven's 2000 season was cut short by an injury in early August. If he is healthy for a full season a .270-30-100+ is reasonable to expect.

Backing Stevens up was slated to be either/or both Fernando Seguingnol and Andy Tracy. Both players are very similar and can play other positions. Both players could also find themselves back in the minors for a period of time also.

Tracy and Seguingnol are both power hitters who would not hit for average if they played every day. Both strikeout a lot and have little speed.

Besides first Seguingnol also plays a shaky outfield and would only see only spot starts in left. Although Tracy is a third baseman by trade, he is below-average defensively and reminds many of Shane Andrews; not a good player to be compared with. Tracy has the better shot at playing time because he also plays third and the Expos did not have a proven year-long starter going into spring training. Seguingnol is stuck behind incumbents Stevens at first and Bergeron in left.

On the horizon is Talmadge Nunnari. Nunnari received a brief callup at the end of the season after having a good year at Double-A Harrisburg. He is a Mark Grace type first baseman, who needs to prove he can hit for power before he becomes a serious contender for a major league first base job. He is at least another year away from a shot at the major league roster, where he would be used as a bat off the bench and defensive replacement.

RECOMMENDATION REVIEW: Stevens is the only Expos first baseman who has any value. In a deep league he is a solid pickup, but should not be looked at until the pool of first baseman thin considerably in your league. Seguingnol and Tracy could add some pop to your lineup in case of an emergency. Both players are wait and sees, if one is playing more as the season progresses then he may be a suitable fill-in for an injured player.

NEW YORK METS

Todd Zeile made a successful transition across the diamond from third base in his first year with the Mets. With help from Keith Hernandez, the 35-year-old Zeile handled the defensive transition well, but didn't produce at an acceptable level to help a Rotisserie team (.268-22-79. He slumped horribly after the All-Star break, batting just .224-8-27.

Matt Franco may be nearing the end of the line at age 31. He had his second consecutive poor season (.239-2-14). He batted only .213 in his primary role as a pinch hitter. He'll draw a walk, but doesn't do much else.

Jorge Luis Toca, like Zeile, is a righthanded batter. Toca is listed as 26 years old, but the Cuban probably is older. He's 4-for-10 in his major league career, but was a more modest .272-11-70 with Triple-A Norfolk. He also can play left field.

The Mets' search for a lefthanded bat last season for a time reached Mark Johnson. The 33-year-old wasn't successful with the Mets last year, but he could be a candidate to take Franco's pinch hitting role. At Norfolk, Johnson batted .270-17-60. Despite his 6'7" frame, he played some left field, stole 14 bases and walked more often than he struck out.

Dan Held batted .312-11-69 at Double-A Binghamton, but he's 30 years old already and not a prospect. Bryon Gainey, a 25-year-old lefthanded batter, also played at Binghamton, but slipped to .203-11-49.

The slugging prospect in the Mets' system is Earl Snyder (.282-25-93 at high Class A Port St. Lucie), but at 24, he's too old not to have played as high as Double-A.

RECOMMENDATION REVIEW: There is no Mets first basemen worthy of a Rotisserie recommendation, except for Zeile as a third corner infielder.

PHILADELPHIA PHILLIES

The Phils entered the offseason with no proven offensive performer at first base, unlike virtually every other team in baseball. Though a free agent (Mark Grace, Rico Brogna) or trade acquisition could not totally be ruled out, the Phils had deemed other areas, such as the bullpen and the leadoff spot in the batting order, as higher priorities. They are likely to hinge their 2001 hopes at the position on the considerable shoulders of faded recent high-impact prospect Travis Lee.

The 6'3", 214, lefthanded hitter retains the obvious raw physical talents that prompted the Diamondbacks to lure him with a $10 million loophole free agent contract before he had been to the plate as a professional. However, he has not progressed one iota with the bat since getting off to a huge start in his rookie season in 1998, finally resulting in his trade to the Phillies in the Curt Schilling deal last July. His athleticism makes him an above average defender at first base, he is capable of playing any of the three outfield positions in a pinch, and he has well above average speed.

As we all know, however, major league first basemen earn their keep at the plate, and Lee has seen his production slip dramatically since 1998. His .366 slugging percentage was light years below the major league average for starters at his position of .489. Despite his well above average plate discipline, Lee's .341 on-base percentage was well below the major league average of .370 for starting first basemen. By any standard, the 26-year-old Lee falls short of the substantial standards for his position.

What does he need to do to get there? Stop insisting on pulling the ball at all times, especially against lefties, for one. He's barely a .200 career hitter against southpaws, and had a grand total of one hit to the left side of the field against them in 2001. He simply must learn to hit the ball where it's pitched against lefties, and keep his hands back on breaking stuff instead of trying to crush it for distance. Against righties, Lee is too patient - he works deep counts, which is fine, but then becomes exceedingly cautious as the count builds. The Phils need him to drive in runs, so a major mental adjustment is necessary. He has also shown a maddening tendency to fall apart in the second half of seasons, a habit he simply needed to kick by this stage in his major league career. Lee also fell in love in 2000, and got married just after the season ended. Rightly or wrongly, Lee seemed a distracted young man at times last season, and needs to begin 2001 with a renewed focus to salvage his career and fulfill his promise.

I like Lee as a sleeper Rotisserie pick for 2001. Expectations will be low, but RBI opportunities will abound as he likely assumes a position behind Bobby Abreu, Scott Rolen, Pat Burrell and Mike Lieberthal in the Phillies' order. He might even be a candidate to bat second, where he will get lots of pitches to hit. He'll never be a high average hitter, but should become a 20-plus homer threat with some mechanical fine-tuning. Toss in his multipositional qualifier status and his decent speed for a corner man, and you have an interesting low-dollar Rotisserie asset.

Brian Hunter served as the Phils' primary first base backup last season, but became a free agent at the end of 2000 and is unlikely to be back in 2001. He's a low average hitter who will occasionally clobber a mistake fastball for distance. There isn't much of a Rotisserie ball market for 33-year-old career .234 hitters who have never batted as many as 300 times in a season, however.

It's always possible that Pat Burrell (see Outfielders section) could move back from left field to first base if the Phils needed him, but his strong throwing arm would be wasted there. Kevin Jordan (see Second Base section) has routinely logged some first time over the years, but that simply has to change if the Phils are to change their losing ways. He makes Travis Lee look like Lou Gehrig.

The Phils' only viable first base prospect in the minors is Nate Espy, 23, and he has yet to bat above the Low-A level despite his relatively advanced age for a prospect. He's a patient righthanded hitter who can hit for average and power, but will have to excel at the Double-A level by the end of this season to certify himself as a potential future major league contributor.

RECOMMENDATION REVIEW: Look for Lee to breakout in 2001. He will give you the bonus of stolen bases from a first baseman too.

PITTSBURGH PIRATES

If Kevin Young wasn't disappointed with his performance in 2000 his Rotisserie owners certainly were. He lost forty points off his batting average, some power and only stole a third as many bases as in 1999. Fielding difficulties cost him playing time and new threats to his regular job emerged. Further adding to Young's decline, catcher Jason Kendall signed a six-year contract in the offseason. The Pirates don't want to lose Kendall for any length of time during that expensive deal so their stated intention of periodically using him at first base in order to extend his career and prevent injury must be taken seriously.

What does it all mean for Young's immediate future? He has played in the outfield and at third base in the past, so he could shift to another spot on the diamond. He may go elsewhere to play full-time. More likely, though, he'll simply see his playing time erode as the Bucs put Kendall in the lineup at first base occasionally and as they try out some of their youngsters such as Alex Hernandez and Craig Wilson (discussed at length in the "Catchers" section).

Young can still hit and still has positive Rotisserie value; however, there are a lot of danger signs here for alert Rotisserie owners to read. Young can no longer be classed among second-tier first basemen. Instead, he must be considered as a player with moderate power and little other positives in a position where phenomenal offensive production is the norm, leaving Young near the bottom of the list of first basemen to be selected on Draft Day.

John VanderWal (discussed in the "Outfielders" section), Keith Osik ("Catchers"), Mike Benjamin ("Third Basemen"), and Ivan Cruz also saw a little time at first base last year. All but Cruz will primarily play at other positions in 2001. Cruz can't cut it in the majors; last year was his third try and it was his worst performance of the three.

Triple-A Nashville split their first base duty between Hernandez, Tim Laker ("Catchers") and Brent Brede ("Outfielders). Laker and Cruz will mostly play other positions in 2001. Hernandez hit .337 and slugged .487 in two months at Double-A Altoona to earn a promotion. His second half at Triple-A Nashville included eight homers and 37 RBI in 75 games and, although he fanned 50 times against just 11 walks, Hernandez was rewarded with his first promotion to the majors where he batted .200 and struck out more frequently than hitting safely. He's not an especially good prospect but he could lower Young's value by taking some at-bats away in a platoon arrangement. Hernandez himself has no Rotisserie value.

Switch-hitting catcher Lee Evans and lefty Eddy Furniss shared first base duty at Altoona after Hernandez's promotion. Both hit for a poor average and although Furniss showed some power hitting and decent on-base ability, neither is considered a strong prospect. There is no Rotisserie value here.

Hitting 14 homers in just 57 games made Dan Meier one

of High-A Lynchburg's top sluggers. Lefthanded-hitting Meier batted .307 and slugged .594 with an impressive .410 on-base percentage, too. Meier has emerged as a prospect; he'll move to Altoona in 2001 and with another good season like 2000 he could be worth inclusion on Ultra squads.

J. R. House tore up the South Atlantic League, batting .348 with 23 homers and 90 RBI in 110 games for Low-A Hickory. He is primarily a catcher, but many scouts feel his defensive skills aren't strong enough for that position; he will likely shift to first base as he advances. House is beginning to emerge as a viable Ultra candidate.

RECOMMENDATION REVIEW: Get Young only if there are no other regular first basemen available at the end of the draft. Avoid Hernandez and Cruz, but consider Wilson or possibly House for your Ultra roster.

ST. LOUIS CARDINALS

Is it even necessary to write about Mark McGwire? He may be the greatest home run hitter of all time and is certainly one of the most dangerous offensive players of the current generation. In addition to have Paul Bunyan-like power, McGwire is a good hitter capable of being at or near .300. He also draws more than 100 walks per season, which sets up the hitters behind him. He hit 32 home runs in just 236 at-bats last season, which is a rate of one every 7.4 at-bats, a pace that would have had him right back in the neighborhood of 70 home runs last year.

Eduardo Perez did a fine job of filling in when called upon last year, hitting .297 with 3 homers and 10 RBI in 91 major league at-bats. He was sold to a team in the Japan during the offseason.

Larry Sutton, who spent most of last year at triple-A, could also be a useful role player at the major league level if used as a pinch-hitter and once-a-week starter. The fact that he's lefthanded also helps.

None of the Cardinals' first basemen in the minors are considered top prospects and as of the end of last year none were close to reaching the majors.

RECOMMENDATION REVIEW: The only hang-up with McGwire is his health, which should be fine in 2001. He had his knee surgically repaired at the end of the 2000 season and was expected to be one hundred percent by spring training. Jump on him as fast as you can -- he's one of the 20 best Rotisserie players in the game today.

SAN DIEGO PADRES

If it weren't for Ryan Klesko and Phil Nevin you'd have to wonder how the Padres would ever score any runs at all. Klesko was one of the club's steadiest producers in 2000, batting .283 with 26 homers, 92 RBI and a surprising 23 steals, four times his previous career high. There is some concern that the weak Padres' lineup would allow opponents to pitch around Klesko. Nevin's presence has lessened that concern. Klesko is not one of the league's top first basemen, unable to rival Mark McGwire, for example, but he is still one of the better second-tier players and now that he's begun to steal bases he's even more valuable. His power and batting average should remain, but don't bet on him stealing 23 bases again. Often, baserunning for players in the middle of a batting order, like Klesko, is a function of situation and of the manager's predilection for the running game. If the circumstances aren't right or the manager has a different approach to running his offense, Klesko could easily return to his five or six steals per year. The best Draft Day approach is to set your price on Klesko based upon his homers, RBI and batting average; if you buy him and he steals bases, that's an added bonus.

When Klesko was out of the lineup, the Padres used a variety of bench substitutes, including Ed Sprague, Joe Vitiello and Dave Magadan. Sprague got the most use, cracking ten homers before an All-Star break trade sent him to contending Boston. Sprague was a bust in Beantown, hitting .216 with very little of the power the Red Sox wanted, then returned to San Diego for the final month of the season. At this point in his career he's just a one-trick pony; put him in to crank one out of the park. Otherwise, Sprague has no value; he strikes out far too much for regular play and is not a strong fielder, either.

Dave Magadan was one of the best pinch-hitters of the 1990s, seeming to always manage to get on base in a late-inning, pressure situation. He's still an extraordinary pinch-hitter, even though he's rapidly approaching his 40th birthday. Still, Rotisserie baseball requires more from a first baseman, leaving Magadan with no value. This bench player is a good one, but has no chance of winning a regular job.

Vitiello hit .350 with eleven homers and 46 RBI as a regular at Triple-A Las Vegas to earn a recall to the big leagues. He can certainly make contact, but Vitiello can

no longer run (the result of several injuries and surgeries to his knees while in the Royals' farm system) and since he doesn't hit the ball out of the park very often, his value as a first baseman in the majors is limited. Vitiello, like Sprague and Magadan, is a bench player at best.

At Las Vegas, John Roskos was primarily an outfielder, but also spent a great deal of time at first base, too. Roskos is not a prospect, by any means, but he does have intriguing power. If given a regular job or even a platoon role, he could hit a few homers in a short time. Because he can play in the outfield or at first base he may spend a significant portion of the 2001 season on a major league bench. Unless he gets that chance to start, though, Roskos has no more value than Sprague, Magadan or Vitiello.

Once a hot prospect as a third baseman, Gabe Alvarez has become a minor-league reserve first baseman. He hit .305 for Las Vegas in 2000, with nine homers and 26 RBI in 43 games, but that was in the Pacific Coast League, where .300 averages are common. He's no longer anything special; he'll need to re-prove himself before he can garner any Rotisserie interest.

Former top draft pick John Curl also spent some time at first base for the Vegas team; he's primarily an outfielder, but his versatility might help him advance even more quickly.

Double-A Mobile featured Kevin Eberwein at first base. Eberwein led the Bay Sox with 18 homers while hitting .263 in 100 games. Eberwein is not an especially good prospect, although he should advance to Las Vegas in 2001.

At High-A Rancho Cucamonga, Graham Koonce led the Quakes in most hitting categories, including homers (18), RBI (93), and on-base percentage, an impressive .425. Koonce struck out more than 100 times but also drew more than 100 walks, remarkable patience for a player at that level. If Koonce can repeat that performance at higher levels he'll be a true prospect.

RECOMMENDATION REVIEW: Get Klesko if the top-line first basemen are unavailable; he's a steady producer, but price him based upon his power and batting average only, not on his newfound running game. Few of the Padres' prospects are worthy of consideration here, although Koonce may be worth a look in another year or so.

The Giants maintain that even if J.T. Snow never got a hit, his defense saves them one to two runs per game. Unfortunately, that is not a stat that will help in any rules configuration. But, Snow's bat is essentially pretty steady, and he plays at a position where his modest totals should make him much of a bargain at first. Snow, who has abandoned his switch hitting, puts out numbers in the .280-20-80 range, and though those these stats hardly compare with those of a Jeff Bagwell, they are, nonetheless, steady. Snow is potentially an excellent bargain in mixed leagues as a corner infielder, and his abilities even bode well in NL only leagues, where his moderate price, coupled with other higher caliber stars at the scarcity spots, could make for a solid, potent lineup. Note to, that Snow is quite durable, averaging 151 games played over the past six seasons.

Giants second sacker, Jeff Kent, was Snow's primary backup in 2000, playing 16 games at the first base spot. Clearly, Kent's value is at second, but don't be surprised if he finishes his career at first (he is covered among the second sackers).

Felipe Crespo, who led the squad with 56 pinch hit at-bats last year, has had a solid career in the minor league (.290-78-363), and will also see playing time at first, and some in the outfield. As a starter Crespo, who made a splash in the Toronto camp as a second baseman several years back, might show some value as a fifth outfielder or corner infielder.

At Fresno, Damon Minor assembled a fine (.290-30-106) season, and he will likely make the squad (or potentially be trade bait) as an extra corner player, as he has little left to learn as a "minor" leaguer. Sean McGowan, had solid totals, starting with his ..327-12-106 numbers at San Jose, then .348-0-12 during a 69 at-bat spree at Shreveport. Jeremy Luster (.282-14-99, with 17 steals) fared well at Bakersfield.

RECOMMENDATION REVIEW: J.T. Snow is an average Rotisserie first baseman. No one else on the roster is of any value at this time.

TOP 2001 HOME RUN HITTERS

NAME	HR
Mark McGwire	45
Jeff Bagwell	44
Todd Helton	38
Richie Sexson	31
Eric Karros	30
Matt Stairs	27
Ryan Klesko	26
Pat Burrell	26
Derrek Lee	26
Sean Casey	23
Kevin Young	21
Todd Zeile	21
Lee Stevens	21
Rube Durazo	21
J.T. Snow	20
Fernando Seguignol	18

TOP 2001 RBI PRODUCERS

NAME	RBI
Todd Helton	132
Jeff Bagwell	128
Mark McGwire	115
Pat Burrell	104
Richie Sexson	104
Eric Karros	102
J.T. Snow	94
Ryan Klesko	93
Sean Casey	91
Matt Stairs	90
Kevin Young	88
Dmitri Young	87
Mark Grace	85
Todd Zeile	81
Rico Brogna	78
Derrek Lee	72
Lee Stevens	70
John Vanderwal	69
Rube Durazo	64
Craig Paquette	55
Travis Lee	55

TOP 2001 RUN SCORERS

NAME	RUNS
Jeff Bagwell	147
Todd Helton	125
Mark McGwire	94
Richie Sexson	87
Mark Grace	86
J.T. Snow	84
Ryan Klesko	82
Matt Stairs	81
Sean Casey	81
Kevin Young	80
Eric Karros	76
Dmitri Young	76
Pat Burrell	75
Derrek Lee	72
Todd Zeile	69
Rico Brogna	68
Rube Durazo	67
Lee Stevens	60
Travis Lee	56
John Vanderwal	52

HIGHEST 2001 AVERAGES

NAME	AVG
Todd Helton	.351
Sean Casey	.330
Greg Colbrunn	.315
Jeff Bagwell	.304
Dmitri Young	.303
Rube Durazo	.303
Julio Zuleta	.298
Mark Grace	.293
Hal Morris	.287
Ryan Klesko	.286
John Vanderwal	.286
Derrek Lee	.285
Mark McGwire	.282
Pat Burrell	.280
J.T. Snow	.279
Richie Sexson	.277
Nate Rolison	.277
Kevin Young	.273
Fernando Seguignol	.273
Wally Joyner	.272
Kevin Millar	.270

TOP 2001 BASESTEALERS

NAME	SB
Ryan Klesko	17
Jeff Bagwell	16
Kevin Young	12
Travis Lee	11
John Vanderwal	7
Eric Karros	6
Rico Brogna	6
Todd Helton	5
Matt Stairs	4
Craig Paquette	3
Alex Hernandez	3
Todd Zeile	3
Pat Burrell	2
Andy Tracy	2
Tyler Houston	2
Richie Sexson	2

STRATEGIES FOR SECOND BASEMEN

Prepare for Turnover

by John Benson

The major league population will see a lot of changes at second base in 2001. This position offers more cases where age, injuries, slumps, friction with managers, and emergence of young talent will produce changes in lineup cards as the season goes on. In this situation there will be a shortage of reliable picks on draft day.

In the National League the stars and reliables include Luis Castillo, Rafael Furcal, Eric Young, Jeff Kent, Edgardo Alfonzo, Pokey Reese, Jose Vidro, Mark Grudzielanek, Jay Bell, Warren Morris and Ron Belliard, making 11 players with 12 owners pursuing them. And as second base is the first place to look for MI fillers, the shortage will be intensified by the middle rounds of the draft.

The American League situation is even tougher, with only five guys who are high value and reliable: Roberto Alomar, Delino DeShields, Ray Durham, Adam Kennedy and Damion Easley. Many of the spring training battles worth watching closely will be among second basemen (and the Private Pages at www.johnbenson.com are the best place to look to see who's winning, why, and with what certainty. If a published value is a bell curve with upside and downside possibilities around the most likely outcome (which it is of course) the values of most second baseman for 2001 will have some wide, flat bell shapes worth understanding before drafting.

One obvious strategy is to make a serious effort to get one the proven players. With a strong team, especially, you want to come out of the draft with the largest possible number of no-question no-problem players, and the second base slots will be difficult to fill using that method this year. A pre-draft trade (before everyone sees how tough the player pool will be) is a particularly good idea this year, if you don't have one of the good picks already on a freeze list.

Chaos always creates opportunities as well as problems. For people who don't have a proven second baseman, the mistake to avoid is becoming over-aggressive about getting an "almost desirable" player after the truly good ones are all taken. This method requires great patience, and can be helped by bringing up name after name of the elderly, oft-injured, problem-plagued question mark play-

ers, and letting other people fill their slots early with the uncertainties. Then the draft pool will offer an assortment of interesting upward possibilities at low prices with little competition.

Some good names to bring up early (and then sit back and watch the others bid) are Chuck Knoblauch with his throwing errors and injuries, Miguel Cairo with his uninspired play, Carlos Febles with immense talent and a long injury history already at a young age, Bret Boone now reunited with the manager who shipped him out for failing to run out grounders, the oft-injured Homer Bush, the elderly and oft-injured Randy Velarde, and Jose Offerman who face unprecedented competition for playing time.

In the NL the toss-out names include Craig Biggio, Quilvio Veras, Damian Jackson, Fernando Vina and Bill Spiers. Lots of second-tier players will be available for a buck. These are the cases where the bell curve works in your favor. Players with a projected value of $1 offer a safety net on the downside with opportunities to soar to higher levels of value. Going for youth will be the first pass at this group: Santiago Perez, Chad Meyers, Pablo Ozuna, Brent Butler, Jack Wilson and Edwards Guzman head a list of guys who might make the majors and surprise. Looking at opening day rosters and career batting averages will produce some upside possibilities with minimal risks. Just be sure: except for Perez and Meyers, stick to $1. Players in this group are fliers with little risk; if they end up in the minors you can just replace them with any .270-hitting off-the-bench type.

In the AL the supply of worth-a-dollar players will be richer. The following are good pickups in the $1 to $5 range: Frank Catalanotto, Jerry Hairston, David Bell, Russ Johnson, Mike Lansing, Luis Rivas, Jeff Frye, Tony Graffanino, Frank Menechino, Bobby Smith and Justin Baughman. What you don't want to do is pay full value for Randy Velarde as a healthy full-time regular. At age 38 he isn't going to show any improvement, and the best you can do, if you assume he is healthy and playing, is to get what you pay for, and that is not a victory of any kind. So stick to the low prices with upward potential after the stars are gone.

AMERICAN LEAGUE SECOND BASEMEN

ANAHEIM ANGELS

Second base is safely in the hands of Adam Kennedy, who will be the everyday starter at the position. His rookie season was generally a success, as he handled his position well and added some much needed speed to the Angels' lineup. He doesn't have much power and didn't get on base as much as the Angels had hoped, but Kennedy will improve in those areas in the coming seasons. He performed much better hitting in the bottom third of the order, which is where he should be this season. Expect a .275-12-75 season with better than 20 steals from Kennedy.

On those rare occasions where Kennedy sits out, Scott Spiezio (discussed in the first base section) or Benji Gil (discussed with the shortstops) could fill in. Anaheim also has a number of fringe-type players at second base, including Keith Johnson, Trent Durrington and Justin Baughman. Johnson is a veteran minor leaguer who is unlikely to see much action in the majors. Durrington is fine defensively but cannot hit. Baughman is a speedy infielder who missed the entire 1999 season with a broken leg, but has now recovered. Baughman has a decent chance of sticking as a backup infielder this season, and could be a source of cheap steals.

David Eckstein was claimed on waivers from Boston late last season. A smallish player without outstanding athletic abilities, Eckstein compensates by playing the game intelligently and hustling. A patient hitter, Eckstein can get on base and has decent speed. He could get the call if Kennedy were to miss an extended period of time.

Alfredo Amezaga is the Angels' best second base pros-

pect, but he is at least two to three years away. Blazing speed is Amezaga's stock in trade; if he can hit in the mid-.200s, he could make it all the way to the majors. Double-A is his destination for this season.

RECOMMENDATION REVIEW: Kennedy is a safe choice at second base, and he should steadily improve over the next season or two. Baughman, if he makes the club, could contribute stolen bases for a small investment. Avoid Johnson and Durrington. Eckstein could be a good late-round reserve pick. In a league with a deep Ultra list and long term keepers, Amezaga might be worth a flyer.

BALTIMORE ORIOLES

Veteran Delino DeShields and hustling young Jerry Hairston got most of the playing time at second base last year with DeShields moving to the outfield to make room for Hairston. DeShields will be an outfielder in 2001, making Hairston the starter at second.

DeShields is a fast slap hitter whose best offensive talent is the stolen base. He's a good leadoff man, even though he doesn't meet the desired .400 on-base-percentage level. He has also hit well in the third slot in the order. He's a valuable offensive force who can swipe a base at any time. He can hit .300 and swipe 40 bases, and can lead off or contribute hitting in other slots in the order. His offense slipped a little when he was shifted to the outfield, but he's a veteran and can easily bounce back in 2001. He's a little inconsistent at second, making an outstanding play; but also flubbing a routine grounder, but he played well in the outfield.

The Orioles management and fans love Jerry Hairston. He has a little power, his hitting is improving, and he can swipe bases, but best of all he's energetic and he hustles. He's a dirty-uniform type of player, a throwback to the old days. In parts of two years, he's hit .257-9-36 in 362 at-bats with 18 stolen bases. It's easy to project that to a full season of 500 at-bats, and with continued improvement, he could hit in the .280 area with 12-15 homers and 25 stolen bases. His defense is excellent, and a *Baseball America* of league managers voted him the best defensive second baseman in the International League. He's not well known outside the Baltimore area, so he can be a good sleeper in many parts of the country. Hairston is only 24, so he's still maturing and gaining power, and in a year or two, he could be a 20-20 man.

The Orioles also like veteran Mark Lewis as the utility man. He's been in the majors off-and-on for 10 years, hitting .264 in over 2700 at-bats. Lewis can also pop an occasional home run and swipe a base, so his Rotisserie value is a little higher than many utility players. He won't hurt you as a replacement for a player that's on the DL.

The second basemen at the Orioles Triple-A club were Francisco Matos and Howie Clark, both older non-prospects who are career minor leaguers. Eddy Garabito was the second baseman in Double-A, but he needs to improve his hitting and defense to move up.

RECOMMENDATION REVIEW: Stolen bases and a good average make Delino DeShields a valuable Rotisserie commodity. Jerry Hairston should be acquired cheaply before he becomes a valuable 20-20 man. Mark Lewis is a good replacement player in time of need.

BOSTON RED SOX

Jose Offerman played more at second base than anyone else for the 2000 Red Sox, but he fell off to .255-9-41. The home run total was a career high, but he had a career-low zero stolen bases (in eight attempts) because of an injured left knee that required surgery in October. He was expected to be ready for the start of spring training. He stole 45 bases as recently as '98, and could run more this year — if he can find a regular job at age 32.

Mike Lansing was expected to take over the second base job after Boston acquired him in a trade from Colorado, but he batted just .194-0-13 in 49 games for the Sox. The 32-year-old Lansing wasn't a whole lot better with the Rockies (.258-11-47, 8 stolen bases). He also seemed to lose some range in the field, so he's likely to lose playing time.

Jorge DeLeon was the starting second baseman with Double-A Trenton, where he batted .307-2-38. However, the righthanded batter is 26, and he stole bases at an Offerman-like 1-for-10 rate.

RECOMMENDATION REVIEW: Choosing Offerman or Lansing could be a gamble. Look to see who wins this job in spring training. Also, see if Offerman is stealing bases, which could give him some added value.

CHICAGO WHITE SOX

Ray Durham is locked in at second base for the White Sox and he's a very good player. His defense is shaky at times, but that won't keep him out of the lineup. He's a legit top of the order hitter, though he is probably better off batting second rather than leadoff. Either way, Durham combines better than average power with better than average speed. He also hits in front of guys like Frank Thomas and Magglio Ordonez, meaning he'll score lots of runs. There has been talk in Chicago about the Sox possibly moving Durham to the outfield someday, but nothing concrete has surfaced and that would only increase his roto value by giving him another eligible position.

Tony Graffanino was a backup infielder with the Sox last year and he did well enough to keep a utility job for the time being. He can play second, third and shortstop, but he's not capable of being a major league starter.

Jackie Rexrode played at Double-A Birmingham last year and he's got above average speed and good discipline at the plate, but he's nowhere near a major league regular right now. He's worth keeping an eye on for the future, especially if Durham is moved to the outfielder, but for now he's not significant.

RECOMMENDATION REVIEW: Durham is a worth pickup in any roto league, especially considering the strength of the hitters behind him. He sees lots of fastballs, scores lots of runs and is a candidate for an appearance in the All-Star Game. Graffanino and Rexrode won't help much unless Durham gets hurt.

CLEVELAND INDIANS

Roberto Alomar is one of the best second baseman in baseball. He had another great season last year, hitting .310-19-89 with 39 stolen bases, and winning a Gold Glove. His 39 stolen bases was good for second in the league, and his 90.7 percent stolen base success rate lead the league. His 12 steals of third base was also tops in the league. He did all that despite being hobbled for a time with a sore elbow in May that limited his hitting from the right side, and a sore ankle in July that slowed his base stealing for a time.

Alomar swiped 37 and 39 bases in 1999 and 2000 respectively, running with the abandon of his younger years. He had not pilfered more than 30 since 1993 when he was with Toronto. He was once a top base stealer, but a severe injury in winter ball some years ago slowed him down. He now looks like the Alomar of old.

The Alomar brothers may be broken up with catcher Sandy unlikely to be signed by the Indians. The impact, if any, on Roberto's play won't be felt until the season. He's had excellent seasons away from his brother in Toronto and Baltimore, and he could easily have another great year. He's never hit over .333, and at age 33, he's unlikely to break out with a monster career-best year.

All-around utility man Jolbert Cabrera is the backup at second, but Alomar will play most of the games. Weak hitting Scott Pratt is the Triple-A second baseman, but he's unlikely to see any major league time.

RECOMMENDATION REVIEW: With the high number of stolen bases, a good over-.300 average, some homers, and a high number of RBI, Roberto Alomar is one of the most valuable Rotisserie players in the game. All Rotisserie players are aware of his value, so he's likely to be overbid in many leagues.

DETROIT TIGERS

Damion Easley is entrenched as the starter at second base in Detroit and he can be a very good player. He's one of the more inconsistent players at his position, but he's also got a good power-speed combination. He's reached double-digits in home runs and steals during each of the past four seasons and during three of those seasons he played in at least 150 games. 2000 was a disappointment for him in that he missed 36 games due to injury, which kept him from reaching the 20 home run barrier for the

fourth consecutive season. If Easley can remain healthy, you can count on 20-plus home runs and double-digit steals, though his average won't be all that exciting.

Jose Macias was the Tigers' rookie of the year for the 2000 season, but that's not saying much—he hit just .254 over 73 games and hit just 2 home runs. Macias projects as a good utility man that can play several positions well enough to not hurt the team. He won't be much of an offensive threat, however.

The best second base prospect the Tigers have is Pedro Santana. He's a contact hitter with excellent speed but no power. He hit .281 with 6 home runs, 53 RBI and 40 steals at double-A Jacksonville last year and is at least a year away from getting a legitimate shot at major league duty.

RECOMMENDATION REVIEW: Easley will be a solid rotisserie player as long as he's healthy. The combination of power and speed that he brings to the table outweighs his .258 career batting average and at the moment he has no competition for the starting job. Neither Macias nor Santana will help a roto team for this season.

KANSAS CITY ROYALS

Despite consecutive seasons of double-digit steals, Carlos Febles remains somewhat an unknown. A variety of injuries have removed 100 games from Febles' schedule over the last two years, reducing his production and leaving a false impression of low-range productivity. Given a full season of play, he is easily capable of producing 30 steals to go with a dozen homers; think "Ray Durham" for an impression of what Febles can accomplish offensively. Because he is a dazzling fielder, Febles will stay in the lineup even when his bat is not cooperating. Fortunately for his Rotisserie owners, his speed will remain even in the down times, and, because he's still underappreciated, Febles can be a tidy little bargain on Draft Day. Febles has often been used in the ninth spot of the lineup, to let the club take advantage of his speed while using more consistently productive hitters in the top part of the order. He is viewed by the club as a number two hitter, though, and could jump into that spot for good this year.

Febles' .256 and .257 batting averages over the last two seasons provide a false sense of established production. At the age of 24 but with two-plus seasons of major league experience under his belt, Febles is likely to make major strides as a big-league player in 2001 and 2002. Because he is unchallenged for his starting job, Febles will play every day and is poised for a big breakthrough in the next couple of years.

When Febles isn't in the lineup, the Royals will turn to a variety of defense-oriented middle infielders. In 2000, Jeff Reboulet, Luis Ordaz and Wilson Delgado each saw some playing time at second base. For Rotisserie purposes Reboulet and Ordaz are to be avoided. Switch-hitting Delgado could eventually develop some Rotisserie value as a fifth infielder. He's not the kind of player to draft for your lineup, or even for your Ultra squad, but if he is called upon to temporarily take over for an injured infielder, he would be an interesting choice as he has a bit of speed.

Triple-A Omaha used a rotation of non-prospects — players like Ray Holbert, Emiliano Escandon, Alejandro Preito and Tony Medrano who, at best, will win a utility infield job in the bigs; there is no Rotisserie value here. Switch-hitting Rod Metzler was the Double-A Wichita second sacker; Metzler has a little speed and not enough power to offset his strikeout tendencies; he is a dim prospect. Mark Ellis, starting shortstop for High-A Wilmington, is a better prospect; Ellis switched to second base upon arrival in Wichita after a late-season promotion. Ellis has both contact-hitting ability and good speed; he's at least two years away from the bigs.

RECOMMENDATION REVIEW: Middle infield is a good place to collect some speed, and still-undervalued Carlos Febles has enough to make him valuable even without any advance in other offensive areas. Let people believe he has already reached his peak, then pick him up mid-draft for a low sum. The best bet is to acquire Febles before he becomes the last positive-value middle infielder or the last potential basestealer left in the draft. Only Wilson Delgado is worth consideration among the backup players, and only for replacement use, not for drafting to start the season. There are no farm players who have yet proven to be worthy of Rotisserie consideration.

MINNESOTA TWINS

Remember this name: Luis Rivas. The young product of the Twins' Venezuelan academy has a chance to become a factor at second base for years to come.

The Twins got a glimpse of Rivas in a late season callup. He did not look overwhelmed, despite being 21 years old. He hit a respectable .310 in a month's work and showed

the speed and fielding ability the club hoped to see.

Rivas came up as a shortstop, but, since Cristian Guzman is entrenched there, Rivas was moved to second base just over a year ago. On problem with the switch is that Rivas has to learn the positioning required of a second baseman, while he adjusts to the overall speed at which the game is played.

Defensive adjustments will land him on the bench a few times during the season, but the Twins are clearing the way for him to start at second base in 2001. He's fast and can hit for average. Some Twins officials feel that Rivas will be able to drive the ball and use his speed to leg out extra base hits.

He hasn't shown much power through the minors, but there's a chance he can hit a few out. The Twins feel they have an offensive player who can also field well in Rivas, and they hope that he pairs with Guzman to be the Twins middle infield combo for years and years. Rivas could bat second in the order, but likely will hit near the bottom of the order as he settles in. His ability to steal bases and drive the ball a little makes him worthy of a late-round selection.

If Rivas flops, there are a couple of fall-back options. Jay Canizaro, a late bloomer at 27, enjoyed a decent season in which some Twins officials admired his tenacity and ability to compete despite not being the best skilled option. Still, he did not receive unanimous support of the coaching staff. His hands were not the greatest, and he swung at too many high fastballs, many of which he was unable to catch up with.

Canizaro will see time at second, the question is how much. He also could play some at third base. A platoon player, at best.

Denny Hocking, a long time Twin, will play some second base. He has good range, and outstanding arm, and almost hit .300 in 2000, which could earn him time in 2001. Actually, Hocking plays every position, expect pitcher and catcher, and will get 400 plate appearances. He doesn't, however, provide enough offense to be a reliable roto player.

RECOMMENDATION REVIEW: Rivas is going to be special. Grab him now before he becomes a household name like Rafael Furcal became last season. They are the same type player.

NEW YORK YANKEES

The Yankees used Chuck Knoblauch at second base more than any other player, but hardly at all during the season's second half, when his throwing problems became too severe for a team in a pennant race to take a chance on. Along with his playing time, the 32-year-old Knoblauch's offense fell off — to .282-5-26, with 15 steals. He batted .338 in 71 at-bats as a DH.

After being released by the Pirates, Luis Sojo was an unlikely World Series hero. But the Yankees always liked him as a utility player, and regretted having allowed him to leave as a free agent. Between the two teams, he received his most playing time since 1995 and finished at a combined .286-7-37, with similar success in each league. At 35, the righthanded batter can't be considered an everyday player.

The future at second base could be D'Angelo Jimenez — or he could become a latter-day Andre Robertson. Jimenez missed most of last season after being involved in an auto accident. The 23-year-old switch hitter had just 124 minor league at-bats in 2000, and his .233 average with Triple-A Columbus was nearly 100 points below what he did in a full season for the '99 Clippers.

The second baseman at Double-A Norwich was Marc Mirizzi, a 25-year-old switch hitter who is not a prospect. He batted just .239-6-29.

RECOMMENDATION REVIEW: The only player in this group who would be worthy of any consideration is Jimenez, and only if he shows during spring training that he's well enough to play. Knoblauch doesn't provide enough offense to be a good Rotisserie DH.

OAKLAND ATHLETICS

Surprise, surprise, surprise. Just when you thought Randy Velarde was a good safe selection amidst the sea of young, run-producing Athletics, the team goes and swaps him to Texas. Why? Well, part of the deal was cost cutting, as Oakland gears up to sign their MVP first baseman to a long and big deal.

But, mostly they felt that Jose Ortiz was ready to join the ranks of the Eric Chavezes and Miguel Tejadas. "Why," you ask. Well, the 23-year old had enjoyed steady progress, advancing a level a year in the minors, starting with his 1995 Dominican League debut (.300-9-41, over 217 at-

bats). At Triple-A in 1999, Ortiz registered respectable .284-9-45 totals, with four steals, but last year, the youngster positively exploded, with a .351-24-108 season, that included 22 steals. He sparked the team as well down the stretch over a couple of starts the last week of the season, hence the starting job.

That means Ortiz will likely be undervalued in most leagues. Over a first full campaign, Ortiz is likely to hit in the .260's with ten or so homers, RBI in the high 50's and 6-10 steals (he is capable of more, but that is not the Athletics game). That makes Ortiz a deal as a $1-2 middle infielder-maybe a little more in traditional AL only leagues. Be careful, though not to spend too much on a rookie, and that includes Ortiz, even though his future looks a lot like that of his NL Jose counterpart: Jose Vidro.

Backing up Ortiz in the event of injury or inconsistency will be Frank Menechino. He is really just a journeyman utility player at this point (actually, Menechino always was), but he is a veteran, and will be called upon to help the team in a pinch. Menechino will generate little interest, and should be cheap, and he could be a decent backup as such. He did hit six homers last year over just 145 at-bats, so should Menechino emerge with a starting role, he could hit 15 or more long balls on this high scoring team.

Mark Bellhorn, once a highly touted prospect, has dropped into minor league oblivion. At Double-A, however, Esteban German is an interesting player. His totals, especially walks, dropped some last year as the 22-year old spent his second year in the California League, although he did swipe 78 bags in 2000.

RECOMMENDATION REVIEW: If you want to take a chance at second base Ortiz is not a bad choice. Keep an eye on Bellhorn. He resurrected his career last season and could be a sleeper if Ortiz falters.

SEATTLE MARINERS

David Bell saw time at both second base and third base last season, but with Mark McLemore's testing of the free agent market after 2000, he's the man on the spot in Seattle. Bell put up big numbers playing in the Kingdome, but has been far less effective as an offensive player since the move to Safeco Field. He's not the type that strikes out a lot and he's got some pop, but he's not much of a hitter for average and he doesn't steal bases. His production last year, .247 with 11 homers and 47 RBI, is about what you can expect from him in the future.

Free agent Bret Boone was signed to play second base. The Mariners expected him to be their starting second baseman going into spring training. See more on Boone in the Padres second basemen section.

Carlos Guillen has seen time at second base in the past, but will probably be their starter at third base. The M's didn't have a major league utility infielder of any value heading into this past Winter and none of their top prospects are second basemen at the moment.

Jermaine Clark is the Mariners' top prospect at second base and he could show up in the majors by the end of the 2001 season. There is an outside chance he could earn a job in Spring Training, but since he's never played above double-A that may be pushing it. Clark is a good hitter that has displayed outstanding patience and tremendous speed. Last year at double-A New Haven he hit .293 with 2 home runs and 44 RBI, but he stole 38 bases and posted a .421 on-base percentage. He was also very consistent in the field, which could lead to a promotion to the majors in the near future.

RECOMMENDATION REVIEW: Barring a trade or free agent signing, Bell appears to be the choice for the Mariners. He's a good defender and serviceable as a hitter, but he isn't much of a rotisserie player. Clark is a good player to pick up in leagues with deep benches or with minor league rosters. In other leagues, Clark is someone to watch during Spring Training and early in the season as he figures to get at least some major league time during 2001.

TAMPA BAY DEVIL RAYS

Three candidates on the Devil Rays' 40-man roster will make a bid for the starting second base job: Brent Abernathy, Russ Johnson and Bobby Smith. Gone is Miguel Cairo, who has been the team's regular second baseman during the franchise's first three seasons.

Cairo's status was up in the air during the winter. He was expected to sign with someone who need a backup middle infielder. He has little Rotisserie value besides his stolen bases. He regressed last season.

Abernathy looks like the guy who will win the starting job. Acquired from the Blue Jays in a deal before the trade deadline, Abernathy hit .290 in 119 games with five home runs and 50 RBI at the Triple-A level. The youngster then excelled as the starting second baseman for the gold

medal winning U.S. Olympic baseball team. According to scouts, Abernathy is not a flashy player, he just gets the job done and does the little things well.

Smith looked as though he'd finally found what it took to play at the major-league level once he was promoted midway through the 2000 campaign. He hit for power, showed his speed and range, and generally displayed an athleticism unfamiliar to the Devil Rays' infield. Unfortunately, after being shelved with a knee injury, Smith returned to his 1999 form to finish with a .234 average with six home runs, 26 RBI and two stolen bases. Included in Smith's portfolio were 59 strikeouts in 175 bats. In short, all of Smith's immense athletic skills don't appear as though they ever will add up to a major-league player.

After playing second, shortstop and third in 2000, Johnson went to spring training with the pitchers and catchers to spend some time learning the catching position in case of emergencies. Johnson's toughness and gamesmanship could land a starting job if Abernathy falters, otherwise he'll be the Devil Rays' utilityman.

RECOMMENDATION REVIEW: Stay away from all three. The position has been unstable throughout the Devil Rays' history and it appears it will continue to be unstable. Even if Abernathy lands the job, his numbers won't be worth investing much money into. As for Smith, he might not be in the majors in 2001. Johnson won't have enough at-bats to interest anyone.

TEXAS RANGERS

The Rangers traded two Class A pitchers for Randy Velarde in the offseason, and he'll play every day for Texas. Expect Velarde to bat leadoff and get 600 plate appearances if he stays healthy. At the age of 38, Velarde is still in superb condition, although he has a tendency to get hurt. With Texas, Velarde should score over 100 runs while hitting in the high .200s. Velarde still has some speed, but won't steal more than ten bases or so.

Frank Catalanotto is the primary backup. Catalanotto is a fine hitter and can back up at every infield position except shortstop. For draft purposes, he will qualify only at second base in most leagues. Catalanotto tends to get overexposed if played too frequently, and his defensive limitations also militate against getting lots of playing time. Depending on individual league rules regarding positibnal eligibility during the season, Catalanotto can be a valuable commodity — a player who can be moved around quite a bit and who will help a little across the board in all the hitting categories. Just don't expect more than 300 at bats from him. Scott Sheldon, who is discussed with the shortstops, also will see some action at second base.

Luis Alicea became a free agent at the end of last season, but Texas was not expected to re-sign him. Alicea had a career year in 2000 and will be hard pressed to repeat it. He is a decent hitting second baseman, but his below average defensive play and age (35 on Opening Day) will work against him getting anywhere near the 540 at bats he saw last year.

The top second base prospect in the Texas system is Jason Romano, who didn't dominate Double-A last season as he had at lower levels. His ETA has been pushed back to 2002 or 2003, but the Rangers still see him as the second baseman of the future. Romano has good speed and line drive power to the gaps. He's young and will get another season at Double-A.

RECOMMENDATION REVIEW: Velarde could be a little undervalued, but carries more than the average risk of injury. Don't overpay for Alicea, whose value will certainly decline this season. Catalanotto is a good choice for a third middle infielder at a modest price. Romano is a decent late Ultra pick.

TORONTO BLUE JAYS

This was a difficult position to fill for the Jays in 2000 because Homer Bush was either bad or injured and the Jays did not have a major league option available, forcing them to trade for Mickey Morandini late in the year.

Bush is a tough one to figure. Coming off a .320 season with 32 steals in 1999, he seemed poised for stardom as the Jays had finally found their first true second baseman since Roberto Alomar. Instead, Bush spent half the season on the disabled list and the other half of the season hitting .215 for the Jays with 1 home run and 9 stolen bases. It couldn't have been a worse year. That said, it did appear as the 2000 season ended that Bush would start 2001 as the Jays' everyday second baseman.

A Blue Jays' team that went with Homer Bush as the everyday second baseman this year would watch him carefully and given his recent propensity for nagging injuries, he would be a longshot to top 110 games for Toronto, even if he were not competing to keep his job. He's certainly not a .215 hitter but chances appear good

now that he's not a .320 hitter either and given his speed and swing, he looks to be a .270 type with little power that can steal 15-25 bases in a full season. His glove is not a concern. Because he hasn't played that much in the majors, people often think Bush is young but in fact he starts the 2001 season twenty-eight years old. Bush also has never been one to take a walk and that will cost him playing time as his career progresses.

Morandini is a longshot to be much of a contributor at the major league level at this stage, and may be without a job now that the Jays signed Jeff Frye, though he always hustles and gives every defensive play his all. His average is likely to continue its decline and he has never hit for power. His basestealing speed is quickly disappearing too though he still fields second base well and has sure hands and a quick throw to first.

Jeff Frye was signed as a free agent. He was expected to push Homer Bush for playing time and could be the main guy if Bush continues to struggle as he did in 2000. Frye is an underrated hitter and has a little value, especially if you need someone to fill-in when one of your starters is out.

Veteran utilityman Craig Grebeck went into this past offseason as a free agent and the Jays were eager to bring him back for another year. Grebeck, at thirty-six, is older than most people think but he is comfortable at any infield position and he doesn't kill a team with his bat though he's never a power threat and doesn't steal bases. His playing time possibilities continue to shrink and he would be fighting to play 50 games this year.

Utilityman Chris Woodward (covered in the shortstop section) could also play here in an emergency. There are no near-ready second base prospects in the farm system at this point and the playing time at this position is likely to be filled from players that appeared in the majors in 2000.

RECOMMENDATION REVIEW: Bush is a risky pick not only because he is a longshot to stay healthy for the whole season but he's on a short leash when it comes to how he starts the season. New manager Buck Martinez will be watching closely to determine which, if any, of 1999 or 2000 was the fluke. Regardless, Bush is an option if you need to take a risk and are looking for some stolen bases. The Jays don't have anyone at Triple-A ready to play second base at this level and so any other possibilities are almost certain to come from outside the organization. If you take Bush, you may also want to keep an eye on Frye.

TOP 2001 HOME RUN HITTERS

NAME	HR
Bret Boone	20
Roberto Alomar	20
Damion Easley	17
Ray Durham	16
David Bell	14
Frank Catalanotto	13
Delino DeShields	11
Chuck Knoblauch	10
Adam Kennedy	9
Randy Velarde	8
Jay Canizaro	8
Jerry Hairston Jr.	8
Bobby Smith	7
Mike Lansing	7
Jose Offerman	7

TOP 2001 RBI PRODUCERS

NAME	RBI
Roberto Alomar	95
Delino DeShields	80
Bret Boone	73
Adam Kennedy	72
Ray Durham	70
Damion Easley	64
David Bell	57
Frank Catalanotto	49
Jay Canizaro	45
Chuck Knoblauch	42
Denny Hocking	42
Jose Offerman	42

TOP 2001 RUN SCORERS

NAME	RUNS
Ray Durham	118
Roberto Alomar	117
Chuck Knoblauch	93
Delino DeShields	87
Damion Easley	79
Adam Kennedy	79
Bret Boone	75
Mark McLemore	75
Jose Offerman	69
David Bell	67
Carlos Febles	63
Frank Catalanotto	62
Randy Velarde	59
Miguel Cairo	53

TOP 2001 BASESTEALERS

NAME	SB
Delino DeShields	34
Roberto Alomar	33
Ray Durham	29
Miguel Cairo	25
Mark McLemore	22
Chuck Knoblauch	21
Adam Kennedy	19
Carlos Febles	18
Homer Bush	15
Jerry Hairston Jr.	15
Damion Easley	13
Bret Boone	10
Randy Velarde	9
Justin Baughman	9
Denny Hocking	8
Jose Offerman	8
Luis Rivas	7

TOP 2001 BATTING AVERAGES

NAME	AVG
Roberto Alomar	.311
Jeff Frye	.303
Brent Abernathy	.291
Homer Bush	.288
Frank Catalanotto	.286
Ray Durham	.285
Randy Velarde	.284
Chuck Knoblauch	.284
Delino DeShields	.284
Justin Baughman	.282
Dangelo Jimenez	.276
Jose Offerman	.276
Mike Young	.275
Adam Kennedy	.275
Jose Ortiz	.274
Jay Canizaro	.273
Denny Hocking	.273
Miguel Cairo	.273

NATIONAL LEAGUE SECOND BASEMEN

ARIZONA DIAMONDBACKS

Over the last 10 years, no major leaguer has evolved more than Diamondbacks' second baseman Jay Bell. The man who led the National League with 39 sacrifice hits in 1990 found power as the decade progressed, capping that shift with 38 homers in 1999, the fifth-highest total at that position in major league history.

Bell tapered off a bit in 2000, although he was again above his career averages in virtually every offensive category while playing regularly.

Bell, in the fourth year of a five-year, $34 million deal, will be the full-time starter in 2001 despite his somewhat limited range at his new position. He has played second base for only two years and a month, moving in September of 1998 to accommodate then-shortstop Tony Batista.

He again was expected to hit No. 2 in the order, a spot that benefits leadoff man Tony Womack because of Bell's proclivity for taking pitches. Bell no longer has the speed that led him to 16 stolen bases in 1993, but he will steal a half-dozen or so, running when matchups are in his favor.

Bell has averaged 26 homers a year over the last four seasons and can be expected to hit another 20 this year. His career average is .269, and he should not stray far from that.

Craig Counsell and Hanley Frias are capable middle infield replacements, and lefthanded hitting Counsell was used to spell Bell against the occasional difficult righty last season.

Counsell, who began 2000 in the minor leagues after being released by Los Angeles in spring training, hit a career-high .316 in 152 at-bats last season and is a capable defender. He runs well but does not have basestealing speed.

Frias, a former expansion draftee, twice stole more than 35 bases in the minor leagues but has not played enough to post those kinds of numbers in the majors. He has a good batting eye — one walk every seven plate appearances over the last two years — and is a capable reserve.

RECOMMENDATION REVIEW: While Bell's reducing range make him somewhat of a hindrance on the playing field, his power numbers at second base make him much better in a rotisserie league than in real life.

ATLANTA BRAVES

It is no coincidence that the Braves struggled more in the second half of the season without Quilvio Veras in the starting lineup. Atlanta simply didn't have the offensive firepower that it did after Veras blew out his right knee in mid-July.

Veras was on the verge of having his best season in the big leagues before the injury. There is not much doubt that he would have set career marks in home runs, RBI, doubles and batting average, and he would have at least come close to his high of 56 stolen bases.

He has improved tremendously as a hitter in the last couple of seasons. He is more patient at the plate and swings at better pitches. He will never hit more than 10 home runs or drive in 100, but he will do everything else. He is the best leadoff hitter in the National League and will hit .300-.320. Veras was expected to be completely healthy by the start of the season, and the latest surgical techniques mean that he will not lose much, if any, of his speed. That means he will again steal about 50 bases.

Rafael Furcal played at second base almost a third of the time last season, but all indications are that he will be a full-time shortstop this year. He is better defensively at short and the Braves would have to have a big reason not to play both him and Veras.

Keith Lockhart is a nice player for a major league team to have coming off its bench, but he has no Rotisserie value. He won't start more than a few times a month, and even if he gets to play regularly because of injury, as he did last season, he won't hit anything close to an accept-able level.

It won't be too much longer before Marcus Giles is ready for big league action. The 23-year-old was second on Double-A Greenville's squad in home runs, RBI and stolen bases, while hitting .290 for the season. The Braves don't have any reason to rush him, but another strong season in the minor leagues will have him knocking at the door at Turner Field.

RECOMMENDATION REVIEW: It will be hard to make any predictions about Atlanta's middle infielders until Alex Rodriguez signs his big contract. If he winds up with the Braves, it would mean that Furcal and Veras will have to fight for playing time at second base and that would diminish the value of both players. If A-Rod goes anywhere else, both will wind up having very good years.

CHICAGO CUBS

Don Baylor brought Eric Young to Chicago, having known EY since both were in Colorado. Young was supposed to add speed and defense and provide the Cubs with their first legitimate leadoff hitter in several seasons. And though Young was not the greatest leadoff hitter in baseball history, he was better than the previous options the Cubs had.

All in all, Young put up decent numbers in his first year in Chicago. Wrigley Field's dimensions — specifically the space it offers down both foul lines — helped Young shatter his previous career mark in doubles. He also stole

54 bases, which marked the second consecutive season he had at least 50.

That is basically the type of player that he is. While he doesn't get on base as much as one might like out of a leadoff hitter, he is a pretty good Rotisserie player and does provide some value. He also is tight with Baylor, which will ensure him a starting spot as long as both remain with the Cubs.

Chad Meyers, Augie Ojeda and Jose Nieves played in a handful of games last year at second base for the Cubs. However, as long as Young is healthy, none of those players will get any real playing time. Meyers is basically the same kind of player as Young, although he cannot come close to stealing 50 bases. Nieves has a little more power, but hits between .260 and .280. Both Meyers and Nieves are going to make the big league club as reserves, though neither will see significant action as long as Young and shortstop Ricky Gutierrez are healthy.

Ojeda might be the best of the three reserves, but he is 26 and has the least amount of big league experience. Expect him to start the year in the minor leagues and receive a promotion only due to an injury.

RECOMMENDATION REVIEW: Your needs will help you determine if Young is the second baseman for you. If you need more of a power hitter, then Young isn't going to help you any. But if you have enough home runs, then Young's speed could help put you over the top.

CINCINNATI REDS

The Reds think so highly of Pokey Reese that their reluctance to let him go held up their trade for Ken Griffey, Jr., for months.

Reese is a fine player and an outstanding defensive performer, as evidenced by the two consecutive Gold Glove Awards he won in 1999 and 2000. However he has some severe limitations as a hitter. His strike zone judgment is suspect at times — he is especially vulnerable to the low pitch outside of the zone — and he tends to try and hit too many home runs.

There are serious doubts about his ability to get much better offensively, as well. He will be 28 in June and has not shown much of a willingness to adjust his batting stance. If he ever learns how to draw more walks and decides to settle for singles and doubles instead of trying to hit home runs he would be fantastic. But until then he will hit .260-.280 with 10-12 homers and about 30 steals.

Chris Stynes is a competent backup, but don't be fooled by his performance in 2000. He is not that kind of player and he won't come close to putting up those kinds of numbers again. He is versatile and can play some in the outfield, but he doesn't have any power and he can't be expected to hit above .300 again. He would be among the worst everyday players in the majors if he gets his wish and becomes a starter. He was trade to the Red Sox and was expected to play third. See more on Stynes in the Sox third base section.

Gookie Dawkins (real name Travis) will get the call if anything happens to Reese to cause him to miss an extended period of time. Dawkins has plenty of experience (he was on the Pan-American team in 1999 and was on the U.S. Olympic team last year) and has made quite an impression. He has a chance to be a special player, but he is still very young (21 on Opening Day) and has a lot of work to do to improve. He was vastly overmatched in his two-week stint with the Reds last season and didn't hit very well at Double-A when he was sent down. He would have to really work to hit .250 in the majors at this point in his career.

RECOMMENDATION REVIEW: Reese will never give you the numbers that Jeff Kent or Edgardo Alfonzo will. He simply is not going to ever be that kind of hitter. He is much more important to his real team than he is to Rotisserie owners because of his defense. There are many other second basemen around who will give Rotisserie players much more value.

COLORADO ROCKIES

The Mike Lansing Era officially ended last July, when Lansing was dealt to Boston in the Rockies' flurry of trading deadline moves. Colorado committed $24 million over four years when they signed Lansing as a free agent in 1998.

The new second baseman is Todd Walker, who fell out of favor in Minnesota last season after trashing manager Tom Kelly. Walker, a lefthanded hitter, stands to open the season as the regular second baseman while Brent Butler and Terry Shumpert offer options from the right side of the plate.

Walker in effect forced a trade when he criticized Kelly's

handling of the Twins' young players, and landed in Colorado on July 16. He took off after joining the Rockies, batting .316 with seven home runs and 36 RBI in only 171 at-bats in Colorado.

Walker was used in a platoon with Jeff Frye over the final two months in Colorado, but showed he might be capable of handling himself on both sides of the plate. He hit .357 against lefties with Minnesota and the Rockies, although that came in only 26 plate appearances.

He will steal a half-dozen bases. Walker is known as more of a hitter than a glove man, and Colorado manager Buddy Bell's emphasis on defense could mean less-than-everyday playing time. While he batted higher in the order in Minnesota, Walker would probably be a No. 7 hitter in Colorado.

Shumpert has proven to be a very valuable commodity in his three seasons with the Rockies, playing seven positions — all but pitcher and catcher — and starting at all four infield positions in 2000. He broke in as a second baseman with Kansas City in 1990, replacing legendary Frank White, and could see a moderate amount of time there this season. He has the ability to steal double-digit bases in only 300 at-bats.

Butler, perhaps the least heralded acquisition in the Darryl Kile trade with St. Louis before the 2000 season, was an all-star at three different minor league levels in the Cardinals' organization as a shortstop but is seen here as a second baseman. He was a likely 2000 Olympian but suffered a broken hand before the selection process was completed.

Neifi Perez also is an option at second base, his position when he broke in with the Rockies in the second half of the 1997 season. But Perez is the reigning NL Gold Glove winner at shortstop, and probably would play second only in an emergency.

The Rockies would have moved Perez to second had they successfully wooed Alex Rodriguez in the offseason.

RECOMMENDATION REVIEW: Walker enters the season as the starter, but it is far from certain that he will play everyday. Butler has hit double-digit homers in three minor league seasons and appears to have a better glove. Draft Walker as a platoon player, not a regular, and you will be better off.

FLORIDA MARLINS

Luis Castillo has turned into one of the premier leadoff men in the National League. He's always displayed a good eye at the plate and great speed on the bases, but he made a big step forward as a hitter last year. Castillo hit .334 with only 2 home runs and 17 RBI, but he got on base at a .428 clip and stole 62 bases while scoring more than 100 runs. He's also a strong defensive player, so he'll play everyday barring injury.

Chris Clapinski is one of the Marlins utility infielders, but he has almost no rotisserie value. He hit .304 for the Marlins last year, but that was in just 49 at-bats. He's versatile, which could keep him in the majors, but he's not much of a hitter.

Pablo Ozuna is one of their top prospects and he's got a chance to be a player much like Castillo. He's a .300 hitter with good gap power for a guy his size and tremendous speed. He could develop double-digit home run power as he matures, but even if he doesn't his speed and ability to make contact will allow him to advance. He does, however, still need a little work on his defense.

RECOMMENDATION REVIEW: Castillo is a no-brainer, so grab him if the opportunity presents itself. Ozuna is a nice player to have in leagues with minor league rosters, but not if you want to get something out of him this season.

HOUSTON ASTROS

Craig Biggio has been the second baseman for the Houston Astros since 1992 when he made the difficult transition from catcher. Over most of that period, he and Roberto Alomar ranked as the two top second basemen in baseball. Biggio had his best seasons in 1997 and 1998 before falling off slightly in 1999. His production declined significantly in 2000 before he suffered a severe knee injury on August 1, which put him out for the season.

Biggio had surgery to repair a torn ACL in August. He was expected to be ready to participate in some spring training activities but may not be ready to begin the regular season. He is a strong competitor and has worked hard on his rehabilitation. However, at age 35, he is not likely to regain the speed and range he had before the injury. He played through some other injuries the last two years and the long layoff may have allowed the rest of his body to recuperate. The maximum that can be expected for

Biggio is his 1999 production (.294-16-73-28).

Julio Lugo was Biggio's primary replacement after his injury. Lugo, a shortstop in the minors, filled in admirably (.283-10-40-22 in 116 games). Lugo played 60 games for Houston at shortstop, 45 at second base and also played all three outfield positions. He is somewhat erratic defensively but at 25, he has established himself as a valuable utility player who can bat at the top of the order. He could open at second base if Biggio isn't ready and should also see action at shortstop.

Keith Ginter, 25, had a surprising breakout season at Double-A Round Rock in 2000. He led the Texas League in both batting average (.333) and on-base average (.457) and was voted the League's Most Valuable Player. With 26 home runs, 92 RBI and 24 stolen bases, he is a complete player. He finished the season in Houston and also played in the Arizona Fall League where he failed to continue his strong offensive showing. He is likely to play at Triple-A in 2001 and may get some time at third base as well as second.

RECOMMENDATION REVIEW: Coming off his injury, Biggio has to be considered a risk for 2001. He should not be expected to approach his peak 1997-1998 performance. Lugo is a versatile performer who should get at least 300 at-bats and around 20 stolen bases while not hurting other categories.

LOS ANGELES DODGERS

So confident that Mark Grudzielanek could move from shortstop to second base, the Dodgers traded first Eric Young, then Jose Vizcaino. They signed Grudzielanek to a long-term contract, gave him the job and removed all competitors. The result: Grudzielanek made the defensive transition, but his offensive numbers slipped.

Batting second in the order, Grudzielanek ironically missed Young's leadoff table-setting. Grudzielanek's batting average dropped 47 points. Although he played 25 more games than the previous injury-marred season, he drove in only three more runs, had the same home-run total (7) and wasn't much of a factor over the second half. The speed that translated to 33 stolen bases earlier in his career has vanished, as he stole only 12 in 2000.

He couldn't use the position switch as an excuse for his lower production, because his offense was fine in the first half, when adjustment to the new position could have had a negative impact. In fact, he confirmed the opinions of many scouts who believed he never had true shortstop skills and was better suited for second base.

But he has always been a bit of an offensive puzzle. He doesn't run the bases well enough to bat leadoff, isn't patient enough or make contact reliably enough to bat second and lacks the power to handle a mid-lineup spot, yet has the type of multi-year contract that would indicate he should be able to fill one of those roles. The contract, combined with the Dodgers' staggering payroll and rumored interest in Alex Rodriguez, led to rumors that Grudzielanek might be traded.

The Dodgers always could move another shortstop named Alex (Cora) to play second base, although it would be a waste of Cora's impressive range and slick hands. No matter what position Cora plays, he is not the type of player you build an offense around. He lacks power and hasn't shown he can handle big-league pitching for average over an entire season. He's a number eight hitter unless the pitcher can really rake. The only hope for Cora is that his brother, Joey, was a late bloomer offensively, too. One troubling aspect to Cora's game is that, despite his reliance on hitting the ball on the ground, he is no factor stealing bases.

Perhaps a more intriguing player to consider is Hiram Bocachica, a former first-round pick by the Montreal Expos, now on his third position after going from shortstop to outfield and now second base. The knock on Bocachica has always been a lack of concentration and focus, but he made enough improvement in Triple-A last year that he was expected to be in the big leagues this year. A .542 slugging percentage is pretty strong for a second baseman, so if he can control his wild throwing arm, Bocachica might become more than just an offensive-minded utility-man.

Although he's still a few years away, remember the name Joe Thurston. He's a Pete Rose-type hit machine who steals bases and ignites a crowd.

RECOMMENDATION REVIEW: You can say this about Grudzielanek: at least he plays a lot. He won't hit a lot of home runs or steal a lot of bases, but he provides enough offense to stay in the lineup.

Handed the everyday job at second base following the offseason trade of Fernando Vina to St. Louis for Juan Acevedo, Ron Belliard took a step backward in 2000. His regression is quite possibly attributable to physical issues. Belliard played most of the second half of the season with a lower back problem. The team medical staff considered post-season surgery but instead determined that Belliard could rehab the injury with a strengthening program.

Belliard's physical conditioning may have played a role in the injury as it was clear that the infielder was carrying extra weight all season. This factor may have also contributed to "Belly's" second half vanishing act.

Belliard plays the game with a confidence that borders on cockiness, which doesn't always play well since he is still overly prone to mistakes in judgment on the bases and in the field.

Manager Davey Lopes cast Belliard as his leadoff hitter for most of the season's first half, but his second half swoon called a halt to that, and he settled into the seventh slot for most of the remainder of the year. It's instructive that Marquis Grissom, he of the lowest on-base percentage among National League full-time players, replaced Belliard in the leadoff role.

Belliard is a disciplined hitter who will work the count and look for a walk, but the stolen base has inexplicably disappeared from his game. After stealing 33 bases at Triple-A Louisville in 1998, Belliard's totals at the major league level dropped to four in 1999 and seven (in 152 games) in 2000. Belliard is an above average runner going from first to third, so the low stolen base total is something of a mystery, particularly on a club managed by one of the game's most aggressive runners in Lopes.

An instinctive and gifted defensive player with outstanding range, Belliard will make the spectacular play with regularity, and turns a nifty double play as well. Belliard will be 26 on Opening Day and is just entering his prime. It is now time for him to add maturity to his game and start to eliminate the mistakes that have marked his play to this point.

Belliard is a solid hitter with gap power who can occasionally go deep. Behind Belliard, about all Milwaukee has at the major league level is journeyman middle infielder Luis Lopez. Lopez brought a well-earned reputation as a light-hitting bench player carried mainly for his glove coming into the 2000 season, but fashioned perhaps his finest offensive season at the age of 29 in Milwaukee. The switch-hitter belted six home runs in 201 at-bats while hitting a respectable .264, and Lopes was utilizing him as a valued pinch hitter in the last two months of the season. Meanwhile, Lopez was at times extremely erratic afield. He has little or no speed.

Besides Santiago Perez, Milwaukee has nobody at the upper levels of the minor league system ready to take the step up to the major leagues in the middle infield. Perez needs to prove he can hit for average in the majors. He has little power, but has stolen over 20 bases in four of the past five seasons. His best chance is as a backup MI.

Jeff Pickler and Mickey Lopez are short-term possibilities in a pinch. Below them, Mark Ernster is a solid defensive infielder who was one of several Brewer prospects who played in the Arizona Fall League.

RECOMMENDATION REVIEW: Belliard will come into the 2001 season with something to prove after a mildly disappointing 2000 campaign. Belliard is an enormously talented player who could still develop into an All-Star. That will take more attention to conditioning than he has shown to this point and a refining/maturing process to begin to take hold along with it. It wouldn't be unreasonable to expect a .290 season out of Belliard, with 12-15 home runs and 10-12 stolen bases. He needs to rediscover the hunger that marked his performance when he first arrived on the scene in 1999 and then to just let the talent flow. Assuming that he is 100% following rehab from the back injury, he will play every day. The Brewers have no other legitimate options, are certainly not giving up on Belliard, and have far more pressing priorities.

MONTREAL EXPOS

Jose Vidro is one of the most underrated players in the game today. He is second in NL second basemen to only Jeff Kent and on the same level as Edgardo Alfonzo in terms of offensive production.

The best part of Vidro is that he has continued to improve in all facets of his game since he has arrived in the majors. His defense was once shaky and threatened playing time as recent as the 2000 Spring Training when the Expos brought in veteran second baseman Mickey Morandini for his glove. The hard working Vidro put any doubts to rest with a very good defensive season. It is no longer a major concern.

Offensively he has improving power and is a high average contact hitter who does not strike out much. Vidro has greatly improved his clutch hitting and run producing abilities. He should push his RBI total past the century mark in 2001. His minor draw back is low steal totals. Vidro has never stolen more than the five bases he stole last season. With more experience he possibly could push that total up to eight or 10.

The only threat to Vidro's playing time in Montreal is if the team moves from Montreal; which is a yearly topic. He is a tough player who plays though injuries and can be expected, barring a severe injury to play every day and bat in the three hole.

Backups at second will have little rotisserie value. Trace Coquillette is a good offensive player with a shaky glove. He had more of a chance to challenge for more third base time than at second.

On the farm there is no player who could step in and produce even acceptable numbers besides Coquillette. Jamey Carroll is a true second baseman who played at Triple-A Ottawa last season, but did not display enough power or speed to be a viable Rotisserie player. He would not even be considered a good ultra pick.

RECOMMENDATION REVIEW: Vidro is entering the prime of his career. He will be 26 for most of the season and has not had his career-year yet. With the expected improvement of Peter Bergeron and Milton Bradley getting on-base at the top of the Expos order in 2001, Vidro could be a more productive RBI man. It is not hard to fathom, Vidro being the best Rotisserie second baseman in 2001.

NEW YORK METS

Edgardo Alfonzo plays virtually every day, and plays well. At 27, the righthanded batter is in his prime. His power numbers fell off to 25 homers and 94 RBI's in 2000, but his .324 average was a career high. He's an above-average second baseman, so he'll continue to get playing time at a position where his Rotisserie value is maximized.

The second baseman for Triple-A Norfolk was career minor leaguer Mitch Simons. The righthanded batter produced an uninspiring .267-0-48 season, with 16 stolen bases in 29 attempts.

Twenty-three-year-old Ty Wigginton offers uncommon

power for a second baseman. His 2000 season at Double-A Binghamton (.285-20-77) was nearly identical to the previous year in high A ball, except that his strikeout/walk ratio took a significant turn for the worse.

RECOMMENDATION REVIEW: After Jeff Kent, Alfonzo is clearly the National League's best Rotisserie second baseman. You might consider Wigginton as a late Ultra pick.

PHILADELPHIA PHILLIES

The Phils entered the offseason with a gaping hole at the second base position, which they have desperately wanted Marlon Anderson to fill for three seasons now. He's 27 now, and is running out of time to develop solid fundamental skills. Though the Phils faced more pressing needs in the bullpen and in the leadoff spot in their batting order entering the 2001 season, they would love to upgrade here as well. The free agent (Luis Alicea?) and trade markets (Quilvio Veras?) offered some possibilities for the Phils to fill the leadoff and second base roles in one fell swoop, but it still appeared better than a 50/50 bet that Anderson would be the man in 2001.

Whenever the Phils are questioned about the slow development of Anderson, they are quick to point out that he's "still young" and "still developing." Hate to break it to you guys, but he's 27. He's older than Darin Erstad. Older than Jason Kendall. Two years older than Alex Rodriguez. Two years older than Vladimir Guerrero. Three years older than Andruw Jones. You get the point. Anderson, a lefthanded hitter, has always intrigued the Phils because of his above average gaps power for a middle infielder and well above average foot speed. He has conclusively proven able to harness those gifts at the Triple-A level, hitting .300 with solid doubles, triples and steals totals there. However, poor plate discipline and a maddening lack of all-around baseball instincts have hampered his development at the major league level. To make matters worse, he has shown absolutely no signs of progress to that end. On the bases, he seems to become timid in clear running situations, and then take chances at inopportune times.

In the field, his footwork remains a mess, and the Phils have thrown up their hands after numerous attempts to refine his technique. He has gotten better at routine plays, but often makes them look a lot harder than they are.

For six seasons now, the Phils have trotted Kevin Jordan,

31, out there as an all-purpose first, second and third base backup. That versatility in itself merits a mention and at least a shred of Rotisserie value, but the Phils must learn soon that they have absolutely no chance of making material progress while doling out 250-plus at bats to this guy on a seasonal basis. He has no speed (he hasn't stolen a base since 1996) and has never hit more than six homers or walked more than 24 times in a season. He's a scrappy tough out as a pinch-hitter, a guy who nibbles at lefties and righties alike, but the Phils are likely to shove him down on their depth chart as they search for more bench power. Despite Anderson's uncertain status as the second base starter, Jordan is not a wise investment at any price in 2001.

The Phils acquired 27-year-old minor league journeyman David Newhan from the A's last season. Like Jordan, he has a little pop to the gaps, and unlike Jordan, has playable speed. If the Phils find themselves a lefty bat short on the bench, Newhan could beat out Jordan for a slot. Don't waste Rotisserie bucks on him, however.

The Phils have high hopes for 2000 first round pick Chase Utley, 22, and expect him to rise through the ranks quickly and possibly start in the majors by 2003. The lefthanded hitter should hit .300 in any league, and could develop 25-homer power. His defensive tools are just adequate, however, and there's a chance that he might not have the quickness to play middle infield in the majors. The Phils need to aggressively promote him to Double-A by the end of 2001 to see what he's got under the hood. If he achieves there, he's for real and could soon make Marlon Anderson a memory.

RECOMMENDATION REVIEW: I'm not going to tell you to avoid Anderson at all costs — there are plenty of worse low-dollar middle infield risks out there, and it wouldn't be a shock to see Anderson hit 10 homers and steal 15 bases if he got a full shot. Don't consider him a high-upside "prospect", however — I never have, and never will. His inability to play other infield positions makes a future as a utilityman unlikely. Don't be surprised if Marlon Anderson fades out of the big league picture in the next two to three seasons.

PITTSBURGH PIRATES

Warren Morris suffered through a disappointing sophomore campaign, causing his Rotisserie owners' tidy little bargain from 1999 to virtually disappear in 2000. Morris' batting average fell thirty points and his power dried up.

However, the news wasn't all bad as Morris ran more often (although less successfully) and still maintained a good on-base percentage despite the mediocre batting average. The underlying message is that he has a very good chance to return to his previous form from 1999.

Using the most simplistic philosophy of buy low/sell high, this would make Morris a "buy" for 2001, presuming he is available in the draft. More likely, he is still tied to a contract by owners who got him cheaply in 1999. However, the sophomore slump by Morris in 2000 leads to an interesting phenomenon which will make Morris available in trade in many leagues this year. Owners who had him at a low salary in 1999 and protected him in 2000 are now faced with the third-year decision of letting him play out his option or extending his contract. Of course, after the down season in 2000 they are less likely to extend his contract. But, teams that are not contenders in 2001 have little to gain by letting him play out his option. This opens a window of opportunity for you if you are a contender in 2001.

If you have a contending team and need to shed a little salary, and Morris is owned by a team that has little chance to contend in 2001, you can make a small gain by offering to trade for Morris. Give them a player who is not in his option year, someone with more potential than proven production, perhaps, at a minimum salary. Let the non-contender carry a prospect while you have Morris play out his option for you. The non-contender gains by getting something useful for 2002 in exchange for something that was relatively worthless in 2001. You get a player who is likely to be at a low salary but who will earn more than that for one final year to help your pennant drive. This tactical ploy can be applied to just about any third-year player who 1) was relatively unknown prior to his rookie season and, therefore, purchased at or near the minimum salary, 2) had a sophomore slump, and 3) is currently owned by a non-contender. Look around your league and you are sure to see at least one player like that. Morris will be that player in many leagues.

When Morris didn't start at second base last year, the Bucs used light-hitting utility infielder types like Mike Benjamin, Enrique Wilson, or Abraham Nunez. Of this group, Wilson has slightly more upside potential, but still not enough to have any Draft Day value.

The Triple-A Nashville group wasn't much better; second base was staffed by fringe major leaguers John Wehner and Eddie Zosky with occasional appearances by third baseman Jason Wood or utility infielder Abrioris

Cleto. None of these players are prospects or have Rotisserie value.

Double-A Altoona used Rob Makowiak, a mediocre prospect who has a little bit of everything on offense and defense both; but he'll probably make it to the majors as a utility infielder, and, therefore, provokes little Rotisserie interest. Rico Washington is a better prospect, but he is primarily a third baseman for now.

Farther down the farm system are Jon Prieto, who can't make contact well enough to use his good speed, and Justin Martin, another a speedy player who is primarily an outfielder. Josh Bonifay had a good season at Low-A Hickory, hitting for power and average, and stealing eleven bases, too. All of these players are a long way from the majors and none are exceptional prospects.

RECOMMENDATION REVIEW: Coming off of a down year as a sophomore, Morris is a bargain hunter's special, and a good bet to rebound; get him for a low price or use the trading tactic described above to get him for one final year. Of all the other potential second basemen within the Pirates organization, Washington provides the best upside, perhaps worthy of an Ultra spot, near the end of the list.

ST. LOUIS CARDINALS

Fernando Vina is a fine roto infielder because he provides a top of the order presence. He's a legitimate .300 hitter that puts the ball in play, gets on base and scores runs. He doesn't provide any power and for some reason hasn't stolen many bases recently, but he runs well and the ability is there. Having guys like Mark McGwire and Jim Edmonds hitting a couple of spots behind him doesn't hurt his roto value either. Vina is also a fine defensive player, which means he'll never be in danger of losing his status as an everyday player due to glove problems.

Placido Polanco turned into one of the best reserve infielders in baseball last year. He's adequate defensively at second, third and short and he became a better hitter during the 2000 season. He hit .316 over 323 at-bats, so the average was no fluke. It's hard to see where he'll get much regular playing time in the future, but he should get two or three starts per week split up amongst the three positions. Tony LaRussa likes him and did his best to find playing time for him last year.

The only minor league second baseman the Cardinals

have that's even close to being a major leaguer is Stubby Clapp, but he's viewed as a future utility man. He makes contact and gets on base, but lacks the raw natural ability of other players.

RECOMMENDATION REVIEW: Vina is a consistent veteran that will hit around .300 while stealing some bases and scoring plenty of runs. Don't go crazy on him, but don't worry if he winds up being your second baseman. Polanco will be worth having in deep leagues or if someone gets hurt on the infield, otherwise you'll only be getting a couple of games per week out of him and he doesn't provide any power or stolen base potential.

SAN DIEGO PADRES

Bret Boone was signed as a free agent by the Seattle Mariners during the winter.

There should no longer be any questions about Bret Boone's limitations as a ballplayer. He's an average fielder, at best, who hits for a mediocre average, has moderate power and strikes out in bunches. Despite not having real fence-busting power, Boone continues to swing for the fences almost all the time, rarely adjusting to count or situation. He managed to avoid his fifth straight 100 strikeout season only because he missed 35 games; he fanned "only" 97 times instead. In today's climate where power hitters also often hit well for average, Boone's .251 batting average in 2000 (close to his career .255 mark) and 97 strikeouts to go with just 19 homers is poor. His season averages the last five years are a .246 batting average, 16 homers, 69 RBI . . . and 103 whiffs. Even for a middle infielder, this is relatively unproductive.

Boone was a free agent over the winter after his 2000 season and there was only lukewarm interest from the Padres in bringing him back for another season. 2001 will bring a fourth team in as many seasons for Boone; maybe the major league community is figuring out that Boone is what he is and won't change — he certainly won't get any better. His increasing strikeout rate suggests he could get worse.

If second base is open in San Diego, look for Damian Jackson or Kevin Nicholson to get the job. The Padres made a winter deal to acquire shortstop Santiago Perez from the Brewers. If Perez starts at shortstop as expected, Jackson will have to move to the outfield or second base, likewise, Nicholson would have to shift someplace else.

Jackson made 80 starts at shortstop, but also played 36 games at second base and another 17 in the outfield as the Padres worked to get his bat in the lineup without compromising their middle infield defense. There is some question about Jackson's ability to handle a demanding infield job. However, they need his speed in their offensive scheme. Jackson will again play an important role in the San Diego lineup and should again be ready to steal 30 bases. Rotisserie owners should acquire Jackson solely for his speed, though, and ignore his other stats; they won't contribute much to Rotisserie totals.

Nicholson is a significantly weaker hitter than Jackson, and lacks Jackson's speed, too. Nicholson is a switch-hitter, and could eventually earn some platoon role. For now, though, Nicholson is a significantly weaker hitter than Jackson and should settle into a fifth infield role in 2001. He presents no Rotisserie value.

David Newhan, Ralph Milliard, Greg LaRocca and Nate Tebbs each made at least 20 appearances at second base for Triple-A Las Vegas. Newhan and Tebbs were traded to Philadelphia and St. Louis, respectively at midseason, and LaRocca is primarily a third baseman. Milliard was formerly a prospect with the Phillies but has had trouble taking the final step to the majors. He may get that chance at last after a good season for Vegas in which he hit .280 with 18 steals. Milliard is being groomed as a utility infielder now; being able to hit a bit and run well will only enhance his chances. He should see some playing time in the majors in 2001, although not enough to be worth any Draft Day money.

John Powers was Double-A Mobile's primary second sacker; he has a fine batting eye, but not much else that would mark him as a prospect. Powers will need to show more pop or hit for a better average if he is to attract Rotisserie interest. Jake Thrower also made some appearances at second base for Mobile, but he's a minor-league utility player at this point.

Clay Snellgrove showed some speed and contact hitting ability at High-A Rancho Cucamonga. Snellgrove should advance to Mobile in 2001 where his prospect status will truly be tested.

RECOMMENDATION REVIEW: Overrated Boone has value only if you can get him for less than $5. Jackson is the better bargain after what appears to be a failed season in 2000 (he was shuttled out of the shortstop job a couple of times); he could be undervalued in 2001 drafts, but make sure to buy him strictly for his speed. Nicholson can't hit enough to have value and the others are utility players at best; avoid them.

SAN FRANCISCO GIANTS

There is not much more you can say about Jeff Kent and his fabulous MVP season, other than he will no longer be a cheap pickup. He is arguably as valuable member of his team as his illustrious counterpart in left field, and at age 33, is still a prime player. Kent has driven in 100 or more runs for four consecutive seasons, an amazing feat for a middle infielder, and has managed over 500 at-bats over each of his four seasons in a San Francisco uniform, despite several difficult injuries.

Ramon E. Martinez is the Giants primary second base backup, with Juan Melo in the wings. Neither has any Rotisserie value going into the draft, but Martinez, who plays all over the infield, could have some value, mostly on your reserve list (and contingent on the health of his team).

San Francisco's minors are thin when it comes to second base prospects. They do have names like Edwards Guzman, Travis Young, and William Otero, but none project to be major league starters at this point, and merit no more than periodic tracking.

RECOMMENDATION REVIEW: Kent is an anchor at second, and is worthy of the high salary he will generate. And, don't forget that there is great depth at the second base/middle infielder spot. In other words, determine a fair value, relative to your league for Kent, but don't make it a mission to walk away from the draft with him, no matter what. A combo of Damion Easley and Randy Velarde could collectively cost half that of Kent (naturally in a mixed league) and potentially deliver as much as Kent at a high price and Jay Cannizaro at a bargain one.

TOP 2001 HOME RUN HITTERS

NAME	HR
Jeff Kent	28
Edgardo Alfonzo	25
Jay Bell	22
Jose Vidro	20
Julio Lugo	13
Craig Biggio	12
Warren Morris	10
Pokey Reese	10
Terry Shumpert	9
Todd Walker	9
Ron Belliard	8
Damian Jackson	7
Mark Grudzielanek	7

TOP 2001 RBI PRODUCERS

NAME	RBI
Jeff Kent	118
Edgardo Alfonzo	97
Jose Vidro	87
Jay Bell	74
Ron Belliard	55
Warren Morris	54
Julio Lugo	54
Craig Biggio	52
Todd Walker	52
Mark Grudzielanek	49
Pokey Reese	46
Eric Young	45
Rafael Furcal	44
Damian Jackson	42
Bill Spiers	42
Placido Polanco	40

TOP 2001 RUN SCORERS

NAME	RUNS
Edgardo Alfonzo	112
Jeff Kent	104
Rafael Furcal	104
Julio Lugo	99
Luis Castillo	99
Jose Vidro	93
Jay Bell	91
Craig Biggio	89
Eric Young	89
Mark Grudzielanek	88
Fernando Vina	78
Ron Belliard	75
Pokey Reese	74
Damian Jackson	70
Quilvio Veras	70
Warren Morris	67
Todd Walker	59

TOP 2001 BASESTEALERS

NAME	SB
Luis Castillo	60
Eric Young	52
Rafael Furcal	48
Damian Jackson	33
Pokey Reese	30
Julio Lugo	27
Quilvio Veras	26
Miguel Cairo	25
Craig Biggio	21
Todd Walker	14
Fernando Vina	12
Jeff Kent	12
Mark Grudzielanek	11

TOP 2001 BATTING AVERAGES

NAME	AVG
Luis Castillo	.320
Edgardo Alfonzo	.313
Rafael Furcal	.305
Jose Vidro	.303
Jeff Kent	.297
Todd Walker	.297
Jack Wilson	.294
Fernando Vina	.293
Julio Lugo	.293
Eric Young	.292
Placido Polanco	.291
Mark Grudzielanek	.287
Quilvio Veras	.282
Warren Morris	.278
Terry Shumpert	.278
Bill Spiers	.277
Santiago Perez	.276
Craig Biggio	.276
Craig Counsell	.275

STRATEGIES FOR THIRD BASEMEN
Filling Your Shopping Cart

by John Benson

Third base, like outfield, offers something for everyone. In both leagues there are proven high value players, middle-of-the-road guys, promising youngsters and veteran hangers-on. There is no big drop-off, nothing to guard against, no way to box yourself in to a bad position. Third base is the position where you can find a way to address whatever contingencies arise in your auction. For these reasons you will not want to buy a third baseman too early (unless your problem is too much money).

In both leagues there is a nice, gentle slope from the top guys down to the last ones who will be drafted. There isn't any particular strategy that will fail, and none that is necessary. My basic method in most leagues would be to go for one of the best third basemen, because the other bidders won't have such a sense of urgency when so many other players, almost as good, are always available. This method would mean bringing up the third baseman you want as soon as prices begin to match fair value. If that point is reached before these guys are gone, buy them at full value without fear: Chipper Jones, Jeff Cirillo and Adrian Beltre in the National League; or in the American League, Troy Glaus is the top guy, followed by Tony Batista and Eric Chavez.

Given the many choices and the absence of risk, third base is a position where the focus can be type of player rather than class of value. My favorite method in general (except for pitchers) is to load up on young players with room for improvement, and third base offers plenty of these. Glaus is just age 24 and is already the best in his league at his position, so getting him accomplishes two purposes: locking in a higher value than any of your competitors can have at the same position, and some upward potential, which is rare combination. Chavez is similar in these virtues; his second half stats, times two, yield .278-28-90-4. Although my forecast is shade under that line, he can move upward at age 23, even move upward dramatically (nice bell curve here). The Yankees have a pair of 23-year-olds in Alfonso Soriano and D'Angelo Jimenez, both of whom may be squeezed for playing time in New York and yet both of whom will become prime trade bait as the Yanks pursue another championship.

In the National League a focus on rising stars would put your attention on Beltre, Scott Rolen and Fernando Tatis. Rolen and Tatis are classic "age 26 and under, with experience" cases (see that essay). Beltre's second half, times two, is .316-26-98-12. If I wanted to produce bold forecasts for marketing purposes to help myself (instead of what is most helpful for you on draft day) I would be issuing numbers like .330-30-110-15 because these are quite attainable (another nice bell curve).

If the youth with potential theme isn't what you want from your third baseman, there are possibilities to go for a specific category that you seem to need at that moment in the draft. Want some unusual speed at the hot corner? Aaron Boone then belongs on your list right up there with Jones, Beltran, Glaus and Tatis. Raw power? Try Dean Palmer, Phil Nevin, Robin Ventura, Mike Lowell or Matt Williams. You get the idea.

Another way to have fun with third base is just to bid aggressively against your arch rivals, hopefully depleting their cash on hand. This method works much better when you have a little more money than they do, putting them into a deeper hole. Carried to its extreme, this method might get you as many as three third basemen, which isn't the worst outcome as long as you are getting good talent (just be sure you have a trading friend with a spare first baseman). The key feature of bidding aggressively against arch rivals is that it can make them nervous, which can affect their other decisions.

If you want the calmest and easiest route, just make third base your "no effort" position, perhaps the last to be filled with whatever is available. It won't be too bad no matter how long you wait. Effort saved on one slot will free up brain cells for use on other problems like sorting through the leftovers in the pitching department. Thus a third base opening on draft day 2001 can be your most flexible commodity.

AMERICAN LEAGUE THIRD BASEMEN

ANAHEIM ANGELS

In a relatively short time, Troy Glaus has broken through to the elite ranks of American League third basemen and should head any draft list at that position. He is the best power hitting third sacker in the league, and has made major strides in his batting average and on base percentage. At the age of 24, he still has room for improvement. Mike Scioscia batted him sixth most of last season, although Glaus performed well in a few games as the number two hitter as well. Check spring training lineups to see where Glaus is being used. Glaus should be good for 100 runs, 100 walks and 100 RBI, while hitting in the high .200s and competing for the home run title. Add in double-digit steals and Glaus will clearly be one of the most expensive American League third basemen in many years. He should be worth it.

Subtract a few RBI but add some runs if Glaus winds up hitting second. One more hidden advantage of owning Glaus; last year, he played more than five games at shortstop, which allowed him to be moved to that position under the rules used by many leagues. There's no guarantee of that happening this year, but it's possible.

Scott Spiezio is the primary backup for Glaus. He is discussed in the first base section, since he will only qualify there on Draft Day in most leagues.

RECOMMENDATION REVIEW: If you can get Glaus for anything less than what he earned last season, go for it.

BALTIMORE ORIOLES

One of the questions marks following last season was Cal Ripken's return for another season. He spent a long time on the disabled list with a back problem last year, playing in only 83 games. He came back strongly after his injury, giving encouragement to his signing for another season.

Now 40 years old, possible injuries are always possible as is a major loss in bat speed and hitting. He's experienced enough to cheat a little on the harder throwing pitchers, starting his wing a little earlier to hit the good fastballs. But it will soon reach the point when experience won't help any longer. With the arrival of hitting coach Terry Crowley several years ago, Ripken stopped changing his batting stance weekly and followed Crowley's recommendation. The result was a resurgence of his bat speed and plate aggressiveness. Ripken's age and injuries make him a risk in Rotisserie baseball.

Mike Kinkade was acquired in a trade with the Mets in the Orioles late-season youth movement. He's 27, and although he's always hit well in the minors, he hasn't gotten many opportunities to play in the minors. It's not really his fault as there were always established major leaguers ahead of him. His defense is a little weak at third, but he can also play first and catch. He has good gap power, and hits for a good average. His defense may not earn him a permanent position, but his bat will keep him in the lineup. Kinkade is a good sleeper, especially if he doesn't appear to have a starting position at the season's onset.

Jeff Conine played 44 games at third last year, doing a good job at bat and in the field. He and the Orioles have been a good match, and his playing first, third, outfield and DH keeps him fresh. He's hit .284 and .291 for the Orioles in the past two years, getting over 400 at-bats in each year, despite not having a permanent position. The Orioles management likes Conine, and he should have another solid year in 2001.

Ivanon Coffie hit well in Double-A last year, but he struggled in short stints in Triple-A and with the Orioles. Ryan Minor was considered as Ripken's heir, but he has poor plate discipline with a weakness for high and outside breaking balls. He's not in the Orioles long range plans.

RECOMMENDATION REVIEW: Cal Ripken's age and possible injuries make him a risky player. Conine will be more valuable than Ripken, and he also provides some roster flexibility because he qualifies at more than one position. Kinkade is a good sleeper.

BOSTON RED SOX

One of the reasons Boston didn't play in the 2000 postseason was that Manny Alexander played more games as its third baseman. The 30-year-old righthanded batter finished at just .211-4-19, and even played below-average defense. A free agent during the offseason, he's best suited to be a utility player.

And one reason Alexander played so much was because John Valentin went out in June after suffering a ruptured tendon in his left knee. He played just 10 games, and batted .257-2-2. He's 34, and his career may be in jeopardy.

Another reason for Alexander's playing time was that Wilton Veras, after a promising major league debut in 1999, was a major disappointment last year. He batted .244-0-14 in 49 games, but a bigger factor in sending him back to the minors was that he committed 13 errors. The 23-year-old righthanded batter didn't do any better at Triple-A Pawtucket (.211-3-25)

The Red Sox ended up reacquiring Lou Merloni from Japan's Yokohama BayStars. He provided a spark by batting .320-0-18 in 40 games. But at 29, the righthanded batter is no more than a stopgap.

A trade with the Reds brought a more viable insurance policy in case Valentin can't play much this season. Chris Stynes, a 28-year-old righthanded batter, received mucho playing time at third base with the Reds after Aaron

Boone was injured, and finished the season at .334-12-40 in more than 400 plate appearances. Once a high-percentage basestealing threat, Stynes stole just five times in seven attempts in 2000. His power numbers should increase at Fenway Park. If he doesn't play regularly at third base, he also can fill in at second base and in the outfield. The Sox are likely to find a place for him whenever they face lefthanded starters. See more on Stynes in the Reds third base section.

Tony DeRosso, a 25-year-old righthanded batter, had a big year (.281-20-85) at Double-A Trenton.

RECOMMENDATION REVIEW: Stynes provides a viable option at this position, and would have greater Rotisserie value in leagues where he can qualify at second base. Alexander isn't even a good Rotisserie shortstop, let alone a third baseman. Even if Valentin receives a clean bill of health in spring training, his physical condition makes him a gamble. Veras has to go back to Triple-A and prove himself.

CHICAGO WHITE SOX

Herbert Perry emerged during the 2000 season as a consistent threat at the plate and won over Jerry Manual with his glove work. He was picked up early in the season and took a while before forcing his way into the lineup, but he proved to be a valuable player. He hit .308 with 12 home runs in 109 games with the Sox. Perry isn't viewed as the team's long term answer at the hot corner, however, and might be relegated to a bench role in the near future. He doesn't have much power and he's 31 years-old; he's not likely to get better than he already is.

Joe Crede is one of the very best third base prospects in baseball and was expected to become a part of the major league picture in Chicago sometime this season. Crede is a strong offensive player with the ability to hit for both average and power. He hit .306 with 21 home runs and 94 RBI last year at Double-A and he could earn the starting job for the Sox in spring training. If he struggles during the spring, however, he'll probably go to Triple-A for a little more seasoning. Crede is also an above-average defender at the hot corner, which never hurts.

The only other player that could see time at third base is Greg Norton, but because of his defensive shortcomings and lack of offensive punch he's really only a possibility in case of emergency.

RECOMMENDATION REVIEW: Perry is worth a shot early in the season, but beware of Crede's progress. Perry is a short-term answer and will lose the job as soon as Crede demonstrates he can play everyday. Crede is a worthy pickup in all leagues that have minor league or reserve rosters and he might be worth drafting in major league only roto leagues if he plays well in spring training.

CLEVELAND INDIANS

Travis Fryman had a great season last year, playing in 155 games, reaching career-highs in average with .321, RBI with 106, and slugging percentage with .516. He hit 22 home runs, missing a career high since he hit 28 in 1998. He also had a great year defensively, and won the Gold Glove Award. To avoid injury, Indians manager Charlie Manuel will occasionally rest Fryman in games played on artificial turf. Fryman is 32, and another solid year can be expected in 2001. He's not a big flashy slugger, so he may be underbid in some Rotisserie leagues.

Russell Branyan is the backup at third. He's been earmarked for right field and DH, and he's covered in the outfield section. Veteran Bill Selby could get some playing time in case of injury, and Mike Edwards is developing in the minors. Edwards is 23, and has a solid minor league record, but he's a few years away.

RECOMMENDATION REVIEW: Fryman is a solid value at third base. He should have another good year in 2001, putting up similar numbers as last year. Keep an eye on Branyan, he can have a breakthrough year if he gets the playing time. Branyan would have more value at third base than in the outfield, if he qualifies for that position in your league. Branyan is a batting average killer.

DETROIT TIGERS

Dean Palmer is a premier power hitter at the hot corner despite the fact that he doesn't hit for much average. His career average per 162 games played is 34 home runs and 102 RBI, which is hard to come by at the hot corner. Suffice to say that if he plays an entire season he'll be one of the premier power players at his position. His defense isn't great and the shoulder problems he had during the second half of the 2000 season could become a problem down the line, but he's still a third baseman for the moment. He may not be one of the elite players at his position, but he's in the next level down and will be a better value in many rotisserie leagues because you won't have to draft him really high or spend a lot of money on him.

The Tigers have two prospects at third base, but neither of them is anywhere near being a major league player. Matt Boone, son of Bob and brother of Bret and Aaron, was at High-A last year and he didn't show much with the bat. He struck out a lot and only hit six home runs. Neil Jenkins was at Low-A last year and he's a strikeout machine, but he has big-time power potential. He's very young and is a minimum of two years away from being a major league player.

RECOMMENDATION REVIEW: You know what you're getting with Palmer; roughly 30 homers and 100 RBI to go along with 140-150 whiffs and a mediocre batting average. Aside from Palmer, the Tigers don't have a major league caliber third baseman anywhere in their system. Jose Macias will be their utility infielder and should backup at third base, though he won't help a rotisserie team at all. If Palmer struggles with his shoulder again they'll probably have to trade for someone to play the hot corner.

KANSAS CITY ROYALS

Joker Joe Randa's offense doesn't stand up to the other American League third baseman ... or does it? No, he's not a big power threat, like Troy Glaus, but he still drove in 106 runs last year, and an average of 95 each of the last two seasons. He doesn't challenge for a batting title, but he has hit over .300 in four of the last five seasons. Throw in a few stolen bases, the fact that he plays virtually every day, and that he is still improving at the age of 31 and you've got one pretty good little offensive threat.

Randa is a streaky hitter who generally starts slow and goes on a lengthy offensive streak in June and July. The trend is consistent enough that it has become good strategy to trade for Randa about Memorial Day. While he can't be counted on for 100 RBI each season, 80 is a safe bet to go along with his .300-plus batting average. Randa represents an opportunity for Rotisserie owners to get a little bit of power and fine batting average at a position usually not known for good batting averages; it's a chance to zig when your Rotisserie opponents zag. If you already have sufficient power at other positions, use Randa to give yourself a batting average advantage your opponents can't get.

When Randa isn't in the lineup, the Royals have turned to Rotisserie zeros like Jeff Reboulet and Ray Holbert.

Wilson Delgado (discussed in the "Second Basemen" section) can also fill in at the hot corner. Only Delgado has value and only as a replacement player in case of injury.

Joe Dillon is an up-and-comer who split the season between Omaha and Double-A Wichita; Dillon can hit for average with some power. Among other Royals' third sackers, only Henry Calderon, at High-A Wilmington, showed potential, batting .263 with 45 RBI and 14 stolen bases.

RECOMMENDATION REVIEW: Don't overlook Randa as a source of everything except power. His lack of power will bring his price down; take advantage before he's the last decent third baseman remaining in the draft pool. Only Delgado has value among the remaining Royals' players, and only as a mid season injury replacement, not a draft day selection. The other prospects have a lot to prove before being worth an Ultra selection.

MINNESOTA TWINS

Corey Koskie is 27 years old. He admits that he is a late bloomer, considering that he didn't pursue baseball full time until he was in his teens. But his hard work should pay off this season as he proves that he is a prototypical third baseman and a productive roto player.

Koskie has had to work harder than others just to be average. He's taken extra ground balls at third and has worked hard to keep his swing short. He batted .310 in 1999 in a limited role and hit .300 last season, his first as the regular at third base.

Koskie spent a chunk of last season hitting the ball to all fields in expense of power. His average hovered around .300 all season, but he did not show the power teams like to see from a third baseman. Koskie has vowed to change this in 2001. He has a good batting eye, and will work on getting ahead in the count and being more aggressive when he has an advantage.

Koskie has a very firm build and has the strength to hit 30-plus homers in the majors. But he's preferred to work on serving the ball to the opposite field. Sabermetrics mavens will notice that his slugging plus on base percentage ranks him favorably among players in his league. He's expected to hit for more power in 2001, which will make him a decent mid to late-round pickup.

The Twins have resisted interest in Koskie dating back to

a year ago, believing that he will deliver the goods. He's expected to provide such a return in 2001. Koskie will play every day, expect for occasional off-days and stints as the designated hitter. There have been whispers about him being moved to first base, but Koskie's fielding percentage at third base was fourth best in the league, and the Twins are expected to leave him there.

There are a few players who will fill in for Koskie when he needs a rest or is injured. Ron Coomer is an adequate offensive player, but is not the answer at third. Coomer is best suited to play first base, designated hitter or even come off the bench as a pinch hitter.

Denny Hocking, plays almost everywhere on the field, but is not an offensive player. Jay Canizaro has played third, too, but there are concerns about his defense. Jason Maxwell has played third too, but provides little offense.

Casey Blake, who hit for average but little power at Triple-A, could be given a look or two during the season, but is not considered a top prospect.

RECOMMENDATION REVIEW: It will be up to Koskie to provide offense from that position. Indications are that he will come through with a breakout season. Now is a good time to pick up Koskie, as he is still relatively unknown.

NEW YORK YANKEES

In 2000, Scott Brosius continued the slide from his career peak as the 1998 World Series MVP. He still can play in the field, but the 34-year-old righthanded batter finished just .230-16-64. Especially alarming was his .210 average after the All-Star break.

Alfonso Soriano has had difficulty finding a position, but played more at third base than anywhere else with the 2000 Yankees. He committed seven errors in 20 games in the field, and didn't hit enough (.180-2-3) to stay in the majors. At Triple-A Columbus, the 23-year-old righthanded batter finished at .290-12-66.

Former prospect Kevin Orie, 28, began the season with the Triple-A Omaha Royals (.280-5-23), then finished it with New York's Triple-A farm at Columbus (.289-4-19). He's a righthanded batter.

Scott Seabol emerged as the Yankees' best third base prospect by making the All-Star team in the Double-A

Eastern League, Norwich. He batted .296-20-78, but the righthanded hitter is already 25. He's a marginal prospect.

RECOMMENDATION REVIEW: Brosius' glove won't help a Rotisserie roster. Soriano could be a steal in a leagues where most owners believe he's a failed prospect, or where he can qualify as a middle infielder.

OAKLAND ATHLETICS

Eric Chavez came out of the blocks hot last April, then stalled in May. Just when it looked like Manager Art Howe was going to go back to a platoon between Chavez and Olmedo Saenz, Saenz was injured and Chavez was forced to work through his problems. That was probably a good thing, as the young third sacker posted new, albeit temporary, career highs. Chavez did hit for a little higher average (.283 to .272) over the second half, although his on-base numbers dropped (.361 to .348) over the same period. His power totals were consistent, so there is no strong second half hiding in his totals to merit big spending. Rather, Chavez is still quite young (he'll still be just 23 Opening Day), and the 26 homers and 82 RBI he banged are the beginnings of what will be steadily improving numbers over the next several years. That means if you can grab him for $15 or less on a 3-year deal, you will have a steal on your hands.

In most leagues, however, especially AL only, he will cost more, but in general prove to be worth it. As with the other Athletics, stolen bases factor little in his game.

Olmedo Saenz assembled his best season in 2000, despite injuries to most of his body. Saenz can flat out hit, and he will spell Chavez at third, Giambi at first, and log a fair amount of DH time. As long as he can stay healthy, Saenz was expected to get a shot at 400 at-bats in 2001, and should respond with numbers in the .280-17-70 range. He too could be a bargain, as Saenz' role is still undefined, hence he is likely to be a bargain corner infielder, available at the end draft for a marginal salary. Keep an eye on him.

1999 Texas League Triple Crown winner Adam Piatt will also be available to play third; a spot he handled in the minors. But, for now the outfield, in particular right field, will be his domain. Piatt is discussed with the outfielders.

Josh Hochsgesang is a 23-year old who had respectable totals at Modesto (.246-20-80, with 20 steals) but he should do well at that level. Give him a 2001 at Midland to see if he has a major league future.

RECOMMENDATION REVIEW: Chavez is a good young player who should improve over the next few seasons. Expect him to put up better numbers from 2000, making him a solid value 2001. He is even more valuable in keeper leagues, due to his age and potential. Saenz is a viable backup to any Rotisserie team, especially if Chavez goes down and he is eligible for third base.

SEATTLE MARINERS

Carlos Guillen was once a prized shortstop prospect, and he was a second baseman after that, but knee injuries have caused the Mariners to move him to third base. He's got good hands and a very strong arm which makes him a nice fit at third. The problem is that Guillen hasn't shown much home run power yet. He's a good contact hitter that should be able to hit .280 or better with consistent playing time and he should display double-digit home run power in the future, but he's not the classic big-banger at the hot corner. Injuries have really taken the juice out of his last two seasons, so proceed with caution. If healthy, Guillen could come on strong in 2001.

Charles Gipson is an athletic player that can play the outfield in addition to third base. He's never played much at the major league level and is probably going to be a utilityman in the future. His speed is an asset, but he hasn't had many opportunities to show it.

RECOMMENDATION REVIEW: Guillen is worth a shot as a late round pick or cheap signing, but don't count on him for too much.

TAMPA BAY DEVIL RAYS

The 2000 season is one Vinny Castilla would love to forget. After establishing himself as a perennial 150-plus games a year guy, the bottom fell out for the veteran third baseman. Castilla was injured most of the season, playing in just 85 games. When he was in the lineup, Castilla's production was far less than what the Devil Rays expected when they traded for him prior to the 2000 season. Castilla hit .221 with six home runs and 42 RBI.

Was Castilla's season an aberration or was it how he will play now that he's away from Coors Field? Could the veteran be over the hill? Chances are the 2000 season was not a true indication of where Castilla is ability wise, which is why he spent the offseason with a personal trainer for the first time in his career.

If Castilla is on the team, he will be the starting third baseman, simple as that. However, given his salary as well as the emergence of youngster Aubrey Huff, there was a reasonable chance Castilla could be traded before the season begins. In which case, the job will fall to Huff.

Huff made great strides in 2000, hitting .316 with 20 home runs and 76 RBI in 108 games at Triple-A Durham before getting promoted to the majors in early August. Once in the majors, Huff showed some lapses in the field, but they are lapses that can easily be overlooked given the power he showed. Huff hit .287 with four home runs and 14 RBI in 122 at-bats and didn't look overmatched against major-league pitchers.

RECOMMENDATION REVIEW: Castilla is a good bet to bounce back from his abysmal 2000 numbers. Just look at the injuries Castilla suffered from and his numbers make sense. He missed the beginning of the season with a pulled oblique muscle; later it was a sore back - both are injuries that take their toll on bat speed. Meanwhile, Huff could be a good buy, but only if Castilla is gone. The kid is ready to hit in the majors even if his glove has not yet caught up to his offense.

TEXAS RANGERS

Ken Caminiti was signed as at least a platoon, and more likely a full-time third baseman, if he can stay healthy. Caminiti's main problem has been staying in the lineup, but when he's been physically OK, he has shown that he is still capable of putting up good numbers. The Rangers were satisfied that his substance abuse problems were behind him, and relocation to Arlington could give Caminiti a bit of a new lease on life. Still, given his recent seasons, expecting more than about 400 at bats is probably a stretch.

Mike Lamb's rookie season was a bit of a surprise on several levels. First that he was in the big leagues at all; second, that he held his own at the plate after a two-level jump; and third, that he struggled so badly on defense at the major league level. It's the latter problem that will probably send Lamb back to the minors to start the season. Expect Lamb to see some time with the big club this year, especially if (or when) Caminiti winds up on the DL. In the minors, Lamb was a high-average hitter with line-drive power. While Lamb kept his average up in his rookie season and generally made contact, he didn't hit for power. He should gradually develop more power over the next few years.

Frank Catalanotto and Scott Sheldon are infield backups who could see some playing time at third base. Catalanotto is profiled with the second basemen and Sheldon is in the shortstop section.

Tom Evans must be tired of that black cloud that keeps following him. After fighting his way back to the majors and winning the Rangers' starting third base job, Evans tore his labrum last May and missed the rest of the season. At season's end, Evans became a free agent and his immediate destination was uncertain. With a major league team, Evans could provide a decent bat off the bench or veteran insurance at Triple-A. Either way, he's a long shot to get much big league playing time.

The Rangers' organization is relatively well stocked at the hot corner. Jason Grabowski should see action at Triple-A at some point in the 2001 season. The lefty power hitter has good strike zone judgment despite a big swing and has some chance of seeing major league duty by the 2002 season. An even brighter, but longer-term prospect is Hank Blalock, a Class A third sacker who has put up good numbers since being drafted in 1999. He won't arrive in the majors until late 2003 at the earliest, but could eventually be a solid everyday big leaguer.

RECOMMENDATION REVIEW: Caminiti could be a nice purchase at a low salary, but don't pay for a full season's worth of stats from him. Lamb has some upside for the future, but won't get anywhere near as many at-bats this season as he did last year. If Lamb is on the roster but doesn't start on Opening Day, he becomes a very good buy-and-hold at a low salary. If he's in the minors, he makes a good Ultra pick. Evans could produce in the right situation, but is likely no better than a reserve round pick. Grabowski is a marginal Ultra pick. For teams that can hold on to minor league players indefinitely, a flyer on Blalock could eventually pay off.

TORONTO BLUE JAYS

Tony Batista made a smooth transition from shortstop to third base and in fact, looked more comfortable as a third baseman. With a good glove and sure hands for a player new to third, Batista filled the hole vacated by the departed Tony Fernandez. Beyond all expectations, Batista picked up on his excellent 1999 campaign and actually tied Carlos Delgado for the team-lead in home runs with 41. With his incredible open stance, the ball flies off his bat. Though Troy Glaus got most of the attention at third base, Batista actually led American League third basemen in

RBI with 114.

Batista has hit 72 home runs in the past two years and it's hard to believe that the Diamondbacks traded him for Dan Plesac. He has become one of the better power hitters in the American League and though it's uncertain where he'll bat in the 2001 lineup, he seems to be a good fit as a number five hitter.

Because Batista played almost every game at third last year, the Jays didn't get a look at any of their minor league options. Though there are several candidates for future work at third base, most of the strong ones are in the lower minors.

The senior member of the farm system is likely Luis Lopez, not to be confused by the other veteran major leaguer of the same name. Lopez year after year shows that he can hit for average and he made a relatively comfortable move from first base to third base for Triple-A Syracuse last year. Lopez hit .328 for Triple-A Syracuse, the fourth straight year he has enjoyed a .300-plus average in the minors. Unfortunately, he's already in his late twenties and his opportunities will get thinner as time advances. He does reserve an outside shot of getting called to the major leagues but for now, he's strictly a Triple-A batting title contender.

More likely to get a major league look is Joe Lawrence, who rose as high as Double-A last year. Lawrence is a walk-taking machine and seems better suited for third base than shortstop, his original position. He looks to be about two years from making his debut but in the right situation or in the event of an injury, Lawrence could make his first big league appearance this year. If he did get the early call, he's not ready to hit for average just yet but should develop into a decent power hitter as his progress continues.

Chris Woodward (detailed in the shortstop section) is a possibility at third in an emergency.

RECOMMENDATION REVIEW: The Jays don't have any major league-ready third base prospects other than Batista. So even a Blue Jays' team that moved Batista back to shortstop would not be able to solidify the position from within. Look for Batista to put up another year of big numbers with 2000 serving as a good guide as to what he is capable of doing this year. Batista can help a Rotisserie team win the home run and RBI category as there is a wide gap between Glaus, Batista and the rest of the American League third basemen.

TOP 2001 HOME RUN HITTERS

NAME	HR
Tony Batista	39
Troy Glaus	39
Dean Palmer	32
Eric Chavez	27
Travis Fryman	21
Shane Andrews	16
Scott Brosius	16
Cal Ripken	16
Carlos Guillen	15
Joe Randa	15
David Bell	14
Vinny Castilla	14
Ken Caminiti	12
Jeff Conine	12
Corey Koskie	12
Willie Greene	11
Aubrey Huff	11
Chris Stynes	10

TOP 2001 RBI PRODUCERS

NAME	RBI
Tony Batista	112
Dean Palmer	103
Travis Fryman	97
Joe Randa	94
Troy Glaus	93
Eric Chavez	90
Carlos Guillen	79
Corey Koskie	75
Scott Brosius	68
David Bell	57
Cal Ripken	57
Vinny Castilla	53
Jeff Conine	51
Herbert Perry	49
Charlie Hayes	48
Mike Lamb	48
Shane Andrews	46
Aubrey Huff	46
Ken Caminiti	40

TOP 2001 RUN SCORERS

NAME	RUNS
Troy Glaus	105
Tony Batista	93
Eric Chavez	91
Joe Randa	86
Travis Fryman	85
Carlos Guillen	84
Dean Palmer	80
Corey Koskie	78
David Bell	67
Chris Stynes	64
Scott Brosius	60
Mike Lamb	57
Herbert Perry	53
Jeff Conine	48
Cal Ripken	48
Aubrey Huff	45

TOP 2001 BATTING AVERAGES

NAME	AVG
Corey Koskie	.299
Joe Randa	.295
Herbert Perry	.292
Eric Chavez	.288
Mike Lamb	.288
Chris Stynes	.288
Travis Fryman	.287
Aubrey Huff	.287
Lou Merloni	.286
Troy Glaus	.280
Carlos Guillen	.277
Dave Magadan	.277
D'Angelo Jimenez	.276
Jeff Conine	.269
Ken Caminiti	.268
Tony Batista	.267
Vinny Castilla	.267

TOP 2001 BASESTEALERS

NAME	SB
Troy Glaus	11
Alfonso Soriano	9
Chris Stynes	7
Russ Johnson	6
Joe Randa	6
Shane Halter	5
D'Angelo Jimenez	5
Corey Koskie	5
Mark Lewis	5
Tony Batista	4
Scott Brosius	4
Dean Palmer	4
David Bell	3
Ken Caminiti	3
Eric Chavez	3
Jeff Conine	3
Carlos Guillen	3

NATIONAL LEAGUE THIRD BASEMEN

ARIZONA DIAMONDBACKS

Matt Williams will be the Diamondbacks' third baseman if healthy, and probably even if he is not, as he demonstrated last season, when he tried to play through a right quadriceps injury and plantar fasciaitis in his left foot that slowed him appreciably.

Williams missed the first seven weeks of the regular season after suffering a fractured second metatarsal when he fouled a pitch off his right foot the final week of spring training, and appeared determined not to let a barking muscle or two sideline him again.

But it showed in his numbers. For the first time in 11 years, Williams did not reach 20 home runs, finishing with 12 in 96 games. Five of his homers came in the final 10 games of the season.

Williams was in such a rut last season that the D'backs moved him out of the No. 4 spot in the order in late August, but he was expected to return to his familiar cleanup spot this season.

He can carry an offense, as he showed with the D'backs in 1999. He was third in the NL MVP race that season, batting a career-high .303 while hitting 35 homers and driving in a career-high 142 runs, the third most by a third baseman in major league history.

Williams opted against offseason surgery on the plantar fascia, a tight band of muscles on the foot. The last day of the season, he said he also suffered from a form of degenerative arthritis that Rico Brogna has as well.

Williams, who has had the condition the last 10 years, said he first felt symptoms last season when it became difficult to grip a bat. He planned to combat the disorder with dietary changes and an offseason program designed to increase flexibility. He does not expect it to factor into the 2001 season.

Danny Klassen filled in admirably when Williams missed the first eight weeks of the season, but he does not bring the same bat. Craig Counsell and Hanley Frias also can play third, but none will see much duty if Williams returns to health.

RECOMMENDATION REVIEW: A very tough call. Williams is capable of monster seasons when he is at full strength. But he has played more than 135 games only twice in the last six years.

ATLANTA BRAVES

Many Braves fans will associate the 2000 season of Chipper Jones for the throwing error he made on the last day of the regular season which cost Atlanta home field advantage in its Division Series against the Cardinals. However it should be noted that Jones had another fantastic season.

Other than hitting nine fewer home runs, it was a virtual duplication of his MVP performance in 1999. And it should be noted that many sluggers (Sammy Sosa for one) hit fewer home runs last year than they did in '99. Jones is a professional hitter who has a great knowledge of the strike zone and a fabulous idea of how to hit, and those are the two main reasons why he is able to avoid prolonged slumps.

Over the past three seasons, Chipper has averaged 40 homers and 109 RBI while hitting about .315. Expect him to at least come close to those numbers again this season.

There was talk shortly after the season ended that the Braves wanted to move Chipper to left field. This move would only help to increase his offensive production since left field would be a much less demanding position defensively than third base. But that's not to say he cannot again be MVP playing in the infield.

If Jones does wind up in left field, the position which he played 20 games at in 1995, the benefactor will be Wes Helms, who hit .288 with 20 homers and 88 RBI last season in Triple-A. Helms, a 25-year-old, has slowly worked his way up through Atlanta's farm system. He has boosted his power numbers in the last couple of years as he finally got stronger, but he would be lucky to hit 20 in the majors as a rookie.

Troy Cameron is a 22-year-old switch hitter who has more raw power than Helms, but needs a lot more seasoning before he can be considered for a big league assignment. He struck out 131 times in 401 at-bats at Single-A Myrtle Beach last year, which offset his team-high 15 home runs.

RECOMMENDATION REVIEW: Jones will hit wherever he plays. If he is at third he will be one of the top players at that position in all of baseball. It would be the same if he were out in left.

CHICAGO CUBS

Third base was a total disaster for the Cubs last year. On paper, the platoon of Shane Andrews and Willie Greene looked to be a good one. Andrews always has been a better hitter against southpaw hurlers, while Greene can be devastating against righthanders. Unfortunately, neither player did much of anything at the plate.

Andrews was sidelined for much of the season with back problems and Greene faded badly in the second half of the season, squandering what might prove to be his last chance to be an everyday player in the major leagues.

Andrews was a decent player in Montreal and had his best season there in 1998, hitting 25 homers and driving in

69 runs. But severe back problems have limited his performance in the last two seasons, including forcing him to miss 96 games last year.

Even when he is healthy, Andrews does not hit for average, which makes it imperative that he hit for power. So far he has shown signs of being able to do that, but has not yet proven he can be a consistent long ball threat. He certainly wouldn't be the worst third baseman to have on your roster, but his history of back problems should make you wary. At least have a solid backup on your roster if you decide to go with Andrews.

Greene was once a highly prized prospect in Cincinnati's farm system and seemed destined for a long and productive career. But he never really got the opportunity he deserved with the Reds and has spent the past three years bouncing around from team to team. He has a lot of talent in his body, but he can't seem to lay off the breaking balls. He hit 26 homers in 1997 with the Reds, in his only full season as a starter. He also has an outstanding batting eye, but his inability to hit much above the Mendoza Line will relegate him to bench duty.

The Cubs traded for Bill Mueller shortly before Thanksgiving, but it is hard to see how Mueller will be much of an upgrade. He has virtually no power, especially for a corner infielder, and his batting average has declined every year except one, dipping to a career low .266 in 2000. He is no better offensively than Mark Grace, who held up Chicago's offense by playing a position normally reserved for a big bopper. Mueller will cost the Cubs in the same way.

RECOMMENDATION REVIEW: Mueller is near the bottom of major league third basemen. Like big league clubs, you are going to need more than 8-10 homers from your third baseman. Avoid Mueller, Andrews, and Greene at all costs.

CINCINNATI REDS

Aaron Boone was having the best season of his still short career last year when he blew out his knee right before the All-Star break. He was hitting for more power than he had before, but it still wasn't overly impressive, especially for a guy playing a corner infield position.

Before he got hurt, Boone's performance was virtually identical to that of right fielder Dante Bichette, which probably says more about Bichette than it does about

Boone. Aaron was hitting for some power, but not a lot, and his batting average stayed between .275 and .290. He is a decent player, however there are many more third baseman out there better than he is.

Boone's rehab went very well and he was expected to be at full strength for the start of the 2001 season.

Chris Stynes filled in for Boone in the second half of last season and did a fantastic job, especially for Chris Stynes. Becoming somewhat of a folk hero in Cincinnati, the diminutive Stynes performed beyond anybody's reasonable expectations. In over 450 at-bats combined between 1998 and 1999 Stynes hit less than .250 with eight homers and 11 doubles. But last year, in close to the same number of times to the plate last season, Stynes hit .334 with 12 homers, 24 doubles, a slugging percentage of almost .500 and scored 71 runs.

Stynes had a hell of a year, there is no doubt about that, but he is not that good. The Reds, partly afraid that his 2000 season would make him a big-money player through arbitration, traded him to Boston for prospects. Boston obviously felt that Stynes would help shore up its problems at third base, but there is no way he will be as good as he was last year. See more on Stynes in the Red Sox third base section.

Chris Sexton, Mike Bell and Juan Castro also appeared in a handful of games at third for the Reds last year, but none of them will see any real playing time there this season. Sexton and Bell will have to struggle just to make the big league roster and Castro will only play there as part of a double switch.

RECOMMENDATION REVIEW: Boone won't embarrass himself on the field, but he is really just holding onto the position until somebody better comes along. He will never be an All-Star, though having his father for a manager will guarantee him the starting job as long as he hits better than .220.

COLORADO ROCKIES

Jeff Cirillo gives the Rockies a reliable third baseman who, as the cognoscenti predicted, increased his numbers by the Coors Field factor in his first season in Colorado last year.

Cirillo is a perfect fit in Coors. (Aren't we all?) He is a line drive hitter with gap-plus power who uses the whole field.

Because the ball carries well in spacious Coors, alleys are larger and gaps are wider. More gaps. More places for line drives to land. Cirillo's .403 batting average at Coors was the best home average in the majors.

Manager Buddy Bell's decision to put Cirillo in the cleanup position proved another perfect fit. Cirillo, who put up solid if underappreciated numbers in Milwaukee, led NL third basemen in hits and batting average for the second consecutive year while setting a career season records with 115 RBI and 53 doubles. According to SABR, Cirillo became the first player in major league history to record at least 45 doubles in each league. He twice had 46 with Milwaukee.

Cirillo is not the prototype No. 4 hitter because he is not a home run hitter, even at home. But he has hit between 10 and 15 homers in each of the last five years. Cirillo does not have basestealing speed can steal a half-dozen bases a year. His career high was 10 with Milwaukee.

Durable, Cirillo has missed an average of only six games a year over the last five years. He is a solid defensive player who will play through a hitting slump because his glove will carry him.

Terry Shumpert can play third, although the Rockies do not have a reserve third baseman per se. Shumpert was one of three National Leaguers to start at every infield position last year. Andy Fox and Geoff Blum were the others.

RECOMMENDATION REVIEW: Cirillo had what at first glance appeared to be a career year last year. Or could it simply be the first season of the rest of his career? Cirillo is a steady, solid pro who seems capable of a string of 2000s. He will be in Colorado through at least 2005 after signing a contract extension after the All-Star Game that includes a team option for 2006.

FLORIDA MARLINS

The Marlins have one of the better young third basemen in baseball, Mike Lowell. He has the ability to improve his batting average in the future and is a legit run producer. He hit .270 with 22 home runs and 91 RBI last year, which was his first full season as a major leaguer. He only struck out 75 times, which is a great sign, and he's got the ability to hit 30 home runs this season if the players around him perform well. He's a good defensive third baseman, so don't expect a position change any time soon. In time he could turn into a Jeff Kent-like player.

Dave Berg is one of several utility players on the Marlins roster that can play third base. He's a good contact hitter with a little speed, but he's beyond the point of becoming an everyday player. His ability to play anywhere in the infield and still hit a little bit makes him a valuable role player, but nothing more.

Veterans Sean McNally and Mike Gulan split up duty at the hot corner for the Marlins' Triple-A Calgary team last year, but they're both too old to be considered prospects. McNally hit .262 with 12 home runs and 41 RBI in 374 at-bats and Gulan hit .317 with 17 home runs and 74 RBI in 426 at-bats. They're both "four-A" players -- too good for Triple-A but not good enough for the majors.

RECOMMENDATION REVIEW: Lowell will be a strong rotisserie player this year and you could do a lot worse at the hot corner - get him if you can. None of the other three figure to help in roto leagues.

HOUSTON ASTROS

The two-part Ken Caminiti era in Houston is over. Third base will be manned by a combination of Bill Spiers, 35, Chris Truby, 27 and possibly Morgan Ensberg, 25. None are likely to be full-time regulars.

Spiers has been one of the top utility players in the major leagues for the last four years. Over this period, his production has been remarkably consistent, averaging 355 at-bats, a .294 batting average, 4 home runs, 43 RBI and 9 stolen bases. More of the same is likely in 2001. He qualifies at second base and shortstop as well as third base and he also played a few games in left field and right field in 2000. He has periodic problems with his back, which prevents him from being a full-time player. He is also a reliable lefthanded pinch-hitter off the bench.

Truby made his major league debut in mid June when he was recalled from Triple-A New Orleans to replace the injured Caminiti. He was the nominal regular at third base for the rest of the season, playing in 78 games. He batted .260 with 11 home runs, 59 RBI and 2 stolen bases. However, his underlying stats give reason for some concern. His on-base average was only .295 and he had 56 strikeouts and only 10 walks. His future as a major league regular is by no means assured. He is strong defensively, which helps his case.

The third candidate, and a decided dark horse for 2001, is Morgan Ensberg. In his third minor league season, Ensberg was a vital part of Double-A Round Rock's success in winning the Texas League championship. He batted .300 with 28 home runs, 90 RBI and 9 stolen bases. He earned a late season promotion to Houston, appearing in four games. Ensberg was an outstanding college player at USC, ranking third in career home runs behind Mark McGwire and Geoff Jenkins. Truby has an edge over Ensberg defensively but Ensberg's bat may ultimately move him ahead. He will likely play at Triple-A in 2001.

RECOMMENDATION REVIEW: The Astros do not have a third baseman that will attract much interest in rotisserie drafts.

LOS ANGELES DODGERS

It got overlooked in the Dodgers' disappointing finish in 2000, but while nobody was looking Adrian Beltre blossomed. Confronted by his agent at the All-Star break, he responded with a more serious preparation routine that vaulted him into a huge second half and the kind of offensive production that could lead to regular appearances in the All-Star Game.

In the second half he hit for average and power. Batting .331 after the break, he had 12 of 20 homers, 47 of 85 RBI and a .538 slugging percentage. Not bad considering his age, whatever that is. We know it's young and we know his birth certificate was altered. But we also now know he can hit in the big leagues. A free swinger, he still makes good contact, avoids the strikeout and is an aggressive, if not daring, base runner. Defense is where he needs the most work. Although he improved from the previous year, he has so much confidence in his rifle arm that he sometimes makes poor choices on throws. But that won't keep him out of the lineup.

He did all of this in his second major league season, a time when his lack of Triple-A seasoning should have showed. He did it under relative cover, batting either sixth or seventh behind the heart of the order: Gary Sheffield, Shawn Green and Eric Karros. If he continues his progress, he'll force his way into that group. If he hits 20 home runs at age 21, no wonder the Dodgers truly believe he can be another Mike Schmidt with the ability to hit the ball out of any part of any park.

On the few occasions that Beltre rests, Dave Hansen is a very acceptable stand-in. The veteran hitter's best role is that of pinch-hitter extraordinaire, as last year's home run record indicates, but third base was his original position and he has enough arm to make an occasional appearance there.

As at most positions for the Dodgers, there are not many top prospects in the organization that can play third base. Luke Allen, who has the power, has had so much trouble with ground balls that he's likely to be sent to the outfield again in 2001. And Ricky Bell, Buddy's son, doesn't have dad's arm or power. Neither is likely to reach the big leagues this year.

RECOMMENDATION REVIEW: Beltre is improving and has almost limitless potential. He meant so much to the Dodgers that they gave him a free-agent type contract to avoid losing him even though he had less than two years major league service. He's got protection in the lineup and a maturity beyond his years, however many he has.

MILWAUKEE BREWERS

In addressing the organization's pressing needs for a solid catcher and a couple of power arms for the starting rotation, new GM Dean Taylor made the decision to trade the club's most marketable "commodity", popular third baseman Jeff Cirillo, along with lefthander Scott Karl. The trade netted catcher Henry Blanco, along with righthanders Jamey Wright and Jimmy Haynes. At the same time, the deal allowed the Brewers to dump some salary, as Cirillo was in line for a considerable raise and Karl was moving up the salary scale as well. To a certain extent then, this made some sense on a fiscal level.

What didn't make much sense was the decision to turn around and spend $10 million on the signing of career utility man Jose Hernandez to a three-year contract to play the hot corner for the Brew Crew. To this point, this move has not worked out. At this writing, Milwaukee enters the 2001 season with two major holes in its everyday lineup, center field and third base.

Hernandez was coming off a reasonably decent year in Atlanta in 1999, where Taylor was the assistant GM, although 19 home runs and 62 RBI are not the numbers you're looking for from a corner infielder in this era of high-octane offense. Josie had 23 homers in 1998 for the Cubs but the career .250 hitter has always struck out far too much, never been one to walk much, and isn't much of a threat to steal (27 stolen bases in a 9-year major

league career). Hernandez's most valuable attribute has always been his versatility and ability to play a number of positions reasonably well. In his best year, 1998, Hernandez appeared in at least two games at every position except pitcher and catcher, including 31 in center field!

Although it might be a luxury for a small market team like the Brewers to carry a $10 million utility man, that is probably the role Hernandez should resume in 2001, whether it be in the Brew Town or somewhere else.

Charlie Hayes saw considerable action at third for Milwaukee in 2000 but is nearing the end of the line and is not expected to be asked back. Tyler Houston also got a shot to claim the hot corner but is an uneven defensive performer and seemingly best suited to a bench/utility role himself at this point of his career. Houston is discussed under Milwaukee catchers and first basemen as well.

In the minor league system, nobody is waiting in the wings to move up to the big club. Jose Fernandez played third base reasonably well for the Brewers' Triple-A club at Indianapolis, but is not considered a prospect.

RECOMMENDATION REVIEW: The third base spot is a position in transition in Milwaukee. The Brewers attempted to trade Jeromy Burnitz to San Diego for third basemen Phil Nevin in the offseason but the trade fell through when Burnitz wasn't satisfied with the Padres' offer on a contract extension. This tipped the hand of Dean Taylor as a clear indication that the organization is looking to upgrade the third base spot. If Jose Hernandez opens the season at third for the Brewers, stay away. The 15-20 home runs, .240-.250 batting average, 65 RBI and 5-10 stolen bases won't make your team a winner unless they come awfully cheap.

MONTREAL EXPOS

Last season the Expos went into the season with Michael Barrett as their starting third baseman. They had very big hopes for him especially since the Expos settled on one position for him. However, it did not turn out to be a breakout season for the young Expos prospect. Instead it became a nightmare as Barrett took his fielding struggles to the plate with him. He has now been move back behind the plate where Manager Felipe Alou said he would never play again: Never say never!

This switch had left a large hole at third for the Expos before they trade starting pitcher Dustin Hermanson and setup man Steve Kline to the Cardinals for third baseman Fernando Tatis. Tatis is going to be the Expos starter at third. See more on Tatis in the Cardinals third base section.

Jeff Blum played 55 games at third, most down the stretch run of the season when Barrett had been sent down to the minors, and proved that he deserved a shot at more playing time in the 2001 season. Blum is a hard nosed player who has average fielding ability and a good stick. He proved last season that he could hit for both average and power. He is a fundamentally sound player who over a full season could hit .280-20-60, and steal ten bases. He was the frontrunner for the full-time third base job before Tatis was signed. Look for Blum to now get his at-bats while moving between third, second, and short.

Both Mike Mordecai and Andy Tracy could also see some time at third. Mordecai is a veteran backup utility-man who's role will not drastically change. Even in the event of a major injury to the starting third baseman, Mordecai will not be an everyday player. He can give a major league team good production in a limited role, but is not a viable Rotisserie player.

If Andy Tracy could improve his defense and cut down on the strikeouts he would have a more significant role at third base and be a potential player to pick off the wavier wire in time of need. As of now he was still expected to be plagued by those problems and will be mostly used as a lefty bat off the bench in pinch-hitting situations. He will probably see more time at first.

On the horizon is both Scott Hodges and Josh McKinley. Both are two years away. Hodges played mainly at High-A Jupiter in 2000 and McKinley played at Single-A Cape Fear. Hodges has more power potential, but McKinley is the more well-rounded player. He is a former shortstop who has developing power and the potential to steal 25-plus bases. Hodges does not have the basestealing ability, but at this point is a little more refined and was due to arrive in the big leagues a year ahead of McKinley if all goes well.

RECOMMENDATION REVIEW: If he is doing well in spring training and looks to be the full-time Expos utilityman (think Tony Phillips type), then Blum is a good choice here in a deep league. Since he played 44 games at short, he can be used there, where he has more Rotisserie value than at third. He would be a good pick for a middle infield spot. Blum would be a wiser choice than taking Orlando Cabrera as the Expos shortstop for your

Rotisserie lineup.

NEW YORK METS

Before last season, Robin Ventura underwent surgery on his right shoulder, but during the year he went on the disabled list because of a bruised rotator cuff. His arm had an impact on his committing the most errors since 1994. His batting also seemed affected; he finished at .232-24-84, and was just .222-8-31 after the all-star break. At age 33, the lefthanded batter could be on a downhill slide.

The Mets Lenny Harris from Arizona in a June trade, then signed him to a two-year contract after the season. A big second half of the season (.342-3-13) allowed him to finish at .260-4-26 with 13 stolen bases. The 36-year-old lefthanded batter played all four corner positions, plus second base, and batted .268 (15-for-56) as a pinch hitter. He could play more if he weren't hopeless against lefthanded pitchers. He would have some value if he could qualify as a third middle infielder.

David Lamb played more at third base than at second base or shortstop during his brief major league time in 2000, but he isn't a good Rotisserie choice even as a middle infielder.

Mo Bruce, a 25-year-old righthanded batter, moved back to third base, but showed more speed than power last season. He batted .274 at Double-A Binghamton, but just .232 with Triple-A Norfolk. He totaled four homers, 33 RBI and 29 steals.

Junior Zamora, once a promising hitter, has been side-tracked by injuries the last couple of seasons. The 24-year-old righty batted just .162-4-11 at Binghamton.

RECOMMENDATION REVIEW: Ventura is hardly a sure thing any more, because of age and that bad shoulder. You'd be advised to bring him up early in the draft to get another owner to overpay, or hope that he'd last until late so you could get him at a lower price as a third corner infielder.

PHILADELPHIA PHILLIES

Despite their recent perennial also-ran status, the Phillies possess some of the best young offensive talents in the game in right fielder Bobby Abreu, left fielder Pat Burrell, and (most of all) third baseman Scott Rolen. He's certainly the best player in the game to never have made an All-Star roster, and has quietly become the premier defensive third sacker in the game despite media celebrations of the play of the likes of Robin Ventura and Scott Brosius during the 2000 postseason.

Rolen came up to the majors around the same time as Andruw Jones, Vladimir Guerrero, Nomar Garciaparra and other young greats. Compared to such a high standard, Rolen's major league performance to date has to be considered a little bit disappointing. His progression in many statistical categories over his four-year career as a regular has been negative. His walk and stolen base totals have declined from 1998 to 1999 to 2000, as his plate discipline has wavered and his durability has been hampered by several nagging injuries, the most serious of which is an arthritic back condition that is aggravated when he plays on artificial turf.

Rolen, still only 26, has all of the skills to be a superior all-around performer. The 6'4", 226, righthanded hitter has lightning-quick bat speed and awesome physical strength, but is not a prototypical power hitter. Many of his homers are rising line drives, and when he is truly locked in, he will bash the ball from gap to gap with authority. Over the last two seasons, however, he has more regularly gotten himself out early in the count, and has focused on pulling the ball too often. He's an exceptionally effective baserunner, but has cut down on his basestealing attempts because of his physical problems. Defensively, Rolen is a shortstop playing third base. He's athletic enough to have once been a prized Division I basketball recruit, and possesses the first-step quickness, flexibility and cannon-like arm strength to make any play a third baseman has ever been asked to make. Think Mike Schmidt with a more accurate arm.

The Phils had better hope that Rolen remains healthy, as there isn't much behind him in the system. His likely 2001 backups (barring the potential offseason addition of a powerful bench bat) include the likes of Tomas Perez (see Shortstop section) and Kevin Jordan (see Second Baseman section). There are no third base prospects of note in the farm system, either.

RECOMMENDATION REVIEW: If he can overcome his physical problems and rack up 600 at-bat seasons (which new manager Larry Bowa will push him to do, unlike cruise director Terry Francona) Rolen is a solid bet to regularly hit .300 with 40 doubles, 10 triples, 30 homers, 120 RBI and 10 steals. At that level, he'd soon surpass Chipper Jones as the most valuable Rotisserie

third baseman in the National League. A rising walk total would be a sure sign of budding superstardom. Pay top dollar for Rolen in 2001.

PITTSBURGH PIRATES

2000 was a season of transition at the hot corner for Pittsburgh. Aramis Ramirez began the year as the regular third baseman, hit .167 and was sent to Triple-A Nashville for a month. Luis Sojo got the bulk of the playing time before Ramirez returned in mid June. Ramirez hit much better over the last few months of the season before losing the last month of the season to injury. Mike Benjamin, John Wehner, Enrique Wilson and Keith Osik finished out the season sharing the job.

For 2001, Ramirez is the front-runner; it's his job to lose. For rotisserie players, Ramirez is an interesting prospect. Because he hasn't established himself yet and because his overall career numbers are relatively poor, he is easily dismissed or ignored by Rotisserie owners who don't look beyond stat lines. Here's a better stat for you: 22. That's Ramirez's opening day age in 2001.

What do we know about players who reach the major leagues at an early age, as Ramirez did in 1998? They have a great likelihood of going on to be good major league ballplayers. Ramirez hasn't done it yet, with the key word there being "yet." All the signs are positive for Ramirez: he's very young, he has not yet provided positive value, he has developed what appears to be an established level of play that is, in fact, deceptively poor, and he has little or no challenge for his playing time. Ramirez will be a cheap bargain for a number of winning Rotisserie teams in 2001 and 2002, and this might be the last time he's cheap on Draft Day.

When Ramirez is out of the lineup, the Bucs can go with other utility infield types as they did in 2000 with Benjamin, Wehner, et al. They can also call upon Jarrod Patterson or Jason Wood, both of whom spent the 2000 season at Triple-A Nashville and shared the job with Rob Makowiak and Shaun Skrehot, who primarily appeared at other positions. None of these players have any Rotisserie value.

A pair of better long-range prospects were at Double-A Altoona in 2000. Rico Washington split the year between second and third base, hitting .258 with eight homers and 59 RBI. He made a bunch of errors, though, and could wind up at another position before he gets much farther along in the Pirates' farm system. Kevin Haverbusch is a better fielder who has a bit of pop in his bat. In 43 games at Altoona, Haverbusch hit .279 with five homers and 21 RBI. Haverbusch is the most likely candidate to advance as a third sacker, and your best bet as a Bucs' infield prospect.

At the A-ball level, Rolando Segura, Luis Lorenzana and Justin Martin are decent prospects, although Lorenzana will probably advance as a middle-infielder and Martin as an outfielder. Segura has some power, but fans rather easily. He can advance on his power potential alone, although he won't be effective at upper levels if he continues to strikeout at a high rate.

RECOMMENDATION REVIEW: Pick up Ramirez cheaply, before he becomes the last living, breathing third baseman, and you'll get yourself a tidy bargain for the next few years. He's only a bargain if you get him cheaply, though, so don't involved in Draft Day bidding wars for Ramirez. Ignore the other Bucs' third basemen; only Washington or Haverbusch have long-range potential and even they are not especially sharp prospects.

ST. LOUIS CARDINALS

Fernando Tatis was traded to the Montreal Expos for pitchers Steve Kline and Dustin Hermanson. Look for both Craig Paquette and Placido Polanco to split time at third.

Tatis is one of the most dynamic third basemen in the National League. He has tremendous power, he runs very well and he's got solid defensive skills at third base. Injuries really hampered his play last year, but he still managed to hit .253 with 18 home runs and 64 RBI. He tore his groin muscle pretty early on in the season and never fully recovered, so his numbers are a bit skewed. He was expected to be totally healthy come spring training and should return to the form he showed in 1999 when he hit .298 with 34 homers, 107 RBI and 21 steals.

Craig Paquette, who is a serviceable utilityman, should serve as one of the backups to Tatis. Paquette also plays first base and the outfield, but probably won't play nearly as much this year as he did last year unless injuries become a problem once again. He hit .245 with 15 homers and 61 RBI last year, but those numbers will come down as he doesn't figure to get 384 at-bats again in 2001.

Placido Polanco may become the primary backup to Tatis

at third base this season. Tony LaRussa will be looking for ways to get him in the lineup, especially if he hits like he did last year, and that will mean some action at the hot corner for him.

Third base prospect Chris Haas is a lefthanded hitter with plenty of raw power, but he's regressed as a hitter the past year or so. He hit 17 homers in about half a season at Double-A last year, but he also struck out 84 times in 291 at-bats against younger competition. He also plays first base, but was far from being a major league player at the end of the 2000 season. Troy Farnsworth hit 23 home runs and drove in 113 at High-A Potomac last year, but his .240 batting average and 133 whiffs are signs he's not nearly ready for the majors.

RECOMMENDATION REVIEW: Tatis should be in for a big year, so grab him quickly if you need a productive third baseman. Paquette and Polanco will only be useful in deep NL only leagues where reserve players have more value. Neither Haas nor Farnsworth merit having at this point of their careers.

SAN DIEGO PADRES

Phil Nevin has finally lived up to his top overall draft pick status; he led the Padres in several primary hitting categories, including homers (31) and RBI (107), and also hit .303, second only to Al Martin's .306 mark. He has finally settled into just one position; for those of you used to sticking Nevin in at catcher: you can't do it anymore — he didn't catch a single inning last year. Still, Nevin's value in Rotisserie and to his major league team is unmistakable. Without Nevin, Ryan Klesko would be the Padres only power threat. Nevin ranks as one of the league's best hitting third basemen and one of the few Padres hitters worth spending any Draft Day money to acquire.

Greg LaRocca was Triple-A Las Vegas' primary third baseman and had a good season including power, speed and batting average. LaRocca makes good contact at the plate, but could shift to another position before reaching the majors. He's not a good prospect; still, he would be somewhat useful in a temporary, fill-in role should he get some kind of major league playing time.

It's interesting that nomadic Nevin has finally settled into a spot at third base just as super-prospect Sean Burroughs comes along . . . as a third baseman. Nevin may have to move again soon. Burroughs didn't do much at Double-A Mobile in 2000, hitting .291 with just two homers and 42

RBI. The telling number to look at, though, is 29 . . . the number of doubles Burroughs whacked in 108 games and a telling sign of developing power. He's a pure hitter who is still learning to make the most of his talents; he was expected to hit for above-average power when he matures. Hitting that well at the age of 19 in the difficult environment of the Southern League identifies Burroughs as a good prospect. He needs another full season in the minors, then should be ready to jump into the big leagues with both feet. Look for Burroughs to earn a cup of coffee in San Diego in September, then give the Padres something to worry about: how to get both Nevin and Burroughs in the lineup at the same time.

Other Padres' prospects don't measure up to Burroughs and, besides, Nevin is in the way at the major league level. None should be considered for Rotisserie purposes.

RECOMMENDATION REVIEW: There are still those Rotisserie players out there who don't consider Nevin the real deal. They remember him as a failure in Houston, Detroit and Anaheim, not as the success he is today in San Diego. Let them believe that; it will only serve to keep the price down. Nevin is a fine buy in 2001, especially for teams that are looking to win now. Don't look for Nevin's value to increase or for him to be a bargain beyond this year. For future prospects, look at Burroughs; he's an excellent choice for Ultra squads and he may actually produce positive value by September of this year.

SAN FRANCISCO GIANTS

With the Thanksgiving swap of Bill Mueller to the Cubs, Russ Davis, amazingly, inherits the third base spot at Pac Bell Park, for now anyway. Davis has changed little since he first appeared as a potential big bopper in the Yankees chain in 1994. Occasional power (he averaged 20 homers per year between 1997-99, and Davis' 2000 numbers over 500 at-bats extrapolate to the same) belies a questionable glove and terrible (.309 for his career) on-base average.

Davis will give you home runs, but little else, however, he could be a cheap corner infielder: A $3-4 investment for 20 homers might be worth it, if you can handle a low average and if strikeouts don't factor into your scoring.

However, the Giants were most likely willing to deal Mueller because they do have some solid youngsters on the way in the minors. Leading the pack is Pedro Feliz,

who went .298-33-105 at Fresno last season. At 23, Feliz has both climbed through the Giants ranks, and improved his average and power numbers since debuting at Scottsdale in 1994. And, he strikes out a lot, with 454 minor league whiffs to just 109 walks.

He could be a player, but Feliz must work on his discipline to succeed in the majors. He could also dazzle with a hot spring, and earn a starting job, but be wary not to spend too much on the free swinging youngster just yet (if he does start, get Davis or someone as back up). Feliz does project to make the team's roster, in any event.

An even better prospect is 1998's #1 draft selection, Tony Torcato. Torcato, who is just 21, played the bulk of 2000 at San Jose, going .324-7-88, with 19 steals and 37 doubles over 490 at-bats (he also hit .500 over eight at-bats at Shreveport). He should spend most of 2001 there, with some time at Fresno a possibility as well. Torcato , who walked 41 times to just 62 strikeouts last year, has a much better notion of the art of hitting than Feliz, so he could indeed earn a starting job (another possibility has Torcato moving to second in the future, with Feliz going to third, as Jeff Kent is eased into the first base spot).

If that is not enough, San Francisco's number one draft selection in 2000, Lance Niekro, fared very well at Salem-Keizer, going .362-5-44 over 196 plate appearances.

Finally, at the bottom of the prospect totem pole, is Tony Zuniga, last year's Shreveport starter at the hot corner. Zuniga turned in respectable .260-17-62 totals at Double-A, and will likely move up to Fresno. Feliz and Torcato are way ahead of him, however.

RECOMMENDATION REVIEW: Davis is not a valuable Rotisserie third baseman. Take him only as a backup, in case of injury, for his home runs. Feliz is a decent late round Ultra pick, who can possibly contribute in 2001, but don't bank on it. Torcato is also a good ultra pick, for down the road, but will most likely end up at second base.

TOP 2001 HOME RUN HITTERS

NAME	HR
Chipper Jones	39
Phil Nevin	28
Scott Rolen	27
Fernando Tatis	27
Robin Ventura	26
Mike Lowell	22
Matt Williams	20
Aaron Boone	19
Chris Truby	19
Adrian Beltre	18
Shane Andrews	16
Jose Hernandez	15
Tyler Houston	15
Russ Davis	14
Craig Paquette	14
Jeff Cirillo	13

TOP 2001 RBI PRODUCERS

NAME	RBI
Chipper Jones	110
Jeff Cirillo	102
Phil Nevin	97
Robin Ventura	96
Fernando Tatis	93
Chris Truby	92
Mike Lowell	90
Scott Rolen	88
Aaron Boone	78
Matt Williams	78
Adrian Beltre	77
Jose Hernandez	62
Craig Paquette	55
Bill Mueller	50

TOP 2001 RUN SCORERS

NAME	RUNS
Chipper Jones	118
Jeff Cirillo	106
Fernando Tatis	90
Scott Rolen	87
Bill Mueller	86
Chris Truby	80
Phil Nevin	75
Adrian Beltre	74
Aaron Boone	72
Robin Ventura	71
Mike Lowell	70
Jose Hernandez	62
Matt Williams	62
Placido Polanco	51

TOP 2001 BASESTEALERS

NAME	SB
Chipper Jones	18
Adrian Beltre	14
Aaron Boone	14
Fernando Tatis	11
Scott Rolen	10
Andy Fox	8
Lenny Harris	8
Bill Spiers	8
Jose Hernandez	6
Jeff Cirillo	5

TOP 2001 BATTING AVERAGES

NAME	AVG
Jeff Cirillo	.325
Chipper Jones	.314
Phil Nevin	.303
Placido Polanco	.291
Scott Rolen	.289
Enrique Wilson	.285
Fernando Tatis	.284
Aaron Boone	.283
Adrian Beltre	.282
Aramis Ramirez	.280
Dave Magadan	.277
Bill Spiers	.277
Geoff Blum	.276
Bill Mueller	.276
Matt Williams	.276

STRATEGIES FOR SHORTSTOPS

Don't Be Shortchanged

by John Benson

The Big Three have become the Big Four, and one of them is a National Leaguer. Rafael Furcal, just age 20, has joined Alex Rodriguez, Derek Jeter and Nomar Garciaparra as the largest number of the best shortstops ever playing in the same era. How good is Furcal? No one yet knows, but his second half stats times two equal .289-8-50-56 for a $35 value. The best way to get Furcal this year is to talk about sophomore slumps. Don't even mention the name Furcal, or it will be too obvious. Just talk about how pitchers share ideas with each other when they gather for spring training (that's why they start early, for all those pitchers-only meetings) and discuss hitters' weaknesses and how to exploit them. Cite the names of other players who have had a falloff after their rookie year, whichever players produced the most humiliating outcomes in your league. The words "sophomore slump" wouldn't be in our vocabulary if the phenomenon wasn't real. Then get Furcal.

It wasn't that long ago that shortstop was a talent-starved position for those of us who care so much about offensive stats. If you didn't get Barry Larkin in the NL or Cal Ripken in the AL, just drop back and punt. How times have changed. Now there are four superstars and plenty of other good ones to go around. In 2001 there will not be any good excuses for having a bum shortstop.

That wonderful quality — youth — is widely available in both leagues. In the NL, Jimmy Rollins is just 22, Adam Everett and Alex Gonzalez are 24, Edgar Renteria and Julio Lugo are 25. While Rollins was not assured of a major-league role going into spring training, he makes a great pick for the future nonetheless. Everett, who beat out Rollins for the job on the 2000 Olympic team, looks like a part-timer for 2001 but has some upward potential too. Lugo has the potential to be a Tony Phillips type: play every day without having any set position; he can play second or short or any of the outfield positions, and his offensive is strong on speed and power.

The AL has even more youngsters worthy of a roster spot, including Cristian Guzman age 23, Miguel Tejada and 24, and Deivi Cruz and Carlos Guillen age 25. Guzman

hasn't hit for average yet, but he will be in the .250-.270 range this year and will mature into a .300 hitter soon. Tejada in the second half hit .299 with 17 homers; he will pass the $20 value level for the first time this year with .290-30-100+ and a handful of steals for good measure. Guillen will surprise a lot of people (but not us) by popping 15 homers this year.

Speed will be up this year as the fastest young shortstops get to play more and improve with experience. We see two passing the 50 mark, Furcal and Tony Womack (29 in the second half) compared to zero shortstops with 50 steals in 2000. And we see 13 shortstops with more than 15 stolen bases, compared to ten above that mark a year ago. This speed in the middle infield will take some pressure off the competition for speedy outfielders, or give you a leg up if you act early and effectively.

In the bargain basement, infant shortstops make good picks for weaker teams needing to take chances, or for any team which can park them on a reserve or Ultra list to wait and see what happens. As shortstops are typically the best athletes on a roster, they often deliver pleasant surprises. Not all good young defensive stars hit as well as Furcal did in his first year. In the good-for-$1 department, D'Angelo Jimenez is the best pick in the AL, while the NL offers a handful including Everett, Geoff Blum, Alex Gonzalez, Alex Cora and Juan Sosa.

Finally, remember that shortstops can play second or third better than a second baseman or third baseman can fill in at shortstop. Thus taking a cheap shortstop for a last-pick MI will usually produce more roster flexibility than taking another second baseman. To see this flexibility at work, and to have a list of multiposition types on draft day, focus on Furcal, Lugo, Damian Jackson, Guillen, Placido Polanco, Jose Hernandez, Santiago Perez, Jimenez, Bill Spiers, Blum, Andy Fox, and Ramon E. Martinez.

AMERICAN LEAGUE SHORTSTOPS

ANAHEIM ANGELS

As the offseason began, the Angels' shortstop position was unsettled. Gary DiSarcina re-signed during the winter and was expected to be healthy and start. Kevin Stocker became a free agent, leaving Benji Gil as the backup for the time being.

Gil was the surprising beneficiary of the season-ending injury to DiSarcina, and he turned in a typical season: low batting average, few walks and scant power. His strike-out rate makes him look like Dave Kingman without the home runs. Not the guy you want on a Rotisserie team. It would be hard to fathom the Angels, or any team, going into the season with Gil as a starter, but he has developed enough versatility to be a backup for somebody.

DiSarcina lost most of last season, undergoing arthroscopic shoulder surgery in May. From a Rotisserie standpoint, DiSarcina is a dangerous proposition: if healthy, he will play a lot, but has no power, no speed and a lifetime batting average of .258. In eight full seasons, he has topped .260 only twice. You could get lucky for $1, but there are better bets out there.

Stocker's career numbers are striking similar to DiSarcina's: a couple of good seasons, but a lifetime batting average of .254 with no power or speed. In a full-time role, he's more likely to hurt than to help a Rotisserie team. He missed time last year with chronic knee problems. At his best, he's never been worth more than a few dollars, and at his worst he's had negative value. The wisest course is to steer clear.

The Angels acquired Wilmy Caceres from the Reds during the offseason for pitcher Seth Etherton. He was expected to start the season at Triple-A. Caceres is a player to keep an eye on for the Angels, especially with the lack of talent at the Angels shortstop position; he could see a midseason callup. He plays solid defense and sprays the ball around the field, but his speed is his main game.

Justin Baughman could see some playing time at short-stop, and could have more Rotisserie value than any of the players discussed above, entirely from stolen bases. His primary position is second base, and he is discussed more fully in that section.

Any of the above players would hit ninth in the Angels' batting order.

RECOMMENDATION REVIEW: Watch Caceres during the spring to see if he can handle major league pitching. Barring a change in the other cast of characters, just say no to Angels shortstops.

BALTIMORE ORIOLES

Mike Bordick was signed by the Orioles in the offseason. He will be the starting shortstop for the O's. See more on Bordick in the Mets shortstop position.

Bordick was a favorite of both the Orioles fans and management. He was in the last year of his contract last year, and was swapped to the Mets as part of the Orioles late season make-over. Among the players obtained in return for Bordick, the Orioles received then 28-year-old

Melvin Mora, who the Mets discovered had an erratic glove. Mora was hitting well for the Mets as an all-around utility man and shortstop fill-in for the injured Rey Ordonez.

Mora has been on the fringes of the major leagues for a number of years, spending four years in Triple-A in the Astros and Mets organization, getting only 31 at-bats prior to last year. He's shown that he can hit Triple-A pitching, but prior to last year, he was never given much of a shot at hitting big league stuff. He came through nicely last year, hitting a solid .275-8-47 with 12 stolen bases, in a combined 414 at-bats for the Mets and Orioles. He has hit well in Triple-A, and now he has shown that he can hit major league pitching.

The Orioles realized that Mora wasn't the answer at shortstop, so they planned to move him to the outfield. The Orioles high minors are devoid of prospects, so they will most likely obtain a veteran to play shortstop, and Mike Bordick was a possibility. Bordick's improving offensive production has been a surprise every year for the past three years as he continues to have new career-high years. Last year he hit a good .285-20-80, setting career highs in average, homers, and RBI. Bordick is now 35, and some decline in his hitting was expected. See more on Mike Bordick in the New York Mets shortstop section.

Jesse Garcia was the Triple-A shortstop, but he's a weak singles hitter whose best role is a utilityman. But even then, some hitting was expected from utilitymen, and Garcia is not in the Orioles long range plans, nor is he a draftable player.

Ivanon Coffie was the Double-A shortstop who also played some in Triple-A and with the Orioles. He's an improving hitter who needs more minor league time, and his best position may be third base. Ed Rogers, from the Dominican Republic shortstop factory in San Pedro de Macoris, is a 19-year-old prospect who some scouts cautiously compare to Alex Rodriguez and Derek Jeter. He was signed at 16, and is moving up quickly. He has a great glove, and he could be in Camden Yards in 2001 if he can hit above .250 in the minors. Rogers is a year away and is a good pick for your farm system.

RECOMMENDATION REVIEW: Look for a fall-off in production from the aging Bordick, who had a career year in 2000. Melvin Mora has shown that he can hit and swipe some bases. He was expected to get a lot of playing time in 2001, but he may be playing the outfield. Mora will provide more value as a shortstop. Ed Rogers is a good long range farm pick.

BOSTON RED SOX

If Nomar Garciaparra can play every day, he can bring enough value to justify the price you'd have to pay for him. However, he has missed at least 19 games in each of the last three seasons. One factor that could reduce his auction price is the continuing development of American League shortstops. Miguel Tejada clearly has moved up near the elite group, though Tony Batista no longer qualifies as a shortstop. Despite missing 22 games last season, Garciaparra again led the league with a .372 average, hit 21 homers and drove in 96 runs. And at 27, the righthanded batter should be in his prime.

The regular shortstop at Triple-A Pawtucket was 29-year-old Andy Sheets, also a righthanded batter. He batted just .228-8-36 in Triple-A.

RECOMMENDATION REVIEW: You want one of the AL shortstop studs. You don't want to overpay for Garciaparra as the first star shortstop brought up in an auction, or as the last of the group. So if you want him, you need to bring his name up after one or two of the other big names are gone.

CHICAGO WHITE SOX

The White Sox acquired Royce Clayton from the Rangers during the offseason. He was expected to be the starting shortstop for the Sox. See more on Clayton in the Rangers shortstop section.

Jose Valentin did a great job for the White Sox during the 2000 season, providing them excellent power and speed out of the second spot in the lineup. He hit 25 home runs, drove in 92 and stole 19 bases, not bad for a shortstop. His defense was very inconsistent, but if he continues to hit like he did last year it won't keep him out of the lineup. He has offered to play another position if need be, possibly the outfield.

Mike Caruso was once the White Sox' shortstop of the future, in fact he was once their starting shortstop, but a two-year batting slump and below average defense have changed that. He's a weak hitter with no power and no patience whose only above average tool is speed. Caruso's future will be as a utility player, not a regular.

At one time, Jason Dellaero was considered a pretty good prospect, but he can't hit. His .185 batting average at Double-A last year took him out of the running for a major league job down the road.

RECOMMENDATION REVIEW: Valentin is a good Rotisserie player, but he comes with some risk. He's been prone to injury and to slumps, he's worth a mid round selection. Don't bank on him too much, however. Caruso and Dellaero have no roto value.

CLEVELAND INDIANS

Omar Vizquel is a steady producer who had another good season last year, hitting .287-7-66 with 22 stolen bases. The 22 stolen bases was his lowest total since he swiped 13 playing part time in 1994. In recent years, he's stolen 35-43, making him a very valuable in Rotisserie leagues. His value is also enhanced by his good batting average, usually in the .280-.297 area, with his .333 in 1999 being his career-best year.

Jolbert Cabrera is the backup shortstop, but Vizquel plays almost all of the games. Cabrera is a reserve infielder-outfielder who has hit for some solid averages in Triple-A. He can also steal some bases. He has no draft-day value, but could have some midseason value.

Zach Sorensen is 24 and will likely spend most of 2001 in Triple-A. Last year in Double-A, he hit .263-6-38 in 382 at-bats. He's a singles hitter who can swipe some bases. John McDonald is 26 and was in Triple-A last year, but he isn't regarded as a prospect. He may get some major league playing time as a utility player. Jeff Patzke is 27 and has had some good years in Triple-A, but he's a singles hitter.

RECOMMENDATION REVIEW: Stolen bases and a good average make Vizquel valuable in Rotisserie leagues. Although his is moving up in age and was expected to run less. He ranks only behind Nomar Garciaparra, Derek Jeter, Alex Rodriguez, and Miguel Tejada in the American League.

DETROIT TIGERS

Deivi Cruz has turned himself into one of the most underrated shortstops in all of baseball. He's always been a consistent fielder with soft hands and a strong throwing arm, but he's also become a very good hitter. His batting average has improved by nearly 20 points between each of his four major league seasons, going from .241 during

his rookie season to the .302 average he posted last year. His RBI totals have also risen during each of his four major league seasons, going from 40 during his rookie year to 82 last season. In other words, he's gotten better as a hitter every single year since he came to the big leagues. He doesn't steal many bases, but he does have double-digit home run power. Cruz will be overlooked in many roto leagues, but he's a solid player.

Shane Halter figures to backup Cruz at the major league level, though he's not much of a shortstop or hitter. His value is as a player that can play multiple infield positions and all three outfield spots in an emergency and he has no rotisserie value.

The only shortstop prospect the Tigers have that's worth mentioning is the switch-hitting Ramon Santiago. He played at Class A West Michigan last season, demonstrating excellent defensive ability and well above average speed. He has a long way to go as a hitter, however, and shouldn't have an kind of major league future for at least two or three years.

RECOMMENDATION REVIEW: Cruz figures to be a big-time bargain in most roto leagues because he's not a big name, but he's a very good player that should post respectable offensive numbers. He may not hit .300 again, but he's a good bet for .275-.280 with 10-15 home runs and 50-plus RBI. If Nomar, A-Rod, Jeter, Vizquel, and Tejada are gone then Cruz is one of the top two or three shortstops left. Aside from Cruz, no Tiger shortstop is worth having.

KANSAS CITY ROYALS

Rey Sanchez has always yearned for a chance to be an everyday major league shortstop and the Royals have given him that opportunity. He hasn't disappointed them, turning in a career-best season at the plate in 1999 and a marvelous season with the glove in 2000. He's a defensive anchor on a relatively young Royals' club, but he's not too shabby at the plate either. Sanchez has very little power and just marginal speed. Still, he hits for a useful average and, with a newly potent Royals' offense, Sanchez can score and drive in a fair amount of runs, too. He's worth more than a buck, although he generally is drafted for just a dollar.

Luis Ordaz, Jeff Reboulet, Wilson Delgado and Ray Holbert were some of the shortstop fill-ins for Kansas City last year; only Delgado has value, and only as an injury replacement; avoid Ordaz, Reboulet and Holbert. It's unlikely anyone except Delgado can produce anything of value for Rotisserie owners in case of Sanchez's absence.

Holbert, Alejandro Prieto and Tony Medrano were the shortstops at Triple-A Omaha; all of them are, at best, major league utility players and have no Rotisserie value. Double-A Wichita featured Nick Ortiz at shortstop; Ortiz is a decent prospect for both batting average and speed, but he was traded near the end of the season to the Yanks. Mark Ellis was a standout for High-A Wilmington another contact hitter with some speed, but he was expected to shift to second base as he advances up the farm ladder. No other shortstops are currently worthy of long-range Rotisserie consideration.

RECOMMENDATION REVIEW: Put Rey Sanchez on your $1 list; he can give you a little more than a buck's worth of value and is unlikely to hurt his Rotisserie owners. Wilson Delgado can be of some value as an injury replacement only (for selection as a replacement during the season, not for drafting). There are no other shortstops in the Royals' system with any Rotisserie value.

MINNESOTA TWINS

Cristian Guzman will enter his third major league season on the verge of becoming another American League shortstop who can field and hit exceptionally.

We will not mention A-Rod, Nomar, Tejada, or Jeter. They are at the top of the list, and it would be insulting to place Guzman in that category. But Guzman, heading into his third major league season, is no slouch.

Guzman showed marked improvement from his first season to his second season. He went from 16 extra base hits in 1999 to 53. He stole nine bases in 1999 to 28 in 2000. Paul Molitor, who knows a thing or two about stealing bases, said during the season that Guzman is still learning how to swipe a bag. For someone with 28 steals, that's alarming.

The Twins gave Guzman a chance to bat leadoff many times in 2000, with mixed results. He worked hard at bunting, and legged out many hits. His walks increased from 22 to 46, but he struck out over 100 times. He's still a work in progress at the plate, but is improving.

The Twins are still figuring out what kind of offensive player Guzman is going to be. They like his speed. He was voted the fastest baserunner by players in the annual *Baseball America* poll. His ability to drive the ball helped him lead the majors with a club-record 20 triples. But he also could end up a sixth or seventh place hitter and drive in runs. Guzman is only 22-years-old, which means his potential is limitless.

There are a handful of shortstops in the majors who can provide offense. Guzman already is better than most of them and has a chance to be among the league's elite. He's worth a high-round pick once the big ticket shortstops are gone. With eight home runs last season, Guzman almost hit double figures in doubles and triples, which doesn't happen often.

He'll likely be at near the top of the order in 2001, which means the chances for stolen bases and runs scored are great. He's a solid fielder, but has the tendency to lose his concentration, but that will not endanger his status.

Denny Hocking will back up Guzman at short, but is far behind offensively. There's no hot shortstop prospect until the Class A level, so this is Guzman's job for years to come.

RECOMMENDATION REVIEW: After the big-four shortstops, Guzman is the next best thing. His power will increase as will his stolen bases.

NEW YORK YANKEES

At age 26, Derek Jeter has been a major league star for five seasons, playing in at least 148 games each year. The righthanded batter doesn't have the Rotisserie impact of Alex Rodriguez or Nomar Garciaparra, but there was nothing wrong with .339-15-73 and 22 stolen bases (in 26 attempts).

Mike Coolbaugh, the shortstop at Triple-A Columbus, is most famous for being the brother of former major leaguer Scott Coolbaugh. Mike, a 28-year-old righthanded batter, finished at .271-23-61. He has little if any major league future.

At Double-A Norwich, Erick Almonte was a better prospect. He batted .271-15-77 and stole 12 bases, but also struck out 129 times. At 23, the righthanded batter has time to improve.

RECOMMENDATION REVIEW: Jeter could move

up higher among the top rank of American League Rotisserie shortstops if the Yankees turn him loose so he can steal more bases. If he were injured, the Yankees wouldn't have a viable alternative.

OAKLAND ATHLETICS

One of the great trivia questions, both within and outside of the Bay Area last year was, "Who had more RBI, the Giants left fielder, or the Athletics shortstop?" Well, it really is a loaded question, but Miguel Tejada drove in eight more runs than Barry Bonds in 2000 (yes, we know, Miguel had more plate appearances) and is now mentioned with the illustrious troika of A-Rod, Nomar, and Jeter. He deserves it, too, as Tejada carried the Athletics and a number of roto teams down the stretch with good power.

That means he will now be an expensive middle infielder, but he will be worth it. Tejada has likely come close to his abilities power wise, but he will be able to improve his batting average and on-base totals, and is also capable of double digits in steals, 20 or more even should that become part of the Oakland game plan. He will be just 24 on Opening Day, going into his third full season as a starter, so, as with most of his teammates, the numbers will generally only get better.

With Tejada entrenched as a durable hitter, there isn't much need to look beyond. In the event of an injury, Eric Chavez can play short, but utilityman Jorge Valendia is the leading candidate to get playing time. He has no roto value.

In the minors, however, there are names to at least watch, starting with Oscar Salazar, a 22 year-old who went .300-13-57, at Double-A Midland (he didn't fare as well at Sacramento, where he should spend 2001). At the Class A level, Caonabo Cosme hit just .241 but banged 33 doubles and stole 44 bases for Modesto, and Angel Berros went .277-10-63 for Visalia.

Freddie Bynum, the Athletics second round selection in the 2000 draft, had a good first go at rookie ball, going .256-1-26 with 22 steals at Vancouver.

RECOMMENDATION REVIEW: Tejada is now in the upper echelon of shortstops and will bring value close to that of Nomar and Jeter in 2001. Look for his average to rise and he can steal more too!

SEATTLE MARINERS

Alex Rodriguez hit the free agent market this past offseason and got the richest contract in baseball history; as you may have heard. As far as rotisserie baseball goes, Rodriguez is perhaps the ultimate player. He's the total package, bringing a .300-plus average, incredible patience, 40-50 home run power, 125-plus RBI potential and the ability to steal anywhere from 10 to 40 bases. There are no questions about his ability to produce. See more on Rodriguez in the Rangers starting shortstop position section.

The M's don't have any proven backup, but they do have one of baseball's best young shortstop prospects in their system. Antonio Perez, acquired from the Reds in the Ken Griffey, Jr. trade, has developed Roberto Alomar-like talent. He's a solid hitter with better power than you would expect from a teenage middle infielder. He runs extremely well and is a good basestealer which, combined with his above average defensive ability, makes him an elite middle infield prospect. He could get a shot and is worth the risk.

Carlos Guillen could be moved back to his original position. He was expected to play third going into spring, but if Perez does not look ready then Guillen could be the Mariners man at short. He is injury prone, but has a very good bat and just needs playing time. He won't be one of the top offensive shortstops, but could be a productive mid-range pickup at short.

RECOMMENDATION REVIEW: Anyone who doesn't know that A-Rod is one of baseball's elite shouldn't be playing Rotisserie baseball. Perez would be a great pickup in leagues with deep benches or minor league rosters. He could be the starter now that A-Rod is gone.

TAMPA BAY DEVIL RAYS

Felix Martinez can make a manager cry for joy with his glove and weep with sincere sadness with his bat.

The slick-fielding Martinez won the shortstop job in 2000 and didn't hit a lick. After hitting over .300 for a prolonged period once he reached the majors, Martinez hit a prolonged dry spell that dropped his average to .214. A switch-hitter, Martinez hit just .101 from the right side while hitting .248 lefthanded. Further bad news in the offensive department comes in the fact Martinez struck out 68 times in 299 at-bats while drawing just 32 walks. The Devil Rays hope he can become more selective and do the little things up to bat like hitting behind the runner and putting down sacrifice bunts.

Fortunately for the Devil Rays, Martinez never let his lack of offense affect his performance in the field. He made just 14 errors and most of those were of an aggressive nature where he tried to make a play that was impossible — even for Martinez.

Given Martinez's glove, he won't have to improve much offensively to convince the Devil Rays to keep him around as long as his glove holds up. Currently there is nobody in the Devil Rays' farm system ready to take the job.

RECOMMENDATION REVIEW: There's little chance Martinez's bat will improve enough to interest anyone at any price. However, if you need stolen bases and want to risk that he can keep his average around .250, Martinez might be worth the gamble.

TEXAS RANGERS

In a stunning move, the Rangers signed Alex Rodriguez to a mammoth $252 million, ten-year contract. So, he should play a little. The Ballpark in Arlington will be a more hospitable hitting environment for A-Rod than pitcher-favoring Safeco Field, and a succession of career years is possible. The one area of Rodriguez' game that will probably be de-emphasized is stolen bases; with Rodriguez batting third in the hitting-oriented Texas lineup and with Johnny Oates calling the shots, Rodriguez probably won't get more than two dozen steals, a factor that wise Rotisserie owners will take into account. Still, A-Rod's best hitting years should be ahead of him in the very near future. See more on A-Rod in the Mariners shortstop position section.

Incumbent shortstop Royce Clayton was traded to the White Sox. Last season, against the advice of everyone who pays attention to these sorts of things, Johnny Oates decided to have Clayton bat in the leadoff position. Predictably, Clayton had little success there and he was returned to the bottom of the order for the balance of the season. In the bottom third of someone's lineup, Clayton he should be able to improve on last year's dismal .242 average. Clayton is becoming more of a power-oriented hitter as the years go by, and less of a basestealer. Part of that has had to do with the Texas offense, which radically de-emphasizes the steal. (Clayton's 11 steals led

the team last season.) In a full season, Clayton should hit around .260 with 15 homers and 60 RBI and stolen bases in the teens.

Scott Sheldon will back up at every infield position, and is the emergency catcher for the Rangers. Johnny Oates doesn't play his bench much at all, so Sheldon probably would not have a significant impact on a Rotisserie team one way or the other. A reasonable guess would be about 100 at-bats for this season. Were he to get an extended chance, Sheldon would hit fairly well, with better power than most infield backups. He's an ideal guy to have for position flexibility, since he'll play most everywhere at one time or another. For Draft Day this year, Sheldon will qualify only at shortstop, since he did not play 20 games at any other position.

Kelly Dransfeldt will spend most of the season at Triple-A but could get the occasional stint in the majors. A fine defensive player, he is a poor hitter and thus of no use to a Rotisserie team.

With Alex Rodriguez on board, Mike Young may need to move back to second base again. Young was the key player in the Esteban Loaiza deal with Toronto last year. Young has good speed and a quick bat and makes good contact. If he masters Triple-A this season, he should be ready for the next step. For this season, a September callup is as much exposure as he's likely to get in the majors.

RECOMMENDATION REVIEW: Rodriguez is a premier Rotisserie shortstop, and will continue to improve, except in the steals category. Clayton should improve a little over last season, and is still in the top half of American League shortstops. Sheldon adds roster flexibility for $1, but not much else. Avoid Dransfeldt. Young is worth a mid-round Ultra pick as a speculation for 2002.

TORONTO BLUE JAYS

Alex Gonzalez re-signed with the Jays after it looked like he was going to leave. The slick-fielding Gonzalez showed that he had completely recovered from an injury-shortened 1999 campaign and his .252 average last year was actually the best season in his major league career, as were the 15 home runs and 69 RBI. On the negative side of the ledger, his stolen base ability appears to be gone at an earlier age than most would expect and he has never developed into the run producer that some envisioned he would be. Regardless, he's a full-time player.

A Blue Jays team without Gonzalez would have been forced to consider varying options, such as moving Tony Batista (covered in the third base section) back to short-stop or trading for a veteran replacement.

Failing those options, the Jays could turn in the short run to Chris Woodward. Woodward has been thrust into a part-time major league role at times the past couple of years, despite never doing anything significant with the bat in the minor leagues. Because he plays major league quality defense at any of the infield positions, he's the kind of player the Jays could use in April while they search for a long-term solution. Woodward would hit in the low .200s at this point with a bit more power than some would expect and no speed.

Also a remote possibility would see the Jays turn to minor league infielder Cesar Izturis, a switch-hitting speedster with incredible range and increasingly sure hands. Izturis rose all the way from Single-A in 1999 to Triple-A last year as Syracuse's regular shortstop. At that level, he was overmatched and hit just .218 with no home runs and only 20 walks. To his credit, he made just 12 errors and made Rey Ordonez-like plays on a consistent basis. A 2001 major league Izturis would be hard-pressed to stick around long unless he surprised everyone with newfound hitting skills. All the defense in the world won't save a .150 hitter from losing his job and to his credit, Izturis did hit .308 a year earlier at Single-A Dunedin, showing some prom-ise. He is just twenty-one years old.

RECOMMENDATION REVIEW: At the end of the 2000 season, there wasn't anyone on the Blue Jays roster at shortstop that could help a Rotisserie team. Alex Gonzalez is worth a bit of power and some RBI but up until last year, he was a consistent .230s hitter and he used to run more. None of the minor league players in the Jays' system projects to be an immediate star and both Wood-ward and Izturis would kill a Rotisserie team's batting average, even though Izturis would steal a few bases.

TOP 2001 HOME RUN HITTERS

NAME	HR
Alex Rodriguez	41
Miguel Tejada	31
Nomar Garciaparra	25
Jose Valentin	23
Derek Jeter	18
Mike Bordick	15
Carlos Guillen	15
Royce Clayton	14
Alex S. Gonzalez	14
Deivi Cruz	11
Melvin Mora	8
Cristian Guzman	6
Omar Vizquel	6

TOP 2001 RBI SCORERS

NAME	RBI
Alex Rodriguez	125
Nomar Garciaparra	105
Miguel Tejada	99
Jose Valentin	85
Derek Jeter	83
Carlos Guillen	79
Deivi Cruz	75
Mike Bordick	71
Alex S. Gonzalez	64
Omar Vizquel	64
Melvin Mora	54
Royce Clayton	53
Cristian Guzman	47
Rey Sanchez	43

TOP 2001 RUN SCORERS

NAME	RBI
Alex Rodriguez	126
Derek Jeter	124
Nomar Garciaparra	108
Omar Vizquel	103
Jose Valentin	99
Miguel Tejada	96
Carlos Guillen	84
Mike Bordick	81
Cristian Guzman	80
Royce Clayton	72
Melvin Mora	71
Deivi Cruz	69
Alex S. Gonzalez	69
Rey Sanchez	65

TOP 2001 BASESTEALERS

NAME	SB
Omar Vizquel	30
Cristian Guzman	24
Derek Jeter	22
Alex Rodriguez	20
Melvin Mora	15
Jose Valentin	15
Royce Clayton	11
Justin Baughman	9
Mike Bordick	9
Felix Martinez	9
Nomar Garciaparra	8
Benji Gil	8
Alex S. Gonzalez	8
Rey Sanchez	8
Miguel Tejada	7

TOP 2001 BATTING AVERAGES

NAME	AVG
Nomar Garciaparra	.344
Derek Jeter	.337
Alex Rodriguez	.312
Deivi Cruz	.293
Omar Vizquel	.290
Miguel Tejada	.287
Justin Baughman	.282
Rey Sanchez	.274
Wilmy Caceres	.268
Melvin Mora	.266
Gary Disarcina	.261
Mike Bordick	.260
Cristian Guzman	.260
Jose Valentin	.257
Royce Clayton	.256
Alex S. Gonzalez	.255

NATIONAL LEAGUE SHORTSTOPS

ARIZONA DIAMONDBACKS

Tony Womack made the return to shortstop, his original position, with grace last season with the Diamondbacks, playing his third position in as many years. Womack began his minor league career as a shortstop before moving to second base in the Pittsburgh chain because Jay Bell was a fixture at short. Funny how things work out, huh.

Womack, who played right field in his first season with the D'backs in 1999, once again led the team in stolen bases with 45, although for the first time in four years he was not the National League leader.

He was troubled by a bothersome Baker's cyst (similar to a hernia) in his left knee for the second half of the season and missed the final week of the season to undergo a surgical procedure in which a hole the size of a fist was sutured shut. He also had cartilage removed but was expected to be at full strength for spring training.

Womack's speed is his best asset. He led the NL with 14 triples last season, setting a team record, and has 235 stolen bases the last four seasons. He is a good bet to approach 60, his league-leading total with Pittsburgh in his rookie season of 1997. He had a career-high 72 in 1999.

Womack is not the quintessential leadoff man because he seldom walks, getting only 30 in 659 plate appearances last season. But his speed is such that he will again man the No. 1 spot in the order.

He set season bests in homers, RBI and triples in 2000 while finishing fourth in stolen bases. His average was a career-low .271, a figure he should be able to maintain.

Danny Klassen was a favorite of the old D'backs regime, and former manager Buck Showalter envisioned him as a major league starter in the near future. It remains to be seen how new skipper Bob Brenly will use him.

Klassen took a three-day crash course at third base after Matt Williams went down late in spring training last year and handled the switch without a hitch, but he is considered a shortstop first. Klassen missed most of the second half of last season with a bothersome turf toe.

Hanley Frias also can defend at shortstop. Prospect Alex Cintron was a Texas League All-Star at Double-A El Paso after making the California League postseason All-Star team at Class A High Desert the year, but he appears at least one more season away. Cintron hit .301 with 30 doubles in the hitter-friendly Texas League.

RECOMMENDATION REVIEW: Womack should get his 600-plus plate appearances and once again finish among the league leaders in stolen bases. His average is not a drain considering the number of stolen bases he gets.

ATLANTA BRAVES

The only thing that would keep Rafael Furcal from being one of the top shortstops in the National League would be if an NL team were to wind up with Alex Rodriguez. But if the NL does not wind up getting the most coveted free agent in the past decade, then Furcal will go on to be an All-Star shortstop.

There weren't many people who thought the diminutive native of the Dominican Republic would play much of a role for the Braves last season. After all, he had never played above Single-A and was listed as being only 19-years-old (although now indications are he might be as old as 23). But a strong spring training camp forced Atlanta to keep Furcal on its big league roster and he used his speed and athletic ability to win the NL Rookie of the Year award.

Furcal is one of the fastest players in the game and used his quickness to steal 40 bases and beat out seemingly that many infield hits. He will steal many more bases than that as he gets more accustomed to life in the big leagues. He stole 96 bases in 126 games in Single-A in 1999, so 60 or 70 steals with the Braves shouldn't be too high a total to expect.

Veteran Walt Weiss started about a third of the time at shortstop for Atlanta in 2000, but he won't see that much playing time again in his career. A couple of years with the Rockies made the Braves overestimate his ability and he wound up with three less than average years in Hot-lanta. It's possible he could stick around for another year as a backup shortstop, but his days of being a regular are over.

Mark DeRosa has appeared with the Braves off and on during the past two seasons, but he is older than Furcal and not nearly as talented. The only way he would get any kind of shot would be with another team.

Chipper Jones played six games at short last season, but his days as an infielder will soon be over. The Braves would like to move him to the outfield, which would mean an end to his token appearances at shortstop.

RECOMMENDATION REVIEW: Furcal is only going to get better as he gets bigger and stronger and in another year or two he will be the best leadoff hitter in all of baseball. If 50 or 60 steals from your shortstop will put you over the hump in your league, then Furcal is your man. You should also put him at the top of the list of shortstops who don't hit a lot of home runs.

CHICAGO CUBS

Ricky Gutierrez got a lot of publicity last year by hitting .355 in April, but he cooled off considerably after that, batting about .265 for the rest of the season. Still, the mighty Cubs PR machine would have you believe that Gutierrez is an All-Star.

That is not the case, although he is hitting much better now that he is out of the dreadful Astrodome. He posted career highs in many offensive categories in 2000, including going from a career-best of five homers to 11 last season.

He missed most of June and July with a separated shoulder, but returned in August and was fine physically the rest of the season. Still, even if he were to play an entire season, he is not likely to hit many more than 11 homers. He hit seven in the first two months of the 2000 season, but managed only four in the last two. Use his performance from August and September as more of a true gauge of what his totals will be this year. Even with Wrigley Field still boosting his offensive output, expect 8-12 homers, a batting average of .270-.285 and only a handful of RBI.

Jose Nieves and Augie Ojeda were Chicago's primary backups last season, and each played fairly well in that role. Nieves is the better player of the two right now, and would have been the Cubs' starter had they not picked up Gutierrez. He has more power, but he doesn't hit for a high average and he is not polished defensively. Ojeda impressed the Cubs last year, but he too has his offensive limitations. Ojeda, for sure, is not good enough to start in the big leagues.

Jeff Huson played in a few games at short for Chicago last season, but he will not be a significant contributor to any team this season.

RECOMMENDATION REVIEW: Gutierrez did little with the bat playing for Houston in the Astrodome, but he improved greatly in 2000 with the Cubs. He is not going to get much better, however, and he is older than one might think. He will turn 31 in May, which is a sure indication that he is in the latter part of his career.

CINCINNATI REDS

Nearly no one expected this last July, but Barry Larkin will again anchor Cincinnati's infield. Larkin returns for his 14th full season with the Redlegs after signing a three-year contract extension last summer, just as it appeared he might be traded to the New York Mets for prospects.

It was a great public relations move for the Reds, who received kudos from the Queen City residents after the signing, but will Larkin be able to justify his nine million dollar salary with a strong on-field performance?

Larkin isn't the same player he was even five years ago. He has lost a step defensively, his arm isn't nearly as strong as it used to be, and he isn't able to drive the ball like he once could. In 1990 or 1995 there wasn't much doubt that he was the best shortstop in the National League and maybe all of baseball, but now there are a few that are heads and shoulders above Larkin. Still, he remains a productive player and should stay high on your list of shortstops to get.

If anything happens to Larkin this season that knocks him out of the lineup for a couple of weeks, the Reds will call on Juan Castro, who came over from the Dodgers early last season and impressed Cincinnati with his defense and his improved bat. Castro can hit for a decent average and steal some bases, but he has very little power and is not a run producer. Chris Sexton played 14 games at short for the Reds in 2000, but he will be lucky to make the big league roster for any team, much less see significant playing time.

Gookie Dawkins, the Reds' 21-year-old wunderkind, seems to be the heir to Larkin's job at this point. He is regarded as one of the top middle infield prospects in all of baseball, as evidenced by his selection to the 1999 Pan-American team and the 2000 U.S. Olympic squad. Defensively, he is ready to play in the major leagues right now, but offensively he has plenty of work to do. He shares some of the same deficiencies as Pokey Reese, in that he hasn't grasped a good knowledge of the strike zone yet and he swings for the fences too much.

The Reds selected David Espinosa, a high school short-stop from Miami, in the first round of the 2000 draft. The club signed him to a major league contract, mostly to keep from having to pay him a multi-million dollar signing bonus. Scouts believe he will become a polished fielder who will hit for average and steal bases, but there are doubts about his ability to hit for power.

RECOMMENDATION REVIEW: Larkin should benefit the most from the Reds' removal of the artificial turf in Cinergy Field. The natural surface will be much more forgiving on his aging body and should help the former NL MVP stay more productive throughout the season. Also, the Reds are moving in the fences in Cinergy Field, which should add a few more homers to his total. Expect 18-20 homers and a .300 batting average again, numbers which would still put him at or near the top of NL shortstops.

COLORADO ROCKIES

Iron man Neifi Perez had the best season of his blossoming career in 2000, when he set season highs in virtually every offensive categories while playing 162 games for the second time in three years. Since replacing Walt Weiss as the starter in 1998, Perez has missed only five games.

Perez, a switch-hitter, packed a lot of punch from the left side of the plate last year, the first time in his career he has shown that ability. He hit .357 against lefties with seven homers in only 154 at-bats. For the third straight season he homered off Randy Johnson, leaving his ability to turn around a fastball not in question.

Shuffled between the 1-2 and 7-8 spots in the batting order his first three seasons, Perez settled into the No. 2 spot last July 21 and excelled there, hitting .298. He is one of the best bunters in the league he hit six bunt hits in September alone and seems an ideal No. 2 man.

Batting ahead of Todd Helton, Jeff Cirillo and a healthy Larry Walker certainly will not hurt Perez's productivity, since he should get plenty of pitches to hit as the lesser of a whole lot of evils.

Perez, who has a tremendous arm and above-average range, won his first Gold Glove in 2000 and will play through hitting slumps because of his outstanding glove.

Perez's speed manifests itself in his ability to bunt and stretch extra-base hits - he has 11 triples for the second season in a row. But he has yet to learn the nuances of stealing bases. He has only 13 steals in his three seasons as a regular, although that part of his game should take a step up in the near future.

While Perez's hold on the job is strong, the Rockies have several quality youngsters in their minor league system - Juan Sosa, Elvis Pena and Juan Uribe. Sosa, 25, had a career-high 69 RBI at Triple-A Colorado Springs last season after stealing 68 bases at Class A Salem in 1998. Pena hit .300 for the second straight year at Double-A Carolina while setting a career high with 48 stolen bases. Uribe hit 13 homers and stole 22 bases in Class A last season and also participated in the Arizona Fall League.

Sosa has the best chance to stick as a backup infielder, but all appear to have long-term promise.

RECOMMENDATION REVIEW: Perez has increased his run producing numbers in each of the last seasons as he has become more comfortable in the major leagues. He could be expected to add stolen bases to his line, since he has the necessary speed. He gives special meaning to the term "every day player."

FLORIDA MARLINS

The Marlins have a gifted shortstop in Alex Gonzalez, but he lacks focus and has just gone through a horrific season. He hit .200 with 7 home runs and 42 RBI just a year after hitting .277 with 14 home runs and 52 RBI and making the All-Star team. Gonzalez has all the tools needed for him to be a star. He's very stubborn and hasn't been very coachable so far, which is his greatest problem. If he would listen to instruction and remain patient he could be a very good offensive player with some power and some speed. He's also got Gold Glove ability in the field, but mental lapses force him into making an unacceptable number of errors.

Andy Fox was re-signed this past offseason as insurance against another collapse by Gonzalez. Fox is more of a utility man by nature, but is a decent shortstop when called upon to play there. He's not much of a hitter, but does have some speed and could reach double-digits in steals if he can garner enough playing time.

The Marlins really don't have any top of the line shortstop prospects in their system unless they move Pablo Ozuna back from second base. The problem is that Ozuna's defense at shortstop could leave a lot to be desired.

RECOMMENDATION REVIEW: Gonzalez will have the job heading into Spring Training, but if he doesn't show marked improvement the Marlins will go to shortstop by committee. They could eventually trade for a shortstop, but they weren't ready to give up on Gonzalez as of the end of the 2000 season. He's worth looking into in most NL only leagues and could be a nice steal if he comes low in the draft or cheap in an auction.

HOUSTON ASTROS

Shortstop has been Houston's weakest offensive position for years. The 2001 season looks like more of the same. The Astros signed Jose Vizcaino as a free agent to solidify the position and he projects as the starter. Tim Bogar opened the 2000 season as the starter but, after a

disappointing year, became a free agent and was not resigned. Julio Lugo played in 60 games at shortstop for Houston in 2000 and his bat may get him that much playing time again. The shortstop of the future is Adam Everett who probably needs at least another half season at the Triple-A level.

Vizcaino, 33, split the 2000 season between the Dodgers and Yankees batting .251 with no home runs, 14 RBI and 6 stolen bases in 113 games. He has essentially no Rotisserie value but will be playing in his 13th major league season primarily because of his versatility and defensive skills. He qualifies at shortstop and second base and also appeared at the other 2 infield positions in 2000.

Lugo (covered in the second base section) considers himself a shortstop and prefers to play there. However, he been erratic both in the minors and majors and the Astros do not regard him as a full time regular at the position. Among the three shortstop candidates, he is by far the strongest offensively, with a clear advantage in both power and speed.

Everett, 24, was obtained from the Red Sox in the Carl Everett trade after the 1999 season. He is exceptionally strong defensively with great range, sure hands and a strong arm. He has been compared with former Astro shortstop, Roger Metzger, who had the same qualities. Unfortunately, Everett also appears to be carrying Metzger's weak bat.

Everett played at Triple-A New Orleans where he started very slowly in his first exposure at the Triple-A level. He batted .245 with 5 home runs, 37 RBI and 13 stolen bases. He was selected for the U.S. Olympic team and was the starting shortstop despite not getting his first hit in the Olympics until the final game.

RECOMMENDATION REVIEW: Lugo is the only Houston shortstop with Rotisserie value but he does not project as the starter so playing time is an issue.

LOS ANGELES DODGERS

Don't believe the Dodgers can go through a season with Alex Cora at shortstop? Well, they pretty much did last year.

It wasn't supposed to be that way. After moving Eric Young out of town and moving Mark Grudzielanek from shortstop to second, the Dodgers brought in Kevin Elster because they didn't think Cora was ready to play short-stop position every day. It turned out Elster couldn't hold the job. Cora, after bombing in a spring training audition, took it from him after being recalled at the end of May and wouldn't let go, although he tailed off badly at the end of the year. Of course, Cora could have hit .400 and Dodgers fans still would have set their sights on the other Alex Rodriguez.

First names are about the only things these Alexes have in common. Cora averages about 100 batting average points and 40 homers a year less than A-Rod. Although he has a flair for late-inning dramatics, he more often is overmatched by big-league pitchers. And he compliments his lack of power with a lack of basestealing ability. So if you're looking for offense at shortstop, look for the other Alex. If Cora plays, it will be because of his glove. He can make all the plays and a few he shouldn't.

So, what will the Dodgers do if Cora's average heads for the Mendoza line? There is no great option. First call might go to Hiram Bocachica, the former first-round pick of the Montreal Expos. The problem with Bocachica is that if he could play shortstop defensively, he probably wouldn't have been moved to center field. Of course, if he could play center field, he probably wouldn't have been moved to second base. Perhaps you get the point that Bocachica really doesn't have a position and shortstop isn't very likely, but his lively bat has kept the Dodgers interested enough to keep trying to find him a spot.

Like most teams, the Dodgers think highly of some of their shortstop prospects. Unlike many teams, the Dodgers don't have any near to being ready for the big leagues. The one in which they've invested the most is Jason Repko, a former first-round pick who hasn't exactly been on the fast track but is progressing and has some tools. The Dodgers think he has Paul Molitor-type tools, a slashing swing with longball power. But he is years away, and then only if he stays healthy.

RECOMMENDATION REVIEW: Unless he sud-denly turns into another version of his brother, Cora does not offer much offensively (single-digit homers and steals) other than he figures to play in a lot of games because his defense is so good. Bocachica would offer more produc-tion, but he probably won't get the chance. Repko is the name to follow, but it could be years before he sees the big leagues.

MILWAUKEE BREWERS

After floating around the infield as a super-utility player type for several years, Mark Loretta was finally ceded the regular shortstop position when Jose Valentin was dealt to the Chicago White Sox in one of GM Dean Taylor's shakier trades.

Certainly the rock-steady Loretta, now the senior mem-ber of the Brewers, had earned a shot at the position, unquestionably. Nor did he disappoint, committing just two errors in 377 total chances at the game's most challenging position for a major league leading .995 fielding percentage, although some range was sacrificed in the bargain.

In addition to the most consistent defense in the game, Loretta brings a huge measure of leadership to the organization both in the clubhouse and on the field and is as solid a citizen as you will find. Lo is a prototype #2 hitter who features excellent plate discipline and who is consid-ered one of the best right field hitters and bat handlers in the game.

For the first time in his career, Loretta missed significant time in 2000 when he fouled a pitch off his left foot and broke a bone in early June. He was out for over two months and was missed both offensively and defensively.

That being said, Loretta is a player whose numbers don't even come close to reflecting his actual value to a club. Loretta has gone deep just 25 times in nearly 2,000 career at-bats, covering parts of six seasons. He is virtually no threat to steal either, having pilfered a scant 21 bags in his career (0 in three attempts in 2000).

A late-season slump last year dropped Loretta's batting average to .281, but Lo is a career .292 hitter who is a good bet to develop into a consistent .300 hitter with his discipline and maturity.

Luis Lopez is the Brewers' primary backup at both middle infield positions. Lopez showed surprising pop last season but his reputation has been earned on the defensive side of the ball and he has below average speed for a middle infielder.

Santiago Perez got a shot at shortstop last year after Loretta's injury and had his ups and downs. Perez is a speedy switch-hitter with gap power who is still young enough at 25 to be considered a prospect. Perez, who was named MVP of the Triple-A World Series for the champion Indianapolis Indians, stole 35 bases in 43 attempts between Indianapolis and Milwaukee last year.

RECOMMENDATION REVIEW: Mark Loretta is a fine baseball player and a critical component of the Milwaukee Brewer baseball club both on and off the field. But the only thing to recommend him in the Rotisserie world is his batting average, which should stay consistently around the .300 level. He did hit seven home runs in 91 games last season, which may mean that his power is on the rise. (He has 25 for his six-year career.) He is no threat on the bases. By today's standards for shortstops, Loretta is a below average offensive performer and should be slotted as such. Barring injury, he will play every day. Luis Lopez is a career middle infield backup with little speed who showed virtually no power prior to the 2000 season. Speedy Santiago Perez might be worth keeping an eye on but may not get a lot of playing time if Loretta and Ron Belliard stay healthy.

MONTREAL EXPOS

Orlando Cabrera has never lived up to his billing as a top basestealing prospect. Once thought of as a potential 30-plus stolen base man, Cabrera has never had more than six in any of his four major league season. Mainly because of poor baserunning instincts and a poor on-base percentage (.295 lifetime). Instead he is more mesmerized by the longball. In order to hit the 13 home runs in 2000, a career high, Cabrera has sacrificed his average and just about every other category.

Cabrera's main short coming is an inability to hit the ball on the ground and use his speed to get on. Instead he hits too many lazy flyballs in order to hit a few more homers.

It would not be much of a surprise to see the Expos replace him in the near future. While it wasn't one of their top priorities during the winter, the team has not been thrilled with his play over the past few years. Cabrera has not showed any growth with maturity and has actually regressed since 1998.

Jeff Blum played a solid shortstop when Cabrera went down with injuries and it was with that opportunity that he show he could hit major league pitchers and play regularly. Unfortunately he does not have the range or glove to play there full-time making him a better fit at third base. See more on Blum in the third base section.

Thomas De la Rosa was expected to make the team as a backup middle infielder because of his glove. On a team with more money De la Rosa would probably see more minor league time, but the cash strapped Expos like using the young, inexpensive talent. He had a good showing during a September callup after a poor Triple-A season at the plate. He has little power and cannot be expected to hit for average.

On the horizon is the hot hitting Brandon Phillips. He has power/speed potential and hits for average. He still needs to work on his plate discipline and basestealing technique, but that should come along as he gains more experience. He has a solid glove and has the potential to be a 20/20 player in the majors. He is about two years away.

RECOMMENDATION REVIEW: Although Cabrera is entering his prime years, he will be 26 for the entire year, he has shown no signs of improvement at the plate. He is a lower rung Rotisserie pick at shortstop. Hype his past history as a stolen base threat and the fact that he is coming into his prime years. Maybe someone will over spend for him. The player you want here is the underrated, and like many Expos, unknown player, Jeff Blum. He would be a solid Rotisserie middle infielder if he is playing full-time at third for the Expos because he was eligible to be used at short. Keep an eye on his playing time during spring training. Phillips is a very good pick for an ultra team.

NEW YORK METS

Mike Bordick signed with his former team the Orioles during the offseason. Rey Ordonez will be the Mets starting shortstop.

After beginning the best offensive season of his 11-year major league career at Baltimore, Mike Bordick went to the Mets in a trade to fill the hole left by Rey Ordonez's broken arm. Bordick's combined totals were .285-20-80 with nine stolen bases. The power totals were career highs the 34-year-old righthanded batter may never match again.

Before he was injured, defensive whiz Rey Ordonez seemed to regress from even his own modest offensive performance. The righthanded batter, who's an old 28, finished just .188-0-9 in 133 at-bats.

Kurt Abbott was one of the stopgap shortstops the Mets used before they acquired Bordick. Abbott, 31, batted just .217-6-12, and was not a very effective pinch hitter.

Kevin Baez was the regular shortstop at Triple-A Norfolk (.278-5-50). The righthanded batter is 34. He completed his 150 at-bat major league trial eight years ago — and batted .179.

At Double-A Binghamton were the light-hitting Gabby Martinez (.248-2-12) and Gavin Jackson (.224-0-9).

RECOMMENDATION REVIEW: Bordick is the only shortstop in this group with any Rotisserie value, and he could be overpriced if people think he can at least match his 2000 season. He would have more value if he stayed in the National League.

PHILADELPHIA PHILLIES

How on earth, you say, can a team featuring the likes of Bobby Abreu, Scott Rolen, Mike Lieberthal and Pat Burrell in its everyday lineup finish last in the major leagues in runs scored? That's an easy one - how about first basemen named Rico Brogna and Travis Lee, second basemen named Mickey Morandini and Marlon Anderson, a center fielder named Doug Glanville, and shortstops named Desi Relaford and Tomas Perez. Though the Phils had yet to address their other offensive short-comings as winter fell, they feel that a needed offensive jolt will come from 22-year-old rookie shortstop Jimmy Rollins in 2001.

The Phils' second round pick in 1996, Rollins is a 5'8", 160, switch-hitter that has always ranked as one of the youngest players at each successive level of minor league competition. Don't be fooled by his relatively unexciting 2000 Triple-A numbers (.273, .336 OBP, .404 SLG), as he had to overcome a poor first two months to drag his numbers up to that level. His extra-base pop is solid for a middle infielder (28 doubles, 11 triples, 12 homers in 2000), and he hits the ball with surprising authority, considering his size, from both sides of the plate. The Phils envision him as a leadoff hitter, quite possibly right away this season. Don't expect him to be an immediate rousing success in that role, as he has never walked more than 52 times in a season or recorded a full-season on-base percentage higher than .341. Still, he should reasonably be expected to exceed that level quite soon, after he fully matures physically and mentally and is - for the first time in his life - no longer the youngest player at his level of competition. He runs extremely well and has above average baserunning instincts, and should quickly evolve into a 40 steal threat at the top of the Phils' lineup. Defensively, Rollins' range is a bit above average, and

though his throwing arm isn't cannon-like, it's plenty strong and he possesses a quick release.

Rollins capped his fine 2000 Triple-A season with 53 impressive major league at bats and a tour de force in the Arizona Fall League. New manager Larry Bowa is likely to see a bit of himself in Rollins, and will give him a very long leash. Down the road, Rollins could record a .400 OBP and steal 50 plus bases per season over an extended period. That's too much to ask for now, but a .280 average, a .350 OBP, 10 homers and 30 steals looks like a reasonable projection for 2001, and should put him squarely in the Rookie of the Year race. If you can add him to your roster for a reasonable price, go get him.

After Desi Relaford cleared waivers and escaped to San Diego last summer, the Phils gave Tomas Perez an extended trial as their starting shortstop. The Phils had tired of Relaford's inability to handle the routine play, and Perez did give them an upgrade in that area. Still, however, Perez' range left quite a bit to be desired, and he was actually a substantially more limited offensive player than Relaford. Perez, 27, unlike Relaford, swings at just about anything, and is virtually incapable of driving the ball for distance, though he did display career-best extra-base pop early in 2000 at the Triple-A level. Perez retains some value to the Phils, as he's an experienced veteran influence behind Rollins at shortstop who affords the Phils some maneuverability because of his ability to also play second and third base. However, his Rotisserie value is nil.

A spot will likely be available for Perez because of the departure via free agency of Alex Arias. A steady offensive player and versatile utility infielder for the Phils in 1998-99, Arias seemingly forgot how to hit in 2000. He's 33 now, about the age where average to below-average hitters tend to lose bat speed. His Rotisserie value can be summed up thusly - he has 16 homers and nine steals in his nine-year career, encompassing 1629 at bats.

Down on the farm, there are a couple of Phillies' shortstop prospects to watch. Nick Punto, 23, is a bit lacking in the raw skills department, but is a blood-and-guts/dirty-uniform type who draws walks, steals bases and slaps the ball around to all fields. In other words, the switch-hitter is a lot like his possible near-term manager, Larry Bowa. Look for Punto to be a fine utilityman in the majors beginning in 2002. Anderson Machado, 20, is a multiskilled athlete with a particularly high defensive upside. He's snazzier with the glove than even Rollins, but must make substantial strides with the bat to eventually challenge him for the starting major league job. He has decent pop to the gaps, fair plate discipline and excellent speed, but needs to make more consistent contact. Also a switch-hitter, Machado will be the regular Double-A shortstop in 2001 - his offensive performance there will go a long way toward projecting his eventual major league upside.

RECOMMENDATION REVIEW: Rollins will most likely start in 2001, but is most likely a year or two away from making an impact.

PITTSBURGH PIRATES

Quick: Who is the Bucs' starting shortstop?

Time's up. The answer is Pat Meares. He may be one of the least recognizable regular in the game today, but Meares is and has been a productive player for his big-league and Rotisserie teams alike. Usually capable of double-digit homers and decent batting average, plus a few steals, Meares is usually available near the end of the draft for a meager salary. He's steady and reliable; he won't win you any championships by himself, but he will give you positive value at a minimal price at a position where negative production is a common occurrence.

When Meares is not in the lineup, the Bucs have used utility infielder players like Mike Benjamin, Abraham Nunez and Enrique Wilson. Benjamin has marginal value. Nunez was once a prospect but has settled into a reserve role; ditto for Wilson, who was once an Indians prospect. Neither has much value although Wilson could be a positive-value player if he got to play regularly.

Jason Wood and Eddie Zosky shared much of Triple-A Nashville's shortstop duties neither is a prospect for any extended major league duty and also split time with Luis Figueroa. Figueroa is a better prospect, primarily for his glove and speed, though. In 94 games at Double-A Altoona, Figueroa hit .284 and stole 14 bases to earn a late-season promotion to Nashville. It's questionable if his offensive skills will carry to the majors, though. Jack Wilson and Shaun Skrehot also played some shortstop at Altoona. Skrehot is primarily an outfielder and Wilson, despite being added to the Pirates' 40 man roster over the winter, is not a great major league prospect. At lower levels, Vic Gutierrez, Luis Lorenzana and Jose Castillo filled the shortstop spot; none are considered top prospects.

RECOMMENDATION REVIEW: Meares is a good player for budget-conscious owners to pursue; he won't hurt you and will give you steady low-level production for a few bucks. None of the other Bucs' shortstops are worthy of drafting or selection for an Ultra roster.

ST. LOUIS CARDINALS

Edgar Renteria is one of the best all-around shortstops in baseball and he seems to be getting better every year. He's a Gold Glove caliber defensive player with good range and a strong arm, but it's his offense that gives him roto value. He's become a better hitter recently, drawing a few more walks than before and showing some more power. He hit .278 with 16 home runs, 76 RBI and 21 steals last year, which is productive for a middle infielder. He also hits right in front of guys like McGwire and Edmonds, which could lead to even better numbers in the future.

Placido Polanco figures to be the primary backup at shortstop, but because Renteria plays everyday that won't mean much. Polanco's value will come from playing several infield positions on an as-needed basis.

Shortstop prospect Jason Woolf is a fine player that should be a major league infielder before long. He's still on the raw side as a hitter, but he's got some pop in his bat and he runs exceptionally well, giving him something to work with. He also has above average defensive ability, but needs to be more consistent.

RECOMMENDATION REVIEW: You could do a lot worse than Renteria at shortstop, especially if McGwire and Edmonds are healthy for the full season in 2001. He's one of the more productive shortstops in the National League. Woolf is still a year or two away from the majors and isn't worth placing on your minor league roster, if you have one, until he shows more at the plate.

SAN DIEGO PADRES

Chris Gomez was lost for the season in June, but it was apparent well before that Gomez was no longer a part of the Padres' long-range plans. He had already been replaced, for all intents and purposes, by Damian Jackson and Kevin Nicholson. Gomez is a weak hitter and had no value to Rotisserie owners even when he was playing regularly. He has negative value now.

Jackson and Nicholson both spent more time at shortstop than at second base, but both are discussed at length as second basemen due to the offseason acquisition of Santiago Perez from Milwaukee. Acquired in exchange for pitcher Brandon Kolb, Perez is the most likely to win the Padres' starting shortstop job in the spring and he represents a great opportunity for Rotisserie owners who need to take chances. Because he hit so poorly in a month of play for the Brewers in 2000, he can easily be written off as a no-hit glove man. But, Perez CAN hit. He batted .275 with five homers and 34 RBI in 106 games for Triple-A Indianapolis. More importantly, he can run; Perez stole 31 bases in 39 tries at Indy. If he is as adept with the glove as he appears to be, Perez will stay in the lineup strictly for defense and, since speed never goes into a slump, he should be able to steal 20 bases just by playing regularly. Don't look for anything else positive for Rotisserie purposes, but get Perez for a buck at the end of the draft and enjoy a bunch of steals.

Light-hitting Desi Relaford also spent some time in the Padres' middle infield; he has since moved on to the Mets.

Kevin Nicholson and Ralph Millard held down the Triple-A Las Vegas Stars' shortstop job in 2000; both are discussed in the "Second Basemen" section.

At Double-A Mobile, Julius Matos hit .264 with 11 steals but is otherwise a mediocre prospect. He should shift into a utility role as he gets closer to the bigs.

Cristian Berroa has a lot of speed; he stole 30 bases for High-A Rancho Cucamonga. However, he didn't run the bases very intelligently, getting caught 16 times. Also, his relatively poor .329 on-base percentage was significantly padded by his getting hit by a pitch 17 times. He doesn't make very good contact at the plate and will have to improve dramatically to be considered a true prospect.

RECOMMENDATION REVIEW: Here's a great place for bargain hunters. Little-known and undervalued Santiago Perez has a chance to win and retain a regular shortstop job in San Diego, and could steal a bunch of bases. If he learns to make contact at the plate like he did in the minors, he could actually produce positive value as a hitter, too. In any case, he's a much better prospect than the usual group of non-hitters that populate the bottom of the player pool when it comes time to fill in the last infielder spot on your roster. Get him at the end of the draft for a buck and enjoy a fine bargain. This advice is applicable only to teams that need to take chances, though; get someone else if you need a sure thing.

SAN FRANCISCO GIANTS

At a time when there are so many great shortstops out there, it is easy to overlook Rich Aurilia. Still, the 29-year old has been among the league's most productive middle players, with back-to-back 20-homer years over 1999 and 2000. He is solid, but he is also a free agent, and though the Giants seem likely to re-sign him, they were also considering trading him for a steadier glove last summer.

Wherever he lands, Aurilia will deliver numbers similar to those of his past two seasons, hitting in the .270s. banging 20 or so homers, and driving in 75 (he doesn't steal), and he could even have a bigger year hiding within that body over one of the coming seasons. He is a good value in the $10-15 range.

The big question for San Francisco, is if Aurilia strays, who plays short? The Giants were interested in Rey Ordonez last summer, and with Mike Bordick in the Mets' wings, the defenseman may be available, although with marginal value.

Ramon E. Martinez is the top backup at short, and though he too could take over for a spell, Martinez projects as a utility player (he will start, most likely, and sometimes some at-bats are better than none).

Juan Melo hit .295-12-50 at Fresno last season, a marked improvement for the 24-year-old, but hitting at Fresno and in the majors is quite different. However, Melo was well thought of as part of the Padres system, so he is worth tracking (and couldn't hit worse than Ordonez).

Cody Ransom (.200-7-47) showed little as a full-timer at Shreveport, while Nelson Castro (.284-5-41, with 27 steals) fared better at Bakersfield last year, but neither has any value at this time.

RECOMMENDATION REVIEW: If you can't get one of the big three shortstops in a mixed league, Aurilla is a good choice. In an NL only league he is one of the top shortstops offensively. He'll give you about 20 HR and 80RBI with a pretty good average.

TOP 2001 HOME RUN HITTERS

NAME	HR
Rich Aurilia	20
Jose Hernandez	15
Julio Lugo	13
Edgar Renteria	13
Orlando Cabrera	12
Barry Larkin	12
Neifi Perez	11
Pat Meares	10
Kevin Elster	9
Alex Gonzalez	9

TOP 2001 RBI PRODUCERS

NAME	RBI
Rich Aurilia	77
Neifi Perez	70
Edgar Renteria	68
Jose Hernandez	62
Barry Larkin	54
Julio Lugo	54
Orlando Cabrera	53
Ricky Gutierrez	52
Tony Womack	51
Mark Loretta	50
Alex Cora	48
Rey Ordonez	48
Rafael Furcal	44
Alex Gonzalez	44
Desi Relaford	44
Damian Jackson	42
Bill Spiers	42
Pat Meares	40
Placido Polanco	40

TOP 2001 RUN SCORERS

NAME	RUN
Rafael Furcal	104
Julio Lugo	99
Tony Womack	99
Neifi Perez	96
Edgar Renteria	92
Barry Larkin	84
Damian Jackson	70
Rich Aurilia	67
Ricky Gutierrez	66
Mark Loretta	63
Jose Hernandez	62
Alex Cora	58
Orlando Cabrera	53
Desi Relaford	52
Placido Polanco	51

TOP 2001 BASESTEALERS

NAME	SB
Tony Womack	54
Rafael Furcal	48
Damian Jackson	33
Edgar Renteria	28
Julio Lugo	27
Barry Larkin	20
Jimmy Rollins	15
Desi Relaford	11
Adam Everett	9
Chris Sexton	9
Andy Fox	8
Ricky Gutierrez	8
Bill Spiers	8

TOP 2001 BATTING AVERAGES

NAME	AVG
Rafael Furcal	.305
Barry Larkin	.295
Jack Wilson	.294
Julio Lugo	.293
Mark Loretta	.290
Neifi Perez	.284
Edgar Renteria	.282
Bill Spiers	.277
Santiago Perez	.276
Rich Aurilia	.274
Tony Womack	.274
Ricky Gutierrez	.271
Jimmy Rollins	.270

STRATEGIES FOR OUTFIELDERS AND DH's

Portfolio Management

by John Benson

Your five outfield slots are 36% of your hitting assets. Even after allowing some money for position scarcity at catcher or middle infield, you will still probably want to spend about $60 on outfielders. There is a good reason to try to stay under this level (adjusted for inflation of course; $60 worth of outfielders can easily cost $80 after all the low-price freezes are taken into account). Fixing an outfield problem is easier than fixing a problem at any other position, because there are so many outfielders. Needing a catcher or shortstop after an injury, you might be tempted to take a .238-hitting, low-power, low-speed free agent and hope for the best, or even trade for such a player. That kind of thinking won't happen with the outfield population, or at least it shouldn't happen.

The first step in getting oriented is to forget about obtaining any particular outfielder. We all got into the habit (I did, anyway) of focusing on Barry Bonds (NL) and Ken Griffey (AL) during the 1990's. We were motivated by the observation that whoever had Bonds or Griffey would often have the best overall offense. Although such observations were consistent with the theory that massive combinations of speed and power in one roster spot will have a significant non-linear value from extremely high marginal utility, that theory is not the way to explain the Bonds-Griffey success phenomenon. The non-linear, exponential accumulation of value is real, but it can be measured as having no more then $1 or $2 effect, even with Bonds or Griffey in their prime. But that is another essay.

The reason for the 1990's Bonds-Griffey success phenomenon is mainly that the extremely high-value players, in an auction environment with high inflation, can achieve real auction values which seem unthinkable and thus are never approached in real bidding. A $45 player with 50% inflation (commoner than most people think) really is worth $67 and with a 99% optimal bid should actually sell for that. Most of us run into a psychological barrier soon after passing $50. Investing one fifth of your team money in one twenty-third of your players (or one twenty-fifth of

your players in the NL) just doesn't seem to make sense, although arithmetic can prove its rationality. Thus we have seen a $65 (inflated) Bonds or Griffey going for (say) $51 year after year for a decade, and note the success that follows. Give a smart guy $14 extra to spend for hitting on draft day, and he will consistently get the best offense, even with some bad luck. That $14 will buy one whole everyday productive outfielder, sometimes even a star, in place of a benchwarmer.

One piece of illumination for 2001 in the above caution about wanting one particular player, is that the highest-value players with high inflation can really be worthy of bids over $50. While Bonds and Griffey are long-faded, Johnny Damon is just coming into his own, and Vladimir Guerrero at $35 is a conservative, uninflated estimate (he is just age 25 this year and will be on the age 26-and-under surge list for yet another year after 2001). So the point is to recognize real in-auction values, and for goodness sake, do not try to guess or estimate what your draft inflation is. Calculate it! (Or get my draft software and let me calculate it for you.) Guesses with a price range of plus or minus $5 to $10 simply won't do for the highest value players.

There is one rational reason to avoid the $50+ bids, and that is simply the risk of all eggs in one basket. A broken arm or torn ACL can happen to anyone, even a DH. The avoidance of $60 players will fit well with the method of not focusing on any big star. Just tell others in your league about draft inflation, and get two or more bidders thinking $60 when the moment arrives. Given the talent available among outfielders, and the likelihood of a $1 catcher (or two) and a $1 MI, many owners will push their outfield budget to $70-$75 or even higher, and wisely. There is no maximum if you are doing OK with cheapies at other positions.

If not pursuing any specific big names, then what? Begin with an idea that you will get your share of the stars. Focus on youth: guys who haven't yet had their career year; give yourself opportunities for pleasant surprises. Be willing to bid aggressively on the most talented players under age 28. And don't be afraid to run out of money. When you have only $1 or $4 to spend on each of your remaining vacant slots, you will have to use all of your knowledge, and you will make wise picks. So leave room (or make room) for some low-priced players. Following are some specific recommendations.

In the Young Stars department: Vladimir Guerrero, Bob Abreu, Andruw Jones, Preston Wilson, Richard Hidalgo, Geoff Jenkins, J.D. Drew, Juan Pierre, Lance Berkman, Jay Payton, Richard Hidalgo, Richie Sexson and Mark Kotsay in the National League; and in the American League, Damon, Darrin Erstad, Roger Cedeno, Magglio Ordonez, Shannon Stewart, Carlos Lee, Gabe Kapler, Jermaine Dye, Juan Encarnacion, Mark Quinn, Terrence Long, Carlos Beltran and Ruben Mateo.

In the bargain basement after your money is (almost) gone, try some of these guys: Torii Hunter, Ricky Ledee, Steve Cox, Adam Piatt, Trot Nixon, Jeremy Giambi, Jason Tyner, Russ Branyan, Jose Guillen and Vernon Wells in the American League; and in the National League, Daryle Ward, Travis Lee, Peter Bergeron, Wilton Guerrero, Corey Patterson, Alex Escobar, Fernando Seguignol, Reggie Taylor, Emil Brown and Roosevelt Brown, to give some examples.

Here is one $70 budget you don't want: five $14 players, or any combination of prices where all of them are over $10. Why not? Because there cannot be any great bargains in such an outfield. (And you won't have a throw-in outfielder for making change in trades.) I am not saying I wouldn't fill my fifth and final outfield slot with Jay Payton or Pat Burrell for $10, but I am saying that it would make me uncomfortable, later in the draft, if good outfielders selling for $2 and $3, and I couldn't bid on them because all my slots were filled. Try to keep your final outfield slot open as long good outfielders remain untaken.

Good athletic outfielders tend to be interchangeable parts. Most center fielders can also play left or right. Most right fielders can also play left, and some of them are fine in center. Most left fielders, on the other hand, are dispensable types who can sit down for a day or a week, or a month. When a manager wants to shake up his batting order, or give a youngster a chance to start, the outfield (and left field especially) is the first place most managers will look for flexibility. So lean toward center and right, and away from left field, if all other factors are close when choosing an outfielder.

An injury to any of three outfielders will mean a promotion for the fourth in line, and the fifth then gets increased usage as a reserve. It pays to know who the fourth and fifth outfielders are. They don't make the starters' charts and aren't featured in the spring training magazines. This year those names include Troy O'Leary, Orlando Palmeiro, Wil Cordero, Russ Branyan, Dee Brown, Denny Hocking, Glenallen Hill, Shane Spencer, Jeremy Giambi, Steve Cox, Randy Wynn, Jason Tyner, Jose Guillen, Ricky Ledee, Chad Curtis and Vernon Wells in the American League, and in the National League, Dave Martinez, Danny Bautista, Corey Patterson, Damon Buford, Wilton Guerrero, Michael Tucker, Terry Shumpert, Daryle Ward, Glen Barker, Devon White, Marquis Grissom, Fernando Seguignol, Timoniel Perez, Alex Escobar, Travis Lee, Brian L. Hunter, John Vander Wal, Adrian Brown, Emil Brown, Chad Hermansen, Bubba Trammell, Ruben Rivera, Eric Davis and Shawon Dunston.

Finally, in the AL you may be required to take a player who qualifies at DH based on 20 games played there in 2000. Do not build your team around the DH slot. With a long enough list, you can use it as an afterthought. Go for players who qualify at two or three positions to keep some roster flexibility (i.e. let someone else have Harold Baines this year).

AMERICAN LEAGUE OUTFIELDERS

ANAHEIM ANGELS

Garret Anderson, Darin Erstad and Tim Salmon are coming off fine seasons as front line outfielders for Anaheim, and will continue as the primary starters.

Anderson came into his own last season, setting personal bests in the power categories without a substantial decline in his batting average. For the last five years, Anderson has been a model of consistency: at least 150 games played, over 600 at bats and an average between .285 and .303. He is firmly entrenched in center field for the Angels. Anderson will bat in the middle of the lineup, most likely fifth, as his on base average isn't all that hot. For the upcoming season, expect a year in line with Anderson's trend - a .295 batting average with 28 home runs, 95 RBI and five steals.

Darin Erstad had the worst year he could possibly have in 1999, and the best year he could possibly have last season. For this season, expect something in the middle, as Erstad will be extremely hard pressed to come up with a repeat performance. Erstad will play every day in left field, and lead off for the Angels. He should hit for average with moderate power, steal bases and score runs in bunches. A reasonable expectation would be .300, with 18 home runs, 88 RBI, 110 runs scored and 17 steals.

Tim Salmon is the Angels' right fielder and cleanup hitter. Last fall, he had his left (non-throwing) shoulder and his right foot operated on, to relieve nagging problems that hampered him last season. He was expected to be ready for spring training, and if the surgeries are successful, Salmon could have one of his better years ahead. When healthy, Salmon has always provided a dependable power/average combination, and is usually among the league leaders in walks. Although it seems as if he's been around forever, he'll only be 32 on Opening Day. Salmon should hit near .300 with over 30 homers and well over 100 RBI this season if can stay off the DL.

Orlando Palmeiro is the primary backup outfielder for Anaheim. He plays both corner outfield positions, but is strictly a singles and, occasionally, doubles hitter. In nearly 1,000 career at bats, he has one home run. To put it in perspective, light-hitting teammates Gary DiSarcina and Kevin Stocker have gone deep nine times as frequently in their careers as has Palmeiro. What Palmeiro does offer is an ability to make contact and hit in the high .200s, but for Rotisserie purposes, most teams need at least a little pop or some steals in the fifth outfield spot.

Edgard Clemente is a candidate for the fifth outfield spot, but has zero discipline at the plate. He doesn't hit for average and has scant power. Although he runs well, Clemente doesn't steal bases. The Angels will, in all likelihood, find better options and so should you.

Jeff DaVanon missed the entire 2000 season due to a shoulder injury. He has some speed, plays good defense and hits for a solid batting average. He would not be likely to get much more than 150 at-bats as a fifth outfielder.

The Angels' system is loaded with so-so outfielders, some of whom could see some time with the big club this season. Scott Morgan, a tall righthanded hitter, was claimed off waivers from the Indians' organization last year. Morgan has good power, but is below average in other respects. He's also a bit old to be a prime prospect. Anaheim has several speedsters in the system who may not hit well enough to advance. Elpidio Guzman and Nathan Haynes are raw youngsters who are at least a couple of years away. Guzman has blazing speed (53 steals at Class A last year) and Haynes is an exceptional athlete who's trying to learn the craft of baseball. Juan Tolentino is a Triple-A speedster who could get a brief cup of coffee under the right circumstances.

RECOMMENDATION REVIEW: Anderson is a solid value; you should get what you pay for. Erstad will probably be slightly overbid based on last year, but is an across-the-board talent. Salmon may be primed for a big year, and is crossing the border into "unsexy player" territory, so he could be a slight bargain. You should be able to do better than Palmeiro for a buck. Clemente and the other outfield candidates from the Angels' farm system this year.

Lacking a full-time DH, the Angels used a variety of players at the DH position last year, and that could be the case this season as well. Scott Spiezio, a switch-hitter, will get a fair share of the DH duties. He is discussed with the first basemen. Mo Vaughn (first base), Tim Salmon, Darin Erstad and Orlando Palmeiro (outfield) will also get an occasional chance to DH. If he makes the club, Shawn Wooten (discussed with the catchers) would have some value as a third catcher/part-time DH.

BALTIMORE ORIOLES

The Orioles 2001 outfield will look much different than it did last year. The overall team youth movement resulted in the trade of veteran B.J. Surhoff, and the shifting of Delino DeShields from second base to the outfield to make room for young second baseman Jerry Hairston. Albert Belle's deteriorating hip condition greatly reduced his production last year. Center fielder Luis Matos was a promising rookie who got substantial playing time.

Albert Belle is normally the regular right fielder, but his hip condition has been likened to that that shelved Bo Jackson. A hip replacement like Jackson's means the end of an athletic career. Belle has a huge long-term contract, and owner Peter Angelos would prefer him to retire on a disability and have the insurance company pick up the contract.

Belle was hurting last year, but to his credit no complaints or whining was heard. His power disappeared around mid-year, shown by his going over 130 at-bats without a home run. If his hip holds up for 2001, it still may not be good enough for him to play the outfield, and he will most likely spend most of his time at DH. However, the last time he had significant playing time at DH was in his Cleveland days when he showed that he didn't have the mental makeup to be a DH. He needs to be into the game mentally to be a productive hitter, and the only way to do that is to play a position. As a full-time DH, Belle could easily slip below .250, and even down to the .220 area with a loss of run production. There is great uncertainty about Belle's performance in 2001, and he should be avoided in Rotisserie. Let someone else take the risk.

After an injury-plagued 1999, Delino DeShields had an excellent comeback year last season, earning the "Most Valuable Oriole" trophy from local sports journalists. The Cardinals considered moving him to the outfield a few years ago, so the Orioles move wasn't new. Although he played some center last year, he is best suited for left field, and should be the starter in 2001. Another good season was expected from him, and his Rotisserie value is primarily in his stolen bases. With fewer stolen bases being available in the American League because of Kenny Lofton not running as much, and Rickey Henderson nearing retirement, DeShields becomes more valuable because of the supply-and-demand situation.

Rookie Luis Matos was prematurely jumped to the majors last year as the Orioles went overboard with their youth movement. He's a pure center fielder with good speed and defense. He hit .271-2-33 with 14 stolen bases in Double-A last year, a solid year, but not nearly enough to warrant a promotion to the majors. He was overmatched with the Orioles, especially against righthanders, and he's likely to spend most of 2001 in Triple-A, earning a promotion if his hitting comes around. Matos is only 22, and is a potential five-tool star and a valuable Rotisserie player because of his stolen bases, but he needs to improve his hitting.

Brady Anderson has a large long-term contract, and center field is his normal slot. If Belle is on the DL or moved to DH, then Anderson will likely move to right field with DeShields playing center. Anderson has lost a step or two in recent years, and his career is in the declining years. He had an up-and-down season last year, hitting a solid .287 in May, followed by a weak .205 in June; and a weak .222 in August, followed by .308 on September. The Orioles shopped him around late last year, but there were no takers. He's now a .250-area hitter with some home run pop, but a long way from his 50 dingers of some years ago. Anderson will have a hard time getting 15 homers and 15 stolen bases.

Veteran Jeff Conine is the reserve outfielder, but he doesn't have the range to play center. He also plays first, third, and DH, and gets 350-400 at-bats, hitting around .280 with a dozen homers and 40-50 RBI. Speedster Eugene Kingsale seems to get injured every year, but if he's healthy he can swipe a ton of bases. But he hasn't proven that he can hit major league pitching, and he can't steal if he can't get on base.

Karim Garcia hits well in the minors, showing good power in Triple-A. But he's failed in numerous trials with the Dodgers, Diamondbacks, Tigers, and Orioles. He now has over 700 major-league at-bats, hitting .220-24-83. Garcia is looking more and more like a Triple-A all-star who can't hit major league pitching. The Orioles left him off their 40-man roster; so another club may pick him up. He's still only 25, so he could still make the necessary adjustments and hit the better pitching.

Over the winter, the Orioles announced that Melvin Mora will be the center fielder. He's the incumbent shortstop, but the Orioles found that he is not the answer at shortstop. Mora is covered in the shortstop section.

Zaire-born Ntema "Papy" Ndungidi is an excellent prospect. He's very athletic, but his baseball skills are a little rough, although he's getting much smoother as he gets more experience. He's already shown some power, and he should develop more as he matures. Ndungidi has a great upside potential, but he's about two years away from challenging for a major league job. Prospect Darnell McDonald struggled in Double-A last year, and is not making progress as quickly as the Orioles would like. Tim Raines, Jr. has his father's speed but needs to hit more to make it to the majors.

RECOMMENDATION REVIEW: The Orioles 2001 starting outfield will likely be Delino DeShields in left, Brady Anderson in right, and Melvin Mora in center. Mora and DeShields are the best Rotisserie values, and Anderson can provide some offense. Albert Belle is a big risk and should be avoided.

BOSTON RED SOX

Manny Ramirez was one of the bigger free agent signings of the winter. He will start in right field and also see some time at DH. Ramirez is an offensive machine and will not be effected much by the change in parks -- even though Fenway is not as good of a hitters park as the Jake. Ramirez' RBI totals and batting average may rise as he peppers the Green Monster with line drives. See more on Ramirez in the Indians outfielders section.

The Red Sox planned to bring back Carl Everett, who had one of the most eventful, bizarre and productive seasons in the majors in 2000. His wacky views and his run-ins with umpires, teammates and manager Jimy Williams brought Everett more attention than the play that made him a viable MVP candidate at the All-Star break. At that point, he was batting .326-24-69. However, the 30-year-old switch hitter tailed off to finish at .300-24-100, with 11 stolen bases. He was Boston's best center fielder in years.

Troy O'Leary also had personal setbacks last season. The 1999 playoff hero plummeted to .261-13-70. At 31, the lefthanded batter still could bounce back.

Boston's starting outfielders all are interesting studies. The most intriguing may be Trot Nixon, who one day seems ready to blossom into a star and the next appears destined to be a career disappointment. Last year, he batted .276-12-60, and stole eight bases (third on the team). Most important, he learned how to hit lefthanders. At 26, Nixon may be ready to break through.

Darren Lewis began the season platooning in right field with Nixon, but by season's end was filling in more often for Everett. The 33-year-old Lewis' game has been built on defense and speed, but he stole just 10 bases in 2000. He batted just .241-2-17.

Midre Cummings, 29, joined the Red Sox for the stretch drive as primarily a lefthanded pinch hitter and DH. His season total for 206 at-bats was .277-4-24.

Bernard Gilkey also was a late-season acquisition. The 34-year-old righthanded batter was a shadow of his Cardinals self, batting just .231-1-9 with the Red Sox.

Israel Alcantara was another head case in the Red Sox outfield for part of last season. The 27-year-old right-handed power hitter made his major league debut last season, but infuriated Williams with his indifferent attitude toward his job. Alcantara, who also played first base and DH, batted .289-4-7 for Boston and .308-29-76 for Triple-A Pawtucket.

James Chamblee, who began his career as a shortstop

and moved to second base, was the regular right fielder at Pawtucket last season. The 25-year-old righthanded batter finished at .258-17-56. However, the gangly size (6'4", 175) that made it difficult for him as a middle infielder, also contributed to 129 strikeouts last season.

Curtis Pride finished the season in the Boston organization. He batted .303-10-35 and stole 15 bases in the International League, but just .250 in 20 at-bats with the big club. The weak-armed veteran is little more than a fringe major leaguer.

Former Dodger Garey Ingram, 30, spent his second season in Pawtucket's outfield, batting .238-10-26. If a team is desperate for a righthanded-hitting outfielder, it can find Ingram.

Rontrez Johnson, a 24-year-old righthanded batter, offers some excitement from the Boston farm system. At Double-A Trenton, he batted .269-6-53 with 30 steals.

Virgil Chevalier also had a good year at Trenton (.309-7-67). However, the chunky (6'2", 240-pound) righthanded batter is 27. He has been at Trenton for three seasons, and should have more power than he has shown.

Tonayne Brown is another outfielder with speed on the way up. And as baseball's new stadiums pass Fenway Park's offensive potential, the Sox may be needing to move away from power toward speed. At high Class A Sarasota, Brown batted .272-2-40 with 33 steals. He's a 23-year-old righthanded batter.

RECOMMENDATION REVIEW: Expect another big season from Manny if he stays healthy for a full season. Nixon is the lowest-risk, highest-potential-reward Boston outfielder. Everett clearly can produce the most, but he also could self-destruct and provide little value at a high price. O'Leary may never get back to his prime — which was nice, but good for little more than a fourth Rotisserie outfielder. None of the 2000 reserves is a good bet for even as much playing time as last season. Johnson could be worth an Ultra roster spot.

CHICAGO WHITE SOX

Carlos Lee has emerged as one of the best young hitters in the American League. He can hit for both average and power, though the 24 home runs he hit during the 2000 season will be on the low end for his career -- he has the ability to reach 40 someday. He's a clutch run producer

that will drive in runs at virtually every opportunity and is also an opportunistic base stealer, having swiped 13 bags in 17 attempts last year. His defense is pretty awful, but his bat will surely keep him in the lineup. On many teams Lee would be a fourth or fifth hitter, but even hitting sixth or seventh for the White Sox provides him with plenty of RBI chances.

Chris Singleton is a good defensive player with some pop and good speed, but he may be destined for a role as a fourth outfielder in the future. He doesn't walk enough to hit near the top of the order and he doesn't have the power to hit in the middle of the lineup, so he'll always be a guy that's on the verge of being replaced. Center field is a strong offensive position in the major leagues and with the White Sox searching for someone that can bat leadoff and allow Ray Durham to hit second, Singleton's future is up in the air. He's been a good player for the Sox, but isn't guaranteed anything.

To put it simply, Magglio Ordonez is one of the very best hitters in baseball today. He's a young Edgar Martinez at the plate, but he's got good speed and is an excellent right fielder. Ordonez hit .315 with 32 home runs, 126 RBI and 18 steals while striking out just 64 times in nearly 600 at-bats. A power hitter that makes contact is the rarest of gems and Ordonez is only going to get better. He's got the swing to challenge for a batting title someday, he's got middle of the order power and he runs the bases extremely well. There aren't many players who provide more for their teams, roto or major league.

Jeff Abbott is a professional hitter that seems to have overcome his horrendous slump from 1999, but he doesn't have much power or speed and probably won't be a full-time player because of those factors. He was traded to the Marlins for outfielder Julio Ramirez. See more on Ramirez in the Marlins outfielders section.

McKay Christensen, Brian Simmons and Jeff Liefer all have a chance to figure into the mix for the backup outfielder spots.

Christensen runs like the wind and can run down pretty much anything in center field, but he's a weak hitter with little patience and no power. Simmons has some speed and some pop, but injuries have held him back. He can be a strong fourth outfielder, however, because he's a switch-hitter that can play all three outfield spots. Liefer is the slugger in the group and because he's lefthanded he may get a chance to play in the White Sox' heavily righthanded lineup -- he could also figure into the mix at first base and designated hitter.

The White Sox also have two top-notch outfield prospects, though neither was expected to have an impact at the major league level this season. Aaron Rowand, who some scouts have compared to a young Tim Salmon, has good power and speed but still needs to improve as a hitter. Joe Borchard is a top outfield prospect with power.

RECOMMENDATION REVIEW: Ordonez is an elite player and should be snatched up as quickly as possible because his production is still on the upswing. Lee is also a top flight run producer worthy of a spot on any rotisserie team. Singleton is a good player, but more of a late pickup than anything else -- his job could be in jeopardy. Abbott is a nice player to have if you're in a deep AL only league, but Simmons and Christensen don't seem to have a shot at much playing time. Keep an eye on Liefer, he could figure into the mix at multiple positions. If your league allows you to have prospects on your roster, both Rowand and Borchard are worthy pickups, though Borchard has mega-star potential and Rowand does not.

CLEVELAND INDIANS

The Indians signed Juan Gonzalez during the offseason. See more on Gonzalez in the Tigers outfielders section.

Injuries to Indians outfielders provided playing time for many last year. In addition to the regulars at last season's onset, Richie Sexson, Kenny Lofton and Manny Ramirez, the Tribe played Jacob Cruz, Mark Whiten, Dave Roberts, Russell Branyan, Jolbert Cabrera, David Segui, Chan Perry, and Bill Selby.

The Indians signed free agent Ellis Burks to play right field when the possibility of signing incumbent Manny Ramirez looked hopeless. Now 36, he has played in 119, 142, 120 and 122 games over the past four years. But they have been in the National League without the benefit of the rest provided by the DH. His batting average was settling in the .280-290 range until he hit an unexpected .344 last year, defying predictability. His quick bat still generates enough power for 20-30 homers and at least 85 RBI. He was once a 20-30 per year stolen-base man, but to protect his health, he runs very little these days. He should have a good year with the Indians, given some DH time and other selected rest.

Following his shoulder injury in the 1999 playoffs and subsequent surgery, center fielder Kenny Lofton wasn't

expected to return to form until mid-year last season. But he surprised everyone, and came back strongly. However, on the side of caution, he didn't run with the abandon of past years. With RBI machine Manny Ramirez driving him in with extra base hits, he didn't need to swipe as many bases as in other years when he swiped over 50 bases, often reaching the 60-75 levels. With Ramirez out of the lineup, he will be called on to run more, and could reach 50 stolen bases again.

Richie Sexson patrolled left field until he was traded to the Brewers. Wil Cordero was acquired from the Pirates to play left, but he was injured and rookie Jolbert Cabrera got his opportunity. Cordero will be the left fielder in 2001. He's only 29, and has many good years still ahead of him. He usually hits in the .280-290 range with enough power for 15-20 homers, but he doesn't get many RBI, probably because of his position down in the batting order. He's also a free swinger, not getting many base on balls. In Rotisserie, Cordero may go for less than he is really worth and can thus be valuable.

Following the injury to Manny Ramirez, David Segui was obtained from the Rangers to play right field and some first base. He had his career best year last season, hitting .334-19-103, the first time he has reached the 100-RBI mark. His .510 slugging percentage was also a career high. A switch hitter, in recent years, he has hit righthanders about 30 points higher than lefties. He has a great glove at first base, and can also play right and left field. He is 34, and could easily have another good year. Segui's Rotisserie value comes from his good batting average, homers and RBI. Just don't expected his batting average to be so high again.

Manny Ramirez is a run-producing machine. Last year, a bad hamstring injury limited him to only 118 games. But in those 118 games, he hit .351 and drove in 122 runs, averaging more than a RBI per game. He was especially tough in the clutch, shown by his hitting .354 with runners in scoring position, and an incredible .444 when the games are close and in the late innings. It was his second great year in a row, following his outstanding 1999 season when he hit .333-44-165. He batted cleanup, following Kenny Lofton, Omar Vizquel and Roberto Alomar setting the table in front of him, and slugger Jim Thome following him. Lofton, Vizquel and Alomar are all excellent hitters with good on-base-percentages, and can steal bases to get into scoring position. Thome provided some protection in the order, so opposing pitchers were less likely to walk Ramirez to pitch to Thome. Without taking away any credit from him, he is less likely to have such great years in a lineup without such hitters around him. Ramirez is 28, so he can easily have another career-best year, but 1999 will be difficult to beat. See more on Ramirez in the Red Sox outfielders section.

Russell Branyan is earmarked for more outfield duty in 2001. He was tried in right field for a few games last season, and since left and center are anchored by regulars, it's right for him, plus whatever DH at-bats he can muster. Lack of making contact is his big problem, and this leads to bunches of strikeouts and wasted at-bats. To show the magnitude of the problem, he played in Triple-A for parts of 1999 and 2000, and struck out an incredible 47 and 41 percent of the time. With the Indians last year, he whiffed 39 percent of the time, despite being platooned. He bats left and has tape-measure home run power when he makes contact. He's only 25, so he can improve dramatically overnight, or he can become the next Rob Deer. The strikeouts will keep Branyan's batting average below .240, thus ruining the Rotisserie value that is produced by his home runs and RBI.

The Tribe is also ear marking Jacob Cruz for sharing right field and DH with Burks and Branyan. Cruz is 28 and a lefthanded hitter who has had some good years in the minors, hitting for a good average and showing a little power. He was formerly in the Giants organization, getting into about 50 major league games in 1996-98, hitting a weak .207 in 106 at-bats. He's hit much better in the 43 games that he got into with the Indians in 1999 and 2000. He would have played more last year, but he injured his knee causing him to miss most of the season. It remains to be seen how he would hit in the majors, given extended playing time, but his minor league hitting provides a clue that he could hit major league pitching for a decent average, say .260-280. Cruz doesn't steal bases, so his Rotisserie value derives from his average.

Speedy Dave Roberts is another outfielder in the mix, and he's number six when counting Lofton, Cordero, Branyan, Cruz and Burks. Roberts is 28, and is largely a singles hitter who has hit well in the high minors, with a decent average but with no power. He has stolen base speed, swiping 39 in the past years in Triple-A. He hit a weak .238 with the Indians last year, swiping 11 in 143 at-bats. Nevertheless, his good Triple-A hitting record provides a clue that he can hit major league pitching. He can play center, and is also a good pinch runner. Roberts will never become another Kenny Lofton, but he has a little Rotisserie value, coming from his stolen bases.

Jolbert Cabrera played all three outfield positions last

year, plus second and short. He's the Tribe's all-around utility man. He's 28, and was a marginal major leaguer until last year when he got 175 at-bats, hitting .251-2-15. He doesn't have any power, but can steal some bases. He's had some good years in Triple-A, hitting for a good average with good plate discipline.

"Hard hittin" Mark Whiten isn't hitting hard anymore, and he had several adventures with flyballs while in center field. He was another stopgap measure, and is not in the Indians plans for 2001.

Following the recent emergence of Richie Sexson and Russell Branyan, the Tribe doesn't have anymore good prospects in the pipeline in the minors. Chan Perry, Jon Hamilton and Chad Whitaker may see some playing time in Jacobs Field, but they will be reserve outfielders or injury fill-ins. They don't have any upside potential.

RECOMMENDATION REVIEW: Manny Ramirez is a valuable run producing machine, and will likely be overpriced in many Rotisserie leagues. David Segui quietly continues to have good years, and he's likely to be undervalued. Based on his stolen bases and good hitting, Kenny Lofton is the most valuable Indians outfielder. He could step it up to swipe more bases, reaching the 50 level again. Ellis Burks is good for 120 games, but with selective rest and DH play, he could get into more games and become more valuable. Once a triple threat, he doesn't steal many bases now to avoid injury. But he can still drive the ball with power, collecting a high number of RBI. Cordero will most likely be undervalued, and is a good Rotisserie pickup. Strikeout king Russell Branyan is a low-average power hitter, and his low average keeps his Rotisserie value down. Dave Roberts swipes bases, and has some Rotisserie value.

DETROIT TIGERS

The Tigers' best outfielder, by far, is Bobby Higginson. He rebounded in 2000 to post numbers more consistent with what he did during the early years of his career. He hit .300 with 30 home runs and 102 RBI last year while also displaying a strong, accurate arm from the outfield. He can play either left or right field, depending on what kind of players the Tigers put out there with him. In a perfect world Higginson would be a right fielder because of his throwing ability. Now that he's healthy, you can expect him to be a consistent middle of the order run producer that will also steal you a few bases here and there.

Juan Encarnacion has the most physical talent in the Tigers' outfield and he's capable of playing all three outfield spots. He runs well enough to be a center fielder and throws like a right fielder, which is always nice. His offense has gotten better since his arrival to the majors, though he hasn't shown the kind of power the Tigers think he should. Encarnacion has the ability to be a 30-30 hitter, though the home runs will be more difficult for him in spacious Comerica Park if the fences aren't brought in. He's not a sure-thing for roto owners, but he's got a lot of potential and would be worth a look after the big name players are gone.

The Tigers received center fielder Roger Cedeno from the Astros to replace free agent Juan Gonzalez who was signed by the Indians. The Tigers were expected to start Cedeno in center and move Encarnacion to right. See more on Cedeno in the Astros outfielders section.

Gonzalez was a free agent and there were many questions about his degenerative back. When his back isn't keeping him out of the lineup, Gonzalez is a power hitter that can drive the ball to all fields and an RBI machine. The problem is, Gonzalez always seems to be hurt or unhappy about something. If he's healthy, he's definitely one of the game's premier offensive players.

Billy McMillon, who had a strong showing at Triple-A Toledo last year, and Wendell Magee were also expected to compete for outfield spots in Detroit. McMillon could start and bat near the top of the order if the Tigers fail in their attempt to either sign Gonzalez or trade for a more proven leadoff man. Magee is more of a reserve player at this point, spelling the regulars from time-to-time.

As far as prospects go, the Tigers have a few worth noting. Chris Wakeland hit 28 home runs at Triple-A Toledo last season, but struckout nearly once in every three at-bats. He's a lefthanded hitter, however, and he could earn a job in Spring Training if he hits well. Rod Lindsay is a speedster who struggled to hit double-A pitching last year, so don't expect more than a cup of coffee for him in 2001. Further on down the line is switch-hitting speed man Andres Torres. He hit .295 with 65 steals at high-A Lakeland last year and he could be the Tigers' center fielder of the future.

RECOMMENDATION REVIEW: Higginson is a sure thing, Encarnacion is a bit of a risk with a big upside and everyone else is up in the air. If Gonzalez winds up healthy, he's one of the best offensive players in the league and might be a bargain given his lack of perfor-

mance last year. McMillon would be worth a look if he has a chance to play regularly, but given his age and lack of success at the major league level he's probably not going to help much. None of the prospects listed can be expected to help much in the near future, but grabbing Torres in a deep league with minor league rosters would be a good idea.

KANSAS CITY ROYALS

Once one of the worst trios in the major leagues, the Royals outfield group is now one of the majors' best. Despite the disappointment of Carlos Beltran's sophomore slump, the Royals outfield sported the American League stolen base leader in Johnny Damon, they also had a leading power threat in Jermaine Dye and a prominent Rookie of the Year candidate in Mark Quinn. Most of the club's DH at-bats for 2001 will come from this group, too, as it is a talented and deep group of players.

Damon was traded to Oakland in a three-way deal that brough a much need closer in Roberto Hernandez to K.C. Damon has improved every single year and showed further improvement across the board last season to become one of the game's best leadoff hitters. As in previous seasons, Damon started slowly, then heated up around mid-May. If you don't own Damon by May 15, and he is struggling, try to trade for him. He is capable of repeating as a stolen base champ and hitting 25 homers with a very good batting average, too. Damon is a free-agent-to-be and the Royals have alternatively attempted to re-sign him or trade him. They are going to have a hard time affording his hefty price tag. So, while it is hard to part with a player of his abilities, the Royals have to get something of value for him before he leaves as a free agent. Since Kauffman Stadium is a hitter's park, it is likely to hurt Damon's overall numbers—slightly—if he plays regularly someplace else. With just the same kind of production as last year Damon is worth $30. And he's still improving . . .

Dye has gone from being notorious as the weaker part of one of the worst trades in recent history to being one of the most consistent RBI threats in the game. After hitting .250 with just 24 homers and 82 RBI in his first three big-league season, Dye has batted over .300 with 60 homers and 237 RBI the last two years. Last year he added 27 points to his batting average, hit six more homers, walked 11 more times and struck out 20 fewer times on his way to his first All-Star berth. It was an outstanding season for a player just entering his prime. What to expect from Dye in 2001 is more of the same, and more of it. He has 40 homer potential, is a sure bet to collect 100 RBI and hit at or above .300, all the while producing very consistently at the plate, day in and day out. It makes Dye worth $25 in Rotisserie terms and, since he's relatively obscure, he can be bought for less in some leagues.

If you're the gambling type, take a chance on Beltran in 2001. After missing half the 2000 season due to injury and a suspension following his challenge of a rehab assignment to the minors, the 1999 Rookie of the Year was on the outs with Royals' management. When he finally returned to the big club in September it was in a reduced role with management stating that he would have to win his job back. Despite his sophomore bust, Beltran remains a talented player and is still very young. If he can put the 2000 season and its distractions behind him, Beltran can again be a very valuable player to the Royals and to Rotisserie owners, too. This is one of the better gambles for Rotisserie. His talents are diverse and obvious; he has proven himself in the majors already; his poor 2000 season was due to injury and off-field distraction, neither of which are likely to be repeated in 2001. All signs point to a rebound season for Beltran, potentially a big rebound. Use his lost season in 2000 as a way to buy Beltran for $10-12 and enjoy a bargain in 2001.

Quinn had all the numbers to win the 2000 Rookie of the Year award, only to see it given to an imported Seattle relief ace. The contrast calls into sharp focus the Royals bullpen problems and also helps highlight the club's attempt to trade Damon for relief help, plus it points to the fact that Quinn would likely replace Damon as the Royals' regular left fielder if Damon were traded. In any case, Quinn has earned a chance to play regularly, either as a left fielder or as a DH. He'll get 550 at-bats, possibly reach 30 homers and drive in 90 runs while sporting a very good batting average. Keep in mind that Quinn regularly hit in the mid-to-high .300s throughout his minor-league career and you get the sense he has potential to be a batting champion. Not winning the Rookie of the Year award will help keep Quinn's price down in 2001 drafts, but not by much. Expect to pay at least $15 for Quinn in 2001, although it may very well be worth it as he is a young player who has earned a full-time job in the majors. If recent history is any guide, consider that runners up and other high finishers in Rookie balloting often go on to produce at much higher levels than the actual Rookie winners. In the American League, consider Garret Anderson who was runner-up to Marty Cordova in 1995, or Manny Ramirez, runner-up to Bob Hamelin in 1994, or Kenny Lofton, who finished second to Pat Listach in

1992. In the National League, Jason Kendall lost to Todd Hollandsworth in 1996 and Chipper Jones was second to Hideo Nomo in 1995. This is not to say the winners were undeserving at the time, but, instead, that the non-winners in many cases have gone on to repeatedly have much more valuable Rotisserie seasons than the award winners. Quinn has the potential to do that in coming years.

The Royals tried a something-for-nothing approach with Todd Dunwoody and Dave McCarty; it worked with McCarty (discussed at length in the "First Basemen" section), but not with Dunwoody. Given a chance to step in as a fourth outfielder, or even more when Beltran was unavailable, Dunwoody hit poorly and struck out frequently; his pinch-hitting appearances were awful, reducing his value as a reserve. Dunwoody is probably a better ballplayer than he has shown the last two seasons. But, even at his best he wasn't worth more than a dollar. Spend your Rotisserie money elsewhere.

Scott Pose has been a useful pinch-hitter in the past, but was awful in 2000. At his very best, Pose cannot crack the starting lineup; at worst he's a weak pinch-hitter. Either way, he has no Rotisserie value.

Dee Brown is ready for the big leagues. He led Triple-A Omaha in homers and steals, while also leading the club in strikeouts. Overall, he's still a raw bundle of talents and is considered one of the club's best young prospects and their only real non-pitching prospect. Laying off bad pitches has been difficult for Brown, who has shown streaks of extremely good and extremely bad play. He's not a good defensive outfielder and would be relegated to left field in the bigs. But, his overall abilities make the potential loss of Damon via trade or free agency not as painful for the Royals. If Damon leaves Kansas City, it is Brown who will pick up a huge portion of those lost at-bats. Should Brown get 400 at-bats in Kansas City in 2001, look for extremely inconsistent play. He'll go for stretches where he hits nothing and strikes out a lot while also looking awful in the field. But, there will also be stretches where he hits everything, hits for power, and runs the bases well, too. As Brown has only an outside chance to get those 400 at-bats this year, he is worth no more than $1. However, his potential says Brown can earn $10 as a rookie if he gets a chance to play. If you can get him for your Ultra squad, do it. If you need to take a potential big-gain long shot, Brown represents a fine risk. However, don't pick up Brown if you need consistent, definable production.

Except for Brown, in 2000 Triple-A Omaha sported

mostly journeyman outfielders like Les Norman, Aaron Guiel, Jeremy Carr and Doug Jennings, or utility types such as Tony Medrano or Alejandro Prieto; none have future value as Rotisserie players. Geof Tomlinson is a potential leadoff hitter who lost all but a month of the 2000 season to injury. A slashing, line-drive hitter with fine speed and a decent batting eye, Tomlinson should reach the majors late in 2001; he's an interesting choice for Ultra teams, but not a sure thing because the Royals' outfield is very crowded.

Jeremy Dodson is a better prospect; he led Double-A Wichita with 18 homers and also added 17 steals, although he also led the team in strikeouts and had a disappointing RBI count. Dodson should spend significant time in the Omaha outfield in 2001 and get his first taste of the bigs later in the year. He has potential and could be a good choice for Ultra teams but has the same drawback as Tomlinson: the crowded Kansas City outfield.

Speedy Mike Curry shared the Wichita outfield with Dodson, stealing 52 bases and hitting .289. Curry could overtake Tomlinson as a potential leadoff hitter and he should also advance to Omaha in 2001. Curry is not considered an especially good prospect as his skill set may not extend to the majors. Curry's Wichita teammate Pat Hallmark has similar skills but is considered a better prospect; Hallmark hit .326 with 41 steals and an impressive .409 on-base percentage, along with leading the club in RBI with 79. Hallmark might reach the majors as a first baseman instead of in the outfield; think Darin Erstad for upside potential, although it'll take at least two years before Hallmark plays regularly in the majors.

Other outfield prospects at lower levels include Brandon Berger, who was High-A Wilmington's biggest power threat and earned a late-season promotion to Wichita, and Alexis Gomez, a speedy hitter who hasn't made consistent contact in the minors. Neither is a great prospect, though, and both have a lot to prove before they can be recommended for inclusion on an Ultra roster.

RECOMMENDATION REVIEW: Any of the Royals' four regulars, plus Brown, are good buys. Damon and Dye are more consistent, established, and higher-level producers, recommended for teams that need to get exactly what they pay for in the outfield, either for Damon's speed and batting average or Dye's power and batting average. Quinn is recommended for his potential growth in terms of power and batting average. Beltran is recommended for his rebound potential. Brown is recommended for teams that need to take low-dollar/high-gain

risks. Dunwoody and Pose are to be avoided, as are Royals' minor-league prospects except for Tomlinson, Dodson and Hallmark, who have potential as late Ultra or farm system candidates, with Hallmark and Dodson better candidates than Tomlinson.

MINNESOTA TWINS

The Twins outfield has a chance to be productive in 2001, with a little power, a little speed and a little hitting for average across the board. The key here is that two of the three starting outfielders, Jacque Jones and Torii Hunter, are entering their third straight seasons of getting consistent playing time, and should start to show their talent at the plate.

Jones, a fast lefthanded hitter, has what they call, "juice." He's a solid, yet slender fellow, but the ball surprisingly jumps off his bat farther than you'd think. He has the potential to hit 30 homers a year, and led the Twins with 19 homers in 2000.

He's a free swinger, striking out 111 times last season. The Twins also were concerned with his habit of diving out over the plate to hit outside pitches. Jones got into trouble during the season half of the season when opponents began to pitch him inside.

Still, Jones looks like the type of player who will hit .290-.300, hit 25-30 over the fence and drive in about 100 RBI. That potential could be seen this season, as Jones approaches 1,000 major league at-bats (he's currently at 845).

Twins manager Tom Kelly kept the pressure off Jones last season, batting him in the bottom third of the order most of the season. While it's realistic to think that Jones could hit sixth or even fifth (where he would be in more RBI situations), his high strikeout rate may keep him out of the top half of the order. Jones is very fast, but hasn't mastered base stealing.

Hunter is a physical specimen who puts on a nice show in batting practice. After being set down to the minors for a month, Hunter made an adjustment at the plate, returned to the majors, and pushed his average from around .200 to .280 by the end of the season.

Hunter enters 2001 with his confidence at an all-time high. He's seeing the ball better at the plate, and is starting to drive the ball. The Twins likely will keep Hunter in the bottom half of the order, but he has the power to hit 25-30 homers in 2001. He has the speed to steal 20-plus bases.

He will play every day. He was benched at times in 2000 when he would miss a sign or overthrow the cutoff man. But Hunter learns from his mistakes. He has a tremendous arm and great range, too, other good attributes that will keep him in the lineup every day. This will be the first year that Hunter is worthy of being drafted, albeit in the late rounds.

Matt Lawton is the Twins' most accomplished offensive player. He sacrificed power for average last season, and responded with his first-ever .300 season. A foot injury late in the season cost him 20 points off his average and grounded his running game.

But Lawton has become a polished hitter. He'll take the outside pitch to the opposite field and drive a few over the fence. He still can turn on an inside pitch and shoot it down the line or over the fence. His bat is quick, and Lawton understands what pitchers are trying to do to him and can make adjustments.

Look for Lawton to hit around .300 again, but he will try to hit for more power in 2001. He's a good basestealer, and could swipe 30 bases. He walked 91 times last season, and, with his speed, is better suited as a leadoff hitter. The Twins, however, need someone to bat third in the lineup, and he's happy to be in a RBI spot.

Denny Hocking is the key reserve off the bench. He'll give one of the starters a day off, as he can play all three outfield positions and has the best arm on the team. There will be a drop off in offensive on the days he plays, because he doesn't drive the ball much.

The Twins were very pleased with minor league player of the year John Barnes, who played well in a September call up. Barnes is not a big power hitter, but can hit line drives up the middle. He's a good outfielder with a strong and accurate arm. He will be an intriguing player this season, but likely will break in as a reserve, since Jones, Hunter and Lawton make up one of the best defensive outfields in the league.

The Twins have a power hitting center field prospect in Bobby Kielty, who could be called up during the season. Kielty is a good defensive player but needs more seasoning.

RECOMMENDATION REVIEW: The most stable player of this group is Matt Lawton, he should provide good value with good overall numbers, with a possible increase in power in 2001. Jones and Hunter are both possible stars in the making, and could both be very good in 2001.

NEW YORK YANKEES

In 2000, Bernie Williams had another excellent, and largely overlooked, season. Even though he played just 141 games, he finished at .307-30-121 with 13 stolen bases in 18 attempts. He has become a higher-percentage base stealer. The switch hitter is 32.

David Justice, 34, may have been the only Yankees acquisition who was a hotter hitter than Glenallen Hill after moving to New York. Playing primarily in left field, Justice batted a combined .286-41-118 with Cleveland and New York. He's a lefthanded batter.

The Yankees re-signed Paul O'Neill to a one-year, $6.5-million contract even though the lefthanded batter is 38 and his production fell off to .283-18-100 last season.

Glenallen Hill also played some left field for the Yankees. There's more about him under designated hitters.

Shane Spencer was platooning in left field and as DH until undergoing season-ending knee surgery. Up to that point, the 29-year-old righthanded batter was off to an excellent start (.282-9-40).

Injuries caused New York to bring Ryan Thompson, a 33-year-old righthanded batter, back to the majors for 50 at-bats. Thompson batted .260-3-14 for the Yankees and .285-23-75 with Triple-A Columbus. He can play all three outfield positions, so he could remain in the majors as a fourth or fifth outfielder.

The righthanded-batting Clay Bellinger, 32, had been primarily an infield reserve until injuries caused the Yankees to add "outfielder" to his resume. Though he came up with some clutch home runs, his overall production for New York was just .207-6-21.

Luis Polonia was part of the gaggle of left fielders/DHs, but batting from the left side. He began the season as the Tigers' leadoff batter, and finished it in the World Series. Polonia, 36, finished the year at .276-7-30 with 12 stolen bases. He hit six of his homers for Detroit. During the offseason, Polonia was a free agent.

Roberto Kelly began the year as the Yanks' righthanded-batting left fielder, but went out because of a sprained right elbow after playing 10 games (.120-1-1). The 36-year-old also was a free agent after the season.

Luke Wilcox, a 27-year-old lefthanded batter, spent three days on New York's roster despite batting just .219-13-49 at Triple-A Columbus. In fact, Wilcox was demoted to Double-A Norwich, where he played 18 games. He doesn't appear to be a prospect anyway.

Felix Jose returned to the majors after a five-year absence. In 20 games, the 35-year-old switch hitter batted .231-1-5. At Columbus, Jose was productive in a .310-11-38 season.

The speedy Kerry Robinson (37 stolen bases at Columbus, where he batted .318-0-32) has been in five organizations during the past four seasons. As a minor league free agent, the 27-year-old was eligible to move on to another.

Mike Frank, 26, hasn't been the same since the Reds rushed him to the majors prematurely. The Yankees obtained the lefthanded batter in last season's Denny Neagle trade. With three minor league teams, he totaled eight homers, 45 RBI's and 13 steals, but batted just .239-2-12 in 45 games at Columbus. The Yankees used 14 outfielders last season, and Frank wasn't one of them.

Donzell McDonald once was considered a good prospect for adding speed to a major league lineup. But at age 26, the switch hitter has played just 24 games in Triple-A. Last season, he totaled three homers, 16 RBI and 25 steals in 68 games. McDonald batted in the .240s at both Norwich and Columbus.

Paul Ottavinia batted a surprising .302-8-58 in his second tour of Norwich, with 15 stolen bases. But the lefthanded batter, signed out of the independent Northern League in '98, is 27 years old. He was eligible for minor league free agency.

RECOMMENDATION REVIEW: The Yankees' starting outfielders all are on the down sides of good-to-excellent major league careers. Among Williams, Justice and O'Neill, the only one who appears capable of providing value for the price required to acquire him could be Williams. He still could increase his stolen-base total, unless he gets worn out trying to cover ground in the

Yankee Stadium outfield. None of the others figures to be more than a platoon or fill-in player. The Yankees don't appear to have any good Ultra prospects among their minor league outfielders.

OAKLAND ATHLETICS

Johnny Damon was traded to the A's who sent Ben Grieve to the D'Rays in a three way trade with K.C. Damon will start in left and hit lead off, moving Terrence Long down in the batting order. See more on Damon in the K.C. outfielders section.

Lost on many last year was the fact that Ben Grieve was not only consistent, but actually drove in 100 runs (104, to be precise) for the first time in his young career. Most owners of Grieve were likely perplexed as he led the world in hitting into double plays, while simultaneously being unable to crack the .300 barrier-something that seemed like a given three years ago.

Well, Oakland was at a crossroads with Grieve. They were heavy with lefthanded hitters, and even in left field, Grieve is a defensive liability. However, he most certainly can hit, and his numbers should continue to improve, particularly his power, average, and on-base totals. Grieve is too young (at 24) to force into a full-time DH role. In Tampa, Grieve will split time between left and DH.

Grieve has underwhelmed some owners with higher expectations, but face it, he did drive in 100 runs, and hit nearly 30 homers last year. That means he could be a bargain relative to some other outfielders (should Juan Gonzalez cost more?), costing anywhere from the high teens to the low 20's in dollar value. He'll be worth it (he is the kind of player you can often sneak through after a lunch break, when owners have a little food in their bellies, and a little less money in their budget totals).

Though he didn't make the Opening Day roster, Terrence Long excelled once promoted, adding some offense to the lead off spot (which he held for most of the year). Long is a strong player, and though he is one who learns, be careful not to overspend based upon the combination of his 2000 totals, and what you may project an improved and full sophomore season to be. Long will be good, and both his steal and runs totals should go up: runs to over 100, and steals to double digits. But, his power totals are right around what he is capable of, and he might endure a drop in average as pitchers get the better of him the second time around. Long is still a solid #3 outfielder and should be available in the $10 range.

With the departure of Matt Stairs to Chicago, right field does indeed open for the platoon of Jeremy Giambi and Adam Piatt. The left handed Giambi, who actually had better minor league hitting totals than his esteemed elder sibling, belted 10 homers last year, several of which came as a pinch hitter, over 260 at-bats. He will probably receive more playing time this year, and if Giambi can avoid the injuries that slowed him in 2000, he can improve on the .254-10-50 totals of last year. Should a deal move Grieve, Giambi becomes the left field heir apparent, and .270-20-70 totals are a reasonable expectation, should Giambi get 500 at-bats. He will get close to 400, playing some right, some first, and some DH. He is a solid pick as a fourth or fifth outfielder, and shouldn't cost too much.

The real name to watch in right, however, will be Adam Piatt, who has shredded all pitching at every level he has played as far. After a .288-20-107 first full season at Modesto, in 1998, the eighth round selection of the 1997 draft (Piatt attended Mississippi State) turned in a stunning 1999 at Midland. Piatt won the Texas League Triple Crown in 1999 at Midland, going .345-39-135, with 48 doubles (it was the first triple crown in 72 years), and followed up with a 2000 spent between Triple-A Sacramento (.283-8-42) and Oakland (.299-5-23). Piatt will get the bulk of right field at-bats for two reasons. First, he is over a year younger, with a greater offensive upside. Second, he has a stronger arm in right field, meaning he at least should start more games. Piatt is an excellent selection as a fifth outfielder, and probably is worth a number four slot on your roster, depending upon the price. As a high potential rookie, he might be a bit pricey, but as a $3-5 flychaser, Piatt will prove to be a bargain.

The Athletics Ryan Christenson will be the extra outfielder/late inning defensive replacement. Christenson has a little pop, and excellent speed. In an AL only league, he can be a valuable fifth outfielder, who could hit a handful of homers and potentially swipe 10 bases, but Christenson's value in most other leagues is marginal.

Oakland is anticipating the arrival of young slugger Mario Encarnacion, but that arrival will likely not be for another year or two, especially with the development of Long, Piatt, and Giambi. Coming off a solid (.309-18-71) season at Midland in 1998, the 23-year old struggled at Triple-A, going .269-13-61, with 15 steals. The big concern continues to be Encarnacion's plate discipline. He walked just 36 times to 95 strikeouts, and those numbers will not be tolerated at the major league level by the club. He does,

however, remain a top prospect, and will spend another year at Triple-A.

Another speedy name to watch is that of Eric Brynes, who earned a September callup following his solid 2000 year, wherein he went .333-9-47 with 12 steals at Sacramento, following .301-5-37 totals (21 more swipes) at Midland. Should Terrence Long falter, and Byrnes get off to a hot start at Sacramento, he is a logical lead-off/center field replacement.

We have been hyping Dionys Ceser (.277-4-37, 13 at Midland last year) for so long that he doesn't seem to be a prospect any longer, but he did just turn 24 last September, and still merits a look. Cesar does project to be a #4 outfielder, at best in the majors, however.

At the A level, Ryan Ludwick (.264-29-102) and Kirk Asche (.247-18-63) are worth watching.

RECOMMENDATION REVIEW: While there are no superstars in this outfield there are some interesting players to watch. Ben Grieve drove in 100 runs last year and should repeat that and improve in the other triple crown categories as well, making him a solid value in the outfield. Terrence Long, after a very good rookie season, should be the A's everyday center fielder while putting up respectable but not All-Star numbers. Adam Piatt has the ability to be one of this year's sleepers, if he gets the playing time.

SEATTLE MARINERS

The Mariners figure to have an athletic outfield with the ability to cover a lot of ground, but they don't figure to get much home run production out there unless they make a change. Al Martin came over in a trade last season and wasn't nearly as useful as the team had hoped, but he's still a good player. His defense sometimes leaves something to be desired, but he's the kind of player that can hit .300 with 15-plus homers and 20-plus steals in a good year. If he gets off to a good start, Martin could have a nice year with the Mariners. Even if he winds up in a platoon situation, he's a lefthanded hitter and would play 70-75 percent of the time.

Mike Cameron took over in center field in place of Ken Griffey, Jr. last year and he was a bit of a disappointment. His raw ability is unquestionable, he has the power to hit 30-plus homers and the speed to steal 30-plus bases, but he's known to be a bit of a head case. Not that he has a bad attitude, he just doesn't seem to learn very quickly when it comes to hitting. He hit .267 with 19 homers and 24 steals last year, but his strikeouts make it difficult to find a place for him in the lineup. Cameron is an excellent defender and should play regularly barring a major slump.

The wild card in the M's outfield for the 2001 season will be Japanese import Ichiro Suzuki. Plenty of pitchers have come over from the "Land of the Rising Sun," but Suzuki will be the first hitter to attempt the transition. He was easily the best hitter in Japan, posting a career average over there of better than .350, but how will that translate to the major leagues? Nobody knows for sure, but scouts have compared him to Johnny Damon and Kenny Lofton. He'll probably hit in the first or second spot in the Mariners' lineup, providing a solid on-base percentage and a bunch of stolen bases. He doesn't have much power, but should still be a decent threat.

Jay Buhner was re-signed and will see his playing time shrink even more. He is not able to play every day, but is still productive and has some Rotisserie value. Do not over bid for the name. He will give you homers and RBI, but little else.

Stan Javier will see significant time as a fourth or fifth outfielder. His value has slipped in recent years and give little more than a good average. He also showed his age by stealing a career low four bases in 2000.

Rickey Henderson was not offered a contract and was a free agent during the winter. He still is a well conditioned athlete and could bounce back even at his age. A wait and see approach should be taken with Henderson. He is no longer a starting left fielder where ever he goes.

Anthony Sanders and Raul Ibanez could figure into the mix. Sanders has been a prospect for a few years, but isn't expected to have a significant role. He runs reasonably well and has some power, but has never demonstrated the ability to be an everyday major league player. Ibanez has pretty much carved out his niche in baseball as a part-time player. He plays the outfield and first base, but doesn't have the kind of offensive ability teams would like to see out of those positions.

The Mariners really only have one top-notch outfield prospect on the way and that's Juan Silvestre. He spent last season at high-A Lancaster where he hit .304 with 30 home runs and 137 RBI. He's still at least a year or two away from reaching the majors, but his ability to hit for power and produce runs should keep him on the fast track.

RECOMMENDATION REVIEW: None of the Mariners outfielders are all that exciting. Suzuki is intriguing, but proceed with caution. He isn't a known commodity at the major league level and comes with significant risk. If you can get him later on in a draft or at a good value, go ahead. Martin and Cameron are known commodities. You aren't like to see any drastic improvement or significant regression from either one this year. Silvestre is worth having in leagues with minor league rosters.

TAMPA BAY DEVIL RAYS

The Devil Rays have a veteran group of outfielders ready to start the 2001 season, but much of how the cards fall could depend on the health of Greg Vaughn's right shoulder. Vaughn brought a much-needed competitive attitude to the Devil Rays, showing a penchant for breaking up double plays, running into walls to catch fly balls and hitting in the clutch. Then an old nemesis, his right shoulder, flared up to force him into the DH role in early August.

Vaughn had his shoulder checked and he didn't need a major overall—just rest, so there's no reason not to pencil him in as the left fielder. If healthy, the Devil Rays can pound on 35-50 homers and 100 RBI, if not it makes for some interesting speculation. Who plays left field if Vaughn is the DH?

Jason Tyner is the leading candidate to play left if Vaughn is out of the mix. After joining the Devil Rays from the Mets, the lefthanded hitting youngster showed quality defense and a capable lefthanded bat that could finally answer the Devil Rays' leadoff problems. Tyner does all the little things leadoff hitters are supposed to do. He can work a count, lay down a bunt, steal a base and make contact.

With Tyner in the lineup leading off, the Devil Rays are free to bat Gerald Williams deeper in the lineup. Williams, who was voted the team MVP for the 2000 season, batted in the leadoff spot in 2000, hitting .274 with 21 home runs and 89 RBI. But Williams is hardly the classical leadoff man as he struck out 103 times in 632 at-bats—and often looked bad doing so. Given the chance to hit further down in the lineup, Williams could be looked upon to produce 100 RBI, while Tyner could set the table at the top of the lineup.

Right field is the biggest question mark in the Devil Rays' lineup. Once again, a lot of what happens in right field is dependent on what happens with Vaughn. If Vaughn is healthy, first baseman Fred McGriff will be used more often at DH, allowing Steve Cox to start more games at first base. However, with Vaughn at DH, Cox will be used more in right and perhaps some in left.

Jose Guillen continues to be an enigma, displaying five-tool skills without the necessary maturity to control his gifts. Guillen hit .253 with 10 home runs and 41 RBI in 105 games, but has yet to maintain a consistent level of play. He continues to fall into ruts where he swings for the fences and strikes looking bad in doing so. And he falls asleep in the field, throwing to the wrong base on occasion. Guillen needs to make strides quickly before the Devil Rays' becomes further frustrated with his wasted talents. Randy Winn continues to hang around, producing decent numbers at the minor-league level — .330, 7, 40 at Triple-A Durham. But he's a longshot given his poor and less than accurate arm and his inability to win the leadoff job when given the chance.

Wild cards to the Devil Rays' outfield picture include Alex Sanchez and Josh Hamilton. Sanchez has improved every year and could finally make the club in 2000. He still strikes out too much, but he is a legitimate threat from the leadoff position. Just check out his 52 steals at Durham in 2000. Meanwhile, Hamilton could be the best talent in baseball not playing at the major-league level. Hamilton is a classic right fielder with speed. He has a strong arm, can hit for average, power and steal bases. What the Devil Rays don't want to do is rush him. However, Hamilton has had no difficulty at any level he's played and might just be one of those rare talents who can handle such a jump. Hamilton is a superstar waiting to happen and might just win the job on the basis of his ability to hit home runs and play quality defense.

RECOMMENDATION REVIEW: If you need stolen bases and Sanchez makes the team, you have a lock. Keep an eye on Williams and where he's batting in the lineup. If he's not the leadoff guy, he could easily produce 100 RBI. On the speculative side, Hamilton is the real deal. If he makes the team his average might dip below the .300 mark but he will produce home runs, RBI and stolen bases.

TEXAS RANGERS

The brightest spot for Texas from the Juan Gonzalez trade turned out to be Gabe Kapler. After a slow start that included a two-month stint on the DL with a torn quadri-

ceps muscle, Kapler had a hot second half (.344-10-48). His role as a starter is a done deal. Kapler could play either center or right field, depending on need. Because his full-season numbers don't look out of the ordinary, Kapler is one player that could be a bargain in many leagues next year. He could easily get 550 plate appearances this season, and another .300 season with 20 homers and 80 RBI is well within his reach. Kapler could bat anywhere from fifth to seventh in Texas' order.

Rusty Greer is coming off his poorest season since 1995. Ankle, hamstring and shoulder injuries slowed him early in the season, and he ended the year out with plantar fascitis in both feet, the same type of injury that ruined a few seasons for Mark McGwire. When Greer is able to play, he is a virtual lock as a .300 hitter, with modest power and a few steals. Johnny Oates was projecting Greer to lead off, which actually makes quite a bit of sense since Greer historically has a high on-base percentage. If he is healthy, Greer will play every day in left field, but the foot problem could be serious. Watch Greer's health in the spring, and act accordingly.

Super-prospect Ruben Mateo's abilities have never been in question, but his health has always been dubious. Last season, Mateo suffered a badly broken right leg that ended his season after only two months. There is some question whether Mateo will be ready to play by Opening Day. The most likely scenario has Mateo rehabbing through the spring, then starting the season in the minors and playing his way back to the big leagues during the season. In that event, Mateo should be ready for the majors within a month after he begins playing. Mateo is a free swinger who nevertheless makes good contact with decent power. His speed may be slow to recover this season. It may be late 2001, or even 2002 before we see what Mateo can do when he is really healthy. He can play any of the three outfield positions.

The Rangers were actively trying to acquire additional outfield help, both in the free agent market and in trade discussions. To the extent they succeed, the playing time of Chad Curtis, Ricky Ledee and Bo Porter would be adversely affected. Curtis should be the first righthanded hitter off the bench for Texas. Capable of playing any of the three outfield positions, Curtis gives it everything he's got. He is at his best in a platoon where he faces lefthanded pitchers exclusively, as he tends to get overexposed playing regularly. Curtis is no longer a big base stealing threat, but will swipe a few here and there. With Mateo's and Greer's injury problems, Curtis could get 300-400 at bats for Texas.

Scouts still like Ledee's potential, and he'll be only 26 on Opening Day. But he hasn't produced in parts of three seasons, and he may have to prove himself off the bench in 2001. Best-case scenario for Ledee would be to tear it up in spring training and get Mateo's lineup spot as the right field starter. Worst-case has him riding the bench for most of the season with Johnny Oates, who is not noted for giving his bench much playing time. Barring personnel changes, Ledee should at least be the first lefty hitter off the bench. A few homers are the likely upside; a low batting average the downside. At number 5 or number 6 on the outfield depth chart, Porter is unlikely to get much playing time for Texas. If injuries or other developments thrust Porter into a major role, he would likely hold his own, hitting an occasional homer to boot.

Speedy Scarborough Green became a free agent at season's end and was uncertain to re-sign with Texas. The occasional steal is not enough to make up for a very low batting average. The best outfield prospect for Texas is Kevin Mench, an Arizona Fall League all-star last fall. Mench has been a high-average power hitter so far and could advance quickly. A cup of coffee this September with a shot to make the team in 2002 is a possibility.

RECOMMENDATION REVIEW: Kapler is a solid value, and could be a bargain this year in many leagues. Greer is downgraded because of health concerns. Mateo is a better bet for 2002 than this season, but could be a good buy-and-hold acquisition with a little upside this year. Curtis is a good fifth outfielder at a low price. At a few dollars, Ledee has some upside. Porter is unlikely to play enough to help. Avoid Green. Mench makes a very good Ultra pick.

TORONTO BLUE JAYS

One area of strength last year for the Jays was the continued development of its outfielders.

Shannon Stewart has become an excellent leadoff hitter, showing improved ability to get base hits and he has underrated and developing power. Few noticed that Stewart hit 21 home runs last year. Of some concern was his apparent decline in walks, thus leading to the dropoff in steals to just 20, down from 51 only two years ago. More realistic an expectation for Stewart would be to see his average dip below .300 with fewer than 20 home runs but 25+ steals this year. Also exceptional is his improved defense as he made just two errors last year.

Jose Cruz Jr, despite constant rumors of his departure the past three years, spent a full season as the Jays' center fielder, actually playing in 162 games. Though he hit just .242, he surprised some by clubbing 31 home runs and stealing 15 bases. Among American League center fielders, Cruz was third in home runs behind Garrett Anderson and Carl Everett. More to his credit were the 71 walks that compensated for his low average. Cruz has become a valuable run producer and deserves to play every day. He's also an intelligent player with underrated defensive skills and a desire to improve. He will bat in the lower part of the batting order, sixth or seventh.

Raul Mondesi turned out to be everything the Jays needed and more when they were forced to trade Shawn Green. Though Mondesi missed most of the second half of the 2000 season, he brought a hustle and determination to the Jays that simply wasn't there before. Mondesi was on pace for his first ever 100 RBI season and despite playing just 96 games, he finished sixth among American League right fielders in home runs. He came back from injury at the end of the season and he should start 2001 healthy and ready to play a full season. He is a good bet to be a 25-25 man, as he would have certainly been had it not been for injury last year. Though new manager Buck Martinez did not say whether he would continue with Jim Fregosi's approach, Mondesi is likely to hit third in the Jays' order this year.

Vernon Wells took a step back of sorts last year when he failed to beat Jose Cruz Jr in spring training for the center field job on the Jays and then proceed to struggle at Triple-A Syracuse. Regardless, he projects as a long-term four category player who should develop an interesting power-speed combination with a good glove. For now, Wells is a Triple-A player at most and has spent much of the past couple of years as a player frequently mentioned by other teams in trade discussions. The Jays will give serious consideration to making Wells a major league backup outfielder. The fact that the Jays briefly brought in Rob Ducey last year demonstrates the team's belief that Wells needs more refinement in the minors at this stage of his career.

Chad Mottola surprised many with an outstanding 2000 Triple-A season and as the season ended, he appeared to have a good shot at making the 2001 Opening Day major league roster as a backup outfielder. Mottola, a former first round pick for Cincinnati, had a 30-30 year with Syracuse and won the International League's MVP Award, the first player in the Jays' organization to do that since Derek Bell in 1991. He is ready to fill in as a backup outfielder and he stands a better than even shot at being the team's fourth or fifth outfielder this year.

Andy Thompson is close to a permanent breakthrough and though he hit just .246 at Triple-A last year, he topped 20 home runs for the second straight season in the minors. Still a step away from being a major league quality outfielder, Thompson fits in as the kind of player who could get called up for a few weeks in the event of injury. His chances of staying in the majors for any length of time this year are slim at best. Were he to be rushed to the majors, he would be a .230s major league type with occasional power.

Though DeWayne Wise spent the season on the Jays' roster (and much of it on the disabled list) last year, he's now ticketed for the minors after fulfilling the Rule 5 draft requirements. He projects to be a speedster with a good glove and little power and his 2001 contribution would appear to be as an emergency callup only. He is a longshot to make the Opening Day roster and if he doesn't make it to start the season, we probably won't see him at all this year.

Todd Greene (covered in the DH section) could play in the corner outfield positions in an emergency.

RECOMMENDATION REVIEW: Both Stewart and Mondesi are excellent picks in Rotisserie leagues with Stewart being the superior pick between the two in leagues that use runs scored. Both are safe bets to top twenty steals and Stewart showed better power than most expected last year, though he's unlikely to top 20 home runs again this year. Mondesi's numbers took a hit because he missed half the season yet Stewart is the greater injury risk. Cruz has good power but always seems to be one slump away from a Triple-A tour. Mottola would be a good major league player now but is not going to play much no matter how much playing time is available. Thompson is not ready and Vernon Wells, though a good long-term choice, is at least two years from being a star and still needs to improve to avoid being a disappointment. Wells is worth only the lowest of gamble picks for 2001.

TOP 2001 HOME RUN HITTERS

NAME	HR
Manny Ramirez	46
Greg Vaughn	35
David Justice	31
Magglio Ordonez	30
Tim Salmon	30
Garret Anderson	29
Albert Belle	29
Jermaine Dye	29
Carl Everett	29
Juan Gonzalez	29
Jose Cruz	28
Bernie Williams	28
Raul Mondesi	27
Ben Grieve	26
Mark Quinn	26
Dante Bichette	25
Russ Branyan	25
Ellis Burks	25
Bob Higginson	24
Glenallen Hill	24
Carlos Lee	22
Jay Buhner	21
Darin Erstad	21
Gabe Kapler	21
Ruben Mateo	21
Henry Rodriguez	21
Mike Cameron	20

TOP 2001 RBI PRODUCERS

NAME	RBI
Manny Ramirez	154
Magglio Ordonez	117
Bernie Williams	117
Jermaine Dye	115
Albert Belle	108
David Justice	106
Carl Everett	105
Garret Anderson	102
Dante Bichette	102
Ben Grieve	97
Paul O'Neill	96
Tim Salmon	95
Juan Gonzalez	94
Carlos Lee	92
Greg Vaughn	92
Ellis Burks	91
Mark Quinn	90

Darin Erstad	84
Bob Higginson	84
Matt Lawton	81
Troy O'Leary	81
Johnny Damon	80
Delino Deshields	80
Terrence Long	79
Raul Mondesi	79
Rusty Greer	78
Gerald Williams	78

TOP 2001 RUN SCORERS

NAME	RUNS
Johnny Damon	118
Manny Ramirez	118
Bernie Williams	110
Kenny Lofton	107
Darin Erstad	106
Shannon Stewart	104
Roger Cedeno	101
Jermaine Dye	100
Magglio Ordonez	98
Tim Salmon	98
Carlos Lee	97
Terrence Long	97
Mike Cameron	94
Jose Cruz	93
Greg Vaughn	92
Brady Anderson	89
Ben Grieve	89
Garret Anderson	88
Delino Deshields	87
Juan Gonzalez	87
Bob Higginson	87
Dante Bichette	86
David Justice	85
Raul Mondesi	85
Mark Quinn	84
Albert Belle	83
Carl Everett	82
Matt Lawton	81
Rusty Greer	80
Gerald Williams	80

TOP 2001 BASESTEALERS

NAME	SB
Roger Cedeno	49
Johnny Damon	44
Delino Deshields	34
Rickey Henderson	33

Kenny Lofton	31
Mike Cameron	30
Luis Matos	30
Shannon Stewart	28
Raul Mondesi	26
Matt Lawton	24
Darin Erstad	23
Reggie Sanders	23
Juan Encarnacion	22
Chris Singleton	20
Carlos Beltran	19
Brian.l. Hunter	19
Jose Cruz	16
Carl Everett	16
Magglio Ordonez	16

TOP 2001 BATTING AVERAGES

NAME	AVG
Manny Ramirez	.324
Darin Erstad	.322
Johnny Damon	.316
Gabe Kapler	.312
Shannon Stewart	.311
Bernie Williams	.311
Magglio Ordonez	.308
Carlos Lee	.307
Mark Quinn	.306
Juan Gonzalez	.305
Jermaine Dye	.299
Rusty Greer	.299
Carl Everett	.297
Terrence Long	.297
Ellis Burks	.294
Garret Anderson	.292
Roger Cedeno	.292
Luis Polonia	.292
Albert Belle	.291
Dante Bichette	.291
Orlando Palmeiro	.289
Kenny Lofton	.288
Ruben Mateo	.288
Adam Piatt	.288
Carlos Beltran	.286
Ben Grieve	.286
Jacque Jones	.286
Tim Salmon	.286
Juan Encarnacion	.285
Bob Higginson	.285
Delino Deshields	.284
Jeremy Giambi	.284
Matt Lawton	.283

NATIONAL LEAGUE OUTFIELDERS

ARIZONA DIAMONDBACKS

With Luis Gonzalez and Steve Finley, the Diamondbacks have left field and center field covered. If Danny Bautista plays the way he did in an extended trial in right field late last season, all three positions would be in capable hands.

First, the givens. Gonzalez, slightly miffed that his 1999 season was perceived by some as a career year, was even better in most offensive categories in 2000. Gonzalez set career season-bests in doubles (47), home runs (31), RBI (114) and walks (78) while starting every game last season, the only National Leaguer and one of three major leaguers to do that. Toronto's Carlos Delgado and Jose Cruz Jr. were the other two who started all 162 games.

Gonzalez set a franchise record with 80 extra-base hits while batting over .300 for the second consecutive year. He has taken off since former manager Buck Showalter inserted him into the No. 3 spot in the batting order one month into the 1999 season, behind Jay Bell and in front of Matt Williams and Steve Finley.

Gonzalez hammers righthanded pitching, hitting .333 against righties last season after going .339 against them in 1999. To think, the original plan in 1999 was to platoon him with righthanded hitting Bernard Gilkey, who was waived in the middle of last season.

Not a blazer, Gonzalez has limited basestealing speed, although he stole 12 in 1998 and nine in 1999. He does not have a great throwing arm but makes up for that by charging balls hit in front of him. His signature play is leaping above the eight foot fence in left field at Bank One

Ballpark to take away home runs. He has done it three times in his two years.

Finley carried the D'backs the first three months of the 2000 season, when third baseman Matt Williams was out with a broken foot.

Finley had 27 homers and 75 RBI by July 21 before finishing with a career-high 35 homers, one more than he hit in 1999, his first season in Arizona.

As in 1999, Finley won a Gold Glove in 2000, his fourth. But also as in 1999, his second half was marred by a back injury. Finley collided with the center field fence while making a running catch in a 2-1 victory at Houston on July 6, aggravating a lower back problem that first flared in 1999, when his left knee jammed into the turf at Bank One while attempting a diving catch in short left-center.

Finley had two epidural applications of cortisone in his lower back to treat the pain last season and had only eight homers and 21 RBI in his last 57 games. He underwent lower back surgery in November and was expected to be pain-free in spring training.

Finley has curtailed his base stealing but can be counted on for about 10 a year at this stage of his career. A dynamic defender, he will be in the lineup even if in a hitting lull.

Bautista, obtained for handyman Andy Fox on June 10, established career bests in virtually every offensive category while moving from a platoon right fielder to the everyday starter the last two months of the season.

After hitting only .191 with the Marlins, Bautista batted .317 with seven homers and 47 RBI in 262 at-bats with the D'backs. He also had 16 doubles, seven triples and five stolen bases with his new team.

Bautista showed no trouble with righthanders when thrust into the lineup full-time, hitting .320 with 19 extra-base hits against them in 181 at-bats last year.

Bautista will get the first shot to be the everyday right fielder again this season, although the D'backs do have lefthanded hitters David Dellucci, Jason Conti and Rob Ryan waiting in the wings.

Dellucci, who missed the final two months of the 1999 season after undergoing right wrist surgery, was hit by injuries again last season. He made the Opening Day roster before being sent to Triple-A Tucson to get work, but while in Tucson suffered a dislocated finger on his right hand while making a diving catch, then tendinitis in his right wrist for which he took eight cortisone shots.

Dellucci returned to the major leagues on August 18 and hit .300, going 7-for-20 as a pinch hitter. He is a career .291 pinch-hitter and will be used in that role if he does not win a part-time outfield position. He does not have a great arm and could lose time in double-switches.

Conti, a member of the D'backs' original draft class of 1996, singled in his first major league at-bat June 29 but at times appeared overmatched at the plate, striking out 30 times in 91 at-bats. He has a strong arm and good range, and with Bautista provides capable backup in center.

Ryan, another 1996 draftee, was 6 for 19 as a pinch-hitter, his most likely role if he makes the major league roster.

Jack Cust was added to the 40-man roster for the first time last winter. He hit .293 with 32 doubles, 20 homers and 75 RBI at Double-A El Paso last season after hitting .334 with 42 doubles, 32 homers and 112 RBI at Class A High Desert the year before. He is seen strictly as a left fielder, perhaps a first baseman (or DH) down the line.

RECOMMENDATION REVIEW: At this point in their careers, Gonzalez and Finley seem capable of maintaining their current production in the near future. Both take care of themselves and have learned how to be successful. Finley might have an even better year if healthy the entire season. Bautista might be worth a gamble, as only Dellucci among the reserve outfielders

seems capable of playing in even a platoon situation.

ATLANTA BRAVES

Andruw Jones makes it look so easy that we sometimes forget that he is still a young player and therefore expect too much. Though he won't turn 24 until after the start of the season, Jones already has played four full seasons for Atlanta and amassed 116 career home runs, despite being the same age as many rookies, and is already regarded as the best defensive center fielder in the game.

Jones had by far his best season in 2000, which should be an indication of what is to come. He easily surpassed his previous career marks with a .303 batting average, 36 home runs and 104 RBI. He also was very consistent throughout the season, although he did bat about 15 points higher before the All-Star break.

Andruw is more comfortable with his role on the team now, and has earned the respect of his manager, coaches and fellow players. A few years ago there were some questions about his hustle and desire, but no longer. Jones is still a kid, but one who has a boatload of experience and one who will be even better this year.

The Braves gave every indication early in the offseason that they were going to move Chipper Jones from third base to left field in 2001. That position has given Atlanta trouble over the past few seasons and having a player of Chipper's caliber certainly would help solve that problem. Jones suffered from bone chips in his elbow last year and that injury is likely another reason why the Braves are thinking about making the move. He has been a fantastic hitter as a third baseman and moving to the left field, a far less demanding position defensively, would only make him better at the plate.

Right fielder Brian Jordan was the subject of trade rumors in the first part of the offseason and he lashed out at Braves management for apparently wanting to get rid of him. Jordan claimed that the reason his stats had been down since coming to Atlanta was that he had been playing hurt. Even so, that should be a big reason to avoid overspending on Jordan. Even if he is healthy, he is not going to hit 45 homers. His career high is 25 and he's bettered 100 RBI only twice in his career. He is definitely better than he was last season, but he is not one of the league's best outfielders.

Reggie Sanders can be a fearsome hitter when he is

healthy, but unfortunately for him, those days are often few and far between. A strong, but fragile individual, Sanders has a quick bat, a lot of power, and good speed, but he has been healthy and truly effective only two of the last six seasons. In those two (1996 with the Reds and 1999 with the Padres), he posted very good Rotisserie numbers (nearly 30 homers and about 35 steals). But in the other years he has struggled to hit his weight and has been disabled more often than not.

Last season was a perfect example. He was hurt most of the season and was batting .193 on September 8. But when he finally got healthy, he was one of Atlanta's most productive hitters during the stretch drive, batting .337 with five homers and 18 RBI over the final month.

It is all right to take a chance on Sanders. But avoid him until the final rounds (if drafting) or make sure you pick him up dirt cheap in an auction.

B.J. Surhoff is a popular player, and a dependable reserve, but he is near the end of his career and cannot be counted on for consistent play. While he has been durable, 14 home runs from a starting outfielder is unacceptable in today's game. His lack of power is one reason why the Braves were thinking about moving Chipper Jones to left field.

The Braves signed veteran fourth outfielder/backup first baseman Dave Martinez during the offseason. He is a capable backup who will give you a good batting average, but as he has aged, he has lost most of his power. He is a good injury replacement during the middle of the season, but not someone you would want for a long time in your starting lineup.

Bobby Bonilla made Atlanta's management look like super geniuses in the early part of last season. Playing for his fifth team in five seasons, and fresh off having been run out of New York, Bonilla tore it up in the first two months by hitting over .300 in 105 at-bats in April and May. But he came back to earth after that and wound up hitting only .255. He hasn't approached hitting .300 since 1997 and has managed only 31 home runs combined in the last three seasons. Having him on your roster would be a huge mistake.

George Lombard has a world of talent, but the Braves seem unwilling to give him more than a cursory look in the big leagues. Part of that is his own doing as he has a poor batting eye and has made little effort to cut down on the number of times he strikes out. He seemed destined for

stardom when he hit 22 home runs for Double-A Greenville when he was only 22-years-old, but even then he struck out 140 times. He received a brief trial with the Braves last year, but struck out 14 times in 39 at-bats and was shipped back to the minors after less than a month in Atlanta. He could still develop into a productive everyday player, but he is not going to get that chance with the Braves.

Steve Sisco is primarily an infielder, but did play in a couple of games last year in the outfield. He is not going to be a contributor at the big league level, however, in either position. Pedro Swan also made a few appearances for the Braves in 2000, but he is 30-years-old and should be considered nothing more than a career minor leaguer now.

RECOMMENDATION REVIEW: This will be the year that Andruw Jones takes his game into the strato-sphere. Now that he is a much more patient hitter, it will become almost impossible for pitchers to get him out on pitches out of the strike zone. And with more good pitches to hit, he will wind up with MVP-type numbers.

<u>CHICAGO CUBS</u>

It is very hard to find anything wrong with Sammy Sosa as a Rotisserie baseball player. If he only stole bases the way he did four and five years ago he would literally be the perfect Rotisserie performer. He has developed into a fearsome power hitter and run producer, while main-taining an ability to hit for average. He strikes out a bunch, but a groundout instead of a whiff makes no difference in our game.

Sosa's home run total dropped by 13 from his perfor-mance in 1999, but it won't fall much further, if it falls at all. If there is any slugger in the game who can be counted on to hit at least 50 homers, it should be Sosa. He also has driven in at least 119 runs in five of the last six seasons, and likely will surpass that number as he has each of the past three.

Sosa managed to stay focused last season even when he was the subject of constant trade rumors. That should be a sign that he is not all of a sudden going to lose his ability to hit the ball even if he leaves the Friendly Confines of Wrigley Field. It is true that Sosa has really blossomed the past few years under hitting coach Jeff Pentland, but Sosa is extraordinarily talented and will not fall apart if either one leaves the Windy City.

The rest of Chicago's outfield isn't nearly that good. In fact, sometimes it borders on barely being passable. Damon Buford played center field most of last season, but he was a major disappointment to the Cubs, even though he set a career high with 15 homers and equaled his career mark with 18 doubles. But he hit only .251, didn't walk much and struck out a lot.

Buford is signed through the 2001 season, which could be the only thing that keeps Corey Patterson out of center field. Patterson is one of the Cubs' best prospects and is regarded as being a true all-around player. He can hit for average and power, and he has speed and defensive ability.

He has only one real weakness at this point, a tendency to swing at anything and everything. Pitchers at Double-A began to exploit that weakness last season and big league pitchers would take even more advantage. Still, Patterson is young enough that it should not be regarded as a critical flaw. He will open the season in Triple-A, but if he has a good first half he will push Buford out of the way and take his place in the Wrigley Field outfield for what could be a long, long time.

The Cubs acquired Rondell White in the middle of last season, but the injury prone outfielder appeared in but 19 games for Chicago before the season ended. White is a fine player, but his history of injuries makes him quite a risk for Rotisserie players. When he is in the lineup he produces, but he has played in more than 130 games only twice in his career.

The Cubs traded for Oakland's Matt Stairs in November. While it remains unclear exactly what the Cubs saw in Stairs, a slow, lumbering, player with no speed or defensive ability and only marginal hitting ability, the rumors started almost immediately after the trade that Chicago got Stairs as insurance in case the club made a deal involving Sosa. Losing Sosa would be bad enough, but to have to run Stairs out in right field every day would be a nightmare. Stairs is a prototypical American League designated hitter, although he isn't a good enough slugger to do that job adequately. His strike zone judgment is bad and he doesn't smack enough homers to compensate for his low batting average.

Gary Mathews, Jr., is the son of the popular former Cubs and Phillies outfielder who helped Chicago to a division title in the 1980s. However, the younger Mathews doesn't have his old man's ability and will have to perform well in spring training to earn a roster spot. In two years he has

almost 200 at-bats in the major leagues and has a career average of .194. That and his age (he will turn 27 this season) mean he will get little opportunities in the big leagues.

Roosevelt Brown is a good player, but not quite good enough to earn a starting spot. The Cubs, of course, prefer to go with name players over rookies, even if the youngsters are better players. Brown's best hope for playing time might rest with Sosa. If Chicago dumps the popular right fielder it could open up a spot for Brown, who hit .404 last September and impressed management with his ability to drive the ball.

RECOMMENDATION REVIEW: Sosa quite possibly is the best Rotisserie player available in either league. He is not nearly the injury risk that Mark McGwire is, and is almost the slugger Big Mac is when he is completely healthy. Sosa shows no signs of slowing down and should be a monster at the plate for several more seasons.

CINCINNATI REDS

Any discussion of Cincinnati's outfielders, of course, will start with Ken Griffey, Jr. A future Hall of Famer for sure, Griffey has been one of baseball's best players for a decade and will remain so for most of the rest of this one.

Much was made about Griffey's "off year" in 2000, but how bad was it really? His batting average was the lowest it had been for a full season since his rookie year in 1989, his 40 homers were his lowest total since 1994 when he also hit 40 long balls, and his on-base and slugging averages also were down.

But his numbers weren't that bad. If you throw out the first two months of the season, when he hit around .200, he was his normal self. And even in April and May, when much was being made of his extremely slow start, he was still hitting plenty of home runs, scoring runs and driving them in.

When Griffey was criticized in midseason for not hustling, he claimed a bad hamstring had bothered him most of the year and was slowing him down. Many questioned this excuse, which didn't appear to hamper his range in the outfield any. Even first base coach Dave Collins said that while Griffey wasn't intentionally failing to give his best, he had developed some poor habits, which included standing in the batter's box too long.

Griffey was flanked in the outfield last year by Dmitri Young in left and Dante Bichette in right. While Bichette has more name recognition because of his days playing in the ultra-hitter-friendly Coors Field, Young is by far the better hitter.

Young is a consistent hitter. While he doesn't have a lot of power, it is as close to a mortal lock as you are going to get that he is going to hit .300 and approach 40 doubles and 20 home runs. He suffers through slumps like every hitter, but invariably makes up for those bad times with stretches where it is almost impossible to get him out. He is a slow player, and that combined with the fact that he came up as a first basemen leads to the impression that he is a bad defensive outfielder. And while he won't win any gold gloves, he is better than most people think, and certainly good enough to keep his starting spot.

Bichette, on the other hand, is one of the most overrated players in the game. Even when he was hitting home runs and driving them in in Colorado, he wasn't nearly as good as he was made out to be. And now that he is removed from the thin atmosphere of Coors Lite Field, he isn't worth very much at all. He won't hit many home runs anymore, even with the Green Monster to shoot for in Boston, and he won't hit for a high enough average to be anything more than a fair run producer. Don't waste your time with Bichette.

Alex Ochoa and Michael Tucker split time in right field after Bichette was traded to the Red Sox last July. Ochoa, especially, performed very well and earned the starting spot by the end of the season. He can do a little bit of everything, he has moderate power, some speed, and has the ability to get on base. It remains a mystery why the Brewers gave up on him so quickly, especially considering how desperate that team is for outfielders, but he proved last year in Cincinnati that he can play.

Tucker is a decent hitter, but he has a reputation of not being able to hit lefthanded pitchers. This may or may not be true, but since Tucker has had only a handful of at-bats against southpaws in the last two years, 63 to be exact, it would be a safe bet that he will not be an everyday player this year either. He has the ability to hit the ball a long way, but his tendency to chase pitches out of the strike zone makes him an even worse risk.

The Reds have about a bazillion other outfielders, including Brian Hunter and Kimera Bartee. Reds GM Jim Bowden loves Hunter, but there simply isn't enough room for him to play. He can steal plenty of bases, as his AL

stolen base crowns in 1997 and 1999 would indicate, but he doesn't get on base nearly enough to be a leadoff man. Bartee is nothing more than a reserve outfielder. If he even makes a big league roster to start the season, he will be mired on the bench.

Chris Stynes can play some in the outfield, but the Red Sox traded for him thinking he could help Boston shore up its problem at third base. He won't provide much value either place he plays, however.

Cincinnati does have several outstanding outfield prospects who are not that far away from making it to the big leagues. Adam Dunn and Austin Kearns both are barely out of their teens, but they tore up the Midwest League in 2000. Both will have to succeed at Double-A, but if they start the season strong they could be in Cincinnati before the end of the season. Ben Broussard hit everything in sight in 1999, but a series of injuries set him back some last season. Still, he is a hitting machine so keep a close eye on him once he gets healthy.

RECOMMENDATION REVIEW: Expect Griffey to be back to his old self this season. He won't feel nearly the amount of pressure this year that he did last, his first playing in his hometown, and a couple of cosmetic changes to Cinergy Field also will assist him. Playing on grass will help his legs and joints tremendously. Add to that the fact that the Reds had to move the fences there in 10 feet to accommodate the construction of their new ballpark, and Griffey's stats are certain to bounce back up.

COLORADO ROCKIES

Colorado will try another outfield incarnation with veteran Larry Walker again as the lead this season.

Walker is the best right fielder in baseball when healthy, but those times are becoming fewer and farther between. Meanwhile, late 2000 additions Todd Hollandsworth and Juan Pierre are expected to be key player in left and center, replacing Jeffrey Hammonds and Tom Goodwin.

Walker was the landslide NL MVP in 1997, when he came within four hits and 10 RBI of the first NL triple crown in 60 years. But that was the only season since 1993 in which Walker played more than 131 games.

He suffered a stress reaction irritation in his right (throwing) elbow the second week of May last year and missed 23 games before returning, although he obviously was bothered the rest of the season. The Rockies even put him in left field when he came back in an attempt to alleviate the strain on his throws. He returned to the DL in late August with right elbow inflammation and missed the rest of the season.

Walker again hit .300 for the sixth time in the last seven seasons he has done that -- but had only nine homers, 40 less than in 1997.

He is the complete package when (add qualifier) his flesh is willing. Walker is a perennial 30-100 candidate. Despite all his down time, he has averaged 29 homers and 87 RBI in his six seasons since signing with the Rockies as a free agent.

Walker stole a career-high 33 bases in 1997 but has been less prone to steal lately, although he is a savvy, smart baserunner who can win games by taking the extra base. His arm is strong and accurate.

Pierre, 23, made the major leagues in only his third pro season and could be the center fielder the Rockies have longed for.

In a two-month trial at the end of 2000, the speedy Pierre showed the ability to cover a lot of ground in Coors Field while fashioning 16 and 15 game hitting streaks. He was the first rookie to have multiple 15 game streaks since Minnesota's Kent Hrbek in 1982.

Pierre, a sleek six footer in the Tom Goodwin mold, has absolutely no power. Only two of his 62 hits last season went for extra bases, and both were doubles. He had one home run in his first two minor league seasons after being selected in the 13th round of the 1998 draft out of South Alabama. But he did have a three-hit game against Randy Johnson, so he can get around on a fastball.

At the same time, Pierre had 68 stolen bases in 1999 and 46 in four months at Double-A Carolina last summer. He had only seven in his first two months in the major leagues but certainly has the ability to steal 30 in the major leagues once he gets a read on the pitchers.

Hollandsworth, the National League Rookie of the Year in 1996, came over in a trading deadline deal with the Dodgers for Goodwin last July 31.

Not surprisingly, his numbers immediately shot up after

the deal. Hollandsworth batted .323 with the Rockies and had a great finish, hitting .357 with 10 (yes, 10) homers and 18 RBI in September. He finished with a career-high 19 homers, 11 with the Rockies.

A good defender, Hollandsworth does not quite have the range to play center field in Coors but is an upgrade in left field for a team that suffered through Dante Bichette's misadventures for most of the 1990s. He was expected to platoon with Ron Gant in left.

Ron Gant was signed as a free agent during the winter. He was expected to be righthanded bat in a righty/lefty platoon with Hollandsworth in left field. Do not expect Coors Field to make Gant the next Jeffrey Hammonds. He will get less at-bats than Hammonds did and he is on the downside of his career.

Terry Shumpert and Butch Huskey provide veteran depth. Shumpert has played seven positions, everything but pitcher and catcher, in his three seasons with the Rockies. A converted second baseman, he is most suited to left field if in the outfield. He will hit 10 homers and steal 10-15 bases while playing half the time.

Huskey hit .348 after coming to the Rockies from Minnesota in mid-July while playing left field, right field and first base. He averaged 18 homers a year while playing 120 games a year with the Mets, Seattle and Boston from 1996-99. Playing time is the only thing that stands in the way of similar numbers this year.

RECOMMENDATION REVIEW: Larry Walker is always a gamble playing time is such a variable because of his predisposition to injury. Catch him in a full season and he is worth every penny spent. Rumor had it that he was working out hard during the offseason, and was in the best shape of his career, so a big year could be in store for Walker if he stays healthy. Based on his September performance, Hollandsworth could project into Bichette/ Hammonds left field numbers over a full season, although he has struggled somewhat since his Rookie of the Year season in 1996. He will be a more valuable rotisserie player than Gant. Pierre is a stolen base threat in the making and should continue to improve as he learns the league. Huskey is a good risk as a backup outfielder because of a) the fragile health of Walker and b) the possibility of some at-bats in left field with Gant, and Hollandsworth, who hit .250 with no homers against lefties last season. Huskey hit .308 against lefties: By midseason, Shumpert will qualify at four or five positions, always a plus.

FLORIDA MARLINS

If Cliff Floyd could just stay healthy for an entire season he'd put up fabulous numbers. He's just now starting to fulfill the promise so many saw in him while a minor league player with the Expos, but injuries keep bringing him down. In just 121 games last year, Floyd hit .300 with 22 home runs, 90 RBI and 24 steals. If he can play 25-30 more games this season, he'll be a 30-30 man threatening the 100 RBI barrier. Floyd is on the verge of becoming a star.

Preston Wilson had a breakout year in 1999 and he followed that up with an even better season in 2000. He only hit .264 and he struck out a whopping 187 times, but his 31 homers, 121 RBI and 36 steals make those numbers acceptable. Throw in the fact that he's an excellent defensive center fielder and you have the makings of an All-Star for years to come. If he ever becomes even a little bit more disciplined at the plate, Wilson could be a 40-40 man.

Mark Kotsay took a little while to get where the Marlins wanted him to be, but he arrived as a consistent offensive threat during the 2000 season. Kotsay doesn't have great home run power, but he hits for average, steals bases and plays Gold Glove caliber defense in right field. He hit .298 last year with 12 home runs, 52 RBI and 19 steals, which is about what you can expect from him this year. He should hit a few more homers and perhaps steal a handful more bases, but his overall impact should be about the same. He's an ideal number two hitter in a major league lineup.

Jeff Abbott was acquired from the White Sox for Julio Ramirez. He was expected to fulfill the same fourth outfielders role as he did with the White Sox. See more on Abbott in the White Sox outfielders section.

The Marlins have virtually no major league ready outfielders. Julio Ramirez is a very gifted young player with some power, tremendous speed and a cannon for an arm, but he struggled at Triple-A last year and was traded to the White Sox for outfielder Jeff Abbott. Ramirez still needs more time at Triple-A.

Manny Martinez played at triple-A for the Marlins last year and could figure into the Marlins' plans as a fourth or fifth outfielder, but don't count on much from him. Cesar Crespo moved to the outfield at Double-A Portland last year, but he needs some time to develop as a hitter. He's got excellent speed, but minimal power and raw

hitting skills at this time. The most talented outfield prospect in the Marlins' system is Abraham Nunez, a player they got from the Arizona system. He's just a baby, but he's got 30-30 written all over him.

RECOMMENDATION REVIEW: Floyd, Wilson and Kotsay are all proven players worth having in most roto leagues. Floyd and Wilson are the better power-speed packages, but Kotsay could contend for a batting title in the near future and should score 100 runs. Look for Floyd to have an exceptional year in 2001. Of the other potential Marlins' outfielders only Nunez has the ability to be a star, but that won't be for at least a year or two. Pick him up if you have a minor league roster, but don't waste a major league roster spot on him.

HOUSTON ASTROS

In 1997, a year in which Houston won the NL Central Division, the Astros used eight outfielders who combined for 40 home runs. In 2000, a year in which Houston had a 72-90 record, the Astros had two outfielders who batted over .300 and reached the 30 home run and 100 RBI level. Richard Hidalgo's 44 home runs in 2000 exceeded the total of all eight Astro outfielders in 1997. And it can't be all due to Enron Field since Hidalgo hit only 16 of his 44 home runs at home.

The Astros may have the best offensive outfield in the major leagues with Hidalgo (.314-44-122-13), Moises Alou (.355-30-114-3) and Lance Berkman (.297-21-67-6 in 353 at-bats). Hidalgo, 25, had a breakout season in 2000 and should be one of the top hitters in the major leagues for many years. He can play all three outfield positions and constantly works to improve his game. Alou, 34, made a remarkable comeback after missing the entire 1999 season with a serious knee injury. A slight drop-off in production might be expected because of his age but Alou still has exceptional bat speed, which allows him to hit any pitcher's fast ball.

Berkman, a 25-year-old switch-hitter, should be a full-time performer in left field in 2001 after sharing the job last year with Roger Cedeno and Daryle Ward. Berkman was Houston's first round draft choice in 1997 and hit well at every stop as he progressed to the majors. He was a first baseman in college but was switched to the outfield early in his professional career. He is not a polished outfielder but has made substantial improvement. Berkman has not yet reached his potential as a hitter and could easily give the Astros a third .300-30-100 outfielder, as early as 2001.

Roger Cedeno was traded to the Detroit Tigers during the offseason. Lance Berkman and Daryle Ward will benefit from Cedeno's departure with more at-bats: meaning more home runs and RBI.

Roger Cedeno, obtained from the Mets in the Mike Hampton trade, began the 2000 season as the Astros' starting center fielder. He started slowly both offensively and defensively and failed to hold the job. His main asset is speed, a natural for a center fielder, but his defensive instincts were so poor that he was replaced in center field by Hidalgo. His playing time in the last half of the season was mostly in left field.

Cedeno, a 26-year old switch-hitter, is young enough to have a productive career. However, he must improve on his 2000 performance (.282-6-26-25), a major drop-off from his 1999 season with the Mets (.313-4-36-66).

Daryle Ward, also 26, is a player without a position as long as he stays in Houston. Like Berkman, he was originally a first baseman who has been moved to the outfield. However, he doesn't have the same all-around athletic skills as Berkman and the transition has been less successful. Ward is essentially a one-dimensional player. Some have speculated that he has 40-home run power if he played regularly. In 2000, he was .258-20-47-0 in 264 at-bats. His on-base average was only .295 and he had 61 strikeouts and only 15 walks. He was not very successful as a pinch hitter and did his best work in inter-league games when he played semi-regularly. This suggests that he could be productive in the American League where could get more playing time as a designated hitter.

Glen Barker, a 30-year old switch hitter, is another one-dimensional player: speed. After spending the entire 1999 season with Houston as a Rule 5 draftee, Barker split time in 2000 between Triple-A New Orleans where he was .271-2-10-11 in 26 games and Houston where he was .224-2-6-9 with only 67 at-bats in 84 games. He was used primarily as a pinch runner and a defensive replacement. He can't hit well enough to get much playing time but his speed gives him some value as a fifth outfielder.

The Astros don't have any other outfielders on the 40-man roster and don't have any outfield prospects far enough along to have an impact in 2001.

RECOMMENDATION REVIEW: The Astros' three starting outfielders should be major contributors to any Rotisserie team. Berkman may still be available at a reasonable price. Ward could have value if he is moved

to an American League team. Barker can be counted on for a few steals.

LOS ANGELES DODGERS

Jim Tracy gets to find out firsthand what Davey Johnson learned the past two years. Managing all these high-paid Dodger outfielders is not all it's cracked up to be. Both good and bad. For example, baseball snickered when the Dodgers essentially traded Mike Piazza for Gary Sheffield, not just because Piazza was destined to be in the Hall of Fame, but because Sheffield was supposedly destined for trouble. He was supposed to be moody and injury-prone. He was supposed to be a problem.

Most Dodger critics have been so eager to blast the club for letting Piazza get away that Sheffield's production has gone almost unnoticed. But it shouldn't. He merely carried the team for a second year, both on the field and in the clubhouse. Even though he missed 21 games with ankle and back injuries, the flu and a five-game suspension, Sheffield still hit 43 home runs (more than Piazza, Ken Griffey or Jim Edmonds), drove home 101 runs and hit .325, the second-highest average in his career. He also walked 101 times for the second consecutive season. All of the numbers are even more remarkable considering the two players supposed to protect Sheffield in the lineup - Shawn Green and Eric Karros hit .250 and .269, respectively.

Sheffield continued to display an amazing combination of power and patience, and is especially punishing to right-handed pitchers. His 70 extra-base hits led to a .643 slugging percentage, but he complements that with a .438 on-base percentage that seemingly would make Sheffield as good a leadoff hitter as the Dodgers have. Except for running the bases. Only 32, his body is brittle to the point that he has become very careful, especially on the bases, where his basestealing totals dipped to a career-low 4. But what he lacks in hustle he makes up for in smarts. Sheffield has baseball instincts. He will take the extra base with the game on the line, but won't do it to pad his stats. All told, Sheffield went from being a supposed overpaid malingerer to a bargain cornerstone without changing a thing.

And there's no telling what Sheffield might do if the real Shawn Green shows up. Of course, one year after signing him for a gazillion dollars, the Dodgers are wondering just which one is the real Green. Is it the one who parlayed a career season in 1999 .309-42-123 into that trade and contract? Or is it the one who seemed to try to justify the money by stubbornly slumping through his first National League season? Green lost 40 points in average, 18 home runs and 24 RBI in his first season at Dodger Stadium. Maybe it was playing in front of the family in his backyard. Maybe it was mental. It couldn't have been the ballpark, considering Sheffield's production. He wasn't hurt, playing all 162 games, and he's only 28 so he can't be losing his skills.

So the Dodgers are counting on Green to rebound even more than they were counting on him to produce last year. If they didn't desperately need a lefthanded slugger in the middle of the lineup, they wouldn't have acquired him in the first place. But Green did not show himself to be a classic lefthanded power hitter, driving many of his extra-base hits to the left-center gap. He was very mediocre against lefthanded pitching, as he has been throughout his career. On the bases, Green knows what he's doing. He knows when to take the extra base, he gets good jumps for steals and has a percentage high enough that he should run more than the 29 attempts he took last year (stealing 24). Defensively, Green did not win a Gold Glove, but those who tested his arm paid for it.

That takes care of the corners, which are a lot more settled for the Dodgers than center. This is a mess, a case of more being less. Devon White or Tom Goodwin? Nobody's sure. White is an aging (38) fraction of his former self. His season was derailed by shoulder surgery, but there was no guarantee he would see a lot of playing time even if he had been healthy with Todd Hollandsworth around. If not for his ridiculously rich contract, White would have been cast adrift long ago. He played in only 46 games last year, with substandard numbers for on-base percentage as well as slugging. Once capable of stealing as many as 44 bases, he as caught six times in nine attempts. His arm was clearly shot by the time he needed surgery, and he must play deep because he's lost a few steps.

Goodwin, who started in the Dodger system then bounced to Kansas City, Texas and Colorado, returned when general manager Kevin Malone finally admitted that with Eric Young gone and White failing, the Dodgers needed a center fielder and leadoff hitter. In Goodwin, they have a center fielder. He can outrun most balls, and he compensates for a below-average arm by hitting the cutoff man. As a leadoff hitter, Goodwin is a good center fielder. His on-base percentage is horrible (.346) because he strikes out too much (117). That might be tolerable if he delivered a Brady Anderson-type 50-home run sea-

son. Goodwin won't hit 50 home runs for his career, no matter how long he plays. His slugging percentage last year was .352. He had more triples, nine, than homers, six.

The strikeouts (many of them looking) means Goodwin has never developed a knowledge of the strike zone. He doesn't walk enough and his .263 average was only 10 points of his career mark. The real frustration is that if he could just get on base, he can wreak havoc. Over the last five years he has more steals than anybody in the major leagues, including 55 last year. Without average and power, Goodwin's only Rotisserie value is the stolen bases, but he wracks them up because he stays healthy and he plays every day because he actually hits lefthanders better than righthanders. Predictably, Goodwin hit about 25 points lower in Dodger Stadium than Coors Field.

The Dodgers are not expecting minor league help for the outfield. Top Taiwan prospect Chin-Feng Chen is coming off a disappointing year at Double-A and shoulder surgery. Tony Mota, Manny's son, needs another year at Triple-A.

F.P. Santangelo, Geronimo Berroa, Chris Donnels and Bruce Aven were to battle for the last bench spots. Santangelo missed most of the 2000 season with injuries, but he is a Malone favorite because of his versatility. Donnels also was hurt for much of 2000, but when healthy he showed increasing power picked up while playing in Japan. Aven was acquired during the 2000 season from Pittsburgh after emerging as one of the best fourth outfielders in the game in 1999. Berroa was signed to give some pop off the bench, but broke a bone in his foot. If any of these get considerable playing time, the Dodgers have big problems.

RECOMMENDATION REVIEW: Sheffield will again be one of the most reliable sluggers in the game, but other Dodger outfielders are a mystery. Green has the work ethic to rebound to his Blue Jays form. White is a player to steer clear of, while Goodwin will steal bases, but that's about it.

MILWAUKEE BREWERS

Any discussion of Milwaukee Brewers' outfielders these days must begin with Geoff Jenkins. Selected in the first round of the 1995 June Free Agent Draft (ninth overall), Jenks is probably the best draft pick the Brewers made under the deposed Sal Bando administration. Always considered a promising hitting and power prospect, Jenkins added gold glove caliber defense while flashing a powerful and accurate throwing arm in left field in 2000, easily leading National League left fielders with 12 assists. Jenkins even stole a career high 11 bases in 12 attempts and though he's no speed merchant, runs the bases with instinct and intelligence. At 26, Jenkins is beginning to assert himself as a team leader and is on track to become the Brewers' next franchise level player. Accordingly, the Brewers are looking to get their future superstar locked up with a long-term contract.

Jenkins was platooned earlier in his career but now plays every day. A broken finger kept him on the disabled list for nearly three weeks in 2000 and affected his power for weeks after that, but Jenks still managed to blast 34 home runs and drive in 94 runs in just 135 games. His only weakness is a tendency to be somewhat of a wild and free swinger at times, and he walked only 33 times (six intentional) compared to 135 whiffs. As he matures, he will learn to cut down on the big swing with two strikes situationally but even now uses the whole field and posted a .303 batting average to go with his .588 slugging percentage. What's not to like...?

By his previous standards, right fielder Jeromy Burnitz had an off year in 2000, seeing his average free fall from the .270 he registered in 1999 all the way down to .232. But a hot September lifted his power totals to 31 home runs and 98 RBI, and he added 99 walks. And for the second time in three years Burnie played in 161 games. He takes a big hack, as evidenced by the 121 strikeouts, is no longer much of a threat to steal a base, and can hurt a team with the occasional week-long slump. But he also can carry a team for a week with a barrage of home runs and his 12 outfield assists ranked him among the league leaders in that category. Though not the most physically conditioned athlete, Burnitz is only 31 and should bounce back with a better year in 2001.

Jeffrey Hammonds was signed as a free agent in the offseason from the Colorado Rockies. He was expected to start in center field when they acquired him. Although Hammonds has always had talent, he has been plagued by injuries throughout his career. Last year he had his career year offensively (Playing your home games at Coors Field tends to help!).

Marquis Grissom, on the other hand, is nearing the end of the line at 33, at least in terms of being a productive everyday player. His on-base percentage of .288 was lowest among full-time National League position players, and his average dropped 23 points to .244. These paltry numbers came largely from the leadoff slot! Consequently, Brewers' management has made it clear that the acquisition of a center fielder and leadoff hitter is the organization's top priority in the offseason. That should relegate Grissom, who still has two years to go on a five million dollars per year contract, to fourth outfielder status. Grip still plays a nice center field, although his throwing arm is probably the weakest in the league, and got his 20 steals for the second consecutive year. But his home runs dropped from 20 to 14 and his RBI from 83 to 62. All these numbers should continue to slide as he is unlikely to play every day from this point on.

James Mouton handled the fourth outfielder role for the Brewers in 2000, until a bad wrist that eventually required surgery deprived him of all but a pinch-running role for the season's final month. Speed is Mouton's primary weapon, and he stole 13 bases in 17 attempts in a part-time capacity. Mouton also plays a competent center field and can handle left and right field as well. He hit just two home runs in 2000 and has just 16 in his seven year major league career. The .233 batting average isn't overly helpful either. Coming off the wrist surgery at 32, a wait-and-see attitude on Mouton would be well advised.

Lou Collier got a late-season callup to Milwaukee in September and was given a shot in center field after Mouton went down, with mixed results. A shortstop by trade, Collier has the speed and athleticism for center field but isn't a disciplined hitter and has little power. His good speed has never translated into the stolen base column as he has but six in his four year major league career. A utility role somewhere probably awaits the former Pirates' prospect.

Down on the farm, you probably have to drop to the rookie-league level to ferret out any outstanding talent in the outfield within the Brewers' organization. Cristian Guerrero, a cousin of Vlad and Wilton, is a slasher who hit .310 with 14 home runs and 62 RBI between Beloit (Low-A) and Ogden (rookie league). Guerrero is still a couple of years away. Also keep a sharp eye on center fielder David Krynzel, the Brewers' top draft pick in 2000 who was hitting .359 at Ogden before a thumb injury prematurely ended his first season. Krynzel was rated the fastest high school player in the 2000 draft by Baseball America, possesses above average tools in every area but power and is as exciting a player as the Brewers have drafted since Paul Molitor. The Brewers have essentially given up on 1996 first-round draft pick Chad Green.

RECOMMENDATION REVIEW: Playing in the anonymity of small market Milwaukee, Geoff Jenkins may still be somewhat underappreciated among even knowledgeable baseball fans. This condition will probably not last for long so take advantage of it while it still lasts. He's for real! Forty home runs, 110 RBI, 10-15 stolen bases and a .280-.300 average likely await this all-star caliber performer. The law of averages says Jeromy Burnitz should bounce back with better power numbers and a higher batting average in 2001. Don't forget he's going to be playing for his next contract as well. Hammonds offensive numbers will drop without the luxury of Coors Field. Do not over pay. A more reasonable expectation for him would be around .285-.290-18-90. Stay away from Marquis Grissom. His playing time should diminish his already fading numbers.

MONTREAL EXPOS

The Expos once had Moises Alou, Larry Walker, Marquis Grissom, and Rondell White roaming in their outfield. While Vlad Guerrero is better than all three of those former Expos, the other two expected Expos' starters in 2001, Peter Bergeron and Milton Bradley, still have a lot to learn and are not as talented at the same age and stage as Alou, Grissom, Walker, and White.

By now everyone knows what Vlad Guerrero can do; Everything! He is going to be only 26, and it is scary to think that he is coming into his prime years now. You can bet the house that he shows up on any "Age 26 with Experience" articles.

Guerrero now has protection in the lineup with Jose Vidro hitting in front of him and Lee Stevens covering his back. If the Expos could find two players ahead of Vlad and Vidro in the batting order who could get on base consistently, then Vlad's numbers will go up even more, especially his RBI.

Vlad went virtually injury free in 2000, and has toned down his all out defensive style in right. So the injury risk, which was high in his first three season, is not as great.

Peter Bergeron had a disappointing rookie season. He failed to hit for average and show off his basestealing abilities. He stole only 11 bases and was caught 13 times. The Expos would also like to see his on-base percentage go up from the lowly .320 in 2000 if he is going to continue to be the Expos leadoff or No. 2 hitter. He is a line drive hitter who can not be expected to hit more than 15 homers

and will not drive in many runs.

During the offseason, there was talk of moving Bergeron over to left field to make room for the moody Milton "Shoots & Ladders" Bradley in center. Bergeron played 32 games in left. Most of those games came when Rondell White was trade to the Cubs.

Bradley is a rising star who has both power and speed, but also has an explosive temper that has gotten him into hot water. He was sent back down to the minors after his initial trip to the majors in 2000 for an attitude adjustment. If he can harness his attitude, Bradley has the talent to be a rookie of the year candidate.

Bradley was going to get every opportunity to win the Expos starting center field job in 2000.

The Expos always seem to bring in an aging veteran free agent to fill a role in their outfield. Two years ago it was Orlando Merced. Last year it was Terry Jones. Who ever it is, do not expect him to be of much Rotisserie value.

Wilton Guerrero is Vlad's older brother. Unfortunately, Wilton does not have the talent of his brother, though he is a better player than he has shown. Wilton is now used only as an outfielder. He was expected to be used mostly as the Expos fourth or fifth outfielder. He is still learning the outfield. His defensive concentration at second base held him back, but his move to the outfield has enabled him to concentrate more on hitting. He turned 26 during the offseason so expect Wilton to have one of his best years to date in limited time. Don't expect more than 300 at-bats unless there is some major injuries.

Terry Jones is a fifth outfielder who is more of a defensive replacement and pinch runner. He is a low .200s hitter with little power, who does not play enough or get on base enough to use his speed.

Fernando Seguignol was also expected to see some time in the Expos outfield. Though the team feels he is better suited for first. See Seguignol in the Expos first base section.

On the very near horizon is 2000 USA Olympic Team member, Brad Wilkerson. In 2000 he had 229 at-bats at Double-A where he hit .336-6-44-8, before being moved up to Triple-A where he hit .250-12-35-5 in 212 at-bats. He could be in Montreal as early as 2001, mainly as a fourth outfielder.

Depending on Bergeron's improvement, Wilkerson could find himself at Triple-A to start the season. If either Bergeron or Bradley falter, Wilkerson would be called up to take their spot and play left field. He has above-average power and is a .280s hitter. He has good speed but is not aggressive on the base and probably won't run as much in the majors.

RECOMMENDATION REVIEW: Vlad will have a bigger year than his 2000 season. Expect his RBI number to be in the Manny Ramirez range of 150, especially with the expected improvement of Bergeron or Bradley in the leadoff spot. If Vlad is available in your Rotisserie draft or auction, take him over anyone except Pedro Martinez, and Alex Rodriguez. Bergeron and Bradley are minor gambles, who will come cheap. They will both be more productive than their 2000 seasons. Bradley will be the better pick over the long run.

NEW YORK METS

Benny Agbayani continued to confound the personnel people who kept him down in the minors for seven seasons. He barely made the opening-day roster, beating out Joe McEwing, but by season's end had worked his way into the starting lineup and was one of the key producers for the National League champions. Agbayani, a righthanded batter, finished the season at .289-15-60. The downside is that he's 29 already.

Jay Payton was kept down, too, but by injuries. Last season, the Mets tried eight players in center field, and finally arrived at Payton as the regular at the position. The righthanded batter was third in Rookie of the Year voting with a .291 average, 17 homers and 62 RBI. He's 28, but he has received so little playing time that he might be able to play at a higher level into his 30s than most players do as long as he doesn't try to steal bases; he was 5 for 16 in 2000.

In contrast to Agbayani and Payton, Timo Perez shot to the majors after beginning last season at high Class A Port St. Lucie. The 23-year-old lefthanded batter tore up the Florida State and International leagues before joining the Mets in time to go on the postseason roster. He batted .289-1-3 and stole a base in September, then started most of the postseason games as the leadoff batter and right fielder after Derek Bell was injured. Perez, who began his professional career in Japan, could struggle against lefthanded pitching.

The streaky Derek Bell became a fan favorite as the Mets' right fielder, but faded to .266-18-69. He was a free agent during the offseason and signed with the Pirates. The righthanded batter is 32; he only looks 52. Look for a platoon of Timo Perez, Darryl Hamilton, and Tsuyoshi Shinjo to take his place.

Speaking of fan favorites, Joe McEwing played six different positions, pinch hit and hustled, but added just .222-2-19 and three steals to the Mets' offense. That was after the righthanded batter played 43 games at Triple-A Norfolk. McEwing is a month older than Payton, with nowhere near as rosy a future.

The Mets acquired another fan favorite, Bubba Trammell, from Tampa Bay for the stretch run. The 6'2", 220-pounder provided some righthanded power on a team where only he, Hamilton and Alex Escobar are 6'0" or taller among the eight outfielders on the 40-man roster. Trammell totaled .265-10-45 last season, and was successful on all four stolen base attempts. Trammell was traded to the Padres for reliever Donne Wall during the offseason.

Darryl Hamilton played in only 43 games after undergoing surgery on his left foot and finding Payton and Agbayani in place where Hamilton might have played. He batted .276-1-6. At age 36, with a bad wheel, the lefthanded batter doesn't appear likely to earn another starting outfield job.

Tsuyoshi Shinjo played in Japan last season. He was a average hitter in Japan with a little power and speed. It is unknown how successful he will be in the majors and has little value at this point.

Chris Sheff batted .259-7-43 at Norfolk. The righthanded batter is 30; he was a minor league free agent during the offseason.

Alex Escobar is considered one of the Mets' top prospects. He finally avoided injury well enough to play a career-high 122 games at Double-A Binghamton. The 22-year-old righthanded batter finished at .288-16-67 with 24 stolen bases.

Another 22-year-old righthanded batter, Brian Cole, joined Escobar in Binghamton's outfield after batting .312-15-61 and stealing 54 bases at Port St. Lucie. In Double-A, Cole batted .278-4-15 and swiped 15 more bases.

Also at Binghamton was Allen Dina (.258-7-46, with 21

steals). At 27, the righthanded batter may be out of time.

Juan Moreno totaled two homers, 39 RBI and 34 stolen bases between Binghamton (.200 in 90 at-bats) and Port St. Lucie (.280). The 25-year-old righthanded batter was a minor league free agent during the offseason.

Another speedy outfield prospect is Endy Chavez (.298-1-43, 38 steals). However, the lefty swinger is a year older than Escobar and Cole.

The Mets' power-hitting outfield prospect is 23-year-old righthanded batter Robert Stratton (29 homers, 87 RBI at Port St. Lucie). However, he batted just .228 and struck out 180 times.

RECOMMENDATION REVIEW: None of the Mets' major league outfielders is a high producer by Rotisserie standards. Payton offers the most potential. Perez is likely to be overpriced after his postseason success. Agbayani is likely to continue to be overlooked, and could make an excellent fourth outfielder for a Rotisserie roster. Escobar and Cole would be very good Ultra selections.

PHILADELPHIA PHILLIES

The Phillies like to believe that they have one of the most productive, best all-around young outfields in the major leagues. They are two-thirds correct. In right fielder Bobby Abreu, they possess one of the game's most underrated offensive forces, a five-tool guy whose numbers sneak up on you. In left fielder Pat Burrell, they possess one of the foremost of the game's next generation of premier power hitters, a perennial long-term league home run leader. In center fielder Doug Glanville, however, they possess a guy who insists on swinging the bat at virtually every pitch within reasonable proximity to the strike zone, regardless of the count or game situation. A guy who basically needs to bat .325 (as he did in 1999) to be considered truly productive.

1998 first round draftee Pat Burrell, 24, made his long-awaited major league debut last season, and showed glimpses of the extreme power that will allow him to rank among big league home run leaders over the next decade. The ball simply explodes off of Burrell's bat to all fields. Just ask Armando Benitez, the fearsome Mets' right-handed closer, who allowed all of 39 hits in 76 innings last season, just 23 to righties. He allowed gargantuan homers to righty Burrell on back-to-back nights last season, one to the opposite field, and the other a mammoth shot to left

in Shea Stadium. Burrell struck out way too much, an amazing 139 times in 408 at bats, in his rookie season, but his minor league track record suggests that he'll likely develop expert plate discipline, with his strikeout and walk totals likely intersecting around the century mark in a couple of seasons.

Last year, he got himself out quite often on high fastballs and low and outside breaking pitches, though his overall offensive performance was just fine for a rookie. He's quite slow afoot, but has worked hard on fitness and flexibility during the offseason, to positive effect. He didn't clog the bases as a runner, and his range was adequate in left field last season, where he showed a strong, accurate throwing arm. He also did some time at first base prior to the acquisition of Travis Lee, but didn't appear comfortable there. For now, his future appears to be in left field.

Look for Burrell to make a strong step forward as the Phils' everyday left fielder and number five hitter in 2001. Look for a .280 average, 35 homers and 105 RBI; and that's only scratching the surface of his upside potential. His dual eligibility at first base and outfield makes him extra attractive for next season. Go get him, and don't be afraid to pay.

It's a shame, but center fielder Doug Glanville, 30, could really be one heck of a baseball player. He possesses a few uncommon offensive traits, but utterly lacks one key, basic one: plate discipline. He's one of the highest-percentage basestealers in the game, tasting success on 87% (65 for 75) of his attempts over the past two seasons. He hits righties much better than he hits lefties, by the tune of .314 to .262 over the last three seasons. On the rare occasions when the count is in his favor, he is apt to hit the ball with authority from gap to gap. He's a fine defensive center fielder, with above average range and a decent arm, though he sometimes took bad at bats with him to the outfield last season.

However, after a brief dalliance with the concept of "plate discipline" early in the 1999 season (he walked 27 times in April and May of that year) he has reverted to his wild-swinging ways, drawing just 52 walks in the season and two-thirds since. This wouldn't be that much of a big deal, you see, if Glanville hadn't been used primarily as a leadoff man during that span. And by the way, Mr. Glanville doesn't consider this an issue; he insists that he's "not one of those on-base percentage guys". 'Oh. New manager Larry Bowa might have something to say about Glanville's approach, or even more likely might take his leadoff job away and hand it to rookie Jimmy Rollins, leaving Glanville to bat second or even seventh. Another option could be a change of locale for Glanville. This guy is much more valuable in a Rotisserie sense than he is to the Phillies. He'll steal his 30 bases, and his .275ish average 10 homers and 55 RBI won't hurt you as much as his low OBP will hurt the Phillies. Anything under $10 is a Rotisserie bargain.

Then there's Bobby Abreu, It is truly amazing how little attention this guy gets. He has a .313 career batting average. A .413 career on-base percentage. A .515 career slugging percentage. And he's done all of that with the benefit of a grand total of only three, that's right, three, career homers against lefthanded pitching. Once this 27-year-old lefty develops a power stroke against south-paws, as switch-hitter Chipper Jones did at about this age, watch out. Abreu has one of the sweetest strokes in the game. He massacres righthanded hurlers, batting .348 and .339 and slugging .612 and .616 against them in 1999 and 2000, respectively. He works the count, rifles the ball with authority to all fields, and will occasionally turn on mistake fastballs for extreme distance. Against lefties, he's more content to serve the ball back through the middle, but showed signs of developing that southpaw power stroke late last season, finally going deep three times. He also has well above average speed and tremendous first-step acceleration, and incorporates his wheels into his offensive game in an efficient manner. He stole 27 and 28 bases in 1999 and 2000, and has always ranked among major and minor league triples leaders. Defensively, his range is solid for an outfield corner and his arm is well above average; his assists ranked among NL outfield leaders last season. Oh, and he plays hurt, and enjoys playing this game as much as any guy around. Despite all of this, and despite the fact that other Phillies basically took the last two months of 2000 off, ex-manager Terry Francona opted to publicly beat up on Abreu for arriving late for practice a few times last season. Larry Bowa, on the contrary, will likely use this guy as an example of how to play the game for the rest of his squad.

Abreu's offensive numbers could jump to a new level in 2001 as he continues to learn to drive the ball against lefties. Look for a .330 average with 30 homers, 100 RBI, and 25 steals in 2001. He'll give you nearly Andruw Jones-equivalent Rotisserie performance for a non-Andruw Jones price. Get him.

The Phils, as usual, were expected to be looking for a few good men to add some pop off of the bench during the offseason, and were likely to add to their current stable of outfielders. Kevin Sefcik, 30, could aptly be described as the poster child for recent backup Phils' outfielders. He's scrappy, will take a pitch, and can play a bunch of positions, but has absolutely zero above average tools and would be unlikely to hit a ball out of the park from second base. In an obvious attempt to exorcise their bench demons of the recent past, the Phils waived Sefcik early in the offseason, though his ghost could return in the spring if they can't sufficiently upgrade.

Rob Ducey's another good story. Truth be told, the 36-year-old lefthanded hitter had a pretty darned good season off of the bench for the Phils in 1999, hitting for unexpected longball power and exhibiting solid plate discipline. Well, only the plate discipline was evident during a woeful 2000 season, leading to his trade to Toronto for a player to be named later. That player to be named later turned out to Ducey himself, who came back to the Phils in the subsequent Mickey Morandini trade. He's likely to reside near the end of the Phils' bench in 2001, and has no Rotisserie value. 1995 first round pick Reggie Taylor, 24, is an interesting player to watch this season. The 6'1", 178, center fielder is a slightly modified, lefthanded version of Doug Glanville. He runs even better than Glanville, has a higher power upside, and possesses equivalent range and a superior throwing arm. However, his plate discipline is at least as poor as Glanville's, and laughably, the Phils have also consistently used Taylor out of the leadoff spot. If Glanville is dealt elsewhere for pitching help, Taylor could play center field for the Phils in 2001. If he batted seventh and made subtle strides with regard to his patience, he could be a surprise success story and a solid low-dollar Rotisserie flyer. More likely, he's a .240-hitting 150 at bat guy who might be worth a buck because of his stolen base potential. Travis Lee (see First Base section) could also see some time in the outfield.

There's a little bit of potential near-term help down on the farm. The best of the lot is corner outfield prospect Eric Valent, 24, a lefthanded hitter with improving patience and a 20-homer stroke. However, players of his vintage who have yet to invade Triple-A generally aren't budding big league studs. He could help in a complementary role in Philly right away, however. Center fielder Josue Perez, 23, is a rather raw athletic specimen who can run and play solid defense, but is still struggling to piece together an offensive game. At this point, this 6'0", 180, switch-hitter looks like a future big league backup, at best. Jason Michaels, 25, was Pat Burrell's college teammate at Miami. He could develop into a solid long-term upper minor league standout, but lacks the power upside or patience to make a serious run at a material big league role. Way down low, the Phils have hopes for Marlon Byrd and Jorge Padilla. Byrd, 23, put up massive, Abreu-like all-around numbers at Low-A Piedmont, but was way old for that level. If he can bat .300 and reach double-digits in everything at Double-A Reading this season, then I'll believe. Padilla, 21, on the other hand, has a real chance to be a good one. The ball explodes off of his bat, and he should also hit for average at higher levels with a material improvement in plate discipline. A successful jump to Double-A for Padilla this season, unlikely in the glacial Phils' system, could mark him as a future star.

RECOMMENDATION REVIEW: Bobby Abreu is the surest thing of this group, he's in the upper echelon of national league outfielders. Watch Pat Burrell, he could be this year's Troy Glaus.

PITTSBURGH PIRATES

The Pirates outfield in 2000 consisted primarily of Brian Giles and a handful of others who were in and out of the lineup throughout the season. Wilfredo Cordero was a regular until traded to Cleveland before the deadline, John VanderWal graduated from a pinch-hitting role into regular right field duty. Chad Hermansen sputtered through a disappointing season to end up back in the minors. Adrian Brown filled in at all three outfield spots when the others weren't playing, and the remaining outfield roles were filled by Alex Ramirez (traded to Japan in the offseason), Bruce Aven, Emil Brown, Tike Redman, and a couple of players who were primarily infielders: Alex Hernandez and John Wehner.

In 2001, Giles is the focal point and a very productive player no matter how you track the stats. He hits for average and power both, steals a handful of bases, and does a marvelous job of getting on base. Giles has emerged from part-time use by the Indians to become one of the most feared hitters in the National League and a model of consistency. Still in his prime and showing a fine batting eye, Giles will maintain this level of play in the near future. Rotisserie owners should expect 40 homers, 110 RBI, and a .310 batting average; they should also expect to pay a pretty penny to get it, too, as Giles and Jason Kendall are the two Pirates hitters who will attract more than a $10 bid in most leagues.

Did the Bucs turn to VanderWal in 2000 because they had to or because he'd earned it? Both, actually. Hermansen's inconsistency opened a spot, but VanderWal kept it by

hitting consistently for power and average. It was the first time in his ten-year career that he'd gotten more than 250 at-bats. 2000 was, by far, his best season. So, what do we expect for 2001? Hey, they don't call them "career years" for nothing. Nearly every sign points downward for VanderWal. He's well beyond prime years. He's severely challenged for playing time from a number of Bucs youngsters. He has a well-defined pinch-hitting role in which he has succeeded in the past, meaning he would probably return to that role quickly if he struggled as a starter. He has never shown this kind of power in the past, so expecting it in the future is a bit of a gamble. In 2001, VanderWal may be given a platoon role. The most likely scenario is that he'll play more often early in the season, then return to a bench job as the Pirates' youngsters get more comfortable in starting roles. If you get VanderWal on Draft Day, be sure to have alternatives available before June.

Rookie of the Year candidate Hermansen must be considered one of the biggest rookie busts of the 2000 season. Rated by Baseball America as the Pirates top prospect and as one of the best prospects in all of baseball, Hermansen hit poorly to start the year, began to press and slumped badly before being sent back to Triple-A Nashville. At Nashville, his struggles continued as he hit .224 with eleven homers and 38 RBI. Despite his struggles in 2000, there is a silver lining for 2001. Hermansen's defense remained top shelf, he still ran the bases successfully at Nashville, and, more important, he maintained a positive approach and didn't let his troubles multiply. Hermansen will have a fresh shot at a starting role in the spring and might just surprise people this year. If you like reclamation projects or taking a chance on a "failed" prospect, Hermansen is your man. The pressure will be off Hermansen this year; no more "Rookie of the Year" expectations to carry. Instead, he'll have to win the job and he has the talent to do that. Rotisserie owners should let others point to him as a poster child for rookie failures, then quietly take a flier on Hermansen for a minimal salary at the end of the draft. Either he'll struggle again and you'll lose a very small sum, or he'll live up to his potential and you'll have a very large gain.

Adrian Brown picked up some of the slack left over by Hermansen, becoming a full-time player over the last two months of the season. He had actually earned the regular role in June before getting hurt. Over his last two months of play, Brown got 206 of his season total of 308 at-bats, hitting .313 with two homers, 20 RBI and seven steals in those two months. Projected to a full-season of play, Brown would put together a season line that looks like this:

.313 batting average, six homers, 60 RBI, 21 steals. Since Brown will be 27 on Opening Day and he now has almost two years worth of major league experience under his belt, he's ready to take on a full-time or nearly full-time role. The best bet is for switch-hitting Brown to play regularly against lefties (whom he hits much better than righties), and occasionally against righthanders, leaving him with about 350 at-bats. Figure a .300 batting average, about ten homers and twenty steals and Brown can be a valuable commodity in Rotisserie circles. Figure, also, that he's relatively unknown and you can get him pretty cheaply. Brown will be a small bargain for a number of Rotisserie owners in 2001.

Derek Bell was signed as a free agent during the offseason. He is a very streaky player and it is hard to predict what you are going to get with him. Our advice is to stay away. He was expected to get the majority of the starts in right field, but the Bucs have a lot of outfielders so his time and at-bats may be less than last season with the Mets.

Tike Redman and Emil Brown are going to each get a chance to win at least a platoon job in 2001. Redman has very good speed, although he hasn't shown an ability to use it effectively on the bases. It's unlikely he'll be able to hit enough for average to hold down a starting job in the big leagues. Brown may be one of those players who is perennially on the outside looking in. He did set a career best in at-bats in 2000; the bad news is that he still only got 119 in the majors. Brown has very good speed but his career .206 batting average suggests he is destined for a fifth outfield job when he is in the bigs. Of this bunch, for Rotisserie purposes, Ramirez is the only interesting choice.

Most of Nashville's outfield was stocked with the aforementioned players and with major league retreads like Brent Brede and Ray Montgomery, and guys who never could make it in the majors like Darryl Brinkley. None of these players are good Rotisserie prospects, although Brede can fill a hole in the unlikely event that he gets regular playing time in the majors.

At Double-A Altoona, Adam Hyzdu was a world-beater; he's a good organizational ballplayer but nothing more. Alex Hernandez and Rob Mackowiak filled in for the regular outfielders, but are both primarily seen at other positions. Darren Burton is a washout from the Royals organization. Garrett Long and Derrick Lankford are better prospects, but are still relatively dim.

The Bucs' best outfield prospect is J. J. Davis, who spent

the 2000 season at High-A Lynchburg, where he led the club in homers (20) and RBI (80) but also fanned 171 times in 485 at-bats while hitting just .243. Obviously, he needs to cut down on his swing a bit in order to make better contact. Tony Alvarez blazed around the bases for Low-A Hickory, stealing 52 bases in 73 tries, while also hitting 15 homers and driving in 77 runs. Aron Weston also ran wild on the bases at Hickory, stealing 28 in 34 chances. It remains to be seen if either player will be able to make productive contact at higher levels so they can make use of their brilliant speed.

RECOMMENDATION REVIEW: Get Giles if you want consistent, high-level, high-priced production. Elsewhere, there are a number of good bargains to be had. Hermansen, and Adrian Brown will turn a small profit for their owners in 2001. Stay away from VanderWal, Bell and any of the other bench players. Among the prospects, Davis, Alvarez and Weston are the best bets although they are all years away.

ST. LOUIS CARDINALS

Ray Lankford has been a Cardinals for a long time and for the most part has been a productive middle of the order hitter. His ability to play everyday has been hampered by continuous health problems and his performance began to decline a bit last year. Lankford hit .253 with 26 home runs and 65 RBI while striking out a whopping 148 times in 392 at-bats. That performance had the Cards thinking about dealing him this past offseason. Even if he remains in St. Louis, it seems like he's headed toward platoon work, playing mostly against righthanded pitchers.

Jim Edmonds strikes out a lot, but is an otherwise productive all-around player. He won a Gold Glove for his play in center field last year and also hit .295 with 42 home runs and 108 RBI. Even though he struck out 167 times, he managed to draw 103 walks and that really makes the strikeouts irrelevant. With Mark McGwire in the lineup next to him, Edmonds figures to see a lot of fastballs and plenty of RBI opportunities over the next several years.

J.D. Drew is on the verge of breaking out in 2001. His rookie season in 1999 was a disappointment, but he bounced back with a strong showing last year. Drew hit .295 with 18 home runs, 57 RBI and 17 steals - that's just the beginning of what he can do. Tony LaRussa took good care of him, playing Drew in situations where he could be successful and building his confidence. His defense is stellar and he could be a Gold Glove candidate someday.

Expect Drew to play even more this year and look for his overall numbers to take another step up.

Thomas Howard was expected to be one of the backups in the outfield, though Craig Paquette should figure into the mix as well. Paquette is a versatile player that can help by filling in at several positions. Howard is more of a pinch-hitter.

The loss of Shawon Dunston to the Giants creates a hole for a backup outfielder. Luis Saturria and former D'Ray Quinton McCracken were the prime candidates to replace Dunston.

McCracken may have something left and could surprise. He has been injured most of the past two seasons.

Prospects Luis Saturria and Andy Bevins are close to being ready for the majors, but they won't be needed this year if everyone stays healthy. Saturria is a five tool player that still lacks discipline. He has power, speed and a tremendous arm, but he needs refinement as a hitter. Saturria managed to hit .274 with 20 home runs, 76 RBI and 18 steals at Double-A last year, but struck out 124 times. Bevins is a good hitter with 25-30 home run power, but he needs to improve his patience at the plate. He hit .321 with 25 homers and 88 RBI last year at Double-A.

RECOMMENDATION REVIEW: Edmonds is an established star who is in the prime of his career. He's surrounded by talent and should be able to come up with numbers similar to those he put up last year again this year. Lankford will hit home runs, but seems to be on the downside of his career and might be better off in the American League where he could split time between left field and designated hitter. Proceed with caution where Lankford is concerned. 2001 will be a big year for Drew. Expect something in the range of .300 with 25-plus homers and 25-plus steals. Dunston and Paquette could have value in deep NL only leagues, but don't expect a heck of a lot. Both Saturria and Bevins are worthy of minor league roster spots, but weren't expected to have major league roles heading into 2001.

SAN DIEGO PADRES

To call the Padres' outfield crew a disappointment would be an understatement. When your fourth outfielder (Eric Owens) leads the outfield group in most hitting categories and garners more at-bats and hits than anyone else on the team, you know there has been some trouble with the

outfielders. Al Martin had a decent year before being traded to Seattle in advance of the trade deadline. Ruben Rivera was a major disappointment as a hitter, an outfielder and a player in general. Tony Gwynn spent far more time on the DL than he did lashing singles the opposite way. Rookie Kory DeHaan didn't make a big positive impression (although rookie Mike Darr did). The rest of the outfield spots were filled by players from other positions: Damian Jackson is primarily an infielder (see "Second Basemen") and Ed Sprague, John Roskos, Gabe Alvarez, Ryan Klesko and Joe Vitiello all are discussed in the "First Basemen" section.

Owens was again a pleasant surprise, leading the team in hits and improving his batting average by 27 points. He played each outfield position flawlessly and also led the Padres in steals with 29. Despite his success over the last two years, it is hard to recommend Owens for 2001. If the Padres had other options they would certainly use them and Owens' playing time would evaporate. Also, despite an overall good year, most of Owens' performance slipped a bit from 1999. He struck out more often, walked less frequently, his power dropped a bit and he ran the bases less successfully. For a 30-year-old who had been a career bench player until 1999, these are not good signs. Owens can still be useful in Rotisserie, but only if purchased at a very small price.

The leading disappointer among the Padres outfielders would have to be Ruben Rivera. His amazingly poor hitting line of .208-17-57 represents career bests, or nearly so, in all three categories. He fanned 137 times in 423 at-bats, bringing his three year total to 232 whiffs in 1006 at-bats, or 28 more strikeouts than hits over that span. Couple this performance, or lack thereof, with an unreachable, unteachable attitude and you've got a major problem. Rivera has — or had — a boatload of talent when he was a prospect with the Yankees oh so many years ago. Occasionally he will display a spark of that talent; usually, however, he just swings as hard as he can at anything near the plate and never learns a thing about hitting. For Rotisserie purposes, Rivera might represent an interesting low-dollar gamble except that he has shown absolutely nothing that can be considered progress; the worst thing about bidding on Rivera is that you might just get stuck with him.

Could you have imagined a Padres' team without Tony Gwynn? It almost happen; Gwynn was considering going elsewhere in pursuit of a World Series ring. If he plays regularly, expect a return to his usual high average hitting with little else of positive value. His best purpose for a

Rotisserie team would be as a last outfield pickup on a Rotisserie team that doesn't expect to contend. If you get Gwynn and he gets a chance to play regularly, trade him to a contender for a prospect. If he doesn't play enough to have value you haven't lost much.

Mike Darr collected nearly all of his at-bats during the last two months of the 2000 season and put up respectable numbers. He showed good speed and a useful average; he didn't hit for much power but still managed 30 RBI. Prorating his two months of play out to a full year leaves the following batting line: .280, three homers, 81 RBI, and 27 stolen bases. Presuming he gets a chance to play regularly, Darr would be a nice surprise to his Rotisserie owners, and with Gwynn's recent injury history and the lack of talent elsewhere in the outfield, it is a good possibility. He could easily push Owens back into a reserve role or knock Rivera out of the lineup altogether. All signs point to Darr emerging as a viable major league hitter in 2001 and giving his Rotisserie owners a fine bargain at the same time.

Kory DeHaan is a better hitter than he showed in 2000. In primarily a bench role, DeHaan batted just .204 with two homers and 13 RBI. While he is not likely to take over a full-time job, DeHaan can win a platoon role, although he'll have to hit above the Mendoza line to do so. Fortunately for DeHaan, he can do that, and hit with a little bit of power, too. Still, even if DeHaan were to get 250-300 at-bats as a platooner, it's a stretch to believe he can earn more than a minimum salary for Rotisserie purposes. There are better, more established part-time players available in most drafts, so DeHaan is not a good selection in Rotisserie ball.

Jack-of-all-trades John Mabry came to the Padres in the Al Martin deal; he was used fairly regularly by a Padres team starving for outfield production. Mabry didn't do much for San Diego, hitting .228 with seven homers in a Padres uniform. Mabry used to be a high-average hitter capable of an occasional homer. He can still hit the occasional homer, but his batting average has slipped gradually each of the last five years. His low batting average now offsets any value provided by his little bit of power making Mabry a useless Rotisserie player.

Bubba Trammell was acquired from the Mets for reliever Donne Wall. He will be a fourth or fifth outfielder. Expect more at-bats than in the past, due to a lack of talent in the Padres outfield. See more on Trammell in the Mets outfielders section.

Fifth outfielder Mike Colangelo was acquired from the Angels at the end of the 2000 season. He missed the entire '00 season with a shoulder injury. He has good speed and hits for a high average.

Considering the lack of depth for the Padres at the major league level and the struggles of some of their regulars, it is certain that at least one of their prospects will graduate to the bigs in 2001, possibly more. The best prospects to get playing time in 2001 are John Curl and Ryan Radmanovich from Triple-A Las Vegas, or A. J. Leday from Double-A Mobile. Curl was a first-round draft pick who hasn't quite developed the way a first-rounder would normally be expected to develop. Still, he has some talent and could jump into a semi-regular role in San Diego before the end of the year. Curl can hit for average and has a bit of power and speed. Radmanovich has regularly hit for a high average in the high minors but hasn't been able to make that final jump to the majors. The most telling thing about Radmanovich is that he was unable to get a major-league callup last year when the Padres were desperate for outfielders. If he gets to the majors it will be as a fifth outfielder and pinch hitter. Leday batted .283 and was one of Mobile's leading power hitters, with 12 homers and 70 RBI. When Leday jumps to Vegas in 2001, he should benefit from the hitter-friend environment of the Pacific Coast League and could put up some impressive numbers. Ryan Balfe, Ethan Faggett and Pete Tucci were other regulars in the high minors, but none are especially good prospects or were especially impressive in 2000.

Better prospects for the Padres reside at lower levels. Jeremy Owens ran like namesake Jesse, swiping 54 bases for High-A Rancho Cucamonga. He was also one of the club's better power hitters, with 55 extra-base hits. Owens will be challenged in 2001 when he moves to the pitching-heavy Southern League. An interesting prospect at Low-A Ft. Wayne last year was Vince Faison. Faison batted just .219 and struck out 159 times in 457 at-bats, but still managed 12 homers and 21 steals. He has very good speed and a quick bat, but his lack of baseball experience has prevented him from making consistent contact at the plate. He can become a prominent prospect in a hurry just through a little more experience.

RECOMMENDATION REVIEW: There are few recommended selections from the San Diego outfield. Owens is likely to have less value if his playing time diminishes. Rivera is such a negative producer it's impossible to take that risk. Gwynn may not play often enough any longer to produce more than minimal value. Most of the reserves are relatively worthless for Rotisserie purposes and most of the minor-leaguers are not especially good prospects. The best bet here is Mike Darr, who can be purchased at a very low price but has potential to hit for a decent average and steal a bunch of bases. Get him cheaply or not at all, though.

SAN FRANCISCO GIANTS

It is tempting to want to write Barry Bonds off each year, thinking he'll get hurt, or he'll drop off in production, but the reality is Bonds is one the best and most consistent players-in fantasy or reality-there is, or possibly has ever been. And, he plays with some sort of personal mission, which however distracting it might seem, allows Bonds to make the big plays.

He had a monster year in 2000, and Bonds doesn't look like he is ready to slow down now, even at his current age of 36. Bonds will no longer steal even 20 bases (10 is more like it), and if he plays 135 games, be happy. He will get his nominal .300-30-100 totals, and if your league counts walks, he'll give a big boost there, too.

The local sentiment was for the Giants to retain the services of Ellis Burks, who had a spectacular .344-24-96 season over just 393 at-bats (five steals, even). The Giants certainly played much better when Burks was in the lineup, but his price tag was greater than the Giants, who have a new ball park to pay for, want to pay. So Burks signed with Cleveland where he will continue to hit. Again, the limited at-bats might point to a lower price for Burks, just as his terrific numbers might push to inflation. There is no secret that he is just a tweaked knee away from being a disappointment, but Burks can and will produce, no matter where he plays. A DH job, in a town with a grass diamond, is going to help keep him healthy, and 20 homers and a .300 average are almost a given at this point. See more on Burks in the Indians outfielders section.

Eric Davis elected not to retire and signed as a free agent. He will take up a lot of the at-bats left behind by Burks. Don't expect much from the aged Davis. Who can't play everyday anymore due to injury problems. He has little Rotisserie value at this point in his career.

Shawon Dunston was signed during the offseason. Like Davis, Dunston is also past his prime and of little help at this point for a Rotisserie team. He will be used as a fifth outfielder/ emergency infielder.

Coming off his breakthrough 1999 (.290-16-64) even bigger things were expected from Marvin Benard. Benard struggled, starting slowly, but Dusty Baker stuck with his center fielder, and Benard turned in a decent follow-up season. With Burks gone, Benard will be depended upon to improve his totals, so look for an upward edge in offense, more in line with his 1999 season. And, if Benard can return to the .396 on-base total he rang up for that year, his stolen bases will increase (note that even with the drop in stats, Benard stole 16 more bases in 2000 than in 1999) dramatically. Benard is capable of 30 or more, registering as many as 42 for Clinton in 1993.

The best bet to earn the starting right field job is diminutive (5'9", 185) but powerful (.528 major league slugging average over 390 at-bats) Armando Rios. Rios, who suffered shoulder problems which limited his playing time last year, does indeed had solid power, having hit .301-26-103 with Fresno in 1998. Projected over 525 major league at-bats, Rios current major league totals would just about match those, at .295-26-110, with 13 steals. If Rios does indeed earn that starting spot, he could be a great value as a $1-2 fifth outfielder, potentially delivering numbers worthy of a #2 or #3 flychaser. Keep an eye on him: Rios could be a real steal.

Calvin Murray starts the season as outfielder #4 (a spot that may also be claimed by Felipe Crespo, covered among the first sackers). Murray, who was a #1 selection in 1992, is the organizational antithesis of Benard, the #50 selection the same year. Murray's primary value is that of basestealer (he bagged nine last year over 194 at-bats), making him a good fifth outfield gamble.

The last spot would belong to Terrell Lowery, who managed .441-1-5 totals at Pac Bell over limited at-bats, yet .199-16-44 over 301 plate appearances. In the minors, Mike Byas (36 swipes at Fresno), Chris Magruder (.282, 33 doubles, and 18 steals at Shreveport), and Carlos Valderrama (.315-13-81, with 54 steals at Bakersfield). Also, keep Ali Cepada, Alex Fajardo, and Clay Greene on your radar.

RECOMMENDATION REVIEW: Bonds is still one of the best. Rios could be a major sleeper. Let someone else bite on the names of Eric Davis and Shawon Dunston. They both are old and faded, and will not be much help.

TOP 2001 HOME RUN HITTERS

NAME	HR
Sammy Sosa	55
Barry Bonds	45
Ken Griffey	44
Vladimir Guerrero	43
Richard Hidalgo	37
Gary Sheffield	37
Brian Giles	34
Jim Edmonds	33
Andruw Jones	33
Jeromy Burnitz	32
Geoff Jenkins	32
Shawn Green	31
Richie Sexson	31
Preston Wilson	31
Moises Alou	30
Steve Finley	30
Juan Gonzalez	29
Luis Gonzalez	29
Matt Stairs	27
Pat Burrell	26
Lance Berkman	25
Ray Lankford	25
Jeffrey Hammonds	24
Bob Abreu	23
Ron Gant	23
J.D. Drew	22
Henry Rodriguez	21
Larry Walker	21
Daryle Ward	21
Benny Agbayani	20
Cliff Floyd	20
Todd Hollandsworth	20
Brian Jordan	20
Ruben Rivera	20

TOP 2001 RBI PRODUCERS

NAME	RBI
Sammy Sosa	139
Ken Griffey	126
Vladimir Guerrero	124
Moises Alou	123
Brian Giles	115
Luis Gonzalez	109
Jeffrey Hammonds	108
Richard Hidalgo	108
Preston Wilson	107
Shawn Green	106

Barry Bonds	105
Pat Burrell	104
Richie Sexson	104
Jeromy Burnitz	102
Larry Walker	101
Gary Sheffield	100
Jim Edmonds	99
Geoff Jenkins	97
Andruw Jones	97
Juan Gonzalez	94
Brian Jordan	90
Matt Stairs	90
Steve Finley	88
Dmitri Young	87
Bob Abreu	85
Cliff Floyd	84
Lance Berkman	79

TOP 2001 RUN SCORERS

NAME	RUNS
Barry Bonds	122
Jim Edmonds	121
Andruw Jones	111
Shawn Green	110
Ken Griffey	109
Sammy Sosa	109
Bob Abreu	106
Luis Gonzalez	106
Brian Giles	105
Vladimir Guerrero	102
Richard Hidalgo	102
Jeffrey Hammonds	100
Geoff Jenkins	97
Gary Sheffield	97
J.D. Drew	96
Marvin Benard	95
Doug Glanville	94
Todd Hollandsworth	92
Moises Alou	91
Steve Finley	91
Jeromy Burnitz	90
Larry Walker	89
Preston Wilson	88
Peter Bergeron	87
Juan Gonzalez	87
Richie Sexson	87
Lance Berkman	86
Tom Goodwin	86
Brian Jordan	83
Derek Bell	82
Ray Lankford	82

TOP 2001 BASESTEALERS

NAME	RBI
Tom Goodwin	49
Rickey Henderson	33
Doug Glanville	31
Bob Abreu	28
Preston Wilson	28
Eric Owens	27
Juan Pierre	26
Shawn Green	24
J.D. Drew	23
Andruw Jones	23
Reggie Sanders	23
Marvin Benard	22
Cliff Floyd	20
Todd Hollandsworth	19
Brian.l. Hunter	19
Corey Patterson	19
Mike Darr	17
Barry Bonds	15
Adrian Brown	15
Marquis Grissom	15
Mark Kotsay	15
Michael Tucker	14
Ken Griffey	13
Jeffrey Hammonds	13
Richard Hidalgo	13
Derek Bell	12
Peter Bergeron	12
Brian Jordan	12
Timoniel Perez	12
Ruben Rivera	12
Glen Barker	11
Vladimir Guerrero	11
Ray Lankford	11
Travis Lee	11
Jim Edmonds	10
Steve Finley	10
Wilton Guerrero	10
James Mouton	10
Luis Polonia	10
Reggie Taylor	10

TOP 2001 BATTING AVERAGES

NAME	AVG
Vladimir Guerrero	.334
Moises Alou	.327
Bob Abreu	.321
Larry Walker	.321
Tony Gwynn	.318
Juan Pierre	.312
Timoniel Perez	.306
Juan Gonzalez	.305
Luis Gonzalez	.305
Jeffrey Hammonds	.305
Lance Berkman	.303
Brian Giles	.303
Dmitri Young	.303
Geoff Jenkins	.302
Gary Sheffield	.302
J.D. Drew	.300
Mark Kotsay	.300
Rondell White	.300
Darryl Hamilton	.294
Cliff Floyd	.293
Adrian Brown	.292
Richard Hidalgo	.292
Andruw Jones	.292
Dave Dellucci	.291
Alex Ochoa	.291
Jay Payton	.291
Jim Edmonds	.290
Doug Glanville	.290
Sammy Sosa	.289
Eric Davis	.287
BJ Surhoff	.286
John Vanderwal	.286
Ken Griffey	.285
Barry Bonds	.284
Daryle Ward	.284
Shawn Green	.282
Armando Rios	.282
Mike Darr	.281
Todd Hollandsworth	.281
Benny Agbayani	.280
Milton Bradley	.280
Pat Burrell	.280

DESIGNATED HITTERS

ANAHEIM ANGELS

Lacking a full-time DH, the Angels used a variety of players at the DH position last year, and that could be the case this season as well. Scott Spiezio, a switch-hitter, will get a fair share of the DH duties. He is discussed with the first basemen. Mo Vaughn (first base), Tim Salmon, Darin Erstad and Orlando Palmeiro (outfield) will also get an occasional chance to DH. If he makes the club, Shawn Wooten (discussed with the catchers) would have some value as a third catcher/part-time DH.

RECOMMENDATION REVIEW: There is no pure DH here. Darin Erstad is versatile and valuable no matter what position he plays. Vaughn and Salmon should provide value for reasonable prices.

BALTIMORE ORIOLES

The Orioles are in rebuilding mode, emphasizing youth. So local favorite and Maryland native Harold Baines is unlikely to be back for another year. Instead, the Orioles will use position players in the DH slot, rotating them to give them a day off from playing in the field. Thus, Cal Ripken, Jeff Conine, Brady Anderson, and others will see some DH time. Promising rookie catcher Mike Kinkade swings a good bat, and the Orioles may want to keep him in the lineup.

Another possible exception is slugger Albert Belle who has a hip injury. If Belle can't play the outfield, and his hip is healthy enough for him to bat and run the bases, then he could become the regular DH. But Belle doesn't have the mental makeup to be a DH. The Indians tried it with him,

but the bench sitting affected his hitting, so much so that he was down in the .220 range. So Belle should be avoided if he's the DH.

RECOMMENDATION REVIEW: Albert Belle could become the O's everyday DH. If so use caution, his hip has been giving him problems, plus he was unsuccessful in a DH role in the past.

BOSTON RED SOX

Dante Bichette found his calling when he became the Red Sox DH down the stretch. As Cincinnati's right fielder, Bichette had batted .295-16-76. He contributed .289-7-14 in 30 games for Boston. But at 37, the righthanded batter is far removed from his Colorado days.

The switch-hitting Morgan Burkhart, 29, batted .288-4-18 in his major league debut. At Triple-A Pawtucket, he produced at a rate of

Freddy Garcia, 28, is a righthanded batter who was disappointing in trials with Pittsburgh and Atlanta. Garcia is an all-or-nothing batter who finished at .262-24-74 at Pawtucket, while striking out about three times as often as he walked.

RECOMMENDATION REVIEW: A Bichette-Burkhart platoon is a possibility. You may want more production from a DH than either can provide separately.

CHICAGO WHITE SOX

He's back, Frank Thomas, that is. Thomas was one of the most feared hitters in baseball during the first half of the 90s but went into an inexcplicable slump for a couple of years before returning to MVP status during the 2000 season. As he did before, Thomas hit for both average and power while consistently driving in runs. With the support around him in the White Sox' lineup, there will be no reason to expect a decline in his performance at any time in the future. Thomas is a legit contender for batting titles that will hit 30-plus homers and drive in 100-plus without a problem.

Paul Konerko, who will mostly play first base, will also see time as the DH. It won't change his value in the least.

Prospect Jeff Liefer could see time here as well, but probably only in the case of injury. He hit 30-plus homers at triple-A last year and swings from the left side of the plate, something the Sox need, but with Thomas and Konerko in the way he won't get much playing time during the 2001 season.

RECOMMENDATION REVIEW: The only thing Thomas won't bring to the table is defense and speed, but only one of those even counts for roto owners. He's a star and will put up monster numbers, so get him if at all possible.

CLEVELAND INDIANS

The Indians don't have a DH-only player like Harold Baines or Jose Canseco, but rotate position players through the slot. The most likely to get DH time are outfielders Russell Branyan, Ellis Burks and Dave Roberts. They are discussed in the outfield section.

RECOMMENDATION REVIEW: Burks has the most Rotisserie value based on is good average and high number of RBI. Roberts can swipe some bases, and Cruz, by far, is the least valuable of the three.

DETROIT TIGERS

The Tigers went into this past offseason searching for a new designated hitter, but if they wind up staying in house the job will most likely fall into the lap of Rob Fick. Fick can also play some at first base and behind the plate, but DH seems like the most likely place for him if he's

healthy. Fick is a professional hitter that can hit for average but is still working on developing his power. Given a chance to hit regularly, Fick could be a really nice pickup.

Tony Clark and Dean Palmer could also figure into the designated hitter rotation in Detroit because of past injury problems that could keep them from playing in the field at times. If they're healthy there should be no problem, but keep an eye out in Spring Training. Also pay attention to what they do in free agency as a the signing of a significant hitter could send Fick to the bench.

The Tigers really only have one minor league player that could figure into the DH spot this year and that's Chris Wakeland. He hit 28 homers at Triple-A last year and is a lefthanded hitter, but so is Fick. Wakeland's greatest weakness is, however, is that he strikes out a lot.

RECOMMENDATION REVIEW: Fick is worth picking up if he looks good in spring training, but proceed with caution.

KANSAS CITY ROYALS

The DH duty was split in 2000 between Mike Sweeney and Mark Quinn, with other players getting a "day off" via the DH occasionally. Sweeney is discussed at length under "First Basemen" and Quinn is discussed in depth in the "Outfielders" section. Either player is a good addition to a Rotisserie squad although Sweeney is a more consistent and, therefore, more expensive choice, while Quinn provides more potential upside and is a greater risk.

RECOMMENDATION REVIEW: Kauffman Stadium is a hitters park and the Royals are a productive offensive bunch. Whomever fills the DH role for Kansas City will produce; get anyone who looks like they will get 400 at-bats among Royals outfielders or first basemen and you won't be disappointed. Sweeney is recommended for strong teams that need consistent, predictable production; Quinn is recommended to owners who need a small bargain at the expense of a small risk.

MINNESOTA TWINS

The Twins tried to upgrade last season, signing Butch Huskey and making him the cleanup hitter. Unfamiliar with having such a responsibility placed on his hulking shoulders, Huskey scuffled, sulked and was gone before the All-Star break.

Designated hitter is one of the most expensive positions on a baseball team. Since the Twins are reluctant to spend on players, they have had poor productions there in recent years. The Twins hope that David Ortiz will hit like a bonafide DH this season, but have a few others to try at the position if he fails to produce.

Ortiz definitely has the power to put up respectable numbers, and enters 2001 with his best chance at getting consistent playing time. Ortiz has a short stroke and a decent eye at the plate. But what makes him effective is that he can hit outside pitches to the opposite field. He does this especially against lefthanders. When pitches adjusted and began to bust him inside, Ortiz was able to adjust with them.

What was most impressive in 2000 was that Ortiz, who bats lefthanded, hit .423 against lefthanders, something that will keep him in the lineup every day. Once inserted into the starting lineup in July, Ortiz was one of the best run producers on the team. With that success under his belt, Ortiz can be expected to have a productive 2001 season.

If Ortiz doesn't come through, look for Ron Coomer to see action as the designated hitter. Coomer's righthanded bat would help balance out a predominantly lefty hitting lineup, and his experience as a cleanup hitter would also be an asset. But Coomer, at best is a 16-20 homer, 65-90 RBI player. On the Twins, that's helpful. To the roto owner, that's a late-round pick or low bid.

Matthew LeCroy, a young slugger with potential, could see some time here as well. LeCroy puts on a show in batting practice, but got in some bad habits last season and had to be sent down. LeCroy is primarily a catcher but he needs work behind the plate. If he shows promise at the plate, the Twins will try to keep his bat in the lineup at either first or DH on a part-time basis.

RECOMMENDATION REVIEW: The Twins don't have one guy that's going to be their DH. More than likely, it will be a combination of several players listed at other positions. Look for David Ortiz to get the lions share of at-bats now that Coomer was released during the winter.

Even though Jose Canseco, also 36, played just 37 games for the Yanks, Shane Spencer was the only righthanded batter who DHed more for them. Canseco batted .252-15-49 with two steals for Tampa Bay and New York.

Glenallen Hill also joined the Yankees during the season, and was one of their hottest hitters down the stretch. He's also 36 and a righthanded batter. With the Cubs and Yankees, he totaled .293-27-58 in just 300 at-bats.

Luis Polonia also played some DH late in the year, but was mostly used as a pinch hitter.

Chuck Knoblauch's throwing problems could cause him to end up as a DH. Read more about him under second basemen.

Darryl Strawberry's career appears to be over after a year of legal, drug and health problems, with no baseball.

RECOMMENDATION REVIEW: The Yankees don't seem likely to have more than a platoon DH. If Knoblauch had the job on a regular basis, he wouldn't be likely to contribute as much power as most DHs, but would steal more bases. David Justice will most likely see some time at DH as well when he's not playing in the outfield.

OAKLAND ATHLETICS

Signed to a two year deal following his stellar 1999, John Jaha returned to form, and was injured for most of the 2000 season. He will make the roster, but has little roto-value, bearing in mind his injuries. In fairness, though Jaha only batted 97 times last year, but walked an amazing 33. If he gets healthy, Jaha is capable of 20 plus homers, an average near .300, and terrific on-base totals, but that is a big "if" these days.

Look more for Olmedo Saenz (discussed with third basemen) and Jeremy Giambi (discussed with the outfielders) to carry the bulk of DH duties, unless Jaha stages another miraculous return. (And, don't rule out the possibility of Ben Grieve logging some serious DH time.)

It is hard to consider scouting a minor league DH, but Todd Mesnick (.265-23-84 at Midland) and Rafael Pujols (.322-9-74, with 11 steals at Visalia) were the minor league leaders at the spot. Being a minor league DH, however, points to little in the roto value world.

RECOMMENDATION REVIEW: Saenz and Giambi can provide some value at the DH position. If they platoon expect Giambi to get more at-bats since he is lefthanded.

SEATTLE MARINERS

Edgar Martinez will see full-time DH duty for the Mariners and he generally doesn't miss too many games. He's played in at least 153 games in three of the past four years, so he's been reliable. The one year out of those four he played less than 153 was 1999 when he played in 142 games. He also hasn't played fewer than 139 games since 1995. An average season for Edgar is .320 with 25 home runs and 97 RBI to go with 100 plus walks. He's a hitting machine coming off career highs in homers with 37 and RBI with 145. Forget about Edgar's age, he's not about to drop off anytime soon and is one of baseball's best hitters.

Raul Ibanez and Jon Olerud could see the occasional game at DH, but that doesn't increase their value in any way.

RECOMMENDATION REVIEW: Get Edgar if it is at all possible.

TAMPA BAY DEVIL RAYS

The Devil Rays began the 2000 season with Jose Canseco penciled in as the team's every day DH; that all changed when Canseco was claimed off waivers by the Yankees in August, leaving this year's DH duties to three and perhaps four players. But DH duties won't be split by four players if Greg Vaughn's shoulder doesn't heal properly. The Devil Rays' everyday left fielder had shoulder problems toward the end of the season which made him the everyday DH. That likely will change this season as the prognosis was good for Vaughn's shoulder. If his shoulder is healthy, he will only serve as the DH on occasion, otherwise those duties will fall mostly to Steve Cox and Fred McGriff, who will find himself in the lineup more often as the DH than he has been the first three years of the franchise's history.

In addition to those three, catcher Toby Hall could find himself in the lineup as the DH against righthanders if he makes the team, as could speedsters Alex Sanchez and Jason Tyner, who could be the DH in the leadoff role.

The only certainty as far as the Devil Rays' DH is concerned is if Vaughn's shoulder is hurt. In that case he will be the DH.

RECOMMENDATION REVIEW: Stay away from Devil Rays DH candidates, none will be able to approach the kind of numbers other DH's are putting up, unless Vaughn is the guy and you need home runs.

TEXAS RANGERS

The Rangers signed Andres Galarraga to be their full-time designated hitter. Galarraga comes with some questions about his health and durability, particularly since his performance tailed off dramatically in the second half of last season. Still, the transition to DH should help keep him fresher for longer into the season. Galarraga's bat has slowed a bit, but the American League is less of a fastball league and Galarraga may find it to his liking. Expect around 400 at bats for Galarraga, with homers in the teens and a solid batting average. See more on Galarraga in the Braves first basemen section.

Rafael Palmeiro, who is the starting first basemen, is sometimes used at DH to rest his knees on artificial turf. Frank Catalanotto (see second base profiles) and Chad Curtis (see outfielders) are also DH possibilities.

RECOMMENDATION REVIEW: As long as you don't pay for a full season's worth of stats, Galarraga should be a solid investment.

TORONTO BLUE JAYS

Brad Fullmer probably breathed a sigh of relief when he was traded to Toronto, where his defensive skills (or lack thereof) became a non-issue with the presence of Carlos Delgado.

With a manager that showed confidence in him and an everyday spot in the lineup, Fullmer responded with his best offensive season, showing that his power stroke, always a presence in batting practice, could translate into major league home runs. Fullmer was at or above .300 for most of the season, finishing at .295, and his 32 home runs and 104 RBI were both career highs. In fact, he hit more home runs than he had hit in 892 major league at bats prior to the 2000 season. For an encore, Fullmer begins the

2001 season with absolute job security as the everyday DH and he can play first base if something should happen to Delgado.

Todd Greene was surprisingly available as the Angels gave up on him in a preseason roster-crunching exercise. No one has doubted Greene's power and the Jays gave him an opportunity, first at Triple-A and then with the major league squad. Greene responded by showing his great power stroke in limited work and then came to terms with the Jays on a 2001 contract immediately following the season. He fits in here as a righthanded hitter to complement Fullmer and in addition to occasional DH duties and pinch-hitting spots, he claims a desire to backup as a catcher. A healthy Greene capable of catching would move to the team's number two catching spot, ahead of Alberto Castillo.

Darrin Fletcher, the team's incumbent catcher, could also see more than his share of work out of the DH spot this year. It's no secret that the years are beginning to take a toll on him and because Fletcher still hits well, he could see a gradually increased number of starts at DH, though with Fullmer present, it will only be a handful at this stage.

RECOMMENDATION REVIEW: Brad Fullmer broke out in 2000 and should repeat that performance in 2001 now that he's settled into the everyday DH role. His power numbers should even improve. Fletcher is much more valuable as a catcher.

TOP 2001 HOME RUN HITTERS

NAME	HR
Manny Ramirez	46
Rafael Palmeiro	40
Jason Giambi	38
Jim Thome	36
Greg Vaughn	35
Edgar Martinez	32
Frank Thomas	32
David Justice	31
Tim Salmon	30
Albert Belle	29
Juan Gonzalez	29
Brad Fullmer	26
Mark Quinn	26
Dante Bichette	25
Russ Branyan	25
Mike Sweeney	25
Glenallen Hill	24
Jose Canseco	21
Darin Erstad	21
David Segui	18

TOP 2001 RBI PRODUCERS

NAME	RBI
Manny Ramirez	154
Jason Giambi	130
Edgar Martinez	123
Rafael Palmeiro	122
Mike Sweeney	121
Frank Thomas	116
Jim Thome	109
Albert Belle	108
David Justice	106
Dante Bichette	102
Brad Fullmer	95
Tim Salmon	95
Juan Gonzalez	94
Greg Vaughn	92
Mark Quinn	90
David Segui	86
Darin Erstad	84
Johnny Damon	80
David Ortiz	73
Chris Hatcher	71
Russ Branyan	62
Jose Canseco	60
Glenallen Hill	57
Brian Daubach	54

TOP 2001 RUN SCORERS

NAME	RUNS
Johnny Damon	118
Manny Ramirez	118
Jason Giambi	109
Jim Thome	107
Darin Erstad	106
Tim Salmon	98
Frank Thomas	98
Mike Sweeney	97
Rafael Palmeiro	95
Edgar Martinez	94
Chuck Knoblauch	93
Greg Vaughn	92
Juan Gonzalez	87
Dante Bichette	86
David Justice	85
Mark Quinn	84
Albert Belle	83
David Segui	81
Brad Fullmer	72
David Ortiz	70

TOP 2001 BASESTEALERS

NAME	SB
Johnny Damon	44
Darin Erstad	23
Chuck Knoblauch	21
Luis Polonia	10
Greg Vaughn	10
Mike Sweeney	7
Albert Belle	6
Dante Bichette	6
Chris Hatcher	5
Mark Quinn	5

TOP 2001 BATTING AVERAGES

NAME	AVG
Manny Ramirez	.324
Darin Erstad	.322
Johnny Damon	.316
Mike Sweeney	.316
Frank Thomas	.315
David Segui	.312
Jason Giambi	.309
Mark Quinn	.306
Juan Gonzalez	.305
Edgar Martinez	.301
Billy McMillon	.296
Scott Morgan	.294
Luis Polonia	.292
Albert Belle	.291
Dante Bichette	.291
Olmedo Saenz	.290
Brad Fullmer	.288
David Ortiz	.286
Tim Salmon	.286
Jeremy Giambi	.284
Chuck Knoblauch	.284
Rafael Palmeiro	.284
Glenallen Hill	.277
David Justice	.276
Jim Thome	.273
Shane Spencer	.271

STRATEGIES FOR STARTING PITCHERS
Finding Your Way in a Minefield

by John Benson

After the 1993 expansion and its experience of starting pitchers with exploding ERA's and arms falling off, things settled down a little as the pitchers regrouped, gained more experience, learned better conditioning methods and benefited from improving forms of surgery. Since the 1998 expansion, however, the problem of bad pitching is just getting worse. The 1999 total league ERA's were 4.86 for the AL and 4.56 for the NL. In 2000 it was 4.91 for the AL and 4.63 for the NL. And it was even worse for the starting pitchers. Last year the total average ERA in the American League was 5.09 for starters, and in the National League starters worked to a collective 4.68 ERA.

One implication is that we must have a new and more liberal definition of a bad starting pitcher. It wasn't that long ago that we looked askance on an ERA over 4.00. If the average for all starters is now 5.09 in the AL, we must revise our thinking to see value in guys like Mark Redman (4.76 last year, 4.81 forecast this year), Ramon Ortiz (5.09 last year, 4.81 this year), Brad Radke (4.45 last year, 4.90 this year), Sidney Ponson (4.82 last year, 4.81 this year), Blake Stein (4.68 last year, 4.85 this year), Brian Rekar (4.41 last year, 4.72 this year), Jeff Suppan (4.94 last year, 4.84 this year), and Pat Hentgen (4.72 last year, 4.53 this year) and so on. You get the idea. The 200-inning guys with unattractive ERA's are likewise numerous in the NL.

The gap between good and bad is growing even more rapidly, and an ERA in the 3's is worth a lot more now than it used to be. How much space should we devote to telling you that Pedro Martinez is a terrific package of value? About that much. Take a longer look at the value of guys like Barry Zito (3.22 ERA this year), Paul Wilson (3.61), Roger Clemens (3.66), Mike Mussina (3.66), Freddy Garcia (3.68), Jarrod Washburn (3.69), Bartolo Colon (3.88), Mike Sirotka (3.89), Tim Hudson (3.81). And in the AL especially, there is solid value in guys over 4.00 like Steve Sparks (4.02), Paul Abbott (4.02), Jose Mercedes (4.11), Albie Lopez (4.11), Ramiro Mendoza (4.12), Juan Guzman (4.21). Chuck Finley (4.27). An ERA over 4.00 and a value of $10 or more can now go hand in hand in the AL.

The same phenomenon is clear in the NL although the numbers come with less sticker shock. Carl Pavano (3.99), Robert Person (4.02), Rick Reed (4.15), Tony Armas (4.27), Jon Lieber (4.29), Elmer Dessens (4.38), Andy Ashby (4.40), Todd Ritchie (4.41), Dustin Hermanson (4.44), Shane Reynolds (4.43), Kirk Rueter (4.43), Scott Elarton (4.44), Todd Stottlemyre (4.44), Javier Vasquez (4.45), Jamey Wright (4.46), Garrett Stephenson (4.51), Brad Penny (4.52), A.J. Burnett (4.53), and Kevin Millwood (4.57) are all among the better SP candidates for 2001. If you had a team ERA in the high 4's or even above 5.00 last year, you know exactly what we are talking about.

Track record is everything when it comes to starting pitching. A bad track record should scare you away from any pitcher, even a famous pitcher. And there is one thing worse than a bad track record: no track record. The most dangerous starting pitchers of 2001 will be the promising youngsters whose managers keep sending them out there once every five days, because they have talent and show some evidence of improvement.

In a normal year on a normal team, a rookie starter would be allowed to keep his spot in the rotation if he pitched well in one third of his outings. In 2001 some rookie starters on average teams will be allowed to keep their jobs if they pitch well in just a fourth of their outings. When a rookie (or any other starter) gives up nine runs in three innings, that's just a one-game setback for him and his team. The hope that he will pitch well the next time can be enough to keep him in the rotation. But nine runs in three innings is the type of performance that ruins a lot more than one day in a stat league. A few bad outings like that can undo weeks or even months of creditable work by other pitchers. So be careful.

Here are some simple methods to find your way safely through the minefield of starting pitchers in 2001:

1. Be willing to spend a more on starting pitchers. Pay $6 instead of $1 for your fifth starter, just to minimize the risk of disaster.

2. Be prepared to spend a lot more for a top starter. Greg Maddux, Kevin Brown, Pedro Martinez and Randy Johnson are in a class by themselves, and everyone knows it.

3. Judge starting pitchers by what they have done badly, not by what they have done well. Be pessimistic. Rate pitchers by their worst season over the last three years.

4. Get some unexciting pitchers who have never had a bad year.
5. Try going with fewer starting pitchers. That's good advice every year, and especially in 2001. One of the biggest, simplest mistakes to make is to guess that you must have a certain number of starting pitchers when the draft ends, which is wholly untrue. There are no innings penalties assessed in April, May or June. You can come out of the draft with only one or two starters, add a third and fourth in May, June or July, and then have five or six or even seven in August-September, and get more innings than you would have had with five starters in place all year. And your numbers will be much better. Waiting has the benefit of giving

more information. By June 1 we will all have a better idea who the good starters are this year. And waiting opens the door to trading opportunities. There is no better method than trading for a proven veteran starter on May 1 when he has a 1-4 record and his owner is unhappy with him.

6. Avoid the fifth starters on major league staffs (except for the Braves and Yankees). The value of a fifth starter is usually negative, and often severely negative, in a typical Rotisserie league (whatever you gain in wins, you will lose in ERA and ratio). There is a simple reason why wins will always be such a tightly-packed category in September: everybody tries to get as close as possible to the edge of that cliff, without falling over. This year, don't be in a hurry and rush to the edge of the cliff; it is closer than you think.

Ultra rules and reserve lists change everything of course. If you can keep a pitcher inactive on a reserve list, he can't hurt you, and you can pick your pitching spots (such as using Dodgers at home, and keeping all pitchers on ice whenever they come anywhere near Colorado). When you can just take a pitcher and see what happens, you can take chances left and right.

In Ultra or with a reserve list, you can even take rookies, boldly. When looking at unproven talent and hoping for a break-through year, we like Tony Blengino's methodology for iden-tifying the best prospects (you can read about it in "Future Stars," available from Diamond Library). We examined 14 of the top prospects he identified using The Rule of 25. That rule says that the best pitchers average at least 2.5 strikeouts per walk while holding opponents to a batting average of .250 or less.

Our recommended rookies: lefthanders Ryan Anderson (Mari-ners) and Bud Smith (Cardinals) and righthanders Paxton Crawford (Red Sox), Roy Oswalt (Astros), Luke Prokopec (Dodgers) and Jon Rauch (White Sox). As always, how well those pitchers can do depends on the opportunities they receive, how much support they get from their teams.

The "Don't Change a Thing" Strategy

We say this because we're pretty doggone proud of the advice we gave you last year. Here are four names for you: Eric Milton, Tim Hudson, Scott Elarton, Javier Vazquez. Those were the four up-and-coming surprises on a list of the 15 major league pitchers who ranked in the top quarter of their league in '99 in strikeout/walk ratio and opponents' batting average. To show you the type of quality on that list, the others were Chuck Finley, Bret Saberhagen, Bartolo Colon, Randy Johnson, John Smoltz, Alex Fernandez, Kevin Brown, Curt Schilling and Sterling Hitchcock.

In 2000, the four surprises did even better than the 11 estab-lished pitchers on the list. Among them, Milton, Hudson, Elarton and Vazquez were 61-32 with a 4.45 ERA and 1.34 ratio. And they averaged 203 innings per man, so they would have helped hold down a lot of ERA's and Ratios. So we think we could use the same methodology, of combining pitchers'

Hittability (opponents' average) and Strikeability (K/BB ratio), to be successful this year. In doing so, of course, we're going against some of our own advice from 1999: "Winning always involves making changes. Last year's winning methods won't work exactly the same with this year's player population. Essentials remain the same, but details keep changing, and details often decide who wins when everyone is using the same essentials."

Bobby McFerrin

You remember Bobby, don't you? He sang, "Don't worry, be happy."

That's what you should be doing in preparing for and attending your draft.

Sure, you can go to spring training or peruse spring box scores for hours, but don't put too much stock into spring pitching performances. Often those who are doing best in exhibition games won't be in a major league rotation by the All-Star break. The best starters usually go into each outing in Florida or Arizona planning to work on one or two pitches, unless they're auditioning a new pitch, or on merely hitting a location. They save their heavy lifting of mixing up their repertoire and pitching in situations until the very last exhibitions or even the beginning of the season itself.

The pitchers you'll see working hardest to get outs in exhibi-tions are the marginal major leaguers or marginal rotation starters. They'll come to camp in excellent shape, trot out a four-pitch repertoire and look terrific—even against veteran hitters, who may be working themselves merely on making contact with breaking pitches or driving balls to the opposite field. But once the season begins, and surely as it unwinds into lilac time, hitters get their timing down and marginal pitchers become . . . well, marginal pitchers.

So even if you go into your auction without a whole lot of knowledge of who's hot and who's not in March — as long as you don't bid on a pitcher who broke his arm — it probably doesn't make much difference who's in your April rotation. Spend as little as possible, and look for bargains from among the pitchers you see in the lists in this essay. Concentrate on building the best offensive team you can. If you can't pick up high-quality pitching aces or even some bargains among the pitchers listed here, you can always get pitching help later. Don't worry, be happy.

AMERICAN LEAGUE STARTING PITCHERS

ANAHEIM ANGELS

While there aren't any sure things on the Angels staff for this season, there are some opportunities to get promising young pitching, potentially at bargain prices. Just remember that any of these young starters could just as easily compile an ERA of 6.80 and a 1.85 ratio by June, and find themselves in the minors for the rest of the season.

Anaheim expected to spend the offseason looking for a couple of veteran starters, and accordingly several of the youngsters discussed below will begin the season in the minors. Best bets for spots in the big league rotation are Ramon Ortiz and Jarrod Washburn.

Pat Rapp was signed as a free agent. See more on Rapp in the Orioles starting pitchers section.

Ortiz reminds some scouts of a young Pedro Martinez. He's a slender righthander who has occasionally been dominant, such as in the game last season where he beat Pedro head to head on a complete game two-hitter. Ortiz has a great deal of upside, and is still finding himself as a pitcher. Like many young pitchers, he has a tendency to have an occasional disastrous start, which really hurts in a Rotisserie format. In three of his 18 starts (oddly enough, all no-decisions), Ortiz gave up 24 earned runs in 10 innings total; take those starts out, and Ortiz would have had an ERA of around 3.50. He should begin to develop more consistency this season and is a good bet for improvement. A full season in the majors could produce 14 wins with a 4.25 ERA and 1.38 ratio. Or not.

Lefthander Washburn suffered through an injury-filled 2000 season. His sore shoulder was finally diagnosed as a fractured shoulder blade, and he had surgery late in the season. Washburn was expected to be ready for Opening Day. Like Ortiz, Washburn is a talented young pitcher whose numbers are inflated by a handful of terrible starts. Take out two of Washburn's 14 starts, and his 2000 ERA plummets to 2.60. If he can stay healthy, Washburn could quickly develop into a reliable number two starter as early as this season. If he stays healthy through September, double-digit wins and an ERA in the low 4.00s are attainable.

Scott Schoeneweis is another lefty candidate for the Angels rotation. Due to all of the injuries suffered by Anaheim's pitchers last season and the late season trade of Kent Bottenfield, Schoeneweis wound up leading the staff in starts. Despite that statistic, Schoeneweis is not a lock for this year's rotation, as the Angels would like to see better consistency from him in the spring before making that decision. He is an extreme groundball pitcher, and getting a shortstop with good range would help Schoeneweis this year. If he doesn't make the rotation, the bullpen is a possible alternative. Either way, Schoeneweis will struggle to have a positive Rotisserie value.

Seth Etherton was traded to the Reds during the offseason. Anaheim's number one draft pick from the 1998 draft, made an impressive debut last season, only to wind up on the DL with tendinitis in his right shoulder. This is never a good sign in any pitcher, especially one as young as Etherton, but if the shoulder responds to an offseason of rest, he has the talent to break out this season and could quickly become a dominant pitcher. Watch him carefully in the spring to determine his physical status.

Brian Cooper got an extended look last season, but faces an uphill climb to regain a rotation spot this year. He has an assortment of decent pitches, but doesn't strike out many hitters. When his control within the strike zone is lacking, Cooper gets hit hard. Cooper has limited upside and serious downside for this season and is not recommended.

Matt Wise is a lanky young righthander who has a history of elbow problems. He's more of a pitcher than a thrower, and relies on control to be effective. If Wise's elbow is OK, which was expected, he'll compete for the last spot in the rotation. In any event, it will be hard for him to match the success he had in his short major league stint last year.

Derrick Turnbow is a very young righthander who spent the entire 2000 season on the Angels' roster as a Rule V draftee rather than being exposed to waivers. Having completed the season, he will return to the minors for further seasoning. He could surface in the majors this season and start a couple of games, but even that is unlikely.

There isn't much else in the way of an impact starting pitcher in the upper reaches of the Anaheim system, since most of the better candidates made it to the big leagues last year.

RECOMMENDATION REVIEW: If you're looking for a money-in-the-bank starting pitcher for this year, look elsewhere. Those with a taste for adventure or who need to gamble a bit could do worse taking a flyer on Ortiz or Washburn at a low salary. Etherton is a health risk, but could pay off handsomely within the next couple of years. Pass on Schoeneweis, Wise and Cooper, who have much more downside than upside. Turnbow is an OK very late Ultra pick.

BALTIMORE ORIOLES

The Orioles management has indicated that they will not be contenders until 2002, leaving 2001 as a continuation of the rebuilding that began with a flurry of trades in late August of last year. The rotation has a small nucleus of largely inexperienced starters, providing plenty of opportunities for rookies, comeback candidates, retreads looking for jobs, and unknowns to step up and succeed just like Jose Mercedes did last year.

The Orioles have a revolving door for pitching coaches with a new one every year, and 2001 will see still another new one. The parade of new coaches and their different approaches and preferences tends to confuse the younger pitchers like Sydney Ponson and Jason Johnson. Some of the coaches also had disagreements with staff ace Mike Mussina. The Orioles have hired Mark Wiley, once Manager Mike Hargrove's pitching coach in Cleveland, so the coaching should stabilize for the next few years.

Pat Hentgen was signed during the offseason to be one of the Orioles top of the rotation starters. Hentgen's best days have passed him by and arm injuries have taken their toll. He is a 12-12 win pitcher now with a high ERA and Ratio. The Orioles are expected to be bad in 2001 so don't even pick him up for wins because they really won't offset any of his other minuses.

The departed Mike Mussina is a small step from the elite class of top pitchers of baseball consisting of Randy Johnson and Pedro Martinez. He has six great pitches: two fastballs, two curves, a slider and a changeup. His great curveball is rated as the best in the American League in a *Baseball America* poll of league managers. His knuckle-curve changeup, 15-18 MPH slower than his fastball, is also highly regarded. His other pitches are a four-seamer fastball that hits the mid-90's on the radar gun, a sinking two-seamer fastball. He has good command of all his pitches, so any can become his "out" pitch, thrown on any count, which baffles hitters even more. He also has the pitching smarts to work around a pitch if he doesn't have it on a particular day. He's experienced enough to win consistently in a homer-friendly stadium like Camden Yards, a park where starters such as David Wells and Kevin Brown had a hard time winning. He has experienced a short midseason funk even in his good years, likely from a temporarily tired arm, consisting of four or five mediocre starts before he gets in the groove again. He's also an excellent Gold Glove-level fielder.

Considering his won-lost record, Mussina had a rough year last season, plagued in part by a minor problem with his mechanics and overthrowing early in the season, a rare problem for the usually consistent ace. At one point in mid-May, he had already given up 14 dingers, a shocking figure considering that he had given up only 16 in all of 1999. Solving that, poor run support then plagued him, aided in part by a late-season Oriole youth movement resulting in an influx of mistake-prone rookies. A poor bullpen also ruined some of his good outings. The result was a poor season when considering his won-lost record, but his 3.79 ERA was third best in the league, and he led the league in innings pitched with 237.2. His other statistics were consistent with his good performances in past years. See more on Mike Mussina in the Yankees starting pitchers section.

The 2001 rotation will include Sydney Ponson and Jose Mercedes. Ponson has a good fastball, curve and slider, plus he added a splitter late last year. His fastball is a plus pitch, hitting 93 MPH, his slider is sharp, and his curve comes over the top with a sharp break. His location is usually good, but he occasionally gets wild in the strikezone and his pitches sometimes get too much of the plate leading to big hits and big innings. He usually ranks among the league leaders in giving up homers. Overall, he's a talented pitcher who has some occasional great games, but he lacks consistency and is prone to having bad outings. But Ponson is only 24, and although he's pitched over 500 innings in the majors, he's still developing. For 2001 can have a big breakthrough year if he improves his command and avoids giving up the longball. He needs to become a more consistently good pitcher, avoiding the big bad outings. Ponson has the potential to win 15 games with an ERA around 4.50, making him a solid number two or three starter.

Jose Mercedes came out of nowhere last year to have a good year. He won the fifth spot in the rotation out of spring training, but pitched poorly, was demoted to the bullpen, and nearly wound up back in Triple-A were it not for an administrative glitch with the waiver procedure. He was back in the rotation in early July and was a pleasant surprise, leading the Orioles starters while posting one of the best second-half records in the American League. His best pitch is a fastball, which he throws with good command at different speeds anywhere from 85-95 mph with the same arm motion. The pitch is an effective changeup when thrown slowly, and he also has a good slider. Mixing locations and speeds keeps hitters guessing and upsetting their timing. He can also gas it up and blow it by hitters. It took him a few years to perfect his craft, with some shoulder problems and Triple-A time slowing his return to the bigs with the excellent form he showed as the Brewers' best starter in '97. He's also a much smarter pitcher now than he was in '97. He's a good number three or even number two starter, and he's capable of winning 15 games with an ERA around 4.00. With the Orioles rebuilding, Mercedes can step up and be their number one starter.

Journeyman Pat Rapp can usually be relied on to provide 150-180 innings, albeit poor ones, as a starter or swingman with an ERA around 5.00 and a record around 7-10. He doesn't have any great pitches, getting by on average stuff and pitching smarts. He relies on a cut fastball and a decent curve, and an 88-90 MPH fastball with a little movement. He's getting more hittable as he gets older and loses velocity. He can start, but he usually doesn't pitch deep into games, with six or seven innings being a good outing. He can also work out of the bullpen. In mid-year last season, he had a string of 12 awful starts with an overall 8.24 ERA. That 8.24 ERA says it all for Rapp's Rotisserie value — stay away from Pat Rapp unless you have some need to finish last. Rapp signed with the Angels during the offseason.

Innings-horse Scott Erickson blew his elbow out last year, and had "Tommy John-type" ligament transplant surgery in August. He's not expected back until late in 2001, if then. But Erickson is a tough competitor so he may come back earlier. It's best to avoid pitchers in the year following major surgery, so stay away from Erickson.

Jason Johnson is an enigma. He has a good arm with good stuff and showed great promise in 1999; and the Orioles were counting on him to be a key member of the rotation in 2000. But he had an awful spring training, and was shipped to Triple-A to get his mechanics and mental approach together. He pitched great in Triple-A, but had difficulty with the Orioles beginning the season at 0-8, although the bullpen killed his wins a few times. Overall, he made 13 starts with a dreadful 7.20 ERA. He was shipped back to Triple-A, and again overwhelmed the Triple-A hitters. He was promoted a second time, got shelled and was demoted to the bullpen where he also struggled. He has good stuff, and is need of a good pitching coach to get straightened out. Johnson is a very risky Rotisserie pitcher.

That Jay Spurgeon made it to the majors last year should have surprised him because he began the year in Class-A where he was 8-2. He was subsequently promoted to Double-A, Triple-A, and eventually the Orioles where he made his debut on August 15. He's 24 years old, and is a risky Rotisserie pitcher.

Twenty-three year old lefty John Parrish was another Orioles farmhand who was given a trial in the rotation. He began the year in Double-A, made 18 starts in Triple-A, and started eight games for the Orioles. He began his Orioles career with some good starts, but his control deserted him and he walked 35 in 36 innings while striking out 28. He didn't walk many in the minors until he hit Double-A where he began to nibble more trying to hit corners and missing out of the strike zone.

The Orioles desperation was indicated by their thrusting of veteran reliever Chuck McElroy into the rotation late in the season. He pitched surprisingly well in two starts, and if the kid pitchers are found to be woefully inadequate in 2001, old Chuck may be starting again. Hard throwing Leslie Brea was acquired from the Mets in July in the Bordick trade. He was listed as 21 years old, but it was learned that he was really 26, making him a much less promising prospect because his fastball is unlikely to get any faster. Nevertheless, he does throw hard, and has been a strikeout pitcher with high walk-counts in the minors. The Orioles would like to show that their trades were successful, so he's likely to get numerous chances. Based on his pitch make-up, his best role may be in the bullpen. Hard throwing pitchers always like Brea have more upside potential and are less risky than the soft tossers, so Brea is worth a shot on rebuilding Roto teams.

Calvin Maduro is a soft-tossing righthander who made 13 starts with the Phils in 1997 with a horrendous 7.23 ERA. The Orioles picked him up after his release, and gave him another trial last year. He made some starts last year, but pitched out of the bullpen most of the time. He came down with elbow problems and was shut down in late June. The 7.23 ERA tells enough of Maduro's potential value as a Rotisserie pitcher.

The minors are almost barren of pitching talent. Veteran lefty Rick Krivda continues to pile up impressive Triple-A seasons, but he doesn't have enough talent to win in the majors. Josh Towers looks like the best pitcher in the Orioles minors. He had a good all-star year in 2000 with Rochester in Triple-A, and Baseball America rated him as the best control pitcher in the league. He's been a winning pitcher everywhere he's pitched, and he's walked very few and posted good ERA's in Double-A and Triple-A. He doesn't dazzle hitters with a blazing fastball, all he does is get guys out. Brad Radke was a similar pitcher in the minors, and Towers could also have a solid major league career.

Top prospect Matt Riley finally got his act together in the second half of last year in Double-A. He matured and finally developed a good work ethic. He pitched excellent ball, but then had the bad luck of blowing out his elbow. He underwent "Tommy John-type" surgery and will be out for the year.

RECOMMENDATION REVIEW: Although not in the Pedro Martinez class, Mike Mussina is one of the top Rotisserie pitchers in baseball. But he has yet to reach a 20-win season, and he's only 32. He's a top starter, and

will be among the top 10 in innings pitched, wins, starts, and ERA. With good run support, something that's been missing in his past, and a few breaks, he could win 20-25 and capture the Cy Young award. Let someone else take Hentgen because of his name.

Jose Mercedes and Sidney are not sure things, with Ponson expected to be inconsistent and prone to a few poor outings. Mercedes looked great for a half-season, and he could step up and be a top Rotisserie pitcher, but he's risky. Avoid the other Oriole starters described here, and also stay away from free agents, especially the fly-ball types who could give up tons of runs in Camden Yards. Also keep in mind that even good starters like David Wells and Kevin Brown struggled in Baltimore.

BOSTON RED SOX

David Cone was signed by the Sox. See the Yankees stating pitchers section for more on Cone.

Pedro Martinez is Boston's undisputed ace, with three Cy Young Awards in two leagues over the past four seasons. He has pitched very well almost every time out, but there are signs that he may be wearing down his 5'11", 170-pound frame a bit. His starts have declined from 33 in 1998 to 31 in '99 to 29 last year. Pedro is a much better pitcher than his older brother, but he'll be 29 this season. When Ramon reached that age, he went from 27 starts, 168 2/3 innings pitched and a 15-6 record to 22 starts, 133 2/3 innings and 10-5. For the record, in 2000 Pedro was 18-6 with a 1.74 ERA and an 0.74 ratio. His control is so good that he'll always have a good ratio. But be prepared to pay a lot to get him on your roster, and know that there's a possibility he may not be able to pitch enough to earn his Rotisserie salary.

Ramon Martinez now is 33. He was 10-8 in 2000, but with a 6.13 ERA and a high ratio.

Pete Schourek's 2000 season (3-10, 5.11, 1.43) wasn't a whole lot better than Fassero's 1999. And Schourek, a 31-year-old lefthander, hasn't had the success Fassero has — just one season in 10 with more than eight victories.

Rolando Arrojo was supposed to help the Red Sox after they acquired him from Colorado during last season. But 5-2, 5.05 1.25 with 10 home runs allowed in 71 1/3 innings wasn't as much as they had hoped. Arrojo, 32, was 5-9, 6.04 with the Rockies. He hasn't matched the rookie of the year success he had with Tampa Bay in 1998.

Tim Wakefield swung back and forth between Boston's rotation and its bullpen last season, and wasn't happy about it. He finished 6-10, 5.48, 1.47. He re-signed with the Sox during the winter. Watch him during the spring to see what type of role he will be used in.

Hideo Nomo was signed as a free agent and was expected to be a mid rotation starter for the Red Sox. Rotisserie owners along with professional GM's and managers have been waiting for the return of the "old" Nomo, but don't you be fooled. It is not going to happen. He is an ERA and Ratio killer.

The Red Sox signed Frank Castillo during the offseason. He was expected to compete for the fourth or fifth spot in the rotation. He may also be used as a swingman. See more on Castillo in the Blue Jays starting pitchers section.

Bret Saberhagen tried to come back in the minors, but couldn't pitch enough even to get a decision in Double-A or Triple-A. At age 36, with his arm in tatters, the two-time Cy Young Award winner may be finished.

Tomokazu Ohka pitched very well at Triple-A Pawtucket (9-6, 2.96), but didn't have enough power to succeed in the majors. The righthander was 3-6, 3.12, 1.38 for Boston, but had just 40 strikeouts in 69 1/3 innings. He's just 25, and knows how to pitch, so he still could have a future — as early as this season.

Paxton Crawford, a 23-year-old righty, pitched at the top three levels in the Boston organization. He was 2-3, 3.10 with Double-A Trenton, 7-4, 4.55 at Pawtucket and 2-1, 3.41 with a 1.31 ratio in 29 innings in Boston.

In a desperation move, the Sox signed ancient righthander Steve Ontiveros from the independent Western League. In three games back in the majors, the 40-year-old was 1-1, 10.13, 2.44. If he pitches in 2001, it probably will be back in independent ball.

Juan Pena, a highly regarded 23-year-old righthander, has missed most of the last two seasons because of injuries. Watch to see if he can take a regular turn in spring training.

Jin Ho Cho, 25, was just 4-3, 4.65 at Pawtucket and 3-5, 5.83 at Trenton. The righthander may need at least part of another season in the minors.

Another part of Boston's Asian connection, righthander Sun Woo Kim, went 11-7 at Pawtucket despite a 6.03

ERA. He's just 23, and that ERA should come down if he has a chance to work in a better pitching environment at Fenway Park.

Jared Fernandez was Pawtucket's answer to Tim Wakefield — a righthanded knuckleballing swingman. But after a 10-4, 3.02 start, with four saves, an injury ended his season with more than a month to go. The Sox don't seem sold on the 29-year-old, but a lot of knuckleball pitchers have succeeded at relatively advanced ages. Watch where Fernandez pitches this season; he could pay off on a small investment.

Justin Duchscherer, another 23-year-old righty, was 7-9, 3.39 at Trenton last season. He could reach the majors this year with a good start in Triple-A.

Farther down the organization, Boston has righthander Chris Reitsma (3-4, 3.66 at high Class A Sarasota and 7-2, 2.58 at Trenton) and lefty Casey Fossum (9-10, 3.44 at Sarasota). However, Fossum, who is very tough on lefthanded batters, was 7-2, 2.33 during the season's second half.

RECOMMENDATION REVIEW: It is very difficult to recommend any Red Sox starter. Pedro Martinez will cost so much in an auction that it will be difficult for him to return anywhere near that value. Once the money is out of your auction, you may be able to pick up a younger sleeper such as Ohka, Crawford, Kim or Pena. However, in many leagues, owners will realize that the Sox will have to fill their rotation somehow, so even those young pitchers may be relatively pricey. Fossum is a good Ultra prospect.

CHICAGO WHITE SOX

The White Sox don't have the strongest rotation in the world, but they do have loads of potential. Lefty Mike Sirotka has been their ace now for a couple of years and he's turned out to be a very good pitcher. He won 15 games last year and had one of the top ERA's in the American League, a respectable 3.79. He's not a power pitcher, but he locates well and changes speeds consistently. He may not last as a number one starter, but he's a good pitcher that will get a lot of wins on a team like the White Sox that scores a lot of runs.

James Baldwin is one of the most enigmatic pitchers in all of baseball. He's got excellent stuff and always has one really strong half during each season, but he never puts it together for an entire year. To illustrate the point, Baldwin was 8-1 at the end of last May with an ERA in the low 3.00's and he finished 14-7 with a 4.65 ERA. He throws in the low 90's and has a knee-buckling curve, but he when he struggles he winds up hanging the curves and falling behind in the count quite a bit. If he ever puts it all together he could win 18-plus games.

Jim Parque has been a part of the Chicago rotation for a couple of years now, but he may be hanging on by a thread these days. With the team almost certainly looking to upgrade the rotation and with several stud pitching prospects nearly ready for the majors, Parque could be on his way to the bullpen in the near future. He walks quite a few batters for someone who isn't overpowering and always seems to be pitching out of trouble. Parque was lucky to have a 13-6 record and a 4.28 ERA; he allowed 279 baserunners in just 187 innings last year.

The rest of the Chicago rotation is completely up in the air. Cal Eldred pitched well for them during the 2000 season, but he finished the year on the DL. Eldred was re-signed by the Sox during the offseason and was expected to be their fourth starter. Kip Wells was given a rotation spot coming out of spring training, but struggled badly finishing with a 6-9 record and a 6.02 ERA. Jon Garland struggled as well, though he did show flashes of brilliance, going 4-8 with a 6.45 ERA. Other candidates for the 2001 rotation are righthanders Rocky Biddle, Matt Ginter and Jon Rauch as well as lefthander Mark Buehrle.

RECOMMENDATION REVIEW: Sirotka is the safest bet on the Sox and Baldwin is worth taking a chance on, though make sure you deal him if he gets off to a good start. Parque should open the season in the rotation, but aside from picking up some wins because of the strong offensive team he plays for, his rotisserie numbers won't be all that impressive. Don't look for Eldred to have the type of run he did in the first half of the 2000 season. It is more likely that he will lose his starting spot by midseason to one of the Sox talented youngsters.

Both Wells and Garland are top pitching prospects and both will get every opportunity to earn rotation spots. They're great pickups in leagues that have deep benches or minor league rosters. Buehrle is a good-looking lefty and he could also win a spot, though there's also a chance he could wind up in the bullpen. Biddle is a middle-of-the-road prospect and probably not worth picking up just yet. Ginter and Rauch are both top prospects, especially the 6'10" Rauch, but they're probably a solid year away from reaching the majors for good. Both, however, are great

pickups in deep leagues or leagues with minor league rosters.

CLEVELAND INDIANS

The Cleveland Indians set a new major league record by using 13 different starters last year, using just about everybody except Phil Niekro and Steve Carlton. The Tribe's big three were Chuck Finley, Bartolo Colon and Dave Burba, with the other slots filled by 10 different starters. Key starters like Charles Nagy and Jaret Wright came down with injuries, and the immediate replacements were found wanting. New replacements were tried, and they couldn't cut it either so more were called on. In desperation, the Tribe even tried old retreads Jaime Navarro, Scott Sanders and Bobby Witt. The rotation wasn't settled until the late-July trade with Milwaukee when they acquired Jason Bere and Steve Woodard.

Veteran Chuck Finley was the Tribe's number one starter, and he had a good year in his first season out of an Angels uniform, going 16-11 in 218 innings with a solid 4.17 ERA and a 1.431 ratio. Except for the 3.39 ERA in 1998, his ERA has ranged from 4.16 to 4.43 since 1994. With the exception of a ratio of 1.364 in 1999, his ratio has ranged from 1.408 to 1.431 since 1997. Now 38, Finley is still a top pitcher, but the below-3.00 ERA's of his early career are gone forever. For 2001, the outlook for the consistent Finley is about the same as in 2000.

Bartolo Colon stepped up and showed his toughness down the pressure-filled stretch, wining his last six decisions and not losing after July 26. Overall, he made 30 starts, going 15-8 with a good 3.88 ERA, fifth best in the league. A short stint on the DL slowed him down a little. Nevertheless, he held opposition hitters to .233, third best in the league. He's getting consistent as it was his third year in a row when he ranked in the top 10 in these categories, and now he's improving to rank in the top five. His ratio in the past three years has been 1.38, 1.27 and 1.39, all excellent numbers. He throws a mean rising fastball, likened by some to that of Tom Seaver's. He normally throws at 92-94 MPH, but he can gas it up to 97-98 when needed. "That's some serious giddyup," said Tigers manager Phil Garner. "And he's not throwing a straight fastball. He was toying with us when he got into trouble."

Veteran righthander Dave Burba is big, tough and durable, in past years making 30-34 starts per year, pitching 191-220 innings with an ERA ranging from 4.11 to 4.73. His ratio varied from 1.37 to 1.51 over the past three years. Last year he went 16-6 with a 4.47 ERA and a 1.51 Ratio. The Tribe's good run support helped him, giving him an average of 6.44 runs per start, good for eighth best in the league. For 2001, Burba, now 34, can be expected to win 15 games with a ratio and ERA about the same as last year.

Veteran Charles Nagy came down with elbow problems last year, making only 11 starts. His poor 8.21 ERA should be written off because of the injury. He underwent surgery, and it won't be known until he begins throwing in spring training if he can come back early in the year, or if he needs more rehab time. The high number of innings over the past nine years are beginning to take their toll. He's been more hittable the past three years, posting ERA's of 5.22 and 4.95 in 1998 and 1999 respectively, with ratios of 1.50 and 1.47. The advice on Nagy is wait and see, until he's regained his effectiveness.

Manager Charlie Manuel said that Jaret Wright has been more mature and composed this year, In prior years, an error or bloop hit would upset him, getting him out of his pitching rhythm and causing him to get hit. Last year, he spent some time on the DL with a rotator cuff problem, making only nine starts. He underwent surgery in August, and he should be ready for spring training. His best year was 1998 when he went 12-10 with a 4.72 ERA with a 1.52 ratio. He throws a 95 MPH fastball, a sharp curve and a good changeup. But he's been inconsistent and plagued by random wildness. He's only 25, with 83 career starts, and he could mature and develop into a consistently effective pitcher. Wright is a risky Rotisserie pitcher but he could pay off nicely, and is recommended only for teams willing to take the risk.

The Indians obtained Jim Brower from Texas several years ago. He has an average fastball and a good slider. He started 11 games last year, with several impressive starts. But he also had some very bad starts, ending up with a poor 6.24 ERA in 62 innings. He was plagued by wildness, walking 31 and striking out 32. He was wild in Triple-A in 1999, but seemed to have things under control last year until he got to the majors. Brower is an inconsistent pitcher, and a contending team like the Indians normally would not use him as a starter unless they were desperate. Avoid Brower.

Tim Drew is a former number one draft pick from 1997 who was called up from Triple-A to fill a hole in the rotation. He has an excellent 94 MPH fastball and a good slider, but he is still lacking consistency of his command. He gets wild in the strike zone and becomes hittable. He

began last year in Double-A, then made 16 starts in Triple-A and three unimpressive starts for the Indians. He was hit hard in Triple-A, posting a 5.87 ERA. He is talented, but he needs to develop a changeup to make his other pitches more effective. He's only 22, and he should become more consistent with experience. Drew is a year or two away from challenging for a rotation slot, and he's a risky Rotisserie pitcher because he's a rookie who may be erratic with a high ERA and ratio.

Steve Woodard came to the Tribe from the Brewers for slugger Richie Sexson in late July. He was ineffective for the Brewers, and was dropped from the rotation. He wasn't much better for the Tribe where he started 11 games, going 3-3 with a 5.67 ERA. His best years were 1998 and 1999 for the Brewers when he started a combined 55 games with a 4.36 ERA. He has an average fastball and curve, but has a terrific changeup. But he loses his command and becomes easily hittable. Woodard is only 25, and could become a good winning pitcher when he becomes consistent. For Rotisserie, Woodard is very risky with a limited upside potential, and it's best to let others take the risk.

To stop the bleeding last year, the Tribe called up almost everyone they thought could win a few games. Two that weren't called up were C.C. Sabathia and Danys Baez, two talented starters that the Tribe didn't want to rush to the majors. Lefthander C.C. Sabathia is one of the top pitching prospects in baseball. He's big at 6-6 and 240 lbs., and throws a mean fastball in the upper 90's, a good curve and a good change-up. He was promoted to Double-A last year, where he found better hitters that he couldn't simply overpower with his heat. Nevertheless, he did strike out 90 in 90 innings, but he walked 48, a little too many, but not unusual for a big power pitcher. Manager Charlie Manuel wanted Sabathia promoted to the Indians last year because of the shortage of live arms in the rotation. But he hasn't pitched much in the minors and Indians management was cautious and didn't move him above Double-A. In a *Baseball America* poll of league managers, he was selected as the best prospect in the Class A Carolina League, and the second best prospect in the Double-A Eastern League, despite spending partial seasons in each league. Indians management is bringing him along slowly and cautiously. Sabathia is a future big league ace.

The Tribe signed Cuban Danys Baez to a big contract, but he wasn't as polished a pitcher as they expected. He also had to adjust to U.S. society. He began the year in Single-A, and was promoted to Double-A where he made 18 starts, going 4-9 with a 3.68 ERA. He's only 23, and could be in Jacobs Field in 2001. As are many rookie pitchers, Baez is a risky pitcher at this point in his career.

Jamie Brown, Zach Day and Jake Westbrook are the other minor league prospects who may see some major league action in 2001. Day and Westbrook came over from the Yankees in the David Justice trade. Day is 23 with a lanky physique at 6-4 and 185. He throws a 90-MPH fastball that could get a few more miles when he matures. He may spend most of the year in the high minors. Westbrook is a ground ball pitcher with a good sinker. He doesn't strikeout many, and walks a little too many. Despite that, he's posted some good records in the minors. His best role in the majors may be as a reliever. The Indians were Westbrook's fourth organization in five years, having been in three trades. Brown spent two years getting it together in Double-A, and if he were any good, the Indians would have promoted him to the majors last year.

Rookie prospect Willie Martinez was waived by the Indians and signed by the Twins. He's covered in the Twins section.

RECOMMENDATION REVIEW: General Manager John Hart is always seeking a big pitching ace like Mike Mussina or Pedro Martinez that the Indians have lacked. The rotation for 2001 will have Chuck Finley, Bartolo Colon and Dave Burba as the anchors with Jaret Wright as the fourth starter. Charles Nagy will be in the mix if he's healthy. Finley, Colon and Burba are consistent starters without any big surprises in their records expected in 2001. Based on his experience, Jaret Wright should be a more consistent and better pitcher at this point in his career. He's a sleeper with some upside potential, but a risky one.

Charles Nagy is in the wait and see category because of the uncertainty associated with his injury. Steve Woodard was not expected to be in the Indians rotation in 2001, but even if he lands a job elsewhere, he should be avoided because of the expected stratospheric ERA and ratio numbers. Woodard could end up in the bullpen. Promising prospects Tim Drew, C.C. Sabathia and Danys Baez can be expected to get some starts. Sabathia is the most talented and is worth a farm league pick.

DETROIT TIGERS

The Tigers have only a few proven major league starters, which is why they spent most of the Winter looking for a top of the line veteran, and they really don't have an ace. Brian Moehler has been their best pitcher over the past few years, but he's more like a third or fourth starter on most good teams. He's got average stuff, but picks up wins when his team scores runs for him. His ERA should be reasonably good if the Tigers don't move in the fences at Comerica, though he doesn't help you in many rotisserie categories. Don't be fooled by the fact that he's at or near the top of the Tigers' rotation, he's really only good for 10-15 wins and nothing else.

Of all the Tigers' pitchers, Jeff Weaver has the highest upside. He's still raw and makes too many mistakes, but he's got the kind of stuff number two starters are made of. He throws a low 90's fastball that really moves and he's got a couple of quality breaking pitches. With improved consistency, which should come with experience, Weaver would be a good middle of the road roto starter. He should be worth 200-plus innings and 10-15 wins in 2001 and his strikeout totals could improve as well.

Chris Holt was acquired from the Houston Astros during the offseason. He was expected to be one of the Tiger starters in the lower part of the rotation. He is a serviceable pitcher, and may have some success the first time around the AL. At the end of the season he will at best be a .500 pitcher with a high ERA and Ratio. See more on Chris Holt in the Astros starting pitchers section.

None of the other contenders for the Tigers' 2001 rotation are guaranteed anything, especially considering the fact that they were expected to sign at least one veteran starter during the offseason. Dave Mlicki will most likely get an opportunity to start for the Tigers, though he was a major disappointment last year, going just 6-11 with a 5.58 ERA. Knuckleballer Steve Sparks pitched pretty well last year, posting a 7-5 record and a 4.07 ERA, but he's more valuable as a swingman than as a full-time starter. Rookie Adam Bernero did a respectable job in his first major league action last year and because of his above average control and impressive poise he has a shot at making the rotation if pitches well during the Spring. He's really just a fourth or fifth starter now, but he has a little upside and could wind up being similar to Brian Moehler down the line.

The Tigers don't appear to have any top flight pitching prospects that will be ready to help them come Opening

Day, but there are a few that could show up by the end of the season. Righthander Mark Johnson has always had a strong right arm, but control problems have really limited his effectiveness thus far in his career; he simply throws too may hittable pitches. Righty Nate Cornejo has a live arm and he keeps the ball down in the zone, but hasn't been dominant against older hitters and probably needs another year of development. Shane Loux has a good fastball and performed well at Double-A during the 2000 season, but he'll also need more minor league seasoning. Lefties Matt Miller and Adam Pettyjohn are advanced pitchers with good control and above average breaking pitches, but neither figures to be a future staff ace.

RECOMMENDATION REVIEW: Weaver will be the best of the bunch this year with Moehler being solid roster filler for most roto teams. If you have Holt on your roster and he starts off well, trade him while his value is high, before he reverts back to his old self. Mlicki and Sparks aren't worth picking up before the season and Bernero is too much of an unknown to get excited about him. Miller and Pettyjohn, both of whom pitched in the Arizona Fall League last year, have a shot at getting to the show this season, but probably not early on. If you have a minor league roster spot, Pettyjohn isn't a bad pickup.

KANSAS CITY ROYALS

Although the Royals' starting pitching was not as much of a mess in 2000 as it was in 1999, it was still a poor place to look for Rotisserie help.

Losing Jose Rosado after five starts hurt the club's depth and the rest of the staff was relatively inconsistent over the course of the season. Mac Suzuki had the most useful season as a starter, although Jeff Suppan was the only double-digit winner. Dan Reichert and Blake Stein were good at times, especially over the last part of the year, and Brian Meadows was a fine surprise after his acquisition from the Padres near the end of the year. Chad Durbin, Miguel Batista and Jay Witasick were early season busts and Chris Fussell was better in a relief role.

Suzuki led the Royals in ERA and strikeouts but couldn't win because he got virtually no run support in his home starts. Occasional trouble locating the plate also hurt Suzuki; he had one start in which he permitted just one hit, but walked seven in five innings and failed to earn a decision. He also failed to win a game in September. Suzuki has the kind of stuff to put him in a top-of-the-rotation spot, but probably not the kind of stamina needed

to stay there even if he conquers his wildness. Unfortunately, that can be said of a lot of the current Royals staff; they are really lacking that one true number one starter. Suzuki would fit well into a fourth or fifth starting spot where he could go hard for five or six innings, then turn the game over to a middle innings guy. It would reduce the number of innings and opportunities for him to suddenly lose the plate as is his wont. Now that Suzuki has learned better control of his plus fastball, though, the possibility of being a winning hurler is good. Suzuki is not going to ever have a good Ratio, but he can have a good ERA and win ten or twelve games. As he is still virtually unknown in Rotisserie circles, Suzuki is a good low-dollar Rotisserie choice, particularly if your league counts strikeouts.

Reichert might actually have the kind of stuff to be a staff ace and he showed it periodically late in the year. He looked like a staff ace before losing four straight games to finish the 2000 season. Like Suzuki, Reichert struggles with his control from time to time. But, when he keeps the ball in the park Reichert can blow people away with his nasty breaking stuff often enough to keep opponents from crossing the plate. He doesn't win easily, but he can be a winner nonetheless. When he's got his good slider, Reichert is nearly untouchable. Reichert is at the age and with the right kind of blend of experience and stuff that he could suddenly emerge as a successful big-league pitcher, seemingly overnight. Of all Royals starters to acquire, Reichert is the best bet and, again due to his low profile, he can be had cheaply.

Stein also has pretty good stuff. A big guy who throws hard, Stein went 7-2 with a 3.69 ERA over his last twelve starts, covering the last two months of the season. While he cannot be expected to win at that rate for a full season, he can post a fine ERA and win 10-12 games. Like Suzuki and Reichert, though, he does occasionally lose control of the plate and he won't put up a good ratio. Stein can be useful to Rotisserie players at a minimum salary, but keep in mind that he's pitching for a second division club which has serious bullpen problems, so wins will be hard to come by. Of all Royals' starters from 2000, Stein might make the biggest leap forward in 2001, especially in terms of strikeouts and wins. Use his status as a fairly unknown starter to get him for a buck, or not at all.

Because Suppan has occasionally been thrust into a top starter role he hasn't enjoyed especially good success in the won/lost column. Still, he has managed double-digit wins with a useful ERA each of the last two years while pitching for bad teams. Suppan is a very valuable starter for the Royals because he eats innings and gives a reliable start each time out. However, he's not nearly as valuable in Rotisserie circles. Workhorses like Suppan have almost no upside value; they pile up a lot of innings that add little to a Rotisserie team's ERA or Ratio. When they pitch for a bad team like the Royals, they have almost no Rotisserie value because they also can't win very often. In Suppan's case, it's even worse because he is often expected to match up against the staff ace for the other team and he is overmatched in that kind of situation. For Rotisserie, Suppan can be a safe choice at the end of the draft if you really need a lot of innings, but don't bid more than the minimum and don't expect a lot of positive value, either.

Rosado was expected to return fully healthy in the spring and resume his role as one of the league's better lefthanders. Long-range success has eluded Rosado partly because he has pitched for some bad teams, but also partly because he tries to do too much himself. Instead of using his natural pitching ability and placing the ball on the edges of the plate, Rosado gets caught up in the pitcher/hitter battles and tries too often to challenge a good hitter with an all too hittable pitch. He has been prone to giving up crucial extra-base hits that cost him victories. If he learns to pitch a little smarter, Rosado can be a winner. Because he hasn't lived up to the expectations following his rookie season in 1996 and because 2000 was such a washout season, Rosado could actually be a surprise for Rotisserie this year and worth more than the few bucks he'll go for in many leagues. Even if he merely maintains his average season stats he'll give good Rotisserie value; he'll post a good ERA and Ratio, but don't count on the wins . . . unless he gets smarter about his approach on the mound.

Don't get caught up in what Meadows did for the Royals over the last two months of the season. Yes, he did win six of ten starts, including four straight in September, but more important are his peripheral numbers. His 4.77 ERA for KC was easily the best of his career and he managed to post a good ratio simply because he briefly cut his walk rate in half. American League batters found his stuff just as hittable as National Leaguers, hitting .293 against Meadows, not far short of his career .305 opposition batting average. He hasn't been a big winner in the past, he has a dreadful strikeout rate due to just mediocre stuff, and he only succeeded in ten AL starts because batters weren't quite used to him yet. That will change in 2001 as Meadows becomes overexposed. Avoid Meadows for Rotisserie purposes.

Because the Royals starters have yet to show much in the way of reliability and due to the injuries that have become increasingly more commonplace for all pitching staffs, the club will delve into a cadre of minor-league pitchers for additional starts. Among this group, Durbin and Fussell are the most likely to get spot starts with vastly different results. In 2000, Durbin made 16 starts and although just two of them were good he was very close in a number of other starts, giving up late runs just before leaving the games; his overall numbers could have been much better if not for a few severe shellackings right before he was sent back to Triple-A Omaha. Durbin has decent stuff and can succeed in the bigs as a starter. When he gets another chance for Kansas City in 2001 he would be a fine choice for a Rotisserie team needing a spot start. He's not worthy of selection on Draft Day, and don't try to keep him around more than a few starts. Instead, put him on your list of potential midseason replacements.

Fussell is a different story. He doesn't have stuff as good as Durbin and has been exposed when used more than once through a batting order. He's a far better long reliever and will be used in that role more often than as a starter. Fussell is exactly the kind of pitcher not to get for Rotisserie. If he has any success in long relief he'll be shifted into a starting role where he can get really crushed, destroying any positive value he may have built in relief. And, in that kind of usage he isn't going to pick up many wins or saves. He has little potential positive value and a whole lot of potential negative risk. Avoid.

Brett Laxton and Dan Murray made a number of starts at Omaha but appear to be seen as relievers by the Royals. Since they won't get saves, neither has Rotisserie value.

The Royals have some very good prospects on the horizon; a couple of which are very close to the bigs. Jeff Austin and Chris George are considered fine major league starting pitching prospects. Olympian George is probably the best of the two, often compared to Tom Glavine as he throws a fastball and changeup each with varying speeds to always give hitters a new look. He went 8-5 with an outstanding 3.15 ERA in the bandbox at Double-A Wichita last year to earn a promotion to Omaha before pitching for Team USA in Australia. George has a good chance to win a starting job in the Royals' rotation this spring. If so, pick him up only if you can hide him someplace. Rookie starters are notoriously deadly to Rotisserie teams, particularly if they pitch for big-league teams as desperate for pitching as the Royals. George is an especially good pick for teams that need to take chances or rebuilding teams.

Austin also has good stuff, a low-90s fastball and a hard breaking ball, although his stuff isn't as good as George's. He had excellent early-season success at Wichita, then was mediocre in his first try at the Triple-A level in 2000. Austin still needs to refine an out pitch. If he can build a little more steam into his heater and keep refining his changeup, Austin can be a successful lower rotation starter. Because he is already a polished pitcher with a highly professional attitude, Austin is less likely to suffer from a typical rookie flame-out although he's also less likely than others to take the American League by storm. For Rotisserie purposes, Austin is a "pass" simply because of his lack of high upside potential. He'll be of much more use to the Royals than to Rotisserie owners.

Jeff D'Amico is another potential callup who will get starts in 2001. A former shortstop, D'Amico got his starting debut on Father's Day, 2000, and was rocked, giving up eight runs in just two innings; his stats never recovered despite some otherwise useful outings later in the year. He made 16 starts for Omaha that were a lot more reasonable and he remains a possible 2001 starter candidate for Kansas City. D'Amico has a volatile fastball that makes him unpredictable. When he is able to throw it over the plate he can be a difficult read for hitters. However, D'Amico often has trouble taming the heater and, therefore, is a big risk for Rotisserie players. His potential for that one terrible outing far outweighs any potential for positive outings, too. Avoid.

Other Royals' youngsters have some long-range potential, too, including Kyle Snyder, Junior Guerrero, Brian Sanches and Mike MacDougal. Snyder and Guerrero both had disappointing seasons in 2000 but remain prospects. Sanches and MacDougal are too far from the majors to properly rate at this point. For Ultra purposes, a better selection may be George or Austin, rather than one of these pitchers who are at least two years away from a big-league impact.

RECOMMENDATION REVIEW: There are no aces in this deck. However, there are a few low-dollar bargains if you shop carefully. Look to pick up one of these guys to round out your pitching staff late in the draft, spending only the minimum or a few bucks more: Reichert, Stein, Rosado, or Suzuki; Reichert is the best choice. Avoid Suppan, Meadows, and Fussell. For Ultra, George is a good selection or possibly Austin. When looking for a midseason replacement, remember Durbin.

MINNESOTA TWINS

Teams frequently inquire about the Twins young pitchers, but the Twins aren't likely to part with any of them. The Twins enter 2001 thinking they have the makings of a very effective starting staff, with experience at the top of the rotation and talent at the back.

Righthander Brad Radke is one of the better pitchers in the American League, but is not one of the elite aces in the game. What Radke can do, however, is pitch 200-plus innings and, for the most part, keep the Twins in games.

Radke is great for owners looking to keep their ratio down. He doesn't walk many batters, as he's one of the better control pitchers in the league. He does give up a lot of hits, especially when good hitting teams are able to wait on his change up and poke it the other way.

His won-loss record is terrible. Some would point to the poor run support he got (4.17) last season. Others would say that Radke is going up against the other team's ace, which hurts him. The truth is that while Radke is a very reliable pitcher, he needs to step up, win the close games, and prove he's worth the $36 million the Twins are giving him over the next four years.

Eric Milton is one of the best young lefthanders in the game and is more like the 1A pitcher on the Twins staff. Some believe he has better makeup to be a staff ace than Radke. Milton is coming off a 13-10 season and looks ready to win 15-plus games in 2001. He's worth drafting early, not in the first couple of rounds, but not too soon thereafter.

Milton has improved a little bit each season. His fastball, needs consistency. It hit 96 mph in a couple of starts, but slumped to 91 late in the season. His curveball has improved greatly, he still has a very good change up and the cut fast ball has given him an additional weapon against righthanded hitters.

When everything is working, Milton will have long streaks of retiring hitters. He threw a no-hitter in 1999 and retired the first 20 Kansas City Royals during one start last season. He's unflappable on the mound, has good stuff and knows how to use it.

Mark Redman went from being on the fringe of the majors to establishing himself as someone to watch in 2001. He's a 6-5 lefthander with a good curve and very good changeup, and should win around 15 games a season for years to come.

Like Radke, Redman relies on good defense behind him. His changeup has a nice downward break to it, and induces plenty of ground ball outs. He does not throw hard, but will his 91-92 mph on the gun. Redman should build on his rookie season of 2000, because he confidence seemed to surge as his good starts piled up. He's worth a late-round selection, especially since it appears he can win 15 games in 2001.

The Twins just don't know what to do with righthander Joe Mays, who has a tremendous arm but has trouble using it. Mays should be part of the 2001 rotation, but it's not clear how long he will stay in it, especially if he continues to be inconsistent.

Mays has a good fastball, curve and changeup and can dominate at times. But he gets in trouble when he nibbles at the corners or doesn't mix his pitches. He doesn't get close pitches called strikes. He'll walk batters, Give up a cheap hit, and it all shows on his face and through his body language. This has angered the coaching staff in the past, and Mays even spent a part of 2000 in the minors when his control really got bad.

No one expects Mays to be sent down again. But the roto owner may want to sit back and wait to see if Mays has things figured out before investing a draft choice in him. There are candidates for the last spot in the starting rotation. Righthander Matt Kinney, grew up in the Northeast, named his cat after Roger Clemens and tries to copy the Rocket's delivery. After an impressive September call up, Kinney could become the power pitcher in the rotation. He has a hard fastball with good movement, improving curveball and good slider. He also showed more poise than some club execs expected when he was called up.

He's coming off a strong stint at the Arizona Fall League, and could be a sleeper pick. He'll have to cut down on his walks if he's going to have a career in the majors, but the tools are there. If he doesn't make the starting staff he will begin the season at Triple-A as the top starting pitching prospect.

Lefthander J.C. Romero throws three pitches well, so the Twins have converted him from a closer to a starter. If he fails, at least he was able to face more hitters. Romero will have to break a bad habit of not using all his pitches. When he spots his fastball and uses his good change up, he can shut a team down. He's the best bet to be the fifth starter, where he can be used out of the bullpen when he's skipped over in the rotation.

As this point in his career, Romero can't be relied on for

much production; he's still an unknown commodity. He may not even make the rotation. Since the Twins have plenty of lefthanders around, Romero could start the season in the minors if he can't make the major league rotation or bullpen.

The Twins have few arms ready to debut in the majors. Kyle Lohse was dreadful at Double-A New Britain last season, going 3-18! But he rebounded in the Arizona Fall League, posting a 1.80 ERA in 30-plus innings. He'll start the season in the minors, but should get a callup during the season.

Righthander Jason Ryan has had two chances to prove himself in the majors, and, each time, has failed. He's gone from being a prospect to suspect. Righthander Mike Lincoln has a good curveball and hits his spots, but a second elbow surgery has set back his bid to reach the majors. Righthander Juan Rincon spent most of 2000 at Double-A, but he has a very good slider and fastball. He needs to master a third pitch, but still could be called up for a start during the season.

RECOMMENDATION REVIEW: The Twins have pretty good pitchers to pick from. Radke and Milton are good mid to upper range starting pitchers, while they are not Rotisserie aces, they are solid pickups if you can get them. Mark Redman had a career year in 2000 and it remains to be seen if he can repeat. Take a chance on Redman, but don't overpay.

<u>NEW YORK YANKEES</u>

By signing free-agent righthander Mike Mussina to a six-year, $88.5-million contract, the Yankees established a rotation that could challenge the Braves' best, with a potential four aces — Mussina, Andy Pettitte, Roger Clemens and Orlando Hernandez. The biggest difference between the two is that the Yankees' quartet is much older than Atlanta's when those pitchers were in their prime.

Mussina, 32, is the closest to Greg Maddux. In an off-year, the righthander was 11-15 despite a 3.79 ERA and 1.19 ratio. The Orioles scored only 3.7 runs per game when he pitched. Though Mussina allowed 28 home runs, only nine came after the All-Star break. He had a career best 4.57 strikeout/walk ratio, and is a Gold Glove caliber fielder. See more on Mussina in the Orioles starting pitching section.

The lefthanded Pettitte is the baby of the staff at 28, but he was the one Joe Torre gave the ball for the World Series' first game. Pettitte doesn't pitch like Tom Glavine, but has had comparable success — in six seasons, Pettitte is 100-55 with a 3.99 ERA. Last year, he was 19-9, 4.35.

At age 38, Clemens remains a power pitcher (188 strikeouts in 204 1/3 innings last season). He went 7-2 with a 3.15 ERA after the All-Star break to finish 13-8, 3.70 and earn a three-year contract extension. The difference between his won-lost record and Mussina's? They had similar ERAs, but The Rocket received 5.4 runs per game from his offense.

Back and elbow injuries contributed to an off year for El Duque (12-13, 4.51). The righthander is at least 31 years old, but is in exceptional physical condition. Like Maddux and Glavine, Hernandez doesn't throw very hard, and is somewhat at the mercy of umpires to call pitches on or off the corners strikes. When they don't, the result can be the 34 homers Hernandez surrendered.

David Cone was a free agent during the offseason and signed with the Red Sox. After a 4-14, 6.91 record in 2000, Cone may be finished at 38.

Ramiro Mendoza, a 28-year-old righthander, was off to a good start (7-4, 4.27) as a swingman before suffering a shoulder injury that required season-ending surgery.

Brian Boehringer was signed as a free agent during the winter. If Boehringer could stay healthy for a stretch he might become an adequate major league starting pitcher. Rotator cuff surgery in 1999 limited him to just 11 starts and only seven outings in 2000. Because he hasn't yet proven to have the stamina for a rotation job and because he has the ability to retire lefthanders as well as right-handed hitters, a long-relief job may be in the offing for Boehringer. In any case, he's not a good Rotisserie selection.

Cuban righthander Adrian Hernandez, 26, shot through the top three levels of the Yankees' farm system. The power pitcher (86 strikeouts in 73 innings) totaled 8-2, 3.95.

Another fast-rising pitcher in the organization is lefthander Randy Keisler, 25. After totaling 14-5, 2.85 at Double-A Norwich and Triple-A Columbus, Keisler won an important start for the Yankees in September. However, his major league record was 1-0, 11.81, so he may need more time in the minors.

The Yankees traded for lefty Ted Lilly, also 25, from the Montreal organization. Coming off elbow surgery, he went 8-11, 4.19 at Columbus. He's a power pitcher who did well in five of seven relief outings for New York.

Another acquisition before last season was 25-year-old righty Brandon Knight. He was the workhorse of Columbus' staff, going 10-12, 4.44.

Also at Columbus, Denny Lail was 7-7, 4.64. The 26-year-old righthander appears to have a limited future.

Jason Beverlin reached 27 years old before he reached the majors. The righthander won 15 games at Norwich in 1999 with a 3.69 ERA. Last year he improved to a 2.82 ERA, but lost his strikeout pitch and was just 8-9. At Columbus, he lost all three starts with an 18.90 ERA. Beverlin was a minor league free agent during the offseason.

The Hideki Irabu trade that brought Lilly to the Yankees organization also delivered 25-year-old righthander Christian Parker (14-6, 3.13).

Brian Rogers, a 24-year-old righthander had by far the best of his three pro seasons last year at Norwich (11-6, 3.94).

Twenty-two-year-old Dave Walling starred at high Class A Tampa (7-2, 1.99). But his performance after a promotion to Norwich (3-9, 5.27) indicated he may need to begin 2000 back in the Eastern League.

At 24, righty Brett Jodie fared better with being promoted from Tampa (11-4, 2.57) to Norwich (2-1, 3.15).

RECOMMENDATION REVIEW: Mussina may be overpriced this year, but for the wrong reason, because he's now a Yankee, not because he pitched in a lot of bad luck in 2000. Pettitte should provide good production; he could still be improving, and he's not the type of flashy pitcher who attracts attention in Rotisserie auctions. Clemens' age makes him a risk. Orlando Hernandez could come back big; he's certainly worth taking if the bidding doesn't get too high. If Lilly makes the team as a reliever, an injury could put him into the rotation and give him increased value. The best Ultra choices appear to be Adrian Hernandez and, down the road, Walling.

OAKLAND ATHLETICS

As with most of their position players, the cost of owning an Athletics starter went up with their fine showing over the last several weeks of last season. Leading the way is 20-game winner, Cy Young candidate Tim Hudson, a pitcher who is simply a winner. He certainly won't cost as much as Pedro, but at this point, considering age, team, and experience, the 25-year old Hudson is now among the elite in AL pitchers, so he will be both costly, consistent, and a solid anchor for your rotation, helping in all categories.

Free agent Kevin Appier signed with the Mets. Appier did continue his workhorse status, pitching nearly 200 innings last year, and also turned in solid performances down the stretch and into the playoffs.

As Appier's walk total went up alarmingly last season, and his hits allowed were above innings pitched, ratio is clearly now an issue with Appier, and that could point to dangerous totals. So, don't write him off pitchers who win 15 games are certainly valuable-but be careful not to overspend or overestimate Appier's abilities. You are better off getting him as a $7 bargain at the end of the draft, than as a $15 main cog in a pitching staff that may go nowhere.

Gil Heredia also put together a career season in 2000, and accordingly put himself of among the top starters in the league. Heredia did pitch well in general, but did much better over the first half (9-7, 3.99) than the second (6-4, 4.29), making four more starts and going 26 more innings prior to the break. Heredia is on a similar scale, both cost and production-wise, to that of Appier, but be wary of taking both on your team unless you can sneak both through cheap at the end of your draft.

If, however, there is a chance for a sleeper or two in this rotation, it would start with Barry Zito. Since Zito did pitch so well during the last month and post season, savvy owners will be hip to one of last year's top rookies despite his accumulation of just a half season's numbers. Make no mistake, Zito has stuff that is as good as it comes, and has control and guile to boot. He would be a much better $15 gamble than Appier, and will deliver numbers that could even exceed those of ace Hudson. Get him now.

If Zito is a known potential sleeper, then Mark Mulder is the Athletics pitcher you can indeed "most likely sneak by for a buck and get a bargain." With a 9-10 mark, 5.44 ERA, and 191 hits allowed over just 154 innings, owner's

might shy away from the lefty who hurt a disk in September, and was shelved for the rest of the year. Mulder was able to last deeper into his starts after July, showing better control and presence. Naturally, back injuries are tricky, so watch Mulder carefully in the spring, but should he be performing well, he is more than worth the few bucks he will cost. Expect 10-plus wins, and dramatically improve strikeout and ratio totals, and expect those numbers to enjoy continued improvement over the next few years.

Lost on the same path (that would be the "signed for two years coming off a great one, only to have a collapse" trail) as John Jaha, Omar Olivares was erratic from spring training on, and never really came through as the Athletics intended when they signed him to the new deal. At this point, his position in the rotation is questionable. Olivares could take Mulder's spot, should the lefty not be ready in spring, but more than likely, Olivares will be the number six starter, or will be dealt to a team that needs pitching. In any event, you need neither his 1.79 ratio, nor the numbers that could accompany it.

Ariel Prieto still looms out there in the Athletics roster, although he has no roto-value. Oakland has a number of starters in the minors worth at least tracking, including Eric Dubose, Chris Enochs, Justin Lehr, Juan Pena, Mario Ramos, Scott Chiasson, and Javier Calzada.

RECOMMENDATION REVIEW: Tim Hudson won 20 games in 2000 and he will only get better for years to come. Be prepared to pay a premium for Hudson, especially in keeper leagues. Gil Heredia is a seasoned veteran who had a career year in 2000, expect him to pitch well enough for 12-15 wins. Barry Zito may have just as much upside as Hudson, and he alread pitches like a vet.

SEATTLE MARINERS

The Mariners might have the deepest collection of starting pitchers in baseball. They have all five members of the rotation from the end of last year back, they have two other young pitchers that have had success as major league starters and a couple of top pitching prospects that appear to be ready for a shot at the bigs. A bonus with Seattle pitchers is the fact that they play 81 games per year at Safeco Field, a noted pitchers' haven.

Freddy Garcia has the best stuff of the established pitchers. A broken leg cost him 10-12 starts last year, but he was clearly their best pitcher come playoff time. He throws in the mid 90's with a good, hard breaking pitch and has very good composure on the mound. Barring injury, Garcia should be good for 15-20 wins and a bunch of strikeouts for this coming season.

Aaron Sele is an established veteran starter that is far from dominant, but he's durable and he picks up wins. He has one of the best curves in the game, but isn't really a strikeout pitcher. The thing you can count on Sele for is innings. Ever since recovering from injury problems early in his career, Sele has been a workhorse and that's an asset to his major league team as well as to many rotisserie teams.

Paul Abbott might have been their most consistent starter last year. He started 27 games for the Mariners despite beginning the year in the bullpen and was a member of their playoff rotation as well. There is some doubt, however, as to whether he'll be back in the rotation for the 2001 season. He could be pushed out by a younger, more talented pitcher during spring training.

Jamie Moyer has been a stalwart on the Mariners' staff for years, but he was awful after the All-Star break last season. He was able to post a 13-10 record, but his 6.50 ERA in the second half raised concerns about his age and his stuff. He could get the benefit of the doubt early in the season, but won't be long for the rotation if he struggles.

John Halama is simply a younger version of Moyer. He relies on locating his fastball and keeping his changeup down to be successful. He's been mentioned in trade rumors for the past couple of seasons and could either be dealt or moved to the bullpen if one of the young guns comes along quickly.

Both Brett Tomko and Gil Meche have had success as major league starters and both have tremendous stuff. Tomko is a little older and has been hampered by inconsistency the past couple of years, but he has a mid 90's fastball and good breaking ball at his disposal. He could be used as a reliever if he's not rewarded with a rotation spot or he could be dealt in their effort to add a power hitter to the lineup. Meche was outstanding last year in his 15 starts before going down with arm problems. If healthy, Meche should rejoin the rotation pretty early on in the 2001 season. Like Tomko, Meche has a mid 90's fastball and outstanding breaking pitch, but Meche has more poise than Tomko. He's a keeper.

The Mariners also have a couple of other young pitchers that will be ready soon. The most notable is 6'10"

lefthander Ryan Anderson. He's called the "Little Unit" by some and the "Space Needle" by others, but no matter what you call him he's got an amazing future. He's got the 97-98 MPH fastball Randy Johnson has as well as a knee-buckling curve, but he's far more polished than Johnson was at that age. Anderson's 2000 season was cut short by arm problems, but he's expected to be healthy for Spring Training and could be one of the best stories in baseball this season. The other young pitcher to watch is Joel Pineiro. He's got a low 90's fastball, a solid breaking pitch, an above average change and outstanding control. He may not be a big name, but he can flat out pitch.

RECOMMENDATION REVIEW: Garcia has the ability to be a top of the line starter and All-Star this season, so grab him if you can. Sele is a proven veteran that will provide in 2001 what he has over the past three or four seasons. Halama, Moyer and Abbott are all wild cards heading into this season; don't place too much value on them based on their numbers from last season. Both Tomko and Meche are excellent talents that are worth picking up, Tomko especially if he's traded. Meche has the talent to be a number two or three starter right away. Anderson, of course, is worth having on any roster heading into 2001 because of his amazing ability and because of the success he had last year at Triple-A.

TAMPA BAY DEVIL RAYS

Devil Rays manager Larry Rothschild was asked how well his staff would do in 2001 when he referenced something Jim Leyland told him when Rothschild was the pitching coach for the Florida Marlins: the best pitching staff usually is the healthiest pitching staff. If any staff in baseball has the right to feel like they're due a break, it is the Devil Rays who have watched injuries claim countless innings from their starting staff. So they're hoping to draw a break in 2001.

Albie Lopez will start the season as the staff's No. 1 starter and the only thing keeping Lopez from attaining the status as a true No. 1 is consitency over the next couple of years. After changing from a setup role in the Devil Rays' bullpen, Lopez made an impact in the starting rotation, finishing the season with an 11-13 record and a 4.13 ERA. Lopez always has had good stuff, but he has learned to pitch while in the Devil Rays bullpen and now appears to have his best days ahead of him.

Having Lopez at No. 1 will take some pressure off Wilson Alvarez, who is coming back from shoulder surgery after not pitching an inning in the majors in 2000. Alvarez's innings will be watched at the beginning of the season as a precautionary measure, but he should back to full speed before the All-Star break. When Alvarez is at his best he is one of the best pitchers in the major leagues, at his worst, he is one of the worst. Leaving consistency as the hurdle he must cross to reach his potential.

Pencil in Ryan Rupe as the No. 3 starter and the righthander should look completely different after having a blockage discovered in his pitching shoulder. If healthy, Rupe should be able to pick up where he left off in 1999 when he was regarded as one of baseball's up-and-coming pitching prospects. He knows how to pitch and he has the stuff to match his knowhow.

Paul Wilson will be a strong No. 4 on this staff after coming back from several years of physical problems to show he is once again ready to pitch at the major-league level. Wilson's 2000 numbers are deceiving as he pitched well after coming to the Devil Rays in a trade with the Mets. Wilson's 1-4 record with a 3.35 ERA in seven starts could easily have seen him post a 5-1 mark. He left several games tied or with the lead because the Devil Rays took a cautious stance on the number of pitches he could throw. He'll be off the pitch counter in 2001, which has the Devil Rays expecting big things from Wilson in 2001. Healthy competition will surround the No. 5 slot in the rotation.

Bryan Rekar will be the top candidate after posting a 7-10 mark with a 4.41 ERA in 2000. Rekar has the stuff to dominate a game, but has a poor makeup.

Juan Guzman also is in the background, but it's not likely the veteran righthander will be healthy enough to be in the rotation until well into the season. Others who will be given a strong shot at earning a spot in the rotation include Tanyon Sturtze, Travis Harper, Matt White and Bobby Seay.

Sturtze was used in mop-up duty after being acquired from the White Sox early in the 2000 season and worked his way into the starting rotation by early August, finishing with a 5-2 record with a 4.74 ERA. Sturtze then finished the season on the disabled list after straining an oblique muscle. Harper was racked up in his first start against the Orioles then was sent back to Durham. Upon his return in September, Harper was a different pitcher, starting five games and pitching a masterful one-hit shutout against the Blue Jays in Toronto. White and Seay are the most talked about minor-league pitchers in the Devil Rays' system

and each could finally get their shot. Rothschild believes the bullpen is a great place for a young hurler to get comfortable, which might be the way these youngsters make their entrance to the major leagues.

RECOMMENDATION REVIEW: Look for Lopez to continue to dominate. With 96 strikeouts in 185 1/3 innings in 2000, he could approach 200 in 2001, which can help any team. None of the other starting candidates have the kind of numbers to help, but keep an eye on Seay and White. Each can put up big strikeout numbers. Otherwise, stay away from the Devil Rays' staff as they won't have the needed wins because the team is likely headed for another season in the cellar.

TEXAS RANGERS

As the offseason began, Rick Helling and Kenny Rogers were the only sure things in the Ranger rotation. The leading candidates for the next three spots were Doug Davis, Ryan Glynn and Darren Oliver, although Texas was actively scouring the market for veteran pitching help. With the newly beefed up Texas offense in place, each of the Ranger starters should expect better run support and more wins than they had last season.

Helling has become one of the major workhorses in the American League, pitching 652 innings over the last three years. These are fairly high-pitch count innings, too, as Helling walks and strikes out a fair number of batters. Last season, Helling threw at least 106 pitches in over two-thirds of his starts, and went over 120 pitches in two out of five starts. Perhaps coincidentally, perhaps not, Helling fell apart in September last season, posting a 9.45 ERA in his last six starts. Few pitchers over the last 20 years have had this kind of workload without ultimately breaking down. Helling has been uncommonly healthy over the past few years, and could be an exception to the rule. But his workload, and the lousy September, are reasons to be wary. He is still much better on the road than in the Ballpark. If he keeps body and soul together, 14 or 15 wins and a 4.80 ERA in 210 innings is a reasonable projection.

Rogers, too, has been a workhorse, with 661 innings since the beginning of the 1998 season, although he's thrown nearly 1,000 fewer pitches than Helling over that span. A groundball pitcher, Rogers is much better suited to pitching at the Ballpark than is Helling. He has been pretty consistent over his career, and he should have another decent year or two in him, but his best years are probably behind him. Expect 190 innings with a 4.40 ERA and double-digit wins.

Beyond the first two members of the rotation, inexperienced hurlers and retreads comprise the remaining candidates. In the former category, the leading candidates are lefthander Doug Davis and righthander Ryan Glynn. Of the two, Davis has the higher ceiling and probably the brighter near term future as well. He still suffers from young-pitcher-itis, in other words maddening inconsistency. When Davis is good, he's usually very good, but his bad outings are real stinkers. He has enough talent to overcome it, and he's a good bet to stay in the rotation all season, but there will be some bumps in the road. If Davis sticks in the rotation, eleven wins, a 4.40 ERA and 1.40 ratio are attainable numbers. Glynn has a couple of partial years of experience in the big leagues under his belt, and should be able to improve over the next two years. At his best, Glynn would probably be a decent middle-rotation pitcher. For this season, expect an ERA over 5.00 with a handful of wins.

Darren Oliver is coming off an abysmal season in which he twice went on the DL for "shoulder fatigue." Presumably, whatever was wrong with his left shoulder had an effect on his pitching, so if the shoulder comes around in the offseason, Oliver should be able to improve on 2000. He is in the second year of a huge contract, so every effort will be made to get him straightened out and in the rotation. Even with significant improvement, Oliver is only a marginal Rotisserie pitcher. He gives up far too many walks and has trouble putting batters away when he gets into trouble. In a full season, expect nine wins, a 5.20 ERA and a ratio over 1.50.

Matt Perisho was the most heralded young pitcher in the Texas system going into last season, but he crashed and burned in a full-season trial. The young lefty could wind up starting some games this season, but long relief is a more likely role, if he is in the majors at all. Last season's debacle really hurts his chances with the Rangers, and he may need a change of organizations to move forward in his career.

Righthander Brian Sikorski will probably spend some time on the big league roster as a spot starter. Sikorski is a pretty good Triple-A starter who doesn't really have the stuff to be a consistent winner in the majors.

Justin Thompson, a key part of the Juan Gonzalez trade with Detroit, is rehabbing from his second shoulder surgery last May and is unlikely to pitch until midseason

at the earliest. Even then, Thompson would be likely to toil in the minors for an extended period before being returned to the majors. He is not likely to have any impact this season.

The two best pitching prospects in the Ranger system are Joaquin Benoit, a righthander who could arrive as early as mid-2002, and Jovanny Cedeno, who is at least three years away from the big leagues. Benoit had a successful stint in the Arizona Fall League and is slated to return to Double-A Tulsa this year. Benoit has terrific stuff but has been dogged by injuries, including a shoulder problem that troubled him early last season. If he can stay healthy, Benoit could be very good. Cedeno has also had shoulder problems, but has been dominant when he does pitch. The Rangers are bringing him along very slowly.

RECOMMENDATION REVIEW: The Ranger rotation is a good place to fish for cheap and ugly wins. Helling and Rogers are solid mid-level starters. Helling in particular has been overworked, however, so caution is advised. The rest of the rotation is a crapshoot. Davis is the best bet to have some immediate upside, while Glynn and especially Oliver are likely to have negative value. Avoid Perisho and Sikorski. Thompson has some possible 2002 upside as a reserve pick. Benoit is a good mid- to late-Ultra pick.

TORONTO BLUE JAYS

Once thought to be the up and coming young rotation in the league, the Jays' so-called "future" rotation took a collective step back last year.

David Wells, the veteran of the staff, was a Cy Young contender for most of the year, slipping out of contention late in the season. Always one to allow his share of hits, Wells' control, endurance and ability to keep the ball down led him to a 20 win season and a major league leading 9 complete games. How much longer it can last is in doubt as Wells turns thirty-eight in May. There were also rumblings after the season ended that he was disappointed in the Jays' firing of manager Jim Fregosi and would consider asking for a trade, though Wells himself would not confirm nor deny the rumors. He starts 2001 as a top pitcher on almost any staff and one of the most reliable lefthanders in the American League.

Steve Trachsel signed with the New York Mets during the offseason. Steve Parris will take his spot in the rotation as the number four or five guy.

Steve Trachsel was supposed to bring stability to the Tampa Bay Devil Rays' rotation and ended up in Toronto by late summer. Though he wasn't a big winner with the two teams, he started 34 games and pitched just over 200 innings of average ball, a valuable commodity in today's market. Just about any staff he ended up on would have him in the middle to end of the starting rotation. Of some concern was that he struck out just 110 batters last year, the second-worst strikeout to inning ratio of any 200+ inning pitcher (with Brian Anderson being the worst).

Joey Hamilton finally made his return to the majors after two injury-shortened years and though he pitched well in his six starts down the stretch, he averaged just over five innings a game in his late-season return. His control looked off, as it had even before he was injured. A healthy Hamilton starts the 2001 season as the number three or four starter but remains a longshot to pitch a full season. Given that he's started a total of 24 games the past two seasons, there's no guarantee of how sharp he will be out of the gate.

Esteban Loaiza proved to be a good fit for the Jays, so much so that it appeared he would start 2001 as the fourth starter. Loaiza, who came from the Rangers in a minor trade in late summer, was glad to get to Toronto, where he immediately joined the rotation. He quietly finished the 2000 season with 10 wins and just fell short of 200 above-average innings. He starts 2001 as a likely candidate to get 25-30 starts with more than his share of wins and a decent ERA.

Steve Parris was a surprise acquisition this past offseason. The Cincinnati Reds, who felt they couldn't afford to keep him, demanded two minor leaguers from the Jays in Clayton Andrews and Leo Estrella. Parris, immediately following the trade, was called the "fourth or fifth starter" by Jays' Assistant GM Tim McCleary. The move to get Parris, which fell into place relatively quickly, gave the Jays some much-needed depth to the rotation. Parris recovered from a slow start last year to finish with 12 wins for a disappointing Cincinnati team. Of some concern was that he walked 71 batters in just over 192 innings. See more on Parris in the Reds starting pitchers section.

Chris Carpenter was supposed to be an ace-in-waiting but instead suffered his worst season in the majors to date. Carpenter was so bad that he not only lost his berth in the rotation but also had the worst American League ERA among pitchers that qualified for the ERA title. Only Jose Lima saved Carpenter from having the worst ERA in the majors. Despite a developing fastball and good curve,

Carpenter is inconsistent at best and can look like an ace for three innings and then promptly self-destruct. He starts 2001 as the precarious favorite in a spring training battle for the fifth starter's job and may be ticketed for the bullpen . . . or worse.

Frank Castillo never did seem to gain respect and despite constantly being on the bubble last year, he put together a fine season out of the Jays' rotation. Ironically, the Jays would have been one of his best situations to get some innings as last year proved that there are plenty to go around when injuries and ineffectiveness strike. He is a much better pitcher than people think but not as good as he showed last year. He was signed be the Red Sox during the offseason.

The Jays signed Canadian Jason Dickson immediately following the end of the 2000 season though it appeared uncertain at best that he could make a meaningful contribution this year. Dickson pitched in just 6 major league games last year and was knocked around in those starts. He appeared headed for Triple-A to start the 2001 season with an outside shot of earning a spot in the bullpen or if healthy, a midseason callup in the event of an injury.

Kelvim Escobar and Roy Halladay (both covered in the relievers' section) remained options to pitch out of the rotation in the event of a longer injury to any of the established starters.

RECOMMENDATION REVIEW: Other than Wells, there aren't any Cy Young candidates on the 2001 squad. A Rotisserie team that needs to gamble for wins could take a chance on Parris or Loaiza. Hamilton is a risk not only in that he could get hurt again but that there's no way to tell whether he'll pitch well if healthy. Steer clear of him unless you have to take chances. Trachsel is good only if you need innings and Dickson is a big risk, even if healthy.

TOP 2001 WINNERS

NAME	W
Pedro Martinez	20
Tim Hudson	19
Andy Pettitte	19
Bartolo Colon	17
Mike Mussina	17
Aaron Sele	17
David Wells	17
Dave Burba	16
Chuck Finley	16
Freddy Garcia	16
Rick Helling	16
Jose Mercedes	16
Roger Clemens	15
Pat Hentgen	14
Orlando Hernandez	14
Jamie Moyer	14
Mike Sirotka	14
Blake Stein	14
John Halama	13
Gil Heredia	13
Mark Redman	13
Kelvim Escobar	12
Esteban Loaiza	12
Albie Lopez	12
Brian Meadows	12
Brian Moehler	12
Steve Parris	12
Brad Radke	12
Kenny Rogers	12
Eric Milton	11
Ramon Ortiz	11
Jim Parque	11
Steve W. Sparks	11
Jeff Suppan	11
Jeff Weaver	11
Rolando Arrojo	10
Kent Bottenfield	10
Sidney Ponson	10
Bryan Rekar	10

TOP 2001 STRIKEOUTS

NAME	K
Pedro Martinez	289
Mike Mussina	195
Bartolo Colon	191
Roger Clemens	189
Chuck Finley	188
Dave Burba	173
David Wells	167
Eric Milton	156
Hideo Nomo	155
Aaron Sele	155
Blake Stein	148
David Cone	146
Freddy Garcia	146
Orlando Hernandez	145
Rick Helling	143
Tim Hudson	141
Brad Radke	135
Sidney Ponson	133
Kelvim Escobar	131
Makoto Suzuki	131
Mark Redman	130
Kenny Rogers	128
Mike Sirotka	127
Andy Pettitte	126
Cal Eldred	125
Rolando Arrojo	122
Wilson Alvarez	119
Pat Hentgen	116
Chris Holt	116
Esteban Loaiza	116
Jamie Moyer	116
Jeff Weaver	116
Dan Reichert	114
Bryan Rekar	114
Chris Carpenter	113
Ramon Ortiz	113
Jeff Suppan	113

NATIONAL LEAGUE STARTING PITCHERS

ARIZONA DIAMONDBACKS

The Diamondbacks' rotation is heavy on top but filled with question marks toward the bottom.

Lefthander Randy Johnson and righthander Curt Schilling give the D'backs the most potent Nos. 1-2 starters in the league, a statement that only Atlanta and perhaps Los Angeles could argue. Lefthander Brian Anderson seemingly has emerged as a solid No. 3, with Todd Stottlemyre hoping to recover from another operation and Geraldo Guzman, Armando Reynoso and Mike Morgan battling for the fifth spot.

Johnson won his third Cy Young Award, his second in two seasons with the D'backs, while going 19-7 with a 2.64 ERA, second in the league. He lost the ERA title on the last day of the season but still dominated the league, striking out 347 in 248 2/3 innings. He gave up only 278 baserunners, a ratio worth its weight in gold considering the amount of innings he throws.

Johnson still can reach 100 MPH with his fastball and can get his killer slider in the 89-91 MPH range, making him tough to hit even if a batter guesses correctly.

He will be the No. 1 starter in a rotation that has two, Schilling being the other. Johnson, 37, has shown absolutely no signs of aging. He posted arguably the best April in major league history last year — 6-0, 0.91 ERA, 64 strikeouts in 49 1-3 innings. He became the third pitcher in history to win six games in April, joining Vida Blue and Dave Stewart.

Johnson also became the 12th player in major league history to record 3,000 strikeouts when he reached that milestone Sept. 10 at Florida. He joined Nolan Ryan as the only pitchers with three straight 300-strikeout seasons last year.

Schilling, obtained from Philadelphia for a package that included Travis Lee and Vicente Padilla on July 27, had 300-strikeout seasons in 1997-98 before undergoing arthroscopic surgery on his right shoulder in December of 1999.

Schilling was 5-6 with the D'backs, 11-12 overall after returning to the rotation the last day of April. He tied Johnson for the NL lead with eight complete games but said he never felt completely back to the form that helped him win 47 games for the Phillies from 1997-99. He planned a rigorous offseason workout regimen to regain his form.

Anderson opened the 2000 season as the No. 5 starter but worked his way up the rotation because of his solid performance and injuries to Stottlemyre. Anderson was 11-7 with a 4.05 ERA last season, pitching better than his record indicates. He had 14 no-decisions, the most in the National League.

His 213 innings were a career-high, and he will be expected to pitch that many again this season after nailing down a spot in the rotation. (He opened 1999 in the bullpen, remember.)

Anderson gives up hits but seldom walks many — his 1.6 walks per nine innings was the second-best ratio in the NL

— so his ratio is acceptable for an innings-eater.

Stottlemyre was off to a great start last season before suffering the latest in a series of disabling injuries. He was 8-3 before leaving a game against St. Louis on May 29 with what was diagnosed as tendinitis in his right elbow. He returned after 15 days on the DL and made three more starts before going back on the DL with a microscopic tear in the flexor mass in his right elbow.

He rehabbed for two months before returning in September, making four starts before undergoing right ulnar nerve transposition surgery to alleviate the discomfort. He was expected to be near full strength at the start of spring training.

If the D'backs opt to alternate lefties and righties, Stottlemyre would open the season as the No. 4 starter. He missed a majority of the 1999 season with a 70 percent tear in his right rotator cuff that he treated with rehabilitation rather than surgery.

The fifth spot appears to be between veterans Mike Morgan, with his record 12th major league organization, Armando Reynoso, and youngster Geraldo Guzman, who was working as a carpenter when D'backs' Latin American guru Junior Naboa signed him in November, 1999.

Reynoso had a disappointing season in 2000, but the D'backs re-signed him anyway. He even spent time in the bullpen. Though he was the top candidate for the fifth spot going into spring training, he is no lock to hold it for the season especially with a few quality arms ready to fill-in when he struggles. He is 35, and on the downside of his pitching career.

Morgan, 41, had a rebirth of sorts with the D'backs last season, appearing in a career-high 60 games in the first extended relief duty of his career. He had only 12 career relief appearances in the 1990s while with Los Angeles, the Cubs, St. Louis, Cincinnati, Minnesota, the Cubs again, and Texas.

Morgan saved for the cycle, saves of one, two, three and four innings in April before settling into a setup role behind Byung-Hyun Kim and Matt Mantei. Morgan was much more effective as a reliever than in his four spot starts, when he gave up 13 earned runs in 19 1-3 innings. He also was more effective early in the season. He is the least likely out of the three to see substantial time in the number five spot. He was expected to be used more as a jack-of-all-trades in case of injuries.

Guzman, 28, shot through the D'backs minor league season before replacing Omar Daal in the starting rotation the first week of July. He gave up four hits and one run in a 2-1 victory at Enron Field in his first start, then threw eight shutout innings in his second start on July 17. He came back down to earth after that, going almost two months without a victory until beating the Giants twice in the final nine days of the season.

There does not appear to be much immediate help in the farm system. Righthander John Patterson and lefthander Nick Bierbrodt, former No. 1 draft choices and among the best young arms in the organization, were felled with injures last season.

Patterson made only three appearances before undergoing Tommy John surgery in May and was expected to miss much of this season, too, as the D'backs will practice patience. Bierbrodt suffered an intercostal strain that caused him to miss two months, then was sent home after one winter league appearance because of a tender shoulder.

RECOMMENDATION REVIEW: Johnson is the most valuable pitcher in the league, not only for his victories but also for his ratio. He is always a candidate to win 20 games, as is Schilling, who has a similarly strong ratio for a power pitcher. Anderson could have won 14-15 games with a little luck last year, but of course that was last year. Stottlemyre, a gamer, remains a gamble because of his injuries. Morgan seemed a perfect fit in middle relief, although his ratio was poor even there. Beware if he is forced into the starting rotation this season. Stay away from Reynoso.

ATLANTA BRAVES

The Braves have the unquestioned best starting staff in the National League, and it seems as if this staff full of veterans will never slow down.

Greg Maddux and Tom Glavine have been Atlanta's best pitchers over the past three or four years. Maddux doesn't look as good on Sportscenter as Randy Johnson, but he is not far behind the Big Unit and remains one of the best pitchers in the league, even at age 35. His control is as good as it's ever been and he keeps hitters off balance by getting fantastic movement on all his offerings.

Glavine, also 35 years old, had one of his best seasons last year, winning 21 games and pitching the second most innings of his career. He never threw exceptionally hard, but he hasn't lost much speed, if any, and can still hit the outside corner better than the rest. And like Maddux, he has never had any major injuries to either his left arm or elbow.

The Braves will get John Smoltz back this year after the hard throwing righthander missed all of last season because of major reconstructive surgery. Smoltz has had chronic problems with his right elbow, which have sent him to the disabled list many times over his long career and required minor surgery. While the "Tommy John" surgery keeps getting more successful, Smoltz will not be able to throw as hard as he did before he first got hurt. However, what he still should have the same amount of zip he did in the late 1990s, when he won 56 games over a three-year span.

Kevin Millwood was as good as any pitcher in baseball in 1999, but suffered through an awful season last year. He attributed that to a change in attitude. Instead of throwing his fastball, Millwood said, he threw more offspeed pitches. He went back to being more of a power pitcher in the second half of 2000 and he improved, although he still wasn't as good as the year before. Still, a 4.66 ERA was about the league average last season. He is a sure bet to rebound this year. As good as the Braves will be, just moderate improvement will put him on track to win 15-18 games.

Atlanta picked up Andy Ashby halfway through the season, and though he pitched better than he had for Philadelphia, he still was not nearly as good as he had been the previous two seasons with San Diego. On the surface, Ashby's stats were not significantly worse than they had been during his time with the Padres. He gave up a few more hits and a handful of more homers, but other than that, everything was pretty much the same. That would indicate that he ran into some bad luck along the way. He is bound to be better this season, although he is not likely to win more than 13-15 games.

Ashby was signed as a free agent by the Dodgers during the offseason. No loss for the Braves, because if healthy, Smoltz will take his spot.

The Braves picked John Burkett off the scrap heap early in the season and he performed admirably for them for a little while. He put together a streak of four consecutive wins in May and was 8-3 in late July before suffering some tough losses in the final weeks of the season. After struggling badly in his first few appearances in an Atlanta

uniform, Burkett was extraordinarily consistent for the rest of the year. His ERA was between 4.70 and 5.14 from June 23 to the end of the campaign.

The big question is can he duplicate his performance again this year? He certainly was a dependable fifth starter in 2000, eating up some innings and generally keeping the Braves in every game in which he started. But this is a 36-year-old pitcher who hasn't had an ERA of less than 4.50 since 1996. He gives up a bunch of hits and if his control is not perfect, he also gives up a bunch of runs. All in all, it is not worth taking the risk.

Terry Mulholland can always be counted on to make several starts over the course of the season, whether it is filling in for an injured pitcher, making an emergency start during a doubleheader, or just filling in if someone needs a rest. Mulholland is what he is, a fairly dependable long reliever who can make a few starts if needed. However, he is not capable at this point in his career of maintaining any kind of consistency if placed in the starting rotation for an extended period of time. Don't pick him up thinking he will solidify your starting staff. Mulholland signed with the Pirates during the offseason and was expected to be used mainly out of their bullpen.

Odalis Perez missed the entire 2000 season after having the same reconstructive surgery as Smoltz. He will miss at least the first half of this season and likely will spend the second half in the minors to make completely sure he is healthy. He wasn't expected to be ready to rejoin Atlanta until the start of the 2002 season.

Damian Moss is the only decent pitching prospect the Braves have left in Triple-A since the club has traded away many of its best young arms in the last two years to acquire veteran players to try and win another World Series title.

Moss, who was 9-6, was the only starter at Triple-A Richmond to win more than five games. He posted a 3.14 ERA and would be considered a prime candidate for the fifth spot in Atlanta's rotation had he not walked 106 batters in 160 innings.

L.J. Yankosky and Matt McClendon were the top starters at Double-A Greenville, but neither has much professional experience and will not be ready for the big leagues for at least another year.

RECOMMENDATION REVIEW: You can't go wrong with either Glavine or Maddux as your No. 1

pitcher. Neither shows any signs of slowing down at all. Of all the other pitchers the Braves had, Millwood would be the best bet to really improve over his 2000 campaign. He is a much better pitcher than he was last year and will rebound tremendously. Watch Smoltz closely during spring training to see if he is fully healthy.

CHICAGO CUBS

There is no doubt that much of the Cubs fortunes will lie on the right arm (and elbow) of Kerry Wood. When Wood blasted onto the scene in 1998, it seemed that he would be one of the dominating pitchers in the National League for many years to come.

However, a torn ligament in his pitching elbow have set Wood, and the Cubs, back a couple of years. While many thought Wood might have earned a Cy Young Award by now, he and the rest of the team are simply trying to get back on the winning track.

Wood blew out his elbow during spring training in 1999 and missed all of that season. The dreamers hoped he might be totally recovered from his surgery, but most realized that he still had some work to do.

Wood's 2000 comeback season wasn't quite what he or the Cubs had hoped for, but it wasn't that bad, either. For a player with only one year of big league experience who missed an entire season with an elbow injury, an 8-7 record with a 4.80 ERA cannot be considered to be bad. Even though he was not back to where he was before the injury, he still struck out a batter an inning and didn't allow many hits. But as one might suspect, he struggled mightily with his control. Even in the minor leagues, he has always experienced difficulties in finding the strike zone.

With another offseason to rest and strengthen his arm, Wood should have no trouble being the ace of Chicago's pitching staff.

Jon Lieber had a fine season in 2000, eating up innings and keeping the Cubs in nearly every ballgame. While he is not a dominating pitcher, he has outstanding control. He gives up a lot of home runs, but part of that is making half his starts in Wrigley Field. However, the home runs are not something that should scare you away from Lieber. He is a solid No. 3 or 4 pitcher on anybody's staff.

Kevin Tapani has been a huge disappointment for the Cubs. Chicago signed the former Twins ace for the 1997

season hoping he would be a dominating presence on the mound. But other than 1998, when he went 19-9, he has been a huge disappointment. A variety of injuries have set him back, including a knee injury last season that sent him to the sidelines in September. He had surgery that month and was expected to be ready for the start of the season. Even if he is healthy, Tapani is a .500 pitcher at best at this point in his career. He is 37 years old and has to rely on guts and guile more than anything else. Occasionally that is good enough to get him into the late innings, but most of the time he will be a six-inning pitcher.

Jason Bere was a good starter with the White Sox back in 1993 and 1994 when he won 12 games each year with excellent ERA's of 3.47 and 3.81 respectively. Since then, he's had elbow problems, surgeries, lengthy stays on the DL and some awful ERA's of 7.19, 5.65, and 6.08. He's also been released several times. He's lost some speed off his fastball, and has been plagued by wildness. His curve is his best pitch, but he needs to throw strikes. He made 20 starts for the Brewers last year, with a 4.93 ERA and 1.54 ratio. He made 11 starts for the Indians, going 6-3 with a 6.63 ERA. Bere is an inconsistent starter, not the type that contending teams would use unless they were desperate as the Indians were last year. Bere became a free agent, but teams weren't breaking down the doors trying to sign him. He will be looking for a job somewhere in spring training. Avoid Bere.

The Cubs signed Jeff Fassero as a free agent during the offseason. Fassero made a comeback last season. But remember that he's 38 and coming off a year when he was just 8-8, 4.78 with a 1.56 ratio. He was expected to get a shot a the fourth or fifth spot in the starting rotation. Injuries over the past few years have been a problem for Fassero and he is quite hittable now. Don't expect much from the 38 year-old.

The Cubs got Ruben Quevedo and Joey Nation from the Braves in 1999 as part of the Terry Mulholland trade. Quevedo is further along now, but it will not be long before Nation is in Chicago's rotation to stay. Nation, only 22-years-old, spent most of last season in Double-A, going 11-10, but he pitched extremely well. The Cubs called him up late in the season and he made two starts, losing both. He will start the season in Triple-A, but the Cubs need pitchers badly and a strong spring could have him in the big league rotation by June.

Quevedo lacks overpowering stuff, but he has good movement on all his pitches and good control. Like Nation, he is only 22 and has plenty of learning to do before he is a polished pitcher. Obviously uncomfortable pitching in relief, Quevedo allowed 13 earned runs in 3 2/3 innings out of the pen. His ERA as a starter was 6.40, but he pitched well enough at times to show that he will eventually be successful at the major league level.

Kyle Farnsworth has an outstanding arm, but he hasn't been able to harness his ability yet. After making rapid progress through Chicago's farm system, Farnsworth was respectable in 21 starts in 1999, but fell on his face last season, going 2-9 with a 6.43 ERA. He has good stuff, but still needs to learn how to use it against major league hitters. He won't be a major contributor this season, but there is still hope that he will get himself straightened out in the long run.

Daniel Garibay split his time last season between the bullpen and the starting rotation. He was 0-5 with a 6.23 ERA as a starter last year, so don't look for him to make more than a couple of starts, and then only in emergency situations.

Todd Van Poppel started two games for the Cubs last year, but he appears to have finally found his niche as a long reliever/setup man. Although he made only two starts last year, his ERA was a run a game less when he pitched in relief. He could get a few starts in emergency situations, but his role will be to pitch in the sixth and seventh innings.

Jeremi Gonzalez has missed all of the last two seasons with severe elbow problems and it is not known if he will ever be able to pitch again.

RECOMMENDATION REVIEW: Most experts say it takes at least two years to regain full velocity and arm strength following major elbow surgery. And since the procedure is more and more successful all the time, there is no reason to back off taking Kerry Wood. Wood has one of the best arms in the National League and he should be back to his old, dominating self this year. Lieber is an underrated pitcher who will give you some wins along with a good ERA and Ratio. He should be a pitcher that other owners undervalue. Stay away from Bere, he is an ERA and Ratio killer. Fassaro is not a lock to make the starting rotation and he is worse than Bere.

CINCINNATI REDS

For the last couple of years Cincinnati's starting pitchers have been accused of being only slightly better than a

Little League staff. And while there are not any big names on the staff, especially now that Denny Neagle is gone, there are plenty of capable pitchers who are better at getting hitters out than increasing their name recognition.

Pete Harnisch is a perfect example. Pete has a career ERA of 3.84, which is more than good in this time in baseball history. He is also a winner, having posted a record better than .500 in each of the last three seasons.

Harnisch has had his share of problems, including a bout with clinical depression that caused him to miss most of the 1997 season, and injuries to his shoulder, which put him on the disabled list each of the last two seasons. But those injuries appear to be behind him, as a serious workout and rehabilitation program has added a good deal of strength to his weakened throwing shoulder.

Harnisch can't overpower anybody any more, but is sneaky in that he will lull hitters to sleep with 90 MPH fastballs only to sneak one past every now and then at 94. His splitter is excellent and he knows how to pitch. And don't be afraid by his groundball/flyball ratio. He will give up some home runs but the long balls never hurt him much overall.

Scott Williamson will be the best starter on Cincinnati's staff this season. Only 25 years old, Williamson spent his first season and a half in the majors pitching out of the bullpen, sharing closing duties with Danny Graves. But injuries gave Williamson a chance to start and he took advantage of it. He excelled in that role, going 3-3 with a 2.93 ERA in the second half of 2000. He should only get better this year, as he will be able to adjust his offseason workout program to build up the endurance he will need to pitch into the late innings.

Steve Parris, much like New York's Rick Reed, succeeds but fails to get the recognition he deserves because he is not a flashy pitcher. Parris doesn't throw hard, but he hits his spots and keeps hitters off balance by changing speeds. Parris was dogged in 2000 because he was among the league leaders in losses for much of the campaign, but that was due more to Cincinnati's tepid offense and lack of run support than it was to Steve's lack of ability. It isn't likely that he will approach 20 victories, but count on 12-15 wins and a decent number of innings. Parris was traded to the Blue Jays during the offseason. The hole in the rotation left by Parris will benefit, Williamson, Etherton, and Bell. See more on Parris in the Blue Jays starting pitchers section.

Elmer Dessens is another overlooked pitcher on Cincinnati's staff. Forced to spend the 1999 season in Japan after getting dumped by Pittsburgh, Dessens came back strong last season. It remains something of a mystery why Pittsburgh gave up on Dessens, because he has good stuff. He is a competitor, keeps the ball down in the strike zone, and can be dominating when his breaking pitches are working. He was 10-1 as a starter last year for the Reds, and while his winning percentage is certain to drop this year, there is no reason to think that he will not be able to win at least 12-15 games. He is a good pitcher.

The Reds think more highly of Osvaldo Fernandez than they do of Dessens, but Fernandez has a long history of arm problems. His elbow problems, which caused him to miss two and a half seasons, were the reason the Giants let him go. When he is healthy he can get hitters out. But those days can be few and far between and there is no way you should count on him being 100 percent for the entire season. He is almost guaranteed to miss several weeks along the way, as he did last season when he was out for most of July and all of August.

The Reds added Rob Bell to their starting rotation only a few days before the end of spring training last March. Bell, like most young pitchers with a lot of talent, had a rookie season with as many ups as downs. He pitched brilliantly in the first three weeks of the season, then fell apart and got sent to Triple-A while the Reds were trying to stay in the pennant race. He was better when he returned, but he still had some bad outings. He is going to improve some this season, but not as much as Williamson. Overall his upside is not as good, but he still has a chance to be a very good pitcher. Winning 10-12 games shouldn't be too much of a stretch.

Villone was Cincinnati's best starting pitcher early last season, but completely fell apart in the middle part of the year. It took him most of the rest of the season to get things straightened out, but when he did he was good again. Villone does not have the stuff to be a No. 1 or 2 starter, but his arm is capable enough to succeed in a swing role, much like the end of the 2000 season when he pitched out of the bullpen, but also made a handful of starts. Going to Colorado will automatically raise his ERA by a point or more, and the thin air there could wind up destroying his confidence. But like Gabe White, another former Cincinnati pitcher, he also could succeed there and wind up a .500 pitcher. See more on Villone in the Rockies starting pitchers section.

Righty Seth Etherton was acquired during the offseason from the Angels. He was expected to be in the Reds starting rotation, most likely as the number four or five starter. He has talent and could be a sleeper if he stays healthy. See more on Etherton in the Angels starting pitchers section.

Chris Reitsma could wind up in the Reds rotation at the start of the season. The Reds like the young righthander, acquired last July from the Red Sox in the deal for Dante Bichette. He pitched in relief in the Arizona Fall League in the fall of 2000, but the club still views him as a starter. It's more likely that he will begin the season in the bullpen, but an injury or a couple of bad outings by another starter could get him his shot. He will be an effective starting pitcher, but it is hard to say exactly when he will move into the rotation for good. It could be in April, but it might not be until 2001.

Cincinnati's minor league pitching staffs are very thin and the club has few prospects in the high minor leagues. Lefthander Ty Howington was the club's top draft pick in 1998, but he struggled badly in the Class A Midwest League and is at least two or three years away from consideration.

RECOMMENDATION REVIEW: Only Williamson has the arm and the stuff to be a truly dominating pitcher, but the rest of Cincinnati's staff certainly is capable of winning 10-15 games. Williamson is young, but beginning the season as a starter will only help him improve. Look for him to have a breakout season.

COLORADO ROCKIES

Everything that is good about Coors Field for hitters is bad for pitchers. The ball travels. There is a large expanse of outfield. Line drives and short pops fall because the outfielders must play deep to account for the fact that the ball travels. And so it goes.

Pitchers' hell? Try Coors Field with a tightly wrapped baseball -- as Mike Hampton and Denny Neagle will soon find out.

You have to wonder Part I:

Besides Mike Mussina, Hampton was the biggest free agent pitcher on the market. You have to wonder what he was thinking when he signed his contract (MONEY???). He will be the Rockies staff ace. Do not pay a ton of money for Hampton or take him to high in the draft. He is a little overrated from his 1999 season with the Astros and pitching home games at Coors Field will not help.

You have to wonder Part II:

While Hampton will still be a successful pitcher, Neagle is a crap shoot. He will be the Rockies number two starter. The one thing on his side, like Hampton, is that he keeps the ball on the ground, but also like Hampton, he is not overpowering. Neagle was very hittable with his brief stint in New York in 2000. He is also an injury risk.

Righthander Pedro Astacio has ascended to the role of staff ace in 2000, although the numbers (when judged in normal light) do not reflect that.

Lefthanders Brian Bohanon and newly acquired Ron Villone will fill two spots in the rotation, while righties Masato Yoshii, Brian Rose, Kevin Jarvis and John Wasdin will compete for the final two vacancies.

Astacio is the franchise's winningest pitcher (47 victories in three-plus seasons) and has the top three strikeout seasons in club history after being acquired late in the 1997 season from Los Angeles. Demonstrably durable, Astacio missed his final three scheduled starts in 2000 because of hand and knee injuries that ended a streak of 239 consecutive career starts.

Astacio has won 17 games with a 3.8 ERA in road games the past two seasons, a truer gauge of his effectiveness. He will be the number one starter and should make the second Opening Day start of his career.

Bohanon bounced back and forth between the rotation and the bullpen last season before regaining his status as a top starter over the final four months of the season, tying tied his season high with 12 victories despite making only 26 starts. Bohanon (2.78) edged Diamondbacks lefthander Randy Johnson (2.79) for the best road ERA in the National League.

Bohanon is the type of pitcher who seems best-suited for Coors; a guy who mixes speeds and locates well who also has the mental toughness not to be intimidated by the conditions. He will open the season as the No. 2 or No. 3 starter, with newcomer Villone the other candidate.

Ron Villone was acquired from Cincinnati for spare parts in the offseason and appears very similar to Bohanon, not only because he is a big, burly lefthander but also because he has bounced back and forth between the bullpen and the rotation in recent seasons.

When Villone is spotting his fastball and has command of his breaking ball, he can be dominating. He tied a Reds' franchise record (nine-inning game) with 16 strikeouts in his final start of the 2000 season against St. Louis, winning 10 games in 23 starts. He beat Randy Johnson, 1-0, with eight innings of one-hit ball the year before. See more on Villone in the Reds starting pitchers section.

Masato Yoshii seems the type who could be effective at altitude, a control pitcher who has average only 2.9 walks per nine innings in his three major league seasons. But he could not put it together in his first season in Colorado last year despite the 10th best run support in the NL last year.

Yoshii got half his six victories — and all three in the first three months of the season — against the Diamondbacks. If pitchers' running mattered, Yoshii's value would be greater. He became the first Japanese-born player to steal a base in the majors when he stole second against the D'backs on June 24.

Brian Rose and John Wasdin were obtained from Boston at the trading deadline in the deal that sent Mike Lansing and Rolando Arrojo to the Red Sox. Rose was immediately placed in the rotation and won four of his 12 starts, while Wasdin was used mainly out of the bullpen.

Jarvis entered the rotation last season when Arrojo suffered an injury and stayed there most of the season, although he won only three of his 19 starts.

Rose, only 25. appears the most likely to win the No. 5 spot, with Jarvis and Wasdin available for spot starting duty out of the bullpen. One or both could start the season in the rotation at Triple-A Colorado Springs.

Righthander John Thomson, a productive member of the starting rotation in 1997-98, underwent surgery to repair a torn labrum in his right shoulder and a recurrent blister on the middle finger of his pitching hand in the offseason and will not begin a minor league rehabilitation program until June. The Rockies hope to have him back in the final half of the season.

Lefthander Josh Kalinowki and righthander Shawn Chacon, both hard throwers, are the best starting prospects in the organization, although each is at least a year away.

RECOMMENDATION REVIEW: The gutty Colorado starters are much better in real life (where heart, mental toughness and the ability to overcome adversity matter) than they are in any pure statistical evaluation. Hampton will win 15 games with an ERA over four; Astasio and Neagle will win 12 games with ERAs over five and Ratios around 1.40; Bohanon and Villone and possibly Yoshii could win 10 apiece, but all of their ratios will rank among the worst third of NL starting pitchers. That doesn't make them bad people, merely products of their environment.

FLORIDA MARLINS

The Marlins have one of the best stables of young arms in all of baseball and their staff will be led by 23-year-old Ryan Dempster in 2001. He broke through with an outstanding 2000 campaign, going 14-10 with a 3.66 ERA and 209 strikeouts in 226-plus innings of work. His control improved enough to make his fastball and slider extremely effective, though he could stand to cut back on the walks a little. Barring a major setback, Dempster appears to be a legitimate top of the rotation starter.

Perhaps the most surprising player in baseball last year was righthander Chuck Smith. The Marlins picked him up from the Rangers' Triple-A club and began using him in their major league rotation out of desperation when several pitchers hit the DL early on in the season. All Smith did was respond by blowing National League hitters away. His 6-6 record didn't indicate how well he pitched. He posted a 3.23 ERA in 2000, allowing 111 hits and 54 walks over 122-plus innings while striking out 118 batters. He showed off a mid 90s fastball, an excellent curve and the ability to use two or three other pitches at times. He did all of this as a 30-year-old rookie.

A.J. Burnett suffered a freak injury near the end of Spring Training last year that cost him most of the season, but he came back late in the year and demonstrated the ability that would have won him a spot in the rotation on Opening Day had he not gone on the DL. His mid 90s fastball and wicked knuckle-curve were overpowering at times, though his control left something to be desired. If he doesn't suffer any more freak injuries, Burnett could really break through in 2001.

Brad Penny was another young Marlins' starter who had some success last year, but an injury cut his season short. He's got the stuff of a number one starter, including a mid 90s fastball and sharp slider. With improved ability to locate his fastball, Penny could emerge quickly as one of the best young starters in the National League. If healthy, he should be able to keep his spot in the Marlins' rotation this year.

The fifth spot in the rotation should be up for grabs in Spring Training with at least five or six pitchers vying for the spot. Lefthander Jesus Sanchez has started a lot of games for the Marlins the past two seasons, but has been extremely inconsistent and could be headed for a bullpen job. 24-year-old lefty Michael Tejera, who missed most of last season with an injury, could compete for the job if he's healthy come Spring Training. He'll probably be handled carefully, however, and spend at least a little time in the minors. Veteran righthander Reid Cornelius made 21 starts for the Marlins last year, but will only be back in the rotation if there are more injury problems or if one or more of the young pitchers falls on his face. Righthander Vladimir Nunez could get another shot at sticking in the rotation after falling apart last year. He had a strong 1999 campaign, but struggled so badly during the first half of the 2000 season that the Marlins had to send him back to Triple-A for the rest of the season. Nunez has a low to mid 90's fastball, a hard slider, a solid change and a deadly split-finger fastball, but he needs to be able to throw more strikes early in counts to be successful.

The other wild card is veteran Alex Fernandez. If totally healthy, Fernandez is an impact pitcher with guts and a four-pitch arsenal. His raw stuff has deteriorated due to numerous arm injuries, but he still knows how to pitch and could help out quite a bit if he's physically sound.

The Marlins have an abundance of top flight pitching prospects in the way soon, but Josh Beckett, Claudio Vargas and Wes Anderson stand out above the rest. Beckett is cut from the Kerry Wood mold - he's a 20-year-old righthander with 95-98 MPH fastball, a brutal curve and a developing changeup. The Marlins have always been aggressive with pitching prospects, so don't be surprised if he moves up quickly in 2001 - he's one of the two or three best pitching prospects in all of baseball. Vargas combines a low 90s fastball, good offspeed stuff and excellent control at the age of 21. He could come on quickly as well. Anderson is a 6'4" fireballer that pitched very well at High-A last year and could finish the 2001 season in the majors if things go well for him.

RECOMMENDATION REVIEW: Dempster is clearly the gem of this group heading into 2001 and he should pitch at least as well this year as he did last year. Smith was a major surprise last year and he could be a great pickup late if you can get him in the right round or at the right price. Both Burnett and Penny are risky, but the upside is high. They could both struggle some this year, but both could pull out performances like Dempster did last year. They've got amazing ability and are worth having, but understand the risk involved before committing to them. The rest of the group is really just a toss-up. Fernandez would be a good pickup if you can get him cheap or really late in a draft, but he's no sure thing. Nunez has the ability, but has to prove himself in Spring Training first. Beckett should be snapped up immediately in leagues with minor league reserve rosters, as should Anderson and Vargas.

HOUSTON ASTROS

The pitcher friendly Astrodome was a good place for Rotisserie League owners to look for starting pitchers. However, Enron Field is a direct opposite. Houston pitchers had the highest ERA in the National League (5.41), which was also worse than all but two American League clubs. The entire blame cannot be placed on Enron Field, however, as the road ERA, 5.26, was not appreciably better than the home ERA of 5.55. Astro pitching was just bad and the starters were even worse (5.52) than the woeful bullpen (5.16).

The Astros did not have a starting pitcher who could legitimately be considered a staff ace. Scott Elarton had an impressive won-loss record of 17-7 especially since he was coming off of shoulder surgery. However, he had an ERA of 4.81 and a 1.46 ratio. He was helped by exceptional run support of 7.10 runs per game. Elarton is still young, 25, and has been considered the Astros best pitching prospect since he was signed as a first round draft choice in 1994. He throws hard and usually has command of a good breaking ball. He has always had exceptional poise, despite his youth. He could become a true staff ace in 2001.

Shane Reynolds has been the nominal staff ace for the last several years. He started the 2000 season strong and made the All-Star team for the first time in his career. However, the second half was a disaster. He began having back problems and tried to pitch through it. His last good start was on June 18. He stayed in the rotation for 7 more games but none were successful. He was shut down for the season at the end of July. He did not have surgery, but with rest and rehabilitation, he expects to be ready to perform in 2001. His 2000 record (7-8, 5.22, 1.49 ratio) was, by far, the worst of his career and is heavily

influenced by his last 7 starts before going on the disabled list. If he is healthy, he should be capable of 12-15 wins, but his back problem makes him a risk.

Jose Lima was the pitcher most affected by the move to Enron Field. A fly ball pitcher, he enjoyed two very successful seasons in the Astrodome, which was made for his pitching style. A case can be made that Lima was the worst starting pitcher in the major leagues in 2000. He had a 7-16 record with a league worst 6.65 ERA and a 1.62 ratio. He set a National League record by allowing 48 home runs and seriously challenged Bert Blyleven's major league record of 50. After a terrible start, Lima did pitch somewhat better in the second half. Before the All-Star Game, he was 2-13 with a 7.36 ERA. After the break he was 5-3 with an ERA of 5.80. However, his problems can't all be blamed on Enron Field. His road ERA of 6.32 wasn't that much better than his home ERA of 6.92.

Lima remained in the starting rotation all season with 33 starts, the most on the team. He will have to show significant improvement in 2001 to retain his position.

Chris Holt was traded to the Detroit Tigers during the offseason. Wade Miller, Tony McKnight, Octavio Dotel, or one of the Astros minor league pitching prospects will be the beneficiaries of Holt's departure.

Holt was the No. 4 starter in 2000 and continued to lose twice as many games as he won, just as he did in his 2 previous seasons. He also stayed in the rotation all season with 32 starts, despite his 8-16 record, an ERA of 5.35 and a ratio of 1.56. Since his best pitch is a sinking fast ball, he was not affected by Enron Field as much as some of the other pitchers. He had a lower ERA at home (4.91) than he did on the road (5.88). His ERA was worse in the second half (5.79) than it was before the All-Star Game (4.99).

With three reasonably consistent full seasons behind him, there is little reason to believe that Holt, now 29, will get appreciably better.

Enron Field will make it unlikely to attract free agent pitchers to Houston. Thus, the Club must rely on trades and their minor league system for improved pitching. Two pitchers from the minor league system showed promise in 2000 in their first significant exposure to the major leagues.

Wade Miller, 24, was promoted from Triple-A New Orleans in early July when Octavio Dotel was moved to the bullpen. He remained in the rotation for the remainder of the season, compiling a 6-6 record in 16 starts with a 5.14 ERA and a 1.39 ratio. He pitched better than his record indicated, allowing less than a hit per inning and recording twice as many strikeouts as walks. His high ERA was heavily influenced by 2 bad starts in which he gave up 12 and 8 earned runs. He finished with 6 strong outings in his last 7 starts. Miller should be a solid middle-of-the-rotation starter in 2001 and has the tools for a successful major league career.

Tony McKnight was Houston's first round draft choice out of high school in 1995. After struggling for 4 years, he had a strong season at Double-A in 1999. He had arm problems in spring training in 2000 and pitched at Double-A and Triple-A where he was 4-10 in 25 starts with an ERA of 4.61. He made his major league debut at the age of 23 when he was recalled for an emergency start in early August. McKnight made 5 starts in September when he and Miller were the two most effective members of the Astros' rotation.

McKnight had a 4-1 record, an ERA of 3.86 and a ratio of 1.26 with Houston in 2000. He has a strong arm and improving command of his secondary pitches. If he can sustain his September performance, he should be in the starting rotation in 2001. He may struggle at Enron since he had a 6.57 ERA in his 3 home starts and a 2.38 ERA in his three road starts.

The Astros had two minor league pitchers who had breakout seasons in 2000, Roy Oswalt and Tim Redding. Oswalt, 23, was 4-3, 2.98 at high Class-A Kissimmee before being promoted to Double-A Jackson where he was 11-4 with an ERA of 1.94 and was named the top pitcher in the Texas League. He topped off the year by being named to the U.S. Olympic Team where he pitched two strong games against Korea.

Oswalt throws in the mid 90s despite his 6' 0", 170 pound stature and has excellent control. He recorded 188 strikeouts and only 33 walks in 2000. He should start the season at Triple-A New Orleans but could find himself in Houston sometime during the season if he builds on his 2000 success.

Redding also began the season at high Class A Kissimmee where he was 12-5 with a 2.68 ERA. He led the league in strikeouts and was named to the Florida State League All-Star team. He was promoted to Double-A Round Rock when Oswalt left to join the Olympic Team where he was 2-0, 3.46 in 5 starts. He was even better in Round

Rock's successful run in the playoffs, picking up 2 wins while allowing no earned runs in 16 innings.

Redding, 23, throws in the mid 90s and has recorded impressive strikeout totals in each of his three seasons. The big improvement in 2000 was in cutting down on his walks. He needs another year or two in the high minors to refine his command but he appears to be on track for a major league career.

Brian Powell, 27, obtained in a trade with Detroit prior to the 1999 season, was promoted to Houston from Triple-A in early August. He stayed in the rotation for 5 starts, compiling a 2-1 record with a 5.74 ERA. Once a prospect in the Detroit organization, he was rushed to the majors by the Tigers in 1998 and, after hurting his shoulder in 1999, has not been the same. He was removed from Houston's 40-man roster after the 2000 season.

The Astros have five other starting pitchers on their 40-man roster. None have pitched in Triple-A. and they are not expected to be in Houston this year. The most prominent is Wilfredo Rodriguez, a hard throwing lefty who was ranked Houston's No. 1 prospect prior to the season by Baseball America. However, the 2000 season was a lost one for Rodriguez as he had persistent arm problems. He was 3-5, 4.75 at high Class A Kissimmee and 2-4, 5.77 at Double-A Round Rock. He is only 22 and should be able to get back on track, probably starting the season at Double-A.

Brad Lidge, 24, the Astros' No. 1 draft choice in 1998 turned some heads in spring training last year with his overpowering stuff but, for the third straight year, experienced arm problems. He has won only 2 games since signing in 1998. Carlos Hernandez, 21, is a small, hard throwing lefty who pitched at the low Class A level in 2000. He already has a no-hitter and an 18-strikeout game in his brief career. Two other lefties, Kyle Kessell, 25, obtained in the Mike Hampton trade, and Greg Miller, 21, obtained in the Carl Everett trade, need strong seasons at Double-A to stay on the radar screen.

RECOMMENDATION REVIEW: Selection of any Astro starter should be considered a risk. Elarton will probably be overpriced because of his deceiving 17 wins. Reynolds could be a bargain and Wade Miller and McKnight could be good, cheap picks for the future but will probably experience some rough spots until they gain more experience. Lima should be avoided by all but big-time risk takers. Oswalt and Redding should be good Ultra picks.

LOS ANGELES DODGERS

Lets start with one of the best pitchers in baseball, Kevin Brown. And let's make a case for why being one of the best pitchers in the game did not necessarily make him one of the best Rotisserie choices in 2000.

A surprising comment? Well, let's check the numbers. If you had him last season, you were probably as frustrated as Brown. He led the league in ERA, but won only 13 games in 33 starts and only three of his last 13. That's a reflection of the disappointing team around him, a team that supported him with five runs per start, 1.5 runs per start fewer than it provided teammate Darren Dreifort, admittedly a better hitter than Brown, but not that much better. The strikeouts, of course, still count. It's hard to argue with his .213 opponents batting average, a 2.58 ERA or a 4:1 strikeout:walk ratio. Those numbers scream ace, even if he has only one 20-win season and that came nine years ago. The numbers breakdown show Brown was unhittable at home. Teams that got to him pretty much had to do it in the first inning. Not to be overlooked is the fact that he is a workhorse, with at least 230 innings each of the last five seasons.

Many teams would like to have a No. 1 starter as good as the Dodgers' No. 2, Chan-Ho Park. His 2000 season could be considered a breakthrough year, except that's what we all thought in 1998, only to regress dramatically the next year. So the big question with Park is consistency? And with so much credit for his improvement attributed to catcher Chad Kreuter, one must wonder what happens if Krueter gets hurt? Does Park slip back into the fog that supposedly hampered him when Todd Hundley was behind the plate? It's something to think about, although the Dodgers believe his maturity and familiarity with a new country have given Park confidence he lacked earlier in his career. One thing about Park for sure is, be patient, he finishes strong. He was 5-1 in September in 1999 and went 7-2 in his last nine starts last year.

Andy Ashby was signed as a free agent and will be the Dodgers third starter. See more on Ashby in the Braves starting pitchers section.

Now let's turn to a pitcher who has never won more than 13 games in any season. He's never had an ERA below 4.00 as a starter. He has three complete games, lifetime. He's already had Tommy John surgery. And in some kind of statement about the condition of major league pitching, Darren Dreifort was one of the hottest commodities on the free-agent market over the winter. Whether he will be an equally hot property among Rotisserie players depends on buying into the projections of his potential rather than buying into a study of his performance. Because in cold, hard numbers, Dreifort hasn't delivered. His lifetime record is six games below .500. He's never struck out more than 168 in a season. For all of the wicked movement on his pitches, he hasn't really put it together. Give him credit, however, for putting to rest the notion that he can't last an entire season. He went 8-2 after the All-Star break and didn't even have to be shut down with a sore shoulder as in the past.

Look who's back, Carlos Perez. And you thought for sure he had pitched himself off the team by going 2-10 in 1999. Not only did his guaranteed contract give him a free pass on cutdown day, but Perez improved a little in 2000, trimming his ERA to 5.56. Actually, after bombing again as a starter, Perez actually found a role as an effective middle-relief lefthander. It seemed not knowing when he would pitch helped Perez. His ERA as a reliever was 4.5 runs lower than as a starter. Granted, many of his appearances were blowout games, but he still had to get batters out. He actually threw strikes, cut down on walks and fooled hitters with that roundhouse curve. But when he gets hit, he gets whacked. Worth a gamble? At your risk.

A more enticing play would be Luke Prokopec, the Aussie righthander who passed on a chance to play in the Olympics at home to debut in the big leagues. Granted, it was September, but it was impressive. After two scoreless relief appearances, he got three starts and didn't look like he just came out of Double-A. He didn't show the control he displayed in the minor leagues, perhaps the one concession to nerves, but he did more than management expected. He was hit hard by righthanders, not a good trend for a righthanded starter.

A worse trend was demonstrated by Canadian Eric Gagne, who made his impressive September debut in 1999 look like a fluke by struggling throughout 2000 until coming to life in September. He walked almost as many as he struck out and was hit equally well by lefties and righties. He did win three of four starts the final month, which means he either finally got straightened out or he just likes to pitch in September.

RECOMMENDATION REVIEW: There is no reason not to feel confident about Brown or Park this coming season (the Dodgers will be much improved). They are warriors, power pitchers who rack up strikeouts and innings. Just how many wins you get out of them depends more on the supporting cast, and we know what they've been up to recently. Dreifort has never even come close to a blowout season, so we'd like to see one first before betting it will happen, but his 2000 second half may be an indication that 2001 could be it. Teamed back up with his buddy Kevin Brown, look for Ashby to have a solid season. Perez is just way too erratic, but Prokopec is intriguing, even if he lacks an overpowering pitch.

MILWAUKEE BREWERS

Nearly given up for dead after two years of shoulder problems had limited him to one inning total in the 1998 and 1999 seasons, Jeff D'Amico put together a beautiful run in the second half that rivaled any two-month pitching performance in franchise history. The highlight was a 5-0 record and 0.76 ERA in six starts that earned "Big Daddy" National League pitcher-of-the-month honors for July. Combining pinpoint control of his 90 MPH fastball with a devastating slow curve, the 6-7 righthander kept hitters off balance and consistently worked deep into games while fashioning a 12-7 record and 2.66 ERA that was good enough for third in the league (behind future Hall-of-Famers Kevin Brown and Randy Johnson). If it weren't for the fact that Big Daddy stumbled somewhat in his last two starts, he would have been the first Brewer in history to claim an ERA title. Still just 25, D'Amico clearly comes into the 2001 season with ace of the staff status.

Jamey Wright, 26, opened the 2000 season on the disabled list with a slight rotator cuff tear that he rehabbed through an exercise program and didn't make his first start until May 23. After that he showed flashes of becoming a serviceable #2 starter with a low-90's sinker and slider repertoire. Wright sometimes gets into trouble when his ball moves too much and he can't keep it in the strike zone. He keeps the ball in the park and induces lots of ground balls and double plays with a heavy two-seamer that bores in on righthanded hitters. Wright was just 7-9 in 2000 with a respectable ERA of 4.10 in 25 starts (164.2 innings). He should have a better year in 2001.

Righthander Jimmy Haynes, 28, was the Brewers' work-horse in the 2000 season, making 33 starts and logging 199.1 innings to go with his 12-13 record and 5.33 ERA. Haynes seemed to falter somewhat in the season's second half, as has been his career pattern. On several occasions he would open a game with four or five dominating innings only to suddenly lose it or surrender a big inning before reinforcements could arrive to right the listing ship. This is a tendency that makes it difficult for Haynes to be a big winner. Though a power pitcher, Haynes struck out just 88 batters to go along with his 100 walks. He enters the 2001 season as Milwaukee's #3 starter but the upcoming year will be a pivotal one for Haynes, who has previously worn out his welcome in Oakland and Baltimore.

26-year-old John Snyder had a season to forget in 2000 after coming over to the Brew Crew along with Jaime Navarro in a preseason trade that sent Jose Valentin and Cal Eldred to the Chicago White Sox. GM Dean Taylor probably wishes he could take a mulligan on that one as Navarro was released after five hideous starts and Snyder went 3-10 with a 6.17 ERA in 23 uneven starts. It's difficult to imagine Snyder figuring prominently in the Brewers' plans for 2001.

Righthander Paul Rigdon, 25, appeared to be a throw-in when he came to the Brewers in late July along with Kane Davis and Richie Sexson in the trade that sent Bob Wickman, Steve Woodard and Jason Bere to Cleveland. But Rigdon pitched intelligently and consistently in posting a solid 4-4 mark and 4.52 ERA in 12 Milwaukee starts. Rigdon isn't overpowering but features excellent control and command and probably earned himself a shot at the #4 spot in the rotation in 2001.

Although the cupboard was left virtually bare in terms of position players when Sal Bando was asked to ride into the sunset, the organization had begun to address the Brew-ers longstanding shortage of quality starting pitching. Righthander Ben Sheets is the closest Brewer pitching prospect to the major leagues and will have to pitch very poorly not to leave spring training as the Brew Crew's #5 starting pitcher. Sheets was Milwaukee's first-round draft pick in 1999 out of Northeast Louisiana University and features a mid-90s fastball and sharp overhand curveball to go with a decent change. He is best known for pitching the U.S. Olympic team to the gold medal in the 2000 Olympics in Sydney and has top of the rotation potential. Horacio Estrada is a 25-year-old lefthander who went 14-4 with a 3.33 ERA to lead the International League in wins in 2000. He was called up to the big club twice during the 2000 season, including a start at the end of the year in Houston in which he pitched reasonably well. Estrada is the classic crafty lefthander who does the little things well and will be in the mix for a rotation spot in spring training. Nick Neugebauer features high-90's heat and is at times unhittable but needs to develop command. Also worth watching are righthanders Jose

Mieses (17-7, 2.56 between Mudville and Beloit) and Jose Garcia.

RECOMMENDATION REVIEW: The issue with Jeff "Big Daddy" D'Amico is health. He has the stuff, makeup and pitching savvy to be a frontline starter but his ongoing injury problems have got to be cause for concern. Jamey Wright is a young power pitcher with nasty stuff who could develop into a big winner if he can stay away from arm problems. Jimmy Haynes is on the verge of moving into "suspect" status but takes the ball every fifth day and has a good arm. It's difficult to project whether Horacio Estrada can make the transition from successful Triple-A starter to the major league rotation but the Brewers would like to add a lefty to the rotation in 2001 to combat St. Louis and Cincinnati's lefty dominated lineups. Forget John Snyder. The jury is still out on Paul Rigdon but he could make the rotation with a solid spring training and might be worth a shot at the right price. Ben Sheets is an ace waiting to happen, it's just a matter of when.

MONTREAL EXPOS

The Expos went into the offseason with a lot of young, quality arms in their starting rotation. However most of them were also recovering from an injury. The Expos expected to start the season with ace Javier Vazquez, Dustin Hermanson, (if he is not traded), Carl Pavano, Tony Armas, and then the No. 5 spot is up for grabs between Scott Downs, Mark Thurman, and Hideki Irabu.

The 24 year old Vazquez came into his own during the 2000 season; already his third big league season. During the season it became apparent that he was the new Expos staff ace. He is a smart pitcher with a knack for pitching "big" in big games, especially when matched up with the top pitchers in the league like Randy Johnson.

Vazquez has gotten better each of his first three seasons and is still improving. He has lowered his ERA almost a run each of the past two seasons. He is an innings eater who goes almost seven innings each time out. His strike-out to walk ratio is better than 3:1, but he tends to give up a lot of hits, leading to a higher Ratio than would be expected from a pitcher who strikes out 196 and walked only 61. There is room for improvement there and you can expect his 1.41 Ratio to drop more when he stops putting the ball over the plate. Vazquez held his own with a bad team, and finished 11-9 with a 4.05 ERA in 217 innings pitched. Watch for the young Expos, along with Vazquez,

to improve overall during the 2001 season.

After a breakout season in 1998 with the Expos, Dustin Hermanson has regressed. There were rumors that Hermanson was on the way out during the offseason. He has been a major disappointment the past two seasons and has past the stage of being an "en vogue" Rotisserie pick.

Hermanson was traded to Cardinals during the offseason. The move opens up a hole in the Expos starting rotation. The candidates to fill the hole are Irabu, Reames, and Thurman.

In 2000, he started as the Expos staff ace before being moved to the closer's role when Ugueth Urbina went down with elbow problems. That surprising experiment did not work out as Hermanson blew three of his seven save opportunities and was generally very shaky each time out as the closer. Hermanson went back to the starting rotation and again had better success at the end of the season, than in the beginning. A trend he's had the past few season.

Hermanson was expected to be in the starting rotation for the 2001 season, but there is always that chance the team may decided to use him out of the pen, especially because he has only two quality pitches and poor stamina for a starter. He has been working on a change to improve his arsenal. Overall, Hermanson only gives you wins for your Rotisserie pitching staff.

Like Vazquez, Carl Pavano was fashioning a breakout season before arm trouble shut him down right before the All-Star Break. He was the Expos best pitcher up until that point and has the potential to be the Expos ace if he could ever get over his reoccurring arm problems.

He was expected to be in camp healthy, and if so, he has the most talent on the staff. Pavano is only 25 and coming into his prime years. Pavano will give you wins, Ratio, ERA, and strikeouts; assuming he stays healthy.

Tony Armas is a rising star. Like Pavano he has had his fair share of arm troubles during his young career. In 2000, Armas was 7-9, with a 4.36 ERA, and a 1.31 Ratio in 95 innings. He was pitching strong when he first was called up during the early part of the season before arm troubles landed him on the DL. Look for Armas 2001 numbers to improve across the board, especially if the Expos young team improves; as expected.

The Expos 5th starter will come from either the lefty Scott

Downs, or the two righties, Hideki Irabu or Mike Thurman.

Downs has the best chance to be the 5th starter. He has the highest upside of the three and he would be the only lefty in the rotation. Downs came over from the Cubs in the Rondell White trade. He is not overpowering, but knows how to pitch and is considered a Maddux-type pitcher.

Irabu's star has fallen in Montreal. He showed up out of shape in 2000 and then was shut down during the middle of the year due to arm trouble. The Expos have tried to trade him, but have had no takers. A bad sign in a pitching starved time! Unless he is in shape, he will again have stamina and health problems. He just does not have the fire to match his talents. Let someone else draft him because of his name.

Thurman is a capable fill-in and was expected to be a swingman type pitcher in times of need. He is average across the board and is not going to surprise anyone. He is a workhorse who will not win over 10 games, while producing a high ERA and Ratio, with low strikeout totals. He is one of those pitchers who is valued more in real life than in Rotisserie baseball.

Donnie Bridges is a name to keep an eye on for your Ultra Roster. He has been moved back and forth from closer to starter. He has hard stuff and seemed to over come his control problems and injuries. If the Expos are hit with a rash of pitching injuries, as they were in 2000, Bridges could see a callup. He was expect to fulfill a competent role in 2001 by the Expos if all goes according to plan.

RECOMMENDATION REVIEW: One through three have the potential to have a breakout season. Because they all pitch in Montreal, they will come cheap. Expect the same from Hermanson: 10-plus wins with a high ERA and Ratio for the Cards. While Vazquez, Pavano, and Armas all have the potential to be real bargains, especially if the team improves as expected. Remember the Expos were a surprise team for the first month and a half of the season before injuries to their pitching staff took its toll. They are a year wiser and healthy so expect more wins for Vazquez, Pavano, and Armas. Do not expect much from any 5th starter, unless they are on the Yankees or Braves. Let someone else take Irabu!

Al Leiter has established himself as the Mets' staff ace. In 2000, the 35-year-old lefthander was 16-8 with a 3.20 ERA and 1.21 ratio. He had a career-best 2.63 strikeout/walk ratio. He didn't appear to be losing any power; he had his second season of 200 strikeouts. Leiter held lefthanded batters to a .119 average.

The Mets faced anxious moments in trying to keep their pennant-winning rotation together during the offseason. They lost Mike Hampton to the Rockies, but re-signed Rick Reed and added righthanders Kevin Appier and Steve Trachsel through free agency. Bobby J. Jones remained a free agent into mid-December.

Reed, a 35-year-old righthander, overcame a series of injuries to match his 11-5 record from 1999 while lowering his ERA from 4.58 to 4.11. The control pitcher managed a 1.23 ratio despite giving up 28 home runs.

Jones' season highlight—quite likely his career highlight—was his one-hit shutout of San Francisco in the Division Series. It was surprising because he had pitched so poorly during the regular season that he was sent down to Triple-A Norfolk for a time. The 31-year-old righthander finished 11-6 despite a 5.06 ERA and 1.42 ratio by going 8-2, 3.98 after the All-Star break. A note of caution: Jones was 4-3, 6.44 away from Shea Stadium in 2000.

Appier was 15-11 with a 4.52 ERA and 1.55 ratio last season. The ratios could be expected to come down a bit in the National League, but the 33-year-old was helped by his home park in Oakland. He's also a late-season risk; he has performed worse after the All-Star break in each of the last six seasons. A motion that makes it look as if he'll throw his entire arm along with the ball at some point also is a concern. See more on Appier in the A's starting pitchers section.

Trachsel, 30, was no more successful with Toronto than with Tampa Bay last season. He does give a major league team innings; Trachsel has worked at least 200 innings each of the last five years. But they're the kind of innings a Rotisserie owner doesn't need (8-15, 4.80 ERA, 1.52 ratio in 2000; 52-62 since '96). See more on Trachsel in the Blue Jays starting pitchers section.

Glendon Rusch, a lesser-known 26-year-old lefthander, gave the 2000 Mets 190 1/3 innings that were far more productive than Trachsel's (11-11, 4.01, 1.26).

Grant Roberts is the pitcher from New York's farm system closest to being ready for the majors. The 23-year-old righthander was 7-8 with a 3.38 ERA at Triple-A Norfolk, but gave up nine earned runs in seven innings with the Mets.

Lefty Bobby M. Jones, 28, was a stalwart at Norfolk (10-8, 4.32) and pitched reasonably well in 11 major league appearances (0-1, 4.15, 1.50). He could be a useful swingman.

Dennis Springer and Willie Banks were minor league free agents after last season.

Mark Corey, a 26-year-old righthander, regressed in 2000. He was 3-7, 6.79 at Norfolk, but straightened himself out in the bullpen back at Double-A Binghamton (0-0, 1.05).

For the second consecutive year, Tyler Walker fared well after a midseason promotion. The 24-year-old righthander was 7-6, 2.75 at Binghamton and 1-3, 2.39 with Norfolk.

At age 22, righthander Dicky Gonzalez is one of the best control pitchers in the minors. He was 13-5, 3.84 at Binghamton, with 138 strikeouts and just 36 walks in 147 2/3 innings. He has added velocity as he has matured. Watch what he does at Norfolk this year; he could be a midseason callup.

Pat Strange is considered the best overall pitching prospect in the Mets organization. Just 20, the big, hard-throwing righty made it all the way to Double-A last season. After a 10-1, 3.58 start at high Class A Port St. Lucie, he was 4-3, 4.55 at Binghamton, but had some control trouble at the higher level.

J.D. Arteaga, who has a very wealthy friend in Alex Rodriguez, turned his own career around last season. The 26-year-old lefty was 10-7, 3.45 at Binghamton, then won his only start at Norfolk.

Former independent leaguer Pablo Ochoa was 9-12, 5.22 at Binghamton. The righthander is 25.

Marino Cota, 24, was 6-3, 3.89 at Binghamton. He's also a righthander.

Twenty-two-year-old righthander Nick Maness continued his steady climb through New York's farm system. He was 11-7, 3.22 at Port St. Lucie, then 1-0, 1.93 in two starts for Binghamton.

Lefthander Rene Vega, 24, didn't do especially well in stepping up from low Class A to high A ball last season. He was 11-6, 4.40 at Port St. Lucie, but his strikeout rate was down by about a third.

RECOMMENDATION REVIEW: The Mets appeared to be losers in the free agency game. Appier and Trachsel together may not equal Hampton's contribution. Reed was in such poor financial shape five years ago that he had to go to spring training as a replacement player; the Mets now are overpaying him $22.5 million for three years. Don't you overpay for him. If Leiter can handle the load as the undisputed ace, he could produce more than he'll cost. Rusch is likely to be a productive bargain. Gonzalez and Strange would be the Mets' best Ultra selections, and Roberts could have some future value.

PHILADELPHIA PHILLIES

For the first time in recent memory, the Phillies will not be able to count upon Curt Schilling for a potentially dominant effort every fifth day. Ironically, however, all that now stands between the Phillies' development of a well above average corps of starting pitchers is the acquisition or development of a Schilling-like ace. In Bruce Chen, Randy Wolf, Omar Daal and Robert Person, the Phils possess a promising supporting group of starters that should be capable of keeping the Phils in most ballgames in 2001. If a staff anchor doesn't materialize, however, it's doubtful that the Phils will actually win enough close ballgames to propel themselves into contention for a playoff spot.

Though the Phils have been deservedly razzed for yielding promising rookie righthander Adam Eaton to the Padres last season in the Andy Ashby deal, they likely have done more than simply save face by parlaying Ashby into young lefthander Bruce Chen, 24, who was acquired from the Braves last July. In truth, Chen has more than a fair chance of being an even better major league pitcher than Eaton. The 6'2", 210, southpaw is not a power pitcher, but is a strikeout pitcher. His fastball only reaches the upper-80's, but he mixes it expertly with a darting curveball and an excellent changeup, both of which make his heater seem much faster than the radar gun suggests. His command within the strikezone is quite good, though he is a fly ball pitcher that at times will leave offerings up in the strike zone in the late innings as he tires. His toughness was questioned at times during his tenure with the Braves, as he was handed a rotation spot several times but couldn't hold onto it. He quickly dispelled such concerns with the Phils, however, as he consistently kept them in ballgames despite abysmal run support. Chen's ability to maintain low pitch counts should make a consistent seven-inning threat in the near-term, and a candidate to complete 10 games per season before too long. Look for a breakout 200 inning, 15 wins, sub 4.00 ERA campaign from Chen in 2001. Don't be surprised if he emerges as the Phils ace, in the absence of an unexpected free-agent or trade acquisition.

While we're on the topic of promising 24-year-old lefthanded starting pitchers, let's discuss Randy Wolf. Wolf has more major league experience and is arguably more polished than Chen, but is not as precise a crafts-man, and likely lacks the former Brave's upside potential. Truth be told, Wolf and Chen are similar in many respects. Wolf too has maintained a higher than league average strikeout rate despite his lack of a single overpowering pitch. His fastball also reaches the upper 80s, occasionally tipping 90 MPH, and is routinely mixed with a curve and changeup. Wolf's control is not as precise as Chen's, however, and he doesn't possess a single pitch that is as impressive as either Chen's curve or changeup. When they're both on their game, Chen can cruise through nine innings in 90 pitches, while Wolf might throw nearly 120 pitches. Over time, that will take a toll, and make a difference in their overall numbers. Wolf has also endured an extended period of extreme ineffectiveness late in both of the last two seasons — most recently, he logged a miserable 8.89 ERA last August. Like Chen, Wolf gets into trouble when he leaves his pitches up in the strike zone, particularly against righthanded hitters. He needs to paint the corners consistently to experience material success. Wolf too should post 15 wins and record a sub-4.00 ERA in 2001, giving him solid Rotisserie value. Bear in mind, however, that Wolf's upside might not be all that much higher than those 2001 projections, while Chen looks like a future 20-win guy.

Go ahead — laugh at them if you must. Omar Daal's numbers for the 2000 season — 4-19, 6.14 — came complete with the farce of 20-game loser Brian Kingman nomadically touring NL ballparks as Daal inexorably marched towards his 20th loss. Well, Daal circled the wagons just in time, pitching well enough in the second half of September to avoid a Kingman-like fate. Folks, this guy isn't a bad pitcher. He was one of the more effective lefthanded starters in the National League in 1998 and 1999, and is still only 29 years old. What happened in 2000? Well, the King of Winter Ball actually skipped his November-January ritual after the 1999 season, and reported to spring training in less than peak physical condition, with two or three MPH missing from his fastball. As any of you who may have witnessed the rapid, horrific decline of former Phils' closers Al Holland or Mitch Williams as they lost a few inches off of their respective fastballs, such results often aren't very pretty. Daal also suffered through a crisis of confidence last season, nibbling early in the count and then paying the price when forced to deliver room-service, mid-80's fastballs. Hitters batted a lusty .462 when ahead 2-0 in the count against Daal in 2000. He played winter ball this season, and is a pretty fair bet to report to spring training with his full repertoire — an upper-80's fastball, curve and changeup — intact. The Phils and Daal showed a belief in each other by tearing up his hefty 2001 contract and replacing it with a lower base ($2.75 million) for this year and a $4.5 club option for 2002. Daal's pitching for his professional life this season, and is a good bet to at least approach his 1998-99 ceiling. Look for 200 respectable innings, around 12 wins and a 4.00 ERA from Daal in 2001. He'll be a very nice low-dollar addition to your staff.

We're down to starter number four, and at long last, we encounter our first righthander, Robert Person. Watching Person pitch is like going to the dentist. It's a long, tedious and sometimes painful process, but hey — that laughing gas sometimes makes the visit quite pleasurable. Nothing Person does is easy — his pitch count usually approaches 100 by the fifth inning, and he's bathed in sweat before he gets once around the lineup. He can be quite nasty, and often overpowering to the opposition, however. Person, 31, relies almost exclusively on hard stuff, featuring a low-to-mid-90s fastball and a sharp slider. His dominance is best evidenced by his success against lefties - who batted just .179 against him — a group that is often the undoing of righty power hurlers. On the down side, however, Person never pitched enough innings to even qualify for an ERA title until last season, at age 30. He has managed to complete all of one start in his major league career. He is one of the easiest pitchers to run on in the major leagues. He has also battled nagging shoulder soreness in recent seasons. That's a whole lot of question marks that Person has to positively answer to become a big winner. On paper, he looks like an ideal closer, but blew up in that role as a Blue Jay in 1998. The Phils will run him out there as a starter again in 2001, and though it's tempting to be tantalized by his raw stuff, he's a good bet to simply offer more of what he has shown since becoming a Phillie. Look for 10 wins, 170 innings, 150 strikeouts, a 4.00ish ERA, and a whole lot of no-decisions. Be willing to pay a few bucks, and be on alert to spend more on the odd chance that the Phils acquire a name starter and shift Person to the bullpen.

Fifth starter options abound. The trade and free agent markets could yield some new faces by spring training, though the bullpen and the top of the lineup were considered higher priorities as winter dawned. Righty Kent Bottenfield, 32, came over from the Angels for Ron Gant late in the 2000 season, and became a free agent at the end of the year. The Phils have expressed some interest, but at nowhere near the 3-year, $15 million price tag set by Bottenfield. Both the Angels and Phils were deceived by his misleading 18-7 campaign with the Cards in 1999. He was the prime beneficiary of very generous run support in that, the only season in which he has qualified for an ERA title in either league. He's a low-ball pitcher who combines a high-80s fastball, slider and changeup, who is big trouble when he isn't precisely locating his offerings, especially against lefty hitters. His command has been subpar in 1999-2000, but not nearly as subpar as his conditioning. He's a frequent bunt target because of his, shall we say, girth. I can't envision anyone meeting Bottenfield's initial financial demands, but could see him re-upping with the Phils at a much lower number. In any event, six to eight wins and a 5.00 ERA is all that appears to be in store for Bottenfield in 2001.

There are other in-house options for the fifth starter slot. The best of them might be righthander Cliff Politte. Politte, 27, reaches the low-90s on a semi-regular basis, a feat that only Person can boast of among the aforementioned big league incumbents. He has made strides with his breaking ball repertoire, showed better control, and appeared much more comfortable in his third venture at the big league level last season. He'd be best used in a swingman role, and could steal five wins and the odd three-inning save over 80 innings, with a respectable 4.00ish ERA. Paul Byrd, 30, was an All Star as recently as 1999. His star has fallen so much that he was dropped from the Phils' 40-man roster after the 2000 season, one featuring equal parts ineffectiveness and injury. An older, righthanded, poor-man's Bruce Chen, Byrd only reaches the mid-80's with his fastball, and is a fly ball pitcher who gets killed when he doesn't paint the corners with precision. He wasn't a very good painter last season, as his 17 homers allowed in only 83 innings would attest. Toss in right shoulder surgery, and you've got one washout of a season. The Phils might bring him back as a non-roster invitee in 2001, and he has an outside chance to make the staff. His high Rotisserie risk outweighs any potential value, however. Righthander Dave Coggin, 24, also got a brief audition in the Phils' rotation last season. He showed good stuff — his fastball reaches the low-90's, and he adds a curve, slider and changeup. However, he doesn't seem to have any idea as to how to set up hitters, and his

pitches lack movement because of his inconsistent mechanics. His upper minor league strikeout rates have been poor, and time is growing short, leaving major doubts as to whether he'll ever make it. I'd pass on Coggin. Ditto righty Nelson Figueroa, 27, a journeyman minor leaguer tossed into the pile of stuff the Phils got for Schilling. His command is sound, but none of his offerings qualifies as a true out pitch, and he would likely be eaten by major league lefthanded hitters.

Amaury Telemaco, 27, once looked like a super starting pitcher prospect, and continues to show flashes of excellence in the upper minors and majors in a variety of roles. However, if he couldn't impress the Phils in the last year and a half, he likely never will. I'm still betting he'll stick somewhere, however, and be a big league contributor.

Sinkerballer Mark Brownson, 26, has great control and keeps the ball low in the zone, but lacks a true out pitch and has never fared well with men on base in the upper minors or majors. He's a sleeper to succeed in a complementary relief role in the majors, but I just don't see it happening as a starter.

Other 2000 upper minor leaguers with a chance to start a game in the majors this season include righties Brandon Duckworth and Geoff Geary, and lefty Jimmy Osting. Duckworth is already 25 and has yet to toil a single Triple-A inning, and his fastball rarely ventures above 85 MPH. However, he really knows how to pitch, has a great changeup and is a gritty battler on the mound. The Phils love him, but he's older than Chen and Wolf already, for goodness sake. I'll pass, and would avoid using a reserve list spot on this trendy pick. Geary, 24, has impeccable control but rather pedestrian stuff. He'll never last multiple times around the order at upper levels, but could be a decent situational bullpen righty in the future. Osting, 24, came over from the Braves with Chen in the Andy Ashby deal, and has an outside shot to make it as a fifth starter type in the majors, possibly in 2002. His command is solid and he maintains low pitch counts, but he needs to find a true out pitch and ramp up his strikeout rate a bit to become a true prospect.

The Phils' best starting pitcher prospects are a couple of years away. Leading the pack are righties Brad Baisley, Brett Myers and Ryan Madson. Baisley, 21, is a 6'9" righthanded version of Randy Johnson who lost part of last season to shoulder soreness. He hasn't blossomed into a power pitcher yet because of inconsistent mechanics and the slow development of his breaking pitches, but he could be primed for a breakthrough Double-A season in 2001. Myers, 20, is a 6'4", 210, bulldog who combines a mid-90's heater with a hard curve and an improving changeup. He has 220-inning Andy Benes-like workhorse - at the very least — written all over him. If reaches Double-A by late 2001, then he's ahead of schedule. Ditto Madson, 20, a 1998 ninth round pick. He's likely more polished than either Baisley or Myers at this point, expertly mixing a low-90's heater, a hard curve, a solid slider and a changeup, throwing them all for quality strikes. The 6'6", 180, righty is a seven-inning guy already, and will likely be a consistent complete game threat before long.

RECOMMENDATION REVIEW: Chen will be looking to finally breakthrough and have a big year. Coming off a disastrous 2000, Daal will most likely bounce back, although not to his 1999 level. Person is a quality lower Rotisserie rotation pitcher who will give you 10-plus wins along with a good ERA and Ratio. Wolf is also a late quality pick, who could have a big year along with Chen.

PITTSBURGH PIRATES

Bucs starting pitching is relatively sound. Kris Benson is an ace and has ample support from Todd Ritchie and Francisco Cordova. Jason Schmidt and Jimmy Anderson round out the staff with Dan Serafini, Bronson Arroyo, Jose Silva and newly acquired Terry Mulholland also available as swing starters.

Despite a disappointing second half in 2000, Benson is still one of the league's best young hurlers. Last year he lowered his ERA and stepped up his strikeout rate. He has been a steady performer the last two years and is living up to his status as a top draft choice. For Rotisserie players, Benson falls between the cracks. He doesn't pitch for a winning team and is unlikely to win 20 games so, despite his good peripheral numbers, he won't command top dollars on Draft Day. But, because he's a steady young pitcher near the top of his game he also won't go cheaply. Benson is the kind of pitcher that winning Rotisserie teams should pursue, however. With hitting reaching new heights the need for quality, reliable pitching is acute. Benson is established as a quality pitcher and, yet, is still cheap because he hasn't yet been a big winner. Put Benson on your "ace" list and be willing to go that extra mile to acquire him.

It should have been no surprise that Ritchie couldn't live up to the expectations set by his 1999 breakout season. His ERA went up nearly a run and a half and he managed

just nine wins after winning 15 games in '99. What happened was simple; he became the pitcher he was before 1999, allowing hitters a .282 batting average and 26 homers to almost double his previous career total. The real Todd Ritchie was shown in 2000; he just doesn't have the stuff to fool all the hitters all the time. That doesn't mean he can't be a successful pitcher in the majors, though. He will make adjustments and find more success in 2001 than in 2000. While he won't return to the same level of success he enjoyed in 1999, he will be a winner and will make his Rotisserie owners happy. Ritchie is a good choice for teams that have very little money to spend for that last starter. Because he was likely protected in 2000 by his 1999 owners he is also coming upon his option year in many Rotisserie leagues and giving his owners a difficult choice... and the astute player an opportunity. Read the strategy outlined in the Pirates Second Basemen section, apply it to Ritchie and you'll get yourself a nice cheap bargain in 2001.

The Pirates gave Cordova a multi-year contract over the winter, so they obviously are unconcerned about the injuries that limited him to just 17 starts in 2000. A bigger concern for Rotisserie players might be Cordova's rising ERA and Ratio, and dropping strikeout rate. The innings he piled up in 1997 and 1998 appear to be coming back to haunt Cordova. Perhaps the limited work he got in 2000 will be the cure, though, and let Cordova return to a productive level. If you want Cordova this is a good time to get him, but do it only as a long shot. Pitchers with this kind of track record often cannot recover their former level of success.

One of the National League's most consistent starters from 1996 to 1999, Schmidt was lost to injury after just eleven starts in 2000. Considering his overall consistency for many years and writing off last year due to injury would indicate Schmidt is ready to rebound. He may have been a disappointment to his Rotisserie owners in 2000, but his failure last year provides an opportunity in 2001. People who look solely at last year's stats or who perceive Schmidt as no longer reliable will discount his value leading to a lowering of his overall pricing in many leagues. Put Schmidt on your low-priced bargain list and be patient as you wait for his name to be brought up in the draft.

Lefty Anderson emerged as a positive force in 2000, suffering through a tough September which skewed his overall stats; he was usually better than his 5-11, 5.25 ERA line looks. Anderson threw the ball over the plate and kept it in the park, two things that young pitchers often fail to do. It augurs well for his future. Anderson hasn't yet developed his strikeout pitch and that will hold him back. Still, he can be a successful lower rotation starter and may take that big step up in 2001 to become a good Rotisserie pick. For now, though, he's still just an unknown youngster without a proven track record. Anderson is recommended only to teams that aren't in contention in 2001; take a one-dollar chance on him only if you have to take risks to find a diamond in the rough.

Another lefty, Serafini, took a circuitous route to Pittsburgh. Once a Twins' prospect, Serafini pitched for the Cubs and Padres before ending up in the Bucs rotation over the last two months of 2000. He didn't set the world on fire, but he did acquit himself well enough to have another shot at starting this year. Although Serafini was trained as a starter he had been primarily pitching in relief for several years. It may take some time before he is ready to pitch deep into ballgames with regularity. It's hard to recommend Serafini to Rotisserie players; he'll help the Pirates a lot more than his Rotisserie owners in 2001.

Arroyo is considered a good prospect, despite his poor showing early in 2000. He rebounded later to make some good starts and a few useful bullpen appearances, too. He has a starter's repertoire and has good stuff although he hasn't yet learned to take command of a game or dominate with a particular pitch. Arroyo is still learning and will continue to improve; he'll do that at Triple-A Nashville for most of 2001 and can return to Pittsburgh whenever the need for a starter arises. Arroyo is a decent pick for Ultra teams.

Desperate for healthy arms at the end of the season, the Pirates thrust Silva into a starting job. It was a poor match as he got lit up several times in his eleven starts. As a reliever, Silva had a bad stretch near the end of April that caused him to drop in the bullpen pecking order. Overall, though his performance was very much in line with a closer; he fanned a batter per inning in relief, with a good ERA and without walking a lot of hitters. He should return to a short relief job in 2001.

Needing a veteran presence on their staff, the Pirates signed Mulholland over the winter — you can't get much more veteran than that! Mulholland is well past his prime but he'll be a big help to Pittsburgh as he can pitch in several different roles. This will squelch any value he may have had to a Rotisserie team, of course.

Jose Parra and Brian O'Connor each made it to Pittsburgh's starting rotation with vastly different results.

Parra was hit hard in six appearances early in the year; his outings at Nashville weren't much better and show why Parra had been exclusively in the minors since 1996. O'Connor is a better prospect who dominated Double-A hitters at Altoona, then made five starts for Nashville before finishing the year in Pittsburgh. O'Connor has decent stuff for a lefty and is an outside shot to win a starting role out of spring training. Should he be sent back to the minors, he will be one of the first to be recalled when the Pirates need a replacement starter. Rotisserie players should put O'Connor on their list of potential midseason replacements; he can be a winner.

Other regular Triple-A starters in 2000 included Chris Peters, Paul Ah Yat and Travis Baptist. Peters has never recovered from his arm injury and the other two simply lack major league stuff. The Pirates have better prospects lower in their chain, including Luis Torres and Bobby Bradley. Torres throws exceptionally hard but hasn't yet succeeded due to lack of quality secondary pitches. Bradley is just the opposite, having a number of quality pitches at his disposal which he can throw at varying speeds to pinpoint locations. His 2.28 ERA, 5-to-1 strikeout-to-walk ratio and 118 whiffs in 82.2 innings for low-A Hickory last year attest to Bradley's star potential.

RECOMMENDATION REVIEW: Be willing to spend a few extra bucks to get Benson; he's an ace. Ritchie will rebound and be worth more than he might be valued in short-sighted leagues. Avoid Cordova, Mulholland, Serafini, and Parra. Chase Schmidt for a few bucks late in the draft and take Anderson as a late-draft one-dollar starter. Arroyo, O'Connor and Bradley make good Ultra picks, especially Bradley. Consider Silva a potential reliever; don't draft him as a starter.

ST. LOUIS CARDINALS

Darryl Kile won 20 games last year after finally getting out of pitcher's purgatory, better known as Coors Field. Kile may not be an elite pitcher, but he's a workhorse that keeps his team in games and piles up some nice strikeout totals. He's as good a rotisserie pitcher as he is a major league pitcher because he gives himself a chance to earn a lot of wins, he strikes people out and he's difficult to hit against. The one drawback he has is that he gives up a bunch of home runs each year. He may have the best overhand curveball in the game today and he uses it well with his low 90s fastball.

The Cardinals received Expos starter Dustin Hermanson

as part of the Fernando Tatis trade. He was expected to be their second or third starter. See more on Hermanson in the Expos starting pitchers section.

Garrett Stephenson was a pleasant surprise in 1999 and he followed that up with another strong showing in 2000. He went 16-9 with a 4.49 ERA before going down with an injury right near the end of the season. He's established himself as a workhorse, much like Kile, that will keep the Cards in games and pick up lots of wins because the team will score a lot of runs.

Rick Ankiel burst onto the scene as a rookie this past season and really turned some heads. Sure he had his problems in the post season, but he's a tough minded pitcher with amazing stuff that won't suffer any long-term effect from his bouts with wildness in the playoffs. Ankiel went 11-7 with a 3.50 ERA and 194 strikeouts in just 175 innings last year and those numbers will only get better. Tony LaRussa and Dave Duncan did a nice job of limiting his innings to make sure they don't wear him down and he paid them back with success. Ankiel has a mid 90's fastball that really moves, a dominant curveball and an improving changeup. He could blossom into a number one or two starter this year.

Andy Benes is a veteran starter more known for durability than performance these days. He was 12-9 with a 4.88 ERA last year, which is nothing special, but he's a veteran that gives the team a chance to win. He's no longer considered a frontline starter, but most teams would love to have a fourth starter like him.

The fifth spot in the Cardinals' rotation appeared to be up in the air at the end of the 2000 season because of the uncertainty surrounding the future roles of Matt Morris and Alan Benes. Both Morris and Benes have displayed top-of-the-rotation stuff in the past, but both spent the 2000 season working out of the bullpen trying to rehab injuries. If one or both of them wind up returning to their previous form, the team may have to deal a starter to make room. Both guys throw in the low to mid 90s with good secondary pitches; Morris has a hard curve and Benes a nasty slider.

Bud Smith and Chad Hutchinson are the Cardinals' top pitching prospects now that Ankiel is a major league and both appear to have bright futures. Smith is the polished pitcher, a lefthander with a slightly above average fastball who gets by with guts and the ability to change speed and locations well. He went 5-1 with a 2.15 ERA at triple-A at the end of last season and could push one of the

righthanders out of the rotation in the near future. Hutchinson has one of the strongest arms in baseball, occasionally topping out near 100 MPH. The problem is that he's a one dimensional pitcher that has some control problems. Even though he's been working as a starter recently, Hutchinson seems better suited to a future as a short reliever.

RECOMMENDATION REVIEW: The best of this group for 2001 with be Ankiel. He could be a 15-20 game winner that contends for the ERA and strikeout title, so get him on your team. Kile is a safe bet to have similar numbers to the ones he posted last year and Stephenson seems to be on course for the same kind of success, though you might want to exercise caution with him. Benese is nothing special in rotisserie terms and don't be surprised if the Cards deal him. Morris and Benes are wild cards that had no defined 2001 role heading into the offseason, but if they look strong in Spring Training they could be terrific pick-ups. Both Hutchinson and Smith are worth having if you have a minor league roster, though Smith might be worth a look even if you have to hide him on your major league bench.

SAN DIEGO PADRES

The 2000 Padres starting staff was in disarray for most of the season but produced very good results nonetheless. Without the emergence of rookies Brian Tollberg and Adam Eaton its hard to say what the starters may have done. Matt Clement was the only starter to go wire-to-wire. Sterling Hitchcock, Brian Meadows, Woody Williams and Brian Boehringer began the year as part of the rotation, but none made it through the whole year in the San Diego starting five. Hitchcock and Boehringer were lost for the season early on, Williams missed two months in the first half of the year, and Meadows was traded to Kansas City at the deadline. Stan Spencer, Rodrigo Lopez and Jay Witasick each made a number of starts for San Diego, with varying results.

Clement and Williams will be the backbone of the 2001 staff with Eaton and Tollberg filling the three and four spots. The fifth spot is wide open. If Hitchcock is fully healthy as early reports say he is, he would be the odds on favorite for the job. If not, Witasick, Scott Karl or Spencer could get the job. Rumors have it that the Padres are looking to deal pitching. If so, look for Clement or Hitchcock to move for offensive help.

Clement is a better pitcher than he showed in 2000. He

was overused and pushed too far, too often as the beleaguered Padres staff needed innings. He has excellent movement on his stuff and enough stamina to be a staff ace; Clement may take that next step forward in 2001 or 2002. As he is coming off a down year this is the opportune time to grab him. Take care not to get into a bidding war for Clement as he can only produce a profit if purchased cheaply.

One of the better underrated starters in baseball, Williams gave the Padres a consistent start every time out after returning to the rotation at midseason. He made 17 straight starts of at least six innings while posting a 3.30 ERA over the last half of the season. Williams has always been a pitcher that escapes the notice of many Rotisserie owners. Pitching for second-division clubs most of his career and not being a big winner or strikeout pitcher have kept him out of the spotlight. But he's always produced good numbers and last year was the first time he'd missed any significant number of starts since 1996. Look for Williams to be available near the end of the draft for a few bucks; buy him and get a small bargain.

Its unlikely either Eaton or Tollberg is available in any "keeper" leagues after they came to the forefront last year. Eaton blew through Double-A Mobile just like Tollberg did at Triple-A Las Vegas, then each pitched very well in the bigs, too. For 2001, neither is a recommended "buy", though. Both will be subject to some hard times in their sophomore seasons as they make their second and third trips around the National League. An occasional bad outing can be expected until they make the necessary adjustments. Even if they are available, they will be priced beyond their ability to perform. Unless you can get them cheaply, which is highly unlikely, spend your starter dollars elsewhere.

Hitchcock is reportedly ahead of pace in his recovery from an elbow problem that limited him to just eleven starts in 2000. If so he could open the season in the Padres rotation. A more likely scenario is that he starts the year on injury rehab, providing astute Rotisserie owners an opportunity to get something for nothing. Buy Hitchcock on Draft Day for a buck at the end of the draft, then replace him immediately after the draft with whomever had a good outing or two the week before, placing Hitchcock on reserve. When Hitchcock returns he'll be ready to replace your temporary fill-in at about the time that pitcher comes back to earth. You'll get the best of both pitchers, for a minimal price.

Witasick had a few good outings with the Padres after his

July 31st trade from Kansas City but mostly was a repeat of his former self, too often wild within the strike zone and eminently hittable. Witasick is a poor choice for Rotisserie ball even if he wins a regular starting spot, which he would not likely hold in any case. He walks far too many batters for a pitcher who also permits a .300 opposition batting average. He has allowed 47 homers in his last 300 innings, too many for a pitcher who doesn't blow hitters away. Witasick is not going to get much better and will not help a Rotisserie team.

Scott Karl was signed during the offseason after a horrible 2000 season. He needs to prove, that his confidence and stuff is back before he has any Rotisserie value.

Spencer has spent a number of years on the major league fringe and appeared to be on his way to capturing a big-league job for good in 2000 when he was felled with a sprained shoulder. He did a phenomenal job of keeping opponents off base, which is a good thing because once there they tend to run wild against Spencer's slow delivery. Former Padres catcher Carlos Hernandez had worked with Spencer to reduce baserunner leads, but now he is gone to the Cardinals and it remains to be seen if the lesson in holding baserunners will stick with Spencer. Although he's not high on the Padres pitching depth chart Spencer will get more time in the bigs in 2001. Don't draft him, but put him on your midseason replacement list.

In the midst of a fairly good season for Las Vegas, Lopez was called up to make a spot start against National League champion Atlanta. He looked fantastic, allowing just one run over seven innings. That represented his peak, however, as Lopez was hammered in his other five big-league appearances and returned to Las Vegas for the rest of the season. He's not an especially good prospect although he may eventually earn a lower rotation or long-relief job in the bigs. For Rotisserie purposes, Lopez has no value.

Lopez, Tollberg, Buddy Carlyle, Will Cunnane and Junior Herndon made up the bulk of the Vegas starting staff, Carlyle has since been sold to Japan and Cunnane is viewed as primarily a long reliever. Herndon is a better prospect, although he had a mediocre year at Las Vegas in 2000. His stuff is not especially outstanding but he can pinpoint his pitches where he needs them to be. Herndon does not appear to have the make up to be a big winner in the majors although he could succeed in a lower rotation or long relief role. He has no immediate Rotisserie value.

A better prospect, Wascar Serrano, got as far as Las Vegas in 2000, also, with disappointing results in four starts after an outstanding 20-start season for Double-A Mobile. Serrano can throw in the mid-90s with developing offspeed pitches and two different fastballs. Last year was his first stumble since turning pro, so he remains a good prospect. Sharper command of his offspeed stuff could get Serrano to the majors in a hurry; look for Serrano as a potential Ultra selection.

The top lefty prospect in the Padres system is Mike Bynum, who owns a good, low-90s fastball and a nasty slider that puts righthanders away. At High-A Rancho Cucamonga, Bynum fanned a batter per inning over 21 starts to earn a late-season advance to Mobile where his success continued. Bynum will be on the fast track to the big leagues and should reach San Diego by 2002; he's a fine Ultra pick.

Jason Middlebrook was considered a good prospect but had an awful year at Mobile in 2000, going 5-13 with a 6.13 ERA. He'll have to reverse that trend to stay on the prospect list. Gerik Baxter and Jacob Peavy are also good prospects with a long ways to go before pitching in the majors.

RECOMMENDATION REVIEW: Clement and Williams are good choices for low-dollar prices with probable moderate production. Eaton and Tollberg will be unavailable or overpriced in most leagues following their rookie successes; get them for a few bucks or not at all. Hitchcock can be a good one-dollar choice for risk takers or as a late-draft selection. Avoid Witasick, Karl and Lopez; look for Spencer as a midseason replacement only. Among the prospects, Serrano and especially Bynum are good Ultra candidates.

SAN FRANCISCO GIANTS

Underrated for a number of years, the Giants starting staff came though with flying colors last year, and promise some solid value this year as well. Leading the pack is the resurrected Livan Hernandez, who went 240 innings (five complete games) en route to culling 17 wins last year. Hernandez is still just 26 years old, and with the backing of Dusty Baker and Dave Righetti, has regained his command and his confidence. Hernandez is a solid, dependable pitcher who should generate a solid value in the $15-20 range, and one who likely could improve his numbers over last season.

Speaking of resurrections, Shawn Estes gathered himself and put together his best season since 1997. Be a little wary of Estes, for though he has great stuff, and a world of talent, he is injury prone. More important, he can be frustratingly erratic (note the 108 walks he allowed last season). At a price around $10, Estes could be a bargain, but should a bidding war arise, let another owner assume the risk.

On the other hand, Russ Ortiz, who slumped over the ladder portion of his big 1999, predictably started slow last year, but his second half numbers (10-4, 3.22, as opposed to the 4-8, 6.22 first half) show a pitcher who has probably adjusted and is ready to resume his dominance. If you compare the numbers of Ortiz and Estes, Estes looks better, but Ortiz is probably a better way to go, and one that will cost less.

Sneaky lefty Kirk Rueter continues to sniff out wins, and post solid numbers as a starter. He has averaged 32 starts and 187 innings, not to mention 14 wins a year since joining the Giants in 1997, but doesn't get as much press-in fact the Giants starters in general are not household names-so again he could be a bargain. If you own Rueter, who inked a contract extension through 2003 last season, try and avoid watching him pitch. He is a nibbler, and though the final numbers are usually acceptable, the stress in watching is far too great.

The fifth starter spot belongs to talented Joe Nathan who had his moments, pitching well at times, getting hammered at times, and spending time on the injury list. Nathan, a former shortstop, has terrific stuff and knows how to pitch, but he is still a stretch as a #5 starter. Be careful not to spend more than a $1 on Nathan, if that. He is a great reserve list selection, however.

Free agent Mark Gardner is never worth drafting and always worth watching in the event of an injury. It was uncertain, at press time, if he would re-sign with the Giants, but wherever Gardner goes, he will pitch 100 or so innings, kill your ratio, and maybe get a couple of wins. Gardner does generally go through a hot streak of three to four starts, and he can turn them in at any time. Watch his numbers if you need a replacement, grab him when he is hot, and be ready to dump him without hesitation.

The Giants have three excellent pitching prospects to track who could move it up and take the place of either Gardner, or Nathan. First is Ryan Vogelsong, San Francisco's #10 pick of the 1998 draft. Vogelsong, 23, completed a first full season at Fresno, going 6-10, 4.23

over 155 innings (153 hits, and 147 strikeouts). Next is 1999 #1 selection, Kurt Ainsworth, who went 10-9, 3.30 over 28 starts at Shreveport (158 innings, 138 hits, 130 strikeouts), and finally, Jerome Williams, a 19-year old starter who went 7-6, 2.94 at San Jose last year, striking out 115 over 126 innings (89 hits).

RECOMMENDATION REVIEW: The Giants are an interesting place to find pitchers. Livan Hernandez seems to be on the verge of becoming a true ace. He eats up innings and picks up wins. Russ Ortiz has the stuff to be a dominate pitcher, but still lacks the control. Kirk Reuter, Shawn Estes, and Joe Nathan are all up and down pitchers who can be very good or be inconsistent and have poor seasons.

TOP 2001 WINNERS

NAME	W
Tom Glavine	21
Greg Maddux	20
Scott Elarton	18
Livan Hernandez	18
Daryl Kile	18
Russ Ortiz	18
Kevin Brown	17
Ryan Dempster	16
Elmer Dessens	16
Mike Hampton	16
Randy Johnson	16
Chan Ho Park	16
Andy Ashby	15
Darren Dreifort	15
Shawn Estes	15
Al Leiter	15
Denny Neagle	15
Javier Vazquez	15
Kevin Appier	14
Pedro Astacio	14
Brian Bohanon	14
Jeff C. D'Amico	14
Curt Schilling	14
Rick Ankiel	13
Matt Clement	13
Pete Harnisch	13
Kevin Millwood	13
Kirk Rueter	13
Garrett Stephenson	13
Bruce Chen	12
Mark Gardner	12
Bobby J. Jones	12

Brian Meadows	12
Rick Reed	12
Jose Silva	12
Woody Williams	12
Andy Benes	11
Dustin Hermanson	11
Jon Lieber	11
Glendon Rusch	11
Julian Tavarez	11
Steve Trachsel	11
Kerry Wood	11

TOP 2001 STRIKEOUTS

NAME	K
Randy Johnson	350
Kevin Brown	222
Rick Ankiel	202
Chan Ho Park	202
Pedro Astacio	190
Jon Lieber	185
Al Leiter	182
Kevin Millwood	179
Curt Schilling	176
Greg Maddux	175
Bruce Chen	169
Ryan Dempster	167
Livan Hernandez	167
Daryl Kile	166
Javier Vazquez	165
Kerry Wood	165
Matt Clement	164
Darren Dreifort	163
Russ Ortiz	157
Kris Benson	152
Tom Glavine	148
Jose Lima	147
David Cone	146
Glendon Rusch	144
Shawn Estes	143
Robert Person	143
Mike Hampton	142
Andy Benes	141
Todd Stottlemyre	132
Rob Bell	131
Jeff.c Damico	131
Denny Neagle	131
Randy Wolf	131
Jesus Sanchez	129
Sterling Hitchcock	128
Kevin Tapani	125

STRATEGIES FOR RELIEF PITCHERS
MIND-READING, TREND-SPOTTING AND CAUTION

by John Benson

There is no job in baseball where a player's value can change so dramatically, so quickly, and so easily, as the relief pitcher. All it takes is a tiny, subtle shift in the manager's mind. One minute the manager is thinking of a player as his ace reliever, and the next minute, he isn't.

A case in point will illustrate. On March 29, 2000, Jose Mesa was the Mariners' ace reliever. He had been announced and reannounced. Twice after a bad outing by Mesa in mid and late March, Lou Piniella had said the usual things: this is just spring training. We begin the season with veterans who have proven themselves year after year. We always begin the season with veterans. During the season we are always open to reconsidering, but spring training is just for getting tuned up, not for changing roles that have been established long before. Mesa is the man, and that's that. No more questions. On March 29 Mesa pitched the ninth inning, and only the ninth inning, of a spring training game, and he produced a line of zeros across.

On March 30 Mesa came in again to pitch the ninth and only the ninth again, the classic spring training workout of the ace in back-to-back games, just to get tuned up. He pitched the inning, and when he got done, he wasn't the ace reliever any more. He didn't walk anyone but gave up some hits and blew a lead. It wasn't the hits or the blown lead that cost him his job; it was the look on his face while he was pitching. He didn't look confident enough. After the game, in front of the dugout, while Mesa walked toward the clubhouse, Piniella explained that a closer has got to look fearless, and Mesa didn't look fearless. Piniella and the pitching coach had discussed the look on Mesa's face. His face didn't look tuned-up, and that was that. Kazuhiro Suzuki became the closer.

The same thing can happen in midseason. Usually a change in the ace role follows a series of failures, but it can also be subtle things like the look on the face. Mike Stanton 7/16/93 pitched a perfect ninth inning with two K's for his 24th save. On the 17th the Braves lost while Stanton sat and watched. On the 18th Stanton got his 25th save with one hit, no walks and no runs, lowering his ERA to 3.15. On the 19th the Braves lost again while Stanton

sat. On the 20th Stanton got his 26th save with a perfect ninth, his ERA dropping to 3.06. On the 21st the Braves won 14-1 as Stanton spectated. On the 22nd Stanton came into a save situation in the ninth, gave up a walk and a hit and was promptly pulled in favor of Jay Howell who gave up two more hits, a walk and two runs. Howell was charged with the blown save, Stanton got credit for a hold, and it was the end of Stanton's career as a closer. His face didn't look right, either, and Greg McMichael's did. McMichael was the closer the rest of the year.

Not every manager is as quick to change his mind as Bobby Cox is. Piniella is in fact a loyal manager when it comes to staying with his closer, as evidenced by the years of patience with Bobby Ayala and Mesa. The point is that saves are not like home runs or RBI. The manager can simply decide to take them away, and they disappear immediately and permanently. If a team loads up on power hitters, there will be many more home runs, with no ceiling or limit; when a team loads up on ace relievers, the number of saves will remain capped by the number of save opportunities.

The job of "ace" reliever doesn't even exist on paper. When the manager turns in his lineup card, there is no line to write in the closer's name. Asking "Who gets the saves?" is like asking, "Who's the pinch hitter?" It is whoever the manager says it is at the moment of making the decision. And what the manager says can change whenever the manager wants it to change. Meanwhile, the Rotisserie world is maniacally eager to know, for all 30 teams, who will get the ball in a save situation on August 1, 2001. The real answer is, nobody knows, not even the manager. Every team has at least six relievers, half a dozen "pinch pitchers" who might be called upon.

If you go to your draft planning to get Trevor Hoffman or Robb Nen or any other established ace for a bargain price this year, you will be disappointed. Not since the dark ages of Rotissehistory have saves been underrated. Long, long ago, there were some leagues where everyone used last year's numbers and most owners didn't notice when the departure of one ace reliever meant the promotion of another.

Times have changed. If there is a common trend in the drafting of relief pitchers in the third millennium, it is to pay full price for the established known aces, to pay almost full price for the newer closers, and to pay too much for the promising "probable" closers. Top setup men used to sell for $1 to $3. Now they cost $5 and higher in most leagues.

Paying full price for Trevor Hoffman, Robb Nen, Derek Lowe, Suzuki, Mariano Rivera or any of their peers remains a popular method, because it's simple and effective. Shelling out $35 for 35 saves may be a sure way to miss getting a bargain, but it accomplishes a number of other purposes:

1. You won't have to worry about saves during the remainder of the draft, and you won't have to worry much during the season. Getting one committee reliever in addition to your ace will generally assure that you score well in the saves category.

2. Your draft will be simpler. You won't have to assemble a "care package" of saves from the many relievers who are new, unproven, fading, broken down, or merely stuck behind a Top Gun who gets all the save opportunities. Searching for bargains in the $2 to $9 range is sometimes rewarding, but it is also complicated and time-consuming, on a day when you might have a better draft by putting all your mental energy into sifting through starting pitchers and assembling an offense.

3. If you do get lucky while filling out your bullpen with $1 leftovers in addition to the ace, and draft a longshot who ends up getting saves, you will have some nice trade bait.

There are plenty of alternatives to the "pay what it takes" strategy to get saves. Most of these alternatives involve risks with the whole saves category. There is no such thing as a strategy to "pay $9 each for four relievers who will get nine saves apiece," because the population of relievers who get nine saves apiece is even scarcer and more volatile than the population of true ace relievers.

Whatever alternative you pursue, if you decide to spend little on relief pitching, don't call your strategy "dump saves." Planning to avoid spending on relievers does not mean you are planning to finish last in saves. Keep thinking that it would be good to score some points in the saves category, and you will do better than you would by adopting a "give up" mentality. You can plan to spend just $1 each on five relievers and still score something in saves by making good $1 choices.

One popular alternative is to skip getting an ace, and spend $1 to $6 each on four or five relievers who just might figure prominently in their team's saves picture. There is a large number of such pitchers, so the chance of getting some at a reasonable price is a fair chance indeed. Byung Kin, Scott Williamson, Doug Creek, Paul Shuey, Arthur Rhodes, Felix Rodriguez, Jason Christiansen, Mike Stanton, Jeff Nelson, Shawn Sonnier, Mike Trombley, Bob Howry, Jeff Zimmerman, Kyle Farnsworth, Matt Anderson, Felix Heredia, Travis Miller and Rich Garces are some examples. All fit the description.

The most extreme strategy to avoid spending on relief is to get all starting pitchers. This method is not inexpensive in total, and it is more popular than it deserves to be, appearing with increasing frequency in leagues that count strikeouts or innings as a fifth category for pitching stats. The whole strategy includes getting Greg Maddux or Pedro Martinez (for example), four more high-quality starters for $15 to $20 apiece, and filling out with less expensive starters while hoping that the stars will control the ERA and ratio. The method doesn't always work; just one thing is certain: you will score a zero in saves. Getting some $1 relievers would give you at least some hope for saves, and do a lot less harm than filling out with cheap starters, so my recommendation is to get a minimum of two or three relievers.

AMERICAN LEAGUE RELIEF PITCHERS

ANAHEIM ANGELS

Here are Troy Percival's blown save percentages for the last five years, ending with 2000: 8%, 13%, 13%, 21% and 24%. Also, Percival's ERA has increased every year since he entered the majors. Having said that, Percival has saved a lot of games during that five-year period and should continue to do so as long as he gets the ball in the ninth inning. He did finish strong last season, with seven saves in eight September opportunities. Expect Percival to save 20-25 games this season with an ERA in the mid-4.00s.

Shigetoshi Hasegawa is the primary setup man and backup closer for Anaheim. In two of the last three years, including last season, he has pitched very well, earning 16 saves over the three seasons. Most of these saves were earned during periods in which Percival was unavailable, however, and Hasegawa is not a threat to muscle his way into the closer's role, unless Percival totally falls apart. The way Hasegawa is used gives him ample opportunity to snag seven to ten wins and saves, so he can be a valuable part of a Rotisserie bullpen.

There are players whose value to their ballclub does not translate to the Rotisserie scoring system. Exhibit "A" is Al Levine. Staff saver, spot starter, setup guy, deputy clubhouse attendant (OK, maybe not that), Levine is a good guy to have in a big league bullpen. Unfortunately, most of that doesn't get you any standings points. Levine won't win a lot of games and rarely gets a save chance. His control really isn't good enough to make him a ratio guy. So get his baseball card if you want, but leave him off your Rotisserie draft list.

Mark Petkovsek isn't too different from Levine as a pitcher. He has a little better control and is generally used in shorter outings. Petkovsek became a free agent at the end of last season, and it was uncertain as to whether he would return to the Angels. Wherever he winds up, Petkovsek will be a versatile bullpen performer with minimal Rotisserie value.

Mike Holtz is a little lefty who fits the situational role well. Tough on lefthanded hitters but vulnerable to righties, Holtz will be used in very short outings that will deny him the opportunity to get many wins or saves.

Kent Mercker also became a free agent after last season. Talented but maddeningly inconsistent throughout his entire career, the lefty will find a spot in someone's bullpen or as a spot starter. Stay away.

Mike Fyhrie, Ben Weber and Lou Pote are journeymen righthanders who enjoyed good partial seasons out of the Angels' pen last year. Of the three, Pote is more likely to have positive value this year, although neither pitcher was used in many win or save situations. Pote has minor league closer credentials, but as we all know those guys seldom get to close games in the big leagues.

RECOMMENDATION REVIEW: Percival should be a source of saves again, but no longer provides much help for ERA and ratio. If you draft Percival, get Hasegawa, and even if you don't have Percival, Hasegawa at a low salary is an excellent buy. The rest may be safely ignored, although if you need a hopefully innocuous $1 pitcher to round out the staff, Petkovsek, Levine, Holtz and Pote are worth a look.

BALTIMORE ORIOLES

The 2001 season will be the third year in a row for major changes in the Orioles bullpen. Last year, the Orioles pen posted a 5.58 ERA, the worst in the league. They also blew 24 saves. The 2001 season should be even a greater challenge as two key 200-plus-innings starters from last year, Mike Mussina and Scott Erickson won't be in the rotation. Other less effective starters are much less likely to pitch deep into games, thus putting greater pressures on the middle relievers who may be burned out by the All-Star break.

Erratic closer Mike Timlin and his proclivity for blowing saves was shipped to the Cardinals in a late-season house cleaning. Mike Trombley, once an effective closer for the Twins, could not step up into the closer role, so the Orioles turned to rookie Ryan Kohlmeier, a virtual unknown at the time. He was the bright spot of a dismal season, surprising everyone with some great pitching, posting 14 saves, including pressure situations against tough contending teams like the Indians and Red Sox. He has a good fastball and a sharp late-breaking slider, but it took him three years to develop it, finally getting it working last summer in Triple-A and accelerating his promotion to the Orioles. He also has a deceptive arm motion, making his pitches even more effective. He's an aggressive pitcher who throws strikes, quickly getting ahead of hitters. He has always been a reliever in his pro career, and has shown that he has the mental makeup to handle the pressures of being a major league closer. The only uncertainty about Kohlmeier is that his deceptive motion may not be so deceiving the second and third time hitters face him, making him more hittable.

One negative indicator about Kohlmeier's performance last year was that hitters reached base at a .291 clip, whereas good closers have on-base numbers below .260, sometimes as low as .220. As a comparison, even setup man Mike Trombley held hitters to a .247 on-base average. The Orioles have some second thoughts about Kohlmeier as a closer because they shopped for a closer over the winter.

Mike Trombley isn't the closer, but he can be an effective setup man. He works fast, throws strikes, and gets a lot of ground balls, making him the ideal type of pitcher for Camden Yards where many fly balls turn into home runs. Southpaw Buddy Groom is a situational reliever and lefty setup man. Alan Mills is back with the Orioles again, and he can be a good middle reliever. Chuck McElroy had another bad season last year, and only pitching surpris-

ingly well in two late-season starts provided some optimism. Jason Johnson had mechanical and confidence problems and was very erratic. Calvin Maduro was hit hard and has a limited future.

Last year, the Orioles believed hard-throwing lefty B.J. Ryan was their future closer, but his mechanics got out of kilter and he needed more Triple-A time. Ryan is prone to wildness, and needs to become consistent. It's not clear if he can handle pressure-packed closing situations.

Late season trades brought the Orioles prospects Luis Rivera and Lesli Brea. Both throw very hard, but Rivera has had health problems in the past. He can be a closer candidate in a few years. Farm-hand Sean Maloney had a good year in Triple-A last year and is another bullpen candidate. All three are long shots for any significant roles in the bullpen.

RECOMMENDATION REVIEW: The Orioles bullpen is not the place to be shopping for relievers. Ryan Kohlmeier was the closer at season's end, pitching well over the last month. But the Orioles shopped for another closer over the winter, indicating that they don't have confidence in him. He could revert to a setup role. It's recommended that if you need a closer, look elsewhere. If necessary, bid very cautiously on Kohlmeier.

BOSTON RED SOX

Derek Lowe, 27, beat out Tim Wakefield for the role of Boston's closer after Tom Gordon went down in 1999. Last season, Lowe took the ball 74 times and ran with it. He finished 64 of those appearances, and saved 42 of 47 opportunities. Lowe was not overpowering, but finished 4-4 with a 2.56 ERA and 1.23 ratio. Jimy Williams showed few qualms about bringing Lowe in before the ninth, so he pitched plenty of innings.

Hector Carrasco joined the Sox from Minnesota late in the season, but didn't add a lot to Boston's bullpen. His season totals were 5-4, 4.69 and 1.63. He saved just one game in six chances.

Hipolito Pichardo had a good season in a number of roles last season. He was 6-3, 3.46 with one save and a 1.37 ratio in 65 innings.

One of the most popular Red Sox in 2000 was Rich "El Guapo" Garces. The rotund righty setup man, 29, was 8-1 with a 3.25 ERA, 1.17 ratio and a save. He's 13-2 the last two seasons, so he should be able to continue adding relief wins to a Rotisserie roster.

Though two-thirds of Tim Wakefield's appearances were in relief, Pedro Martinez was the Red Sox only pitcher who threw more innings. Wakefield is discussed under starting pitchers.

Bryce Florie's season and perhaps his career ended when a line drive struck him in the face. At the time, the 30-year-old righthander was 0-4, 4.56 with a save and a 1.54 ratio.

Former National League closer Rod Beck blew all three opportunities with the Red Sox. The righthander, 32, was 3-0, 3.10, with a 1.13 ERA in 34 appearances.

Tom Gordon has missed most of the last two seasons, including all of 2000, because of arm trouble. The 33-year-old righty was an offseason free agent. See more on Gordon in the Cubs relievers section.

Boston's most active lefthander was Rheal Cormier, 33. He was 3-3, 4.61 with a 1.33 ratio in 64 appearances. He signed with the Phillies during the offseason and will be used as a lefty specialist out of the pen.

The Sox obtained Jesus Pena, 26, from the White Sox. He was the only Red Sox lefty to earn a save. Between the two legwear teams, he was 2-1, 5.13, with one save and a 1.78 ratio. Control is a problem for him.

Rich Croushore, who began the season with the Rockies, was a combined 2-1, 7.88 with a 1.88 ratio in 11 major league appearances. The 30-year-old righthander also was 0-1, 3.43 at Triple-A Pawtucket.

Sang-Hoon Lee may have the most potential of any lefthanded reliever in the Boston organization. He pitches with an attitude, as well as a Rod Beck haircut. In nine games with the Red Sox, Lee was 0-0, 3.09, with a 1.11 ratio. He began the year 5-2, 2.03 with two saves at Pawtucket.

Tim Young was another lefty reliever who split time between Boston (0-0, 6.43, 1.29 in eight games) and Pawtucket (1-1, 2.40, 6 saves). He's 27.

Hard-throwing Rob Stanifer, 29, was the primary closer at Pawtucket (3-4, 1.89, 16 saves), but he was hit hard in eight appearances for Boston (0-0, 7.62, 2.00).

RECOMMENDATION REVIEW: Lowe is about as reliable as any American League closer. Beck pitched well in spots, and could return to saving some games in the right situation. Of the younger pitchers, Lee might be the best bet for a few saves.

CHICAGO WHITE SOX

One of the strengths of the White Sox' team in 2000 was their bullpen, led by closer Keith Foulke. He doesn't have classic "closer stuff" but he throws strikes and has what may be the very best changeup in all of baseball. Foulke also has a low 90s fastball, but it's the change that allows him to be successful. He had 34 saves and a 2.97 ERA last year.

Bobby Howry is a very hard-thrower that could also close some games for the Sox. He had 7 saves and a 3.17 ERA last year and could save more games in 2001 if Foulke struggles a bit. He throws in the mid 90's with a hard slider, though he sometimes runs into trouble when he falls behind in the count.

Both Bill Simas and Sean Lowe are capable middle relievers that are durable and dependable. Neither will put up particularly exciting rotisserie numbers, but they'll pitch a lot. Lowe also started some games for the Sox during the 2000 season and that could happen again in a pinch.

The guy people really need to keep an eye on in the White Sox bullpen, however, is Lorenzo Barcelo. He's a huge righthander with a mid to upper 90s fastball and a good splitter. He had a 3.69 ERA in 39 innings as a rookie last year and he could have a much more significant role in 2001. There are some who feel Barcelo is the team's closer of the future, though there is also a chance he could pitch as a starter some as well.

Kelly Wunsch is the only lefthander the Sox will be able to count on for the 2001 season, but he's a good one. He was 6-3 with a 2.93 ERA last year as their lefthanded late-inning specialist. He should perform well again this year.

Other candidates for bullpen work include lefthander Mark Buerhle and righthanders Chad Bradford and Kevin Beirne. Buerhle can also start, Bradford is a sidearm specialist that can be tough on righthanders and Beirne is a sinker-baller that could also start.

RECOMMENDATION REVIEW: Foulke and Howry are both worthy pickups and they should both pitch in important late-inning situations. Foulke is more of a sure thing than Howry. Of the others, Barcelo is the one that has a chance to put up big rotisserie numbers, though it could be another year or so before that happens.

CLEVELAND INDIANS

The Indians bullpen had a revolving door last year, with 19 relievers making an appearance wearing Chief Wahoo on their hat. Injuries and ineffectiveness were the main problems, and if things had gotten any worse, Ernie Camacho would have been brought out of retirement. The pen went 25-22 with a 4.33 ERA, the fifth best in the league, but they saved only 34 games in 58 save opportunities, blowing 24. Looking back, more than anything else, the blown saves can be blamed for the Indians missing the playoffs.

Without a clear and dominant closer early in the season, Manager Charlie Manuel said that both Paul Shuey and Steve Karsay would get plenty of late-inning opportunities. At that point, Shuey was expected to get 15-20 saves. But that situation evolved into one where Shuey became the setup man for Karsay, and he led the league with 28 "holds" despite spending a lot of time on the DL. Karsay picked up 20 saves, but the blown saves caused the Tribe to look for another closer. In May, Shuey incurred a serious hip injury requiring surgery and a long rehab time. Overall, Karsay led the league with nine losses in relief, and he was fourth in the league with nine blown saves. To shore up the pen, the Indians traded for Brewers closer Bob Wickman in late July.

Both Shuey and Karsay have blown their opportunities to be the Tribe's closer, so Bob Wickman has the job for 2001. But he's regarded as a second-rate closer, an undeserved label attributed to his lack of flashiness and glamour. To his credit, he picked up 37 saves for a poor Brewers team in 1999. He doesn't throw heat, relying on a sinker and a slider. He just gets the job done. For the 2001, Wickman can be expected to see more save opportunities than he did with the Brewers, and 40 saves is possible.

Steve Reed was a setup man and middle inning reliever, getting into 57 games last year. His Rotisserie value is low because he doesn't get many saves, and wins 2-4 games each year. His ERA is usually over 4.00, lowering his Rotisserie value even more.

Justin Speier was a pleasant surprise last year, getting into 47 games, pitching 68.1 innings with a 3.29 ERA. He throws hard, and he strikes out an average of almost one batter per inning. Wildness has been his problem in the past. He's only 27, and has already been in the Cubs, Marlins, and Braves organizations. He pitched briefly in the National League in 1998 and 1999, but last year with the Indians was his breakthrough season where he showed that he belongs in the majors. He's primarily a middle reliever, and usually pitches an average of more than one inning per appearance. Last year, he was 5-2 with six holds and no saves. Speier could be a valuable reliever, and could become a reliever who gets a few breaks and wins 8-10 games with a few saves and a low ERA, making him more valuable to a Rotisserie team than many starters.

Jamie Brewington was another well-traveled reliever who got a good opportunity to pitch as a result of the Tribe's revolving door. He was formerly in the Giants and Royals organizations where he was a wild and easily hittable starter. Prior to last year, his only major league experience was with the Giants in 1995 when he made 13 starts going 6-4 with a 4.54 ERA, providing some optimism but it was short lived. He throws hard, and has a good strikeout rate, the only good statistic on his record as a starter. Signed to a minor league contract by the Indians in 1999, he blossomed nicely, and earned a promotion to the Indians last year. But he hit some rough spots with the Tribe, giving up 56 hits in 45.1 innings. Brewington is 29, and could hang on as a middle reliever and mop-up man, but he doesn't look like he will become a bullpen mainstay unless he harnesses his wildness.

Roberto Rincon's season was limited because of elbow surgery and a lengthy rehab assignment. He's the lefty setup man and situational reliever, usually getting into 60 games every year. He would be more valuable if he pitched more innings than his usual 60-65. Despite the fact that Rincon usually has an ERA below 3.00, he has little or no Rotisserie value because he pitches less than 65 innings and he doesn't get many wins or saves.

Tom Martin, Sean DePaula, Cam Cairncross, Andrew Lorraine, Chris Haney, Mike Mohler, Alan Newman, Chris Nichting, Mark Watson, Brian Williams, Steve Woodard, and Bobby Witt also made relief appearances last year. Nichting was the Triple-A closer, and he will be in the Indians organization in 2001, most likely again in Triple-A. He's a long shot for the Indians closer job. Lefty Tom Martin is 30 years old but the Indians regard him highly enough to keep him on their 40-man roster. Situational relief and setup are his best roles. Andrew Lorraine, Bobby Witt, Chris Haney, Alan Newman and Mark Mohler are job hunting. Brian Williams is a nine year veteran, having appeared in 256 major league games with a poor overall 5.36 ERA, and that's saying enough about him. Sean DePaula is a hard throwing 27-year-old with an impressive minor league record with lots of strikeouts. He had some elbow problems last year, limiting him to 26 major and minor league games. He's another long shot for a future closer role. He has some upside Rotisserie potential, but it may not be realized for a year or two. Lefty Cam Cairncross is a 29-year-old veteran of the minors who made his major league debut last year. He gets a lot of strikeouts in the minors, and could latch on as a situational lefty.

The Indians tried all of their top minor leaguers last year in an attempt to find somebody who could get a few guys out once in a while. Prospects remaining in the pipeline are J.D. Brammer, Martin Vargas and David Riske. They may see some major league action in 2001, but in minor roles with no Rotisserie value.

RECOMMENDATION REVIEW: Closer Bob Wickman is the most valuable Cleveland reliever. Steve Karsay can be valuable especially if he gets lucky and picks up some wins in relief as he did in 1999 when he won 10. He can also become the closer again if something happens to Wickman. Shuey's blown his chances to be he closer, and role is setup, not very valuable for Rotisserie unless he gets some saves and has a low ERA. Sean DePaula and Chris Nichting are long shots for the closer's job, and a lot of things need to happen before they close.

DETROIT TIGERS

The Tigers have a strong bullpen led by Todd Jones who was one of the best closers in baseball last season. Jones had 42 saves last year and a respectable 3.52 ERA, so he's a pretty safe pickup for this year. He's got the job all to himself and barring injury should put up excellent numbers once again. He averaged more than a strikeout per inning last year, which is a nice bonus for a reliever.

The Tigers have a very nice group of righthanded setup men for Jones. Danny Patterson has great stuff, but is very inconsistent. He will pickup the Doug Brocail's innings and will win around five games.

The guy to watch in the Tigers' bullpen is Matt Anderson. He's got a 100 MPH fastball and a low 90s slider, but he

struggles with his control. Anderson could be an elite closer, but for now still has Jones in the way.

Neither of the Tigers' lefthanders will have much roto value, but C.J. Nitkowski and Sean Runyan will get the job done. Nitkowski could start a few games here and there, but probably won't amass many significant rotisserie numbers. Runyan is a soft-tossing lefthander that will only face a lefthanded hitter or two at a time.

RECOMMENDATION REVIEW: Jones is a great pickup, but don't pick him up too high in the draft or at a high price in an auction. He has had a history of up-and-down seasons back-to-back and while he was great last year, proceed with just a bit of caution. Anderson is the only one of the rest of the group worth picking up, but even he is a risk. Anderson is a great guy to have in deep leagues with room on the bench and he could eventually supplant Jones as the closer if there is an injury.

KANSAS CITY ROYALS

Roberto Hernandez was acquired during the offseason in a three-way trade from the D'Rays. He will be the Royals closer. See more on Hernandez in the D'Rays relief section.

You need look no farther than the win column to see why the Royals were dissatisfied with Ricky Bottalico's performance in 2000; you never want your closer to be one victory shy of leading the team. He collected several of his nine wins after blowing seven of 23 save chances last year. For Bottalico, the problem was familiar: walks. After walking at least one batter in six straight outings, Bottalico was demoted from his closer job in June. He later recovered the job when Jerry Spradlin and others failed, and was much better over the last three months. Still, Royals management never felt the confidence in Bottalico often shown in a primary closer. Rotisserie owners may have enjoyed Bottalico's wins but they had to be disappointed to spend closer dollars for a guy who only got 16 saves all year to go with an inflated ERA and Ratio. Unless Bottalico has regular access to saves he is going to be a poor choice in Rotisserie Baseball.

Kansas City signed Doug Henry over the winter. He was once the Brewers closer, but more recently has been a reliable setup man for several National League teams. Henry could easily be thrust into the Royals closer role in 2001 as the team continues to search for an answer in the bullpen. Because he can pile up the strikeouts, Henry seems to have the stuff to close. However, he does have a problem with control from time to time, so he may simply be a repeat of Bottalico. For Rotisserie purposes, Henry can be an excellent bargain if he gets a chance to close games. Few Rotisserie owners will recognize him as a potential saves candidate unless he piles them up during the spring schedule. Even then his lack of a recent track record in that role will keep the bidding to a minimum. Henry could be a fine choice for teams that need to take a long shot at saves.

Looking at his overall numbers you'd think Jose Santiago would be a good choice to try as a closer. But, his inability to prevent inherited runners from scoring will keep him in a setup role. Increasingly, he has been used to start the seventh or eighth inning, rather than being brought in to face batters in mid-inning. He'll remain in short, non-save role in 2001 and, although he can get an occasional win or even a multi-inning save, Santiago has only minimal value with no upside potential.

Another short reliever who won't get saves is Kris Wilson. He has decent stuff and a nice bounce-back arm but lacks the strikeout ability often required to succeed as a closer. The Royals seem to like him in a longer role, often using him for two innings at a time as a bridge to the closer. In this role Wilson, like Santiago, can get wins but few saves. He has a little more upside potential but not enough to be worth a Draft Day bid.

Other short-relief candidates are Paul Spoljaric and Scott Mullen. Spoljaric has been a valuable setup man in the past but has fallen on hard times recently. He could rebound to again take on an important setup role, but he won't close games. Mullen could fill the lefty specialist role the Royals have been lacking for years. He had a good year in 2000, starting at Double-A Wichita, then advancing through Triple-A Omaha to pitch eleven games in Kansas City. While he could be an important pitcher for the Royals, he won't save games and, therefore, has no Rotisserie value.

Erstwhile starters Chris Fussell, Dan Murray and Brett Laxton will be seen far more often pitching long relief. These kinds of pitchers are to be avoided for Rotisserie use because when used in a spot start they tend to get lit up and when used in a preferred long relief role they can't get wins or saves, rendering them virtually useless. For winning teams, long relievers may be a source of an occasional win; look to someplace other than Kansas City if you choose to go that route.

In the minors, Spoljaric, Santiago, Archie Corbin, Tim Byrdak and Lance Carter got saves for Omaha. Cordin is no longer with the Royals and Byrdak has failed in previous chances in the majors. Carter has decent stuff, but has a frightening tendency to leave his fastball up over the plate, resulting in an high rate of homers. He could get to the bigs in an unimportant relief role at some point in 2001.

Orber Moreno was once considered the Royals closer of the future. However, serious injuries over the past two years have sidelined Moreno; he didn't pitch at all in 2000 and may never pitch again. At Wichita, Shawn Sonnier made such an impression he will be given a big chance to open the 2001 season in the Royals bullpen. He posted a 2.25 ERA and saved 21 games with an outstanding 90 strikeouts in 64 innings as opponents hit .177 against him. Sonnier would make a good choice for Ultra teams.

RECOMMENDATION REVIEW: Only pitchers with a chance to get saves should be considered here, so that lets out everyone except Henry and Bottalico. Because neither pitcher is an odds-on favorite to reach double-figures in saves neither will command more than a few bucks on Draft Day. An interesting strategy would be to pursue both pitchers, getting them both at nearly the minimum and then keeping the one who actually gets saves. This would be a successful strategy for a team that needs to take chances, not for a contending team that needs a sure thing from its closer. Ultra players may want to look at Sonnier.

MINNESOTA TWINS

The Twins were able to get by without Rick Aguilera in their first full season without a true closer. Part of the reason was that the Twins weren't involved in many games that needed closing. The other reason was that LaTroy Hawkins came through late in the season.

Hawkins, who lost his spot in the rotation at the beginning of the season, converted 14 of 14 save opportunities and heads into the season as the closer. Hawkins has a good fastball, but the key to his success is that he has to perfect his splitter or curve and throw it over the plate. When he doesn't do that, opponents just wait on the fastball and hammer it. That was a big reason why Hawkins lost his starting spot.

The Twins don't want to give up on Hawkins yet, and will find a way to for him to contribute. Hawkins liked the new role and warmed to it immediately. But roto owners should be aware of his save conversion rate - he created jams in many of them before pitching out of trouble.

Hawkins is the Twins best option, and will be allowed to sail or fail with the role. Hawkins has a golden arm, and could enter games in the eighth inning for saves. His fastball has movement when he keeps it low in the strike zone. He worked on improving his split-fingered fastball during the second half of the season, and was somewhat successful. This move is a clear gamble on the Twins' part, but they really have no choice. Closers cost plenty of money these days, and small revenue teams have to develop their own relievers.

If Hawkins fails, the Twins could use two others in the role. Righthander Bob Wells has ranked among the league leaders in appearances over the last two seasons. He throws a decent sinking fastball, but he also gave up 14 homers in 86 innings. Not good. Eddie Guardado is one of the better lefthanded setup men in the league. He will close a game now and then (he saved nine games last season), but he is not the long term answer.

Wells is a reliable setup man who will not give in to hitters. He gets in trouble sometimes when he gets too much of the plate, but he keeps his walks down, which is important for a reliever.

Guardado is tough on lefthanders and was healthy last year after being hampered by a sore elbow in 2000. He would be the one most likely to close games if Hawkins falters, but the coaching staff prefers him in the set up role.

So Hawkins will start the season as the closer. J.C. Romero actually may be the best closing prospect in the organization, but he has been lengthened out to be a starter. Saul Rivera, a 5 foot 7 flamethrower, just reached Double-A in 2000 and may not be ready this season. If Hawkins falters, expect Romero to be return to his short relief role. The Twins also may try to go with a closer-by-committee setup.

Lefthander John Santana was a Rule V pickup last season who was kept on the 40-man roster throughout the entire season. He was in over his head, but has a nice fastball and slider. Although he improved as the season went along, he will likely start the season in the minors as a starter.

Lefthander Travis Miller is the lefthanded specialist out of

the pen. He'll come in to face one lefthanded hitter, and then he's gone. Miller excelled in this role in 1999 and the logical step up this season would be for him to improve his success against righthanded hitters. He's far from being a closer, however, and should not be drafted.

Highly regarded rookie prospect Willie Martinez made his major league debut as a reliever with Cleveland last year. In a surprise move, the Indians waived him after the season and he was claimed by the Twins. He's been a starter in the minors, showing good potential. He spent almost all of last year in Triple-A, going 8-5 with a 4.46 ERA in 135.1 innings. It's significant that he pitched in Triple-A at age 22, a rather young age for a Triple-A starter, where he was one of the youngest starters in the league. He's not quiet a power pitcher at this point, but he can gain a few miles on his fastball as he matures, and if his command comes around, he can be a solid member of the Twins rotation.

RECOMMENDATION REVIEW: Aside from Hawkins and Wells, none of the Twins relievers should be selected on draft day. Hawkins and/or Wells should get 20 or so saves on a team that, again, will rarely need a closer. Are bet is on Hawkins. Guardado is a good pickup during the season if one of your pitchers go down. He will give you some wins, saves and a good ERA and Ratio.

NEW YORK YANKEES

At 31, righthander Mariano Rivera is baseball's best pressure relief pitcher. However, he hasn't been as good as he could be because the Yankees have had so many blowout victories in which they don't need him. He also slipped some in 2000. He was 7-4 with 36 saves and a 1.10 ratio, but his ERA was up more than a run — to 2.85, his highest since 1995.

New York felt Ramiro Mendoza's absence last season after he underwent shoulder surgery. The 28-year-old righthanded swingman was 7-4 with a 4.25 ERA and 1.31 ratio. He has shown he can fill any role but closer.

Jason Grimsley was a middle reliever and the man the Yankees called on when they absolutely, positively had to have an emergency starter. The righthander, 33, was 3-2 with a 5.04 ERA, 1.47 ratio and one save. He has tended to fade after the All-Star break.

Lefty Allen Watson, 30, was up and down between New York and Triple-A Columbus because of a series of injuries. In the majors, he was awful in 22 innings (0-0, 10.23, 2.18).

Watson's unavailability gave 25-year-old Randy Choate a chance as a situational lefty. He was 0-0, 4.76 with a 1.42 ERA for New York and 2-0, 2.04 at Columbus. His extreme sidearming delivery makes him a liability against righthanded batters.

Dwight Gooden has little Rotisserie value anymore and will be used mainly as a swingman.

Jay Tessmer would be the righthanded Choate if Tessmer had any power behind his pitches. In the minors, the 29-year-old is a killer closer (4-8, 3.80, 34 saves at Columbus in 2000), but he has been hammered in the majors (0-0, 6.75, 1.50 for the Yankees).

Twenty-eight-year-old righty Darrell Einertson didn't make it to the majors until last season. Injuries have held him back. In 2000, he was 5-3, 3.24 with a save at Columbus and 0-0, 3.55, 1.58 in New York.

Craig Dingman, 27, is another righthander whose likely career path screams "potential middle reliever." He was 6-1, 3.05 with a save at Columbus, and 0-0, 6.55, 1.91 with the Yankees.

Lefties Randy Keisler and Ted Lilly could end up in New York's bullpen, but you can read more about them under starting pitchers.

Ryan Bradley is a 25-year-old righthander who was rushed to the majors prematurely and hasn't been the same since. In middle relief at Columbus, he was 5-1, 5.82.

Domingo Jean, 32, returned to the Yankees organization after a seven-year absence. At Double-A Norwich, the righthander was the bullpen ace, going 9-4, 3.13 with 28 saves. He could be a late bloomer, but probably not with the Yankees.

Jake Robbins was a minor league free agent after the season.

Jeremy Blevins is a 23-year-old righthander who was the closer for high Class A Tampa. He was 3-7, 4.44 with 20 saves. A positive was that he struck out better than a batter an inning, but the biggest negative was that he was a long way from the majors.

RECOMMENDATION REVIEW: A good strategy would be to bring up the negatives about Rivera and hope you can acquire him late at a reduced cost. He is as close to a sure bet as there is in Rotisserie, barring injury. Mendoza can add wins and possibly saves if he's physically able to pitch.

OAKLAND ATHLETICS

Jason Isringhausen picked up where he left off in 1999, and took the closer role to solid totals last year. Isringhausen did struggle in September, and was temporarily replaced by Jim Mecir and Jeff Tam, depending upon circumstances.

In his second full year as a closer, Isringhausen should improve upon most of his numbers, and thus generate top-flight closer costs (don't forget, he is on a team that should win 90 plus games) and risks. The risk, however is pretty good, as "Izzy" should log 30 plus saves, along with good ratio and ERA totals.

In the event Isringhausen struggles, both Tam and Mecir make decent insurance, although both are better suited to setup (and both are terrific for the few bucks each setup players should fetch). In the wings, Chad Harville, who is short (5'9") but still tossing in the 100 MPH range, and Bert Snow (27 saves at Midland, with 98 whiffs over 68 innings) are the most likely to watch.

T.J. Mathews is no longer a closer in the waiting. He is a career middleman who has little control. He has no Rotisserie value.

RECOMMENDATION REVIEW: Izzy established himself last season as a solid closer, barring injury he should get at least 30 saves in 2001. Mecir and Tam are quality rotation filler picks for a better ERA and Ratio. They both might even pick-up some saves. Mecir could go on draft day. Tam would be a good in-season pick-up in case of an injury to your staff.

SEATTLE MARINERS

The Mariners had struggled mightily in the bullpen throughout the 90s, but the 2000 season brought some relief to Lou Piniella. The arrival of Kazuhiro Sasaki from Japan proved to be a godsend. He picked up 37 saves in 40 opportunities while posting a 3.16 ERA over 63 appearances during his first season in North America and he was named American League Rookie of the Year. Sasaki features a low-to-mid 90s fastball and a filthy forkball that hitters routinely whiffed on. He's a veteran pitcher with outstanding stuff and good control, so there was no reason at the end of 2000 to expect any kind of decline for this season.

The Mariners' best reliever other than Sasaki last year was Jose Paniagua. He's always had electric stuff but never put together a consistent season until 2000. He's got a 95 MPH fastball and a hard slider, both of which can be considered "out" pitches. He managed to pick up 5 saves last year and should be in line for a similar number this year if Sasaki doesn't get hurt. Brett Tomko, Kevin Hodges and Ken Cloude were candidates for the other righthanded spots in the bullpen during the offseason and barring an free agent signing or a trade, they should all figure in somehow.

Jeff Nelson was signed as a free agent from the Yankees during the offseason to help the Mariners bridge the gap to Sasaki. The vet was expected to be the M's righty setup man. Nelson is good for five or more wins and a handful of saves.

Lefthander Arthur Rhodes was fine all season long, but he blew up in the playoffs. He's a power pitcher that either pitches really well or gets hammered in a given outing. Most of the time he's fine, but when he's bad, he's ridiculously bad. Rob Ramsay also performed quite well out of the pen for Lou Piniella last year. Ramsay had bounced around as a Triple-A starter before being moved to the bullpen full time last year. He responded by posting a 3.40 ERA over 50-plus innings despite the fact that he allowed 43 hits and 40 walks in those innings.

Todd Williams picked up 32 saves last year at Triple-A and did a fine job pitching in relief for the gold medal U.S. Olympic Baseball Team in Sydney, but he's never had much success in the majors. He could, however, emerge as a middle man or setup man at some point.

RECOMMENDATION REVIEW: Sasaki was an elite closer last year and he gave no indication that he would experience any problems in the near future, so treat him just like other top flight closers. Tomko and Paniagua could have some value, as could Rhodes, but none of them will be impact pitchers. Tomko would have more value as a starter and Paniagua's value would go through the roof if Sasaki got hurt. None of the others would help a roto team very much.

TAMPA BAY DEVIL RAYS

Roberto Hernandez was traded to the Royals during the offseason. Estaban Yan, Doug Creek and possibly one of the Rays younger arms are replacement candidates.

Say what you will about Roberto Hernandez making it interesting in the ninth inning, he continues to have the dominating stuff that allows him to close games. He has 75 saves in the past two season despite pitching for the lowly Devil Rays. Hernandez was entering the final season of his contract with the Devil Rays, which made him a lot more attractive to contending teams.

A big question for the Devil Rays' bullpen concerns who will set up Hernandez. Jesus Colome might be the answer to this question. The young righthander was the critical piece in a deal that sent Jim Mecir to the Oakland A's prior to the trade deadline and it's easy to see why the A's were reluctant to part with the overpowering Colome, who has been a starter throughout his tenure in the A's system. Colome registers triple digits on the radar gun during most starts, which has led some Devil Rays' organizational people to speculate that his ultimate destination will be the team's future closer. What better way to break him in than setting up Hernandez? Should all look well, Colome could end the season as the Devil Rays' closer.

Doug Creek returns as the Devil Rays' lone lefthander in the bullpen. He can be dominating at times, but gets too excited from time to time and falls out of his rhythm. Impressive are his 73 strikeouts in 60 2/3 innings.

Esteban Yan returns to the bullpen after struggling as a starter in 2000. Yan continues to be overpowering, which is apparent from his 111 strikeouts in 137 2/3 innings. But he continues to let his big fastball sail into the top half of the strike zone, resulting in 26 home runs. In addition, Yan always seems to have healthy questions by the second half of the season.

Cory Lidle was a valuable pitcher on the staff in 2000 pitching in long relief and spot starting. The righthander relies on a mixed bag of junk to record a surprising number of strikeouts. In 2000 he struck out 62 in 96 2/3 innings.

Other candidates for the bullpen include Dan Wheeler as well as the guys who don't win starting jobs. Tanyon Sturtze and Travis Harper are likely starting candidates not to win starting jobs (see Devil Rays starting pitching). Wheeler has good stuff, check out his 17 strikeouts in 23 innings pitched. But he doesn't have a great makeup and loses concentration as witnessed by the 35 home runs he surrendered in 150 1/3 innings at Triple-A Durham before being recalled by the Devil Rays in September. He does seem to pitch better coming out of the bullpen.

Lefthander Ronni Seberino has an outside shot at winning a spot in the Devil Rays bullpen. He has a quality fastball and slider that he uses to overpower hitters, he had 14 strikeouts in 17 innings at Durham in 2000. If the Devil Rays decide they need a lefthanded specialist out of the bullpen other than Creek, Seberino could be the guy.

RECOMMENDATION REVIEW: Hernandez continues to be a lock when for saves. If he gets traded prior to the trade deadline, he could have even more than usual. Keep an eye on Colome. If indeed he gets put in the bullpen, the strikeout numbers could be eye popping. Creek and Lidle are good for strikeouts.

TEXAS RANGERS

John Wetteland became a free agent at the end of last season, and was contemplating retirement due to continued back problems. Since Texas did not offer him salary arbitration, he could not pitch for them until May 1 of next season. The Rangers were uncertain as to who would close games if Wetteland did not return to Texas. The primary candidates include righthanders Tim Crabtree, Mark Petkovsek, Francisco Cordero and Jeff Zimmerman, and lefty Mike Venafro, none of whom has much experience closing games at the big league level.

Crabtree, along with the rest of the Texas bullpen, had an off year last season, but is the most experienced returning member of the group. That alone may give him the first shot at closing games for Johnny Oates, even though he has but five career saves. Crabtree is a hard thrower who sometimes has trouble getting enough movement on the ball. He has a solid chance to improve on last season's performance and could be a pleasant surprise. Ideally, he would set up a more established closer if Texas acquires one.

Petkovsek is a versatile reliever, able to start, or pitch in middle or short relief. His outstanding changeup gives him a chance to get lefties out, which makes him a good candidate for longer relief outings. With Texas, he could scavenge a good number of wins and even a few saves.

Cordero was a key part of the Juan Gonzalez trade with Detroit a year ago, and Texas had penciled him in as

Wetteland's successor. However, he has yet to fix the control problems that dogged his early efforts with the Tigers. At his best, Cordero can be dominating, but when he fails to get ahead in the count, he tends to give up the key hit. In two seasons, he does not have a big league save.

Zimmerman was one of the best stories of 1999, but faltered badly in his sophomore season. He has an outstanding slider, but the league caught up to him. Zimmerman is working to make his fastball a better setup pitch; if he succeeds, he could be an effective part of a committee to close out games. Like Crabtree and Cordero, he has little experience in the role, with four saves in his two major league seasons.

Ideally, Venafro would continue as a lefty matchup specialist, as his sidearm style is quite effective against lefty hitters. He doesn't have the weapons to get righties out on a regular basis. Used in his optimal role, Venafro could provide nice numbers, a handful of wins and a save or two for $1. If forced to face a lot of righthanders, he'd be a liability.

Bullpens tend to rise and fall as units, and individual relief pitchers are notoriously hard to project on a season by season basis. All of the above mentioned pitchers have decent stuff (Cordero's is well above average) and are capable of having a good season, but they're each just as capable of blowing up.

Other possibilities to fill out the big league bullpen include Matt Perisho and Brian Sikorski, both of whom are discussed with the starting pitchers, and Jonathan Johnson, Danny Kolb and Darwin Cubillan. Johnson is a failed starter who is trying to find a niche in long relief. Kolb is a former flame-thrower who missed most of last season with elbow surgery. Cubillan is a righthander who was obtained from the Blue Jays in the Esteban Loaiza deal last season and got hammered in a late-season trial with the Rangers. None figure to have any Rotisserie value in 2001.

RECOMMENDATION REVIEW: Wetteland could pay huge dividends as a reserve pick if it looks like he will return to Texas on May 1. If the Rangers go into the season without an established closer, pay attention to spring training boxes, especially "games finished", to get an idea of whom Johnny Oates might use as a closer. Don't overpay for Crabtree, Cordero, Zimmerman or Venafro if any of them is anointed with the "closer" title; they are just as likely to fail as succeed in the role. Any of them at a very low salary would be a decent speculation, especially Crabtree. As setup men, any would be worth a buck or so. Don't bid on Johnson, Cubillan, Kolb or any other rookie member of the pen.

TORONTO BLUE JAYS

With a solid young closer and some veteran arms to complement him, the Jays have the makings of a decent bullpen for 2001. The Jays admitted as the 2000 season ended that they would look to strengthen their pitching staff for 2001 but it was unclear whether that meant adding veteran arms to the bullpen or accomplishing tasks such as the Steve Parris trade.

Billy Koch anchors the staff, coming off an excellent year that saw him save 33 games and pick up nine wins, wins worth noting for Rotisserie leaguers. In fact, the 100 MPH Koch was eighth in the league in saves and he should only continue to get better as his heat hasn't translated to the number of strikeouts he should punch up in the long run. His control has also been dramatically better than advertised from his days as a minor league starting pitcher and he has almost absolute job security at this stage, even should he struggle early.

Kelvim Escobar, who spent most of last year as a starter, almost certainly begins the season as the main setup man. Escobar, who was a closer for the second half of the 1997 season, has the makings of a dominant reliever and he is far better suited for this role than as a starting pitcher. As a starter, he tinkers and nibbles and never really shows hitters his best stuff. As a reliever late last season, he fooled veteran hitters by mixing up his overpowering fastball with an assortment of good, off speed pitches. What particularly benefits Escobar in the relief role is that an injury to Koch would move Escobar up to the ranks of closer and that should mean a handful of saves and perhaps more if Koch can't answer the bell for some reason. Given his brief experience as a closer and Escobar's mental makeup, he would be a top choice as the alternate closer in Koch's absence.

Paul Quantrill used to have exclusive hold on the setup man's job but he never really had the stuff expected from a pitcher that goes in the late innings. He always allows more than his share of hits and though he has good control, it isn't sharp enough to fool hitters. Quantrill gets his outs by letting hitters put the ball in play and keeping them in the park. He remains a good seventh inning man and as always, should get plenty of work out of the Jays' pen.

John Frascatore had a late-season dispute with then pitching coach Dave Stewart but put it behind him to finish up on a strong note. Though his ERA didn't reflect it, he actually pitched reasonably well and if anything haunted him, it was his propensity for walking batters. He remains an important part of any bullpen though he is not likely to see much work beyond the seventh inning.

Lance Painter proved to be the most reliable lefty in the Jays' bullpen and one bad outing in September made his ERA look much worse than it should have been. He actually spent most of the season getting hitters out and stepped in for a couple of starts. His control is underrated and his poise is solid. In that regard, Painter is a critical part of any bullpen and he fits in as a primary situational lefty and emergency starter.

Pedro Borbon was the disappointment. Coming over to the Jays in the Pat Hentgen trade, Borbon struggled from the start and never really got into a groove. He walked more batters than he struck out and was rarely used late in a game. At thirty-three years of age and with only a few good seasons in the books, Borbon takes a step back on the bullpen ladder. Regardless, he fits in as a lefty who is better than he looked last year. The Jays spent much of the winter pursuing free agent and former Blue Jay Dan Plesac, demonstrating their desire to replace Borbon in the bullpen.

Mark Guthrie came to the Jays in the Steve Trachsel trade and like Trachsel, appeared to be on his way out after the 2000 season. Guthrie is a veteran lefthander who can be counted on to get out tough lefties, which means he's assured of plenty of appearances no matter which team he pitches for. He hasn't pitched fewer than 50 games since 1993 and that trend should continue in that he gets plenty of short outings.

Roy Halladay is one of the fallen stars in that he was projected to be a future ace starter and now begins 2001 fighting for his major league roster spot. Even the best of situations for Halladay probably earns him nothing more than a long relief role at this stage. Though he could be called into emergency starting service, he was so inconsistent and unreliable in 2000 that he's on short notice right now. It's entirely possible that he needs to go back to Triple-A to get more work and reestablish what seemed to be a promising career as a starter. That he continues to walk about as many batters as he strikes out remains a disturbing sign.

The Jays picked up Scott Eyre from the White Sox after the 2000 season ended. Eyre fits into the Jays as yet another lefthanded specialist, a commodity Toronto seems to covet in recent years. Eyre's 2001 pitching prospects appeared to hinge on whether Mark Guthrie would return to Toronto. A Guthrie-less Toronto could fit Eyre in as a sixth or seventh reliever and situational lefty out of the bullpen. Though Eyre was a starter with the White Sox back in 1997 and 1998, he would have only the rarest of opportunities to fill that role in Toronto.

The Jays also signed Dan Plesac. See more on Plesac in the Diamondbacks middle relievers section.

The Jays' bullpen, though crowded, is surprisingly light on prospects. Though Escobar and Halladay remain likely to improve, they have pitched too much to be called unknowns. Clayton Andrews and Leo Estrella, perhaps two of the superior short-term pitching prospects in the organization, were shipped off to Cincinnati in the Steve Parris deal.

Matt DeWitt remains an interesting candidate to break through a crowded bullpen situation. Coming over from St. Louis just over a year ago, DeWitt is young enough and has the stuff to become a quality major league pitcher, likely as a starter. He seems well-suited to make a major league breakthrough to the bullpen as a long reliever and could appear in a handful of games in relief this season.

RECOMMENDATION REVIEW: Obviously, Koch is the prime choice in this bullpen but Kelvim Escobar is the sleeper here and could earn a number of cheap saves, and there's always the chance that Escobar ends up back in the rotation and wins 10 games. None of the other veterans have much chance to make meaningful Rotisserie contributions, though Guthrie and Quantrill won't kill a team. Halladay is overrated and overvalued by most, at least for what he will do in the near future. Skip over Eyre and DeWitt as neither will have much of an opportunity to pitch and both are suspect as to what they can contribute even if they do get some innings.

TOP 2001 SAVES LEADERS

NAME	SV
Derek Lowe	40
Kazuhiro Sasaki	39
Mariano Rivera	37
Todd Jones	36
Roberto Hernandez	35
Billy Koch	34
Keith Foulke	33
Bob Wickman	32
Jason Isringhausen	29
Ryan Kohlmeier	27
Troy Percival	26
Rick Aguilera	22
Jeff Brantley	21
Latroy Hawkins	15
Bob Wells	15
Steve Karsay	12
Tim Crabtree	10
Shigetoshi Hasegawa	10
Eddie Guardado	8
Jim Mecir	8
Jose Paniagua	6
Jeff Zimmerman	6
Bob Howry	5
Jose Santiago	5
Mike Trombley	5
Mike Venafro	5
Doug Henry	4
Mark Petkovsek	4
Lue Pote	4
Jerry Spradlin	4
Travis Miller	3
Orber Moreno	3
Steve Rain	3
Shawn Sonnier	3
Lance Carter	2
Buddy Groom	2
Scott Kamieniecki	2
Rudy Seanez	2
Bill Simas	2
Joe Slusarski	2
Jeff Tam	2
Matt Anderson	1

NATIONAL LEAGUE RELIEF PITCHERS

ARIZONA DIAMONDBACKS

The Diamondbacks' bullpen played a large role in the team's first-half success last season, but mirrored the team's struggles down the stretch.

The main components return, and the D'backs can hope for a healthy season from closer Matt Mantei, who was on and off the field the first three months before regaining his 1999 form the second half of the year.

Mantei started the season on the DL after suffering ankle laxity in spring training and later missed time because of biceps tendinitis and shoulder laxity before finally hitting his stride around the All-Star break.

Mantei, who finished with 17 saves, converted 15 of his final 16 attempts from July 2. He was scored upon in only four of his final 28 appearances while posting a 1.57 ERA in that span. He did not give up a hit in 19 of those appearances, at times seeming almost unhittable when coupling a slider taught by former pitching coach Mark Connor to a 98 MPH fastball.

He will be the closer, barring injury, despite an encouraging step forward by righthander Byung-Hyun Kim.

Kim, 22, was a long shot to make the team in spring training. But he deserved an NL All-Star berth (he was snubbed) after a dazzling first half with 14 saves with a 1.94 ERA and 71 strikeouts in 41 2-3 innings through July 5. He set a franchise record by striking out eight straight batters May 4-9, then did it again in late June. His ratio of 14.1 strikeouts per nine innings was the best in the NL.

He faltered a bit in the second half, however, failing to convert any of his final four save opportunities. He was sent to the minor leagues to speed up his delivery from the stretch, which at times was an unacceptable 1.7 seconds.

Kim has long said he hoped to be a starter like Korean countryman Chan Ho Park of Los Angeles, but he was expected to begin the season as a setup man. If others fail, however, Kim would be a candidate for the rotation. His one start last season did not go well, he gave up four runs, four hits and four walks in 2 1-3 innings at Colorado's Coors Field on Sept. 26.

Lefthander Greg Swindell had another quality season as a setup man, his ERA marred by giving up eight earned runs in two appearances covering a combined 1 2/3 innings. He converted his only save opportunity when the D'backs went to a bullpen by committee in the early absence of Mantei, and saved his teammates' runs, permitting only four of his 26 inherited runners to score.

Lefties hit only .157 against Swindell last season, the lowest average on the staff.

Righthander Russ Springer was brought in to fortify the setup position but had a miserable year by his standards, giving up 63 hits and 34 walks in 62 innings and failing to convert his only two save opportunities. The D'backs expect him to rebound and will keep him in a setup role.

Veterans lefthander Dan Plesac, 39, allowed an earned run in only one of his last 22 appearances as the second lefty out of the bullpen last season, but filed for free agency after the 2000 season and signed with the Blue

Jays. He is no longer a closer candidate and is strictly middle relief.

The best young bullpen arm in the organization, righthander Jeremy Ward, underwent Tommy John surgery in mid-season last year and is likely to miss most of the 2001 season. He is a potential closer, however, with Bob Wickman-like movement on his late-breaking slider.

Righthanded closer Bret Prinz had a breakthrough season in 2000 after altering his delivery from overhand to sidearm. He gained velocity, to the low 90s, and finished second in the Texas League with 26 saves while at El Paso. He appears more suited to a setup role at the major league level, and may not be far off.

Youngsters Chris Cervantes, Jason Martines and Mike Koplove acquitted themselves well in the Arizona Fall League for top prospects, but all are considered at least a year away.

RECOMMENDATION REVIEW: When healthy, Mantei is an overpowering closer, although his ratio will never be outstanding because of the number of walks he allows. He has a hard time avoiding injury, however, because of genetic looseness in his joints. Kim would get the majority of save opportunities if Mantei were to go down again, but the D'backs do not see Kim as a full-time closer, at least at this stage of his career. When Kim and Mantei are on, the D'backs can shorten games to seven innings. Swindell has developed into one of the best setup men in the NL, but because of the way he is used seldom has an opportunity for victories.

ATLANTA BRAVES

Just how much did John Rocker's moronic comments to Sports Illustrated hurt himself and the club? Well, it certainly didn't do either one any favors.

Rocker was suspended for the first two weeks of the season and took the rest of the first half of the year getting himself back in shape. He couldn't throw a strike to save his life when he was reinstated, and ultimately had to get shipped back to the minor leagues before he got things straightened out.

His 24 saves were split equally between the first and second halves of the season, though he was a far better pitcher after the All-Star break. He had an ERA of 4.62 before the break, but cut that by more than three runs per

nine innings after that. Much of the difference can be attributed to cutting back on his walks. He walked more than a batter an inning through the first three months of the season, but gave only 14 free passes in 27 2/3 innings in the latter half.

It is a shame Rocker has such a big mouth, because he truly could be one of the top two or three relief pitchers in the game. But problems seemed to follow him last year, and they are likely to hound him again in 2001.

Another flare-up by Rocker would be horrible news for the Braves, who don't have anybody else who is really qualified to be a closer. Mike Remlinger is a very good setup man, who did fairly well when called upon in save situations last year. But the lefty is 35 years old and doesn't quite have the velocity to be effective as a stopper for an extended period of time.

Kerry Ligtenberg saved 30 games in 1998, but missed all of the 1999 season because of elbow surgery. He returned to duty at the start of last season, but he needed nearly three months before he was effective. His control and velocity were just a little off from where they were in 1998, and hitters were able to pick up on that. As a rule, pitchers are much better the second year back from elbow surgery, so Ligtenberg should be able to regain the speed he lost on his fastball and once again be a top-notch reliever.

Kevin McGlinchy missed much of last season with shoulder problems, but pitched well in September after his return from the disabled list. He is only 23 years old and still has a bright future in front of him. He was a starter in the minor leagues before being a surprise addition to Atlanta's big league roster in 1999. He might find his way into the starting rotation in a couple of years, but for now he will pitch in relief.

Atlanta called up 22-year-old Jason Marquis in June and he pitched very well for six weeks before one bad outing against the Marlins ruined his ERA for the rest of the season. He got in 15 games last year for the Braves and had only two really bad appearances, which is a good indication that he has a bright future ahead of him. He was a starter in the minor leagues, but he will pitch out of the bullpen this year.

The Braves got Scott Kamieniecki early last April, and while he pitched reasonably well for a while, he was hit hard in the second half of the season. He has nothing to offer any Rotisserie owners at this point in his career.

Rudy Seanez was surprisingly effective for the Braves in 1999, but he suffered a season-ending elbow injury in June, which required reconstructive surgery. He will not be back until at least the All-Star break, and can't be counted on to be effective until the start of the 2002 season.

David Cortes was yet another Atlanta pitcher to blow out his elbow. As a result he missed most of last year, returning in late August and appearing in only four games. The 27-year-old saved 22 games in Triple-A in 1999, but will not pitch in the late innings in the big leagues.

RECOMMENDATION REVIEW: Yes, John Rocker is always a liability due to his self inflicted case of diarrhea-mouth, but he and his 35-plus saves are just to hard to pass up on. His talent will overshadow his mouth in 2001. Both Remlinger and Ligtenberg are good back-ups if you have Rocker on your team. Cox is never afraid to go to the "hot-hand" in the pen and Remlinger and Ligtenberg would be first in line to get some saves.

CHICAGO CUBS

It is safe to say that the best days are behind Rick Aguilera. The former All-Star closer with the Twins came to the Cubs in 1999, but has not made any real impact for the club. He pitched reasonably well overall in 1999, but last year was close to a total disaster.

Though he had stretches when he was effective he saved eight games and had a 2.00 ERA in June and posted a 1.29 ERA in August he got pounded the rest of the season and finished up allowing nearly five runs a game. He also ended the season on the disabled list with a broken thumb.

Aguilera is 39 years old and will have to have an impressive spring if he is going to regain his spot as closer. Like many veteran pitchers at the end of their careers, he has enough experience to get by in spring training, but he doesn't have enough left in his tank to keep things going good once the regular season starts. Be very wary of good stats during spring training. Until the last week of camp he would be facing a lineup consisting of many minor leaguers, especially in the late innings, and that is no way to judge the effectiveness of any pitcher.

Aguilera stayed as the closer in Chicago because the Cubs did not have any other options. Tim Worrell, Todd Van Poppel, Felix Heredia, Kyle Farnsworth, Brian Williams and Jamie Arnold all recorded a save or two, but none of them is closer material at this point.

Tom Gordon was signed as a free agent during the winter. Depending how his arm holds up, he could be in line to close. Gordon will need close attention during spring since his situation during the winter was still iffy. If he is fully healthy the Cubs intended to give him every opportunity to be their closer. He is a well conditioned athlete and has always taken care of himself, so it would not be a surprise to see him with 25 saves by season's end.

The Cubs signed free agent Julian Tavarez, formerly of the Colorado Rockies. Tavarez came on strong in 2000, especially as a starter. The Cubs were expected to try and use him as a starter. If not he will be a valuable reliever for them. He is heading into his prime as a pitcher and his ground ball style suits Wrigley well.

Heredia would wind up being the best option if the Cubs have to choose between those other pitchers. He is a hard-throwing southpaw who has the arm and stuff to be a good stopper. His main problem so far in his career has been a lack of control. He has walked about a batter every other inning throughout his professional career, and has shown no real signs of learning how to throw more strikes. He will not turn 25 until June, so he still has some time to learn. If he ever masters his control, he will be an extremely effective relief pitcher.

Only 10 years ago it was thought that Van Poppel was going to be a dominating starting pitcher. But things never panned out and he was left for dead after getting numerous chances with several teams. The Cubs picked him out of the scrap pile a year ago and he turned in a very impressive 2000 campaign. Were it not for his control problems (48 walks in 86 1/3 innings) his numbers would have been even better. It isn't likely that he will have a 3.75 ERA again if he doesn't demonstrate more control, and he will not get more than a few saves this season.

The Cubs would love for Farnsworth to develop into a starting pitcher, but he hasn't shown any signs of that in the past two seasons. He was truly awful last year and will have to go back to the minor leagues to prove that he can get hitters out.

Arnold is a former Dodgers farmhand and is hanging on to his big league career for dear life. He has had chances to be a starter and a reliever, but he has not proven he can pitch at the major league level.

RECOMMENDATION REVIEW: Take a pass on Aguilera. He will get some saves, but not more than any other full-time closer, and his other stats will bring down the rest of your pitching staff. He will have a high ERA, especially for a closer, and simply is not worth keeping on your roster. Take a couple of dollars risk with Gordon. He may surprise you. Do not over pay for Tavarez' second half surge as a starter. He will need to be able to carry his second half success through the entire 2001 season to be considered "for real".

CINCINNATI REDS

The main reason why Danny Graves isn't a superstar is because he doesn't throw hard. The stopper for the Cincinnati Reds is just as effective as Billy Wagner or Trevor Hoffman, but because he doesn't throw 100 miles an hour it is sometimes easy for broadcasters and analysts to overlook him.

But like the other top closers in baseball, Graves gets hitters out. Only he gets them out with a sinking fastball instead of an overpowering one. But since racking up saves is the most important thing a Rotisserie owner is concerned with, there is no reason not to count Graves among the top few closers in all of baseball.

Helping get Graves saves situations will be Scott Sullivan, Mark Wohlers, Dennys Reyes and John Riedling.

Scott Sullivan is a workhorse of a pitcher who never seems to get the credit he is due. Year after year he piles up innings (and effective innings at that), never complains about his role as a setup man, and yet it seems as if many people think he is at the bottom of the barrel. That couldn't be further from the truth.

The side-arming righty is devastating on righthanded batters and has improved tremendously against lefties. Add to that the fact he can pitch multiple innings on consecutive days and it should be easy how valuable a reliever he is. He has thrown more than 100 innings each of the last five years, when his minor league innings are included, without a hint of arm problems, so don't let that deter you from getting him on your roster. He would be a great addition to any Rotisserie team.

Wohlers made a sterling recovery from reconstructive elbow surgery last year, rejoining the Reds in midseason. The fact that he also made it back from the mental disorder that prevented him from throwing the ball near

the plate in early 1998 was even more impressive. Still, Wohlers is not the pitcher that he was in the mid 1990s. He doesn't throw quite as hard and he doesn't have the command of his pitches that he did while with the Braves. If he were given a chance he would be able to close out games, but he will need another year of good pitching before he can think about being a closer again.

Reyes is a very good pitcher who essentially had his season last year wasted. Reyes can throw in the mid 90s and has a big-breaking curve ball and nasty slider, but the Reds decided he would only pitch to lefthanded hitters. He sometimes went a week or more between appearances, and even when he did get to pitch, often it was to only one hitter. With Bob Boone taking over in Cincinnati, Reyes should at least get more of a chance to pitch, but he still won't get any save situations.

Riedling has a tremendous arm and made quite an impression on the Cincinnati front office in the second half of last season. He got called up in late August and all he did was throw strikes and get people out. He quickly moved up on the bullpen's depth chart and was used in the late innings most of September. He will only get more chances this season, and would be the team's second choice to save games. He should get at least a few saves by filling in when Graves is unable to pitch.

Ron Villone spent half of last season in Cincinnati's bullpen, but only because he got bumped from the starting rotation. He pitched very well in relief, but regained his spot on the starting staff late in the year. He was traded to Colorado in November, but look for him to swing back and forth between starting and relieving this year. He is good enough to be able to handle either job, although his long-term success likely will be in the rotation.

Larry Luebbers, Hector Mercado and Scott Winchester also saw duty for the Reds in 2000, but none is likely to make the opening day roster. Winchester has a decent arm but has been beset with arm problems over the years. Mercado has promise, but is fighting a weight problem, and Luebbers is nothing more than a mop-up guy.

Scott Williamson was a co-closer in 1999, but he has been moved to the starting rotation and it is very doubtful that he will be a relief pitcher again in the near future. If he were moved back to the bullpen he would be a dominating closer, but that isn't going to happen soon.

RECOMMENDATION REVIEW: There are few closers in the National League who will be more automatic or guaranteed to get more saves than Graves will in 2001. He is the main man out of the bullpen and will get 99 percent of the save opportunities. He is a mortal lock to get 30 saves and if the Reds wind up with a contending team he will have no problem picking up another 10.

COLORADO ROCKIES

Quick. Which pitcher had the best season in 2000?

If you said Colorado lefthander Gabe White, you might be hooted out of the room. But you also might be right.

White, righthanded closer Jose Jimenez and lefthanded situational specialist Mike Myers helped give the Rockies one of the most efficient bullpens in baseball last season.

White, obtained from Cincinnati the first week of the 2000 season, blossomed in his first season at Coors Field, winning 11 games while saving four others. His relief ERA (2.36) and ratio of baserunners per nine innings (8.8) were second in the NL to Robb Nen. White pitched 29 1-3 scoreless innings from May 6 to July 9. Considering he did all that while playing half his games in Coors Field makes it all the more remarkable.

Jimenez again will be the closer after inheriting that role late in the spring when nominal closer Jerry Dipoto was sidelined for most of the season because of a bulging disk in his neck.

Jimenez, who beat Randy Johnson with both a no-hitter and a two-hitter in 1999, had the first 24 saves of his career in 2000, spending the whole season in the bullpen after coming over in the Darryl Kile trade in the winter of 1999.

Jimenez throws a heavy ball and has good late life on a slider, making it difficult for hitters to get the fat part of the bat on the ball. He was one of three Colorado relievers — White and Myers, yes, were the others — to give up less than one hit per inning.

Look up situational specialist in the dictionary and Myers' picture is there. A lefthander with a sidearm motion, can be simply brutal against lefthanded hitters. He held lefties to a .120 batting average in 99 plate appearances last season. He pitched only 45 1-3 innings in 71 appearances, so he was not around long enough to get much in the way of decisions — no victories, one loss, one save.

Myers, who was unscored upon the first half of the season, will be used in exactly the same role this season, giving manager Buddy Bell an early option against tough lefthanders at Coors Field.

Dipoto, who survived thyroid cancer in 1994, pitched briefly in April and then had disk surgery on May 3 that was expected to keep him out for the rest of the year. But he returned to the Rockies in September and made 12 appearances, posting a 1.93 ERA.

Healthy again, Dipoto remains an option at closer, although Jimenez enters spring training with the job.

Righthander Bobby Chouinard, released by Arizona after he was charged with aggravated assault on his wife on Christmas Day, 1999, pitched effectively out of the bullpen after joining the Rockies on July 17.

Chouinard is a capable setup man, and his career will not be hampered by the domestic violence incident. In November, Chouinard was sentenced to serve one year in jail, but a Phoenix judge ruled that Chouinard can serve four three-month terms in the offseason so that his career is not interrupted.

Mike DeJean, David Lee and Craig House offer righthanded help in the bullpen. DeJean will be used mostly as a setup man, although in Coors Field that can translate into victories. Lee had a solid 1999 season but was hammered in a brief callup last season and may be fading in the organization's eye. While he had 68 minor league saves from 1997-99, he does not the stuff to be a closer in the majors.

House, 23, is the most intriguing of the second group. He has been clocked at 100 mph out of a unique motion in which he almost seems to jump off the rubber while delivering a pitch. He made the majors last August, in only his second year in the organization, and his first three pitches were timed at 95, 97 and 99 mph. He walked 17 in his 13 2-3 innings, however, and the Rockies sent him to the Arizona Fall League for further work.

If they do not make the starting rotation, John Wasdin and Kevin Jarvis will be available in the pen.

RECOMMENDATION REVIEW: The bullpen is one of the strengths of the Rockies' team. Jimenez appears to have the stuff to be a quality closer in the near future, and White and Myers are very capable. Jimenez will have more saves as the everyday closer. It would seem impossible for White to repeat his stellar 2000 season, when he had 10 of 11 victories in Coors Field. But someone has to win those 11-10 games. Why not White, who will be used when the games are close? House is not worth a gamble until he can show some semblance of control.

FLORIDA MARLINS

Even though Antonio Alfonseca saved 45 games last year, he did it by pitching ugly. He gave up 82 hits and 24 walks in 70 innings of work and he only struck out 47 batters. The potential for a downward trend in 2001 is very high with Alfonseca. He'll be their closer heading into the season, but with all the other good arms in their bullpen he could be out of a job if he struggles.

Dan Miceli and Braden Looper both performed extremely well for the Marlins in setup roles last year. Miceli was coveted by many contending teams for the stretch run, but arm problems cooled them off and wound up landing him on the shelf. He's a proven reliever with plenty of experience who could close in a pinch. Looper has the big fastball and a developing slider, but he throws too many hittable pitches to be a closer at this point. He doesn't get many strikeouts, which is unusual for a hard thrower, which means he needs to be more fine with his pitches. Manny Aybar, another righthander with a big-time arm, performed really well while with the Marlins last year and could be a valuable part of their bullpen in 2001. He posted a strong 2.63 ERA in 21 games with Florida, perhaps earning himself a job for this season. Veteran Ricky Bones also performed well last year, earning a new contract and a job of some sort with the major league team.

Lefthanders Vic Darensbourg and Armando Almanza also performed well. Darensbourg was 5-3 with a 4.06 ERA and held lefthanded hitters to a .190 average last year. Almanza was 4-2 with a 4.86 ERA and he held lefthanders to a .179 average. Neither figures to have a big impact on roto teams, but they're both useful major leaguers.

Minor league closer Bobby Rodgers has a big arm and had plenty of success at Double-A last year, saving 22 games and posting a 3.25 ERA, but he'll have to prove himself again at Triple-A before he gets a shot at major league time. High-A righthanders Blaine Neal and Tim McClaskey blew away Florida State League hitters while sharing the closing job, but neither was believed to be

close to the majors as of the end of 2000.

RECOMMENDATION REVIEW: Alfonseca is a closer and should get a bunch of saves, but don't draft him too high or overbid on him because he's a risk. Miceli and Looper could get a handful of wins and saves, especially saves if Alfonseca struggles at all. Manny Aybar is also worth paying attention to, though his role was unclear at press time. None of the others will help much unless you're in a really deep NL only league.

HOUSTON ASTROS

The Astro bullpen was one of the main reasons for the team's disappointing performance in 2000. The 5.16 ERA was better than only the Cubs and Phillies and the 30 saves (in 55 opportunities) were better than only the Brewers and Pirates.

In 1999, lefthander Billy Wagner had the finest season ever by a Houston reliever. He broke Doug Jones' club record with 39 saves and set a major league record for most strikeouts per nine innings for the third straight year with 14.94. He was 4-1 with an ERA of 1.57 and a ratio of 0.78. He won the Rolaids Relief Man Award as the top relief pitcher in the National League and finished in a tie for fourth in the Cy Young Award voting.

More of the same was expected from Wagner in 2000 but it didn't happen. While still throwing in the mid to high 90s, Wagner was hit hard and converted only 6 of 15 save opportunities. He had a 2-4 won-loss record with a 6.18 ERA and a ratio of 1.66. In late June, Wagner revealed that he had been pitching with pain in his elbow. An examination revealed a partial tear in a tendon, which required surgery ending his season. His recovery has gone well and he was expected to be ready for the 2001 season.

If his arm is sound, Wagner, 29, should again take his place as one of the top closers in the major leagues. He relies almost entirely on his fastball but he also has a hard slider, which he uses sparingly.

Octavio Dotel began the season in the starting rotation before he became the closer when Wagner went down. Dotel considers himself a starter and has a strong preference for that role. However he was much more successful as a reliever. As a starter, he was 1-5 with an ERA of 5.84 and a ratio of 1.57. As a reliever, he was 2-2 with an ERA of 4.24 and a ratio of 1.32. He converted 16 saves in 23 opportunities.

Dotel, 25, has a strong arm and relies almost entirely on his mid 90s fastball. This limits his effectiveness as a starter but his high strikeout ratio (142 in 125 innings) is desirable in a closer. If Wagner is unable to resume his duties as a closer, Dotel is the obvious alternative. Otherwise, he is likely to be a setup man and should get a reasonable share of the save opportunities.

Doug Brocail was acquired from the Detroit Tigers during the offseason. He is a good middle reliever to take when rounding out your pitching staff and will not cost much. He helps in ERA, Ratio and will win four or five games. He was expected to be the righty setup man to the Astros closer and may pickup a save or two because of that.

Nelson Cruz was acquired with Brocail from Detroit, but has little Rotisserie value and is not much more than a mop-up middleman.

Former closer Mike Jackson was signed after missing the entire season with arm trouble. Do not expect him to return to his closer's role with the Astros. It is anyones guess if he will be even effective when he returns. Watch Jackson close during the spring. If he is back he may get a few saves, but was not expected to see any extended time in the closers role.

The remainder of the bullpen has no appreciable Rotisserie value. Jose Cabrera, 29, was expected to be a setup man in 2000 but had a disappointing 2-3, 5.92 season. Jay Powell, 29, was 1-1, 5.67 before being shut down for shoulder surgery. He was expected to be ready for the 2001 season. Journeyman, Joe Slusarski, 34, started the season at Triple-A but became one of Houston's most reliable relievers with a 2-7 record and an ERA of 4.21. Marc Valdes, 29, was acquired from Tampa Bay in a trade for Russ Johnson in May. He was initially effective but faded and finished with a 5-5 record and a 5.08 ERA.

Wayne Franklin, 27, was the lefthanded relief specialist after Trever Miller and Yorkis Perez failed in that role. He pitched in 25 games without recording a win, loss or save. His ERA was 5.48 but he averaged a strikeout per inning. Scott Linebrink, 24, acquired from the Giants in a trade for Doug Henry, showed some promise and will compete for a spot in the Astro bullpen in 2001.

The Astros typically bring several non-roster pitchers to spring training as bullpen candidates and 2001 will be no exception. Slusarski was in such a position last year and

appeared in more games than any other Astro pitcher in 2000.

RECOMMENDATION REVIEW: Wagner and Dotel are the only two Astro relievers that merit any serious consideration. Wagner could be a bargain because of his injury last year. Dotel is still young and has some upside potential. Brocail has some value, but is not much of a save guy.

LOS ANGELES DODGERS

Almost completely ignored amidst the anarchy that became the Dodgers last year was the fact that manager Davey Johnson asked for a better bullpen and general manager Kevin Malone gave it to him. As a result, while there was plenty to criticize about the 2000 Dodgers, the bullpen wasn't a target. In fact, even when Jeff Shaw went down with a tired arm, the spare parts that Malone collected and Johnson implemented more than picked up the slack.

Still, it was Shaw who recorded 27 saves. He did that in what would be classified as an off year for him, as evidenced by seven blown saves and a bloated 4.24 ERA. But to get a real read on Shaw, look at the numbers behind the numbers. It was a season of two seasons. Before the All-Star break, he blew seven of 19 save opportunities, had an ERA of 8.00, barely struck out more than he walked and went on the disabled list. Once healthy, he was untouchable, converting all 15 save chances after the All-Star break with a 0.89 ERA and a strikeout: walk ration of 4:1. Don't worry about Shaw being too old at age 34 based on the way he finished the season.

Terry Adams fought off nagging minor injuries to be the workhorse of a busy bullpen after coming to the Dodgers in the Eric Young trade. The Cubs decided he would never be the closer they envisioned and he did nothing to make the Dodgers think otherwise, effectively handling a middle relief role. His ERA dropped a half-run while his strikeout ratio dropped and he blew five of seven save opportunities. He was much better in the first half of the season than the second, never a good sign for the future. Some live arms lack the intangibles needed for the pressure of a closer job, and Adams might be in that group.

Antonio Osuna is definitely in that group. He's been given plenty of chances to be a closer because of his heat, but the fastball is straight and if he misses a little it's a gopher ball. Osuna blew all three save opportunities and won't get many more, but he is a serviceable major leaguer who tantalizes scouts because of his fastball.

Without the tools, Mike Fetters has done much more than some of his teammates because he has the intangibles, as well as a splitter and a fastball showing more life than it has in several years. That is why Fetters was given the chance to save games when Shaw was sidelined and he converted five of seven chances. For the year he held opponents to a .205 average, and when you get people out you get more chances to get people out. Fetters was re-signed because the Dodgers expect to use him plenty, and it's not bad having an insurance policy that has a 32-save season on his resume.

The Dodgers aren't quite sure what they have in Matt Herges, but they'll take whatever it is. In 2000, they almost had a rookie of the year candidate. Not really considered much of a prospect, he made the team and got batters out in every situation. Initially he was used in meaningless roles, but as he succeeded the situations got tougher and he continued to respond. He wound up 11-3 out of the bullpen with a 3.17 ERA. He struggled in four starts, so he's likely to remain in the bullpen, perhaps to be groomed as Shaw's heir apparent.

Onan Masaoka could have been the situational lefthanded reliever with his live fastball, but he wound up on the Albuquerque shuttle for three round-trips because of mechanical inconsistency that led to 15 walks in only 27 innings. Masaoka was a starter in the minor leagues and that might be his future. Another lefthander who disap-pointed, Aussie Jeff Williams, will be dueling Masaoka for a big-league job. Williams could be passed by countryman Adrian Burnside, also a southpaw who throws hard. Don't laugh, but the Dodgers had not given up on righthander Robinson Checo, who was on the verge of a callup when he was injured. A real sleeper could be Kris Foster, who throws bullets when his arm is right.

RECOMMENDATION REVIEW: Shaw is the prize in the Dodgers bullpen, and managers judging him off his raw numbers might overlook how well he finished up. As a backup, Fetters has closer experience and proved he can still be trusted in those situations. And the rising star could be Herges, although those 11 wins won't let him slip under the radar.

MILWAUKEE BREWERS

It's not often that a team can trade its All-Star closer and actually get even better production out of the pitcher who is promoted into that slot, but that's exactly what hap-pened when setup man Curtis Leskanic took over as the Brewers' closer when Bob Wickman was traded to the Cleveland Indians last July. Leskanic used a 96 MPH fastball complemented by a hard slider to convert 12 of the 13 save opportunities entrusted to him over the season's final two months, and was dominating much of the time.

The Brew Crew will enter the 2001 season with a closer every bit as intimidating as the squad's lone All-Star representative in 2000. Leskanic is also a perfect example of what can happen when a pitcher is able to escape the thin air of Coors Field in Denver. His ERA dropped from 5.08 at Colorado in 1999 to 2.56 in Milwaukee's pitcher-friendly County Stadium. The latter figure was good enough for fourth place among National League relievers who worked a minimum of 50 innings. The free-spirited Leskanic's goofball antics also kept his bullpen mates loose during games and the righthander was credited with uniting the group into a cohesive unit over the season's second half.

David Weathers appeared in 69 games as a late-inning setup man and posted a creditable ERA of 3.07 in 76.1 innings of work. Weathers is your basic inning-eating blue collar type who uses a sinker/slider repertoire to keep the ball down and the hitters guessing as to which way it's going to break. Weathers seems to have settled into the setup role on a permanent basis after having been used as a part-time starter earlier in his career.

27-year-old Ray King developed into one of the more pleasant surprises in the league in the second half of the 2000 season after being plucked from the Chicago Cubs system in a minor league trade for righthander Doug Johnston on April 14. The hard-throwing lefthander turned in one scoreless outing after another in the season's second half before completing the season with a micro-scopic ERA of 1.26 in 28.2 innings of work. In the process, King became Davey Lopes' top lefthanded setup pitcher and will enter 2001 as the frontrunner for that role, although Lopes would like to see him get his weight down.

Coming over in an offseason trade for second baseman Fernando Vina, Juan Acevedo was initially considered for every pitching role from the starting rotation to closer, but ultimately settled in nicely as a late-inning complement to

Weathers in setup and middle relief. The righthanded power pitcher turned in a respectable ERA of 3.81 in 82.2 innings and was expected to fill the same role in one of the league's better bullpens again in 2001.

Longtime closer-in-waiting Valerio de los Santos got off to a rocky start when he was lit up for five home runs in an April start in St. Louis and was quickly shuttled back into the bullpen. In that role, he was at times difficult for Lopes to deploy as he struggled to retire lefthanders in the first half of the season and was most often consigned to long relief work. But "de los" got his confidence back in the second half as he gained command of his low 90s heater and split finger pitch to record nearly a strikeout per inning. Though the 25-year-old is no longer considered the Brewers' closer of the future, he should be a serviceable member of the relief corps in 2001.

Swingman Rocky Coppinger went down in spring training with an elbow injury and ultimately underwent Tommy John surgery before pitching a single inning for the Brewers in 2000. The big righthander should return sometime in 2001 but may not regain effectiveness for another year. Righthander Everett Stull pitched much more effectively in middle and long relief than he did earlier in the season as a starter and may get a shot at a setup role in 2001. Stull has a great arm but has lacked command. The explosive slider of Chad Fox apparently has taken too severe of a toll on the reliever's right elbow. Though virtually unhittable when he's healthy and on his game, Fox underwent his third major elbow operation in recent years and may be done.

Worth keeping an eye on in the Brewers minor league system are Allen Levrault, Mike Penney, Ryan Poe and Gene Altman. Levrault is the most advanced and may get a shot in middle relief in 2001 after spending most of last season in Triple-A, where he worked as a starter. He has a closer's mentality but may lack the power arsenal for the role. Penney pitched in the Arizona Fall League. He jumped from Class-A to Triple-A and had success at each level. Poe was impressive for the Mudville Nine of the Class-A California League and earned a promotion to Double-A, where he remained effective, leading Brewers minor league pitchers with a 2.25 ERA and whiffing 118 in 104 innings between the two stops. Altman picked up 17 saves for Class-A Beloit. Veteran Bob Scanlan led the league with 35 saves at Triple-A Indianapolis but was torched for six runs in 1.2 innings during a brief callup to Milwaukee and failed to resurface at the major league level after that.

RECOMMENDATION REVIEW: Curtis Leskanic will be the Brewers closer in 2001. Depending on how well the Brewers play, and how many opportunities he gets, he should have a fine season with anywhere from 25-35 saves.

MONTREAL EXPOS

One of the bigger questions during spring train will be how closer Ugueth Urbina is throwing after having bone chips removed from his throwing elbow. His option was picked up for the 2001 season and the Expos expected him to be ready for the start of spring training.

After being shutdown early in the 2000 season with only 13 innings pitched and only eight saves, Urbina will be a risk for the 2001 season. Especially since he relied on being a power pitcher before his second major surgery in the past five seasons to his elbow. It remains to be seen if he will be again able to hit the high 90s with his fastball and throw his nasty slider.

On his side to make a successful comeback is the fact that he is in his prime as an athlete, being only 27, and that he had elbow surgery back in 1997 and was able to rebound quickly from that. Ugie will gain strength and his dominance as the 2001 season progresses.

Here is where you can find a real bargain because many owners will be wary of his arm troubles. Mention to your fellow owners that he is just coming off elbow surgery. It will help lower his draft day value. Whereas last season he was valued around the low to mid $30 range, this season he may be had for the low to mid $20 range. And because the Expos fully expect him to be their closer in 2001, there is no reason you should not want him, especially at a bargain rate.

If there is some unforeseen problem with Urbina, the Expos have a few alternate choices to fill-in for closer. The closer role would change from one guy to a committee of relievers. The hot hand at the time would be called in to close the game. All are very capable.

Lefty Steve Kline was the head candidate before being traded to the Cardinals. He saved 14 games after Urbina went down last season. He is a workhorse who was normally the Expos top lefty setup man and one of the better middle innings reliever in the game today. He will pitch around 70 to 80 innings, win five to eight games, with a few saves, and a low ERA and Ratio. Graeme Lloyd will benefit the most from Kline's departure and will now be the main lefty setup man in the Expos pen.

Scott Strickland has the potential to be the Expos next closer. He has solid control to go a long with a mid 90s fastball and a hard slider. Anthony Telford and Strickland were expected to be the Expos top righty setup men. Strickland was used as the closer when Kline tired at the end of the season. Strickland held his own as the closer; saving eight games, winning four, with a 3.00 ERA and a 1.13 Ratio.

He was expected to be healthy, but shoulder problems plagued him in parts of 1999 and in 2000. There was a point in 2000 when it was thought that he was going to be lost for the season with a partial tear in his throwing shoulder, similar to Todd Stottlemyre.

Anthony Telford has been a very successful righty setup man since he has come to the Expos. He was expected to continue in a similar role, but was expected to share more time with other Expos relievers for that job. Expect a decrease in his win totals and the few saves that he gets. He helps in the ERA and Ratio categories.

Last season the Expos new owner Jeffery Loria wanted to make a statement that the Expos were going to spend a little money on free agents. So the Expos went out and overpaid for the little needed bullpen help of lefty Graeme Lloyd. It was especially odd since the Expos already had a better lefty middle reliever in Steve Kline.

Unfortunately, Lloyd did not pitch at all for the Expos in 2000 due to arm trouble. If he can return to his old form then he may be of some help to the Expos and a Rotisserie team, especially in the ERA and Ratio stats. He is also good for around five wins and a few saves. He is a risk because of his arm trouble and age. Go after Kline first, he is younger, better, and will see more opportunities to help your team.

Britt Reames was acquired from the Cardinals in the Fernando Tatis trade. He was expected to compete for a starting job, but could also be a valuable reliever. He was stellar in the pen during the end of the season for the Cardinals and during the 2000 playoffs. He could be a sleeper either in the starting rotation or in the pen.

The other Expo relievers from 2000 have little draft day value. Julio Santana, Scott Forster, Mike Johnson, J.D. Smart, Sean Spencer and Felipe Lira are middle inning fillers in blowout games. They are all ERA and Ratio

killers, with little opportunities for wins or saves.

While Guillermo Mota has a lot of potential and was once seen as the Expos future closer, he has yet to learn how to pitch. He is getting up there in age to still be looked at as a prospect so his time to contribute is now. He needs to work on his control, but because he has the raw talent, he will get a few more chances. Keep an eye on him during spring and in the free agent pool during the start of the season. If he makes the Expos out of camp and pitches well, then he may be a quality pickup to fill an injury need for a few weeks.

Look for the losers of the fifth starter spot to work as long relievers and swingmen. Read more about Scott Downs, Hideki Irabu, and Mike Thurman in the Expos starting pitching section.

On the horizon is closer Jim Serrano. It was expected that he was another year away and would spend his 2001 season at Triple-A Ottawa unless the Expos were hit with a lot of injuries like they were last season.

RECOMMENDATION REVIEW: Urbina is a risk well worth taking. Just make sure that he is healthy and throwing all his pitches at the time you draft him. If you do take Urbina, it would be smart to try and get either Lloyd or Strickland because they will pickup the majority of Urbina's saves if something were to happen to Ugie. Both Lloyd and Strickland are intelligent sleeper picks to round out your Rotisserie pitching staff. Both will come relatively cheap due to playing in Montreal.

NEW YORK METS

In the court case of Baltimore fans vs. Peter Angelos, Exhibit A is Armando Benitez. Clearly, the 28-year-old is better than anyone the Orioles have had closing for them since he was traded. But last season, he was even the number one closer in New York. Aside from his won-lost record, Benitez outperformed Mariano Rivera. The Mets righthander was 4-4, 2.61 with a 1.01 ratio and a team-record 41 saves.

The Mets re-signed two other key components of their bullpen who were free agents: John Franco and Turk Wendell.

Franco apparently preferred staying home to going somewhere else to become a closer once again. The 40-year-old lefthander appeared capable of closing last year. He finished 5-4 with a 3.40 ERA and 1.26 ratio. He also saved four games in four attempts.

The wacky Wendell is bringing his animal-tooth necklace back to Shea Stadium. The 33-year-old righthander pitches a bit deeper in New York's bullpen. In 2000, he went 8-6, 3.59 with a save and a 1.22 ratio.

At age 38, lefty Dennis Cook is nearing the end of the road. In the last two years, his ERA has more than doubled (to 5.34) and his strikeout/walk ratio is down about 40 percent. In 2000, he was 6-3 with a 1.59 ERA and two saves — but in eight opportunities.

Donne Wall was acquired from the Padres in a trade for outfielder Bubba Trammell. He will be one of the Mets middle relievers and could see time as the setup man. He is good for a few wins and possibly a few saves.

Rich Rodriguez, another lefthander, was never as good as Cook. But the 38-year-old Rodriguez was so bad last season (0-1, 7.78, 2.00 ratio) that he spent part of it in Triple-A. Can he return for an 11th major league season?

Pat Mahomes' golden touch was somewhat tarnished in 2000. Unbeaten the year before, Mahomes slipped to 5-3, 5.46 with a 1.70 ERA. After the All-Star break, he was 3-2, but with a 6.97 ERA. He may have to battle to stay in the majors in '01. In December, the Mets designated him and 24-year-old righty Lariel Gonzalez (5-5, 4.18, five saves at Triple-A Norfolk) for assignment.

Rick White picked up some of the slack after coming over from Tampa Bay at the trade deadline. The 32-year-old righthander was a combined 5-9, 3.52 with a 1.21 ratio and three saves.

At the winter meetings, the Mets also acquired righthander Donne Wall, 33, from San Diego in a trade for Bubba Trammell. Wall finished 5-2, 3.35 with a 1.06 ERA and a save for the 2000 Padres.

A younger righthander, 25-year-old Eric Cammack, pitched well at Norfolk (6-2, 1.70, nine saves), but struggled with his control (10 walks in 10 innings) for the Mets. He was 0-0, 6.30 with a 1.70 ratio.

A better relief prospect could be hard-throwing Jerrod Riggan, who jumped from Double-A Binghamton (2-0, 1.11, 0.94 ratio, 28 saves) to pitch two innings and give up no earned runs for the Mets. However, Riggan already is 26 years old.

Another 26-year-old righty, Corey Brittan, complemented Riggan as a closer at Binghamton — with a 7-1 record, 2.30 ERA and 12 saves.

Also at Binghamton, righthander Juan Cerros, 24, was 10-4, 3.50 with three saves.

Jim Mann and Oscar Henriquez were minor league free agents during the offseason.

The closer for high Class A Port St. Lucie was Heath Bell, a 23-year-old righthander. He finished 5-1, 2.55 with 23 saves.

RECOMMENDATION REVIEW: Benitez could be a bargain because he isn't considered in the same class as the elite relievers such as Rivera and Trevor Hoffman. Franco still can save games and pitch effectively, but if Benitez were injured or ineffective, it doesn't seem likely Franco still could handle the workload of a major league relief ace.

PHILADELPHIA PHILLIES

How bad was the Phillies' bullpen last season? Well, their cumulative 5.72 ERA was by far the worst in the National League, a full 0.53 worse than the second worst pen, which belonged to the Cubs. The Rockies, you ask? A mere 4.74 bullpen ERA, at altitude. You couldn't blame the Phils' relief pitching shortcomings on the workload — only three NL pens logged fewer than the Phils' 434 1/3 innings. The Phils fell short in every bullpen slot — their closers were downright horrible, and their middlemen were even worse, leading the way to a horrific 21-37 relief won-lost record. The Phils promptly made upgrading their pen a major offseason priority — and then arguably made their pen even worse early on by adding the washed-up Jose Mesa to the mix. They also barely fell short in their efforts to land the Mets' John Franco as their new closer.

I guess one needs to begin this discussion by focusing on Mesa, 35, the early offseason leader in the clubhouse in the race for the Phils' closer job. He was last seen being waxed by the Yankees in the postseason. Mesa's career progression has been, shall we say, negative at best over the last three seasons. His seasonal ERA's have blown up from 2.40 in 1997 to 4.57, 4.98, and 5.36, respectively, over that span, and he has allowed well over a hit per inning in all three campaigns. His conditioning (he's charitably listed at 6'3", 225) and control have been quite inconsistent in recent seasons as well. He still throws hard

— his heater still approaches 95 MPH on occasion, and he also mixes in curves and splitters with varying levels of success. To top it off, he's not all that great with the glove or in the art of holding baserunners. However, he does have "closer experience", something that apparently trumps all of his shortcomings in the Phils' eyes. The two-year, $6.8 million contract extended to Mesa by the Phils could go down as the offseason's most laughable signing. Look for a 4-8 record, a 5.00-plus ERA and 20 ugly saves, as Mesa becomes Philly fans' designated whipping boy for the 2001 season. Bear in mind, however, that the Phils were expected to continue their closer search through the remainder of the offseason as we went to press.

The Phils signed closer Ricky Bottalico from the Royals. He will fill-in as a middle reliever and could get some saves if Mesa fails (which is a good possibility). Like Mesa, he is not someone you want to rely on for the majority of your saves. See more on Bottalico in the Royals relievers section.

The Phils consider Vicente Padilla, 23, as arguably the most significant long-term asset acquired from Arizona in last year's Curt Schilling deal. While the righthander certainly has a live arm, there are numerous reasons to be only lukewarm about his future. He relies heavily on a low-to-mid-90s fastball and a hard curve, a combination that appears to be sufficient against righthanded hitters. However, he rarely fools lefthanded hitters with either offering — they batted .337 against him last season, and a whopping .420 after the late July Schilling trade. His performance gradually deteriorated after his move to Philadelphia, as he got careless with his mechanics, and the movement on all of his pitches evaporated. Also, there are significant concerns about his conditioning, and doubts about his listed age. I must admit that he is one of the older looking and more unfit 23-year-olds I've seen. The Phils hope that new pitching coach Vern Ruhle can coax more output from Padilla. Look for a 5-5 record, five saves and a 4.00 ERA in 60 or so outings. His upside is much higher, however -- if he shows up in Florida in shape, and blows away the opposition, he could be in position to pick up the closer pieces should Mesa implode.

Righthander Wayne Gomes, 28, served as a part-time closer for the Phils for portions of the 1999 and 2000 seasons. Like Padilla, Gomes possesses a traditional two-pitch power closer repertoire, featuring a low-90s fastball and a hard curve. Uneven command, especially early in the count, and spotty mechanics and conditioning have prevented Gomes from holding the closer job for any material length of time. It normally takes only two or three

pitches into an outing before you can tell whether Gomes is "on". When he's missing with his curve early in the count, he's dead, and hitters know it. He has tired late in each of the last three seasons, and his strikeout rate has consistently dropped over that span. Gomes has reached a crossroads in his career, but could benefit — like Padilla — from a change in pitching coaches this season. Look for a 5-5, five save, 4.00 ERA season from Gomes as well in 2001, though, like Padilla, improved conditioning and a solid spring training performance could bump him into late-inning duty, increasing his value.

Righthander Chris Brock, 31, had mixed success in a swingman role with the Phils last season, hurling 93 1/3 representative innings that could have been downright exceptional if he didn't allow — get this — an amazing 21 home runs. Brock is a durable workhorse who mixes his high 80s fastball with a decent slider and a changeup, all of which he throws for strikes with some consistency. Hitters batted just .239 against him last year, with south-paws hitting a mere .224. However, he's a flyball pitcher who can get into big trouble when he leaves pitches out over the plate. All things considered, the Phils can't expect much more than they got out of Brock in 2000, when they often asked him to work in the late innings. He'll more likely function in long or middle relief in 2001, and five wins and 4.50 ERA in 70 relatively unexciting innings would seem to be a reasonable expectation.

Jeff Brantley, 37, was the Phils' primary closer for most of 2000, and became a free agent at the end of the season. Once a bulldog competitor with a live fastball and a nasty splitter as well as a couple other passable breaking pitches, Brantley is now, well, a bulldog competitor. His oft-cut right shoulder is shot, his command is spotty, and his fastball checked in around 85 MPH late last season. He might get a spring training invitation from someone, but it probably won't be the Phillies. Ditto Mike Jackson, 36, who was signed to be the Phils' closer last season, only to hurt his shoulder warming up in the bullpen on opening day. He then underwent season-ending shoulder surgery, to go with his recent ongoing elbow and knee woes. When healthy, Jackson featured a low 90s fastball and a nasty slider, both of which he could throw for quality strikes consistently. Teams appeared to be lining up to give Jackson a chance in 2001, and the Phils weren't at the front of the queue as the offseason opened. Other departing free agents included lefties Scott Aldred and Ed Vosberg.

Other bit bullpen players for the Phils last season included righties Jason Boyd and Doug Nickle and lefthander Tom

Jacquez. Boyd, 28, has long teased multiple organizations with his low 90s fastball and smooth motion, but failed his first extended major league test in 2000, posting a horrifying 6.55 ERA and walking almost a batter per inning not to mention breaking his hand during a dugout tantrum. I'll pass, and so will the Phillies. Nickle, 26, was an afterthought acquired from the Angels in the 1998 Greg Jefferies salary dump. His fastball reaches the low-to-mid-90's, but is fairly straight. Also, Nickle has yet to pitch a Triple-A inning at his relatively advanced age, and has been slow to develop his breaking stuff. I'm not a believer. Jacquez, 25, could carve out a niche as a situational lefty, however. His fastball only reaches the mid-to-upper 80s, but he varies speed and location well and can confound hitters once around the order. Don't be shocked if he makes the big club and posts a respectable 3.50 ERA and a handful of wins in 40-50 innings. The Phils were also courting the likes of Rheal Cormier to man the left side of their pen as the offseason began to heat up.

Other 2001 bullpen possibilities include righties Paul Byrd, Cliff Politte, Amaury Telemaco, and Mark Brownson (see Starting Pitcher section).

RECOMMENDATION REVIEW: Jose Mesa will get his shot to close again, this time with the Phillies. If Mesa blows up, which he has in the last several years, Vicente Padilla will be next in line. Gomes is no longer a long term solution at closer. Padilla is their closer of the future.

PITTSBURGH PIRATES

Mike Williams was one of the 1999 closers thought to be least likely to retain his job in 2000, yet he surprised his critics by again serving the Bucs in that role and saving 24 games in 29 chances. While he did a good job last year, Williams doesn't have the bounce-back arm needed to succeed as an everyday closer. He was hit fairly hard when pitching on consecutive days, posting a 5.89 ERA in those appearances compared to a 2.68 mark when he had at least one day's rest. The best use for Williams could be as a multi-inning closer who would then be shut down for at least a day after each outing. This would limit his save chances to about 25 per season although he'd be far more likely to convert the saves and, therefore, it wouldn't cut into his save total much. For Rotisserie purposes, Williams is near his peak in value. He won't advance to the level that most closers reach, getting 35-40 saves. Therefore, he's not worth typical closer dollars. Williams is best used as a supplemental closer, in addition

to a true bullpen ace; keep the bidding under $20 and you'll be happy with your results.

Lefty Scott Sauerbeck has gotten a handful of save chances over the last two years and will get a few more again in his situational role. However, despite his fairly good results it is unlikely he'll be promoted into a shared closer role; he's simply too valuable as a lefty setup man — opposition lefties have hit .198 against Sauerbeck the last two seasons. Because he's used in this limited role he has only marginal upside potential. He also has less risk, too, because he's not going to be over-used and exposed too often to righthanded hitters, thus limiting the number of blowout outings he'll suffer. In his present role he could get a handful of wins and saves, with little risk, making him worth a couple of bucks. Put Sauerbeck on your "safe $1 reliever" list for the end of the draft.

Former closer Rich Loiselle bounced back from the elbow surgery that sidelined him for part of 1999. He's not all the way back, though, having lost a bit off his fastball. Still he has shown an ability to get batters out and he's regaining strength. He's not that far away from being ready to close games again. Whether or not he gets that opportunity is up to Bucs management, of course, and they aren't likely to do that unless Williams stumbles. Still, Loiselle is a good bet to get at least a handful of save chances in 2001, making him worth a flier at a buck.

Jose Silva is discussed more closely in the "Starting Pitchers" section. He's got good stuff that may be better suited to a short relief role. Whether he gets used in that role is problematic, though, making Silva a "pass" for Rotisserie drafts.

The Pirates long-relief staff will see a major overhaul for the 2001 season. Gone are Brad Clontz, Marc Wilkins and Jeff Wallace (all waived or released). Terry Mulholland has been brought in to be a reliever and provide veteran stability. He is a reliever who will get both a few wins and saves. If used in small doses, he can be effective. Mulholland may also see a few starts throughout the season. See more on Mulholland in the Braves "Starting Pitchers" section.

Josais Manzanillo and Mike Garcia will return from the 2000 club and will be joined by whomever doesn't make the starting staff from the group that includes Bronson Arroyo, Dan Serafini, Chris Peters and Jose Parra. Although some of these guys are decent pitchers who can help the Pirates, none will get enough saves or wins to have any Rotisserie value.

Closing games at Triple-A Nashville were Cory Bailey, Dave Pavlas and Luis Andujar. Each are best described as Triple-A insurance; none is good enough to be a big-league closer for any length of time and none would advance to that role should Williams be unavailable. Brian Smith was outstanding at Double-A Altoona in 2000, posting an ERA below 1.00, saving 12 games and striking out almost a batter per inning. He's at least a year from the big leagues, but keep an eye out for him if he gets a midseason jump.

RECOMMENDATION REVIEW: Because he's still the closer, Williams retains some value. But, he's not of the caliber of other closers, so discount the usual dollar-per-save bidding just to be on the safe side. Better yet, get Williams as a supplemental closer instead of your primary bullpen ace. If he goes in the tank you haven't completely been wiped out in saves but if he has a great year all the better for you. Sauerbeck and Loiselle are worthy of one-dollar bids late in the draft. Avoid the rest of the relief corps in Pittsburgh.

ST. LOUIS CARDINALS

Dave Veres did a nice job closing for the Cardinals last year and was yet another player that benefited from getting out of Coors Field. He had 29 saves in 36 chances last year and posted a solid 2.85 ERA in 71 appearances. He's not overpowering and there are times where he'll blow the occasional save, but he's been pretty reliable and is on a good team that should provide him with plenty of save opportunities.

Steve Kline came over from the Expos in the Fernando Tatis trade. He will be the Cardinals main lefty setup man. See more on Kline in the Expos relievers section.

Mike James and Mike Timlin should both have setup roles for the Cardinals this season based on their contributions in 2000. James has a 3.16 ERA in 51-plus innings of work and did a nice job after being recalled from Triple-A during the first half of the season. Timlin was 3-1 with a 3.34 ERA after being acquired from the Orioles during the second half of last season. He had his usual control problems, but did a respectable job all the same.

Jason Christiansen was the only lefthander assured of a job in the Cardinals' bullpen before they got Kline and he's got tremendous ability. He struggled last year and got hit pretty hard for both the Pirates and Cards, but he's got a low to mid 90s fastball and can be really overpowering

when he's throwing strikes.

The other bullpen jobs were up in the air during the Winter. Righthanders Luther Hackman, Gene Stechschulte and Mark Thompson could all figure in somehow, as could Matt Morris, and Alan Benes. Lefthanders Mike Mathews, Justin Brunette and Jose Rodriguez should compete for a job as well.

RECOMMENDATION REVIEW: Veras is a dependable reliever, but don't draft him too high or overbid on him. James, Timlin, Morris, Benes and Reames could help in deep leagues, but Morris, Benes and Reames would be more valuable as starters. Christiansen will pick up strikeouts and is a candidate for a strong comeback, but he probably won't win or save many games.

SAN DIEGO PADRES

The Padres best pitcher and possibly their best player is ace reliever Trevor Hoffman; the only player on the Padres roster worth $30 or more. Hoffman converted 43 of 50 saves in 2000 to get 40-plus saves for the third straight year and 30-plus saves for the sixth straight year. Despite an unusually high 2.99 ERA in 2000, Hoffman continues to blow hitters away at a high rate; all signs are good that he'll again be a top-flight ace reliever in 2001 and worthy of the expensive Rotisserie salaries he'll earn.

The biggest question for San Diego won't be who gets saves but who sets Hoffman up for them. Donne Wall and lefty Kevin Walker collected the bulk of the Padres holds last year. Wall is gone via trade to the Mets leaving the righthanded setup job wide open. Carlos Almanzar, Tom Davey and Heathcliff Slocumb are the best bets to win the job although, in reality, the most likely scenario is a rotating share of this job.

After experiencing a few shaky outings following his mid-April callup, Walker settled down to have one of the better rookie seasons in the National League, winning seven games and making seventy appearances out of the Padres bullpen. He actually handled righthanders better than lefties, leaving the Padres still searching for a true lefty setup man after Matt Whisenant was tried and found wanting. Another lefty, Dave Maurer, also couldn't retire lefthanded hitters with any regularity. For 2001, Walker will get the first chance at the platoon specialist role; in any case he'll get a long look again simply based upon his success in 2000. Because Whisenant and Maurer have little chance at saves, none have any immediate Rotisserie value. Walker has minimal value only because he'll get a shot at a handful of wins and saves both.

Almanzar is the most ready and proven righthanded setup man; he doesn't walk a lot of batters and he gets ground balls. He lacks closer's stuff, though, and would not be the best choice to get saves if Hoffman were unavailable. Davey might be a better candidate as he has a decent fastball. Lack of short-relief experience is the primary thing holding him back; he had been used in a starting and long-relief role the last few years. Slocumb has been a closer in the past, but hasn't had more than three saves in a season since 1997. His past experience might lead to more save chances if Hoffman becomes indisposed. Slocumb or possibly Davey would be a potential insurance pick for whomever buys Hoffman.

Long-relief and middle innings work will be filled by pitchers like Will Cunnane, Matt Whiteside, Carlos Reyes and Todd Erdos. They are not especially bad pitchers but have no Rotisserie value as they will not get wins or saves with any regularity. Since they could be tapped for an occasional spot start, which often has disastrous consequences, all are to be avoided for Rotisserie use.

Triple-A Las Vegas' top closer, Brandon Kolb, was traded during the winter. Jayson Durocher picked up saves at Double-A Mobile, but he doesn't have big-league stuff and would not close games in the majors. There are no Ultra picks among the Padres minor-league relievers.

RECOMMENDATION REVIEW: There are few pitchers who have as much certain value as Hoffman. He's the real deal and worth every penny he commands on Draft Day. Because he's so expensive, though, he is best pursued only by teams hoping to contend. Why spend that much money on one closer if you have no chance to win this year? Among the remaining relievers, only Walker, Davey, and Slocumb have value. Walker is a good one-dollar selection while Davey and Slocumb are insurance against an injury to Hoffman.

SAN FRANCISCO GIANTS

Robb Nen signed a four-year contract extension with the Giants in September, and he will continue to be among the elite closers in baseball, and he will generate a roto salary commensurate with that job. Nen was a perfect 24 for 24 in second half saves last season, registering a 1-0 record and ERA of 0.85 over 31.2 innings (50 strikeouts, to 14 hits). He'll cost, but be worth it.

Nen's primary backup will be Felix Rodriguez. Rodriguez, coming off an excellent 1999 (2-3, 3.80) improved even more in 2000. Rodriguez saved three, allowing just 65 hits over 81.2 innings, striking out a fabulous 95 hitters. He did blow five saves, but in general pitched extremely well, He is an excellent selection as a middle reliever for a buck, and the former Arizona closer of the spring of 1998 will get some chances to convert, especially if Nen is injured or overworked.

Alan Embree, coming off elbow surgery, should be ready to fly, but as a spot lefty, he will not generate much in the name of numbers.

The Giants traded third baseman Bill Mueller to the Cubs for bullpen help in the form of middle reliever Tim Worrell. Worrell had one of his better seasons in 2000. Worrell was expected to see time as the Giants setup man to Nen. Don't bank on Worrell repeating his ERA and Ratio success on 2000.

Also in the Giants stable are Miguel Del Toro and Aaron Fultz. Del Toro is a 28-year-old with limited prospects, if that.

At 27, Fultz has a little more potential. He had an excellent second half as a middleman for the Giants and will pitch in the same role in 2001. Expect more innings for him now that Doug Henry signed with the Royals. Fultz will have little value come draft time, but could be one of those relievers who wins eight games.

If you are searching for minor league help at closer within the San Francisco ranks, you must go to Bakersfield, where Jason Bullard converted 30 saves last year (65 strikeouts, over 65 innings). One other name to watch is Todd Ozais, who saved 21, and whiffed 61 over 52 innings.

RECOMMENDATION REVIEW: Rob Nen will continue to be one of the top closers in the game. Expect him to be among the league leaders in saves, ERA and Ratio. Should Nen get hurt, Rodriguez has the stuff to be a closer. Worrell could also vulture some saves and a few wins, but his career year was last season.

TOP 2001 SAVES LEADERS

NAME	SV
Robb Nen	43
Trevor Hoffman	42
Antonio Alfonseca	40
Armando Benitez	40
Danny Graves	33
Jeff Shaw	33
Matt Mantei	29
Dave Veres	28
Ricky Bottalico	25
John Rocker	25
Billy Wagner	25
Mike Williams	24
Rick Aguilera	22
Jose Jimenez	22
Ugueth Urbina	22
Jeff Brantley	21
Jose Mesa	21
Curt Leskanic	20
Octavio Dotel	15
Kerry Ligtenberg	11
Scott Strickland	11
Steve Kline	9
Mike Remlinger	8
Felix Heredia	6
Mike Fetters	5
Byung Kim	5
Todd Van Poppel	5
Gabe White	5
Jason Christiansen	4
Kyle Farnsworth	4
John Franco	4
Tom Gordon	4
Jerry Spradlin	4
Mike Timlin	4
Juan Acevedo	3
Jamie Arnold	3
Wayne Gomes	3
Mike Morgan	3
Matt Morris	3
Steve Rain	3
Felix Rodriguez	3
Scott Sullivan	3
Anthony Telford	3
Terry Adams	2
Dennis Cook	2
Jerry Dipoto	2
Aaron Fultz	2
Scott Kamieniecki	2
Rich Loiselle	2
Danny Miceli	2
Rudy Seanez	2
Heath Slocumb	2
Joe Slusarski	2
Turk Wendell	2
Rick White	2
Scott Williamson	2
Mark Wohlers	2
Tim Worrell	2

IN SEARCH OF THE IDEAL DRAFT PICK
"AGE 26 WITH EXPERIENCE"

by John Benson

The best stars at bargain prices in 2001 will be the same type of players who have been the best stars at bargain prices for many years: the improving young stars who don't look like improving young stars on paper.

Rookies always look like the youngsters they are. Sometimes an old rookie will look young on paper, because he has no track record in the majors. Rookies will be overbid for two reasons. One reason is that we look at rookies and see what they have done in the minors and tend to believe their success will translate immediately into major league production. Bill James proved long ago that minor league stats really do indicate major league potential, if you know how to interpret minor league stats. Some youngsters never get a chance, although they are deserving based on talent. Sometimes youngsters do get a chance, but it still takes a while for them to realize their potential; even Barry Bonds hit .223 as a rookie.

The second reason that rookies get overrated is because of all the publicity they get. Think how good Ruben Mateo looked two years ago. (He hit .238 as a rookie.) Even dark-horse rookies get overrated. At least one rookie will come out of nowhere and hit ten home runs in spring training this year, win a job, and sell for $20 on draft day, when he doesn't look like more than a $5 player today. That is the nature of excitement about rookies and the peculiarity of spring training stats.

The well-established superstars will all sell for high prices — higher than ever — because we have come to know them and love them. The star hitters will thrive like never before in 2001, and the star pitchers have all been elevated in stature by the arrival of a new lower class at the bottom of the pitching profession. So prices of star pitchers will also soar.

The bargains, and there will be plenty of them in 2001, will come from a mixture of true sleepers and also from players who will be systematically underrated by the Rotisserie world of 2001. The rest of this essay deals with some of those most likely to be underrated, and why.

The most probable bargains have a definite profile. First and foremost, they have not yet had their career year. If there is one simple method to separate good picks from bad picks, it is this: players who have not yet had their career year tend to make good picks. Not only we do know that such players are likely to improve; also we can't put any ceiling on how good they might become. There is lots of room for a pleasant surprise. Players who have already had their career year have a known ceiling, and the limit of a pleasant surprise from them would be a return to their past peak level.

So we are talking about younger players. And because most of the rookies and newcomers will be over-touted and many of them will struggle and fail, we want young players who have been around the major leagues for a couple of years or longer, but still haven't reached their full potential. The experience factor is key. After a couple of years, we think we know what a player can do. In most cases that's true, because in most cases, players don't become major league regulars until age 26 or 27, and by the time they have two years experience, they really have reached their peak.

The players who become major league regulars at younger ages are better players. They have achieved major league competence earlier, with less experience. They are the best athletes and the quickest learners. They are likely to be stars, and all superstars have this characteristic of reaching the majors and getting two or more years experience before age 27. And so all superstars pass through this list on their way up.

The typical player peaks around age 27 or 28. Those age 26

and under are still improving, but if they have been in the majors long enough to give an impression that they have reached an "established" level, they will be underestimated in most Rotisserie drafts (those without owners who have read this essay). The following players all fit this ideal profile: enough experience to give a false impression of having reached their peak or passed it, and enough youth to prove big talent and to offer big upward possibilities.

There are still some analysts who don't believe that players age 21 to 26 will continue improving after they have shown what they can in a couple of years in the majors. These analysts told you last year that Johnny Damon, age 26, had proven his full potential in his first two years, hitting .277-18-66-26 and then .307-14-77-36. They told you to look for numbers like .292-16-72-31, an average of the his two years. But here in this essay last year, we told you that Damon ought to steal 40 bases for the first time in 2000 and ought to hit .320 for the next five years. And if you got Damon, you enjoyed the stats already: .327-16-88-46.

This method is called "Age 26 with Experience." The method has been explained in past editions of the Rotisserie Baseball Annual. The list has grown longer in recent years as more of the youth influx from expansion has moved up the minors and into the majors and now have two years experience. These are the leading picks, according to this method, for 2001:

1. ADRIAN BELTRE - With a .272 average over the last three years, no year higher than .290, no season with more than 20 homers, and no season with more than 85 RBI, Beltre's forecast here of .300-25-90 (all career highs) with 14 stolen bases to boot, might appear optimistic. It's actually a bit cautious. One of the fun parts of doing this essay every year is telling how much better these players might be than their base case, most likely forecast. Beltre's second half 2000, times two, is .316-26-98-12. So if we believe that Beltre improved during the year 2000, and might easily improve a bit more at his tender age, then it's easy to see .320-30-100+ for Beltre this year and .330-30-110 one year soon.

2. GABE KAPLER - The $14 value in 2000 based on his .302-14-66-8 performance doesn't tell the story. We're looking for a 50% surge in value to $21 (uninflated) with a base case forecast of .312-21-80-11. And he can easily go higher, like .335-20-100-8 which is his second half 2000 times two.

3. MIGUEL TEJADA - If you think .275-30-115 was a career year last year, hold on to your hat. Looking at the second half of that output, times two, yields a .299-34-110 season. So we can see 35 homers and a .300 average in the offing. And his defense isn't bad, either. Like most of the guys on this list, he is improving continuously while we just try to get a read on how good he is in a full year. And we still don't know how good that is.

4. RICHARD HIDALGO - Making his second annual appearance in these pages, Hidalgo at age 25 is still improving quite visibly. He's a five-tool player with smarts growing rapidly. If you think 2000 was a bust-out season with a .314-44-122-13 line, try his second half times two: .332-42-124-16.

5. TROY GLAUS - The guy who broke all of Mark McGwire's home run records in the PAC-10, Glaus soared to 47 homers and 102 RBI last year. Can he go higher? Yes. Glaus has a 50-homer bat in his hands, and this .257 career hitter won't hit as low as .257 again until he's age 40.

6. ERIC CHAVEZ - Expect career highs across the board for this talented 23-year-old. Tell people about his .267 career average and career high of 86 RBI, and then don't be surprised when he hits .300-30-100 this year. Even at .288-27-90 he will be a bargain in any auction where all owners (but one) think they already know what he can do. This career is just beginning.

7. CRISTIAN GUZMAN - In his two years of stumbling toward a .239 career average, Guzman has nonetheless shown steady improvement in strike zone judgment and ability to drive the ball more consistently. Whether he's a leadoff batter or a number three, Guzman will reach career highs in every category in 2001.

8. DEIVI CRUZ - Using the second half times two method, look for .317-12-102 in 2001. Even if he doesn't reach those levels, Cruz will be a bargain for anyone bidding against folks who look at his three-year average of .284-9-62.

9. JUAN ENCARNACION - If we just take some things he's done already in one of his first two seasons, Encarnacion looks like .289-19-74-33. He is still learning to play center field with fluidity, still learning to read pitchers' moves so he can get a better jump on steals, and still learning what to look for when at the plate. Seeing a .300-100-30-30 year isn't just wild imagining, though it may not come until 2002 or 2003.

10. ANDRUW JONES - Still just age 24, The Next Willie Mays just passed .300 for the first time in 2000. Has he had his breakout year yet? No. While it may not be 2001, Jones has the skills to be a 40-40 guy. Getting 40 homers and 30 steals with a .300 average and 100+ RBI will be a good deal for whatever he costs this year.

11. VLADIMIR GUERRERO - More evidence that all superstars pass through this list, Guerrero is making his third consecutive annual appearance hear, and he will be back for one more year in 2001. Putting him here two years ago probably helped more people by a wider margin than will this year's appearance. Just be confident while bidding. Amazingly, he really does have some remaining upward potential.

12. DEREK JETER - Hitting .351 in the second half of 2000 says something.

13. SEAN CASEY - So does hitting .372 in the second half.

14. GEOFF JENKINS - The young slugger popped 21 of his 34 homers after July 1 last year.

15. PRESTON WILSON - His second half times two is .282-28-122-48, which was worth $41. Check the stolen bases especially.

16. ALEX RODRIGUEZ - The Rangers new shortstop seems like he's been on this list forever, and 2001 isn't his last year, either. Don't forget he stole 46 bases in 1998.

17. DERREK LEE - The man who struck out profusely while hitting .233 and .206 in 1998 and 1999 respectively, produced a .290 average in the second half of 2000. We haven't yet seen a 30-homer year, but it's coming.

18. CARLOS LEE - The .324 average in the second half is a clue of things to come. Defense remains an issue, and scouts generally feel that getting adjusted to the majors in his mind will get him better adjusted with his bat.

19. TORII HUNTER - Yes it's true, for guys on this list we do get a bit obsessive about second half stats from last year. Hunter's effort times two is .332-10-70-8, which was worth $15. As a just reward for his sterling defense, Hunter will play more in 2001 than ever before.

20. CARLOS FEBLES - After an injury-riddled season, sitting on a .261 career average, and having never produced more than 20 steals with his good speed, Febles is primed to be among the pleasant surprises of 2001. Within reach are 30 steals, double-digit homers, and a .270-.280 batting average.

Honorable mention:

ARAMIS RAMIREZ - With a reputation for bad fielding, demotions back to the minors in each of the last three years, and with a .239 career average, Ramirez is not on anyone's "rising stars" list — except ours. A talented young hitter like this will not be held back for defense; he is just age 22. Left field is always a possibility, and improved fielding with the benefit of major league coaching at third base is an even better possibility. And as so often works for these youngsters, let's go to the second half stats, times two: .281-10-52 in 306 at-bats. So whatever is says for the base case forecast in our tables in the back pages, picture a ball curve that includes a 35% probability of a .280-15-70 season for 2001 and some .300-20-90 seasons coming soon.

CARLOS BELTRAN - Coming off a disappointing .247-7-44-13 season, with injuries and a bad rep for refusing a rehab assignment, Beltran's stock will be down for draft day this year. So buy him cheap. Returning to the .290-20-100-20 levels that he passed in 1999 is clearly within easy reach, and we still don't know how good he can be when he's mature, healthy and out of the doghouse.

ALEX GONZALEZ - Another victim of the sophomore slump, Gonzalez should be available for a dollar or two this year. His .200 average last year ought to scare off most bidders. He improved to .246 in the second half, and is just one year removed from his .277-14-59 season in 1999.

Rounding out the list are Richie Sexson, Scott Rolen, J.D. Drew, Ben Grieve, Fernando Tatis, Jose Vidro, Brad Fullmer, Jose Cruz, Jacque Jones, Neifi Perez, Paul Konerko, Mark Kotsay, Luis Castillo, Edgard Renteria, Roger Cedeno, Placido Polanco, Frank Catalanotto, Wilton Guerrero, Trot Nixon, Randy Winn, Orlando Cabrera, Jeremy Giambi, Bobby Estalella, Bobby Smith, Enrique Wilson, Michael Barrett, Jose Guillen, Ron Belliard, Travis Lee, Todd Dunwoody and Mark L. Johnson. Just missing the list on account of experience requirements (two years experience, but not full seasons) are Ben Davis and Jerry Hairston.

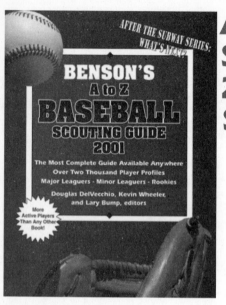
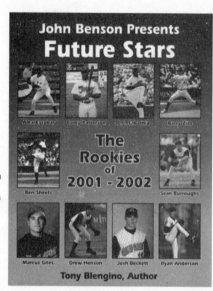

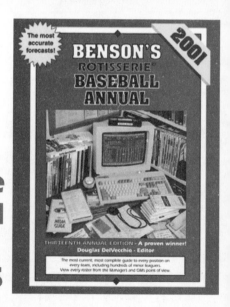

THE ARIZONA FALL LEAGUE WHO'S REALLY WHO:
The Insiders Talk
by Tony Blengino

In one of the more pleasant rituals of fall developed in the past decade, the best young baseball talent again trooped to the Great Southwest to participate in the Arizona Fall League in October. Six prospects were sent from each of the 30 major league organizations to fill out the rosters of the Grand Canyon Rafters, Maryvale Saguaros, Mesa Solar Sox, Peoria Javelinas, Phoenix Desert Dogs and Scottsdale Scorpions. The AFL has established itself as a unique testing ground for the game's foremost young prospects -- for many, it is their first crack at an advanced level of competition, and has often served to certify top prospects' pedigrees. Below are the 2000 AFL All-Star (based upon current-year AFL performance) and All-Prospect (based on long-term potential) teams.

FIRST BASE:
All-Star: Hee Seop Choi (Mesa; Cubs) - This young man is the reason that the Cubs let Mark Grace walk. He only has 122 at bats of Double-A experience under his belt, and is likely not yet quite ready for the majors. He's close, however -- say, a half season away -- and will be immediately productive when he arrives. He batted .298 for Mesa, and drilled over half of his hits for extra bases, compiling a hefty .577 slugging percentage. He also showed a good eye at the plate, easily leading the league in walks with 24.

All-Prospect: Choi

SECOND BASE:
All-Star: Marcus Giles (Mesa; Braves) - Yup, Brian's little brother is on his way to being a star in his own right at the major league level. This 5'8", 180, block of granite tore up the AFL at a .359 clip, driving nearly 40% of his hits for extra bases en route to a .543 slugging percentage. He put the ball in play consistently, striking out only 12 times in 93 at bats. He continues to make great strides with the glove, and is on track to be an above average defender in the majors. He'll likely log a full year at Triple-A in 2001, and will then settle in for a long run with the Braves.

All-Prospect: Giles

SHORTSTOP:
All-Star: Jimmy Rollins (Maryvale; Phillies) - This 5'8", 160, switch-hitting catalyst was quite possibly the most exciting player in the AFL this season. Though clearly not a home run hitter, Rollins has surprising pop to the gaps for his size, can dominate with his speed and aggressiveness on the bases, and has worked hard to become an above average defender. He batted .286 in Arizona despite a late-season slump, and ranked among league leaders with four triples and 11 steals. Rollins is a near shoo-in to be the Phillies' starting shortstop and leadoff man this season, and will be a strong contender for NL Rookie of the Year honors.

All-Prospect: Rollins, as Mariners' stud Antonio Perez only had 59 at bats, and was used primarily as a designated hitter.

THIRD BASE:
All-Star: Albert Pujols (Cardinals; Scottsdale) - A strong AFL campaign capped a whirlwind initial full pro season for this top Cards' prospect. After dominating the Low-A Midwest League, Pujols wound up being a key factor in the Triple-A World Series, and then batted .323 with 10 extra-base hits, a .527 slugging percentage, and only seven strikeouts in 93 Arizona Fall League at bats. He's also well above average with the glove, and could press Fernando Tatis for the hot corner job in St. Louis by late 2001. Pujols' stock is rising sharply.

All-Prospect: Sean Burroughs (Padres; Peoria) - It sure seems like this guy has been around forever, but believe it or not, he's still only 20 years old. Sure, he may have batted only .219 in the AFL, but he did show trademark plate discipline (14 walks), and managed to crack as many homers (two) in 73 at bats as he did in a full Double-A season last year. This guy hit .291 with gaps power as a 19-year-old in Double-A last year -- he's just beginning to develop into a man, and the eventual results are likely to be scary. Hopefully, the Padres won't rush him to the majors this April - he's not ready to achieve there yet. He will be in 2002.

OUTFIELD:
All-Star: Kevin Mench (Rangers; Grand Canyon), Donzell McDonald (Yankees; Maryvale), Tike Redman (Pirates; Peoria) - Ladies and gentlemen: Kevin Mench is becoming a monster. The Rangers' 1999 fourth round draftee from that noted baseball factory -- the University of Delaware -- assaulted High-A Florida State League pitching last year in his first full pro season, and kept right on going in Arizona. He batted a lusty .354 for Grand Canyon, with nearly 40% of his hits going for extra bases as he compiled a lusty .596 slugging percentage. Oh -- and the Rangers used the names of Mench and fellow top Ranger prospect Carlos Pena effectively to help lure Alex Rodriguez to Texas, holding their development up as evidence of the club's commitment to winning over the duration of A-Rod's megacontract. Now that's an endorsement.

Faded 26-year-old speedster Donzell McDonald was a last-minute addition to the Maryvale roster, and he just might have saved his professional future with a command AFL performance. He finished second in the league in hitting at .354, and led the AFL in runs scored (29), hits (45), triples (5), stolen bases (18), and on-base percentage (.435), thanks in part to his 18 walks. McDonald has been quite injury-prone throughout his pro career, but the switch-hitter has now clearly marked himself as one who could provide the Yanks -- or someone else -- with a dangerous multipurpose threat off of the bench in the majors this season.

Pirates' outfield prospect Tike Redman showed signs of developing into a credible leadoff-hitting prospect in the AFL. After walking only 32 times in 538 Triple-A plate appearances last season, Redman drew 15 walks in 130 times to the plate in the AFL. Combined with his .304 batting average, those free passes gave Redman a fine .385 on-base percentage, and he also showed gaps power, nailing nearly a third of his hits for extra bases en route to a .470 slugging percentage. Look for him to be a primary outfield backup for the Bucs at the major league level in 2001 - he has a shot to be their near-term leadoff man.

All-Prospect: Mench, Brian Cole (Mets; Scottsdale), Dee Brown (Royals; Grand Canyon) - Brian Cole is one exciting player to watch, a 5'9", 168, bolt of lightning with surprising extra-base pop. He batted .289 and stole seven

bases in the AFL, and drove fully half of his hits for extra bases, compiling a .530 slugging percentage. However, he is often miscast as a top-of-the-order prospect, which is inconsistent with his total lack of patience at the plate -- he walked just three times in 86 AFL plate appearances. He's likely in line for a full Triple-A season in 2001, but could well be the Mets' center fielder in 2002.

No one can argue with Dee Brown's raw power potential. Though he only went deep twice in Arizona, he drilled over a third of his hits for extra bases, batting .277 and slugging .436 for Grand Canyon. However, Brown's output continues to be limited by his insistence on swinging at darned near every pitch thrown to him. He drew just 37 walks in 516 Triple-A plate appearances last season, and compounded matters by drawing only five free passes in 106 AFL trips. If Johnny Damon isn't a Royal in 2002, Brown will likely make the club and play a complementary role. He won't thrive, however, unless he suddenly develops some patience.

CATCHER:
All-Star: Brandon Inge (Tigers; Scottsdale) - Inge was a shortstop until fairly recently, and continues to make rapid progress towards contention for at least a share of the Tigers' big league catching job as soon as late this season. His defense is solid -- he moves well behind the plate and has a strong arm. The switch-hitter is beginning to pick up the pace with the bat -- he hit .293 in the AFL, with improved plate discipline (11 walks in 86 plate appearances) and decent extra-base pop (three homers, .467 slugging percentage). With a big spring, he'd be a sleeper to break north as the backup to Mitch Meluskey.

All-Prospect: Inge, narrowly over Diamondback power prospect Brad Cresse, who batted .169 and struggled defensively as Inge's Scottsdale backup.

PITCHER:
All-Star: Joaquin Benoit (Rangers; Grand Canyon), Matt Kinney (Twins; Grand Canyon), Kyle Lohse (Twins; Grand Canyon), Chris Reitsma (Reds; Grand Canyon), Matt Miller (Tigers; Scottsdale) - At 21, Benoit was one of the younger AFL pitching prospects, and arguably its most impressive. He's always had above average stuff and decent control, but put it all together for the first time in Arizona. He went 2-2, 1.91, for Grand Canyon, allowing just 22 hits in 33 innings while fashioning an excellent 28/6 strikeout/walk ratio. He appears to be learning how to set up hitters, and could be pretty scary with a bit more mechanical

fine-tuning. He could help Texas this year, and might be a frontline starter fairly soon.

Matt Kinney went from the Red Sox to the Twins along with high-average outfield prospect John Barnes a couple of years back in exchange for the illustrious Orlando Merced. Ouch. Once a wild thrower with good stuff, Kinney has gradually tamed his low-90s fastball and nasty slider to a large extent -- he walked only eight batters while striking out 22 in 23 innings in the AFL en route to a 1-2, 1.57, record. He will do battle for a low rotation spot with the Twins this spring. If that doesn't pan out, he could thrive as a late-inning reliever.

It wasn't the greatest of regular seasons for Kyle Lohse, a key part of the return received from the Cubs in the Rick Aguilera deal, at Double-A New Britain in the Twins' system last year. In fact, 3-18, 6.04, is downright awful. How then, does one explain his subsequent 3-0, 1.80, 35/7 strikeout/walk ratio in 35 innings tour de force in the AFL? A little mechanical tinkering gave his pitches more bite, turning line drive singles into tame infield outs. He did post a solid 124/55 strikeout/walk ratio in 167 innings along with his horrible 2000 regular season numbers, so the ability has clearly been there all along. He'll take a regular turn at age 22 at the Triple-A level this season, so he's on schedule for eventual big league success. The Pacific Coast League will provide a clear litmus test of his ability in 2001.

Former Red Sox #1 pick Chris Reitsma was dispatched to the Reds in last year's Dante Bichette deal. Though he has been plagued by injuries and never developed the power once hoped for by the Bosox, he appears to be developing into quite a craftsman on the mound. He fashioned an excellent 21/4 strikeout/walk ratio in 25 innings in the AFL, allowing only 18 hits en route to a 2-0, 1.44, record. His fastball only reaches about 90 MPH, but his pitches move sharply and he keeps the ball down. He's likely a year away from the majors, but could be a fit as a low-end starter or situational righty reliever.

Matt Miller of the Scottsdale Scorpions is the only non-Grand Canyon Rafters' hurler on the All-Star squad. Sure, this Tigers' lefty is already 26, and lacks the high-octane stuff to be truly considered a top prospect. However, Miller consistently throws strikes, and appears to be learning how to better locate the ball within the strike zone. He took well to a lefthanded setup role in Arizona after starting throughout his minor leaguer career -- how's 5-0, 1.25, with a 20/4 strikeout/walk ratio and only 17 hits allowed in 21 2/3 innings

grab you? He's a sleeper to steal a lefty relief slot with the Tigers this season, and could be a pleasant surprise.

All-Prospect: Benoit, Kinney, Nick Neugebauer (Brewers; Maryvale), Danys Baez (Indians; Phoenix), Chad Hutchinson (Cardinals; Scottsdale) -- Nick Neugebauer -- one of the youngest 2000 AFL players at 20 -- is one scary, albeit quite raw pitcher. In fact, thrower might be a better word at this point. He combines an upper-90s heater with a devastating slider, and his changeup should eventually be a credible third pitch. He has routinely struck out and walked over a batter per inning throughout his pro career, but really focused on throwing strikes in Arizona. He only walked 14 in 28 innings -- great for him -- but allowed 30 hits and "only" struck out 23, quite poor for him, en route to a 1-3, 5.14, record. He's making progress, but will likely need one to two more years of minor league seasoning before getting to Milwaukee. He could be an ace starter or top closer in the majors, but could just as likely implode.

The Indians dumped a whole lot of cash into Danys Baez, 23, but all he has shown since being signed a year ago has been occasional flashes of brilliance. His mid-90s fastball and power curve could develop into centerpieces of a top major league starter's repertoire, but he still has work to do with regard to mechanics and pitch sequencing, and could really stand to develop his changeup into a quality third pitch. His 22/8 strikeout/walk ratio and total of 21 hits allowed in 24 AFL innings were positives, but struggles with men on base resulted in a 1-2, 4.01, record. He'll likely start 2001 at the Triple-A level, but the Indians need him to make major strides very soon and help out in the major league stretch run this year.

Months before Rick Ankiel's control blew up in the 2000 postseason, the Cards' other top pitching prospect, Chad Hutchinson, similarly melted down at the Triple-A level, walking an incredible 27 batters in eight innings before a well-deserved demotion. Though he's still not Greg Maddux by any means, Hutchinson appears to have navigated that rocky stretch of terrain without major incident, however. He unfurled a respectable 38/23 strikeout/walk ratio in 33 AFL innings, allowing 26 hits while posting a 2-1, 4.64, record. Hutchinson still has the mid-90s heater and hard slider that once made him every bit as attractive a prospect as Ankiel, but needs to dominate Triple-A hitters right away in 2001 to remain in the forefront of the Cards' starting rotation plans. A career in short relief could be a viable backup option -- either way, look for him in St. Louis by late this season.

TABBING THE BEST LONG-TERM PROSPECTS EARLY
by Tony Blengino

What do the names Cliff Floyd, Jim Thome, Manny Ramirez, Carlos Delgado, Chipper Jones, Roger Cedeno, Dmitri Young, Alex Rodriguez, Shawn Green, Bob Abreu, Mike Sweeney, Darin Erstad, Vladimir Guerrero, Johnny Damon, Andruw Jones, Adrian Beltre, Scott Rolen, Nomar Garciaparra, Paul Konerko, Ben Grieve, Russell Branyan, Lance Berkman, Eric Chavez, Troy Glaus, Carlos Beltran and Pat Burrell have in common? Or pitchers such as Bartolo Colon, Billy Wagner, Jeff D'Amico, Sidney Ponson, Kerry Wood, Eric Milton, Carl Pavano, Tony Armas, Scott Elarton, Brett Tomko, Rick Ankiel, Brad Penny, and Bruce Chen? These players are both a veritable Who's Who of current and near-future major league stars, and a partial list of alumni from my Relative Production Potential and Relative Control/Power Potential lists from recent years. Many other RPP and RCPP alumni are on the verge of joining their peers on that list after they make noisy big league entrances in the near-term future.

Relative Production Potential ranks minor league hitters by combined on-base and slugging percentage, adjusted for league context and prospect age in relation to minor league level. Relative Control/Power Potential ranks minor league pitchers by combined strikeout/walk and strikeout/nine innings pitched ratio, also adjusted for league context and prospect age in relation to minor league level. These methods allow an 18-year-old's Class A hitting or pitching performance to be meaningfully compared to a 22-year-old's Triple-A performance. These methods identify the prospects with the most long-term - -but not necessarily near-term -- potential. The end result is ordered lists of approximately 300 position player and 200 pitching prospects.

Let's check out this year's Top Ten hitting and pitching prospects.

THE HITTERS

1 - Mariners' High-A shortstop Antonio Perez is this year's top ranked hitter, following in the footsteps of such luminaries as Alex Rodriguez, Andruw Jones, Adrian Beltre and others. A key part of the return received from the Reds in the Ken Griffey deal. Perez torched the High-A California League at the tender age of 18 last season. As that circuit's youngest player, he batted .276 with 36 doubles, six triples, 17 homers, 28 steals and a .527 slugging percentage. Though he stands just 5'11", 175, he's still growing and could well evolve into the AL's next great power shortstop. And coincidentally, shortstop now appears to be wide open in Seattle -- one more year of seasoning, and Perez will step into A-Rod's considerable shoes.

2 - Pirates' 1999 fifth round pick J.R. House, 20 in 2000, led a prospect-studded Low-A Augusta roster last season. He took to the wooden bat quite easily, carving up South Atlantic League pitching to the tune of a .348 average, 29 doubles, 23 homers and a .586 slugging percentage. The 6'1", 202, House needs quite a bit of work behind the plate, but could evolve into an average big league receiver with the glove, or a solid first sacker. However, this high school football legend is considering whether to play football -- as the University of West Virginia's starting quarterback -- in addition to baseball next season. He'll likely be a star at whichever sport he chooses, and should arrive in Pittsburgh in late 2002 or 2003, depending on his level of commitment to baseball.

3 - Rangers' 1999 fourth round draftee Kevin Mench has exploded onto the scene and become one of the game's foremost power prospects. He was a bit old at 22 for the High-A Florida State League last season, but confirmed any doubts about his legitimacy as a prospect by torching the Arizona Fall League after the season. He hit .334 with 39 doubles, nine triples, 27 homers, 121 RBI, 19 steals and a .615 slugging percentage during the regular season, and then hit .354 and slugged .596 in the AFL. This former NCAA home run champ has obviously taken to the wooden bat quite well, and his existence (along with first base prospect Carlos Pena) was cited as one of the reasons above and beyond the $252 million that Alex Rodriguez decided to go to Texas. He should fly towards the majors and arrive to stay this September.

4 - Mariners' Low-A outfielder Chris Snelling was one of the youngest players in a full-season minor league in 2000 at 18. He didn't just hold his own, excelling in the Low-A Midwest League, batting .305 with nine doubles, five triples, nine homers and a .483 slugging percentage in 259 at bats before losing the second half of the season to a thumb injury. The 5'10", 165, lefthanded hitter possesses a solid combination of on-base and power skills, and is likely to be a snug fit in any of four or five different slots in a major league batting order. If his power continues to intensify as he advances through the system, his upside will expand. Look for him in the majors by sometime in 2003, at the latest.

5 - Reds' Low-A outfielder Austin Kearns, their 1998 first round draft pick, is one of the best pure power prospects in the game today. He ravaged the Low-A Midwest League at age 20 last season, batting .306 with 37 doubles, 27 homers, 104 RBI, 90 walks, 18 steals, a .415 on-base percentage and .558 slugging percentage. That, my friends, is a well-rounded offensive package. Toss in his howitzer right field throwing arm and you've got a slam-dunk for future major league success. Homering in his first spring training at bat last season didn't hurt his standing with the Reds' front office either. He'll likely be a Double-A standout this year, and could do battle for a starting job in Cincy as early as 2002.

6 - Expos' and US Olympic team outfield prospect Brad Wilkerson earned this high ranking on the strength of his 229-at bat tour de force at Double-A Harrisburg, where he batted .336 with an amazing 36 doubles at age 23 last season. On the other hand, however, the Expos' 1998 first round draftee struggled in Triple-A after a midseason promotion, and then in the Olympics and the Arizona Fall League after the 2000 season, and he has not developed the expected home run power envisioned by his parent club. He was mentioned quite often in trade rumors early in the offseason, and doesn't appear to be a lock to make the big club should he remain an Expo. His upside is lower than most of the other prospects on this list, but he could develop into a steady .280, 40-double, 20-homer type, and should arrive in the majors sometime this year.

7 - The Marlins got both pitcher Brad Penny and this year's #7 finisher, outfielder Abraham Nunez, in 1999's Matt Mantei deal. At age 20, Nunez was one of the youngest players in the Double-A Eastern League last season. He's a power/speed threat who batted .276 with 17 doubles and six homers in just 221 at bats at that level, while drawing 44 walks, stealing eight bases and recording a .392 on-base percentage and .462 slugging percentage. While those numbers are fine, especially for his age, he has only begun to scratch the surface of his potential. He was limited to predominantly designated hitter duty by a shoulder injury last season, but still projects as a fine center or right fielder because of solid range and arm strength. He likely needs another full year of seasoning, hopefully injury-free, but should battle for a job in South Florida in 2002.

8 - After finishing at #3 on this list in 1999, Padres' third base prospect Sean Burroughs checks in here this year. Critics like to point out Burroughs' lack of home run power at this stage in his development -- in 2000, he managed just two homers in 450 plate appearances at Double-A Mobile. A closer look reveals that Burroughs, at age 19, was the youngest regular at his level last season, and batted a lusty .291 with 29 doubles, many of which will become homers as his physical maturation continues. He struck out only 45 times while drawing 58 walks -- a truly remarkable ratio for a teenager at such a high level of competition. There have been some rumblings that the Padres might run him out there at third base at the major league level this season -- while I consider that misguided, I don't believe he is far from ready. In a best-case scenario, Burroughs would have a power-laced first half at the Triple-A level, then move in for the long haul in San Diego.

9 - Diamondbacks' catching prospect Brad Cresse is the only 2000 draftee in this year's Top Ten. Consider this fifth round pick's immediate impact - he batted .324 with an amazing 17 homers in 173 at bats and a .659 slugging percentage at High-A High Desert at age 21 before wrapping up the season at the Double-A level. Consider that very few other 2000 draftees even played at either of those levels, let alone starred to that extent. Sure, High Desert is a hitters' paradise, and Cresse did strike out 50 times in his short stint there, and he is a very raw defensive receiver. You simply cannot teach this kind of power potential, however, and his bat will carry him to a sizeable role in the Diamondbacks' lineup by sometime in 2002, whether at catcher or a corner infield position.

10 - It's a double-shot of Diamondbacks in the last two slots in this year's Top Ten, with outfielder/ slugger Jack Cust nailing down the last berth. He ranked second on last year's list, and remains highly rated on the strength of a Double-A campaign in which he batted .293 with 32 doubles, 20 homers, 117 walks, 12 steals, a .440 on-base percentage and .526 slugging percentage at age 21. The many comparisons of the lefthanded Cust to the Indians' Jim Thome are quite apt -- he has that kind of extreme power and an excellent eye, but swings incredibly hard and through a lot of pitches, resulting in extreme strikeout rates (150 last season). He's worked hard on his defense, but remains a borderline passable left fielder whose future could lie, like Thome, at first base. He'll likely make a play for a full-time job in Arizona in late 2001 or early 2002, and will be a long-term big league run producer.

THE PITCHERS

1 - The Mariners' Ryan Anderson finished 11th on the 1998 RCPP list, seventh in 1999, and now rises all the way to the top of the 2000 list. The 6'10", 215, Randy Johnson-like lefty overpowered Triple-A Pacific Coast League hitters at the tender age of 20 last season, compiling an amazing 146/55 strikeout/walk ratio in only 104 innings, allowing just 83 hits. He was a bit shaky with men on base, causing his record to be a subpar 5-8, with a 3.98 ERA. The sky is the limit if he tweaks his mechanics a bit and gets a little more sharpness on his breaking pitches - he's so far ahead of Johnson command-wise at a similarly age that it's scary. Look for him to take a regular turn for Seattle this season, and show flashes of brilliance in advance of a long run as an All Star. He should be a prime 2001 AL Rookie of the Year candidate.

2 - Red Sox' righthander Paxton Crawford earned this high ranking on the strength of nine excellent Double-A starts at age 22, in which he posted a stellar 54/6 strikeout/walk ratio in 52 innings en route to a 2-3, 3.10, record. While I will be the first to admit that Crawford is simply not as good as those particular numbers suggest, he still looks like a long-term keeper for the Red Sox. The

6'3", 205, righty has four viable major league pitches, and while his high-80's fastball won't blow major league hitters away, he will place it on the corners with some regularity, and set it up well with his breaking pitches. Crawford is not a budding staff ace, but should earn a mid-rotation slot in Boston this year and hold it for the foreseeable future.

3 - Twins' righthander Adam Johnson is the only 2000 draftee on this Top Ten list of minor league pitching prospects. The Twins supposedly snagged him with their first round pick -- the second overall selection -- because of his signability, not his upside. Well, he apparently has quite bit of talent to boot. He overwhelmed High-A Florida State League hitters right out of the chute at age 20, allowing just 45 hits in 69 innings and posting a spectacular 92/20 strikeout/walk ratio en route to a 5-4, 2.47, record. The 6'2", 210, righty combines a live 90 MPH fastball and a tight slider, and could develop into an ace-level prospect with improvement of his changeup. Double-A will be a telling test for Johnson in 2001 - if he continues to strike out a batter per inning there, he'll be good bet to slide right into the Twins' rotation for the long haul in 2002.

4 - Astros' Double-A righthander Roy Oswalt devastated the opposition in both the Double-A Texas League and the Olympic Games last season at age 22. After making the scary two-level jump from Low-A ball that has defeated many above average pitching prospects, Oswalt excelled by any measure, recording an 11-4, 1.94, mark with a scintillating 141/22 strikeout/walk ratio and only 106 hits allowed in 130 innings. He kept it rolling in the Olympics, recording a 1.38 ERA and a 10/3 strikeout/ walk ratio over 13 innings. He relies on extreme precision and change of speeds for his success, as he stands just 6'0", 170. While his low-90s fastball moves well, it is not overpowering. His nasty curve is a lethal out pitch, even against lefty hitters. He could help out in Houston later this season, and should be successful if he keeps the ball down at Enron Field.

5 - Pirates' 1999 first round draft pick Bobby Bradley overwhelmed the Low-A South Atlantic League last season as a 19-year-old. The 6'1", 164, righthander's biting curveball would be one of the best in the majors right now, and it just wasn't fair to lower level competition -- he compiled an excellent 118/21 strikeout/walk ratio while allowing only 62 hits in 83 innings at Hickory, posting an

8-2, 2.29, mark. His fastball peaks around 90 MPH, and he places it well. Improvement of his changeup into a viable third pitch for use against lefthanded hitters will complete the package, and pronounce him ready to dominate Double-A hitters this season. Look for him in the major leagues by sometime in 2002 -- he should be a long-term big league force.

6 - Flamethrowing righthander Chin-Hui Tsao should test the hypothesis that a pure power pitcher should be relatively unaffected by the high altitude of Coors Field when he arrives in the majors, likely by late 2002. The 6'2", 178, Tsao tore through Low-A South Atlantic League hitters at age 19, compiling a 187/40 strikeout/walk ratio while allowing only 119 hits in 145 innings en route to an 11-8, 2.73, record. He features a heavy mid-90s fastball and already has developed an advanced slider and changeup for his age. A little more natural physical development should add still more velocity, and could make him one truly scary customer. Look for him to excel at the Double-A level by the end of this year, and crash the big league party by late 2002.

7 - Angels' righthander Francisco Rodriguez was one of 2000's breakthrough prospects, overmatching High-A California League hitters at the tender age of 18. He allowed just 43 hits in 64 innings, compiling a gaudy 79/32 strikeout/walk ratio and a 4-4, 2.81, record in a hitters' league. The 6'0", 165, Rodriguez generates top-shelf velocity from his relatively small frame because of very smooth mechanics -- he consistently reaches the mid-90s with his heater, and also has an advanced slider. He's a changeup away from utter dominance, and has plenty of time to develop one. He should taste Double-A success as a teenager in 2001, a leading indicator of major success in the bigs. He'll arrive by late 2002, and could be a staff ace or top closer down the road.

8 - 1999 White Sox' third round draft pick Jon Rauch has amazingly relegated 6'10" Ryan Anderson to second-tallest status among this year's Top Ten. The 6'11", 230, Rauch came out of nowhere to win a multitude of honors in 2000, including the coveted Baseball America Minor League Player of the Year Award. He also drew raves at the Olympics, where he posted an otherworldly 21/0 strikeout/walk ratio while allowing only six hits in 11 innings, posting a 1-0, 0.82 record. He doesn't throw as hard, but is more polished than Anderson, combining a low-90's fastball that moves well with an above average

curve and slider. His deceptive motion is a major asset, and his mechanics are pretty sound for such a massive guy. He could break north with the Sox with a big spring, and has the look of a future staff ace for a very good White Sox club.

9 - You won't find a cooler customer in the population of minor league pitching prospects than Cardinals' lefty Bud Smith. He sliced through two levels -- including Double-A, where the pretenders are weeded out -- in 2000, going a combined 17-2, throwing two no-hitters, and compiling an excellent 102/27 strikeout/walk ratio and allowing only 93 hits in 109 Double-A innings, going 12-1, 2.32, for Arkansas. He doesn't overpower hitters, but consistently keeps them off balance with his high-80s fastball, nasty curve and above-average changeup, all of which he can throw to the corners with regularity. He did all of this at age 20, by the way. The Cards' major league pitching depth will allow them to give Smith a full Triple-A season in 2001, but he will be more than ready for big league action in 2002.

10 - Indians' lefty C.C. Sabathia rounds out this year's Top Ten. At 6'7", 235, he might be able to box out either Ryan Anderson or Jon Rauch, and he's got the stuff to pitch with them as well. He was overpowering at times at the Double-A level at age 19 last season, but got on this list courtesy of his command performance at High-A Kinston, where he went 3-2, 3.54, with a loud 69/24 strikeout/walk ratio in 56 innings over 10 starts. He's a power pitcher to the core, combining a mid-90s fastball and a power curve. He has made great strides with his control and mechanics, but still needs a little tinkering. A better changeup wouldn't hurt, either. He might win a starting rotation spot in Cleveland this season, but he more likely needs a bit more seasoning. In the near future, he'll become either a top-flight starter or big-time closer.

TOP 30 MINOR LEAGUE HITTERS

NAME	LEVEL	ORG	POS
1-Antonio Perez	HI-A	SEA	SS
2-J.R. House	LO-A	PIT	C
3-Kevin Mench	HI-A	TEX	OF
4-Chris Snelling	LO-A	SEA	OF
5-Austin Kearns	LO-A	CIN	OF
6-Brad Wilkerson	AA	MON	OF
7-Abraham Nunez	AA	FLA	OF
8-Sean Burroughs	AA	SD	3B
9-Brad Cresse	HI-A	AZ	C
10-Jack Cust	AA	AZ	OF
11-Albert Pujols	LO-A	STL	3B
12-Dan Meier	HI-A	PIT	1B
13-Travis Hafner	HI-A	TEX	1B
14-Jorge Moreno	LO-A	CLE	OF
15-Adam Dunn	LO-A	CIN	OF
16-Nate Rolison	AAA	FLA	1B
17-Jeremy Cotten	LO-A	PIT	1B
18-Corey Patterson	AA	CUB	OF
19-Hee Choi	HI-A	CUB	1B
20-Aubrey Huff	AAA	TB	3B
21-Alex Escobar	AA	NYM	OF
22-Willie Bloomquist	HI-A	SEA	2B
23-Brian Cole	HI-A	NYM	OF
24-John Buck	LO-A	HOU	C
25-Jose Ortiz	AAA	OAK	2B
26-Nate Espy	LO-A	PHL	1B
27-Ntema Ndungidi	HI-A	BAL	OF
28-Hank Blalock	LO-A	TEX	3B
29-Scott Hodges	HI-A	MON	3B
30-Carlos Urquiola	HI-A	AZ	OF

TOP 30 MINOR LEAGUE PITCHERS

NAME	ORG	LEVEL
1-Ryan Anderson	SEA	AAA
2-Paxton Crawford	BOS	AA
3-Adam Johnson	MIN	HI-A
4-Roy Oswalt	HOU	AA
5-Bobby Bradley	PIT	LO-A
6-Chin-Hui Tsao	COL	LO-A
7-Francisco Rodriguez	ANA	HI-A
8-Jon Rauch	CWS	AA
9-Bud Smith	STL	AA
10-C.C. Sabathia	CLE	HI-A
11-Jacob Peavy	SD	LO-A
12-Luke Prokopec	LA	AA
13-John Stephens	BAL	HI-A
14-Ruben Quevedo	CUB	AAA
15-Matt Belisle	ATL	HI-A
16-Andy Pratt	TEX	HI-A
17-Nick Neugebauer	MIL	AA
18-Jerome Williams	SF	HI-A
19-Mike Nannini	HOU	HI-A
20-Josh Towers	BAL	AAA
21-Dennis Tankersley	SD	LO-A
22-Ricardo Aramboles	NYY	LO-A
23-Dicky Gonzalez	NYM	AA
24-Josh Beckett	FLA	LO-A
25-Eric Gagne	LA	AAA
26-Colby Lewis	TEX	HI-A
27-Sun-Woo Kim	BOS	AAA
28-John Lackey	ANA	AA
29-Joaquin Benoit	TEX	AA
30-Buddy Carlyle	SD	AAA

The 2000 Amateur Draft Report
by James Bailey & Will Lingo

In the weeks before the 2000 draft, Major League Baseball convened a meeting with the scouting directors for all 30 teams, encouraging everyone to do their part to keep signing bonuses in line.

MLB described it as a negotiating seminar, in which information was provided to help teams when the time came to start dickering dollars after the draft. The word some others used to describe it was collusion. Regardless, the meeting was credited months later with helping some teams hold the line on spiraling bonuses, though the cost in many cases was summer-long holdouts that delayed the pro debuts of numerous early-round picks until 2001.

The tactic many teams used come draft day to ensure signability was to seek out players who were willing to agree to terms ahead of time. Though this type of negotiating is technically against the rules, it was obvious it had occurred when several teams announced the signing of their first-round picks almost immediately after the draft. The Florida Marlins, who held the No. 1 overall pick, were rumored to be seriously considering about a half-dozen players in the week before the draft. They finally settled on first baseman Adrian Gonzalez, who signed on draft day for $3 million.

Texas prep phenom Jason Stokes was one of the players the Marlins were said to be strongly looking at before the draft. Unlike Gonzalez, he refused negotiate before the draft, and he slipped accordingly. But when the Marlins' second turn came at pick No. 41, he was still on the board and they took a stab at him. He did not prove to be an easy sign, holding out for two months before choosing to sign instead of going to college.

Thirteen first-round picks signed within two weeks of the draft, by which point the average signing bonus had decreased nearly 10 percent from 1999. The commissioner's office was pleased. The top agents,

including Scott Boras who represented nine early-round picks, were not. Many teams seemed content to just wait out negotiations on their top picks, figuring this would be the year the other side blinked.

Then along came the Joe Borchard deal. Borchard, an outfielder who doubled as the starting quarterback of the football team at Stanford, signed a record $5.3 million deal with the White Sox in mid-July. His bonus was the largest ever given to a player who signed with the team that drafted him. (Several loophole free agents in 1996 received more.) Though no one came close to Borchard's bonus the rest of the summer, negotiations got creative in many cases, as several players signed deals that included major league contracts, requiring them to be placed on the 40-man roster (though not on the 25-man active roster) in 2001.

By the end of the summer, most of the teams had come to terms with their top picks, though not before at least a dozen players skipped the first days of classes at colleges around the country. Once a player attends classes, he's no longer eligible to sign. The Twins lost two of their top three picks when righthander Aaron Heilman and first baseman Taggert Bozeid chose to return to school after a summer of grueling negotiations.

They were consoled somewhat, however, by the sensational debut of their first selection, righthander Adam Johnson, whom they selected with the second overall pick in the draft out of Cal State Fullerton. Johnson jumped right into the high Class A Florida State League and immediately showed he was up to the competition.

Here's a look at some 2000 draftees, who, like Johnson, seem to have bright futures ahead of them. Players who signed late and did not play were not considered.

AMERICAN LEAGUE

Catcher:

Scott Heard, Rangers: Heard was strongly considered by the Marlins as the No. 1 pick in the draft but his signability and a poor offensive showing in the spring caused him to slip all the way to the Rangers at No. 25. He refound his stroke in the Rookie-level Gulf Coast League, hitting .351 with 16 doubles. But what makes Heard an outstanding prospect is his defense which some scouts say is already near major league average. If he can continue to hit even a little as he climbs, he will reach the big leagues, though it will probably take several years as most high school catchers move a level at a time.

First Base:

Sean Swedlow, Indians: This would be Bozeid had the Twins signed him, but instead Swedlow takes it by default. All of the first basemen who were drafted early went to NL teams. Swedlow, who was a catcher in high school, made the transition to first at Rookie-level Burlington and has a lot of work to do defensively. The Indians' third-round pick has a nice lefthanded stroke, though he hit just .226 without a home run in his debut. Like Heard, he could take awhile to reach the big leagues, but he's also capable of showing dramatic improvement as early as next year.

Second Base:

Chris Amador, White Sox: An eighth-round pick out of Puerto Rico, Amador played shortstop in high school. He came to the White Sox with a reputation as a slap hitter who could run and that's what he showed in the Rookie-level Arizona League. Amador hit .302 without much power and tied the league record with 40 stolen bases. He's already willing to take a walk and could develop into a fine top-of-the-order hitter. When he fills out he'll add a little pop, but that's really not his game.

Third Base:

Corey Smith, Indians: A teammate of Swedlow's at Burlington, Smith showed dramatic improvement as the summer progressed. Though he was error-prone defen-

sively, he has all the tools to become a fine third baseman when he learns how to play the position. A shortstop in high school, he owns a strong arm and he's athletic enough to make just about any play. He's got tremendous power potential and will knock his share of home runs, though he managed only four in his debut while hitting .256. Smith's name was tossed around early as the top high school prospect in his draft class, but others passed him during the spring. The early reports might have been right, however, and he could prove a steal with the No. 26 overall pick.

Shortstop:

Freddie Bynum, Athletics: The A's didn't have a first-round pick thanks to their signing of free agent lefthander Mike Magnante. That was acknowledged later as a front-office snafu. When Oakland called Bynum's name in the second round it was viewed by many as a reach—a big reach. The Pitt County (N.C.) CC product might have been an unknown in June, but by September everyone in the Northwest League knew who he was. He batted just .256 for Vancouver, but stole 22 bases and displayed all-round athleticism that made him the No. 1 prospect in the league. He's raw and could take awhile to get to Oakland, but he definitely has an interesting tool box.

Outfield:

Rocco Baldelli, Devil Rays; Joe Borchard, White Sox; Jamal Strong, Mariners: Baldelli was a four-sport star in high school and had scholarship offers in basketball and volley ball as well as baseball. His athleticism was so attractive that the Devil Rays took him with the No. 6 overall pick even though they have another center fielder named Josh Hamilton who is one of the top prospects in the game. Baldelli can do everything but throw, but he won't move as quickly as Hamilton or some of the other top high school prospects because he comes from Rhode Island where the weather—not to mention his other sporting pursuits—cut into his development in high school. He batted just .216 at Rookie-level Princeton. Borchard, on the other hand, climbed all the way to Double-A Birmingham in his debut. Several teams regarded him as the top talent in the draft, and his fall to 'No. 12 can be chalked up almost entirely to money, though no one expected him to walk away with the $5.3 million deal. He batted .311 with two homers in 103 at-bats at three different stops and is likely to begin the 2001 season back at Birmingham. He's a strong candidate to be the first player from the 2000 draft to reach the big leagues. The Mariners lost their first three draft choices due to free agent signings, so sixth-rounder Strong was their third pick. The speedster from the University of Nebraska was the co-MVP of the Northwest League after hitting .314 and stealing an eye-popping 60 bases.

Righthander:

Adam Johnson, Twins: As mentioned earlier, Johnson enjoyed one of the best debuts of any 2000 draftee, and he did it at a higher level than most of his classmates. Ironically, he was viewed as a signability pick when the Twins chose him second overall. He quickly came to terms on a $2.5 million deal and began wowing the Florida State League almost immediately. In 13 appearances for Fort Myers Johnson went 5-4 with a 2.47 ERA and struck out a staggering 92 hitters in 69 innings. That came with just 45 hits and 20 walks. He had a reputation as a cocky competitor at Fullerton, often showing up opponents after a strikeout. But he's proven he can back it all up. His fastball reaches 94 mph and he certainly knows what to do with it.

Lefthander:

Joe Torres, Angels: Torres struck out a mind-boggling 128 hitters in 55 innings in the spring, so it's easy to see why the Angels were interested in him with the 10th pick in the draft. They had enough confidence to start him at Boise in the Northwest League, which can be a tough assignment for a high school draftee. He was definitely up to the task, going 4-1 with a 2.54 ERA and striking out 52 in 46 innings. The Angels have shown a willingness lately to move pitchers rapidly through the system, jumping 1999 draftee John Lackey twice during his first full season. Torres could be on the express soon himself.

NATIONAL LEAGUE

Catcher:

Brad Cresse, Diamondbacks: Cresse may have had the best debut of any 2000 draftee, starting at high Class A High Desert, where he hit .324 with 17 homers in 173 at-bats, and finishing at Double-A El Paso. High Desert is a notorious home run haven, but Cresse's ratio of a homer every 10 at-bats was sensational nonetheless and proved he was not an aluminum-bat hero. He had an outstanding senior season at Louisiana State, hitting .388 with 30 homers and 106 RBIs to lead the Tigers to the national championship. Baseball America named him to its All-America Team as the DH. The Diamondbacks selected him in the fifth round of the draft, though he'd likely have gone higher if he weren't a senior.

First Base:

Garrett Atkins, Rockies: Atkins, another fifth-round find, was a third-team All-American last spring after hitting .352 with 17 homers and 72 RBIs for UCLA. He had been projected as a higher pick, but questions about his power pushed his stock down. He didn't conclusively answer them over the summer, hitting seven homers in 251 at-bats for Portland in the short-season Northwest League. But he showed enough to share co-MVP honors in the league with Strong by batting .303 with 47 RBIs and drawing 45 walks. Atkins will have to hit for power, as he doesn't have the athleticism to play anywhere but first.

Second Base:

Chase Utley, Phillies: A teammate of Atkins' at UCLA, Utley went to the Phillies with the 15th overall pick in the draft. He was one of the top prospects to appear in the New York-Penn League in 2000, hitting .307 with 13 doubles for Batavia. He managed just two home runs after hitting 22 and earning All-America honors in the spring, but the belief is that he will still have above-average power for a second baseman as he develops. He's adequate defensively, though his bat will be what carries him. If Marlon Anderson can't claim the Phillies job for once and for all in 2001, it could be Utley's before long, because there's no one else in the organization to stand in his way.

Third Base:

Lance Niekro, Giants: His father Joe and uncle Phil made their livings baffling big league hitters with knuckleballs, but Lance is aiming to make his mark with a bat in his hands. He broke onto the scene with a tremendous season in the Cape Cod League in the summer of '99, then followed up with a poor spring at Florida Southern. The Giants put enough stock in their old scouting reports to spend their second-round pick on him and he made them look smart in his debut. Niekro won the Northwest League batting title with a .362 mark for Salem-Keizer. He showed enough power and defensive ability to project as a solid third baseman down the road.

Shortstop:

Luis Montanez, Cubs: The third overall pick in the draft, Montanez has the tools to someday join the upper echelon of run-producing shortstops. He could bring the full package to the position and give the Cubs their best shortstop in a generation. Montanez certainly got off to a good start, earning MVP honors in the Rookie-level Arizona League, where he was also the best prospect. He hit .344 with 16 doubles and seven triples. Much has been made of the rejuvenated Cubs' farm system, led by center fielder Corey Patterson, but the organization lacked a bona fide middle infield prospect until Montanez came along.

Outfield:

Josh Kroeger, Diamondbacks; Dave Krynzel, Brewers; Grady Sizemore, Expos: Krynzel is the class of the outfield as far as NL teams go. He's got all the tools to become an outstanding leadoff man and was turning the Pioneer League on its ear when he went down with a thumb injury midway through the season. The 11th overall pick in the draft, he hit .359 in his brief debut. Kroeger was the only high school player the Diamondbacks took with their first 10 picks. He started his career by hitting .297 and leading the Arizona League Diamondbacks with four homers and 28 RBIs. The Expos stunned everyone by granting a $2 million bonus to Sizemore, the fifth pick in the third round of the draft. They had to buy him away from a football scholarship to the University of Washington, but the negotiations were short and sweet and he was under contract within days of the draft. He showed good speed and though he didn't hit for much power, he has the size to do so in the future. He's a center fielder now, and could eventually move to a corner, following the career path of former Expos phenom Cliff Floyd.

Righthander:

Adam Wainwright, Braves: Atlanta is typically conservative with its young pitchers and they tried to be with Wainwright, the first of four Braves first-round picks in 2000. The Braves began him in the Rookie-level Gulf Coast League, but it just wasn't a fair match, as he tore through the competition, posting a 4-0 record and 1.13 ERA in seven appearances. In 32 GCL innings he allowed just 15 hits and 10 walks while striking out 42. He was on such a roll when he moved to the Appalachian League that it took four starts for him to issue his first walk. As it was, he finished with just two walks and 39 strikeouts in 29 innings for Danville, while going 2-2 with a 3.68 ERA. He ranked among the top prospects in both leagues and secured himself a spot on the pitching pipeline to Atlanta.

Lefthander:

Mark Phillips, Padres: Cardinals prospect Chris Narveson had a better debut, going 2-4 with a 3.27 ERA at Rookie-level Johnson City, but Phillips has a higher ceiling. He was one of the multitude of young players the Marlins were said to have had their eye on in the weeks before the draft, but he slid to the Padres at No. 9. He's a power pitcher with a mid-90s fastball and lefthanders with that kind of heat are truly coveted. He was on a tight pitch count at Rookie-level Idaho Falls and managed just 37 innings in 10 starts, posting a 1-1 record and 5.35 ERA. He did, however, strike out a batter per inning.

THE PRICES IN THIS BOOK ARE <u>NOT</u> RECOMMENDED BIDS

YOU MUST ADJUST FOR:

OPTIMAL BIDDING, INFLATION, AND BUDGETING

Three concepts that we pioneered and explained in these pages, years ago, have a big impact on what you should bid on draft day. Other than failure to do homework, there are no mistakes more common than forgetting these three vital elements. Consistent with the introductions in the front of this book, we are not going to write the lengthy "how to" explanations in this Annual again every year. Detailed essays covering all three subjects — Optimal Bids, Draft Price Inflation, and Auction Budgeting — appear in the volumes *Rotisserie Baseball Playing for Fun* and *Rotisserie Baseball Playing for Blood*, which belong in your library if you want to win (these books of course cover many other topics as well).

For those who need a quick refresher, these are the key concepts:

OPTIMAL BIDS

Optimal bids are the bids most likely to yield the biggest profits on each player. The lower you bid, the bigger will be the "value profit" (V) if you buy the player in question. If you buy a $20 player for $15, that's a "V" of $5. The lower your bid, the higher your V will be. However, low bids have a poor probability of success in acquiring the player. The higher you bid, the better will be your probability (P) of getting that player. If you bid half or less of the player's value, you will have a low P. If you bid 100% or more of the player's value, you will have a high probability of getting that player (but little or no value profit). We know the actual probability that certain bids will succeed, by examining hundreds of actual auctions, to see what each player actually sells for (in most cases it is a normal bell curve distribution). Since we know the probability and know the value of each bid, we can calculate the expected result. Your overall

expected profit from each bid is the probability P, times the value of the purchase V, or P x V. Optimal bids are based on calculations of the actual P x V for various types of players.

To summarize the results briefly, the optimal bid for an established star hitter or an established healthy ace reliever is about 85% of the player's value. The optimal bid for a solid star starting pitcher or an average everyday position player is about 70% of value. The optimal bid for an average starting pitcher or a hitter with an obscure role is about 60% of nominal value. The optimal bid for a rookie starting pitcher, or a middle reliever, or mediocre hitter with an injury history, is about 40% of nominal value.

DRAFT PRICE INFLATION

In leagues that retain players from one year to the next, owners tend to keep those players that have high salaries relative to expected value, such as Barry Bonds at $22 or John Wetteland at $10 or Brady Anderson at $2. Each one of these retentions removes a great deal of talent (value) from the draft pool, but only removes a small amount of money from the total auction spending allowance. The result is that lots of money remains in the auction, but not much talent, and prices must rise.

It is easily possible to calculate draft price inflation for your unique league. Simply take your total auction allowance (e.g. 12 teams x $260 = $3120 total) and subtract the total salaries of players being retained ("frozen") or expected to be retained. The balance is the money in your auction. Then subtract the value of players being retained (use my values in this book, or use your own) and subtract that amount from your auction allowance. That is the value of the players remaining in your draft pool.

For example, if your league freezes $1200 worth of players, at salaries of $900, then your money in the auction equals $3120 minus $900, or $2220; and your value in the auction equals $3120 minus $1200, or $1920. Divide the money by the value (2220/1920) and the inflation rate in this example is 15.6%.

The actual average inflation rate in most auctions is about 15%, but can vary from a negative amount (if owners freeze players at salaries higher than true values) or can go as high as 80% or even 100% in extreme cases.

DO NOT USE ESTIMATES OR AVERAGES. CALCULATE THE ACTUAL INFLATION RATE FOR YOUR LEAGUE.

Your bids could be off by as much as 50% if you don't adjust for inflation, and adjust correctly. Once you know your league's inflation rate, you should increase every value in this book by that percentage.

It is an unfortunate coincidence that the average inflation rate (+15%) is often equal to the optimal bid discount (-15%). That coincidence hides these offsetting factors and leads to a great deal of misunderstanding and unsuccessful auctions. Please: do your homework! I hate for people who read my books to do poorly in their leagues. I want you to win. OK?

The world's top expert on draft price inflation, in my opinion, is Mike Dalecki. Almost everything you ever see or hear about DPI derives from Mike's work, often without credit given where it is due. Mike wrote the first explanations, and the best and clearest.

AUCTION BUDGETING

A somewhat more elusive concept than optimal bids and draft inflation, auction budgeting cannot be "calculated" and requires the use of judgment. Budgeting works this way: make sure you spend all your money and get your fair share of big talent. Early in the auction, it's fine to sit back and stubbornly refuse to bid higher than the optimal bid times the inflated value. You must, however, pay attention as the talent disappears.

Make a list of those players you hope to acquire at each position, with an estimate of the price you are willing to pay; and when the list gets short you must bid more aggressively (higher). And for people who have a really good freeze list with a lot of profits locked into star players: forget optimal bids altogether. Once you have more profits than anyone else in your league, your only concern is getting your fair share of the talent in your league.

Like I said, all of these concepts are worthy of deeper exploration, and I hope you will look in to them. Just please: don't look at my dollar values in this book and think they are "recommended bids"—because they're not. There is much more to this game than calculating values.

POSITION SCARCITY

If you compare the dollar values in the alphabetical listing of hitters with the dollar values in the ranking by position, you will see that I have added $1 to the value of several catchers (and $2 to a couple more). The reason that I do this is to provide 24 catchers with a value of $1 or more. Personally, I make this adjustment mentally during the auction; but for the sake of those who have enough to think about already, I have given you lists with 24 "+" value catchers in each league.

FREE AGENTS

Finally, you will see that my rankings by position include free agents listed in both leagues. You can see what a player would be worth IF he ended up playing in that league. In a few cases there is a difference of $1 or even $2. Forecast stats are based on the league in which a player last played; so for example a pitcher moving from the AL to the NL should be expected to have a lower ERA and fewer baserunners per inning.

DOLLAR VALUE "ADJUSTMENTS" — TRYING TO USE STANDARD VALUES IN NON-STANDARD LEAGUES ?

Many people call me to talk about player values and valuation methods. Especially during the winter, when the stats finally stop changing long enough to do some in-depth analysis. People get their stats on disk, load 'em into the computer, and start calculating.

Many of the questions that people ask are not susceptible to short answers. For example:

> "My league uses both AL and NL players. How do I adjust your values so I can use them in a mixed league? Do I just take 50% of your values?"

> "My league uses strikeouts as a category. How do I adjust your values to include strikeouts?" [Same question for runs scored, innings pitched, etc. as additional categories.]

Everybody wishes they could simply adjust the standard dollar values. "Give me a formula," they say, "and I will do the arithmetic." The formula is in those permanent advice books presented on the page following the next ("Blood" if you care to know which one). The only way to calculate dollar values is to begin with the raw baseball stats.

When you build a house, you start with the foundation; you don't buy a pre-fab roof and then build the pieces underneath. To build a truck, you start with a chassis;

you don't start with a car and then take off some parts while adding others. When you build Rotisserie dollar values (for any league using any rules) you start with baseball stats. You can't take dollar values that were founded on different rules and adjust them to your league, unless you want to un-calculate everything, and then re-calculate everything. Trust me: it's easier to start from scratch.

Take the Mixed League case for example. Here's what I tell people who want to know why they can't quickly change one-league values into both-league values:

1. THE PLAYER POPULATION

Standard Rotisserie rules and dollar values are based on a population of 552 active major league players, 276 National League and 276 American League. Standard value methods therefore provide 552 names with a positive value. In a mixed format with, say, 10 teams and 23 players per team, you only need 230 players with positive value. If you have 240 or 250, that's no big problem, but with 552 "valuable" players on your list, you're going to be making some weird bids.

Cutting all values in half will not cut the number of positive-value players in half. In fact, cutting every value in half won't have any significant impact on the number of players valued $1 or higher. A tiny number of players previously valued at $1 will drop below 50 cents and fall off your list, but all of the players worth $2 or more will continue to look valuable, even though they are nowhere near good enough to be selected in a 230-player league.

One major concern in a 230-player league is the 230th player. If you take standard dollar values and cut them in half, the 230th player on your list is going to be worth about $5. If you pay $5 (or even $4 or $3) for the 230th player, you are making a stupid purchase, and you are going to lose. The 230th player is never worth more than $1, because there is only one bidder.

About this point in our conversation, most of the mixed-leaguers introduce one hopeful assertion before giving up: "Well, I can just count 230 players, and if the last guy is worth $5, then I can subtract $4 from every player. And then I can add up the total value of all the positive-value players, and make it conform to my league's auction allowance. If my league allows $260 per team and the total spending limit is $2600, then I just look at the total positive value for my 230 top players, and if it's $1000 for example, then I just multiply every value by 2.6. Wouldn't that work just fine?"

For those who are determined to minimize their work effort, the method: "divide by two, subtract X, and multiply by Y" will get you an answer. But you will end up doing almost as much work as you would have done by starting from scratch, and your answers will not be nearly as accurate. And you will *surely* lose you league. I can even tell you what your team will look like! Your starting pitchers will all be American Leaguers. Your hitting will feature speedsters from the AL (like Shannon Stewart and Kenny Lofton) and you will have a disproportionate share of home run hitters from the National League (like Eric Karros and Brian Giles). If you have tried the divide-subtract-multiply method for your mixed league, look at your roster and see for yourself if I didn't describe it pretty well. The problem is that you forgot to consider…

2. LEAGUE CONTEXT

To value a starting pitcher for an AL Rotisserie league, you compare that pitcher to his peers in the AL population. You don't compare him to National League pitchers. The average ERA in the American League in 2000 was 4.91. In the National League in 2000, the average ERA

was 4.63. Very often the difference between the two leagues is nearly half a run in ERA. How much is half a run in ERA worth in the standings in your league? About five or six points? And then consider the same difference in ratio, and you can see that 10 or 12 standings points depend entirely on league context. If you ignore league context, you lose, unless you have twelve points to throw away on just two pitching categories.

If you just divide-subtract-multiply standard dollar values and think you are getting anything useful for a mixed league, think again. The same distortions occur in the hitter population. A stolen base is worth more than a home run in the American League, but the opposite is true in the National League. Your simple method will gloss over these AL/NL differentials, put you in the dark, and give a huge advantage to your opponents who know how to deal with these factors and take the time to do it right. Conversely, if you do the work and your opponents don't, you get a huge advantage for yourself.

Now consider your mixed league context, and the differentials get even bigger. If you are making ten 23-man rosters using both AL and NL players, a pitcher with a 3.90 ERA can actually be a liability! Your rosters need 90 pitchers in this mixed league. Assume that the ace reliever from each of the 28 major league teams will be selected by somebody. And assume that a few co-closers and top setup men also get chosen. Suppose only about one third of the 28 major league teams have a co-closer or setup man worth choosing. That makes 10 more relievers, or 38 relief pitchers in total. For your league with 90 pitchers, you need only 52 starters for your ten teams, less than two starters from each major league team, on average. Many of the "good" number three starters, worth about $10 in a standard American League, will be zero value or even negative in your league. How are you going to "adjust" for that, without doing the arithmetic, the hard way? If you try to take a pitcher's standard value, and "convert" it to fit your league, you will go nuts. Take my advice. Start with baseball stats. Compare them to the stats in your league. Count the numbers of players needed, and compute real values. Don't try to "convert" or "adjust" anything.

3. THE EASY WAY OUT

For Just $69.00 (repeat buyer, new customer $99) you can buy my draft software which will do all these calculations for you: mixed leagues, non-standard rosters, and 25 different baseball stats to choose from. There is an ad shamelessly promoting this product in the back of the book — but it's there because it will help you win. I want my clients to win! Seriously, software experts tell me this program should sell for $200 or more, but we are crazy enough to give it away cheap.

Questions and answers about player valuation appear in every issue of my *Private Pages* (formerly the *Baseball Monthly*: only on the web). If you don't see what you need in the preceding essays, and don't want to invest a little time and money calling me, you can always write a letter to the editor and get a free answer in the monthly. Finally, all my valuation methods appear with examples in the "*Playing for Blood*" book advertised here. So you can do it yourself from scratch, use the software, or call me. Your choice. Just make sure you do it, one way or another.

12-TEAM MIXED LEAGUE 2001 DOLLAR VALUES

HITTERS

NAME	TM	VAL	NAME	TM	VAL	NAME	TM	VAL
A			Lance Berkman	HOU	$10	Juan Castro	CIN	-$15
Jeff Abbott	FLA	-$12	Sean Berry	CLE	-$17	Ramon Castro	FLA	-$5
Kurt Abbott	ATL	-$11	Dante Bichette	BOS	$9	Frank Catalanotto	TEX	-$1
Bob Abreu	PHI	$30	Craig Biggio	HOU	$4	Roger Cedeno	DET	$23
Benny Agbayani	NYM	$2	Casey Blake	MIN	-$13	Eric Chavez	OAK	$6
Manny Alexander	FA	-$14	Henry Blanco	MIL	-$5	Raul Chavez	HOU	-$5
Edgardo Alfonzo	NYM	$17	Geoff Blum	MON	-$7	Guisep Chiaramonte	SF	-$4
Luis Alicea	FA	-$13	Hiram Bocachica	LA	-$15	Ryan Christenson	OAK	-$16
Chad Allen	MIN	-$14	Tim Bogar	FA	-$18	Jeff Cirillo	COL	$17
Roberto Alomar	CLE	$32	Barry Bonds	SF	$18	Brady Clark	CIN	-$15
Sandy Alomar	CHW	$2	Bobby Bonilla	STL	-$18	Tony Clark	DET	$0
Moises Alou	HOU	$23	Aaron Boone	CIN	$7	Royce Clayton	CHW	-$2
Clemente Alvarez	PHI	-$6	Bret Boone	SEA	-$4	Edgard Clemente	FA	-$18
Rich Amaral	ATL	-$14	Mike Bordick	BAL	-$1	Ivanon Coffie	BAL	-$17
Brady Anderson	BAL	-$4	Milton Bradley	MON	-$6	Mike Colangelo	SD	-$15
Garret Anderson	ANA	$11	Darren Bragg	NYM	-$17	Greg Colbrunn	AZ	-$6
Marlon Anderson	PHI	-$11	Jeff Branson	LA	-$14	Michael Coleman	CIN	-$15
Shane Andrews	STL	-$16	Russ Branyan	CLE	-$11	Jeff Conine	BAL	-$8
Alex Arias	SD	-$13	Rico Brogna	ATL	-$5	Jason Conti	AZ	-$15
Rich Aurilia	SF	$1	Scott Brosius	NYY	-$12	Ron Coomer	CHC	-$12
Brad Ausmus	HOU	$7	Adrian Brown	PIT	$0	Trace Coquillette	CHC	-$17
Bruce Aven	LA	-$11	Brant Brown	MIL	-$16	Alex Cora	LA	-$14
B			Dee Brown	KC	-$5	Wil Cordero	CLE	-$5
Jeff Bagwell	HOU	$29	Emil Brown	PIT	-$12	Marty Cordova	CLE	-$15
Harold Baines	CHW	-$12	Roosevelt Brown	CHC	-$12	Craig Counsell	AZ	-$12
Paul Bako	ATL	-$6	Brian Buchanan	MIN	-$17	Steve Cox	TB	-$5
Rod Barajas	AZ	-$4	Damon Buford	CHC	-$12	Joe Crede	CHW	-$12
Glen Barker	HOU	-$11	Jay Buhner	SEA	-$13	Felipe Crespo	SF	-$12
Kevin Barker	MIL	-$15	Morgan Burkhart	BOS	-$16	D.T. Cromer	CIN	-$15
Michael Barrett	MON	$1	Ellis Burks	CLE	$6	Deivi Cruz	DET	$10
Tony Batista	TOR	$6	Jeromy Burnitz	MIL	-$4	Jacob Cruz	CLE	-$17
Justin Baughman	ANA	-$11	Pat Burrell	PHI	$4	Jose Cruz	TOR	$0
Danny Bautista	AZ	-$4	Homer Bush	TOR	-$1	Midre Cummings	AZ	-$15
Rich Becker	FA	-$15	**C**			Chad Curtis	TEX	-$13
David Bell	SEA	-$11	Alex Cabrera	FA	-$16	Johnny Damon	OAK	$45
Derek Bell	PIT	-$2	Jolbert Cabrera	CLE	-$12	Mike Darr	SD	$0
Jay Bell	AZ	-$2	Orlando Cabrera	MON	-$7	Brian Daubach	BOS	-$10
Mike Bell	COL	-$16	Miguel Cairo	OAK	$2	Ben Davis	SD	-$1
Albert Belle	BAL	$11	Mike Cameron	SEA	$8	Eric Davis	SF	-$5
Mark Bellhorn	OAK	-$14	Ken Caminiti	TEX	-$3	Russ Davis	SF	-$12
Ron Belliard	MIL	-$4	Jay Canizaro	MIN	-$6	Travis Dawkins	CIN	-$13
Clay Bellinger	NYY	-$16	Jose Canseco	FA	-$8	Kory Dehaan	SD	-$16
Carlos Beltran	KC	$8	Javier Cardona	DET	$0	Tom De la Rosa	MON	-$11
Adrian Beltre	LA	$17	Mike Caruso	FA	-$15	Carlos Delgado	TOR	$23
Marvin Benard	SF	$4	Raul Casanova	MIL	-$4	Wilson Delgado	KC	-$11
Mike Benjamin	PIT	-$12	Sean Casey	CIN	$25	Dave Dellucci	AZ	-$13
Gary Bennett	PHI	-$3	Vinny Castilla	TB	-$8	Delino DeShields	BAL	$18
Dave Berg	FLA	-$10	Alberto Castillo	TOR	-$7	Einer Diaz	CLE	$2
Peter Bergeron	MON	-$9	Luis Castillo	FLA	$37	Mike DiFelice	TB	-$3

NAME	TM	VAL	NAME	TM	VAL	NAME	TM	VAL
Gary DiSarcina	ANA	-$10	Ross Gload	CHC	-$16	A.J. Hinch	KC	-$4
J.D. Drew	STL	$14	Chris Gomez	SD	-$14	Denny Hocking	MIN	-$6
Rob Ducey	PHI	-$18	Alex Gonzalez	FLA	-$12	Todd Hollandsworth	COL	$16
Shawon Dunston	SF	-$9	Alex S. Gonzalez	TOR	-$5	Tyler Houston	MIL	$0
Todd Dunwoody	CHC	-$16	Juan Gonzalez	CLE	$10	Thomas Howard	PIT	-$16
Rube Durazo	AZ	$1	Luis Gonzalez	AZ	$14	Trenidad Hubbard	FA	-$16
Ray Durham	CHW	$17	Wiki Gonzalez	SD	-$4	Ken Huckaby	AZ	-$5
Jermaine Dye	KC	$11	Tom Goodwin	LA	$14	Aubrey Huff	TB	-$6
E			Mark Grace	AZ	$1	Todd Hundley	CHC	$4
Damion Easley	DET	$1	Tony Graffanino	CHW	-$10	Brian L. Hunter	PHI	-$10
Kevin Eberwein	SD	-$15	Craig Grebeck	FA	-$12	Brian R. Hunter	PHI	-$17
Angel Echevarria	MIL	-$15	Chad Green	SD	-$16	Torii Hunter	MIN	$3
Jim Edmonds	STL	$13	Scarborough Green	CHC	-$16	Butch Huskey	FA	-$9
Kevin Elster	FA	-$13	Shawn Green	LA	$19	**I**		
Juan Encarnacion	DET	$11	Charlie Greene	SD	-$6	Raul Ibanez	FA	-$16
Darin Erstad	ANA	$28	Todd Greene	TOR	-$17	Brandon Inge	DET	-$4
Alex Escobar	NYM	-$9	Willie Greene	FA	-$14	**J**		
Bobby Estalella	SF	-$1	Rusty Greer	TEX	$1	Damian Jackson	SD	$4
Johnny Estrada	PHI	-$5	Ben Grieve	TB	$6	John Jaha	OAK	-$16
Tony Eusebio	HOU	-$1	Ken Griffey	CIN	$16	Stan Javier	SEA	-$10
Tom Evans	FA	-$16	Marquis Grissom	MIL	-$10	Reggie Jefferson	PIT	-$13
Adam Everett	HOU	-$8	Mark Grudzielanek	LA	$2	Geoff Jenkins	MIL	$16
Carl Everett	BOS	$17	Vladimir Guerrero	MON	$35	Marcus Jensen	LA	-$7
F			Wilton Guerrero	CIN	-$7	Derek Jeter	NYY	$36
Jorge Fabregas	ANA	-$5	Carlos Guillen	SEA	$1	D'Angelo Jimenez	NYY	-$6
Sal Fasano	OAK	-$4	Jose Guillen	TB	-$11	Brian Johnson	LA	-$5
Carlos Febles	KC	$2	Ozzie Guillen	TB	-$14	Charles Johnson	FLA	$10
Pedro Feliz	SF	-$12	Ricky Gutierrez	CHC	-$2	Mark L. Johnson	CHW	-$4
Robert Fick	DET	-$12	Cristian Guzman	MIN	$8	Nick Johnson	NYY	-$12
Steve Finley	AZ	$1	Edwards Guzman	SF	-$5	Russ Johnson	TB	-$10
John Flaherty	TB	-$3	Tony Gwynn	SD	-$3	Andruw Jones	ATL	$24
Darrin Fletcher	TOR	$10	**H**			Chipper Jones	ATL	$30
Cliff Floyd	FLA	$13	Chris Haas	STL	-$16	Jacque Jones	MIN	$2
Brook Fordyce	BAL	$8	Jerry Hairston Jr.	BAL	-$2	Terry Jones	MON	-$15
Andy Fox	FLA	-$9	Shane Halter	DET	-$14	Brian Jordan	ATL	$4
Matt Franco	FA	-$17	Darryl Hamilton	NYM	-$6	Kevin Jordan	PHI	-$15
Ryan Freel	TOR	-$14	Jeffrey Hammonds	MIL	$15	Wally Joyner	FA	-$12
Hanley Frias	AZ	-$13	Dave Hansen	LA	-$14	David Justice	NYY	$3
Jeff Frye	TOR	-$12	Lenny Harris	NYM	-$9	**K**		
Travis Fryman	CLE	$4	Bill Haselman	TEX	-$2	Gabe Kapler	TEX	$15
Brad Fullmer	TOR	$5	Chris Hatcher	TB	-$17	Eric Karros	LA	$2
Rafael Furcal	ATL	$33	Scott Hatteberg	BOS	-$1	Jason Kendall	PIT	$33
G			Charlie Hayes	HOU	-$16	Adam Kennedy	ANA	$6
Andres Galarraga	TEX	-$3	Nathan Haynes	ANA	-$17	Jeff Kent	SF	$18
Ron Gant	COL	-$6	Wes Helms	ATL	-$15	Brooks Kieschnick	COL	-$15
Karim Garcia	CLE	-$15	Todd Helton	COL	$36	Gene Kingsale	BAL	-$18
Luis Garcia	STL	-$13	Bret Hemphill	FA	$9	Danny Klassen	AZ	-$15
Nomar Garciaparra	BOS	$33	Rickey Henderson	FA	$1	Ryan Klesko	SD	$12
Jason Giambi	OAK	$19	Chad Hermansen	PIT	-$15	Chuck Knoblauch	NYY	$5
Jeremy Giambi	OAK	-$8	Alex Hernandez	PIT	-$14	Paul Konerko	CHW	$4
Benji Gil	ANA	-$11	Carlos Hernandez	STL	-$3	Corey Koskie	MIN	$4
Brian Giles	PIT	$16	Jose Hernandez	MIL	-$6	Mark Kotsay	FLA	$8
Bernard Gilkey	STL	-$18	Ramon Hernandez	OAK	$1	Chad Kreuter	LA	-$5
Charles Gipson	SEA	-$18	Richard Hidalgo	HOU	$17	**L**		
Joe Girardi	CHC	-$2	Bob Higginson	DET	$8	David Lamb	ANA	-$15
Doug Glanville	PHI	$15	Glenallen Hill	NYY	-$3	Mike Lamb	TEX	-$8
Troy Glaus	ANA	$16	Shea Hillenbrand	BOS	-$5	Tom Lampkin	SEA	-$4

NAME	TM	VAL	NAME	TM	VAL	NAME	TM	VAL
Ray Lankford	STL	$1	Aaron McNeal	HOU	-$15	**P**		
Mike Lansing	BOS	-$11	Pat Meares	PIT	-$12	Orlando Palmeiro	ANA	-$11
Barry Larkin	CIN	$6	Adam Melhuse	COL	-$4	Rafael Palmeiro	TEX	$12
Brandon Larson	CIN	-$16	Mitch Meluskey	DET	$16	Dean Palmer	DET	$1
Jason LaRue	CIN	-$1	Frankie Menechino	OAK	-$12	Craig Paquette	STL	-$10
Joe Lawrence	TOR	-$4	Lou Merloni	BOS	-$12	Corey Patterson	CHC	-$9
Matt Lawton	MIN	$12	Chad Meyers	CHC	-$13	Josh Paul	CHW	-$3
Matt LeCroy	MIN	-$4	Doug Mientkiewicz	MIN	-$3	Jay Payton	NYM	$4
Ricky Ledee	TEX	-$6	Matt Mieske	FA	-$17	Angel Pena	LA	-$2
Carlos Lee	CHW	$16	Kevin Millar	FLA	-$10	Carlos Pena	TEX	-$14
Derrek Lee	FLA	$3	Damian Miller	AZ	$4	Elvis Pena	COL	-$13
Travis Lee	PHI	-$6	Damon Minor	SF	-$15	Danny Peoples	CLE	-$15
Darren Lewis	BOS	-$14	Ryan Minor	MON	-$19	Eddie Perez	ATL	-$3
Mark Lewis	FA	-$12	Doug Mirabelli	SF	-$5	Eduardo Perez	FA	-$14
Jim Leyritz	FA	-$18	Chad Moeller	MIN	-$5	Neifi Perez	COL	$4
Mike Lieberthal	PHI	$9	Ben Molina	ANA	$6	Santiago Perez	SD	-$5
Jeff Liefer	CHW	-$14	Raul Mondesi	TOR	$11	Timoniel Perez	NYM	$0
Cole Liniak	TOR	-$16	Melvin Mora	BAL	$1	Tomas Perez	PHI	-$14
Keith Lockhart	ATL	-$12	Mickey Morandini	TOR	-$14	Herbert Perry	CHW	-$5
Paul LoDuca	LA	-$5	Mike Mordecai	MON	-$16	Ben Petrick	COL	$11
Kenny Lofton	CLE	$15	Hal Morris	FA	-$13	Adam Piatt	OAK	-$5
Terrence Long	OAK	$10	Warren Morris	PIT	-$3	Mike Piazza	NYM	$30
Javy Lopez	ATL	$14	Chad Mottola	TOR	-$16	Juan Pierre	COL	$12
Luis Lopez	MIL	-$12	James Mouton	MIL	-$13	A.J. Pierzynski	MIN	$1
Mark Loretta	MIL	-$2	Lyle Mouton	FA	-$16	Placido Polanco	STL	-$1
Mike Lowell	FLA	$0	Bill Mueller	CHC	-$7	Luis Polonia	FA	-$5
Julio Lugo	HOU	$11	Calvin Murray	SF	-$11	Jorge Posada	NYY	$10
Fernando Lunar	BAL	-$6	Greg Myers	BAL	-$6	Todd Pratt	NYM	$0
M			**N**			Tom Prince	MIN	-$6
John Mabry	STL	-$15	Phil Nevin	SD	$11	**Q**		
Jose Macias	DET	-$15	Kevin Nicholson	SD	-$12	Mark Quinn	KC	$12
Dave Magadan	SD	-$15	Jose Nieves	CHC	-$12	**R**		
Wendell Magee	DET	-$11	Dave Nilsson	FA	-$4	Aramis Ramirez	PIT	-$5
Eli Marrero	STL	-$2	Trot Nixon	BOS	-$7	Manny Ramirez	BOS	$27
Al Martin	SEA	-$4	Greg Norton	COL	-$10	Joe Randa	KC	$7
Dave Martinez	ATL	-$8	Abraham Nunez	FLA	-$14	Jeff Reboulet	FA	-$18
Edgar Martinez	SEA	$14	Abraham O. Nunez	PIT	-$13	Mike Redmond	FLA	-$3
Felix Martinez	TB	-$14	Jorge Nunez	LA	-$13	Jeff Reed	FA	-$6
Ramon E. Martinez	SF	-$8	Jonathan Nunnally	FA	-$18	Pokey Reese	CIN	$7
Sandy Martinez	MON	-$5	**O**			Desi Relaford	NYM	-$13
Tino Martinez	NYY	-$3	Troy O'Leary	BOS	-$6	Edgar Renteria	STL	$15
Henry Mateo	MON	-$16	Paul O'Neill	NYY	$5	Chris Richard	BAL	-$12
Ruben Mateo	TEX	$8	Alex Ochoa	CIN	-$1	Armando Rios	SF	-$3
Mike Matheny	STL	-$5	Jose Offerman	BOS	-$5	Cal Ripken	BAL	-$8
Luis Matos	BAL	-$4	Augie Ojeda	CHC	-$13	Luis Rivas	MIN	-$11
Gary Matthews	CHC	-$18	John Olerud	SEA	$4	Ruben Rivera	SD	-$17
Jason Maxwell	MIN	-$15	Joe Oliver	NYY	-$3	Alex Rodriguez	TEX	$35
Brent Mayne	COL	$5	Luis Ordaz	KC	-$12	Henry Rodriguez	FA	-$8
David McCarty	KC	-$10	Magglio Ordonez	CHW	$23	Ivan Rodriguez	TEX	$28
Quinton McCracken	STL	-$16	Rey Ordonez	NYM	-$16	Scott Rolen	PHI	$10
Jason McDonald	MIL	-$17	William Ortega	STL	-$16	Jimmy Rollins	PHI	-$1
John McDonald	CLE	-$13	David Ortiz	MIN	-$2	Jason Romano	TEX	-$14
Joe McEwing	NYM	-$12	Hector Ortiz	KC	-$4	Wilken Ruan	MON	-$13
Fred McGriff	TB	$3	Jose Ortiz	OAK	-$13	Rob Ryan	AZ	-$16
Mark McGwire	STL	$11	Keith Osik	PIT	-$3	**S**		
Mark McLemore	SEA	-$4	Eric Owens	SD	$5	Donnie Sadler	CIN	-$12
Billy McMillon	DET	-$4	Pablo Ozuna	FLA	-$13	Olmedo Saenz	OAK	-$9

NAME	TM	VAL	NAME	TM	VAL
Oscar Salazar	OAK	-$13	**V**		
Tim Salmon	ANA	$5	Mario Valdez	OAK	-$8
Rey Sanchez	KC	-$4	Javier Valentin	MIN	-$4
Reggie Sanders	AZ	$3	John Valentin	BOS	-$15
FP Santangelo	LA	-$18	Jose Valentin	CHW	$5
Benito Santiago	FA	-$1	John Vander Wal	PIT	-$1
Dane Sardinha	CIN	-$6	Jason Varitek	BOS	$2
Luis Saturria	STL	-$17	Greg Vaughn	TB	$0
Brian Schneider	MON	-$5	Mo Vaughn	ANA	-$1
Kevin Sefcik	PHI	-$14	Randy Velarde	TEX	-$1
David Segui	BAL	$9	Robin Ventura	NYM	-$4
Fernando Seguignol	MON	-$8	Quilvio Veras	ATL	$6
Scott Servais	FA	-$5	Wilton Veras	BOS	-$16
Richie Sexson	MIL	$10	Jose Vidro	MON	$10
Chris Sexton	CIN	-$11	Fernando Vina	STL	$1
Gary Sheffield	LA	$16	Joe Vitiello	SD	-$16
Scott Sheldon	TEX	-$11	Jose Vizcaino	HOU	-$12
Terry Shumpert	COL	-$3	Omar Vizquel	CLE	$17
Ruben Sierra	TEX	-$17	**W**		
Chris Singleton	CHW	$1	Matt Walbeck	CIN	-$5
Bobby Smith	TB	-$13	Larry Walker	COL	$12
Mark Smith	FA	-$16	Todd Walker	COL	$6
J.T. Snow	SF	-$4	Daryle Ward	HOU	-$4
Luis Sojo	NYY	-$12	Turner Ward	PHI	-$18
Alfonso Soriano	NYY	-$7	Lenny Webster	FA	-$7
Juan Sosa	COL	-$10	John Wehner	PIT	-$17
Sammy Sosa	CHC	$23	Walt Weiss	FA	-$13
Shane Spencer	NYY	-$12	Vernon Wells	TOR	-$12
Bill Spiers	HOU	-$6	Devon White	LA	-$10
Scott Spiezio	ANA	-$12	Rondell White	CHC	$4
Ed Sprague	SD	-$12	Chris Widger	SEA	-$2
Matt Stairs	CHC	-$3	Bernie Williams	NYY	$21
Mike Stanley	OAK	-$13	Gerald Williams	TB	$0
Lee Stevens	MON	-$5	Matt Williams	AZ	$1
Shannon Stewart	TOR	$21	Craig Wilson	KC	-$16
Kelly Stinnett	CIN	-$5	Dan Wilson	SEA	-$4
Kevin Stocker	FA	-$14	Enrique Wilson	PIT	-$8
Chris Stynes	BOS	-$3	Preston Wilson	FLA	$24
BJ Surhoff	ATL	$2	Vance Wilson	NYM	-$5
Ichiro Suzuki	SEA	-$16	Randy Winn	TB	-$7
Mark Sweeney	MIL	-$18	Tony Womack	AZ	$23
Mike Sweeney	KC	$20	Chris Woodward	TOR	-$13
T			Shawn Wooten	ANA	-$4
Fernando Tatis	MON	$10	**Y**		
Eddie Taubensee	CLE	$2	Dmitri Young	CIN	$8
Reggie Taylor	PHI	-$10	Eric Young	CHC	$26
Miguel Tejada	OAK	$16	Kevin Young	PIT	$5
Frank Thomas	CHW	$20	Mike Young	TEX	-$12
Jim Thome	CLE	$6	**Z**		
Jorge Toca	NYM	-$15	Gregg Zaun	KC	$1
Andy Tracy	MON	-$11	Todd Zeile	NYM	-$7
Bubba Trammell	SD	-$8	Julio Zuleta	CHC	-$14
Chris Truby	HOU	-$3			
Michael Tucker	CIN	-$8			
Chris Turner	PHI	-$6			
Jason Tyner	TB	-$10			

PITCHERS

NAME	TM	VAL	NAME	TM	VAL	NAME	TM	VAL
			Dave Burba	CLE	-$1	Scott Erickson	BAL	-$10
			John Burkett	ATL	-$8	Kelvim Escobar	TOR	-$9
Paul Abbott	SEA	$2	A.J. Burnett	FLA	-$6	Shawn Estes	SF	-$6
Juan Acevedo	MIL	$3	Paul Byrd	FA	-$4	Horacio Estrada	MIL	-$9
Terry Adams	LA	$0	Tim Byrdak	CLE	-$6	Seth Etherton	CIN	-$5
Rick Aguilera	FA	$14	**C**			**F**		
Scott Aldred	CLE	-$4	Jose Cabrera	HOU	-$4	Kyle Farnsworth	CHC	$0
Antonio Alfonseca	FLA	$25	Chris Carpenter	TOR	-$11	Jeff Fassero	CHC	-$8
Armando Almanza	FLA	-$5	Hector Carrasco	FA	-$4	Alex Fernandez	FLA	-$1
Carlos Almanzar	SD	-$4	Frank Castillo	BOS	-$1	Osvaldo Fernandez	CIN	$2
Wilson Alvarez	TB	-$6	Bruce Chen	PHI	$10	Mike Fetters	LA	$1
Brian Anderson	AZ	$7	Randy Choate	NYY	-$4	Nelson Figueroa	PHI	-$7
Jimmy Anderson	PIT	-$6	Bobby Chouinard	COL	-$2	Chuck Finley	CLE	$0
Matt Anderson	DET	-$3	Jason Christiansen	STL	$0	Bryce Florie	BOS	-$5
Clayton Andrews	CIN	-$6	Mark Clark	FA	-$6	Scott Forster	NYM	-$8
Rick Ankiel	STL	$9	Roger Clemens	NYY	$6	Keith Foulke	CHW	$29
Kevin Appier	NYM	-$6	Matt Clement	SD	-$8	John Franco	NYM	$2
Tony Armas	MON	$2	Dave Coggin	PHI	-$7	Wayne Franklin	HOU	-$4
Jamie Arnold	FA	-$5	Bartolo Colon	CLE	$5	John Frascatore	TOR	-$6
Rolando Arrojo	BOS	-$7	David Cone	BOS	-$9	Aaron Fultz	SF	$3
Bronson Arroyo	PIT	-$7	Dennis Cook	NYM	-$2	Chris Fussell	KC	-$6
Andy Ashby	LA	$3	Brian Cooper	ANA	-$7	Mike Fyhrie	ANA	-$3
Pedro Astacio	COL	-$7	Francisco Cordero	TEX	-$9	**G**		
Manny Aybar	FLA	-$4	Francisco Cordova	PIT	-$4	Eric Gagne	LA	-$6
B			Rheal Cormier	PHI	-$3	Rich Garces	BOS	$2
James Baldwin	CHW	-$8	Reid Cornelius	FLA	-$5	Freddy Garcia	SEA	$4
Lorenzo Barcelo	CHW	$0	Tim Crabtree	TEX	$0	Mark Gardner	SF	-$1
Miguel Batista	AZ	-$5	Paxton Crawford	BOS	-$2	Daniel Garibay	CHC	-$10
Rod Beck	BOS	$0	Doug Creek	TB	-$1	Jon Garland	CHW	-$6
Kevin Beirne	TOR	-$5	Jack Cressend	MIN	-$5	Tom Glavine	ATL	$16
Tim Belcher	ANA	-$6	Nelson Cruz	HOU	-$1	Ryan Glynn	TEX	-$16
Stan Belinda	FA	-$6	Darwin Cubillan	TEX	-$7	Wayne Gomes	PHI	-$2
Rob Bell	CIN	-$3	Will Cunnane	MIL	-$4	Doc Gooden	NYY	-$7
Alan Benes	STL	-$5	**D**			Tom Gordon	CHC	$4
Andy Benes	STL	-$9	Omar Daal	PHI	-$7	Danny Graves	CIN	$26
Armando Benitez	NYM	$33	Jeff C. D'Amico	MIL	$16	Seth Greisinger	DET	-$4
Kris Benson	PIT	$3	Vic Darensbourg	FLA	-$5	Jason Grimsley	FA	-$3
Jason Bere	CHC	-$12	Tom Davey	SD	-$4	Buddy Groom	BAL	-$2
Sean Bergman	TB	-$9	Doug Davis	TEX	-$8	Eddie Guardado	MIN	$4
Adam Bernero	DET	-$4	Mike DeJean	COL	-$8	Mark Guthrie	OAK	-$5
Rocky Biddle	CHW	-$7	Valerio De los Santos	MIL	-$4	Geraldo Guzman	AZ	-$4
Willie Blair	FA	-$7	Miguel Deltoro	SF	-$4	Juan Guzman	TB	-$1
Brian Boehringer	NYY	-$6	Ryan Dempster	FLA	$0	**H**		
Brian Bohanon	COL	-$6	Elmer Dessens	CIN	-$1	John Halama	SEA	-$7
Ricky Bones	FLA	-$6	Jerry Dipoto	COL	-$3	Roy Halladay	TOR	-$9
Pedro Borbon	TOR	-$6	Octavio Dotel	HOU	$4	Joey Hamilton	TOR	-$5
Ricky Bottalico	PHI	$12	Scott Downs	MON	-$8	Mike Hampton	COL	-$4
Kent Bottenfield	HOU	-$7	Darren Dreifort	LA	$5	Pete Harnisch	CIN	$6
Jason Boyd	PHI	-$6	Chad Durbin	KC	-$8	Travis Harper	TB	-$4
Chad Bradford	OAK	-$3	**E**			Shigetoshi Hasegawa	ANA	$6
Jeff Brantley	TEX	$6	Adam Eaton	SD	-$3	LaTroy Hawkins	MIN	$4
Jamie Brewington	FA	-$5	Derrin Ebert	TB	-$5	Jimmy Haynes	MIL	-$14
Doug Brocail	HOU	-$2	Dave Eiland	OAK	-$9	Rick Helling	TEX	-$2
Chris Brock	PHI	-$3	Scott Elarton	HOU	$1	Doug Henry	KC	-$1
Jim Brower	CIN	-$7	Cal Eldred	CHW	-$10	Pat Hentgen	BAL	-$5
Kevin Brown	LA	$26	Alan Embree	SF	-$2	Felix Heredia	CHC	$1
Mark Buehrle	CHW	-$2	Todd Erdos	SD	-$6	Gil Heredia	OAK	$1

NAME	TM	VAL	NAME	TM	VAL	NAME	TM	VAL
Matt Herges	LA	$2	Sean Lowe	CHW	-$6	Darren Oliver	TEX	-$11
Dustin Hermanson	STL	-$2	Larry Luebbers	CIN	-$5	Gregg Olson	LA	-$3
Livan Hernandez	SF	$10	**M**			Ramon Ortiz	ANA	-$2
Orlando Hernandez	NYY	$6	Greg Maddux	ATL	$22	Russ Ortiz	SF	-$4
Roberto Hernandez	KC	$24	Mike Magnante	OAK	-$4	Antonio Osuna	LA	-$1
Ken Hill	FA	-$8	Ron Mahay	SD	-$6	**P**		
Sterling Hitchcock	SD	-$1	Pat Mahomes	FA	-$6	Vincente Padilla	PHI	-$3
Trevor Hoffman	SD	$35	Matt Mantei	AZ	$17	Lance Painter	TOR	-$3
Chris Holt	DET	-$10	Josias Manzanillo	PIT	-$2	Jose Paniagua	SEA	$3
Mike Holtz	ANA	-$4	Jason Marquis	ATL	-$4	Chan Ho Park	LA	$12
Craig House	COL	-$7	Pedroj Martinez	BOS	$34	Jim Parque	CHW	-$6
Bob Howry	CHW	$4	Ramon Martinez	LA	-$6	Steve Parris	TOR	-$3
Tim Hudson	OAK	$8	Onan Masaoka	LA	-$4	John Parrish	BAL	-$10
I			TJ Mathews	OAK	-$4	Danny Patterson	DET	-$4
Hideki Irabu	MON	-$5	Dave Maurer	SD	-$3	Carl Pavano	MON	$3
Jason Isringhausen	OAK	$17	Joe Mays	MIN	-$9	Jesus Pena	BOS	-$5
J			Chuck McElroy	BAL	-$5	Brad Penny	FLA	-$3
Mike Jackson	HOU	-$3	Tony McKnight	HOU	-$1	Troy Percival	ANA	$16
Mike James	STL	$1	Brian Meadows	FA	-$9	Carlos Perez	LA	-$8
Kevin Jarvis	SD	-$5	Gil Meche	SEA	-$2	Yorkis Perez	LA	-$4
Jose Jimenez	COL	$12	Jim Mecir	OAK	$7	Matt Perisho	DET	-$8
Jason Johnson	BAL	-$16	Ramiro Mendoza	NYY	$0	Robert Person	PHI	$0
Jonathan Johnson	TEX	-$7	Jose Mercedes	BAL	$1	Chris Peters	FA	-$3
Mike Johnson	MON	-$9	Kent Mercker	BOS	-$6	Mark Petkovsek	TEX	$1
Randy Johnson	AZ	$19	Jose Mesa	PHI	-$7	Andy Pettitte	NYY	-$2
John Johnstone	SF	-$2	Danny Miceli	FLA	$0	Hipolito Pichardo	BOS	-$2
Bobby J. Jones	FA	-$2	Travis Miller	MIN	-$2	Joel Pineiro	SEA	-$6
Bobby M. Jones	NYM	-$8	Wade Miller	HOU	-$4	Dan Plesac	TOR	-$2
Todd Jones	DET	$22	Alan Mills	BAL	-$5	Cliff Politte	PHI	-$1
K			Kevin Millwood	ATL	$6	Sidney Ponson	BAL	-$4
Scott Kamieniecki	FA	-$6	Eric Milton	MIN	$2	Lue Pote	ANA	$2
Scott Karl	SD	-$14	Dave Mlicki	DET	-$7	Brian Powell	HOU	-$5
Steve Karsay	CLE	$9	Brian Moehler	DET	-$5	Jay Powell	HOU	-$4
Daryl Kile	STL	$12	Trey Moore	ATL	-$5	Jeremy Powell	SD	-$7
Byung Kim	AZ	$0	Orber Moreno	KC	-$4	Ariel Prieto	OAK	-$5
Ray King	MIL	$1	Mike Morgan	AZ	-$8	Luke Prokopec	LA	-$3
Matt Kinney	MIN	-$6	Matt Morris	STL	$3	**Q**		
Steve Kline	STL	$5	Guillermo Mota	MON	-$4	Paul Quantrill	TOR	-$2
Billy Koch	TOR	$26	Jamie Moyer	SEA	$1	Ruben Quevedo	CHC	-$9
Ryan Kohlmeier	BAL	$15	Mark Mulder	OAK	-$14	**R**		
L			Terry Mulholland	PIT	-$4	Brad Radke	MIN	-$4
Andy Larkin	COL	-$7	Peter Munro	TEX	-$7	Steve Rain	FA	-$4
Al Leiter	NYM	$10	Mike Mussina	NYY	$13	Robert Ramsay	SEA	-$5
Curt Leskanic	MIL	$12	Mike Myers	COL	$0	Pat Rapp	ANA	-$12
Al Levine	ANA	-$2	**N**			Britt Reames	MON	$0
Cory Lidle	OAK	-$4	Charles Nagy	CLE	-$8	Mark Redman	MIN	-$3
Jon Lieber	CHC	$6	Joe Nathan	SF	-$6	Rick Reed	NYM	$4
Kerry Ligtenberg	ATL	$7	Jaime Navarro	TOR	-$7	Steve Reed	CLE	-$2
Jose Lima	HOU	-$14	Denny Neagle	COL	-$4	Dan Reichert	KC	-$13
Mike Lincoln	MIN	-$9	Jeff Nelson	SEA	$1	Bryan Rekar	TB	-$4
Felipe Lira	MON	-$6	Robb Nen	SF	$35	Mike Remlinger	ATL	$7
Esteban Loaiza	TOR	-$2	C.J. Nitkowski	DET	-$6	Alberto Reyes	LA	-$4
Rich Loiselle	PIT	-$4	Hideo Nomo	BOS	-$4	Dennis Reyes	CIN	-$4
Braden Looper	FLA	-$3	Vladimir Nunez	FLA	-$6	Shane Reynolds	HOU	-$1
Albie Lopez	TB	$0	**O**			Armando Reynoso	AZ	-$4
Andrew Lorraine	FA	-$6	Tomokazu Ohka	BOS	-$2	Arthur Rhodes	SEA	-$1
Derek Lowe	BOS	$32	Omar Olivares	OAK	-$10	John Riedling	CIN	-$4

NAME	TM	VAL	NAME	TM	VAL	NAME	TM	VAL
Paul Rigdon	MIL	-$3	Todd Stottlemyre	AZ	-$2	Mike Williams	PIT	$15
Todd Ritchie	PIT	$0	Scott Strickland	MON	$7	Woody Williams	SD	$6
Mariano Rivera	NYY	$31	Everett Stull	MIL	-$5	Scott Williamson	CIN	$3
John Rocker	ATL	$16	Tanyon Sturtze	TB	$4	Kris Wilson	KC	-$4
Felix Rodriguez	SF	$2	Scott Sullivan	CIN	$5	Paul Wilson	TB	$7
Frank Rodriguez	FA	-$6	Jeff Suppan	KC	-$4	Matt Wise	ANA	-$4
Rich Rodriguez	NYM	-$7	Makoto Suzuki	KC	-$9	Jay Witasick	SD	-$14
Kenny Rogers	TEX	-$1	Greg Swindell	AZ	$2	Mark Wohlers	CIN	-$2
J.C. Romero	MIN	-$12	**T**			Randy Wolf	PHI	-$5
Jose Rosado	KC	$1	Jeff Tam	OAK	$2	Kerry Wood	CHC	-$2
Brian Rose	COL	-$7	Kevin Tapani	CHC	-$2	Steve Woodard	CLE	-$6
Kirk Rueter	SF	-$2	Julian Tavarez	CHC	$1	Tim Worrell	SF	-$1
Ryan Rupe	TB	-$8	Amaury Telemaco	PHI	-$5	Jamey Wright	MIL	-$7
Glendon Rusch	NYM	$4	Anthony Telford	MON	$1	Jaret Wright	CLE	-$4
B.J. Ryan	BAL	-$5	Justin Thompson	TEX	-$6	Kelly Wunsch	CHW	$0
Jay Ryan	MIN	-$7	Mike Thurman	MON	-$10	**Y**		
S			Mike Timlin	STL	$1	Estaban Yan	TB	$4
Bret Saberhagen	BOS	-$3	Brian Tollberg	SD	$1	Masato Yoshii	COL	-$6
Jesus Sanchez	FLA	-$11	Brett Tomko	SEA	-$3	**Z**		
Johan Santana	MIN	-$7	Steve Trachsel	NYM	-$6	Jeff Zimmerman	TEX	$2
Julio Santana	NYM	-$8	Mike Trombley	BAL	$1	Barry Zito	OAK	$9
Jose Santiago	KC	$1	Derrick Turnbow	ANA	-$5			
Kazuhiro Sasaki	SEA	$29	**U**					
Scott Sauerbeck	PIT	-$3	Ugueth Urbina	MON	$13			
Curt Schilling	AZ	$15	**V**					
Jason Schmidt	PIT	-$5	Ismael Valdes	ANA	-$8			
Scott Schoeneweis	ANA	-$9	Marc Valdes	ATL	-$4			
Pete Schourek	BOS	-$5	Todd Van Poppel	CHC	$0			
Steve Schrenk	OAK	-$4	Javier Vazquez	MON	-$2			
Rudy Seanez	FA	$0	Mike Venafro	TEX	$0			
Aaron Sele	SEA	-$1	Dave Veres	STL	$19			
Dan Serafini	PIT	-$9	Ron Villone	COL	-$8			
Scott Service	LA	-$5	Ed Vosberg	PHI	-$5			
Jeff Shaw	LA	$23	**W**					
Paul Shuey	CLE	$1	Billy Wagner	HOU	$17			
Brian Sikorski	TEX	-$8	Tim Wakefield	BOS	-$9			
Jose Silva	PIT	-$11	Kevin Walker	SD	-$2			
Bill Simas	CHW	-$2	Donne Wall	NYM	$1			
Mike Sirotka	CHW	$3	Jeff Wallace	TB	-$6			
Heath Slocumb	FA	-$4	Bryan Ward	BOS	-$4			
Joe Slusarski	ATL	-$2	John Wasdin	COL	-$3			
Chuck Smith	FLA	$2	Jarrod Washburn	ANA	$4			
John Smoltz	ATL	$1	Allen Watson	NYY	-$9			
John Snyder	MIL	-$15	Dave Weathers	MIL	$0			
Shawn Sonnier	KC	-$1	Jeff Weaver	DET	$0			
Steve W. Sparks	DET	$3	Ben Weber	ANA	-$5			
Justin Speier	CLE	-$2	Bob Wells	MIN	$12			
Stan Spencer	SD	-$4	David Wells	CHW	$5			
Paul Spoljaric	TB	-$5	Kip Wells	CHW	-$7			
Jerry Spradlin	FA	-$3	Turk Wendell	NYM	$2			
Dennis Springer	FA	-$7	John Wetteland	FA	$18			
Russ Springer	AZ	-$4	Dan Wheeler	TB	-$4			
Jay Spurgeon	BAL	-$7	Gabe White	COL	$5			
Mike Stanton	NYY	-$2	Rick White	NYM	$0			
Gene Stechschulte	STL	-$6	Bob Wickman	CLE	$21			
Blake Stein	KC	-$5	Marc Wilkins	PIT	-$6			
Garrett Stephenson	STL	$0	Brian Williams	BOS	-$7			

HITTERS 2001 FORECAST STATS AND VALUES

AMERICAN LEAGUE

NAME	TEAM	AB	RUN	HR	RBI	SB	AVG	OBA	SLG	$VAL
A										
Manny Alexander	FA	116	16	2	11	2	.229	.276	.336	-$3
Luis Alicea	FA	209	35	3	24	1	.267	.346	.388	$0
Chad Allen	MIN	102	14	2	17	4	.259	.327	.407	$0
Roberto Alomar	CLE	594	117	20	95	33	.311	.388	.486	$34
Sandy Alomar	CHW	296	37	7	37	1	.277	.307	.405	$3
Brady Anderson	BAL	488	89	19	55	14	.253	.365	.427	$10
Garret Anderson	ANA	636	88	29	102	6	.292	.317	.498	$20
B										
Harold Baines	CHW	178	21	8	33	0	.271	.352	.466	$1
Tony Batista	TOR	607	93	39	112	4	.267	.314	.522	$17
Justin Baughman	ANA	62	10	0	4	4	.282	.322	.378	-$1
Rich Becker	FA	272	50	7	33	4	.243	.384	.378	$1
David Bell	SEA	394	53	11	45	2	.257	.321	.403	$3
Albert Belle	BAL	559	83	29	108	6	.291	.367	.524	$20
Mark Bellhorn	OAK	90	16	2	14	2	.250	.325	.397	-$1
Clay Bellinger	NYY	124	23	4	13	3	.206	.281	.364	-$3
Carlos Beltran	KC	512	77	13	72	19	.286	.340	.440	$18
Sean Berry	CLE	61	8	1	8	0	.240	.296	.401	-$3
Dante Bichette	BOS	569	86	25	102	6	.291	.344	.480	$18
Casey Blake	MIN	118	21	7	23	2	.245	.332	.468	$0
Tim Bogar	FA	211	25	4	22	1	.209	.290	.321	-$4
Bret Boone	SEA	499	72	19	70	10	.253	.320	.423	$9
Mike Bordick	BAL	546	81	15	71	9	.260	.318	.397	$9
Russ Branyan	CLE	248	39	19	48	0	.247	.321	.541	$3
Scott Brosius	NYY	460	60	16	68	4	.243	.309	.397	$4
Dee Brown	KC	340	58	14	53	7	.269	.326	.469	$8
Brian Buchanan	MIN	147	18	6	15	0	.247	.317	.418	-$2
Jay Buhner	SEA	303	41	20	61	0	.234	.354	.480	$3
Morgan Burkhart	BOS	34	6	2	6	1	.268	.362	.417	-$2
Ellis Burks	CLE	372	68	24	87	6	.294	.385	.546	$15
Homer Bush	TOR	316	43	2	27	15	.288	.325	.360	$9
C										
Jolbert Cabrera	CLE	181	28	3	14	8	.258	.306	.366	$2
Miguel Cairo	OAK	416	53	2	36	25	.273	.320	.346	$13
Mike Cameron	SEA	548	94	20	74	30	.259	.357	.440	$20
Ken Caminiti	TEX	307	57	19	63	5	.268	.381	.506	$9
Jay Canizaro	MIN	356	45	8	45	5	.273	.322	.419	$6
Jose Canseco	ANA	335	53	21	60	4	.249	.353	.490	$6
Javier Cardona	DET	196	30	9	33	1	.260	.311	.452	$1
Mike Caruso	FA	152	17	0	12	2	.228	.274	.288	-$3
Vinny Castilla	TB	338	37	14	53	2	.267	.310	.439	$5
Alberto Castillo	TOR	126	10	1	13	0	.231	.302	.288	-$4

NAME	TEAM	AB	RUN	HR	RBI	SB	AVG	OBA	SLG	$VAL
Frank Catalanotto	TEX	346	60	13	48	6	.286	.357	.456	$9
Roger Cedeno	DET	505	101	8	45	49	.292	.384	.396	$31
Eric Chavez	OAK	552	91	27	90	3	.288	.366	.512	$16
Ryan Christenson	OAK	195	37	4	22	3	.244	.333	.364	-$1
Tony Clark	DET	406	59	25	73	1	.280	.356	.518	$11
Royce Clayton	CHW	531	76	15	56	12	.256	.316	.399	$9
Edgard Clemente	FA	46	5	1	5	0	.249	.280	.370	-$3
Ivanon Coffie	BAL	56	6	0	6	2	.208	.269	.317	-$3
Jeff Conine	BAL	387	48	12	51	3	.269	.323	.441	$6
Wil Cordero	CLE	456	64	15	64	1	.279	.332	.468	$8
Marty Cordova	CLE	111	14	3	15	2	.264	.341	.415	-$1
Steve Cox	TB	420	55	15	45	2	.281	.359	.450	$7
Joe Crede	CHW	211	30	4	33	1	.271	.322	.405	$1
Deivi Cruz	DET	581	75	11	85	1	.309	.325	.435	$15
Jacob Cruz	CLE	31	5	1	5	0	.277	.350	.442	-$3
Jose Cruz	TOR	590	93	28	74	16	.253	.350	.466	$15
Chad Curtis	TEX	207	33	5	29	4	.256	.348	.404	$1
D										
Johnny Damon	OAK	612	118	16	85	47	.336	.398	.511	$45
Brian Daubach	BOS	302	37	14	50	1	.261	.327	.479	$4
Carlos Delgado	TOR	556	110	41	132	1	.317	.435	.623	$27
Wilson Delgado	KC	176	27	2	14	4	.256	.311	.334	$0
Delino DeShields	BAL	578	87	11	80	34	.284	.361	.426	$26
Einer Diaz	CLE	322	37	5	31	5	.275	.324	.379	$4
Mike Difelice	TB	201	22	6	22	0	.257	.297	.412	-$1
Gary DiSarcina	ANA	440	47	3	44	4	.261	.294	.332	$2
Ray Durham	CHW	616	118	16	70	29	.285	.365	.446	$24
Jermaine Dye	KC	594	100	29	115	1	.299	.366	.521	$20
E										
Damion Easley	DET	533	84	18	68	14	.263	.347	.429	$13
Kevin Elster	FA	162	21	9	23	0	.228	.336	.436	-$2
Juan Encarnacion	DET	550	74	17	75	22	.285	.315	.456	$21
Darin Erstad	ANA	635	106	21	84	23	.322	.377	.490	$32
Tom Evans	FA	53	10	0	5	1	.270	.386	.341	-$3
Carl Everett	BOS	484	82	29	105	16	.297	.364	.552	$24
F										
Jorge Fabregas	ANA	173	15	3	19	1	.240	.296	.330	-$2
Sal Fasano	OAK	115	18	7	19	0	.229	.302	.434	-$2
Carlos Febles	KC	480	80	6	48	22	.270	.340	.381	$13
Robert Fick	DET	193	22	5	29	3	.267	.359	.414	$2
John Flaherty	TB	361	36	10	42	0	.249	.285	.370	$0
Darrin Fletcher	TOR	404	43	18	62	1	.288	.324	.468	$10
Brook Fordyce	BAL	416	51	15	65	1	.282	.323	.451	$8
Matt Franco	FA	136	13	3	16	0	.242	.351	.333	-$3
Ryan Freel	TOR	32	6	1	5	2	.276	.360	.425	-$2
Jeff Frye	TOR	203	30	1	11	4	.273	.338	.368	$0
Travis Fryman	CLE	547	85	21	97	2	.287	.359	.475	$14
Brad Fullmer	TOR	504	72	26	95	3	.288	.334	.516	$16
G										
Andres Galarraga	TEX	359	52	17	73	3	.272	.326	.479	$8
Karim Garcia	CLE	112	16	6	19	2	.238	.310	.470	-$1
Nomar Garciaparra	BOS	557	108	25	105	8	.349	.409	.586	$31

NAME	TEAM	AB	RUN	HR	RBI	SB	AVG	OBA	SLG	$VAL
Jason Giambi	OAK	535	109	38	130	2	.309	.437	.573	$24
Jeremy Giambi	OAK	307	45	11	51	0	.284	.366	.453	$5
Benji Gil	ANA	233	25	5	21	8	.237	.295	.358	$1
Charles Gipson	SEA	52	5	0	4	1	.223	.278	.288	-$3
Troy Glaus	ANA	560	107	44	100	12	.280	.386	.556	$24
Alex S. Gonzalez	TOR	534	69	14	64	8	.255	.315	.399	$7
Juan Gonzalez	CLE	506	87	30	94	1	.305	.354	.557	$19
Tony Graffanino	CHW	135	23	2	14	4	.269	.339	.390	$0
Craig Grebeck	FA	209	32	2	20	0	.289	.347	.378	$0
Todd Greene	TOR	154	18	7	19	0	.241	.276	.432	-$2
Willie Greene	FA	287	34	11	40	3	.236	.319	.414	$1
Rusty Greer	TEX	453	80	12	78	3	.299	.388	.467	$12
Ben Grieve	TB	580	92	27	100	3	.286	.366	.498	$17
Carlos Guillen	SEA	530	84	15	79	3	.277	.339	.407	$10
Jose Guillen	TB	333	43	8	42	2	.269	.308	.426	$3
Ozzie Guillen	TB	157	22	2	15	2	.236	.285	.330	-$2
Cristian Guzman	MIN	605	86	7	50	33	.260	.307	.393	$17
Jerry Hairston Jr.	BAL	311	46	8	33	15	.269	.335	.397	$9
H										
Shane Halter	DET	263	27	3	29	5	.251	.294	.336	$1
Bill Haselman	TEX	142	16	4	18	1	.267	.316	.431	-$1
Chris Hatcher	TB	36	4	1	7	0	.249	.271	.526	-$3
Scott Hatteberg	BOS	211	22	7	31	0	.268	.371	.430	$1
Nathan Haynes	ANA	53	6	1	5	2	.249	.300	.346	-$2
Bret Hemphill	FA	266	46	10	63	0	.308	.412	.492	$7
Rickey Henderson	FA	368	69	6	32	33	.248	.375	.348	$14
Ramon Hernandez	OAK	412	49	13	62	1	.256	.321	.401	$4
Bob Higginson	DET	533	87	24	84	11	.285	.369	.498	$18
Glenallen Hill	NYY	295	46	24	57	2	.277	.325	.546	$9
Shea Hillenbrand	BOS	33	5	1	4	0	.262	.299	.373	-$3
A.J. Hinch	KC	175	23	3	17	1	.251	.306	.346	-$2
Denny Hocking	MIN	359	49	5	42	8	.273	.341	.377	$6
Trenidad Hubbard	FA	117	21	2	9	5	.240	.316	.334	-$1
Aubrey Huff	TB	310	45	11	46	1	.287	.336	.465	$6
Torii Hunter	MIN	489	64	9	57	8	.271	.315	.411	$8
Butch Huskey	FA	307	43	12	51	2	.267	.338	.442	$5
I										
Raul Ibanez	FA	157	21	4	18	3	.242	.305	.379	-$1
Brandon Inge	DET	34	4	1	6	1	.240	.294	.409	-$3
J										
John Jaha	OAK	117	21	6	22	1	.234	.389	.429	-$1
Stan Javier	SEA	306	51	3	33	8	.270	.347	.374	$4
Derek Jeter	NYY	607	124	18	83	22	.337	.409	.503	$33
Dangelo Jimenez	NYY	200	30	5	29	5	.276	.336	.415	$3
Mark L. Johnson	CHW	135	18	2	13	2	.245	.354	.342	-$2
Nick Johnson	NYY	81	18	3	15	2	.304	.383	.473	$0
Russ Johnson	TB	256	37	5	26	6	.266	.359	.373	$3
Jacque Jones	MIN	530	72	18	76	6	.286	.321	.465	$14
Wally Joyner	FA	245	27	5	36	0	.272	.365	.392	$1
David Justice	NYY	497	85	31	106	2	.276	.379	.513	$15
K										
Gabe Kapler	TEX	539	74	21	74	11	.312	.372	.506	$22

NAME	TEAM	AB	RUN	HR	RBI	SB	AVG	OBA	SLG	$VAL
Adam Kennedy	ANA	580	79	9	72	21	.275	.307	.419	$17
Gene Kingsale	BAL	139	19	0	14	2	.241	.289	.314	-$3
Chuck Knoblauch	NYY	451	87	9	39	20	.284	.376	.416	$15
Paul Konerko	CHW	502	76	22	87	1	.293	.356	.484	$14
Corey Koskie	MIN	520	80	12	76	5	.299	.380	.443	$14
L										
David Lamb	ANA	100	13	2	13	1	.268	.318	.390	-$1
Mike Lamb	TEX	305	43	6	37	1	.288	.335	.425	$4
Tom Lampkin	SEA	55	8	3	10	0	.249	.306	.463	-$2
Mike Lansing	BOS	308	44	7	36	5	.253	.302	.391	$2
Joe Lawrence	TOR	31	6	1	3	1	.244	.283	.428	-$3
Matt Lawton	MIN	554	83	13	83	25	.283	.380	.430	$22
Matt Lecroy	MIN	201	22	6	20	0	.247	.315	.400	-$2
Ricky Ledee	TEX	434	60	13	71	11	.254	.336	.429	$9
Carlos Lee	CHW	554	95	21	90	10	.307	.343	.496	$22
Darren Lewis	BOS	202	31	2	16	8	.245	.315	.317	$1
Mark Lewis	FA	213	23	4	28	5	.252	.301	.392	$1
Jim Leyritz	FA	108	10	4	13	0	.221	.313	.370	-$3
Jeff Liefer	CHW	135	21	5	23	1	.258	.338	.466	$0
Cole Liniak	TOR	71	7	1	6	0	.275	.314	.380	-$2
Kenny Lofton	CLE	545	111	12	64	32	.288	.382	.424	$24
Terrence Long	OAK	610	97	19	79	10	.297	.345	.456	$19
Fernando Lunar	BAL	62	4	0	6	1	.209	.245	.274	-$4
M										
Jose Macias	DET	175	27	3	25	2	.243	.307	.360	-$1
Wendell Magee	DET	193	33	8	33	2	.278	.316	.445	$3
Al Martin	SEA	404	68	14	37	11	.271	.326	.447	$9
Edgar Martinez	SEA	540	94	32	123	4	.301	.407	.541	$22
Felix Martinez	TB	410	56	2	24	13	.229	.302	.321	$0
Tino Martinez	NYY	541	75	20	93	4	.262	.335	.449	$10
Ruben Mateo	TEX	486	79	21	69	14	.288	.327	.499	$18
Luis Matos	BAL	459	55	4	46	30	.240	.286	.327	$12
Jason Maxwell	MIN	120	16	2	13	2	.243	.306	.360	-$2
David McCarty	KC	260	33	11	51	0	.268	.326	.452	$3
John McDonald	CLE	91	12	0	8	3	.225	.268	.284	-$3
Fred McGriff	TB	535	76	27	99	2	.277	.376	.469	$14
Mark McLemore	SEA	455	75	4	41	22	.251	.356	.324	$9
Billy McMillon	DET	310	50	8	52	4	.296	.384	.464	$8
Mitch Meluskey	DET	408	57	17	80	2	.304	.402	.502	$13
Frankie Menechino	OAK	140	27	5	23	2	.259	.346	.438	$0
Lou Merloni	BOS	196	19	0	25	2	.286	.319	.382	$1
Doug Mientkiewicz	MIN	424	59	11	59	5	.280	.358	.422	$9
Matt Mieske	FA	108	15	4	14	0	.244	.299	.402	-$2
Chad Moeller	MIN	142	15	2	14	0	.248	.294	.347	-$3
Ben Molina	ANA	434	53	12	64	1	.279	.317	.408	$7
Raul Mondesi	TOR	471	85	27	79	26	.265	.329	.508	$22
Melvin Mora	BAL	483	71	8	54	15	.266	.324	.382	$10
Mickey Morandini	TOR	260	31	1	20	4	.257	.329	.336	$0
Hal Morris	FA	179	22	2	17	0	.287	.374	.388	$0
Chad Mottola	TOR	31	5	1	6	2	.273	.319	.482	-$2
Lyle Mouton	FA	67	10	2	11	1	.272	.344	.463	-$2
Greg Myers	BAL	182	16	5	19	0	.233	.298	.358	-$3

NAME	TEAM	AB	RUN	HR	RBI	SB	AVG	OBA	SLG	$VAL
N										
Dave Nilsson	FA	347	54	17	60	2	.284	.370	.481	$9
Trot Nixon	BOS	332	53	11	46	5	.274	.364	.462	$6
Jonathan Nunnally	FA	66	14	2	6	2	.200	.334	.368	-$3
O										
Troy O'Leary	BOS	548	76	19	81	1	.268	.327	.445	$9
Paul O'Neill	NYY	529	71	17	96	12	.279	.343	.431	$16
Jose Offerman	BOS	407	69	7	42	8	.276	.373	.395	$7
John Olerud	SEA	549	89	15	96	1	.296	.408	.457	$14
Joe Oliver	NYY	184	25	7	28	2	.233	.284	.408	-$1
Luis Ordaz	KC	140	21	1	14	5	.242	.295	.330	-$1
Magglio Ordonez	CHW	584	96	29	115	16	.308	.360	.523	$29
David Ortiz	MIN	473	67	12	70	2	.286	.374	.462	$9
Hector Ortiz	KC	155	15	2	12	1	.261	.309	.350	-$2
Jose Ortiz	OAK	76	14	1	11	3	.274	.359	.404	-$1
P										
Orlando Palmeiro	ANA	257	39	0	24	4	.289	.378	.356	$3
Rafael Palmeiro	TEX	540	95	40	122	3	.284	.390	.551	$20
Dean Palmer	DET	540	80	32	103	4	.261	.333	.481	$13
Josh Paul	CHW	187	39	4	19	4	.246	.290	.389	$0
Carlos Pena	TEX	57	11	2	11	1	.284	.352	.453	-$1
Danny Peoples	CLE	92	12	3	13	0	.258	.337	.433	-$2
Eduardo Perez	FA	81	9	3	12	1	.278	.335	.424	-$1
Herbert Perry	CHW	319	53	9	49	2	.292	.346	.453	$7
Adam Piatt	OAK	286	43	12	47	4	.288	.369	.496	$7
A.J. Pierzynski	MIN	202	27	3	27	3	.281	.315	.404	$2
Luis Polonia	FA	266	37	6	24	10	.292	.338	.426	$7
Jorge Posada	NYY	503	84	24	83	2	.269	.384	.479	$10
Tom Prince	MIN	83	9	1	10	1	.215	.292	.335	-$3
Q										
Mark Quinn	KC	548	84	26	90	5	.306	.361	.536	$20
R										
Manny Ramirez	BOS	537	118	46	144	2	.324	.429	.659	$30
Joe Randa	KC	602	86	15	94	6	.295	.340	.437	$17
Jeff Reboulet	FA	130	21	0	8	2	.220	.325	.272	-$4
Jeff Reed	FA	230	28	4	26	0	.236	.346	.346	-$3
Chris Richard	BAL	259	46	9	44	5	.245	.299	.428	$3
Cal Ripken	BAL	345	48	16	57	0	.266	.312	.454	$5
Luis Rivas	MIN	235	34	2	27	7	.256	.287	.370	$2
Alex Rodriguez	TEX	552	126	41	125	20	.312	.400	.603	$34
Henry Rodriguez	FA	356	49	21	64	1	.257	.331	.498	$6
Ivan Rodriguez	TEX	406	74	26	83	10	.320	.351	.578	$22
Jason Romano	TEX	37	6	1	5	1	.271	.345	.406	-$2
S										
Olmedo Saenz	OAK	205	36	9	32	1	.290	.359	.483	$3
Oscar Salazar	OAK	37	5	1	0	0	.280	.333	.405	-$3
Tim Salmon	ANA	533	98	30	95	1	.286	.398	.529	$16
Rey Sanchez	KC	521	70	1	47	9	.274	.310	.339	$7
Benito Santiago	FA	259	22	7	38	2	.257	.311	.397	$1
David Segui	BAL	529	81	18	86	1	.312	.360	.481	$17
Scott Servais	FA	157	14	3	18	0	.240	.301	.339	-$3
Scott Sheldon	TEX	114	20	4	17	0	.271	.325	.479	-$1

NAME	TEAM	AB	RUN	HR	RBI	SB	AVG	OBA	SLG	$VAL
Ruben Sierra	TEX	36	3	1	4	1	.228	.269	.381	-$3
Chris Singleton	CHW	455	71	12	59	19	.269	.310	.417	$14
Bobby Smith	TB	222	24	7	30	3	.246	.305	.402	$1
Mark Smith	FA	208	24	6	29	3	.240	.305	.412	$0
Luis Sojo	NYY	233	27	5	28	2	.263	.299	.381	$1
Alfonso Soriano	NYY	180	28	6	30	9	.275	.313	.433	$5
Shane Spencer	NYY	217	29	9	33	1	.271	.324	.465	$2
Scott Spiezio	ANA	293	43	14	44	1	.250	.334	.446	$2
Mike Stanley	OAK	225	29	11	37	0	.252	.356	.440	$1
Shannon Stewart	TOR	630	112	18	72	21	.311	.367	.473	$27
Kevin Stocker	FA	316	40	2	25	4	.240	.327	.330	-$2
Chris Stynes	BOS	357	64	10	37	7	.288	.345	.428	$8
Ichiro Suzuki	SEA	348	56	7	57	1	.244	.309	.391	$0
Mike Sweeney	KC	572	97	25	121	7	.316	.382	.516	$25
T										
Eddie Taubensee	CLE	265	33	9	39	0	.280	.334	.439	$3
Miguel Tejada	OAK	579	104	32	110	7	.290	.357	.520	$21
Frank Thomas	CHW	543	100	34	127	2	.315	.424	.577	$25
Jim Thome	CLE	556	109	37	111	1	.273	.407	.538	$16
Jason Tyner	TB	220	25	0	24	12	.266	.315	.318	$4
V										
Mario Valdez	OAK	234	39	9	36	0	.290	.361	.464	$4
Javier Valentin	MIN	115	13	2	16	1	.253	.293	.357	-$2
John Valentin	BOS	145	21	4	18	0	.256	.330	.417	-$2
Jose Valentin	CHW	540	99	23	85	15	.257	.338	.467	$14
Jason Varitek	BOS	416	54	12	62	1	.261	.340	.429	$4
Greg Vaughn	TB	499	92	35	92	10	.247	.352	.505	$14
Mo Vaughn	ANA	537	78	31	104	1	.261	.340	.523	$12
Randy Velarde	TEX	369	62	9	37	10	.284	.357	.400	$9
Wilton Veras	BOS	104	13	1	9	0	.260	.292	.355	-$3
Omar Vizquel	CLE	598	103	6	64	30	.290	.362	.373	$23
W										
Lenny Webster	FA	95	8	1	9	0	.220	.285	.291	-$4
Walt Weiss	FA	184	28	1	17	2	.246	.337	.321	-$2
Vernon Wells	TOR	245	38	8	33	6	.253	.312	.432	$3
Chris Widger	SEA	262	28	11	34	2	.244	.309	.433	$1
Bernie Williams	NYY	549	110	28	117	12	.311	.399	.538	$27
Gerald Williams	TB	512	77	18	75	13	.267	.309	.432	$13
Craig Wilson	KC	124	17	2	11	1	.254	.313	.333	-$2
Dan Wilson	SEA	308	35	6	31	2	.249	.302	.365	$0
Randy Winn	TB	295	47	2	25	12	.277	.348	.370	$6
Chris Woodward	TOR	140	20	3	18	2	.232	.302	.364	-$2
Shawn Wooten	ANA	34	5	1	6	0	.262	.311	.458	-$3
Y										
Mike Young	TEX	112	15	2	14	3	.275	.327	.398	$0
Z										
Gregg Zaun	KC	228	31	6	30	6	.257	.353	.380	$3

NATIONAL LEAGUE

NAME	TEAM	AB	RUN	HR	RBI	SB	AVG	OBA	SLG	$VAL
A										
Jeff Abbott	FLA	202	27	6	27	2	.280	.345	.441	$2
Kurt Abbott	ATL	179	25	6	20	2	.249	.298	.413	-$1
Bob Abreu	PHI	570	106	23	85	28	.321	.424	.547	$33
Benny Agbayani	NYM	444	73	20	74	8	.280	.370	.483	$14
Manny Alexander	FA	116	16	2	11	2	.229	.276	.336	-$3
Edgardo Alfonzo	NYM	571	112	25	97	5	.313	.405	.518	$23
Luis Alicea	FA	209	35	3	24	1	.267	.346	.388	$0
Moises Alou	HOU	524	95	31	128	5	.327	.397	.583	$28
Clemente Alvarez	PHI	37	4	0	4	0	.201	.294	.293	-$4
Rich Amaral	ATL	91	15	0	7	7	.253	.328	.316	$0
Marlon Anderson	PHI	337	30	4	37	7	.255	.299	.368	$3
Shane Andrews	STL	169	20	10	29	1	.217	.313	.435	-$1
Alex Arias	SD	156	19	2	19	1	.251	.326	.348	-$2
Rich Aurilia	SF	524	67	20	77	2	.274	.336	.441	$11
Brad Ausmus	HOU	472	67	8	49	11	.269	.359	.378	$8
Bruce Aven	LA	215	29	8	38	2	.271	.332	.442	$3
B										
Jeff Bagwell	HOU	577	143	44	128	16	.304	.424	.603	$33
Paul Bako	ATL	147	12	1	13	0	.241	.319	.332	-$3
Rod Barajas	AZ	112	17	3	21	0	.246	.286	.411	-$2
Glen Barker	HOU	62	18	2	7	11	.247	.335	.403	$2
Kevin Barker	MIL	155	20	6	20	2	.243	.345	.395	-$1
Michael Barrett	MON	415	46	4	41	0	.280	.334	.398	$3
Danny Bautista	AZ	377	58	11	58	7	.279	.319	.446	$9
Rich Becker	FA	272	50	7	33	4	.243	.384	.378	$1
Derek Bell	PIT	543	82	17	72	12	.263	.338	.414	$12
Jay Bell	AZ	521	91	22	74	6	.262	.348	.451	$11
Mike Bell	COL	68	8	2	7	0	.264	.318	.397	-$3
Ron Belliard	MIL	530	75	8	55	6	.277	.367	.406	$8
Adrian Beltre	LA	540	83	25	90	14	.295	.364	.456	$22
Marvin Benard	SF	533	95	12	56	22	.275	.350	.415	$16
Mike Benjamin	PIT	134	16	1	12	3	.252	.289	.348	-$2
Gary Bennett	PHI	138	13	4	19	0	.256	.347	.381	-$2
Dave Berg	FLA	235	28	2	22	3	.270	.347	.370	$1
Peter Bergeron	MON	540	87	5	32	12	.265	.342	.377	$7
Lance Berkman	HOU	423	86	25	79	9	.303	.396	.563	$19
Craig Biggio	HOU	443	82	11	48	19	.276	.367	.424	$14
Henry Blanco	MIL	280	29	7	30	0	.241	.327	.397	-$1
Geoff Blum	MON	236	29	9	31	1	.276	.334	.438	$3
Hiram Bocachica	LA	52	10	1	4	1	.248	.312	.375	-$3
Tim Bogar	FA	211	25	4	22	1	.209	.290	.321	-$4
Barry Bonds	SF	470	122	45	105	15	.284	.419	.637	$26
Bobby Bonilla	STL	201	20	5	26	0	.238	.338	.380	-$2
Aaron Boone	CIN	524	72	19	78	14	.283	.345	.457	$17
Milton Bradley	MON	534	70	6	52	6	.280	.338	.411	$8
Darren Bragg	NYM	42	5	1	5	1	.247	.335	.371	-$3
Jeff Branson	LA	50	7	1	7	0	.233	.298	.380	-$4
Rico Brogna	ATL	513	68	15	78	6	.261	.315	.422	$9

NAME	TEAM	AB	RUN	HR	RBI	SB	AVG	OBA	SLG	$VAL
Adrian Brown	PIT	398	76	6	33	15	.292	.359	.408	$11
Brant Brown	MIL	134	15	5	18	2	.238	.290	.428	-$1
Emil Brown	PIT	180	18	5	23	5	.266	.325	.396	$2
Roosevelt Brown	CHC	114	12	3	17	2	.297	.324	.486	$1
Damon Buford	CHC	408	54	12	44	6	.251	.319	.392	$4
Jeromy Burnitz	MIL	539	90	32	102	6	.245	.366	.488	$12
Pat Burrell	PHI	540	75	26	104	2	.280	.383	.506	$15
C										
Orlando Cabrera	MON	444	53	12	53	5	.255	.304	.397	$5
Jose Canseco	FA	335	53	21	60	4	.249	.353	.490	$7
Mike Caruso	FA	152	17	0	12	2	.228	.274	.288	-$4
Raul Casanova	MIL	236	20	7	36	2	.234	.311	.375	-$1
Sean Casey	CIN	522	85	30	115	2	.340	.405	.540	$28
Luis Castillo	FLA	559	99	1	23	60	.320	.404	.378	$36
Juan Castro	CIN	287	27	5	27	2	.234	.277	.350	-$2
Ramon Castro	FLA	173	12	4	17	0	.249	.333	.370	-$2
Raul Chavez	HOU	70	6	1	7	0	.240	.304	.318	-$4
Guisep Chiaramonte	SF	42	6	2	8	0	.245	.314	.448	-$3
Jeff Cirillo	COL	601	106	13	102	5	.325	.396	.469	$23
Brady Clark	CIN	52	8	1	5	3	.268	.358	.402	-$2
Edgard Clemente	FA	46	5	1	5	0	.249	.280	.370	-$3
Mike Colangelo	SD	72	10	0	6	3	.292	.353	.396	-$1
Greg Colbrunn	AZ	225	33	8	39	1	.305	.378	.498	$5
Michael Coleman	CIN	41	6	1	6	2	.290	.358	.496	-$2
Jason Conti	AZ	119	20	3	15	4	.251	.312	.402	-$1
Ron Coomer	CHC	219	25	7	32	1	.269	.312	.417	$2
Trace Coquillette	CHC	34	3	1	4	0	.221	.298	.323	-$4
Alex Cora	LA	537	58	5	48	5	.243	.293	.348	$0
Craig Counsell	AZ	187	26	2	15	2	.275	.356	.383	$0
Felipe Crespo	SF	141	17	5	22	3	.276	.334	.432	$1
D.T. Cromer	CIN	55	8	2	9	1	.268	.322	.453	-$2
Midre Cummings	AZ	127	17	3	16	1	.276	.342	.418	-$1
D										
Mike Darr	SD	427	44	3	59	17	.281	.352	.408	$12
Ben Davis	SD	298	30	7	32	2	.260	.328	.379	$1
Eric Davis	SF	305	47	10	50	4	.287	.361	.430	$7
Russ Davis	SF	298	41	14	41	1	.253	.303	.440	$3
Travis Dawkins	CIN	32	5	0	3	2	.231	.306	.375	-$3
Kory DeHaan	SD	111	20	2	14	4	.234	.295	.337	-$2
Tom De la Rosa	MON	89	9	0	11	4	.259	.326	.367	-$1
Dave Dellucci	AZ	112	12	2	15	2	.291	.362	.407	$0
J.D. Drew	STL	473	87	20	62	21	.300	.395	.483	$22
Rob Ducey	PHI	157	24	6	25	2	.216	.336	.391	-$2
Shawon Dunston	SF	257	36	10	46	7	.257	.273	.454	$5
Todd Dunwoody	CHC	206	19	4	23	3	.244	.282	.369	-$1
Rube Durazo	AZ	334	61	19	59	2	.298	.400	.548	$11
E										
Kevin Eberwein	SD	58	9	3	11	0	.253	.334	.462	-$2
Angel Echevarria	MIL	91	11	4	15	0	.263	.340	.435	-$2
Jim Edmonds	STL	541	123	33	101	10	.290	.386	.536	$22
Kevin Elster	FA	162	21	9	23	0	.228	.336	.436	-$2
Alex Escobar	NYM	152	27	6	26	6	.288	.370	.466	$4

NAME	TEAM	AB	RUN	HR	RBI	SB	AVG	OBA	SLG	$VAL
Bobby Estalella	SF	310	45	14	52	3	.238	.356	.453	$3
Johnny Estrada	PHI	32	4	1	4	0	.247	.268	.447	-$3
Tony Eusebio	HOU	206	21	5	28	0	.271	.348	.388	$0
Tom Evans	FA	53	10	0	5	1	.270	.386	.341	-$3
Adam Everett	HOU	255	39	5	26	10	.243	.335	.346	$2
F										
Pedro Feliz	SF	311	44	8	43	1	.261	.409	.437	$2
Steve Finley	AZ	519	91	30	88	10	.259	.333	.499	$15
Cliff Floyd	FLA	416	70	20	84	20	.293	.365	.512	$21
Andy Fox	FLA	255	31	5	24	8	.247	.326	.355	$2
Matt Franco	FA	136	13	3	16	0	.242	.351	.333	-$3
Hanley Frias	AZ	95	16	2	7	2	.239	.347	.339	-$3
Rafael Furcal	ATL	545	104	7	49	50	.305	.401	.402	$32
G										
Ron Gant	COL	453	81	23	63	8	.251	.345	.471	$9
Luis Garcia	STL	35	5	1	3	1	.244	.271	.354	-$3
Brian Giles	PIT	527	105	34	115	6	.303	.418	.571	$24
Bernard Gilkey	STL	176	21	4	22	2	.224	.312	.355	-$2
Joe Girardi	CHC	286	36	5	33	2	.257	.311	.363	$1
Doug Glanville	PHI	638	94	9	58	31	.290	.330	.399	$23
Ross Gload	CHC	52	7	2	8	0	.261	.300	.474	-$3
Chris Gomez	SD	159	15	1	11	0	.250	.330	.331	-$3
Alex Gonzalez	FLA	408	46	9	44	5	.240	.271	.377	$1
Luis Gonzalez	AZ	580	101	28	104	5	.305	.378	.521	$23
Wiki Gonzalez	SD	330	29	7	37	2	.245	.309	.395	$0
Tom Goodwin	LA	490	86	5	48	49	.265	.344	.348	$23
Mark Grace	AZ	503	80	12	79	2	.293	.393	.449	$12
Craig Grebeck	FA	209	32	2	20	0	.289	.347	.378	$0
Chad Green	SD	43	6	1	5	3	.246	.320	.384	-$2
Scarborough Green	CHC	98	18	0	6	6	.238	.294	.282	-$1
Shawn Green	LA	613	110	31	106	24	.282	.369	.514	$27
Charlie Greene	SD	35	0	0	0	0	.192	.230	.255	-$5
Willie Greene	FA	287	34	11	40	3	.236	.319	.414	$1
Ken Griffey	CIN	527	103	39	119	12	.285	.385	.564	$25
Marquis Grissom	MIL	352	44	9	40	10	.253	.299	.382	$5
Mark Grudzielanek	LA	576	88	7	49	11	.287	.332	.392	$12
Vladimir Guerrero	MON	588	102	44	124	11	.334	.396	.639	$37
Wilton Guerrero	CIN	338	40	2	29	9	.287	.324	.369	$6
Ricky Gutierrez	CHC	449	66	8	52	8	.271	.366	.376	$8
Edwards Guzman	SF	31	4	0	3	0	.284	.341	.368	-$3
Tony Gwynn	SD	306	42	6	45	2	.318	.365	.454	$8
H										
Chris Haas	STL	47	8	2	9	0	.263	.361	.488	-$3
Darryl Hamilton	NYM	371	63	5	30	5	.294	.373	.394	$7
Jeffrey Hammonds	MIL	507	100	24	108	13	.299	.363	.493	$23
Dave Hansen	LA	105	15	5	21	0	.268	.400	.495	-$1
Lenny Harris	NYM	199	25	3	22	8	.268	.318	.372	$3
Charlie Hayes	HOU	134	16	3	19	1	.244	.335	.362	-$2
Wes Helms	ATL	109	12	3	10	1	.255	.329	.413	-$2
Todd Helton	COL	574	125	38	132	5	.351	.436	.640	$36
Bret Hemphill	FA	266	46	10	63	0	.308	.412	.492	$8
Rickey Henderson	FA	368	69	6	32	33	.248	.375	.348	$13

NAME	TEAM	AB	RUN	HR	RBI	SB	AVG	OBA	SLG	$VAL
Chad Hermansen	PIT	180	23	6	20	4	.240	.291	.427	$0
Alex Hernandez	PIT	113	13	3	16	3	.257	.296	.391	-$1
Carlos Hernandez	STL	149	14	2	21	1	.257	.319	.360	-$1
Jose Hernandez	MIL	449	59	14	59	6	.252	.322	.400	$6
Richard Hidalgo	HOU	541	102	37	108	13	.292	.374	.576	$25
Todd Hollandsworth	COL	513	94	23	78	19	.301	.361	.489	$24
Tyler Houston	MIL	250	26	13	34	2	.248	.301	.450	$2
Thomas Howard	PIT	76	7	3	14	1	.242	.293	.405	-$2
Trenidad Hubbard	FA	117	21	2	9	5	.240	.316	.334	-$1
Ken Huckaby	AZ	51	5	1	5	0	.239	.270	.322	-$4
Todd Hundley	CHC	295	44	21	58	1	.253	.343	.482	$6
Brian L. Hunter	PHI	245	40	1	15	16	.249	.308	.316	$4
Brian R. Hunter	PHI	130	16	6	21	0	.221	.321	.422	-$2
Butch Huskey	FA	307	43	12	51	2	.267	.338	.442	$5
I										
Raul Ibanez	FA	157	21	4	18	3	.242	.305	.379	-$1
J										
Damian Jackson	SD	487	70	7	42	33	.247	.338	.362	$13
Reggie Jefferson	PIT	197	22	6	25	0	.281	.348	.447	$1
Geoff Jenkins	MIL	538	97	32	97	9	.302	.359	.570	$24
Marcus Jensen	LA	94	11	2	9	0	.211	.327	.352	-$4
Brian Johnson	LA	101	9	4	14	0	.220	.262	.378	-$3
Charles Johnson	FLA	406	64	24	73	1	.273	.352	.488	$10
Andruw Jones	ATL	629	116	34	105	25	.292	.362	.536	$31
Chipper Jones	ATL	578	118	39	110	18	.314	.415	.584	$33
Terry Jones	MON	181	28	0	13	8	.241	.287	.315	$0
Brian Jordan	ATL	523	83	20	90	12	.276	.334	.448	$16
Kevin Jordan	PHI	331	31	4	40	0	.255	.293	.360	$0
Wally Joyner	FA	245	27	5	36	0	.272	.365	.392	$1
K										
Eric Karros	LA	556	76	30	102	6	.264	.331	.480	$15
Jason Kendall	PIT	535	105	13	61	24	.318	.398	.477	$26
Jeff Kent	SF	558	104	28	118	12	.297	.372	.520	$24
Brooks Kieschnick	COL	105	13	5	17	0	.254	.335	.448	-$1
Danny Klassen	AZ	77	12	3	8	1	.253	.324	.386	-$2
Ryan Klesko	SD	495	82	26	93	17	.279	.381	.516	$20
Mark Kotsay	FLA	524	77	11	56	15	.300	.346	.429	$17
Chad Kreuter	LA	297	37	6	37	1	.241	.349	.346	-$1
L										
Ray Lankford	STL	458	84	25	75	11	.264	.364	.491	$14
Barry Larkin	CIN	356	64	9	41	15	.295	.381	.443	$13
Brandon Larson	CIN	66	9	2	10	1	.242	.302	.473	-$3
Jason LaRue	CIN	254	34	12	32	3	.244	.303	.462	$2
Derrek Lee	FLA	527	73	27	75	1	.285	.362	.456	$14
Travis Lee	PHI	411	56	10	55	11	.260	.358	.399	$8
Mark Lewis	FA	213	23	4	28	5	.252	.301	.392	$1
Jim Leyritz	FA	108	10	4	13	0	.221	.313	.370	-$3
Mike Lieberthal	PHI	418	62	19	76	1	.277	.339	.480	$10
Keith Lockhart	ATL	250	30	2	29	4	.263	.329	.350	$1
Paul LoDuca	LA	69	7	2	8	0	.241	.305	.356	-$3
Javy Lopez	ATL	411	54	21	78	1	.292	.343	.499	$12
Luis Lopez	MIL	178	21	4	22	1	.253	.309	.388	-$1

NAME	TEAM	AB	RUN	HR	RBI	SB	AVG	OBA	SLG	$VAL
Mark Loretta	MIL	431	63	6	50	2	.290	.353	.401	$7
Mike Lowell	FLA	529	75	23	93	6	.266	.338	.460	$13
Julio Lugo	HOU	430	80	12	44	22	.290	.347	.447	$17
M										
John Mabry	STL	222	31	7	30	1	.248	.298	.396	$0
Dave Magadan	SD	115	10	1	16	0	.277	.394	.367	-$2
Eli Marrero	STL	222	31	6	27	9	.225	.280	.370	$1
Dave Martinez	ATL	399	55	4	43	9	.270	.344	.356	$6
Ramon E. Martinez	SF	175	28	5	23	2	.282	.340	.431	$1
Sandy Martinez	MON	32	4	1	4	0	.241	.279	.411	-$4
Henry Mateo	MON	37	5	0	4	1	.232	.301	.339	-$3
Mike Matheny	STL	311	31	5	34	0	.246	.297	.334	-$1
Gary Matthews	CHC	204	31	4	22	4	.225	.312	.349	-$2
Brent Mayne	COL	325	36	5	53	1	.289	.375	.401	$5
Quinton McCracken	STL	87	13	1	11	3	.248	.325	.324	-$2
Jason McDonald	MIL	60	9	1	6	2	.226	.337	.329	-$3
Joe McEwing	NYM	298	38	5	30	5	.265	.309	.385	$3
Mark McGwire	STL	389	94	45	115	1	.282	.444	.663	$20
Aaron McNeal	HOU	76	8	2	15	0	.270	.305	.410	-$2
Pat Meares	PIT	390	47	10	40	1	.248	.310	.377	$1
Adam Melhuse	COL	45	7	1	5	1	.271	.319	.378	-$3
Chad Meyers	CHC	74	10	1	8	5	.237	.311	.351	-$1
Matt Mieske	FA	108	15	4	14	0	.244	.299	.402	-$2
Kevin Millar	FLA	261	36	11	45	0	.270	.363	.472	$3
Damian Miller	AZ	349	44	12	49	1	.274	.337	.443	$5
Damon Minor	SF	84	11	4	15	0	.251	.339	.429	-$2
Ryan Minor	MON	63	5	1	4	0	.198	.232	.280	-$5
Doug Mirabelli	SF	211	22	5	25	1	.236	.336	.375	-$2
Mike Mordecai	MON	112	14	2	11	1	.249	.303	.388	-$2
Hal Morris	FA	179	22	2	17	0	.287	.374	.388	$0
Warren Morris	PIT	527	67	10	54	6	.278	.356	.397	$9
James Mouton	MIL	138	23	2	15	10	.239	.345	.351	$1
Lyle Mouton	FA	67	10	2	11	1	.272	.344	.463	-$2
Bill Mueller	CHC	526	88	8	51	4	.276	.359	.388	$7
Calvin Murray	SF	190	33	3	23	9	.258	.353	.392	$2
N										
Phil Nevin	SD	485	75	28	97	2	.303	.374	.530	$19
Kevin Nicholson	SD	99	10	2	12	2	.244	.269	.367	-$2
Jose Nieves	CHC	187	16	5	22	1	.249	.290	.408	-$1
Dave Nilsson	FA	347	54	17	60	2	.284	.370	.481	$9
Greg Norton	COL	181	24	10	23	1	.278	.366	.514	$2
Abraham Nunez	FLA	79	15	2	13	3	.267	.360	.424	-$1
Abraham O. Nunez	PIT	118	12	2	9	3	.239	.319	.343	-$2
Jorge Nunez	LA	31	4	0	4	1	.266	.310	.377	-$3
Jonathan Nunnally	FA	66	14	2	6	2	.200	.334	.368	-$3
O										
Alex Ochoa	CIN	299	57	12	58	8	.291	.364	.492	$10
Augie Ojeda	CHC	80	10	2	10	1	.247	.334	.390	-$2
Rey Ordonez	NYM	506	44	0	50	5	.240	.306	.290	-$1
William Ortega	STL	60	9	2	11	0	.270	.303	.447	-$2
Keith Osik	PIT	134	11	3	18	2	.247	.321	.364	-$1
Eric Owens	SD	491	70	6	49	27	.276	.330	.370	$16

NAME	TEAM	AB	RUN	HR	RBI	SB	AVG	OBA	SLG	$VAL
Pablo Ozuna	FLA	67	8	1	6	3	.272	.328	.398	-$2
P										
Craig Paquette	STL	301	38	13	52	3	.252	.296	.434	$4
Corey Patterson	CHC	192	32	9	34	10	.251	.305	.464	$5
Jay Payton	NYM	557	71	19	71	6	.291	.331	.446	$15
Angel Pena	LA	133	19	4	19	2	.264	.294	.417	$0
Elvis Pena	COL	41	7	0	4	2	.240	.333	.419	-$3
Eddie Perez	ATL	135	14	3	15	1	.257	.312	.390	-$2
Eduardo Perez	FA	81	9	3	12	1	.278	.335	.424	-$1
Neifi Perez	COL	652	95	11	69	6	.284	.320	.420	$13
Santiago Perez	SD	207	30	2	21	10	.276	.330	.412	$4
Timoniel Perez	NYM	303	45	5	36	12	.306	.337	.436	$10
Tomas Perez	PHI	212	25	3	20	3	.231	.290	.347	-$2
Ben Petrick	COL	275	60	10	41	3	.320	.404	.525	$9
Mike Piazza	NYM	506	93	38	116	3	.309	.378	.597	$25
Juan Pierre	COL	451	77	0	45	26	.312	.355	.360	$19
Placido Polanco	STL	413	58	5	46	5	.291	.328	.373	$8
Luis Polonia	FA	266	37	6	24	10	.292	.338	.426	$7
Todd Pratt	NYM	145	26	6	23	1	.279	.361	.443	$1
R										
Aramis Ramirez	PIT	304	22	6	41	2	.280	.331	.421	$4
Jeff Reboulet	FA	130	21	0	8	2	.220	.325	.272	-$4
Mike Redmond	FLA	180	15	1	15	0	.273	.324	.338	-$2
Jeff Reed	FA	230	28	4	26	0	.236	.346	.346	-$3
Pokey Reese	CIN	510	74	10	46	30	.266	.323	.386	$17
Desi Relaford	NYM	299	39	3	33	8	.229	.330	.323	$0
Edgar Renteria	STL	554	90	13	67	27	.282	.350	.408	$21
Armando Rios	SF	296	53	13	62	6	.282	.367	.490	$9
Ruben Rivera	SD	448	68	20	59	12	.204	.297	.401	$2
Henry Rodriguez	FA	356	49	21	64	1	.257	.331	.498	$7
Scott Rolen	PHI	476	87	27	88	10	.289	.372	.542	$19
Jimmy Rollins	PHI	332	40	4	34	15	.270	.314	.410	$8
Wilken Ruan	MON	97	14	0	9	7	.267	.307	.000	$0
Rob Ryan	AZ	41	5	1	5	1	.272	.350	.390	-$3
S										
Donnie Sadler	CIN	104	16	1	9	3	.250	.284	.336	-$2
Reggie Sanders	AZ	366	57	15	46	23	.265	.338	.462	$14
FP Santangelo	LA	200	31	2	16	6	.224	.357	.308	-$2
Benito Santiago	FA	259	22	7	38	2	.257	.311	.397	$1
Dane Sardinha	CIN	36	4	0	5	0	.215	.266	.294	-$4
Luis Saturria	STL	39	5	1	5	1	.233	.291	.421	-$3
Brian Schneider	MON	169	10	3	17	0	.244	.285	.361	-$3
Kevin Sefcik	PHI	133	16	1	9	5	.269	.352	.386	$0
Fernando Seguignol	MON	282	38	17	36	0	.273	.336	.529	$5
Scott Servais	FA	157	14	3	18	0	.240	.301	.339	-$3
Richie Sexson	MIL	530	95	32	107	3	.290	.352	.521	$19
Chris Sexton	CIN	88	9	1	9	5	.246	.359	.330	-$1
Gary Sheffield	LA	489	97	37	100	8	.302	.417	.573	$24
Terry Shumpert	COL	259	53	10	38	10	.278	.349	.484	$8
Mark Smith	FA	208	24	6	29	3	.240	.305	.412	$0
J.T. Snow	SF	533	84	20	94	1	.267	.353	.445	$10
Juan Sosa	COL	112	16	2	10	4	.266	.310	.344	-$1

NAME	TEAM	AB	RUN	HR	RBI	SB	AVG	OBA	SLG	$VAL
Sammy Sosa	CHC	604	109	55	139	8	.289	.375	.629	$30
Bill Spiers	HOU	279	36	2	32	6	.277	.360	.371	$3
Ed Sprague	SD	291	37	13	43	1	.250	.315	.444	$2
Matt Stairs	CHC	497	81	27	90	4	.254	.356	.475	$11
Lee Stevens	MON	429	60	21	70	1	.266	.336	.480	$8
Kelly Stinnett	CIN	217	24	8	30	1	.227	.298	.403	-$2
Kevin Stocker	FA	316	40	2	25	4	.240	.327	.330	-$2
BJ Surhoff	ATL	513	71	17	72	7	.286	.334	.448	$14
Mark Sweeney	MIL	72	9	2	7	0	.240	.345	.380	-$3
T										
Fernando Tatis	MON	499	90	27	93	11	.284	.378	.513	$19
Reggie Taylor	PHI	160	17	4	23	10	.263	.290	.409	$3
Jorge Toca	NYM	37	8	1	9	1	.268	.344	.432	-$2
Andy Tracy	MON	221	33	9	37	2	.260	.339	.483	$2
Bubba Trammell	SD	282	38	12	47	2	.275	.358	.482	$5
Chris Truby	HOU	424	55	17	86	3	.270	.307	.466	$10
Michael Tucker	CIN	227	43	11	30	9	.259	.361	.472	$5
Chris Turner	PHI	61	6	1	4	0	.228	.308	.321	-$4
V										
John Vander Wal	PIT	287	49	15	64	6	.286	.385	.514	$10
Robin Ventura	NYM	497	68	25	92	2	.259	.353	.468	$10
Quilvio Veras	ATL	373	70	5	39	26	.282	.380	.378	$15
Jose Vidro	MON	593	93	20	87	3	.303	.353	.484	$18
Fernando Vina	STL	487	78	4	34	12	.293	.344	.390	$11
Joe Vitiello	SD	70	8	3	10	0	.239	.343	.369	-$3
Jose Vizcaino	HOU	264	30	1	20	5	.255	.310	.321	$0
W										
Matt Walbeck	CIN	158	17	4	14	1	.233	.285	.355	-$3
Larry Walker	COL	395	89	21	78	9	.321	.404	.578	$20
Todd Walker	COL	411	59	9	52	14	.297	.362	.456	$14
Daryle Ward	HOU	304	37	21	55	0	.284	.334	.546	$8
Turner Ward	PHI	94	9	2	12	2	.223	.299	.327	-$3
Lenny Webster	FA	95	8	1	9	0	.220	.285	.291	-$4
John Wehner	PIT	68	8	1	8	0	.232	.294	.304	-$4
Walt Weiss	FA	184	28	1	17	2	.246	.337	.321	-$2
Devon White	LA	233	33	7	29	8	.263	.312	.410	$4
Rondell White	CHC	412	66	16	62	8	.300	.350	.490	$14
Matt Williams	AZ	522	70	23	88	2	.276	.319	.460	$13
Enrique Wilson	PIT	302	36	5	30	4	.285	.335	.398	$4
Preston Wilson	FLA	583	88	31	107	28	.270	.331	.496	$26
Vance Wilson	NYM	37	4	1	5	0	.233	.303	.370	-$4
Tony Womack	AZ	586	94	6	48	51	.274	.316	.377	$27
Y										
Dmitri Young	CIN	550	76	18	87	1	.308	.354	.485	$17
Eric Young	CHC	546	89	5	45	52	.292	.367	.388	$30
Kevin Young	PIT	502	81	22	90	12	.273	.339	.468	$16
Z										
Todd Zeile	NYM	530	69	21	81	3	.256	.337	.439	$8
Julio Zuleta	CHC	65	12	3	11	0	.298	.334	.529	-$1

Players not listed are projected to have under 50 at-bats in 2001.

PITCHERS 2001 FORECAST STATS AND VALUES

AMERICAN LEAGUE

NAME	TEAM	W	L	SV	IP	ERA	RATIO	H	BB	K	$VAL
A											
Paul Abbott	SEA	9	8	0	162	4.02	1.32	142	71	102	$10
Rick Aguilera	FA	3	3	22	49	4.10	1.19	45	13	37	$20
Scott Aldred	CLE	2	2	0	32	4.86	1.56	35	16	27	-$1
Wilson Alvarez	TB	8	10	0	175	4.83	1.49	181	80	139	$0
Matt Anderson	DET	4	3	3	72	4.79	1.50	60	48	67	$2
Jamie Arnold	FA	1	3	3	44	5.85	1.62	47	25	30	-$2
Rolando Arrojo	BOS	10	10	0	166	5.26	1.48	180	65	122	-$1
B											
James Baldwin	CHW	9	8	0	168	5.10	1.51	189	65	108	-$2
Lorenzo Barcelo	CHW	4	3	0	73	3.78	1.26	71	21	47	$5
Rod Beck	BOS	3	2	2	46	3.90	1.28	44	14	37	$4
Kevin Beirne	TOR	2	4	0	61	5.48	1.40	61	24	50	-$1
Tim Belcher	ANA	4	6	0	56	6.10	1.56	65	22	27	-$3
Stan Belinda	FA	2	3	1	47	6.45	1.52	50	21	48	-$3
Sean Bergman	TB	2	2	0	45	6.95	1.76	63	16	22	-$6
Adam Bernero	DET	2	2	0	32	5.45	1.47	34	13	20	-$1
Rocky Biddle	CHW	1	1	0	31	7.12	1.68	42	10	12	-$5
Willie Blair	FA	9	9	0	152	5.41	1.45	181	40	78	-$1
Brian Boehringer	NYY	2	2	0	72	4.83	1.52	76	33	55	-$2
Pedro Borbon	TOR	2	1	1	40	5.56	1.74	39	31	27	-$3
Chad Bradford	OAK	1	1	0	33	3.90	1.40	36	10	19	$0
Jeff Brantley	TEX	2	5	21	54	6.25	1.66	61	29	56	$10
Jamie Brewington	FA	3	3	0	48	4.97	1.61	58	19	36	-$2
Mark Buehrle	CHW	4	2	0	88	4.08	1.42	93	32	63	$3
Dave Burba	CLE	16	7	0	201	4.36	1.46	204	90	173	$7
Paul Byrd	FA	4	4	0	56	5.32	1.41	58	21	33	$0
Tim Byrdak	CLE	1	1	2	36	6.22	1.70	44	17	25	-$3
C											
Chris Carpenter	TOR	10	13	0	170	5.55	1.57	196	71	115	-$6
Hector Carrasco	FA	4	4	1	68	4.68	1.57	76	31	54	$0
Frank Castillo	BOS	4	4	0	64	3.98	1.27	56	26	48	$4
Randy Choate	NYY	1	1	0	35	4.88	1.40	38	11	21	-$1
Mark Clark	FA	2	2	0	38	6.09	1.66	49	14	21	-$4
Roger Clemens	NYY	15	10	0	202	3.66	1.33	183	86	189	$17
Bartolo Colon	CLE	17	7	0	195	3.88	1.35	174	89	191	$15
David Cone	BOS	7	9	0	152	5.33	1.54	162	72	129	-$4
Brian Cooper	ANA	3	5	0	61	5.75	1.59	70	26	26	-$4
Francisco Cordero	TEX	2	3	0	65	5.13	1.77	72	43	44	-$5
Tim Crabtree	TEX	3	4	6	75	4.54	1.43	80	27	54	$5
Paxton Crawford	BOS	3	3	0	48	3.63	1.38	44	22	30	$2
Doug Creek	TB	2	3	6	67	4.87	1.49	55	45	80	$3

NAME	TEAM	W	L	SV	IP	ERA	RATIO	H	BB	K	$VAL
Jack Cressend	MIN	1	1	0	31	4.97	1.68	35	17	22	-$2
Darwin Cubillan	TEX	1	1	0	36	6.41	1.76	47	16	27	-$5
D											
Doug Davis	TEX	7	8	0	130	4.67	1.64	141	72	88	-$3
Chad Durbin	KC	3	4	0	59	5.90	1.65	68	30	31	-$5
E											
Derrin Ebert	TB	1	1	1	40	5.13	1.56	41	21	31	-$1
Dave Eiland	OAK	2	4	0	57	6.60	1.67	76	19	26	-$6
Cal Eldred	CHW	7	7	0	155	5.35	1.55	159	81	125	-$4
Scott Erickson	BAL	5	6	0	99	5.80	1.62	117	43	50	-$6
Kelvim Escobar	TOR	11	14	0	181	5.37	1.53	193	84	141	-$3
F											
Chuck Finley	CLE	16	9	0	210	4.27	1.45	206	98	188	$8
Bryce Florie	BOS	2	3	1	67	4.64	1.55	77	28	50	-$1
Keith Foulke	CHW	3	2	33	80	2.79	0.96	58	18	86	$37
John Frascatore	TOR	2	3	0	70	4.97	1.52	79	28	32	-$2
Chris Fussell	KC	3	3	1	58	5.46	1.58	58	34	47	-$2
Mike Fyhrie	ANA	0	1	0	47	3.26	1.40	51	15	34	$2
G											
Rich Garces	BOS	3	3	1	62	2.91	1.15	49	21	55	$8
Freddy Garcia	SEA	16	8	0	200	3.68	1.40	187	93	146	$14
Jon Garland	CHW	3	5	0	52	5.52	1.63	57	28	31	-$3
Ryan Glynn	TEX	7	11	0	142	5.97	1.73	174	71	64	-$12
Doc Gooden	NYY	5	5	1	111	5.07	1.57	123	51	68	-$2
Seth Greisinger	DET	4	5	0	55	5.04	1.46	60	20	38	$0
Jason Grimsley	FA	4	2	1	80	4.64	1.45	80	37	47	$1
Buddy Groom	BAL	5	3	2	58	4.85	1.42	61	21	42	$2
Eddie Guardado	MIN	5	4	8	58	4.19	1.31	51	25	52	$9
Mark Guthrie	OAK	2	3	0	66	4.76	1.46	65	31	56	-$1
Juan Guzman	TB	9	9	0	151	4.21	1.40	162	49	99	$7
H											
John Halama	SEA	13	8	0	157	5.11	1.54	188	54	86	-$1
Roy Halladay	TOR	5	6	0	87	5.67	1.62	100	41	52	-$5
Joey Hamilton	TOR	6	7	0	149	4.73	1.46	156	62	85	$1
Travis Harper	TB	1	1	0	32	4.90	1.41	30	15	14	-$1
Shigetoshi Hasegawa	ANA	6	10		90	3.86	1.42	93	36	56	$12
LaTroy Hawkins	MIN	3	5	15	95	5.05	1.51	111	32	59	$9
Rick Helling	TEX	15	10	0	218	4.58	1.42	216	93	143	$7
Doug Henry	KC	2	4	2	70	3.86	1.40	56	42	57	$4
Pat Hentgen	BAL	14	12	0	199	4.78	1.49	215	82	119	$3
Gil Heredia	OAK	13	9	0	184	4.31	1.36	201	49	98	$10
Orlando Hernandez	NYY	14	11	0	201	4.28	1.23	184	63	149	$16
Roberto Hernandez	KC	3	6	35	73	3.23	1.35	71	27	63	$31
Ken Hill	FA	2	2	0	45	5.98	1.82	53	29	27	-$6
Chris Holt	DET	9	13	0	188	5.15	1.54	223	66	126	-$3
Mike Holtz	ANA	3	3	0	34	5.61	1.47	34	17	32	-$1
Bob Howry	CHW	3	4	5	68	3.29	1.23	53	31	65	$10
Tim Hudson	OAK	18	7	0	192	3.91	1.26	163	79	167	$18
I											
Jason Isringhausen	OAK	4	4	29	61	4.08	1.45	59	29	49	$23
J											
Jason Johnson	BAL	8	13	0	185	5.93	1.62	202	98	127	-$11

NAME	TEAM	W	L	SV	IP	ERA	RATIO	H	BB	K	$VAL
Jonathan Johnson	TEX	2	2	0	42	5.84	1.69	48	23	34	-$4
Bobby J. Jones	FA	12	7	0	130	4.98	1.38	142	37	72	$4
Todd Jones	DET	3	4	36	65	3.74	1.46	65	29	65	$28
K											
Scott Kamieniecki	FA	3	4	2	57	5.51	1.70	61	37	42	-$3
Steve Karsay	CLE	6	6	12	72	3.56	1.33	72	24	61	$14
Matt Kinney	MIN	3	4	0	65	5.16	1.58	63	40	37	-$2
Billy Koch	TOR	5	3	34	76	2.84	1.25	73	22	61	$33
Ryan Kohlmeier	BAL	2	3	27	54	2.40	1.71	62	31	35	$21
L											
Al Levine	ANA	2	3	1	89	3.77	1.44	88	39	38	$3
Cory Lidle	OAK	3	2	0	60	4.75	1.45	70	16	38	$0
Mike Lincoln	MIN	2	5	0	45	7.10	1.80	61	20	23	-$7
Esteban Loaiza	TOR	14	11	0	198	4.61	1.42	224	58	133	$6
Albie Lopez	TB	12	11	0	174	4.11	1.43	184	65	94	$8
Andrew Lorraine	FA	1	3	0	44	5.70	1.57	48	21	30	-$3
Derek Lowe	BOS	5	4	40	88	2.76	1.17	81	22	70	$41
Sean Lowe	CHW	3	3	0	72	4.82	1.56	75	37	51	-$2
M											
Mike Magnante	OAK	3	2	0	50	3.97	1.58	56	23	27	$0
Pat Mahomes	FA	3	3	0	66	5.00	1.60	62	44	53	-$2
Pedro Martinez	BOS	20	6	0	218	1.96	0.90	154	42	289	$51
TJ Mathews	OAK	3	4	0	49	5.21	1.45	52	19	35	-$1
Joe Mays	MIN	8	12	0	170	5.14	1.55	195	68	110	-$4
Chuck McElroy	BAL	3	1	0	61	4.70	1.55	61	34	49	-$1
Brian Meadows	FA	12	12	0	189	5.27	1.52	227	60	78	-$2
Gil Meche	SEA	5	5	0	97	4.09	1.40	84	52	63	$4
Jim Mecir	OAK	5	3	8	66	2.94	1.25	53	29	54	$13
Ramiro Mendoza	NYY	7	5	0	111	4.12	1.32	118	29	59	$7
Jose Mercedes	BAL	15	10	0	198	4.11	1.43	201	82	94	$10
Kent Mercker	BOS	2	1	0	44	5.44	1.67	52	22	26	-$3
Travis Miller	MIN	3	3	3	70	3.59	1.58	82	29	63	$3
Alan Mills	BAL	4	2	1	59	4.51	1.67	60	38	42	-$1
Eric Milton	MIN	12	13	0	199	4.81	1.26	199	51	156	$11
Dave Mlicki	DET	9	11	0	169	5.06	1.50	193	61	93	-$1
Brian Moehler	DET	12	12	0	197	4.59	1.50	242	53	111	$3
Orber Moreno	KC	1	2	2	44	4.74	1.54	44	24	37	$0
Jamie Moyer	SEA	14	8	0	184	4.63	1.34	198	49	116	$9
Mark Mulder	OAK	9	9	0	181	5.21	1.69	224	81	103	-$9
Peter Munro	TEX	2	2	0	32	5.98	1.80	43	15	21	-$4
Mike Mussina	NYY	18	9	0	224	3.68	1.20	223	46	195	$25
N											
Charles Nagy	CLE	9	9	0	146	5.36	1.51	175	45	94	-$2
Jaime Navarro	TOR	0	2	0	31	6.12	1.68	39	13	15	-$4
Jeff Nelson	SEA	4	3	1	55	2.83	1.36	39	36	57	$6
C.J. Nitkowski	DET	4	7	0	96	4.91	1.49	98	45	73	-$1
Hideo Nomo	BOS	8	11	0	163	4.69	1.45	160	76	155	$2
O											
Tomokazu Ohka	BOS	3	3	0	68	3.38	1.44	72	26	39	$3
Omar Olivares	OAK	6	8	0	135	5.30	1.61	153	64	66	-$6
Darren Oliver	TEX	7	9	0	165	5.40	1.55	195	61	87	-$5
Ramon Ortiz	ANA	11	8	0	161	4.81	1.39	144	80	113	$5

NAME	TEAM	W	L	SV	IP	ERA	RATIO	H	BB	K	$VAL
P											
Lance Painter	TOR	3	2	0	64	4.69	1.37	64	23	52	$1
Jose Paniagua	SEA	4	3	6	74	3.61	1.40	65	38	66	$8
Jim Parque	CHW	11	9	0	176	4.58	1.54	201	69	108	$1
Steve Parris	TOR	15	10	0	202	4.43	1.48	224	75	128	$6
John Parrish	BAL	4	5	0	82	6.10	1.69	77	62	69	-$7
Danny Patterson	DET	4	3	0	66	4.54	1.49	80	18	38	$1
Jesus Pena	BOS	1	1	0	32	4.98	1.60	31	20	26	-$2
Troy Percival	ANA	4	6	26	54	4.26	1.28	41	28	56	$22
Matt Perisho	DET	4	5	0	77	5.13	1.68	93	36	57	-$4
Chris Peters	FA	2	3	1	53	4.52	1.49	57	22	34	$0
Mark Petkovsek	TEX	5	3	3	81	4.06	1.35	87	22	36	$6
Andy Pettitte	NYY	19	9	0	212	4.43	1.49	230	86	132	$7
Hipolito Pichardo	BOS	3	3	1	50	3.83	1.39	50	19	28	$3
Joel Pineiro	SEA	1	1	0	40	5.24	1.66	46	20	32	-$3
Dan Plesac	TOR	4	2	1	42	4.08	1.46	40	22	48	$2
Sidney Ponson	BAL	10	13	0	210	4.81	1.40	218	76	133	$4
Lue Pote	ANA	2	2	4	63	3.11	1.32	62	22	52	$7
Ariel Prieto	OAK	1	1	0	41	4.89	1.55	50	14	25	-$2
Q											
Paul Quantrill	TOR	3	4	1	78	4.06	1.46	91	23	46	$2
R											
Brad Radke	MIN	13	13	0	223	4.90	1.43	265	54	135	$4
Steve Rain	FA	3	4	3	60	4.97	1.58	63	32	63	$0
Robert Ramsay	SEA	1	1	0	36	3.86	1.66	33	27	23	-$1
Pat Rapp	ANA	8	12	0	167	5.36	1.60	187	81	104	-$6
Mark Redman	MIN	11	13	0	187	4.81	1.38	206	52	145	$5
Steve Reed	CLE	3	1	0	60	4.14	1.36	61	21	44	$2
Dan Reichert	KC	9	12	0	188	4.96	1.67	198	116	114	-$7
Bryan Rekar	TB	10	9	0	204	4.72	1.44	240	54	114	$3
Arthur Rhodes	SEA	4	5	1	65	4.47	1.29	50	34	72	$4
Mariano Rivera	NYY	6	3	37	72	2.47	1.03	53	22	54	$40
Frank Rodriguez	FA	2	2	1	37	6.07	1.70	47	16	20	-$3
Kenny Rogers	TEX	12	10	0	219	4.30	1.42	23773	128		$8
J.C. Romero	MIN	4	6	0	98	6.25	1.65	117	45	81	-$8
Jose Rosado	KC	8	11	0	146	4.34	1.31	143	48	98	$8
Ryan Rupe	TB	6	6	0	118	5.53	1.53	138	4380		-$4
B.J. Ryan	BAL	2	2	0	52	5.36	1.51	42	37	55	-$2
Jay Ryan	MIN	1	1	0	41	6.22	1.67	53	15	23	-$4
S											
Bret Saberhagen	BOS	2	1	0	33	4.56	1.43	35	12	24	$0
Johan Santana	MIN	4	5	0	73	5.12	1.61	76	42	54	-$3
Jose Santiago	KC	4	4	3	66	3.78	1.35	66	23	37	$6
Kazuhiro Sasaki	SEA	2	4	39	64	2.96	1.14	43	30	80	$36
Scott Schoeneweis	ANA	7	10	0	165	5.45	1.49	182	64	77	-$3
Pete Schourek	BOS	4	4	0	88	5.11	1.47	96	33	60	-$1
Steve Schrenk	OAK	2	3	0	33	5.75	1.34	31	13	25	-$1
Rudy Seanez	FA	3	3	2	32	3.64	1.20	26	13	29	$4
Aaron Sele	SEA	17	10	0	210	4.56	1.44	230	72	155	$7
Paul Shuey	CLE	4	3	1	68	3.41	1.29	55	32	78	$6
Brian Sikorski	TEX	2	4	0	65	5.48	1.67	70	39	55	-$5
Bill Simas	CHW	2	3	1	54	3.96	1.43	52	25	37	$2

NAME	TEAM	W	L	SV	IP	ERA	RATIO	H	BB	K	$VAL
Mike Sirotka	CHW	14	10	0	202	3.89	1.38	217	62	127	$13
Heath Slocumb	FA	1	2	1	33	4.90	1.59	34	19	25	-$1
Shawn Sonnier	KC	3	3	2	59	3.85	1.46	59	27	59	$3
Steve W. Sparks	DET	13	10	0	198	4.02	1.36	198	71	104	$12
Justin Speier	CLE	2	2	0	52	3.89	1.29	45	21	50	$3
Paul Spoljaric	TB	1	1	1	32	5.50	1.56	33	17	29	-$2
Jerry Spradlin	FA	4	4	4	81	5.49	1.45	86	30	64	$1
Dennis Springer	FA	1	1	0	56	5.20	1.65	61	31	35	-$4
Jay Spurgeon	BAL	2	2	0	57	5.54	1.60	58	33	26	-$3
Mike Stanton	NYY	2	3	1	70	4.32	1.35	72	23	72	$3
Blake Stein	KC	14	10	0	208	4.85	1.47	191	115	148	$3
Tanyon Sturtze	TB	7	7	0	124	3.43	1.27	113	45	81	$11
Jeff Suppan	KC	12	11	0	201	4.84	1.44	220	69	113	$3
Makoto Suzuki	KC	9	12	0	189	4.73	1.57	200	97	131	-$2
T											
Jeff Tam	OAK	2	2	2	56	2.89	1.25	55	15	31	$7
Justin Thompson	TEX	4	4	0	80	4.86	1.54	86	37	63	-$1
Brett Tomko	SEA	4	4	1	87	4.73	1.37	87	33	62	$2
Mike Trombley	BAL	4	6	5	79	4.13	1.42	77	35	77	$6
Derrick Turnbow	ANA	1	1	0	40	4.55	1.60	39	25	33	-$2
V											
Ismael Valdes	ANA	6	8	0	153	5.02	1.51	176	55	107	-$2
Mike Venafro	TEX	3	2	3	60	3.63	1.40	63	21	33	$5
W											
Tim Wakefield	BOS	5	5	0	139	5.54	1.48	146	60	93	-$4
Jeff Wallace	TB	1	1	0	33	5.86	1.68	31	25	28	-$3
Bryan Ward	BOS	0	0	0	31	4.92	1.45	35	10	21	-$1
Jarrod Washburn	ANA	8	5	0	147	3.69	1.26	122	63	88	$13
Allen Watson	NYY	2	2	0	66	5.97	1.67	75	35	55	-$6
Jeff Weaver	DET	12	12	0	187	4.67	1.32	194	52	128	$9
Ben Weber	ANA	1	1	0	34	5.26	1.44	40	9	21	-$1
Bob Wells	MIN	3	5	15	83	3.85	1.15	77	19	62	$18
David Wells	CHW	17	8	0	218	4.40	1.29	242	39	159	$15
Kip Wells	CHW	5	6	0	70	5.48	1.64	78	37	51	-$3
John Wetteland	FA	5	4	30	62	4.14	1.52	71	23	57	$23
Dan Wheeler	TB	2	3	0	43	4.63	1.52	50	15	37	-$1
Bob Wickman	CLE	3	6	32	74	3.25	1.39	69	34	58	$28
Brian Williams	BOS	1	1	0	36	5.98	1.76	41	23	22	-$4
Kris Wilson	KC	2	2	0	51	4.45	1.43	57	16	25	$0
Paul Wilson	TB	10	11	0	173	3.61	1.24	148	67	136	$17
Matt Wise	ANA	3	3	0	62	4.87	1.46	67	24	33	$0
Steve Woodard	CLE	8	10	0	161	5.21	1.44	192	40	109	$0
Jaret Wright	CLE	6	6	0	144	4.71	1.43	134	72	100	$2
Kelly Wunsch	CHW	4	2	1	37	2.94	1.29	30	17	31	$4
Y											
Estaban Yan	TB	2	2	15	77	5.60	1.41	83	26	92	$9
Z											
Jeff Zimmerman	TEX	5	4	4	71	4.15	1.32	66	28	67	$7
Barry Zito	OAK	11	9	0	178	3.22	1.25	137	86	150	$19

NATIONAL LEAGUE

NAME	TEAM	W	L	SV	IP	ERA	RATIO	H	BB	K	$VAL
A											
Juan Acevedo	MIL	5	7	3	88	3.68	1.26	80	31	51	$7
Terry Adams	LA	3	4	2	72	3.72	1.40	68	33	54	$3
Rick Aguilera	FA	3	3	22	49	4.10	1.19	45	13	37	$19
Antonio Alfonseca	FLA	5	6	40	72	3.90	1.47	80	26	47	$31
Armando Almanza	FLA	2	2	0	33	4.40	1.65	25	28	34	-$2
Carlos Almanzar	SD	3	3	0	56	5.05	1.46	62	20	45	-$2
Brian Anderson	AZ	12	9	0	208	3.92	1.24	223	35	105	$14
Jimmy Anderson	PIT	8	10	0	177	4.82	1.49	192	72	89	-$2
Clayton Andrews	CIN	4	5	0	84	4.90	1.57	95	37	61	-$3
Rick Ankiel	STL	13	9	0	181	3.44	1.24	138	86	202	$16
Kevin Appier	NYM	14	9	0	181	4.77	1.53	191	86	118	-$1
Tony Armas	MON	10	10	0	176	4.27	1.32	140	92	108	$7
Jamie Arnold	FA	1	3	3	44	5.85	1.62	47	25	30	-$2
Bronson Arroyo	PIT	3	5	0	89	5.04	1.53	97	39	66	-$3
Andy Ashby	LA	15	9	0	204	4.40	1.33	213	58	118	$8
Pedro Astacio	COL	14	9	0	202	5.29	1.48	225	74	190	-$3
Manny Aybar	FLA	3	3	1	85	4.86	1.41	85	35	55	$0
B											
Miguel Batista	AZ	3	5	0	66	4.93	1.52	71	29	42	-$2
Stan Belinda	FA	2	3	1	47	6.45	1.52	50	21	48	-$4
Rob Bell	CIN	9	10	0	184	4.74	1.41	165	95	147	$1
Alan Benes	STL	2	2	0	56	4.94	1.55	63	24	40	-$3
Andy Benes	STL	11	10	0	182	5.14	1.55	207	75	141	-$5
Armando Benitez	NYM	4	4	40	76	2.48	1.04	40	39	111	$40
Kris Benson	PIT	9	11	0	190	3.91	1.34	179	75	152	$8
Jason Bere	CHC	9	9	0	156	5.44	1.65	169	89	125	-$9
Willie Blair	FA	9	9	0	152	5.41	1.45	181	40	78	-$3
Brian Bohanon	COL	14	8	0	185	5.00	1.50	196	81	109	-$1
Ricky Bones	FLA	1	3	0	65	4.70	1.59	79	24	47	-$3
Ricky Bottalico	PHI	4	5	25	70	4.95	1.58	69	41	56	$16
Kent Bottenfield	HOU	10	10	0	196	4.85	1.50	207	87	125	-$2
Jason Boyd	PHI	1	2	0	30	6.02	1.74	34	19	28	-$4
Jamie Brewington	FA	3	3	0	48	4.97	1.61	58	19	36	-$3
Doug Brocail	HOU	2	2	1	54	3.91	1.39	57	18	39	$1
Chris Brock	PHI	5	6	1	91	4.72	1.42	91	38	66	$0
Jim Brower	CIN	2	2	0	45	5.94	1.72	56	21	25	-$5
Kevin Brown	LA	17	6	0	239	2.69	1.02	194	50	222	$36
John Burkett	ATL	10	7	0	144	5.22	1.55	175	48	108	-$4
A.J. Burnett	FLA	7	9	0	182	4.53	1.50	173	100	129	-$1
Paul Byrd	FA	4	4	0	56	5.32	1.41	58	21	33	-$1
C											
Jose Cabrera	HOU	2	2	1	45	5.20	1.43	51	13	33	-$1
Hector Carrasco	FA	4	4	1	68	4.68	1.57	76	31	54	-$1
Bruce Chen	PHI	10	9	0	200	3.40	1.20	168	72	169	$17
Bobby Chouinard	COL	3	3	0	62	4.05	1.38	66	20	40	$1
Jason Christiansen	STL	3	4	4	47	4.46	1.35	38	25	49	$3
Mark Clark	FA	2	2	0	38	6.09	1.66	49	14	21	-$4
Matt Clement	SD	13	14	0	204	4.93	1.55	200	116	164	-$4

NAME	TEAM	W	L	SV	IP	ERA	RATIO	H	BB	K	$VAL
Dave Coggin	PHI	3	3	0	78	4.93	1.59	94	30	49	-$4
Dennis Cook	NYM	4	3	2	56	4.55	1.44	54	27	55	$1
Francisco Cordova	PIT	7	8	0	155	4.58	1.43	164	58	103	$1
Rheal Cormier	PHI	3	3	0	66	4.87	1.35	71	18	41	$0
Reid Cornelius	FLA	3	4	0	81	4.95	1.49	91	30	34	-$2
Nelson Cruz	HOU	6	4	0	69	4.23	1.35	71	23	53	$2
Will Cunnane	MIL	1	1	0	33	4.53	1.46	32	16	27	-$1
D											
Omar Daal	PHI	9	12	0	181	4.96	1.48	196	72	115	-$2
Jeff C. D'Amico	MIL	14	7	0	210	2.90	1.18	190	58	131	$24
Vic Darensbourg	FLA	3	3	0	55	4.91	1.51	57	26	48	-$2
Tom Davey	SD	1	1	0	32	4.01	1.53	35	14	23	-$1
Mike DeJean	COL	1	1	0	52	5.77	1.65	59	27	29	-$5
Val. De los Santos	MIL	2	3	0	62	4.46	1.41	60	27	58	-$1
Miguel Del Toro	SF	1	1	0	34	4.65	1.49	37	14	21	-$2
Ryan Dempster	FLA	11	9	0	185	4.01	1.44	177	90	167	$5
Elmer Dessens	CIN	16	8	0	205	4.38	1.45	237	60	118	$5
Jerry Dipoto	COL	1	1	2	55	3.98	1.52	60	24	50	$0
Octavio Dotel	HOU	4	5	15	101	5.39	1.46	97	50	111	$8
Scott Downs	MON	4	4	0	88	4.90	1.67	111	36	57	-$5
Darren Dreifort	LA	15	8	0	194	3.88	1.34	180	80	163	$11
E											
Adam Eaton	SD	4	2	0	81	4.13	1.44	80	36	54	$1
Scott Elarton	HOU	17	8	0	209	4.44	1.39	206	85	159	$7
Alan Embree	SF	3	4	1	59	4.40	1.36	55	25	50	$1
Todd Erdos	SD	0	0	1	35	5.81	1.64	40	18	22	-$3
Shawn Estes	SF	15	8	0	190	4.53	1.58	194	106	143	-$1
Horacio Estrada	MIL	4	4	0	102	4.94	1.68	125	46	57	-$6
Seth Etherton	CIN	7	7	0	130	4.92	1.45	146	42	69	-$1
F											
Kyle Farnsworth	CHC	2	3	4	73	3.84	1.44	71	34	68	$4
Jeff Fassero	CHC	7	9	0	137	5.04	1.56	159	55	102	-$4
Alex Fernandez	FLA	4	4	0	74	3.69	1.32	76	21	44	$3
Osvaldo Fernandez	CIN	5	5	0	89	3.36	1.23	76	33	49	$7
Mike Fetters	LA	2	2	5	45	3.90	1.36	38	24	35	$4
Nelson Figueroa	PHI	1	2	0	35	6.57	1.58	39	16	24	-$4
Scott Forster	NYM	1	1	0	53	5.64	1.66	46	42	38	-$5
John Franco	NYM	3	4	4	52	3.29	1.34	46	24	52	$5
Wayne Franklin	HOU	1	1	1	40	4.68	1.58	43	21	39	-$2
Aaron Fultz	SF	3	2	2	67	2.89	1.21	59	22	60	$7
G											
Eric Gagne	LA	3	4	0	68	4.75	1.57	67	40	55	-$3
Mark Gardner	SF	12	8	0	182	4.75	1.34	186	58	115	$5
Daniel Garibay	CHC	2	6	0	79	5.99	1.64	90	40	51	-$7
Tom Glavine	ATL	21	9	0	238	3.34	1.22	223	67	148	$24
Wayne Gomes	PHI	3	5	3	76	4.33	1.51	74	41	55	$1
Tom Gordon	CHC	1	2	10	31	3.86	1.41	31	13	25	$7
Danny Graves	CIN	5	6	33	96	2.80	1.30	83	42	57	$32
Jason Grimsley	FA	4	2	1	80	4.64	1.45	80	37	47	$0
Geraldo Guzman	AZ	6	6	0	90	4.97	1.45	98	32	78	-$1
H											
Mike Hampton	COL	16	9	0	201	4.90	1.45	199	93	142	$1

NAME	TEAM	W	L	SV	IP	ERA	RATIO	H	BB	K	$VAL
Pete Harnisch	CIN	14	8	0	199	3.82	1.29	193	63	118	$13
Jimmy Haynes	MIL	10	12	0	182	5.54	1.65	207	93	94	-$11
Felix Heredia	CHC	4	3	6	57	4.80	1.43	50	31	52	$4
Matt Herges	LA	5	4	1	70	3.25	1.26	64	24	48	$6
Dustin Hermanson	STL	11	12	0	210	4.43	1.43	228	73	120	$3
Livan Hernandez	SF	18	8	0	240	3.45	1.33	245	74	167	$17
Ken Hill	FA	2	2	0	45	5.98	1.82	53	29	27	-$6
Sterling Hitchcock	SD	7	9	0	137	4.35	1.36	137	49	128	$3
Trevor Hoffman	SD	3	5	43	71	2.59	0.96	55	13	82	$42
Craig House	COL	1	1	0	31	6.22	1.76	36	19	23	-$5
I											
Hideki Irabu	MON	4	5	0	78	5.48	1.43	89	23	60	-$2
J											
Mike Jackson	HOU	1	1	1	32	4.02	1.38	31	13	25	$0
Mike James	STL	2	2	1	60	3.10	1.24	47	28	48	$5
Kevin Jarvis	SD	2	3	0	63	4.97	1.46	74	18	34	-$2
Jose Jimenez	COL	4	4	22	74	4.57	1.40	73	31	49	$17
Mike Johnson	MON	4	4	0	93	5.76	1.57	99	47	69	-$6
Randy Johnson	AZ	17	9	0	245	3.10	1.16	203	82	336	$28
John Johnstone	SF	3	3	1	59	4.56	1.32	60	17	48	$1
Bobby J. Jones	FA	12	7	0	130	4.98	1.38	142	37	72	$2
Bobby M. Jones	NYM	3	4	0	61	5.60	1.70	66	38	45	-$5
K											
Scott Kamieniecki	FA	3	4	2	57	5.51	1.70	61	37	42	-$3
Scott Karl	SD	7	7	0	131	5.78	1.72	171	54	55	-$11
Daryl Kile	STL	17	9	0	220	3.71	1.20	202	62	166	$19
Byung Kim	AZ	5	5	4	64	4.48	1.40	47	43	96	$4
Ray King	MIL	5	4	0	59	2.87	1.25	46	28	36	$5
Steve Kline	STL	3	4	9	78	3.49	1.37	76	30	67	$9
L											
Andy Larkin	COL	1	2	0	33	6.50	1.78	41	17	27	-$5
Al Leiter	NYM	15	8	0	203	3.44	1.26	179	77	182	$17
Curt Leskanic	MIL	5	4	20	80	3.54	1.48	68	49	74	$17
Jon Lieber	CHC	11	11	0	239	4.29	1.24	245	51	193	$12
Kerry Ligtenberg	ATL	2	3	11	59	3.44	1.23	47	25	59	$11
Jose Lima	HOU	9	13	0	190	5.97	1.55	234	60	130	-$11
Felipe Lira	MON	3	4	0	77	5.07	1.53	94	24	40	-$3
Rich Loiselle	PIT	2	3	2	36	4.87	1.70	36	24	28	-$1
Braden Looper	FLA	4	2	1	66	4.18	1.56	72	30	33	$0
Andrew Lorraine	FA	1	3	0	44	5.70	1.57	48	21	30	-$4
Larry Luebbers	CIN	1	2	1	36	5.63	1.62	42	17	14	-$3
M											
Greg Maddux	ATL	20	9	0	241	2.87	1.13	233	39	175	$31
Ron Mahay	SD	1	1	0	33	5.96	1.70	39	17	25	-$4
Pat Mahomes	FA	3	3	0	66	5.00	1.60	62	44	53	-$3
Matt Mantei	AZ	1	2	29	52	3.72	1.38	36	36	68	$22
Josias Manzanillo	PIT	3	3	0	68	3.70	1.40	60	35	51	$2
Jason Marquis	ATL	1	1	0	44	4.62	1.41	45	17	36	-$1
Ramon Martinez	LA	3	3	0	80	5.06	1.54	84	39	58	-$3
Onan Masaoka	LA	1	2	0	36	4.17	1.47	30	23	34	-$1
Dave Maurer	SD	1	1	0	31	4.06	1.45	35	10	19	-$1
Tony McKnight	HOU	5	5	0	90	4.07	1.35	96	26	59	$3

NAME	TEAM	W	L	SV	IP	ERA	RATIO	H	BB	K	$VAL
Brian Meadows	FA	12	12	0	189	5.27	1.52	227	60	78	-$4
Jose Mesa	PHI	3	5	1	78	5.16	1.65	88	40	69	-$4
Danny Miceli	FLA	6	4	2	57	4.19	1.36	53	24	49	$3
Wade Miller	HOU	11	11	0	199	4.97	1.38	199	76	168	$1
Kevin Millwood	ATL	13	11	0	214	4.57	1.20	196	60	179	$12
Trey Moore	ATL	4	4	0	64	5.12	1.55	76	23	47	-$3
Mike Morgan	AZ	3	4	1	78	5.39	1.65	100	29	39	-$5
Matt Morris	STL	4	3	3	78	3.29	1.30	76	26	51	$7
Guillermo Mota	MON	1	2	0	35	4.52	1.36	32	15	23	-$1
Terry Mulholland	PIT	4	5	1	98	4.71	1.47	119	25	49	$0
Mike Myers	COL	1	1	1	40	2.97	1.19	29	18	35	$3
N											
Joe Nathan	SF	5	2	0	83	4.87	1.56	79	51	53	-$2
Denny Neagle	COL	15	8	0	186	5.27	1.42	192	72	131	$0
Robb Nen	SF	4	5	43	70	2.26	1.05	52	22	89	$42
Vladimir Nunez	FLA	1	2	0	33	6.23	1.60	37	16	24	-$4
O											
Gregg Olson	LA	1	1	1	31	4.40	1.52	33	14	26	-$1
Russ Ortiz	SF	18	8	0	189	4.61	1.53	181	108	157	$1
Antonio Osuna	LA	3	4	1	62	3.76	1.36	52	32	65	$2
P											
Vincente Padilla	PHI	4	5	2	80	3.98	1.56	91	34	61	$1
Chan Ho Park	LA	16	8	0	206	2.91	1.30	166	102	192	$19
Carl Pavano	MON	11	10	0	177	3.99	1.32	175	59	116	$9
Brad Penny	FLA	9	9	0	184	4.52	1.42	174	87	123	$2
Carlos Perez	LA	3	4	0	87	5.57	1.54	110	24	40	-$5
Yorkis Perez	LA	0	0	0	31	4.49	1.51	30	17	27	-$2
Robert Person	PHI	10	9	0	172	4.02	1.42	150	94	162	$5
Chris Peters	FA	2	3	1	53	4.52	1.49	57	22	34	-$1
Cliff Politte	PHI	5	5	0	68	3.69	1.40	63	32	60	$2
Brian Powell	HOU	3	3	0	55	5.43	1.48	60	21	26	-$2
Jay Powell	HOU	1	1	1	31	4.64	1.64	32	18	26	-$2
Jeremy Powell	SD	1	5	0	47	5.96	1.63	58	19	26	-$5
Luke Prokopec	LA	1	1	0	33	3.63	1.38	31	15	19	$0
Q											
Ruben Quevedo	CHC	6	7	0	144	5.18	1.56	142	83	113	-$6
R											
Steve Rain	FA	3	4	3	60	4.97	1.58	63	32	63	-$1
Britt Reames	MON	5	5	0	94	3.34	1.38	75	55	77	$4
Rick Reed	NYM	12	6	0	176	4.15	1.26	185	37	119	$10
Mike Remlinger	ATL	5	3	8	85	3.40	1.30	69	42	82	$11
Alberto Reyes	LA	0	0	0	31	4.49	1.44	32	13	22	-$2
Dennis Reyes	CIN	2	2	1	52	4.26	1.58	48	33	51	-$1
Shane Reynolds	HOU	9	10	0	145	4.43	1.36	161	36	115	$4
Armando Reynoso	AZ	10	11	0	179	4.92	1.39	188	61	91	$1
John Riedling	CIN	1	1	0	33	3.98	1.47	36	13	22	-$1
Paul Rigdon	MIL	7	8	0	141	4.74	1.39	142	54	102	$1
Todd Ritchie	PIT	10	8	0	166	4.41	1.36	178	48	109	$5
John Rocker	ATL	2	3	25	57	2.68	1.45	42	42	82	$21
Felix Rodriguez	SF	3	2	3	73	3.16	1.36	63	36	77	$6
Frank Rodriguez	FA	2	2	1	37	6.07	1.70	47	16	20	-$3
Rich Rodriguez	NYM	1	1	0	36	6.25	1.73	47	15	22	-$5

NAME	TEAM	W	L	SV	IP	ERA	RATIO	H	BB	K	$VAL
Brian Rose	COL	3	4	0	73	5.56	1.51	82	28	39	-$4
Kirk Rueter	SF	13	9	0	185	4.43	1.44	208	58	81	$4
Glendon Rusch	NYM	11	9	0	181	3.92	1.30	192	44	144	$10

S

NAME	TEAM	W	L	SV	IP	ERA	RATIO	H	BB	K	$VAL
Jesus Sanchez	FLA	10	10	0	191	5.34	1.56	206	92	136	-$7
Julio Santana	NYM	2	3	0	71	5.79	1.57	76	35	51	-$5
Scott Sauerbeck	PIT	4	3	1	66	3.40	1.66	61	48	66	$0
Curt Schilling	AZ	14	9	0	237	3.48	1.15	222	51	202	$23
Jason Schmidt	PIT	4	4	0	83	4.54	1.52	88	38	61	-$1
Rudy Seanez	FA	3	3	2	32	3.64	1.20	26	13	29	$3
Dan Serafini	PIT	5	8	0	135	4.98	1.58	159	54	73	-$5
Scott Service	LA	1	1	1	34	5.80	1.65	39	17	33	-$3
Jeff Shaw	LA	3	4	33	63	3.48	1.25	63	16	42	$28
Jose Silva	PIT	12	11	0	161	5.50	1.61	199	60	118	-$7
Heath Slocumb	FA	1	2	1	33	4.90	1.59	34	19	25	-$2
Joe Slusarski	ATL	2	2	2	45	4.11	1.38	48	14	32	$2
Chuck Smith	FLA	7	7	0	164	3.62	1.38	151	75	158	$7
John Smoltz	ATL	10	7	0	151	3.79	1.40	163	48	105	$6
John Snyder	MIL	6	11	0	160	5.91	1.65	186	78	86	-$13
Stan Spencer	SD	1	3	0	44	4.88	1.38	46	15	38	-$1
Jerry Spradlin	FA	4	4	4	81	5.49	1.45	86	30	64	$0
Dennis Springer	FA	1	1	0	56	5.20	1.65	61	31	35	-$5
Russ Springer	AZ	2	3	0	57	4.57	1.44	52	29	56	-$1
Gene Stechschulte	STL	1	1	0	33	5.90	1.58	31	21	15	-$3
Garrett Stephenson	STL	13	9	0	197	4.51	1.37	207	63	124	$5
Todd Stottlemyre	AZ	8	8	0	144	4.44	1.40	147	55	116	$2
Scott Strickland	MON	3	5	8	65	3.03	1.17	52	24	68	$11
Everett Stull	MIL	2	3	0	41	5.37	1.55	37	27	31	-$3
Scott Sullivan	CIN	4	6	3	108	3.48	1.19	88	40	90	$10
Greg Swindell	AZ	3	4	1	74	3.06	1.20	68	21	60	$7

T

NAME	TEAM	W	L	SV	IP	ERA	RATIO	H	BB	K	$VAL
Kevin Tapani	CHC	9	12	0	180	4.94	1.32	194	43	125	$3
Julian Tavarez	CHC	11	6	0	165	3.92	1.42	166	68	89	$6
Amaury Telemaco	PHI	3	3	0	45	5.45	1.46	46	21	34	-$2
Anthony Telford	MON	5	4	3	85	3.84	1.36	88	28	67	$5
Mike Thurman	MON	8	11	0	171	5.30	1.55	190	75	99	-$6
Mike Timlin	STL	3	5	4	66	3.84	1.41	63	29	52	$4
Brian Tollberg	SD	7	9	0	191	3.73	1.41	210	59	123	$6
Steve Trachsel	NYM	11	9	0	198	4.99	1.47	222	69	123	-$2

U

NAME	TEAM	W	L	SV	IP	ERA	RATIO	H	BB	K	$VAL
Ugueth Urbina	MON	2	3	22	55	3.88	1.38	50	26	60	$17

V

NAME	TEAM	W	L	SV	IP	ERA	RATIO	H	BB	K	$VAL
Marc Valdes	ATL	3	2	1	38	5.02	1.59	44	16	24	-$1
Todd Van Poppel	CHC	4	5	5	89	4.04	1.49	85	47	77	$4
Javier Vazquez	MON	10	11	0	214	4.45	1.40	236	64	182	$4
Dave Veres	STL	3	6	28	75	3.54	1.32	71	28	68	$24
Ron Villone	COL	4	3	0	81	5.48	1.63	86	46	48	-$5
Ed Vosberg	PHI	2	2	0	43	4.88	1.65	47	24	39	-$3

W

NAME	TEAM	W	L	SV	IP	ERA	RATIO	H	BB	K	$VAL
Billy Wagner	HOU	3	3	25	45	3.41	1.15	32	20	64	$22
Kevin Walker	SD	4	1	0	40	4.18	1.30	29	23	34	$1
Donne Wall	NYM	3	2	1	43	3.14	1.10	31	16	28	$5

NAME	TEAM	W	L	SV	IP	ERA	RATIO	H	BB	K	$VAL
John Wasdin	COL	3	3	1	72	5.01	1.34	76	20	59	$0
Dave Weathers	MIL	3	4	1	75	2.98	1.44	77	31	55	$4
Turk Wendell	NYM	3	3	2	74	3.36	1.26	59	34	65	$6
John Wetteland	FA	5	4	30	62	4.14	1.52	71	23	57	$23
Gabe White	COL	4	3	5	71	3.44	1.19	68	17	70	$9
Rick White	NYM	2	3	2	78	3.72	1.33	76	28	54	$4
Marc Wilkins	PIT	2	2	0	63	4.78	1.56	58	41	44	-$3
Mike Williams	PIT	3	4	24	66	3.80	1.41	56	36	71	$19
Woody Williams	SD	12	9	0	184	3.85	1.26	173	59	123	$12
Scott Williamson	CIN	6	7	2	95	3.03	1.35	71	57	114	$8
Jay Witasick	SD	6	10	0	140	5.74	1.69	168	69	106	-$11
Mark Wohlers	CIN	2	3	2	55	4.55	1.37	45	30	44	$1
Randy Wolf	PHI	9	10	0	203	4.63	1.45	207	87	166	$0
Kerry Wood	CHC	11	8	0	169	4.56	1.40	135	102	175	$3
Tim Worrell	SF	3	3	2	73	3.64	1.44	75	30	61	$3
Jamey Wright	MIL	10	13	0	205	4.46	1.55	209	109	112	-$2
Y											
Masato Yoshii	COL	8	12	0	170	5.21	1.42	188	53	96	-$2

Players not listed are projected to have under 30 innings pitched in 2001.

2001 VALUES BY POSITION

A.L. CATCHERS

NAME	TEAM	$VAL
Ivan Rodriguez	TEX	$24
Mitch Meluskey	DET	$15
Jorge Posada	NYY	$12
Darrin Fletcher	TOR	$11
Brook Fordyce	BAL	$10
Ben Molina	ANA	$9
Jason Varitek	BOS	$6
Einer Diaz	CLE	$6
Ramon Hernandez	OAK	$6
Eddie Taubensee	CLE	$5
Sandy Alomar	CHW	$5
Gregg Zaun	KC	$5
A.J. Pierzynski	MIN	$4
Javier Cardona	DET	$3
Benito Santiago	FA	$3
Chris Widger	SEA	$3
Scott Hatteberg	BOS	$3
John Flaherty	TB	$2
Dan Wilson	SEA	$2
Josh Paul	CHW	$2
Bill Haselman	TEX	$1
Joe Oliver	NYY	$1
Mike DiFelice	TB	$1
Matt Lecroy	MIN	$1

N.L. CATCHERS

NAME	TEAM	$VAL
Jason Kendall	PIT	$27
Mike Piazza	NYM	$26
Javy Lopez	ATL	$14
Charles Johnson	FLA	$12
Mike Lieberthal	PHI	$12
Ben Petrick	COL	$11
Brad Ausmus	HOU	$10
Bret Hemphill	FA	$10
Todd Hundley	CHC	$8
Brent Mayne	COL	$7
Damian Miller	AZ	$7
Michael Barrett	MON	$5
Bobby Estalella	SF	$5
Tyler Houston	MIL	$4
Jason LaRue	CIN	$4
Ben Davis	SD	$3
Benito Santiago	FA	$3
Eli Marrero	STL	$3
Todd Pratt	NYM	$3
Joe Girardi	CHC	$3
Tony Eusebio	HOU	$2
Wiki Gonzalez	SD	$2
Angel Pena	LA	$2
Raul Casanova	MIL	$1
Chad Kreuter	LA	$1
Mike Matheny	STL	$1
Mike Redmond	FLA	$1
Henry Blanco	MIL	$1
Keith Osik	PIT	$1
Carlos Hernandez	STL	$1
Kelly Stinnett	CIN	$1
Eddie Perez	ATL	$1

2001 VALUES BY POSITION

A.L. FIRST BASEMEN

NAME	TEAM	$VAL
Carlos Delgado	TOR	$27
Mike Sweeney	KC	$25
Frank Thomas	CHW	$24
Jason Giambi	OAK	$24
Rafael Palmeiro	TEX	$20
David Segui	BAL	$17
Jim Thome	CLE	$16
Paul Konerko	CHW	$14
John Olerud	SEA	$14
Fred McGriff	TB	$14
Dean Palmer	DET	$13
Mo Vaughn	ANA	$12
Tony Clark	DET	$11
Tino Martinez	NYY	$10
David Ortiz	MIN	$9
Doug Mientkiewicz	MIN	$8
Andres Galarraga	TEX	$8
Steve Cox	TB	$7
Jose Offerman	BOS	$7
Jeff Conine	BAL	$6
Brian Daubach	BOS	$4
Mario Valdez	OAK	$4
David McCarty	KC	$3
Chris Richard	BAL	$3
Scott Spiezio	ANA	$2
Robert Fick	DET	$2
Mike Stanley	OAK	$1
Shane Halter	DET	$1
Nick Johnson	NYY	$1

N.L. FIRST BASEMEN

NAME	TEAM	$VAL
Todd Helton	COL	$36
Jeff Bagwell	HOU	$33
Sean Casey	CIN	$28
Ryan Klesko	SD	$20
Mark McGwire	STL	$20
Richie Sexson	MIL	$19
Dmitri Young	CIN	$17
Kevin Young	PIT	$16
Pat Burrell	PHI	$15
Eric Karros	LA	$15
Derrek Lee	FLA	$14
Mark Grace	AZ	$12
Rube Durazo	AZ	$11
Matt Stairs	CHC	$11
J.T. Snow	SF	$10
John Vanderwal	PIT	$10
Rico Brogna	ATL	$9
Todd Zeile	NYM	$8
Lee Stevens	MON	$8
Travis Lee	PHI	$8
Greg Colbrunn	AZ	$5
Fernando Seguignol	MON	$5
Craig Paquette	STL	$4
Kevin Millar	FLA	$3
Ed Sprague	SD	$2
Andy Tracy	MON	$2
Tyler Houston	MIL	$2
Ron Coomer	CHC	$2
Wally Joyner	FA	$1
Angel Pena	LA	$1

2001 VALUES BY POSITION

A.L. SECOND BASEMEN

NAME	TEAM	$VAL
Roberto Alomar	CLE	$34
Delino DeShields	BAL	$25
Ray Durham	CHW	$24
Adam Kennedy	ANA	$17
Chuck Knoblauch	NYY	$15
Carlos Febles	KC	$13
Miguel Cairo	OAK	$13
Damion Easley	DET	$13
Bret Boone	SEA	$9
Mark McLemore	SEA	$9
Randy Velarde	TEX	$9
Homer Bush	TOR	$9
Frank Catalanotto	TEX	$9
Jerry Hairston Jr.	BAL	$9
Jose Offerman	BOS	$7
Denny Hocking	MIN	$6
Jay Canizaro	MIN	$5
D'Angelo Jimenez	NYY	$3
Russ Johnson	TB	$3
David Bell	SEA	$3
Mike Lansing	BOS	$2
Luis Rivas	MIN	$2
Mark Lewis	FA	$1
Luis Sojo	NYY	$1
Bobby Smith	TB	$1
Jeff Frye	TOR	$1
Tony Graffanino	CHW	$1
Frankie Menechino	OAK	$1
Mike Young	TEX	$1

N.L. SECOND BASEMEN

NAME	TEAM	$VAL
Luis Castillo	FLA	$36
Rafael Furcal	ATL	$32
Eric Young	CHC	$29
Jeff Kent	SF	$24
Edgardo Alfonzo	NYM	$23
Jose Vidro	MON	$18
Julio Lugo	HOU	$17
Pokey Reese	CIN	$16
Quilvio Veras	ATL	$15
Todd Walker	COL	$14
Craig Biggio	HOU	$13
Damian Jackson	SD	$13
Mark Grudzielanek	LA	$12
Fernando Vina	STL	$11
Jay Bell	AZ	$11
Warren Morris	PIT	$9
Ron Belliard	MIL	$8
Placido Polanco	STL	$8
Terry Shumpert	COL	$8
Santiago Perez	SD	$4
Bill Spiers	HOU	$3
Lenny Harris	NYM	$3
Marlon Anderson	PHI	$3
Ramon E. Martinez	SF	$1
Keith Lockhart	ATL	$1
Jose Vizcaino	HOU	$1
Craig Counsell	AZ	$1
Kevin Jordan	PHI	$1
Kurt Abbott	ATL	$1

2001 VALUES BY POSITION

A.L. THIRD BASEMEN

NAME	TEAM	$VAL
Troy Glaus	ANA	$24
Tony Batista	TOR	$17
Joe Randa	KC	$17
Eric Chavez	OAK	$16
Travis Fryman	CLE	$14
Corey Koskie	MIN	$14
Dean Palmer	DET	$13
Carlos Guillen	SEA	$10
Ken Caminiti	TEX	$8
Chris Stynes	BOS	$8
Herbert Perry	CHW	$6
Aubrey Huff	TB	$6
Jeff Conine	BAL	$6
Vinny Castilla	TB	$5
Alfonso Soriano	NYY	$5
Cal Ripken	BAL	$5
Scott Brosius	NYY	$4
Mike Lamb	TEX	$4
D'Angelo Jimenez	NYY	$3
Russ Johnson	TB	$3
David Bell	SEA	$3
Mark Lewis	FA	$1
Joe Crede	CHW	$1
Lou Merloni	BOS	$1
Willie Greene	FA	$1
Luis Sojo	NYY	$1
Shane Halter	DET	$1
Casey Blake	MIN	$1

N.L. THIRD BASEMEN

NAME	TEAM	$VAL
Chipper Jones	ATL	$33
Adrian Beltre	LA	$23
Jeff Cirillo	COL	$23
Fernando Tatis	MON	$19
Scott Rolen	PHI	$19
Phil Nevin	SD	$19
Aaron Boone	CIN	$17
Mike Lowell	FLA	$13
Matt Williams	AZ	$13
Robin Ventura	NYM	$10
Chris Truby	HOU	$10
Aramis Ramirez	PIT	$8
Placido Polanco	STL	$8
Bill Mueller	CHC	$7
Jose Hernandez	MIL	$6
Enrique Wilson	PIT	$4
Craig Paquette	STL	$4
Michael Barrett	MON	$3
Bill Spiers	HOU	$3
Russ Davis	SF	$3
Lenny Harris	NYM	$3
Geoff Blum	MON	$3
Ed Sprague	SD	$2
Andy Tracy	MON	$2
Greg Norton	COL	$2
Pedro Feliz	SF	$2
Tyler Houston	MIL	$2
Andy Fox	FLA	$2
Ron Coomer	CHC	$2
Willie Greene	FA	$1
Mark Lewis	FA	$1
John Mabry	STL	$1
Craig Counsell	AZ	$1
Kevin Jordan	PHI	$1

2001 VALUES BY POSITION

A.L. SHORTSTOPS

NAME	TEAM	$VAL
Alex Rodriguez	TEX	$34
Derek Jeter	NYY	$34
Nomar Garciaparra	BOS	$31
Omar Vizquel	CLE	$23
Miguel Tejada	OAK	$21
Cristian Guzman	MIN	$17
Deivi Cruz	DET	$15
Jose Valentin	CHW	$14
Melvin Mora	BAL	$10
Carlos Guillen	SEA	$10
Mike Bordick	BAL	$9
Royce Clayton	CHW	$9
Alex S. Gonzalez	TOR	$7
Rey Sanchez	KC	$7
D'Angelo Jimenez	NYY	$3
Gary DiSarcina	ANA	$2
Benji Gil	ANA	$1
Felix Martinez	TB	$1
Tony Graffanino	CHW	$1
Wilson Delgado	KC	$1

N.L. SHORTSTOPS

NAME	TEAM	$VAL
Rafael Furcal	ATL	$32
Tony Womack	AZ	$26
Edgar Renteria	STL	$21
Julio Lugo	HOU	$17
Damian Jackson	SD	$13
Neifi Perez	COL	$13
Barry Larkin	CIN	$12
Rich Aurilia	SF	$11
Placido Polanco	STL	$8
Jimmy Rollins	PHI	$7
Ricky Gutierrez	CHC	$7
Mark Loretta	MIL	$7
Jose Hernandez	MIL	$6
Orlando Cabrera	MON	$5
Santiago Perez	SD	$4
Bill Spiers	HOU	$3
Geoff Blum	MON	$3
Adam Everett	HOU	$2
Andy Fox	FLA	$2
Ramon E. Martinez	SF	$1
Alex Gonzalez	FLA	$1
Pat Meares	PIT	$1
Dave Berg	FLA	$1
Alex Cora	LA	$1
Jose Vizcaino	HOU	$1
Desi Relaford	NYM	$1
Kurt Abbott	ATL	$1

2001 VALUES BY POSITION

A.L. OUTFIELDERS

NAME	TEAM	$VAL	NAME	TEAM	$VAL
Johnny Damon	OAK	$45	Troy O'Leary	BOS	$9
Darin Erstad	ANA	$32	Wil Cordero	CLE	$8
Roger Cedeno	DET	$30	Dee Brown	KC	$8
Manny Ramirez	BOS	$30	Steve Cox	TB	$7
Magglio Ordonez	CHW	$29	Luis Polonia	FA	$7
Shannon Stewart	TOR	$27	Adam Piatt	OAK	$7
Bernie Williams	NYY	$26	Trot Nixon	BOS	$6
Delino Deshields	BAL	$25	Randy Winn	TB	$6
Kenny Lofton	CLE	$24	Denny Hocking	MIN	$6
Carl Everett	BOS	$24	Henry Rodriguez	FA	$6
Carlos Lee	CHW	$23	Jeremy Giambi	OAK	$5
Gabe Kapler	TEX	$22	Butch Huskey	FA	$4
Raul Mondesi	TOR	$22	Stan Javier	SEA	$4
Matt Lawton	MIN	$21	Jason Tyner	TB	$4
Juan Encarnacion	DET	$21	Jose Guillen	TB	$3
Mike Cameron	SEA	$20	Russ Branyan	CLE	$3
Garret Anderson	ANA	$20	Vernon Wells	TOR	$3
Mark Quinn	KC	$20	Wendell Magee	DET	$3
Jermaine Dye	KC	$20	Jay Buhner	SEA	$3
Albert Belle	BAL	$20	Orlando Palmeiro	ANA	$3
Terrence Long	OAK	$19	Shane Spencer	NYY	$2
Juan Gonzalez	CLE	$19	Jolbert Cabrera	CLE	$2
Dante Bichette	BOS	$18	Chad Curtis	TEX	$1
Carlos Beltran	KC	$18	Darren Lewis	BOS	$1
Bob Higginson	DET	$18	Rich Becker	FA	$1
Ruben Mateo	TEX	$18	Chad Allen	MIN	$1
Ben Grieve	TB	$16	Jeff Liefer	CHW	$1
Paul O'Neill	NYY	$16			
Tim Salmon	ANA	$15			
Ellis Burks	CLE	$15			
David Justice	NYY	$15			
Jose Cruz	TOR	$15			
Rickey Henderson	FA	$14			
Chris Singleton	CHW	$14			
Torii Hunter	MIN	$14			
Greg Vaughn	TB	$14			
Jacque Jones	MIN	$14			
Gerald Williams	TB	$13			
Rusty Greer	TEX	$12			
Luis Matos	BAL	$12			
Brady Anderson	BAL	$10			
Melvin Mora	BAL	$10			
Al Martin	SEA	$9			
Glenallen Hill	NYY	$9			
Ricky Ledee	TEX	$9			

2001 VALUES BY POSITION

N.L. OUTFIELDERS

NAME	TEAM	$VAL	NAME	TEAM	$VAL
Vladimir Guerrero	MON	$37	John Vander Wal	PIT	$10
Bob Abreu	PHI	$33	Ron Gant	COL	$9
Preston Wilson	FLA	$31	Armando Rios	SF	$9
Andruw Jones	ATL	$31	Danny Bautista	AZ	$9
Sammy Sosa	CHC	$30	Daryle Ward	HOU	$8
Moises Alou	HOU	$28	Milton Bradley	MON	$8
Shawn Green	LA	$27	Tony Gwynn	SD	$8
Barry Bonds	SF	$26	Travis Lee	PHI	$8
Richard Hidalgo	HOU	$25	Terry Shumpert	COL	$8
Ken Griffey	CIN	$25	Eric Davis	SF	$7
Brian Giles	PIT	$24	Luis Polonia	FA	$7
Gary Sheffield	LA	$24	Darryl Hamilton	NYM	$7
Todd Hollandsworth	COL	$24	Peter Bergeron	MON	$7
Geoff Jenkins	MIL	$23	Henry Rodriguez	FA	$6
Doug Glanville	PHI	$23	Wilton Guerrero	CIN	$6
Tom Goodwin	LA	$23	Dave Martinez	ATL	$6
Jeffrey Hammonds	MIL	$23	Bubba Trammell	SD	$5
Luis Gonzalez	AZ	$22	Marquis Grissom	MIL	$5
Jim Edmonds	STL	$22	Michael Tucker	CIN	$5
J.D. Drew	STL	$22	Shawon Dunston	SF	$5
Cliff Floyd	FLA	$21	Fernando Seguignol	MON	$5
Larry Walker	COL	$20	Corey Patterson	CHC	$5
Richie Sexson	MIL	$19	Butch Huskey	FA	$5
Juan Pierre	COL	$19	Damon Buford	CHC	$4
Lance Berkman	HOU	$19	Devon White	LA	$4
Mark Kotsay	FLA	$17	Craig Paquette	STL	$4
Dmitri Young	CIN	$17	Alex Escobar	NYM	$4
Brian Jordan	ATL	$16	Brian L. Hunter	PHI	$4
Marvin Benard	SF	$16	Reggie Taylor	PHI	$3
Eric Owens	SD	$16	Bruce Aven	LA	$3
Pat Burrell	PHI	$15	Joe McEwing	NYM	$3
Jay Payton	NYM	$15	Calvin Murray	SF	$2
Steve Finley	AZ	$15	Ruben Rivera	SD	$2
Rondell White	CHC	$14	Jeff Abbott	FLA	$2
Reggie Sanders	AZ	$14	Emil Brown	PIT	$2
BJ Surhoff	ATL	$14	Andy Fox	FLA	$2
Ray Lankford	STL	$14	Glen Barker	HOU	$2
Benny Agbayani	NYM	$13	James Mouton	MIL	$1
Rickey Henderson	FA	$13	Felipe Crespo	SF	$1
Derek Bell	PIT	$12	Rich Becker	FA	$1
Jeromy Burnitz	MIL	$12	Roosevelt Brown	CHC	$1
Mike Darr	SD	$12	Wilken Ruan	MON	$1
Adrian Brown	PIT	$11	Dave Dellucci	AZ	$1
Matt Stairs	CHC	$11	John Mabry	STL	$1
Timoniel Perez	NYM	$10	Chad Hermansen	PIT	$1
Alex Ochoa	CIN	$10			

2001 VALUES BY POSITION

DESIGNATED HITTERS

NAME	TEAM	$VAL
Johnny Damon	Oak	$45
Darin Erstad	ANA	$32
Manny Ramirez	BOS	$30
Mike Sweeney	KC	$25
Frank Thomas	CHW	$24
Jason Giambi	OAK	$24
Edgar Martinez	SEA	$22
Rafael Palmeiro	TEX	$20
Mark Quinn	KC	$20
Albert Belle	BAL	$20
Juan Gonzalez	CLE	$19
Dante Bichette	BOS	$18
David Segui	BAL	$17
Jim Thome	CLE	$16
Brad Fullmer	TOR	$15
Tim Salmon	ANA	$15
David Justice	NYY	$15
Chuck Knoblauch	NYY	$15
Greg Vaughn	TB	$14
Tony Clark	DET	$11
David Ortiz	MIN	$9
Glenallen Hill	NYY	$9
Billy McMillon	DET	$8
Luis Polonia	FA	$7
Jose Canseco	FA	$6
Jeff Conine	BAL	$6
Jeremy Giambi	OAK	$5
Butch Huskey	FA	$4
Brian Daubach	BOS	$4
Olmedo Saenz	OAK	$3
Russ Branyan	CLE	$3
Scott Spiezio	ANA	$2
Shane Spencer	NYY	$2
Robert Fick	DET	$2
Harold Baines	CHW	$1
Mike Stanley	OAK	$1
Scott Hatteberg	BOS	$1
Jeff Liefer	CHW	$1

A.L. PITCHERS

NAME	TEAM	$VAL
Pedro Martinez	BOS	$51
Derek Lowe	BOS	$41
Mariano Rivera	NYY	$40
Keith Foulke	CHW	$37
Kazuhiro Sasaki	SEA	$36
Billy Koch	TOR	$33
Roberto Hernandez	KC	$31
Todd Jones	DET	$28
Bob Wickman	CLE	$28
Mike Mussina	NYY	$25
John Wetteland	FA	$23
Jason Isringhausen	OAK	$23
Troy Percival	ANA	$22
Ryan Kohlmeier	BAL	$21
Rick Aguilera	FA	$20
Barry Zito	OAK	$19
Tim Hudson	OAK	$18
Bob Wells	MIN	$18
Roger Clemens	NYY	$17
Paul Wilson	TB	$17
Orlando Hernandez	NYY	$16
David Wells	CHW	$15
Bartolo Colon	CLE	$15
Steve Karsay	CLE	$14
Freddy Garcia	SEA	$14
Jim Mecir	OAK	$13
Mike Sirotka	CHW	$13
Jarrod Washburn	ANA	$13
Steve W. Sparks	DET	$12
Shigetoshi Hasegawa	ANA	$12
Tanyon Sturtze	TB	$11
Eric Milton	MIN	$11
Paul Abbott	SEA	$10
Jeff Brantley	TEX	$10
Gil Heredia	OAK	$10
Bob Howry	CHW	$10
Jose Mercedes	BAL	$10
Eddie Guardado	MIN	$9
LaTroy Hawkins	MIN	$9
Jamie Moyer	SEA	$9
Estaban Yan	TB	$9
Jeff Weaver	DET	$9
Chuck Finley	CLE	$8
Jose Paniagua	SEA	$8

2001 VALUES BY POSITION

A.L. PITCHERS

NAME	TEAM	$VAL	NAME	TEAM	$VAL
Rich Garces	BOS	$8	Mark Buehrle	CHW	$3
Kenny Rogers	TEX	$8	Hipolito Pichardo	BOS	$3
Albie Lopez	TB	$8	Mike Stanton	NYY	$3
Jose Rosado	KC	$8	Pat Hentgen	BAL	$3
Lue Pote	ANA	$7	Justin Speier	CLE	$3
Dave Burba	CLE	$7	Brett Tomko	SEA	$2
Aaron Sele	SEA	$7	Paul Quantrill	TOR	$2
Rick Helling	TEX	$7	Steve Reed	CLE	$2
Andy Pettitte	NYY	$7	Paxton Crawford	BOS	$2
Jeff Zimmerman	TEX	$7	Hideo Nomo	BOS	$2
Jeff Tam	OAK	$7	Buddy Groom	BAL	$2
Ramiro Mendoza	NYY	$7	Matt Anderson	DET	$2
Juan Guzman	TB	$7	Jaret Wright	CLE	$2
Esteban Loaiza	TOR	$6	Dan Plesac	TOR	$2
Mark Petkovsek	TEX	$6	Bill Simas	CHW	$2
Paul Shuey	CLE	$6	Mike Fyhrie	ANA	$2
Mike Trombley	BAL	$6	Joey Hamilton	TOR	$1
Jose Santiago	KC	$6	Lance Painter	TOR	$1
Steve Parris	TOR	$6	Jim Parque	CHW	$1
Jeff Nelson	SEA	$6	Danny Patterson	DET	$1
Lorenzo Barcelo	CHW	$5	Chad Bradford	OAK	$1
Mark Redman	MIN	$5	Kris Wilson	KC	$1
Tim Crabtree	TEX	$5	Wilson Alvarez	TB	$1
Mike Venafro	TEX	$5	Mike Magnante	OAK	$1
Ramon Ortiz	ANA	$5	Orber Moreno	KC	$1
Kelly Wunsch	CHW	$4	Steve Woodard	CLE	$1
Sidney Ponson	BAL	$4	Cory Lidle	OAK	$1
Rod Beck	BOS	$4	Bret Saberhagen	BOS	$1
Frank Castillo	BOS	$4	Seth Greisinger	DET	$1
Bobby J. Jones	FA	$4	Matt Wise	ANA	$1
Rudy Seanez	FA	$4			
Doug Henry	KC	$4			
Gil Meche	SEA	$4			
Arthur Rhodes	SEA	$4			
Brad Radke	MIN	$4			
Bryan Rekar	TB	$3			
Jeff Suppan	KC	$3			
Al Levine	ANA	$3			
Doug Creek	TB	$3			
Travis Miller	MIN	$3			
Shawn Sonnier	KC	$3			
Tomokazu Ohka	BOS	$3			
Blake Stein	KC	$3			
Brian Moehler	DET	$3			

2001 VALUES BY POSITION

N.L. PITCHERS

NAME	TEAM	$VAL	NAME	TEAM	$VAL
Trevor Hoffman	SD	$42	Kris Benson	PIT	$8
Robb Nen	SF	$42	Andy Ashby	LA	$8
Armando Benitez	NYM	$40	Octavio Dotel	HOU	$8
Kevin Brown	LA	$36	Scott Williamson	CIN	$8
Danny Graves	CIN	$32	Juan Acevedo	MIL	$7
Antonio Alfonseca	FLA	$31	Chuck Smith	FLA	$7
Greg Maddux	ATL	$31	Matt Morris	STL	$7
Jeff Shaw	LA	$28	Aaron Fultz	SF	$7
Randy Johnson	AZ	$28	Tony Armas	MON	$7
Dave Veres	STL	$24	Tom Gordon	CHC	$7
Tom Glavine	ATL	$24	Scott Elarton	HOU	$7
Jeff C. Damico	MIL	$24	Greg Swindell	AZ	$7
Curt Schilling	AZ	$23	Osvaldo Fernandez	CIN	$7
John Wetteland	FA	$23	Brian Tollberg	SD	$6
Matt Mantei	AZ	$22	John Smoltz	ATL	$6
Billy Wagner	HOU	$22	Turk Wendell	NYM	$6
John Rocker	ATL	$21	Felix Rodriguez	SF	$6
Daryl Kile	STL	$19	Matt Herges	LA	$6
Chanho Park	LA	$19	Julian Tavarez	CHC	$6
Mike Williams	PIT	$19	Garrett Stephenson	STL	$5
Rick Aguilera	FA	$19	John Franco	NYM	$5
Livan Hernandez	SF	$17	Anthony Telford	MON	$5
Bruce Chen	PHI	$17	Ryan Dempster	FLA	$5
Ugueth Urbina	MON	$17	Ray King	MIL	$5
Curt Leskanic	MIL	$17	Robert Person	PHI	$5
Al Leiter	NYM	$17	Todd Ritchie	PIT	$5
Jose Jimenez	COL	$17	Donne Wall	NYM	$5
Ricky Bottalico	PHI	$16	Mike James	STL	$5
Rick Ankiel	STL	$16	Mark Gardner	SF	$5
Brian Anderson	AZ	$14	Elmer Dessens	CIN	$5
Pete Harnisch	CIN	$13	Britt Reames	MON	$4
Jon Lieber	CHC	$12	Mike Fetters	LA	$4
Woody Williams	SD	$12	Mike Timlin	STL	$4
Kevin Millwood	ATL	$12	Shane Reynolds	HOU	$4
Scott Strickland	MON	$11	Todd Van Poppel	CHC	$4
Kerry Ligtenberg	ATL	$11	Felix Heredia	CHC	$4
Mike Remlinger	ATL	$11	Rick White	NYM	$4
Darren Dreifort	LA	$11	Dave Weathers	MIL	$4
Rick Reed	NYM	$10	Javier Vazquez	MON	$4
Scott Sullivan	CIN	$10	Kyle Farnsworth	CHC	$4
Glendon Rusch	NYM	$10	Kirk Rueter	SF	$4
Steve Kline	STL	$9	Byung Kim	AZ	$4
Gabe White	COL	$9	Sterling Hitchcock	SD	$3
Carl Pavano	MON	$9	Alex Fernandez	FLA	$3

2001 VALUES BY POSITION

N.L. PITCHERS

NAME	TEAM	$VAL	NAME	TEAM	$VAL
Danny Miceli	FLA	$3	Manny Aybar	FLA	$1
Kerry Wood	CHC	$3	Terry Mulholland	PIT	$1
Rudy Seanez	FA	$3			
Jason Christiansen	STL	$3			
Dustin Hermanson	STL	$3			
Terry Adams	LA	$3			
Mike Myers	COL	$3			
Tim Worrell	SF	$3			
Kevin Tapani	CHC	$3			
Tony McKnight	HOU	$3			
Antonio Osuna	LA	$2			
Todd Stottlemyre	AZ	$2			
Cliff Politte	PHI	$2			
Nelson Cruz	HOU	$2			
Bobby J. Jones	FA	$2			
Brad Penny	FLA	$2			
Joe Slusarski	ATL	$2			
Josias Manzanillo	PIT	$2			
Wade Miller	HOU	$1			
John Johnstone	SF	$1			
Russ Ortiz	SF	$1			
Dennis Cook	NYM	$1			
Doug Brocail	HOU	$1			
Mike Hampton	COL	$1			
Alan Embree	SF	$1			
Kevin Walker	SD	$1			
Armando Reynoso	AZ	$1			
Mark Wohlers	CIN	$1			
Wayne Gomes	PHI	$1			
Paul Rigdon	MIL	$1			
Rob Bell	CIN	$1			
Dan Plesac	FA	$1			
Vincente Padilla	PHI	$1			
Bobby Chouinard	COL	$1			
Adam Eaton	SD	$1			
Francisco Cordova	PIT	$1			
Chris Brock	PHI	$1			
Jerry Dipoto	COL	$1			
Randy Wolf	PHI	$1			
Mike Jackson	HOU	$1			
Scott Sauerbeck	PIT	$1			
Braden Looper	FLA	$1			
Luke Prokopec	LA	$1			
Rheal Cormier	PHI	$1			

NOTES: Players not listed are projected to have zero or negative value. Listed values are NOT recommended bids (see bidding strategies in the book, *Rotisserie Baseball - Playing for Blood*).

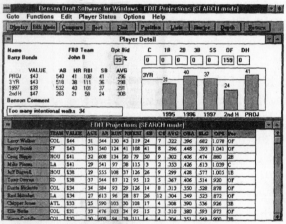

John Benson's Private Pages
(Formerly the Baseball Montly)

In todays electronic/ Internet age, people don't want to wait long periods of time for information -- especially Rotisserie Baseball information! That is why the John Benson Baseball Monthly has been switched to the more "timely and current" Private Pages via the internet only.

When we started 11 years ago, there was no Baseball Weekly, no Baseball Tonight, and hardly any internet outside of universities and military installations. The hard-core box-score browsers were the people willing to walk half a mile if necessary to find a newspaper early every morning. The time period "monthly" seems a lot longer than it did when the inaugural issue came out in September 1989.

The solution is simple: don't call the content a "monthly," don't pick just 12 or 13 (or 14) dates to create big packages; increase the frequency and decrease the size of each issue.

* Instead of 26+ pages 12+ times a year, those same 300+ pages per year will be spread more steadily, and all of them will be more current and timely.

* Simple readable text formated printouts! No more Adobe Acrobat hassels!

* Available only on the internet.

johnbenson.com